THE ENCYCLOPEDIA OF
UNITED STATES SILVER DOLLARS
1794-1804

A source book for the numismatist, dealer, investor, and historian

A catalog raisonné of the early years of America's largest silver denomination

Q. David Bowers

Special contributor
R.W. Julian

Foreword by
Martin Logies

Appreciation by
Warren Miller

STACK'S BOWERS GALLERIES

SPECTRUM GROUP INTERNATIONAL, INC.

ABOUT THE AUTHOR

Q. David Bowers became a professional numismatist as a teenager in 1953, later (1960) earning a B.A. in Finance from the Pennsylvania State University, which in 1976 bestowed its Distinguished Alumni Award on him. The author served as president of the American Numismatic Association (1983-1985) and president of the Professional Numismatists Guild (1977-1979); is a recipient of the highest honor bestowed by the ANA (the Farran Zerbe Award); was the first ANA member to be named Numismatist of the Year (1995); in 2005 was given the Lifetime Achievement Award; and has been inducted into the ANA Numismatic Hall of Fame, today being one of just 12 living recipients with that distinction. Bowers was given the highest honor given by the Professional Numismatists Guild (The Founders' Award) and has received more "Book of the Year Award" and "Best Columnist" honors given by the Numismatic Literary Guild than has any other writer. In 2000 he was the first annual recipient of the Burnett Anderson Memorial Award for writing. In July 1999, in a poll published in *COINage*, "Numismatists of the Century," by Ed Reiter, Bowers was recognized in this list of just 18 names. He is the author of over 50 books, hundreds of auction and other catalogues, and several thousand articles including in *Coin World* (now the longest-running by any author in numismatic history), *Paper Money*, and *The Numismatist*. As Chairman Emeritus of Stack's Bowers Galleries and a numismatic director for Whitman Publishing, LLC, he is in the forefront of current events in the hobby.

**Front cover 1794 silver dollar image provided courtesy of
Professional Coin Grading Service**

PUBLISHED BY

STACK'S BOWERS GALLERIES

A SPECTRUM GROUP INTERNATIONAL COMPANY

1063 McGaw, Suite 100 • Irvine, CA 92614

123 West 57th Street • New York, NY 10019

PO Box 1804 • Wolfeboro, NH 03894

www.stacksbowers.com

ISBN-978-0-9887403-0-3

TABLE OF CONTENTS

STYLE NOTES

Certain original articles and accounts have been lightly edited, but in all instances the meaning has been preserved. Grades of coins such as Very Fine, Extremely Fine, Uncirculated, Proof, etc., are capitalized, per current standard numismatic practice, and quotations from early auction catalogs, etc., have been edited to reflect this. In many if not most instances of catalog listings from the 1970s onward the text has been excerpted to maintain the grade and certain other comments; for expanded descriptions consult the original catalogs.

The terms dexter (the heraldic indication of right) and sinister (the heraldic indication for left) are used to describe the eagle's anatomy in certain issues. For example, on the trade dollar the eagle's dexter leg refers to the eagle's right leg, which is on the left side of the coin (and to the observer's left). Similarly, the dexter wing of an eagle refers to the eagle's right wing (to the observer's left).

Footnotes in all instances, including quoted material, are those of the author of the present work (QDB). Original footnotes are included in parentheses in reproduced quoted material such as Mint reports. The word *government,* when used in a general sense, as in government policies, United States government, etc., is not capitalized. The same applies to *federal.* In original quotations capitalization was inconsistent. *Catalog* is used instead of *catalogue.* Earlier spellings varied. *Luster* is uniformly used instead of lustre.

Grading: American Numismatic Association. In addition to numerical grades such as EF-40, MS-60, etc., adjectival grading is used in connection with older prices, sale results, and catalog listings (as numerical grading for silver dollars was not standardized in its present form until 1986). Certain grades have been abbreviated: Very Good = VG, Very Fine = VF, Extremely Fine = EF, About Uncirculated = AU, Uncirculated = Unc., Mint State = MS. These grades have also been standardized in price quotations, such as listings in advertisements reproduced from *The Numismatist.* For example, in the present text, EF (for Extremely Fine) is used for consistency, although original listings also included such variations as EF, E. Fine, Ex. Fine, Extra Fine, Exceedingly Fine, etc.; what is standardized in the present text as AU (About Uncirculated) sometimes appeared in advertisements as Nearly Uncirculated, Almost Uncirculated, Uncirculated with rubbing, "slider," "super slider," etc. The terms Uncirculated and Mint State are synonyms. For many coins, particularly at the AU and Mint State levels, grading is more liberal in the early twenty-first century than it was in the twentieth century. For this reason many coins listed years ago as MS-63, as an example, have been certified as MS-64 and MS-65 today.

ACKNOWLEDGMENTS
(FIRST AND SECOND EDITIONS)

John W. Adams generously offered the use of books from his library. • **The American Numismatic Association** lent numerous publications from the Dwight Manley Library and photographs of the Class III 1804 silver dollar. • **The American Numismatic Society** provided much information and also made arrangements for Margaret Gray to study library materials, including auction catalogs, for the first edition. • **Mark Borckardt,** on the staff of Bowers and Merena Galleries in the early 1990s (later with Heritage), assisted with many technical details regarding die varieties and die states; his initial B is part of the BB nomenclature. • **Wynn Bowers** read sections of the manuscript and also did research in the Boston Public Library. • **Walter H. Breen** provided detailed data concerning die varieties and also granted permission to use information in his *Encyclopedias,* one on Proof coins and the other on colonial and other U.S. coins. In addition, he reviewed much of the manuscript and made many valuable suggestions. • **Kenneth E. Bressett,** editor of *A Guide Book of U.S. Coins,* read parts of the manuscript and made many valuable suggestions. • **Roger W. Burdette** corresponded concerning 1795 dollars with silver plugs. • **Francis Campbell,** American Numismatic Society librarian when the first edition was being prepared, helped with Mint reports and other data and made arrangements for Margaret Gray to be "in residence" studying auction catalogs on my behalf. • **Armand Champa** provided access to certain publications in his library of numismatic books. • **Lynn Chen,** American Numismatic Association librarian in the early 1990s, responded to numerous inquiries concerning the borrowing of catalogs, Mint reports, and books. • **Elvira Clain-Stefanelli,** curator of the National Numismatic Collection, Division of Numismatics, American Museum of History, Smithsonian Institution, in the early 1990s, furnished information. • **Jack Collins** furnished advice in several areas, copy-read part of the first edition manuscript, and sent information concerning his specialty, 1794 silver dollars. • **William Creech,** National Archives, assisted with research. • **Tom DeLorey** corresponded on various matters. • **Hamilton Dix,** U.S. Mint, was helpful in many ways with the first edition. • **David Fell** reviewed the manuscript section for 1794-1804 dollars and made suggestions. • **John J. Ford, Jr.** reminisced concerning silver dollars, rare and common, that he handled with New Netherlands Coin Company. • **Roberta French** did most of the typesetting for the first edition, much of which was used in the second. • **Kathy Helgesen Fuller** read much of the manuscript and made many valuable suggestions. • **Jeff Garrett** and the museum staff for provided details of early dollars in the National Numismatic Collection, Museum of American History, Smithsonian Institution. • **Margaret Graf** assisted the author with research during the early 1980s when the book was in its initial manuscript stages in the early 1980s. • **Margaret Gray** assisted with historical and numismatic research, including in the library of the American Numismatic Society. • **Stella Hackel,** director of the Mint 1977-1981, made arrangements for the author to visit the Philadelphia Mint and take photographs and do research there. • **David Hall,** founder of the Professional Coin Grading Service, granted permission to use information from the *PCGS Population Report* and from his various articles on silver dollars. • **Michael J. Hodder** assisted with coordinating several aspects of data gathering during the early stages. • **R.W. Julian** wrote the narrative giving the historical background of silver dollars and trade dollars. In addition, he questioned me on numerous statements, made numerous corrections, and suggested further areas of inquiry. Further, he provided mintage figures, die production figures, and other data from Mint records. My debt to him is immense. • **Christine Karstedt,** utilizing select advisors, coordinated the update of this manuscript, the update of all images, and other aspects of publication. • **Gerald L. Kochel** provided a 1795 dollar for examination. • **John Kroon** reviewed sections of the manuscript and provided many valuable suggestions. • **Fred L. Lake** provided out-of-print numismatic publications. • **David W. Lange** sent information about a 1798 dollar variety. • **Russell J. Logan,** John Reich Collectors Society, granted permission to use certain information published in the *John Reich Journal.* In addition, he reviewed the manuscript for 1794-1804 dollars and made many valuable historical and numismatic comments and suggestions. • **Martin Logies** provided illustrations and information for the second edition, including provenance links for of market appearances of condition census specimens and data on 1794 dollars. • **Jim Loyd** reviewed the manuscript in its entirety and made many valuable technical, numismatic, and style suggestions, including in "The Year In History" compilations. • **Andrew P. Lustig** corresponded concerning silver dollar rarities. • **James R. May** sent a 1798 dollar for study. • **Warren Miller** provided illustrations, information, and other help with the second edition. • **Clifford Mishler,** president of Krause Publications, granted permission to reprint descriptions from the Bolender book on early silver dollars, of which Krause is the copyright holder. • The late **Stephen K. Nagy** told of his experiences with 1801-1803 restrikes, and other items. • **The National Archives** provided much Mint data. • **The Nevada Museum** in the former Carson City Mint building), provided photographs of the Carson City Mint. • **Eric P. Newman** read portions of the manuscript. • **Donald Nigro** sent information about an 1876 trade dollar. • **The Numismatic Guaranty Corporation of America, Inc.** made population data available from its *Census Report.* • **Robert Paul** corresponded about early dollars. • **Richard Peloquin** sent a 1796 dollar for examination. • **Dale R. Phelan** reviewed sections of the manuscript and made valuable comments concerning population estimates and other areas, including history and economics. • **Jim Pinkerton** sent information about an 1876 trade dollar. • **Andrew W. Pollock III** helped with certain technical information, read the manuscript, studied the market for 1794-1804 dollars for the years since 1860, and made many valuable suggestions for the first edition and also helped with the second. • **Donna Pope,** director of the Mint 1981-1991, arranged for several visits to do research at various U.S. mints. In addition, through her office in Washington she and her staff helped in many ways. • **The Professional Coin Grading Service, Inc.** made population data available from its *Population Report.* • **Jules Reiver** helped in many ways with research concerning early silver dollars 1794-1803, provided negatives of specimens of in his collection, discussed various die varieties and the rarity thereof, and commented on the manuscript draft. • **Stephen T. Richter** shared information concerning his 1795 dollar overstruck on a dollar of 1794. • **P. Scott Rubin** helped with price data and pedigree chains for certain rarities. • **Harry E. Salyards, M.D.,** made many valuable suggestions and additions concerning early dollars and read most of the manuscript; he helped greatly with the "year in history" entries as well. • **The Smithsonian Institution** provided images for the Class II 1804 silver dollar • **Harvey G. Stack** made several suggestions re the 1804 silver dollar and other rarities, and gave permission to use information and prices from past catalogs. • The late **Norman Stack** granted permission to quote his recollections concerning the Lord St. Oswald sale and to use his writings in various catalogs. • **Dr. Robert Stark** furnished information on varieties and pedigrees of 1794-1803 dollars, and reviewed the manuscript for this section of the book. • **Don Taxay,** for a period of years in the 1960s, conversed and corresponded concerning restrikes, Mint history, and other matters. • **Douglas Winter** provided valuable information on silver dollars 1794-1803, Liberty Seated dollars, and trade dollars.

R.W. Julian credits: These people helped with research and information on certain narratives: Q. David Bowers, Walter H. Breen, Mary T. Brooks, Carl W.A. Carlson, John J. Ford, Jr., N. Neil Harris, Eleonora Hayden, Alan Herbert, Michael J. Hodder, Hope Holdcamper, Ernest E. Keusch, Donald King, Eric P. Newman, William E. Sherman, and Samuel M. Upton.

FOREWORD

BY MARTIN LOGIES

As a collector, researcher and curator for a numismatic museum, I have had the great opportunity to have been the custodian of some of the world's most important coins. These have included a number of condition census and finest known examples of early Philadelphia Mint issues. As I write these words I think of the finest certified (MS-68 NGC) 1792 half disme with a pedigree linking it to David Rittenhouse, the first director of the Mint. The word incredible is certainly appropriate for my 1793 Wreath cent certified MS-69 BN by PCGS, the single highest graded 19th century American coin of any denomination or type. The Neil-Carter 1794 dollar is of course a landmark. Graded Specimen-66 and with a prooflike surface, the die characteristics indicate it may have been the first federal dollar struck. The extraordinary preservation—points above the next finest 1794—may indicate that it was set aside as a memorial of the occasion.

I remember as a young boy reading coin books in the library and daydreaming about maybe someday collecting coins myself. I received an early gift of a common Peace silver dollar and set out on research, even writing a sixth-grade paper about the coin and featuring a pencil rubbing image of it. Through my research, I learned about silver dollars of earlier times—even the fanciful legend that young George Washington once threw a silver dollar across the Potomac River (rather hard to do in reality!). I thought that one day, maybe when I was older, maybe when I made some money, I would search out and find one of those dollars. And find them I did! Not Spanish-American dollars that were circulating in Washington's day, but the first federal dollars from 1794 onward. Using *A Guide Book of United States Coins* as a wish list I set about trying to find the finest example of each early variety through 1803, the last date made for circulation in that early era. To this day, that set known as the Cardinal Collection remains the single finest such group recorded in the PCGS and NGC Registry Set journals. It was during the creation of that set that I became acquainted with your author Q. David Bowers and his vast knowledge regarding the early silver dollars of the United States. Indeed, absent your author's influence and his first edition of this book, the Cardinal Collection of Early Dollars might never have been.

To be sure, there were reference works regarding early dollars before Dave's. The Haseltine *Type Table* of 1881 and the Bolender book published in 1950 were each standard references in their day, but there is a reason your author was named "Numismatist of the Century" by *COINage* magazine, for he has the ability to unlock the hidden essence of knowledge and explain it in a way that can actually be understood and used.

John W. Haseltine and Milferd H. Bolender were both experts in the field and highly respected in their day, but with terms like "bifurcation" and "suction marks," their descriptions were more understandable to those who were already experts than those who were learning. By contrast, Dave's descriptions instantly make sense and enable the beginner and expert alike to recognize and distinguish the nuances of individual die varieties. The additional information he provides allows the reader to understand each variety in its proper context, history and rarity. Rather than just assess the rarity of a variety overall, as those before had done, Dave has further identified the rarity levels of these varieties across the spectrum of grade quality. So, while it may be interesting to know that a certain variety is rather scarce overall, it is exceedingly helpful to know that the variety is relatively unknown above the grade of "Extremely Fine," for example; and, thus, if one was afforded the opportunity to acquire an "About Uncirculated" specimen, that itself would be a very rare opportunity, one not to be passed over lightly.

It is in this regard that Dave's work creates true "added value" for the collector. Before I was able to obtain a copy of the first edition of this book, I had the opportunity to bid on a truly choice "AU" example of a scarce variety ("BB-93") dated 1798. I had received the auction catalog, I placed some bids in the sale, and I was successful on a number of the coins. I was there; I was in the moment. But, lacking Dave's book, I did not realize just how extraordinarily rare that one coin was in such choice condition, and did not pursue it, choosing to wait for another. The coin sold for a modest sum then, but in the more than 15 years since, that specimen has not re-appeared on the market, nor has any specimen of that variety of comparable quality. Unknowingly, the opportunity had been squandered!

Soon after, I was able to purchase Dave's book and pore through its pages, arming myself with new knowledge. The following year, I recognized an example at auction as being likely the finest known example of a very scarce variety, and I set about to secure it. I was successful, winning my prize for about $4,000. Ten years later, when that piece was sold as part of the Cardinal Collection of Early Dollars by American Numismatic Rarities, a well-remembered antecedent of Stack's Bowers Galleries, it was indeed recognized for being the finest known and realized a price of $23,000. Confident with Dave's sage knowledge, this had been an opportunity exploited! I could cite many, many more examples of how Dave's work has enriched the lives of collectors everywhere.

I heartily commend the study of early dollars and this most enlightening book to you. It is one that you will enjoy reading time and again and profit from greatly, and one that I have referred to most often of any reference in my own library. Indeed, my copy of the first edition is now well worn and tattered, but still its pages live on in my memory and Dave's words continue their inspiration. May it lead you to great achievements in your collecting endeavors, and perhaps one day, as I have, you too can look back upon your time and success, and smile broadly at the amazing collection you have assembled, the incredible places you have been, the extraordinary individuals you have met, and the exhilarating experiences that have filled your life.

— Martin A. Logies, Director and Curator
The Cardinal Collection Educational Foundation

AN APPRECIATION

by Warren Miller

I rekindled my interest in coin collecting around 1983. My brother and I had collected Lincoln cents when we were kids searching through change in my dad's store. We both stopped for several decades until my brother asked me to find some Lincoln cents for his collection. I stopped at a local coin dealer who had separate tubes of each date and let me pick what I needed. As the cost of the rare dates increased dramatically, my brother's interest started to wane. At the same time, the collector instinct in me was reawakened and I started to focus on acquiring the rarer dates.

During one of my visits I asked the dealer, Jess Lipka, if he had any Draped Bust dollars, something I had been fascinated by as a teenager, but did not have the resources to acquire. He had three EF examples, all with different dates: 1798, 1799 and 1800. He had priced each one separately and to his shock—and probably mine—I asked if I could get a better price if I bought all three. Sensing a potential good future customer, he presented me with a copy of Bolender's book on my very next visit. After reading the book, I decided to try to acquire an example of each date, except for the 1794 and 1804, which were way out of my price range. After meeting this goal, I then tried to acquire all of the varieties listed in *A Guide Book of United States Coins*.

My collecting began in the era right before PCGS and NGC began certifying coins. In the early years a lot of coins were artificially toned in order to hide defects, old cleaning, etc., in order to obtain higher grades. Jess had a good eye and taught me to look for nice coins that had original surfaces rather than to always go for the highest grades. I carried out this philosophy as best as I could throughout my collecting. I can think of several occasions when I passed on a problem coin, usually harshly cleaned, but with very little wear. I chose to wait for a nice high-grade EF-45 or AU specimen, only to later find out that the problem coin was reworked and now resided in an MS-61 or MS-62 holder. I still do not regret my decision to pass on problem coins. I feel that the condition census is useful but very subjective because of altered coins and "gradeflation." Unless two coins are compared side by side, no one can determine from the auction records or the grade on a holder which is the more desirable specimen. Obviously for unique or very rare coins, it was not always possible to collect totally original specimens and I collected what was available.

Jess also advised me to buy nice original-surface coins when I had the opportunity, not to just try to fill a specific hole in my collection. In the end I ended up with a complete set of much nicer coins. His advice served me well.

As coins became more expensive through the 1990s up to the present, it became apparent to me that I could not afford to own the finest known example of every variety and die state. I made a conscious decision to find nice examples of the common varieties and not try to acquire MS-63 and higher grades of type coins. Instead I concentrated on finding the best, including great rarities.

In one instance I received a call that a beautiful 1798 Small Eagle dollar was available at a Boston show. If I wanted it I was told, I had to take a shuttle to Boston and buy the coin that day or it would be gone. I raced to the airport. The advice of more than one dealer was that the price was way too high and that I would be better off to pass on it. Against their advice I purchased it anyway and it is still one of my favorite coins in the collection! It is the finest known 1798 B-2 15 Star Small Eagle dollar in MS-63 from the Ostheimer Sale.

During my collecting over the last 30 years, I never had a goal to complete a set with all 118 die marriages. However, occasionally a nice original specimen of a variety that I already had would come up for auction. If it was a dramatically different die state I would add it to my collection. I also collected any unusual one-of-a-kind coins, such as double struck specimens, when they came up for auction.

Many of the rarest varieties and unique coins were in the hands of older collectors and were off the market for over 50 years. Eventually coins with famous pedigrees such as Eliasberg, Willasch, Blevins and Reiver came up for auction and some of these coins became available in a possibly once-in-a-lifetime event. It was in these instances that I became a more aggressive bidder. I could now see that completing the set was within reach, something that had never before been done.

The last coin that I acquired was the 1795 B-19 Flowing Hair dollar with a silver plug. It was originally in the Frank Stirling Collection and was off the market for 60 years. David Perkins knew that I needed the coin to complete the set and spoke to the current owner. He managed to acquire the coin on my behalf and I added it to my set at the Central States Show in Columbus, Ohio, in 2005. Needless to say, I treated all to dinner that night!

I also upgraded my 1795 B-8 Flowing Hair dollar, the only gradable example of this Rarity-7 coin, a few years ago. I was the underbidder the first time it came up for auction at a Superior sale over 20 years ago. It again came up for auction in the San Marino sale at the Goldbergs about ten years ago and again I did not acquire it, since I felt that the reserve was too high. After being haunted for another ten years for letting it get away not once, but twice, I finally purchased it from the owner at a price over ten times the original selling price! A valuable lesson learned: if you let something you really want get away, you may not get a second chance, and if you do, it likely will cost a great deal more!

I decided to participate in this revised early dollar book because I believe that there is a strong need for an updated version with up to date auction records. I also feel that the photography in this book will be a valuable tool in attributing die varieties and die states. In many cases the extreme differences between early and late die states are readily apparent thanks to the excellent photography. The old saying that a picture is worth a thousand words is exemplified in this book!

I feel that Dave Bowers did an outstanding job with the overall manuscript, a standard since 1993, and that Martin Logies made excellent suggestions and updates for the present second edition. The result is by far the most complete and useful book on early dollars that has been published to date. The historical information and up to date auction records will be useful for both novices and advanced collectors of this fabulous series of early American coins.

As I reflect upon the present book, the information and rich history imparted, I cannot resist mentioning that the unique completion of my collection of 1794 to 1803 circulation strike silver dollars has brought me many hours of enjoyment. The exciting quest was a combination of the thrill of the hunt, working with many fine dealers and collectors, and closely studying the fascinating series. With pleasure and delight I realize that these coins will ultimately go to new owners, who, I am sure, will in their own way enjoy the tradition and desirability of each piece.

It was a pleasure and a privilege to participate in this book by both editing and supplying photographs as needed.

— Warren Miller

INTRODUCTION

The first edition of *Silver Dollars and Trade Dollars of the United States: A Complete Encyclopedia*, published in 1993, had its inception in the 1960s when I started keeping notes on many of the silver dollars that went through my hands. A serious start was made on the manuscript in the early 1980s, when my then-secretary, Margaret Graf, coordinated many of my notes and ideas. Then, several other book projects intervened, especially the creation of *The American Numismatic Association Centennial History*, which, when all was said and done, amounted to 1,766 pages in two volumes and saw the light of day in the summer of 1991.

In the meantime, I had commissioned two of America's most accomplished numismatists, R.W. Julian and Walter H. Breen, to supply certain information for a forthcoming book on silver dollars. Bob Julian created a truly great historical overview of the series, and Walter H. Breen provided technical notes on die varieties which had come to his attention (many of which had been described in *Walter Breen's Complete Encyclopedia of U.S. and Colonial Coins*). In addition, in 1991 and 1992, Walter H. Breen supplied much other data in correspondence and went over the manuscript with a fine-tooth comb.

Utilizing the efforts of other numismatists past and present, and using much information from the vast fund of publications enumerated in the text and in the Bibliography, I endeavored to create a two-volume study which on a coin-by-coin basis will aid the serious collector and historian to learn a great deal about any issue in the series. The first edition was thus comprehensive in its coverage, from the first dollar in 1794 up to the "minidollars" in the Susan B. Anthony series.

In 2012 the present second edition was created, this being a revision and updating of the information on the early series of Flowing Hair and Draped Bust dollars from 1794 to 1804. Offered in a single volume with much new information, including updated rarity data, color pictures, and state-of-the-art knowledge, this book will be your passport to one of America's most interesting coinage specialties.

Since 1993 there have been new series including the Sacagawea "golden dollars" commencing in 2000, supplemented later with presidential dollars (issued at the rate of four per year). In addition there have been various commemoratives.

There have been many changes in the marketplace as well. Certification of early dollars, especially by the Professional Grading Service (PCGS) and the Numismatic Guaranty Corporation of America (NGC), just beginning to be accepted back then and not an important part of the historical record, is now central to public offerings of scarce and rare issues at auction or placement by private treaty. Many important coins and collections have been dispersed in the past two decades, the most notable of which was the Louis E. Eliasberg Sr. Collection, the only holding ever formed that was complete from the 1793 half cent to the 1933 double eagle. The John Reich Collectors Society (JRCS) has been publishing research and other information since 1986, the vast majority of which has appeared since the first edition of the present book. Accordingly, much new information not available earlier has contributed more to the early dollar specialty.

CHAPTER 1
EARLY SILVER DOLLARS 1794-1804

HISTORICAL BACKGROUND

by R.W. Julian

Coinage Background

With the fall of Rome in the fifth century of our era, there arose in Europe a collection of petty kingdoms. It was not until the age of Charlemagne (768–814) that the practical concept of the great nation once more was seen in Europe. Under this ruler trade was encouraged, and coinage was used by the common man for the first time in centuries.

Prior to Charlemagne, traders and merchants were more accustomed to using gold coins, but beginning about A.D. 755 the French issued small thin coins of silver called deniers. A few years later, King Offa of Mercia (an early English kingdom) struck pennies of high quality. For centuries the English had the reputation of issuing the best coinage in Western Europe, and it was widely imitated in other countries.

As European trade began to expand there was a need for a larger coin than just the simple penny—or one of the numerous equivalents struck throughout the continent. In 1202 the city-state of Venice introduced the grosso. By the end of the century most European nations had issued similar coins. Beginning in 1280, for example, King Edward III of England struck the groat, equivalent to four pennies.[1]

With the introduction of the grosso and its imitations, trade became less confined. Payments were made easier for larger amounts. Gold began to be struck in quantity during the thirteenth century, although West Europeans had used Byzantine gold for centuries. However, the power of Constantinople was visibly declining during this period, and its coinage was increasingly debased.

Silver thaler of Augsburg, 1641, with city view reverse. (Davenport variety 5039).

The First "Silver Dollar"

A combination of small gold coins and larger silver served Europe reasonably well into the fifteenth century, but the ever-growing trade within the Continent and abroad mandated increased supplies of coin. In 1486 Archduke Sigismund of Tyrol struck the first dollar-sized silver coin. Its formal name was *guldengroschen*, but this was soon shortened to *gulden*. It was meant to be equivalent with the gulden, one of the important European gold coins.

Sigismund was a pioneer in the field of large silver coins and proved to be well ahead of his time. It was not until about 1520 that the counts of Schlick in Bohemia (later part of Czechoslovakia) took the guldiner concept to its logical conclusion and began the striking of large silver coins on a regular basis.

Most of the silver for the Schlick coinage came from rich mines in the valley of St. Joachim (Joachimsthal). These coins became known as *Joachimsthalers*, which was soon shortened to *thalers* (or *talers*). By the middle of the sixteenth century large silver coins, based on the thaler, were being struck all over the continent. Many of the countries simply used a derivative name to show the value of their coinage. Sweden, for example, struck *dalers* while Holland coined *daalders* from 1575 to about 1690. Petty German states in particular coined thalers, and even multiple thalers became almost common. These coins were frequently used as commemoratives and royal propaganda for the ruling house.

Spanish-American Silver Coins

In Spain, where vast wealth from the New World was pouring into her coffers, the government chose to coin pieces of *eight reales*, roughly equivalent to the thaler. Mints were established in the Americas to coin silver, and

---

[1] The groat is minted today for special ceremonial purposes, for use in British Maundy sets. It has not been used as currency since the nineteenth century.

Silver eight reales minted in Mexico City (Mo mintmark) in 1738. "Pillar dollar," so called from the Pillars of Hercules on the obverse.

it was not long before the eight reales denomination was struck there also. However, most of the silver struck until the middle of the eighteenth century at Spanish-American mints was in the form of the extremely crude "cob" coins, well known to collectors. Such silver pieces were made by slicing planchets off the end of long silver bars, or "cobs."

Mexico City was the first (in 1732) of these mints to abandon the old hammered coinage in favor of the screw press. In the eighteenth and nineteenth centuries other Spanish-American countries also issued eight-reales coins and other denominations in silver.

Coins of the American Colonists

In what is now the United States permanent settlements from England were established as early as 1607 at Jamestown, but it was decades before the colonists had

A silver NE shilling authorized by the Massachusetts Bay Colony in 1652. These were stamped NE on one side, then turned over and stamped XII (for 12 pence or a shilling). (Variety Noe 1-A)

The Pine Tree shilling maintained the 1652 authorization date but was struck later. Nathaniel Hawthorne wrote a romantic tale about these famous coins. (Variety Noe 1).

much in the way of coined gold or silver. Prior to 1650 most trade in this country was on the barter system, and coins were as rare as the proverbial hen's teeth.

In 1652, in an effort to bring stability to the marketplace and also provide a circulating medium to the hard-pressed colonists, the Massachusetts General Court authorized the famous "NE" silver coinage. These first crude coins, which were struck for only a short time, used Spanish 8 reales as well as Dutch daalders for their raw material. The Massachusetts coins were lighter than their British counterparts because the shilling as a money of account in New England was worth less than an English shilling (sterling). Later issues of Massachusetts silver had a tree on the obverse ("pine tree shillings," etc.). The coinage ended about 1682.

Five-shilling 1658 silver shilling of Oliver Cromwell.

This first coinage by the English colonies in America was due to the interregnum in England. King Charles I had been beheaded in 1649 and the government was effectively controlled by Oliver Cromwell, soon to become the Lord Protector. Cromwell did not especially concern himself with colonial affairs, unlike the royal government, and many of the colonies were virtually independent until Charles II recovered the throne in 1660.

Most of the Spanish and Dutch silver coins that were brought to the colonies came from the well-known—and illegal—commerce with the West Indies and Africa, the so-called triangular trade. Slaves and rum were key ingredients, and profits were taken in silver and, to a lesser extent, gold. The English government had enacted strict mercantile laws to keep the colonists from trading with areas reserved for English merchants, while Spain forbid all Englishmen from trading with their colonies. Neither prohibition was very effective against the Yankee ship captains, however.

By the 1690s at the latest, the term "dollar" was in widespread use throughout the English colonies in America to describe the Spanish 8 reales and the Dutch daalder. The latter was usually called a *Lion Dollar* to distinguish it from the Spanish dollar of 8 reales. Contracts requiring monetary payment in silver coin almost always stipulated the Spanish or Lion dollar by name because of their reputation for quality.

The Dutch, for internal political reasons, began to strike fewer Lion dollars toward the end of the seventeenth

A 1767 Maryland note of $4. This series was the first to be denominated in dollars.

century, and by 1700 they were virtually a thing of the past. In America the Spanish dollar gradually became the single accepted standard of value and the yardstick by which all other monies were judged. Colonies had begun to issue paper currency in the 1690s, and its circulating value depended upon the rate of conversion into Spanish silver coin.

It should be noted that the Spanish dollar was not the only silver coinage to be used in the colonies. The Mexico City Mint—as well as several others—struck a considerable number of fractional pieces, such as half real, real, and 2 reales coins.[1] Other denominations were made but never achieved widespread use.

American Paper Dollars

In November 1766 Maryland authorized the issuance of paper money with dollar denominations. These were issued early in 1767 and constitute the first official use of the dollar as the name for a monetary unit in the colonial American economic system. Values from 1/9th of a dollar to $8 were printed. It was an historic moment when the Maryland government officially recognized what the public had been using in terminology for decades.

For some curious reason little numismatic attention has been paid to this first issue of "dollars." There were 12,000

printed of the $1 value. For those who collect the dollar, there could be no finer way to begin a collection than with the Maryland issue of 1767. In due course other colonies adopted this policy, and in 1775 the Continental Congress ordered currency printed in dollar denominations.

One of the great numismatic mysteries of the colonial era is the so-called Continental "dollar" of 1776. It could have been that the original dies were prepared in order to strike a silver dollar, equivalent to the Spanish eight reales. It did not take long for those behind this issue to realize that bullion was going to be a problem, not to mention the potential of inflation from ever-increasing amounts of paper being issued. Those who believe that the 1776 Continental dollar was semi-official can point to the fact that the Continental Congress did not issue a one-dollar bill from 1776 to 1778, perhaps in hopes that a dollar coin could circulate.

It is likely that the dies were executed with official sanction, and possibly encouragement as well, but in silver only pattern pieces were struck. The relative abundance of pewter specimens almost certainly indicates that they circulated widely in their era as fiat money, as the paper dollar had been as well.

The rapid inflation in the United States after 1777 doomed any proposals for a hard currency until the rebellion was over. With the coming of peace in early 1783, official thoughts turned to coinage once more. Minister of Finance Robert Morris, on his own authority, had patterns of silver and copper made. None of these, however, was of dollar size.

Continental dollar in pewter, 1776. E.G. Fecit = E.G. "made it," thought to refer to Elisha Gallaudet, per the research of Eric P. Newman.

Nova Constellatio silver pattern 1000 units or mark.

---

[1] These coins were the basis for the nicknames of certain coins in this country: the 2 reales was one fourth of a dollar, or "two bits." The frequent pricing of 12½ cents or 6¼ cents seen up until the time of the American Civil War simply refers to the real and half real coins and their value in terms of a dollar.

The inauguration of President George Washington in New York City in 1789. At the time New York was the capital of the United States.

Federal Mint Proposals of the 1780s

Various proposals were made in the 1780s for a federal mint. All foundered on a lack of money as well as general opposition to such plans by those with a vested interest in producing large quantities of copper coins, such as state governments. One of the most interesting suggestions, however, was formulated by Thomas Jefferson in 1785–1786. He recommended a coinage of gold, silver, and copper. The largest silver coin was to be a dollar, containing 375.64 grains of pure silver while the ratio of gold to silver in the coinage system was set at 1 to 15.47. In 1786 the Confederation government formally adopted the Jefferson proposals but nothing came of this law due to a lack of money.

Throughout the 1780s, during an era of hard times, the Spanish dollar—and its fractions—remained the money of choice for the broad mass of citizens in America. These coins were always in short supply, but used by the common people in purchasing the necessities of life. Copper coins from a variety of sources[1] were also used.

In 1787 the Constitution was adopted by delegates in Philadelphia. Over the next few months a majority of state legislatures did likewise. The new government, under President George Washington, took office in New York City during the early spring of 1789, but in early 1790 moved to Philadelphia. (The capital was removed to Washington, D.C. in 1800.) It was not long after the arrival of delegates in Philadelphia that Congress began seriously to consider the state of the nation's economy in general and its monetary system in particular.

Major events sometimes need but a tiny push to become reality and thus it was with our monetary system. An obscure South Carolinian named John Hinckley Mitchell was well acquainted with Matthew Boulton, the famed English private coiner and inventor.[2] Mitchell decided, with very little input from Boulton, to become the latter's agent in America in an effort to obtain a lucrative minting contract for American coinage.

Mitchell sent the proposal for contract coinage to the government and, in due course, this was forwarded to Secretary of State Thomas Jefferson, newly returned from his diplomatic post in France. Jefferson was asked to pass on the proposal for several reasons, including his involvement in the 1786 coinage schemes and his known dislike of having money coined abroad.

As expected, Jefferson advised Congress to disregard the Mitchell effort although the Secretary of State admitted that Mitchell's coinage (*i.e.*, Boulton's) was the best in the world. Because Boulton was not mentioned in Jefferson's report to Congress, some numismatic writers were later misled in believing that Mitchell had his own mint in Europe. One wonders what Boulton thought about all of this.

Hamilton Reports on the Monetary System

Congress, as a result of Jefferson's message, asked Secretary of the Treasury Alexander Hamilton for a complete report on a mint and monetary system. Hamilton and his small group of employees worked on this project for the next several months and asked many experts, such as merchants and importers of gold and silver, searching questions designed to collect the maximum amount of information.

The secretary also ordered careful assays of silver and gold coins to be made, especially on those of Spain. It was clear that the Spanish silver dollar, or 8 reales, would be the basis of our silver coinage, and Hamilton was determined to learn all that he could. The Spanish, because of internal problems with their economy, were somewhat secretive about their coinage and had reduced the amount of silver in the dollar and its fractions without making this fact known. One source indicates that the Spanish dollar in 1791 was supposed to contain about 375 grains of pure silver, though it is not clear if all their mints were that accurate in the final product.

In determining the precise weight of the pure silver in the Spanish 8 reales coin, Hamilton had to consider two

---

[1] Including pieces struck by under contract of or by the states of Connecticut (1785-1788), Vermont (1785-1788; actually, Vermont did not join the Union until 1791), New Jersey (1786-1788), and Massachusetts (1787-1788).

[2] Boulton, who was associated with James Watt (well-known maker of steam engines), developed sophisticated presses and other coining devices which permitted coins to be struck at high speeds to standards more uniform than could be accomplished in the past.

Alexander Hamilton portrait by John Trumbull.

points: the weight and fineness of the coins being issued in 1791 and the amount of pure silver in the average piece of eight circulating in the western hemisphere. Because of the change in the purity prior to 1791, the secretary decided to use the amount of pure silver in the average coin. Some scholars later charged that this was a mistake, and the 1791 Spanish mint purity ought to have been used, but this view has equal problems. Hamilton was forced to work in a vacuum. However, his study was the best that could be done in a nation far removed from the money markets of the world, London and Amsterdam.

Federal Mint Authorized

Hamilton's report was presented to Congress on January 28, 1791, and has long been considered a classic in its field. Because of the complex nature of the report and the several different topics covered, it took the congressmen considerable time to digest all that had been presented. At length, on March 3, 1791, Congress passed a resolution authorizing the president to establish a mint and hire those persons necessary to carry out the work.

Although, in close scrutiny, the resolution actually was of little direct value and nothing was accomplished under its mantle, still it showed the resolve of the legislators to have a mint and national coinage. (It is interesting to note that nineteenth-century Mint directors, especially those in office before 1850, considered the March 1791 resolve to be the basis of the mint system and not the law of April

1792.) The president was simply unable to accomplish much under the terms of a joint resolution.

President Washington's annual address to the joint Congress for 1791 came on October 25, and he pointed out to the assembled legislators that the resolution was hardly what was needed; instead a law should be passed that would spell out in necessary detail what was to be done. Merely saying that there should be a mint was not enough. The Senate responded by appointing a special committee, chaired by Robert Morris, to draft the necessary legislation.

The Morris committee, after its own investigation, proceeded to write a draft bill for consideration by the full Senate. On December 21, 1791, Morris formally presented the bill but parliamentary considerations dictated that little real debate would occur until after the third reading, although it is not clear if the bill actually was read in its entirety; then as now, it is likely that such regulations were honored more in the breach than in reality.

At any rate the committee agreed with Hamilton that the dollar would contain 371.25 grains of silver, but on the other hand should have a gross weight of 416 grains, producing the odd fineness of 1485/1664 (892.4+/1000). Congressmen felt that this was necessary, one would assume, in order to have the prestige of a dollar coin equal in size and weight to the famous 8 reales of Spain.

New Coins to Portray Washington?

When real debate began on the bill in the Senate, on January 9, 1792, the question of the pure silver in the dollar was barely broached, if at all. (The official record in that era merely reported the general thrust of speeches, not the actual words.) The most controversial section of the Morris draft legislation concerned the placing of the current president's head on the obverse of the silver and gold coins.

After heated debate, the Morris draft bill was accepted by the Senate more or less intact; it was then sent to the House of Representatives. The House chose to read the legislation with great care and it was not until March 24 that Representatives got around to formal discussion of the bill and its merits.

The House rejected the concept of the president's head on the coinage and replaced it with one of their own: the head of Liberty. The revised version of the bill was returned to the Senate, which refused to accept the Liberty head provision and reaffirmed the original stand. The House now did the same as before and the bill was returned once more to the Senate; the latter finally gave in and accepted the House version. President Washington signed the bill into law on April 2, 1792.

There is a tradition that the president personally lobbied House members in order to kill the provision about the

A pattern cent proposal of 1792 by Peter Getz depicting George Washington, president of the United States.

presidential profile appearing on the coinage. While this may well be true, it also seems likely that the chief executive would at least have been consulted by Senator Morris before the draft bill had been submitted and thus given his approval of the idea. Perhaps Washington, after the House debate, had a change of heart and persuaded key senators to vote for the House version.

With the adoption of the April 2 law the nation was now on the road toward a mint and coinage. It would be many years before the system worked for the benefit of all citizens, but the seed had been planted and would grow into an impressive tree as the years passed.

David Rittenhouse

Well before the adoption of the new Mint law on April 2, 1792, President Washington had chosen David Rittenhouse, an eminent scientist of international renown, as the first director of the new institution. Because of poor health, Rittenhouse had been loath to accept the post and even then had agreed only to a temporary directorship.

Once the Mint law had been signed by the president, Rittenhouse was free to proceed, although he had already taken some tentative steps toward putting the new institution on a sound footing. In particular he had engaged, probably in March, an artist named Birch to engrave cent dies; this same artist would also do the half disme and disme dies in the weeks following the adoption of the law.[1]

One of Rittenhouse's early choices for his staff was Henry Voight (or Voigt), a watchmaker of Philadelphia,

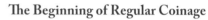

Portrait of David Rittenhouse by Charles Willson Peale.

---

[1] One of the minor mysteries of the early Mint is the correct name of this artist. In the nineteenth century it was thought to be "Bob" Birch, but this was based on the appearance of that name in the 1793 fiscal records, where he is recorded as selling medicine for horses to the Mint.

to be the first chief coiner. Born in Pennsylvania, Voight had gone to Germany before the Revolution to serve an apprenticeship in a small German mint. According to his own statement, he had learned all the skills necessary for a mint except that of engraving. It is thus ironic that Voight also served as unofficial engraver at the Mint between December 1792 and July 1793.

Although somewhat more than 1,500 half dismes were struck in July 1792, from silver believed to have been supplied in part by the president, nothing was said of striking dollars or even half dollars. Until September 1792 the institution was housed in the cellar of a private Philadelphia building—at 6th and Cherry Streets—owned by John Harper. The latter not only sold items of value to the Mint, but had been one of the coiners of the New Jersey copper cents in the 1780s.

On July 31 a foundation stone (not cornerstone as is sometimes stated) was laid by David Rittenhouse, and construction of the coinage building, or "shop" as it was to be called by Chief Coiner Voight, got underway. There was also a double building at the front of the Mint lot (facing Seventh Street) whose remodeling was started shortly thereafter. In early September 1792 progress was so far advanced that Rittenhouse was able to move staff and machinery into the new location.

The Beginning of Regular Coinage

Cent coinage at the new Mint began in late February 1793. The symbolic ceremony may have been held on February 22 (even in those days Washington's birthday was widely honored), and full-scale striking was underway within a few days. The first official delivery of coined money was made on March 1, 1793.

Albion Cox joined the staff of officers in May 1793 as assayer and was to serve until his death in late November 1795. Cox was born in England, but had been in this country during the 1780s as a partner of John Harper in the New Jersey coppers; he had been forced to flee to Britain at the end of the decade to avoid imprisonment for debt and probably made it a point to keep out of New Jersey after his return to this country.

Congress had stipulated in April 1792 that the bonds of the chief coiner and assayer be for $10,000 each, an enormous sum for the period. Because of these high amounts, neither Voight nor Cox was able to find sureties to meet the requirement, and thus only copper was coined in the first year of regular operations, 1793. Rittenhouse turned to Thomas Jefferson to solve the impasse. Toward the end

Above: The first authorized federal coinage under the Mint Act of April 2, 1792, was the silver half disme, struck in a private shop before the Philadelphia Mint was ready.

Right: The Philadelphia Mint in the 1790s depicted in a 1914 painting by Edwin Lamasure.

of 1793 the Secretary of State appealed to Congress to lower the amount of the bonds.

Although Treasury Secretary Hamilton should have been placed over the Mint, Secretary of State Thomas Jefferson was instead chosen by the president. He had, after all, been involved in a significant way with the coinage schemes of the 1780s, but the president also felt that Hamilton was far too busy with other matters to be involved with the Mint. This turned out to be a mistake as the Treasury refused to cooperate when the Mint needed bullion in periods of low coinage during the 1790s.

Design for the 1794 Dollar Created

Once Jefferson had made the request to Congress, it was clear that the decision would be favorable, but then as now the legislators were in no hurry. Well before the Congressional action of March 3, 1794, however, reducing the bonds for the chief coiner and assayer, respectively, to $5,000 and $1,000, Engraver Robert Scot had begun work on designs for the silver coinage. Just when this process began is uncertain, but it is likely that the engraver was at work no later than the middle of January 1794.

Judging from the adopted design, it seems clear that Scot was told by the powers-that-be (the president, Jefferson, and Rittenhouse probably made all key decisions regarding design elements) to use the Liberty head designed for the cent by Engraver Joseph Wright in August 1793. Scot's copy is not exact, but the overall relationship is reasonably clear. The head is gazing at a somewhat higher angle, and the liberty cap has been removed, but otherwise there is little real difference. The government obviously considered Wright's Liberty head to be an outstanding artistic success.

Copper cents for circulation were first coined at the Philadelphia Mint in February 1793. The engraver, fearful that the name in full of our nation would not artistically fit on the coin, abbreviated it to AMERI. Later, the legend was adjusted and AMERICA was used.

Scot also was told to use Wright's eagle from the pattern quarter dollar of 1792, although the head was turned and the base changed to a rock instead of the earlier globe. The Scot eagle was somewhat less refined than that executed by Wright, but under the circumstances was well done for the period. Appropriate lettering encircled the eagle and the design was complete; no wreath was present on this first approved drawing by Scot. (It is assumed that the dies for the "1792" quarter dollar pattern were actually completed in the summer of 1793 and it was almost certainly then that the patterns were struck.)

One of the great misconceptions of American numismatics is that the engraver was solely responsible for a particular design. With minor exceptions, primarily while James B. Longacre served as engraver in the 1850s and 1860s, the designs were almost always dictated by higher authorities—the director played a key role in this work—and the engraver then produced drawings to match his instructions as closely as possible. A typical example of the director ordering a particular style of artwork was to occur in 1891 when Mint Director Edward O. Leech ordered Chief Engraver Charles E. Barber to use certain

French coins and medals as a guide in the preparation of the Liberty head coinage. Barber had some freedom of artistic expression, but only to the extent that it was permitted by Leech.

Little is known of the precise dates that dies and patterns were made in 1794, but it is known that Frederick Riche was hired for 18 days' work in May, and it is likely that Riche worked on the dies for copper coins while Scot executed hubs for a half dime pattern.

How Dies Were Made

At this point it is necessary to explain just how dies were created prior to 1907, when an entirely new system was introduced. (The system in effect during 1794 was heavily modified in 1837 and again, to a lesser extent, in 1867, but the general idea remained the same.)

After the artwork was accepted for use, the engraver carefully cut in relief the head of Liberty (the head appeared just as it did on the finished coin) or eagle as was required. For the obverse the head of Liberty was punched into a blank die, and then the necessary lettering and date were also punched in. For the reverse a similar operation took place except that the hub was of an eagle. The dies were then hardened and made ready for use in the coining press.

Pattern Half Dimes

Pattern half dimes from designs by Scot, but based on the Wright work of 1793, appear to have been struck in May or June 1794. The only known specimen, in copper, is in the National Numismatic Collection in the Smithsonian Institution. There is no question of the denomination as it is written out as *half disme* on the reverse. The pronunciation is now known with certainty to be *dime* as at present; the spelling was modernized at the Mint in the late 1820s. Changes of this type invariably reflect public usage.

The patterns were examined very carefully by top government officials and it was decided that the design was not quite all that was wanted. Someone, probably Jefferson or the president, decided that a wreath was necessary on the reverse and that the spelled-out denomination was no longer wanted. Britain did not put written denominations on its coinage while France did. It is likely here that we see the influence of the pro-British party (Jefferson favored France) in which Hamilton played a key role. It appears to be one of the few times that the Treasury secretary was able to decide a matter affecting the coinage before he left office at the end of January 1795.

A regular-issue 1794-dated half dime, shown twice actual size. Although the dies were made in 1794, coinage of this denomination did not begin until early 1795.

Not only was it felt that the half dime design had flaws, but this denomination was not even to be the first silver coin struck officially under the provisions of the 1792 law. Someone, perhaps Hamilton again, persuaded the president that only the largest coins commanded respect in foreign eyes and that the dollar should be the first coin struck. It is also likely that the public demand for half dimes had lessened since 1792; perhaps more Spanish-American coins of low value (the half real was worth 6 1/4 cents) had been imported into the country.

Creating the 1794 Dollar Dies

After the decision had been made to scrap the proposed coinage of half dimes and begin with the silver dollar, Scot went back to the drawing board to produce sketches of the changes required by the top officials. The fully written-out denomination was duly eliminated (on the dollar and half dollar it would be found only in the edge lettering until 1807) and a wreath was added around the eagle. The new sketches were approved in due course, perhaps in June or July 1794, and Scot began to cut the necessary hubs for the dollar dies.

The hubs for the dollar, being intended as a coin of prestige for the United States, were executed with great care by Scot, who also had to contend with his more ordinary duties of producing dies for the copper coinage. No doubt he was visited by Jefferson and Washington from time to time to see how the work was progressing. (The President's official residence was on High Street, only a few blocks from the Mint.)

It is likely that the hubs were finished by mid-September 1794. The Liberty head, being the most important, would have been completed first and inspected very carefully for flaws, especially by Director Rittenhouse. Scot then began work on the eagle punch.

The letter punches used to put in the necessary wording on the obverse and reverse were executed by Frederick Geiger, who had been hired in early 1794 by Rittenhouse to improve the quality of the letter fonts then being used. Geiger, an expert in cutting type for books and newspapers, had been an indentured servant and had been brought over from his native Germany in the 1780s by Benjamin Franklin Bache, grandson of Benjamin Franklin. (Geiger did not stay all that long at the Mint, leaving in search of greater wealth. He sought to invent a perpetual motion machine, but died while working on it.)

Copper Patterns Struck

Scot's first obverse dollar die had no stars, and but a single specimen, in copper, is now known to exist. It was long thought that this pattern was struck from the unfinished regular dies, but it is now realized that a completely different obverse die was involved. In retrospect, of course, the discovery makes sense as it is very rare that an unhardened die is used to strike anything but the softest of metals; otherwise the die is easily damaged.

The copper patterns, of which possibly a half dozen or so might have been made for official inspection, were carefully examined and found wanting in the balance scale of artistry. One of the top officials suggested putting stars on the obverse, perhaps as a form of replacement for the rejected chain design on the 1793 cent. Fifteen stars, to symbolize the number of states then admitted to the Union, were added to the obverse die. This may have been attempted on the first obverse but almost certainly failed as it is very difficult to make changes on hardened dies, especially those which have been used to strike coins or patterns.

Illegal Standard Adopted for Silver

A new dollar obverse was soon executed by Scot, probably in late September or early October. All that was now needed to strike the first silver dollars was a sufficient supply of planchets for the coining press.

The first deposit of silver was made by the Bank of Maryland on July 18, indicating that Rittenhouse had made known, in May or June 1794, to the banking community and merchant/importers that deposits of silver would be accepted for coinage. The first such deposit was composed of French coin, a considerable part of which was of billon (a mixture containing less than half silver). Assayer Albion Cox said that it was worth $80,414.30-1/2; well, he said it was worth that much, but actually it was worth more than that—and thereby hangs a tale....

In the spring of 1794, when all was being put in readiness for the beginning of silver coinage, Assayer Cox carefully considered the strange fineness mandated by Congress (1485/1664 = .8924+) and decided that he really didn't think much of their work. Instead he felt that .900 was much easier to work with and the computations would be far less complicated. Cox approached Rittenhouse and persuaded him that silver coinage of .8924+ would turn black in daily use but .900 would not. Incredibly, the director accepted the bizarre argument and ordered that coinage begin at .900.

In an even more incredible move, and to hide the illegal standard, Rittenhouse accepted another of Cox's arguments: to leave undisturbed the gross weight of 416 grains. The dollar would now contain 374.4 grains of fine silver in place of the 371.25 mandated by law. This effectively changed the ratio of gold and silver from the legal 15 to 1—as adopted in 1792—to an illegal 15.13 to 1. (The change was not made just for the dollar, but for all silver coinage.) The secret was well kept, with only Henry Voight at first being told. In late 1794 the new melter and refiner pro tem, David Ott, also had to be informed. Neither Edmund Randolph (who replaced Jefferson as Secretary of State) nor Washington was told, both men learning of it in the autumn of 1795.

Supply of Silver is Obtained

On August 22 David Rittenhouse and Charles Gilchrist each brought two deposits of silver, in ingot form, to the Mint for coinage; the four deposits were probably made from melted-down Spanish dollars. The two Rittenhouse entries were for $1,706 and $295, respectively, while those for Gilchrist were worth $1,307 and $47. Why both men made such odd deposits on the same day is unclear, but they were close friends which might help explain it.

There are two possible reasons for the curious small deposits, both of which have merit. The most likely explanation is that each man was acting for a friend or relative who wished to remain anonymous. The second is that Rittenhouse wanted to have more deposits as this would impress Congressmen generally opposed to the Mint. On the day following the four deposits, the Bank of North America also brought in silver ingots, worth more than $22,000. This was the final deposit of silver in 1794.

The French coin was slow to be refined and the process was very expensive. In January 1795 congressional investigators were told that it had cost more than $2,500 to refine the Maryland deposit and the melter and refiner were not yet finished with it. The law required that silver be coined and paid off in the same order as deposited, but Rittenhouse realized that strict adherence to the law would seriously delay the start of coinage, hence the deposits by himself and Gilchrist.

Rittenhouse asked the Maryland Bank for written authority to coin their silver out of the proper legal order, which meant that the director's could be used first. Permission was quickly granted as Rittenhouse had explained the problems that were involved.

Silver deposits Nos. 2 through 5, those by Rittenhouse and Gilchrist, were almost certainly of ingots so that the first regular coinage could not be identified as coming from Spanish or French coins. In this way the first American silver dollar would not have an origin, but rather be of "new" metal, just like the nation itself. This kind of symbolism was quite popular in the early Republic.

Preparing Silver for Coinage

There were many operations to be gone through before the Rittenhouse and Gilchrist silver became coin

A beautiful Mint State 1794 silver dollar from the Boyd and Cardinal collections, much like those featured in the so-called Lord St. Oswald Collection auctioned in London in 1964 by Christie's. Two examples were discovered in a group of coins brought back from America in 1795 and kept in the same family ever since. As the faces of the dies were not completely parallel in the coining press the lower left of the obverse and the upper right of the reverse are lightly defined on all examples.

of the realm. After the alloy was checked for accuracy (*i.e.*, at the illegal standard of 900/1000), the ingots were melted and poured into new molds. The new ingots were gradually flattened between powerful rollers until the thickness of the remaining strip was that of the dollar itself. Planchets (blanks) the size of the dollar were now punched out.

Once the planchets had been made, there were still several operations before coinage could take place. The blanks were annealed (heat softened) before coinage so that they would take a good impression from the dies. One of the last steps was to put each blank in the Castaing machine, which rolled the planchets between a set of parallel bars, impressing into the edge the legend "HUNDRED CENTS ONE DOLLAR OR UNIT" and ornamentation.

The last step (before the edge was lettered) was to individually weigh each planchet; those which weighed more than 416 grains had a file applied to remove metal from one of the faces until the weight was correct. Those which were too light were rejected and later melted, to go through the process all over again.

Coinage of 1794 Dollars

On October 15, 1794, all was in readiness, and a ceremony was almost certainly held, celebrating the beginning of silver dollar coinage as well the regular coinage of precious metals in the Mint. Chief Coiner Voight delivered 1,758 silver dollars, all dated 1794. Voight also had on hand, but did not deliver, a considerable number (perhaps several hundred pieces) of coins that had not struck up well and would thus have brought discredit on the Mint had they been released.

The pieces officially delivered by the chief coiner had a characteristic well known to modern-day specialists

in the dollar coinage of 1794–1795. The lower left part of the obverse, as well as the corresponding area of the reverse, was weakly struck because the die faces were slightly out of parallel (from the first strikes onward; the only known 1794 trial piece from regular dies in copper shows this weakness). The weakness was also due to the use of a press designed to strike coins no larger than a half dollar. There was simply no way to get the necessary strong blow required to bring up the dollar design in full.[1] Chief Engraver Robert Scot had cut the dies in very shallow relief for just this reason, but the problem still remained.

Of the 1,758 coins delivered on that long-ago day, it has been estimated that fewer than still exist, mostly in lower grades.[2] Any 1794 appearing at auction is a signal event and usually brings out dedicated collectors who appreciate the beauty and history behind this famous coin. Rather than detract from the numismatic value, however, the weakness at the lower left is a mark of the problems faced by Rittenhouse and his fellow officers.

Every one of the dollars struck on October 15 was paid over directly to David Rittenhouse, although the Mint books showed for legal purposes that he was not paid until after the Maryland deposit had been cleared from the accounts in 1795. The director made every effort to spend the coins or exchange them for Spanish dollars so that as many persons as possible would learn of the new American silver dollar.

It has been speculated that it was standard policy at the early Mint to have a selection of coins on hand for sale to visitors at face value. English tourists in 1795, for example, are said to have been able to purchase various early U.S. coins, including dollars of 1794. It is known that at least by the late 1820s coins were furnished at face value to numismatists. Coins were sold to visitors until after 1900, although of course the kind of coins depended upon the year in which the visitor asked to purchase souvenirs and the supply of available coins on hand.[3]

Dollar Coinage Suspended

Rittenhouse ordered dollar coinage to cease until a better press could be found. To this end he contracted with

---

[1] These coins were struck by a screw-type press using manpower.

[2] By December 1992 Jack Collins had identified 118 different specimens by photographs; today over 130 have been thus attributed.

[3] When the Mint Cabinet was instituted in 1838, the curator had on hand coins of the preceding decade or two which were available for sale or exchange to interested collectors. Later, Proof coins were available at a premium. At the turn of the twentieth century, Mint visitors could buy circulation strikes for face value. It was reported at that time that Indian Head cents and gold quarter eagles were popular in this regard.

Samuel Howell, Jr., to construct a new and more powerful press for "dollars and medals in particular." It would not be finished for some months and in the meantime depositors had to be paid in silver coin. It was necessary to proceed with all due speed in order to encourage others to bring silver for coinage. The director did report, however, on October 28 that "a large parcel" of dollar planchets was on hand waiting for the new press.

Half dime dies were prepared in 1794 at some unknown time, but were not used in that year. Instead, they were held over until February and March 1795. The director had decided in November 1794 that the half dollar, for the time being, was to be the most important coin and ordered that preparations be made for a major mintage of this denomination. Coining had just gotten underway in late November 1794 when the rolling mills (which flattened the ingots) broke down. It required considerable time and trouble to repair the damage.

While the Mint was gearing up to renew silver coinage, public criticism of the Mint had grown to the point that there was a congressional investigation chaired by Representative Elias Boudinot of New Jersey. The congressmen were not told of the illegal standard although their final report made in February 1795 did suggest changing the standard to 900/1000 along with a corresponding decrease in the gross weight. The report cleared the Mint officers of incompetence, but did state that further work was necessary to bring the institution to a point where it could better serve the public.

The Draped Bust motif was first used on the silver dollar in late 1795. In 1796 the design was extended to the cent, half dime, dime, quarter dollar, and half dollar. It was not until 1800 that it was first used on the half cent.

New Dollar Press Completed

Chief Coiner Voight was able to resume half dollar coinage in January 1795, still using the dies of 1794. This coinage was very heavy, with about 270,000 pieces being struck by the middle of April. About 250,000 of these were dated 1795. A few were made after the beginning of May, when the dollar press was finally completed, but half dollar coinage soon trickled off to nothing. Half dimes were coined on occasion throughout the year, but were not of great economic value.

On May 6, 1795, the first delivery of silver dollars from the newly-completed press was made, amounting to 3,810 pieces. These almost certainly included, as planchets, some of the lightly-struck dollars from October 15 that Chief Coiner Voight had refused to deliver to the treasurer of the Mint. One 1795 dollar

is known with the clear undertype of 1794. More may have been made, but many of the originals were very weakly struck and the undertype would have been easily obliterated when recoined with dies of 1795. The belief that 1794 dies were used in 1795 is without foundation.

For reasons that are presently unclear, the first silver dollars reserved for the annual meeting of the United States Assay Commission were not laid aside until May 16, 1795, when three pieces were put into a special chest in the treasurer's vault. No meeting had been held in 1795 and none was to come in 1796. The first meeting, which tested all of the silver coinage struck since May 1795, was not held until March 1797. More than 100 silver dollars were tested at that time.

Dollars of 1795

There is little in the way of real variation for the Flowing Hair dollars of 1795. Two reverse dies have three leaves beneath the wings, in place of the normal two. Breen reports that many of the planchets used for the 1795 dollar coinage are defective in some way or other, which is understandable in view of the relatively crude operations of the early Mint.[1]

From May through October the coinage of silver dollars was heavy, but not all of these were the Flowing Hair type introduced in October 1794. At some unknown date, probably at the end of September, the design was changed to the Draped Bust obverse, which continued to be coined through March 1804. Existing Mint records are silent concerning this all-important change in design.

DeSaussure Named Director

Director David Rittenhouse, worn out by bouts of ill health and increasingly sharp criticism of the Mint, notified the president in the spring of 1795 that he would resign his post as of June 30. He was replaced by Henry William DeSaussure of South Carolina, an old friend of Washington's. DeSaussure did not arrive until July, but soon threw himself into the work. He expedited the

---

[1] In 1991 Q. David Bowers wrote several accounts concerning multiple specimens of 1795 Flowing Hair dollars that had been struck with silver plugs at their centers, possibly from adding metal to underweight planchets.

beginning of gold coinage, the first delivery of which, 744 half eagles, took place on the last day of July.

Upon his arrival at the Mint, DeSaussure was informed of the illegal standard for silver coinage then in use. The new director, as he later stated, decided to continue the 900/1000 fineness based on the great reputation and "weighty precedent" of David Rittenhouse. It was also a convenient way of shifting blame to someone else.

DeSaussure also took steps to redesign the silver coinage, though it is not clear just why this was done. He may have decided this for himself and then simply cleared the matter with Washington and Randolph, or the idea more likely came from one of these two men. Present thinking is that DeSaussure was responsible for expediting the change. It is likely, of course, that the change was made in order to blunt some of the criticism still being directed at the Mint, primarily by enemies of the Washington administration.

(The design change will be discussed in the section on the Draped Bust dollar.)

Henry William DeSaussure.

Technical Matters—Assaying

In the earliest days of the Mint, deposits came in a variety of shapes and finenesses, and it was the duty of the assayer to test the bullion to find out its value and fineness. Albion Cox became assayer in 1793, but it was not until the summer of 1794 that the first deposit of precious metal was tested.

Until 1835 the Mint assayer tested the fineness by the cupellation method, but in that year the humid system was adopted. A small amount of metal—only a few grains—was scraped from the bullion and the amount of pure metal was then determined.[1] There was some variation in the manner in which gold and silver were assayed.

The assayer did not necessarily test all incoming deposits because some, such as well-known foreign silver and gold coins, had a fixed value by law. The best known examples of these were the Spanish eight reales (dollar) and gold doubloon. French and Portuguese coins were also heavily deposited in the early days.

Once the assayer had certified the weight, fineness, and value of the deposit, the treasurer of the Mint issued a certificate, stating these facts, to the owner. On most occasions the true owner of the bullion would then wait

until coins were made and paid over to him. Sometimes, however, the deposit certificate would be sold to a bank or importer having need of coined gold or silver. The deposit certificates were also used as loan collateral.

The Melter and Refiner

When the assayer had finished with the bullion, it was turned over to the melter and refiner, an office not provided for in the original Mint law of April 1792. The position was, in fact, not created until March 1795, but from the summer of 1794, David Ott served as melter and refiner pro tem. In 1795 Joseph Cloud received the permanent appointment.

The melter and refiner first melted the bullion, although this had sometimes been done by the assayer in order to get good mixture for his tests, and then he added base metal (copper) or silver to bring the bullion to the desired fineness, usually a small amount below the legal standard. Ingots were now made, about a foot in length and from one to three inches in width. The thickness varied, but was usually about one-half inch. The denomination of the coin intended to be made from the particular ingot determined the exact dimensions.

The Coiner

Silver ingots were turned over to the coiner, with the usual receipts being given by all parties concerned. These receipts were preserved for the quarterly accounting so that each officer would have protection against theft or dishonesty on the part of another.

The coiner placed the ingots between powerful rollers and gradually flattened them until the desired thickness was obtained. The ingots were frequently cleaned and annealed (heat-treated to soften the metal) between rollings. The rolling mills in the 1790s were subject to mechanical breakdowns on a fairly common basis, and it was for this reason, perhaps more than any other, that coinage was interrupted in those years.

When the ingots had been properly flattened, the strips were "equalized" (made the same width and thickness) in the *drawing machine*. The strips of gold or silver were again heat-treated and cleaned and then planchets (blanks) were punched out in a special machine designed for just this purpose. The Mint had only one of these machines, capable of about 10,000 pieces per day, in 1795, but more were obtained as time went on.

The assayer had already made the ingots a bit on the low side for fineness. When molten silver or gold hardens there is a tendency for the richer solution to settle toward

---

[1] For those readers interested in the technical aspects of these two ways of assaying bullion, the work by Don Taxay, *The U.S. Mint and Coinage*, Arco, 1966, is highly recommended.

the center of the ingot; the punched-out blank would then have been too high in fineness had the melter and refiner not taken this precaution.

The planchets were weighed after being cut out to see if they were within the legal tolerances. If too light the blank was rejected, melted, and the whole process was started over again. Heavy blanks were filed down by adjusters, who worked in stuffy rooms with little ventilation; breezes would have disturbed the delicate scales required to determine exact weight. After 1862 only gold coins and silver dollars were adjusted by hand. The other denominations were simply remelted if they were too heavy or light.

After being washed and heat-treated once more, the blanks were put through the milling (Castaing) machine to have the edge impressed with the proper markings. Planchets were placed between two parallel bars while workmen cranked the bars in opposite directions. For the silver dollar this consisted of the wording HUNDRED CENTS ONE DOLLAR OR UNIT in capital letters with ornaments between words.

Before being struck, the blank was once more cleaned, but there was also a dilute acid treatment (usually sulfuric) to remove any surface oxidation. The blank was now sent to the coining rooms, to receive the impressions from the dies.

An early hand-operated coining press. (On exhibit at the Philadelphia Mint today)

Coining

Prior to 1836 the Mint used only screw presses, in which weighted arms were swung by strongly-muscled men. The screw was driven downwards with great force, and the planchet was transformed into a coin by being squeezed between the obverse and reverse dies. There was an improved automatic feeding mechanism for smaller coins installed in the presses in 1795, apparently at the suggestion of John Harper. Silver dollars, however, were fed by hand into the coining press from 1794 to 1804.

In March 1836 the steam press was introduced to the Mint but did not strike silver dollars until March 1837. (The knuckle-action steam press operates on a different principle than the screw press.) David Gilbert, an employee of the Philadelphia Mint, invented an improved press in 1858, while in 1874 Coiner A. Loudon Snowden devised additional modifications. Several technical changes have been made since that time, but in essence a device similar in principle to the steam coining press of 1836 remained in use for well over a century after, with later units being operated with electrical motors.

Draped Bust Dollars, 1795–1803

When Henry William DeSaussure became director of the Mint on July 9, 1795, in place of David Rittenhouse, he was faced with a situation few men would have wanted. Attacks on the Mint were still going on, fanned by political enemies of the president. There was widespread belief that the institution had not done its job in providing coins to the public, especially in the precious metal denominations.

There was a certain amount of criticism of the current designs on the silver coins (though modern collectors generally consider the Flowing Hair design a good one). DeSaussure expedited the first coinage of gold (the initial delivery of 744 half eagles was made on July 31) and soon concerned himself with the designs on the silver coinage.

It is not at all clear who instigated the design change although conventional wisdom, based on little more than the fact that DeSaussure happened to be Mint director at the time, says that he was responsible for the new head of Liberty, called the Draped Bust design by modern collectors. It may just as easily have been Edmund Randolph, who, as secretary of state, was the cabinet officer in charge of Mint affairs.[1]

Gilbert Stuart

In the 1850s Mint Director James Ross Snowden became deeply interested in the history of the Philadelphia Mint and interviewed many persons in order to learn as much as possible. One of the individuals with whom

---

[1] In numismatic research and publication, as in other areas of inquiry, one person's theory often becomes the next person's authoritative quotation and the third person's accepted fact. In the present book, R.W. Julian and Q. David Bowers have endeavored to use as much original source material as possible, in preference to existing theories.

he discussed Mint affairs was a descendant of Gilbert Stuart, the famed early American portrait painter. The Stuart family member told Snowden that his ancestor had designed the Liberty head introduced to the silver coinage in 1795. This is the sole known basis on which the Stuart name is attributed.

In the nineteenth century it was quite common for extravagant claims to be made about the doings of ancestors in the Revolutionary War era. Had all of them been true, General Washington would have had an army 10 times its real size and the British would have been defeated in a few weeks, not years. One of the most notorious of these claims was the myth of Betsy Ross sewing the first flag.

However, in dealing with the Stuart family tradition, we are more than likely hearing the truth as it was transmitted over several generations. It must be remembered that in the 1850s there was no great national interest in coins, although several hundred avid collectors were active whereas a handful had existed a decade before. The Stuart descendant would thus have had little incentive to fabricate a story, for the simple reason that little was to be gained and all to be lost should Snowden locate documentary evidence to the contrary.

Whatever the true course of events, it remains highly probable that Gilbert Stuart did redesign the silver coinage as was claimed by his descendant. It is, on the other hand, somewhat unlikely that DeSaussure was the one who approached Stuart to do the work; this would have been Edmund Randolph or the president, either of whom would have known the artist quite well.

It is not, of course, certain when Stuart began the task, but judging from other facts, he probably was at work on the designs by sometime in the latter part of July 1795. The artist realized that he was doing something that could affect how the nation was perceived at home and abroad and would have taken his time. He no doubt prepared several drawings so that the top officials would have something to choose from, rather than just one set. None of this work is known to have survived, however.

Some numismatists believe that Ann Willing (Mrs. William Bingham) was the ultimate model for the Draped Bust figure of Liberty, though this cannot be proven. It may well be that Stuart had her in mind for the profile, but barring further discoveries of documentary material, which is highly unlikely, the best that we can do is to say that this may be possible.

The Mint director was given an early look at the sketches because the engraver, Robert Scot, would have had to examine them also to see if they were suitable for coinage. DeSaussure and Robert Scot gave their nods of approval, probably for more than one drawing, and the several sketches were sent to the president and secretary of state for the final choice. Soon the decision was made

and one of Stuart's drawings was accepted as the new Liberty head.

John Eckstein

Once the drawings had been approved, probably toward the middle of August, they were sent to John Eckstein, who was called by one of his fellow artists a "thorough-going drudge" in his field. Eckstein, who was paid $30 on September 9 for his work, executed a pair of plaster models, not of the whole coin, but just the Liberty head and reverse eagle/wreath combination.

Until relatively modern times it was an accepted practice for artists to prepare relief models of designs for coins or medals as a guide to cutting the dies. At the present time composition models are made as the first step and then used to prepare the dies via a reducing machine. Some engravers in the past prepared their own plasters while others, such as assistant engraver Anthony C. Paquet in the 1850s and 1860s, had them done by specialists in the field.

Robert Scot

At any rate the models were delivered to Engraver Robert Scot for the necessary die work. (John Smith Gardner, an assistant engraver, had been at the Mint since November 1794 and during September would have worked on regular coinage dies while Scot prepared the new dollar hubs. Scot, however, would also have been involved in the regular dies as it is unlikely that he would have worked continuously on the new design without a break. The change was not that urgent.)

In preparing the new dies, Scot used the same technique employed for the Flowing Hair dies of 1794–1795. He first carefully cut a head punch for Liberty, as it was by far the most important part of the design, and then worked on the reverse hub for the eagle. The steel hubs were finished rather quickly, as it is believed that coinage of the Draped Bust dollar began about the end of September 1795.

Because Scot is thought to have worked slowly on most occasions, questions have been raised as to whether he did both hubs (Liberty head and eagle) that were necessary for the new dies. It is quite possible that John Smith Gardner did the reverse hub (the eagle) while Scot did the obverse. This would have still left Scot with the most important part of the work and the credit as well.

Coinage Begins

Whatever the precise way in which the hubs were done, they were soon completed and used to create new working dies for the dollar coinage. There would have been a test, to make certain that all was well, and then Director DeSaussure would have ordered formal coinage to begin. Considering the time needed to prepare hubs from

Eckstein's models, the most likely date for such an order was October 1, which would mean that 78,238 Draped Bust dollars were struck in the remaining days of 1795. However, this is mere supposition and the number may well be above or below that, depending upon the exact date that Draped Bust coinage commenced. Some estimates are less than 50,000 pieces.

For the reader who wishes to choose his own figure, the following list of deliveries for silver dollars in late 1795 will prove helpful:

September 12 – 4,260
September 24 – 4,000
October 3 – 15,000
October 7 – 6,000
October 10 – 14,500
October 17 – 23,368
October 24 – 19,370

The last-named delivery was the final entry for dollars during the year.[1]

By the middle of September, Director DeSaussure decided that he had heard enough criticism as well as family complaints to last him forever and informed the president that his resignation was being submitted. It was not to take effect until the end of October, thus allowing the government a reasonable amount of time to find a replacement. The Mint had not even begun to strike the new Draped Bust dollars when the director sent in his letter of resignation. President Washington must have now wondered to himself if the Mint would ever be a going affair.

In his parting letter to the president, dated October 27, DeSaussure reviewed the problems facing the Mint as well as those matters which he thought had been accomplished. He discussed the illegal 900/1000 silver coinage standard, almost certainly the first time that the president (and thus the secretary of state as well) had been informed of the matter.

It cannot have been an easy time for anyone at that point; the cat was out of the bag and something would have to be done—and soon. DeSaussure suggested that Congress be approached to change the standard to conform with practice but the Administration realized that this would

Elias Boudinot as depicted by J.W. Paradise in the *National Portrait Gallery of Distinguished Americans*, Vol. 3, 1836.

create additional problems, including lengthy explanations of why Congress had not been informed of the whole business in 1794.

Boudinot Named Director

During October, Washington managed to persuade Elias Boudinot to become the third director. Not only had this former congressman been in charge of the Mint investigation during the winter of 1794–1795, but he was also a distinguished statesman who had served as president of the Confederation government in 1782–1783 when the Treaty of Peace with Great Britain had been signed. His list of accomplishments was a long one, and the president could not have made a better choice.

On October 28 Boudinot arrived at the Mint and was immediately informed of the illegal standard for the silver coinage. The new director, known for his strict integrity, ordered that the 900/1000 fineness for the silver coinage be stopped at once and preparations made to resume the coinage on the legal standard, 892.4+/1000.[2] Boudinot

---

[1] Walter H. Breen uses the deliveries of October 17 and October 24, totaling 42,738, for the total of Draped Bust coinage, a figure which is also used by *A Guide Book of U.S. Coins*. However, as indicated, one guess is as good as another and few Mint figures or later interpolations from this era are precise. In general, the coinage figures used in the individual descriptions of early 1794-1804 varieties in the present book are, if yearly, taken from Mint records and, if within a year (such as Flowing Hair and Draped Bust within the year 1795) are from Walter H. Breen.

[2] QDB and Mark Borckardt note for the first edition: Analysis of individual 1795 die varieties to determine their specific silver fineness may be a way to determine which were coined before Boudinot's arrival. Similarly, the presence or absence of trace elements could link certain varieties (of any year) with each other via a common silver deposit source. It would not be surprising if such technology became available on a widespread basis in numismatics within the next decade or two. In other series (such as territorial gold), such analysis could indicate specific mine sources. [Indeed, by 2012 this has happened to a limited extent.]

also directed that all accounts be brought up to date so that his tenure of office would start on a clean slate and not be tainted by actions of the first two years of operation.

The officers made strong efforts to settle their outstanding accounts in the shortest possible time. By the latter part of November all was in readiness to resume the coinage of precious metals, both gold and silver. Boudinot ordered the coinage of half dimes as his first silver coinage. Nearly 34,000 coins of this denomination were struck and then delivered on November 26.

All seemed to be going well, but on the day following the delivery of half dimes, Assayer Albion Cox died suddenly of apoplexy (stroke) in the midst of a dinner party at his home. As this officer was vital to the operation of the institution, Boudinot had no choice except to shut down operations once more and order that Cox's accounts be brought up to date while a successor was being sought. All of this took time and it was not until December 12 that Joseph Richardson took his oath of office as assayer; he was to serve the Mint faithfully for more than 30 years.[1]

At the same time as Cox's death, Boudinot faced another problem: bullion deposits, especially of silver, were beginning to decline. With this falling off, creating smaller amounts of coinage, public criticism once more began to rise. The average person simply did not understand that the amount of silver or gold coinage depended solely on the amount of bullion brought to the Mint. There was no government bullion fund, due in part to the dispute over whether the Treasury should be over the Mint.

Coinage of 1796

The low deposits of bullion, coupled with Boudinot's desire to strike minor silver coins in 1796, led to a greatly decreased coinage of silver dollars in that calendar year (1795: 200,000+ vs. 1796: 72,920). Half dimes, dimes, and quarter dollars were also struck in 1796. The famous half dollars of 1796, however, were actually struck in 1797. It is generally believed that dollar dies of 1795 were used in 1796, though for how long is uncertain. Just under 5,000 dollars were struck in January and February 1796, and this just might cover the final coinage with the old dies.

While the varieties for the 1795 Draped Bust dollar are best described as minor (placement of the head on the obverse), the dollars of 1796 are somewhat more interesting in this regard. There are both large and small dates while the reverse lettering also has large and small varieties. There does not seem to be any chronological significance to these varieties.

The obverse of a 1797 dollar with the stars arranged 10 left and 6 right, BB-71.

The obverse of a 1797 dollar with the stars arranged 9 left and 7 right, BB-73.

There is speculation that John Smith Gardner, the assistant engraver, may have been responsible for some of the reverse dies, and the change of lettering may signal this fact. Gardner left Mint employ in the spring of 1796 but returned in the late summer for a few weeks while Scot was working on the quarter eagle dies.

Coinage of 1797

The minting of all silver coins fell to a very low level in 1797, well under that of the low production of 1796. Only 7,776 silver dollars were delivered by Chief Coiner Voight during the entire year, with nearly all of these coming during the months from May through August. All of the other silver denominations were coined, but mostly in small quantities as well. (The 252 quarter dollars struck in 1797 used dies of 1796 while half dollars dated 1796 and 1797 were struck in 1797.)

So little silver bullion was being deposited in 1797 that Mint officers, especially Assayer Joseph Richardson, went to great lengths to encourage depositors as well as bringing in silver themselves. In June 1797 even Vice President Thomas Jefferson brought 300 Spanish dollars to the Mint for recoinage.[2] Criticism was again building up over the low coinages. (The silver famine at the Mint began to end

---

[1] Joseph Richardson is perhaps better known to numismatists as one of the men who hand-engraved the large oval Indian Peace medals during the Washington administration. Some of these are hallmarked, proving his work.

[2] Philadelphia was capital of the United States at that time (until Washington, D.C. became the capital in 1800), and federal officials, who were nearby, paid more attention to the Mint than any time since.

toward the end of 1797 and by early in 1798 there was a sufficient supply.)

There are some interesting varieties of the 1797 dollar, mostly concerned with the number of stars on the obverse (either 9+7 or 10+6). All dies have 16 stars, which may indicate that no 1797 dollars were struck until after June 1, when Tennessee became the sixteenth state to be admitted to the Union. Of course the admission of Tennessee was a certainty for some time before that, and it is difficult to determine how far in advance the dies were made up. It may be that as few as 2,493 dollars delivered in 1797 actually bore that date; this is the coinage executed in August, when the last silver coins for the year were delivered.

It is probable that many of the known 1797 dollars were actually delivered on January 5, 1798, when the chief coiner brought 30,372 dollars to the treasurer. The maximum coinage from one press, per day, at this time was about 13,000 pieces (the figure is for cents and may be somewhat lower for larger coins such as the dollar), meaning that many 1797-dated coins may have been struck in 1797 but not delivered until the beginning of the new year. Struck coins were sometimes held for several weeks before delivery if there was not enough on hand to pay off the oldest unpaid bullion deposit.

As if the silver famine of 1797 was not enough of a problem, two other disasters struck the Mint during that year. The first of these was in the person of an important Philadelphia merchant and importer named John Vaughn, who had been a heavy depositor of silver in 1795. During 1796 he learned of the illegal standard in effect until October 1795 and calculated that he had been shorted about $2,300 on the payment in coin from his bullion deposits. This was a considerable sum of money in those days, and Vaughn demanded that the government pay him what was his legal and moral due. The Treasury refused to comply.

Mint Director Boudinot played a key role in this refusal to pay Vaughn the money he was owed. The director produced the novel argument that no crime against Vaughn had actually been committed because the 1792 law did not provide penalties for putting *too much* silver in the coinage. Boudinot noted that Vaughn had received all his silver back in the form of coins, it was just that there should have been more coins. Vaughn did not accept this twisted argument and applied directly to Congress for relief. It was not until 1800, along with a great deal of heated debate and delay, that he was paid.

The second major problem during 1797 was the return of the yellow fever epidemic, the first serious attack of the dread disease since 1793. The Mint closed late in August and did not reopen until nearly the end of November. Some coins of the precious metals were apparently struck in 1797, but not delivered until early in 1798, as noted

The first Bank of the United States (1791-1811). Later engraving when the building was used by the Girard Bank. (Engraved and printed by William Birch)

above. There was a considerable coinage of copper cents in December 1797, however.

Director Boudinot was so concerned about the shortage of silver bullion in particular that he searched for a reliable source and, at length, was successful. In April 1797 a formal agreement was signed with the Bank of the United States, a semi-official institution, to supply foreign gold and silver coins for recoinage by the Philadelphia Mint. It was also agreed that these deposits of foreign coins would not include the Spanish dollar because of heavy domestic use; however, this prohibition was only temporary and was later abandoned.

The problem with the Bank of the United States was that during 1797 that institution had almost no foreign silver coins to send to the Mint. In November 1797, however, the Bank of North America delivered nearly $30,000 worth of French silver, mostly in crowns of the old regime. It was not totally a blessing because this bank wanted their bullion returned only as silver dollars, as would most of the depositors during 1798 and 1799. This in turn meant that very little in the way of minor silver would be struck for the benefit of the general public.

Dollars of 1798 and 1799

Even though few of the smaller silver coins were to be made in 1798 or 1799, it was a mixed bag of complaints and benefits. The Mint could stay open because it was receiving deposits, but negative comments also came its way. Yet the minor silver coinage was not always a problem because there was a great deal of Spanish silver coinage in daily use in the United States, mostly in reales (12-1/2 cents) and 2 reales (25 cents). The situation was complex and without a ready solution.

Despite the large November deposit, others were urgently needed, and Director Boudinot decided to put his own money into use by depositing slightly more than 9,000 French crowns (worth $1.10 each). His $10,000 worth of silver was paid off in dollars, but by this time other deposits were beginning to arrive and the director used his money in other ways. In 1800, when fresh problems arose with insufficient deposits, Boudinot was to return with his $10,000.

The Boudinot silver, coupled with increased deposits, especially from the Bank of the United States (which now had a surplus of foreign silver coins), signaled the end of the famine. Coinage of dollars was very heavy in 1798 and 1799 (327,536 and 423,515 pieces, respectively). In 1799 the only silver coinage was of dollars.

As noted above, part of the January 5, 1798, delivery of dollars was probably dated 1797, but there is no certain way of determining the actual number included in this delivery. It is entirely possible that the entire 30,000+ coins of January 5 were dated 1797. Dollars of this date are simply much too common, in a relative sense, for only 7,776 to have been made, the amount reported for the calendar year.

It is not clear precisely when the scarce 1798 Draped Bust dollars with Small Eagle reverse were struck. They may well have made up a small part of the January 5 delivery noted above, or perhaps they were struck in the latter part of January. The mintage was certainly small, whenever the time of striking. Oddly enough, even for this coinage, there are two obverse dies, one with 13 stars and one with 15. The latter is the scarcer of the two.

The Heraldic Eagle Reverse Design

In 1796, as part of a general redesign of American coinage, the government ordered that the new quarter eagles, first issued in the latter part of the year, have the Heraldic Eagle reverse rather than the Small Eagle prepared by Gilbert Stuart a year earlier. Over a period of time all of the gold and silver coin denominations had their reverses changed to include the Heraldic Eagle.

The change to the Heraldic Eagle may seem arbitrary, but almost certainly was done to be in line with standard European practice. Nearly all of those countries used their coat of arms on the reverse of their coins. In the eighteenth century the coat of arms was not so much a sign of royalty as it was a symbol of national pride. The United States gold and silver coins followed Scot's design for the Great Seal of the U.S., in which the national arms were affixed to the displayed eagle's breast.

This decision was misunderstood within a few years. In 1807 when the silver was redesigned by John Reich (as dictated by Mint Director Robert Patterson), a new type of eagle was put on the reverse but the motto "E Pluribus Unum" was kept in the mistaken belief that the new eagle was merely a variation of the official one on the national seal. In the 1830s the 1807 error was rectified by removing the motto but it was gradually returned to the coinage beginning with the 1873 trade dollar.

The silver dollar's turn to get the Heraldic Eagle reverse came in the early weeks of 1798, probably late January or early February. Once more Scot cut a new hub for the eagle (the eagle was separate from the clouds and the stars were punched in by hand) and prepared the necessary working dies.

Dollars Used for Export

The heavy coinage of silver dollars in 1798 and 1799 had an unexpected side effect. It had been normal practice for importers of foreign goods to send Spanish dollars in exchange, but the availability of the American version made it easier to use the domestic product. Many of the American dollars were now sent to the treaty port of Canton in China to pay for Oriental luxury goods. These dollars rarely returned and were thus lost to the nation as coins.

American dollars also went to the West Indies where they were exchanged for Spanish dollars. It has long been an article of faith among numismatists that the trade was done for a profit, but this seems unlikely, especially in view of the fact that freshly-issued United States dollars were roughly equal in pure silver to the average circulating Spanish coin of 8 reales (dollar). It is far more likely that American silver went to the West Indies simply because that is where the Spanish dollars were to be obtained.

Some of the silver dollars that went to the West Indies would eventually return, though of course more worn than when they had left. This left the Orient as the real area that drained American coined silver from our shores, never to return. In 1804 the continuing loss would force the government to stop the coinage of dollars.

In 1798 and again in 1799 the dreaded yellow fever epidemic struck the Philadelphia area in all its fury. People fled for their lives but, even though the Mint was closed for several months in each of these years, coinage resumed soon after reopening with a minimum of trouble. Sometimes dies were used almost at random, thus confusing the order of striking for some issues, but in general the reopenings were more orderly than in 1793 and 1797. After 1799 the Mint was to close but once more (1803) for the terrifying disease.

Varieties of 1798 and 1799 Dollars

There are several varieties of the Draped Bust dollar (Heraldic Eagle reverse) for 1798 and 1799. For 1798 the differences are rather minor for the obverses, primarily consisting of wide or close dates and knobbed or pointed 9s. For the reverse we find the so-called *arc* and *diamond-shaped* star patterns, but these probably do not reflect policy but rather differing individuals in the engraving department helping Scot prepare the dies. One reverse die even has 10 arrows instead of the standard 13. Many of the minor details in the die—such as berries, stars, and arrows—were added by hand after the main design hubs were punched into

Detail of the date on a 1799/8 BB-142 dollar.

a blank die. It appears that there was one or more people lent to the engraving department from other areas of the institution as the need arose.

For 1799 we find the first overdate (1799/8) in the dollar series as well as similar varieties to those of 1798. One that does stand out, however, is a blunder consisting of 15 stars (instead of the regular 13) above the eagle on the reverse; the extra two stars were partially hidden by extra clouds, but not all that successfully.

Silver Dollars of 1800

For 1800 the silver deposits were at first heavy but as the year progressed the quantity of bullion brought to the Mint underwent a serious decline and the amount of coinage, mostly in dollars, went down accordingly. Despite the fall in bullion deposits, the number of dollars struck in 1800 was still substantial: 220,920. The early American economy, increasingly subject to the whims of European politics and wars, often showed sharp swings up and down in the early decades of our independence. During 1800 we were on a downward trend.

Perhaps the most interesting varieties for 1800 are the coins bearing a stray punch mark at the end of "AMERICA." The remaining effect looks like the letter "I", and the word seems to be spelled "AMERICAI."

Dollars of 1801-1803

Despite the virtual dollars-only policy for silver from 1798 to 1800, there was not all that much public outcry over the failure of the Mint to supply sufficient small silver coins to the economy. With the downturn of economic activity in the latter part of 1800 and perhaps some loss of small Spanish silver to the export trade, however, public criticism once more was on the rise. In fact, through 1803 the Mint was under severe attack in Congress over a number of matters, most of which the Mint could not control, such as the amount of bullion deposited for gold or silver coinage.

Even though most of the depositors wanted silver dollars in exchange for their bullion brought to the Mint, Director Boudinot was able to persuade some of them to take an increasing amount of smaller silver coins. Mintage of the dollar dropped to under 55,000 pieces in 1801. A

few thousand dollars' worth of dimes and half dimes were struck in this year but the principal non-dollar coinage in silver was the 30,000+ half dollars struck mostly in December. This was the first coinage of that denomination since May 1797.

For 1802 the situation was even more depressing for silver than in 1801, with only about 42,000 dollars delivered by the coiner. Boudinot continued to twist bankers' arms to get them to take the smaller silver coins they simply did not want. Their main customers wanted dollars, of which Boudinot did not wish to strike any more than necessary.

Interestingly, the dies for dollars show a distinct improvement in quality with differences mostly very minor for 1800 through 1803. There is an overdate, 1802/1, appearing on several different obverse dies, the last such event in the silver dollar series until 1880!

During 1801 came one of those semi-comic interludes which livened up Mint affairs for a few days. An inventor named Leslie had developed a variation of the old European roller die system (in which coins are struck by being squeezed between cylindrical dies rotated on their axes) and announced to the government that he had solved the problems of the Mint. Even President Jefferson, who seems not to have understood why the Mint did not strike more silver and gold coins, thought the invention a good one and sent him to the Mint for a practical trial.

What Leslie got, instead of a practical test, was a mock trial where the assembled officers very pointedly told him that his invention was useless, which was a fair statement. Leslie claimed that his method would speed up production, which was not true because the striking of the coins was only a small part of the overall operation to produce coinage. The inventor was told to bring in bullion, not dies, the next time he wanted to improve the institution.

There was a second affair which was not quite so funny. Benjamin Rush, signer of the Declaration of Independence and famous physician of Philadelphia, became treasurer of the Mint in 1797 after the yellow fever death of his predecessor, Nicholas Way. Rush and Director Boudinot had a mutual relative who died and whose original will left a considerable sum of money to Boudinot's side of the family. There was an all-night death-bed session with physician Rush, however, in which the will was changed to Rush's favor.

By 1800 the two men were barely speaking and Rush even went to the trouble of making formal charges against Boudinot, including theft of Mint property. The "property" in question was horse dung, which Boudinot had arranged to have hauled from the Mint for nothing. The result of the charges was an unpleasant inquiry, but nothing came of the hearings.

In 1805 Boudinot resigned. Rush applied for the post but was told by President Thomas Jefferson that another man, Robert Patterson, had already been chosen. The irony of this was that Rush had been offered the director's post in 1795 (after the resignation of David Rittenhouse) and had declined it at the time because of his lucrative medical practice. To add insult to injury, Rush loaned Boudinot some chemical textbooks to study when the latter became director in October of the same year!

After 1801 the silver dollar started on a roller coaster ride that did not end until suspension of coinage at the end of March 1804. Fewer than 42,000 silver dollars were struck in all of 1802 because of severe problems with declining bullion deposits.

Beginning in 1803 there was some improvement in the amount of silver being brought to the Mint, but in

Benjamin Rush.

the fall Boudinot attempted to stop the coinage of dollars and replace them with half dollars. No dollars were delivered from June 30 through December 12, although it is true that yellow fever interfered with production for several weeks. (1803 was the last year in which this disease forced the closing of the Philadelphia Mint.) The only silver coinage in this period consisted of half dollars, which Boudinot wanted the depositors to take instead of dollars, and a small quantity of dimes consisting of 1,660 pieces delivered in the third quarter of 1803.

Apparently there was enough pressure brought to bear on Director Boudinot that dollar coinage resumed in December 1803 and continued at a strong pace until March 27, 1804, when the last of the Draped Bust dollars was delivered. All of those struck in 1804 bore 1803 or earlier dates. (The 1804-dated dollars are covered in chapter 17.)

CHAPTER 2
ASPECTS OF COLLECTING
EARLY DOLLARS

MARKET HISTORY

Opportunities With Early Dollars

Made in three distinct design types and well over 100 die varieties, early silver dollars of the 1794-1803 years are fascinating to study and collect. (Dollars dated 1804 are treated separately and were not circulating issues, nor were the Proof "restrikes" of 1801-1803) The largest diameter of all United States coins, these "dollars of our daddies," as they have been called, offer an especially large surface on which to study die characteristics, a situation of which the collector of tiny half dimes must surely be envious!

A generation ago Walter H. Breen had this to say about the opportunities awaiting collectors in the early dollar series:

> Only in recent years have early silver dollars begun to attract collector attention as intense as the smaller denominations—despite the shortcomings of available reference books. Were some future researcher to produce a book on this series in a class with Sheldon on 1793-1814 cents, doubtless early dollars would eventually rival the cents' popularity.[1]

Russell J. Logan, an astute observer of the market and collecting scene, commented similarly:

> Bust dollars used to be king for collectors interested in early U.S. silver coins by die variety. I can remember thinking during the mid-1950s how wonderful it would be if half dollars were as organized as dollars were by Bolender. But the bottom line was a Bust dollar cost five times what a comparable Bust half dollar would demand. The world was full of Bust dollar variety collectors.... Today it is a totally different story. There seem to be only a few collectors pursuing the early dollars seriously.... With only half a dozen variety collectors pursuing these lovable cartwheels, there is an opportunity to initiate a collection not only challenging to complete but also financially rewarding.[2]

As early as 1927, B. Max Mehl noted in the first reprint of the Haseltine *Type-Table* catalog: "While practically every series of the American coinage has been covered by works of various kinds, the series of our early silver coinage have remained more or less unexplored."

While the followers of Morgan silver dollars are legion, and while Liberty Seated issues also have a large coterie of enthusiasts, only a few have signed up to follow the early Flowing Hair and Draped Bust coins, although the number now in the second decade of the 21st century is considerably larger than it was when the first edition of this book was published in 1993. I attribute this to several causes:

1. First, unlike the situation with large cents and Capped Bust half dollars of the late 1790s and early 1800s, silver dollars of that era are apt to cost hundreds of dollars just for a specimen in Very Good or Fine grade. In higher grades such as EF and AU, the values of large cents and early dollars draw closer together, except that prices of rare varieties of cents far outdistance those of dollars in any and all grades. As low grade cents and half dollars are inexpensive, the price of entry to those series is low; it costs little to break the ice, to get acquainted. In contrast, it would cost upward of five figures to make a beginning with an early dollar set.

2. There is a great camaraderie and fellowship among enthusiasts in the cent series, who belong to the Early American Coppers (EAC) club and read its interesting, authoritative, and informative newsletter, *Penny-Wise*. At intervals, including at the annual convention of the American Numismatic Association, EAC members gather and swap ideas and coins, and share their enthusiasm. Ditto with collectors of early Flowing Hair, Draped Bust, and Capped Bust half dollars 1794-1836; many belong to the Bust Half Nut Club (BHNC). The John Reich Collectors Society (JRCS) embraces all collectors of early silver, of the general era pre-1837, but articles about early silver dollars in the *John Reich Journal* have been relatively few over the years. Needed: even more camaraderie and inter-relationships among collectors, plus lively, interesting, and thought-provoking articles.

3. The classifying of early dollars by die varieties is easy and quite enjoyable for the years 1794 through early 1798, but for dollars of 1798-1803 (in particular those

---

[1] *Walter Breen's Complete Encyclopedia of U.S. and Colonial Coins*, p. 428.
[2] "Condition Census: Pre-Turban Bust Dollars." Article in the *JRCS Journal*, October 1990.

of 1798, 1799, and 1800), was tedious prior to the introduction of Bowers-Borckardt numbers and the Easy-Finding Guide in the first edition of this book. Unlike the situation with large copper cents in which many enthusiasts endeavor to obtain as many different die varieties as possible, this can be daunting when it comes to early silver dollars. A popular way to collect early dollars is to acquire one of each variety listed in *A Guide Book of United States Coins*. If the numismatic "bug" bites, you can go onward to collect by BB numbers. One advantage for the early dollar specialist is that rarity for rarity, key early dollars are far less expensive than are comparable large cents.

4. Few dealers have made a specialty of stocking early dollars by varieties. Part of the reason is that early dollars are very rare in comparison to early cents and halves. A new collector in the dollar series, who wants to buy quickly, has to be patient, as quality offerings are few and far between, and are mainly in auctions.

Today, in the second decade of the 21st century, early dollars are akin to the old "acres of diamonds" speech given to high school graduation classes; potentially valuable rarities exist, are often not identified, and await only an alert observer to find them. Curiously, the two leading certification companies—Professional Coin Grading Service (PCGS) and Numismatic Guaranty Corporation of America (NGC)—did not identify the die varieties of the coins they encapsulated in their earlier years in business. Therein lies an opportunity to find rare die varieties at generic prices—one of many in the silver dollar field.

Early dollars—representing as they do the largest silver denomination of the fledgling Philadelphia Mint and America's contribution to the crown-sized or dollar-sized coins of the world—are historical in their context, numismatically interesting in their diverse die varieties, aesthetically appealing in their design, and, if another reason to collect them is needed, they are relatively inexpensive *in relation to their rarity*.

It seems apparent that here, indeed, is a fertile field for the alert, astute numismatist—an area of collector endeavor that was largely overlooked until the 1990s, after which time dozens of new enthusiasts took up the specialty. Even so, excellent opportunities abound, and widespread market recognition has yet to come.

The First Study: Haseltine's *Type-Table*

Detailed descriptions of early silver dollar die varieties were first published in November 1881 in Capt. John W. Haseltine's *Type-Table of United States Dollars, Half Dollars, and Quarter Dollars*. Around 1876, Haseltine first contemplated writing an extensively illustrated book on die varieties of higher denomination silver coins, and he set about building a reference collection for this purpose. In 1881, he decided to sell his holdings, with the result being an auction sale catalog with the *Type-Table* title.

Haseltine had close connections with Mint officials of the era and acted as a conduit for the sale of restrikes, secretly-made patterns, and the like. His ethics seem to have been flexible. Haseltine swiped most of his *Type Table* information from dealer J. Colvin Randall, who in the 1870s had been associated with him in some business ventures. In his June 29-July 1, 1885 sale, W. Elliot Woodward, who was always quite free with his opinions, noted this:

John W. Haseltine was the pioneer publisher of information on early dollar die varieties with his 1881 *Type Table*. In 1908 he was a featured speaker at the American Numismatic Association's annual convention held in Philadelphia, where he kept the audience spellbound with his reminiscences of the older days. (Circa 1908 portrait)

In the collection of American silver coins following there are no duplicates; each piece is distinctly different, and the differences are very briefly noted.... In a private letter Mr. Randall writes me: "The idea of a correct work on types and varieties of United States silver dollars, halves and quarters, originated with me. H. and myself were to publish the work together, but without any consultation whatever with me, he issued for his own benefit what he styles the Type-Table Catalog."

For many years, Haseltine numbers were used by some numismatists to identify varieties of early silver dollars, although the vast majority of auction catalogs and price lists omitted Haseltine's specific die variety attributions. Other catalogs—certain of those issued by B. Max Mehl serve as examples—used Haseltine numbers sporadically.

M.H. Bolender's Landmark Study

In 1950, Milferd H. Bolender published *The United States Early Silver Dollars from 1794 to 1803*, an expansion and updating of the 1881 Haseltine work. In the introduction to his book, Bolender noted that he was able to find 114 distinct die varieties covering the 1794-1803 span.

Bolender, born in 1894, started in numismatics as follows, per his own account: "My first silver dollar, a 1795 with a hole, was acquired by me in 1906 from my grandfather, who gave me a bag of old coins, his collection, because

I made the best grades in school of the seven grandchildren. That started me collecting."

At the age of 15, Bolender became a part-time coin dealer. Later, he worked in construction, and in the World War served with the United States Army. In 1919, he began teaching school, a vocation he followed for the next 13 years, until his coin business grew to the point at which he could enter it on a full-time basis. Totally, he spent 57 years as a rare coin dealer, a tenure equaled by few others in the trade, and conducted 197 auction sales. He lived in Illinois, later (upon retirement) moving to California.

In telling of his life, Bolender went on to say that he became interested in early silver dollars by die varieties, but found that specimens described according to Haseltine numbers were very often attributed incorrectly. "In one large shipment of early dollars to me, *every* Haseltine number was incorrect!"[1] Dealers were often too busy to attribute early dollars by die variety, Bolender continued. Therefore, he took matters into his own hands, and using the Haseltine work as a foundation, prepared an easy-to-use reference complete with illustrations. By his own account, his data were based upon observing 5,000 coins over a period of 40 years. Actually, this amounts to only 125 coins per year, certainly a paltry figure. If the 5,000-coin figure is true, this explains why certain coins that Bolender considered to be very rare are rather plentiful today.

I saw Mr. Bolender at several conventions in the 1950s, before his retirement in 1960. He was a quiet man, but was always willing to reminisce about the "good old days." From 1961 to 1964 he conducted a column, "M.H. Bolender Writes," for *Numismatic News*. His death occurred on November 15, 1977, at the age of 83, in Spring Valley, California.

Where applicable, M.H. Bolender preserved in his book the numerical listings of Haseltine, simply converting H numbers to B numbers. Hence, 1795 H-1 in the Haseltine *Type-Table* is equivalent to 1795 B-1 in the Bolender book. In instances in which numbers assigned by Haseltine were proved by Bolender to be incorrect (in several instances, Bolender found that Haseltine had acted upon incorrect information or had misidentified as a new discovery an already known die), Bolender eliminated the old Haseltine number from his new B-number sequence. Hence, while among 1800 dollars, Haseltine had H-1, H-2, H-3, H-4, H-5, H-6, H-7, H-8, H-9, etc., through H-19, Bolender concluded that H-6 and H-7 were misattributions by Haseltine, as was H-9. Accordingly, the Bolender sequence omits these three numbers, and reads B-1, B-2, B-3, B-4, B-5, B-8, B-10, B-11, B-12, etc. This makes it easy to compare an old-time listing by H numbers, such as the 1945 sale of the F.C.C. Boyd Collection, with Bolender numbers.

In some instances, Bolender was conservative in his rarity estimates. He observed that "in some cases only one or two specimens are known to me, but I have declined to imagine that no other such coins exist." Bolender used an eight-point rarity scale, Rarity-1 through Rarity-8, but did not state what the numbers meant, other than R-1 coins were considered common, and R-8 ones very rare. It is possible that he borrowed Dr. William H. Sheldon's rarity scale, which also culminates with R-8, but if he did, he made no mention of it.

Rarity ratings, including these I give in this book, should always be taken with a grain of salt. There are always new discoveries to be made.

Bowers-Borckardt (BB) Numbers

In the descriptions of individual varieties of 1794-1804 dollars in this book, the BB number (for Bowers-Borckardt) represents the numerical designation of the variety. The assigning of numbers was done by me, with assistance by Mark Borckardt, who in 1993 was a numismatist on the Bowers and Merena Galleries staff.

The numbering system is arranged in approximate order of the manufacturing of the dies and/or the striking of the coins. The system is not precise—nor could it ever be—for often dies were used in a different order from their order of production. However, the system is more chronological than any heretofore utilized for the series. Collectors and dealers are invited to use it, if desired, in connection with attributing these early dollars. It has been a great success in the marketplace and in research articles since its introduction in 1993.

There are a number of other "B people" who are closely connected with this book, and with early dollars, including Walter H. Breen and Kenneth E. Bressett, not to overlook the historical contributions of M.H. Bolender. Thus, in your own mind, the BB can represent more than just two people, if you wish. Thus the BB designation cannot be confused with anything else.

Under the BB numbers, the numerical listings are open. If and when new die combinations are discovered, they can be numbered adjacent to related known varieties. Credit is due to Harry Salyards, M.D., who upon reviewing an early draft of the silver dollar section, suggested that it might be about time for a new classification system.

The structure is as follows:
1794: BB-1.
1795 Flowing Hair: Begins with BB-11.
1795 Draped Bust: Begins with BB-51.
1796: Begins with BB-61.
1797: Begins with BB-71.
1798 Small Eagle reverse: Begins with BB-81.

---

[1] QDB note: For this reason, Haseltine attributions appearing in pre-1950 catalogs must be considered with caution, especially when compiling population data of rare varieties.

1798 Heraldic Eagle reverse, Knob 9: Begins with BB-91.

1798 Heraldic Eagle reverse, Pointed 9: Begins with BB-101.

1799/8: Begins with BB-141.

1799: Begins with BB-151.

1800: Begins with BB-181.

1801: Begins with BB-211.

1802/1: Begins with BB-231.

1802: Begins with BB-241.

1803: Begins with BB-251.

1801-4 Novodels: Begins with BB-301.

WAYS TO COLLECT

Silver dollars from 1794 through 1803 (or 1804) can be collected in at least three different ways:

Collecting by Types

A set of early dollars by design type consists of just three coins: one each of the 1794-1795 Flowing Hair type, the 1795-1798 type with Draped Bust obverse and Small Eagle reverse, and the 1798-1803 style with Draped Bust obverse and Heraldic Eagle reverse. Such a set is easy to put together, and although it will not afford a great deal of stimulation so far as identifying varieties or becoming deeply involved in the series is concerned, it still can make a nice introduction to the series. Such a trio of early dollars can be expanded to form one of the specialized sets described below. Of course, such a set of three can also be acquired as part of an overall type set of United States coins from half cents to double eagles.

Collecting by Major Varieties

A popular pursuit two or three generations ago, less so today (because of the overall higher prices of all early U.S. coins), is the acquisition of one each of the major varieties from 1794 through 1803. Such a listing begins with 1794 and continues with 1795 Flowing Hair, 1795 Draped Bust, etc., through 1803. Often, the varieties listed in the *Guide Book of United States Coins* are used as a basis for forming a want list, as I noted earlier. The rarest major variety within the series is the 1797 with stars arranged 9x7, Small Letters reverse, followed by the considerably more expensive and more famous 1794.

Once the cost of a 1794 is absorbed, the rest of the set can be obtained relatively inexpensively, although a budget into four figures is required to acquire certain of the earlier issues in VF-20 grade. I suggest VF-20 to EF-40 as a goal. Such coins, especially EF-40, are sharp enough to show interesting characteristics, and yet cost much less than AU specimens. For all practical purposes, an MS-60 set cannot be collected, for certain varieties, including the

COLLECTING BY TYPES

The Flowing Hair type of 1794 and 1795 (1795 BB-13). This motif was also used on silver half dimes and half dollars.

The Draped Bust type with Small Eagle Reverse of 1795 to 1798, with most varieties dated 1796 and 1797 (1797 BB-71).

The Draped Bust type with Heraldic Eagle (also called Large Eagle) reverse used from 1798 to 1804 (1798 BB-108).

aforementioned 1797 9x7 stars, Small Letters dollar, are not obtainable at that level.

Among high-grade early dollars, say MS-63 upward, dedicated dollar enthusiasts have a lot of competition in the marketplace from investors and other buyers who do not focus on the characteristics of the dollars, but like to acquire "trophy coins." Since the first edition of this work, David Hall of the Professional Coin Grading Service (PCGS) originated the "Registry Set" program—whereby recognition and awards are given to those who build type sets, date runs, or other collections using PCGS-certified coins. The one with the most "grade points" wins. The PCGS website gives details. The Numismatic Guaranty Corporation (NGC) also has a Registry Set program.

1795 BB-21 dollar graded EF-40. Traces of original mint luster can still be seen in some protected areas. Coins in Extremely Fine grade are usually sharp enough to show all the design details but are priced far less than Mint State examples.

Collecting by Specialized Die Varieties

The third way is to collect by specific specialized die varieties as described in the present book. VF-20 to EF-40 is a good objective, for the grade permits study of minute die differences. Probably, no set will ever consist of evenly matched grades. Typically, commoner varieties are more readily available in higher grades than are rarer ones.

In general, under the Bowers-Borckardt numbers, various states are listed as Die State I, Die State II, etc. If there is a reasonable chance that a perfect-dies specimen may have been struck, it is listed as Die State I. If no example has been seen, the notation "May not exist" is given. If at a later date a specimen comes to light, there will be a listing to accommodate it; no need to rearrange numbers or use them out of sequence.

AN OVERVIEW OF THE SERIES

1794-1795 Flowing Hair Dollars

In 1794 the first silver dollars were struck. The mintage has been widely published as 1,758 specimens, a figure taken from the official Mint report. The design is of the Flowing Hair motif with Small Eagle reverse, similar to that used on the half dimes and half dollars dated the same year. The edge of this and other early silver dollars bearing dates through 1804 are lettered: HUNDRED CENTS ONE DOLLAR OR UNIT with ornaments between the words.

According to the late Jack Collins, who studied the 1794 dollar in detail, examples of this date exist to the extent of somewhere between 120 and 130 coins. Most survivors show considerable signs of wear, and all show at least some signs of light striking, particularly at the

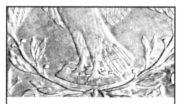

Two leaves below each wing as illustrated by a 1795 BB-14 dollar.

Three leaves below each wing as illustrated by a 1795 BB-18 dollar. The downward lines on the eagle are Mint-caused adjustment marks from the planchet preparation process.

lower left obverse and corresponding part of the reverse. In the early twenty-first century Martin Logies did extensive research on dollars of this date, finding much new information and also tracing the progression of certain specific coins in the marketplace. He was able to identify 134 different coins. Some coins that once had defects were found to have been improved in later years.

In American numismatics, the ownership of a 1794 dollar has always been a badge of distinction. Over the years the frequent auction appearances of this date have furnished occasions for numerous tributes to the coin's rarity and desirability.

The attractive Flowing Hair design was continued in use throughout most of the year 1795. Two main varieties of 1795 Flowing Hair dollars are listed in popular catalogs: the style with two leaves under each wing on the reverse, and that with three leaves, although other characteristics are readily discernible. Nineteen different die varieties are known of 1795 Flowing Hair dollars. However, most demand today comes from collectors desiring but a single specimen for inclusion in a type set. Those acquiring dollars by die varieties are few and far between, due to the basic high cost for even common issues.

Flowing Hair silver dollars of 1795 exist today in all grades. Most often seen on the market are coins in lesser conditions, Good through Very Fine, with Fine to Very Fine being average. Extremely Fine specimens are elusive, AU pieces with original luster are quite rare, and Uncirculated examples are few and far between. Only a few MS-63 or finer pieces are known.

In keeping with other early silver (and gold) denominations, early silver dollars often show mint-caused adjustment marks, due to filing of the planchets to remove excess silver prior to coining, to bring the piece down to the weight required by law. Adjustment marks usually take the form of parallel or crisscross grooves or scratches *recessed* in the surface of a coin, and are most visible near the rims and at the center. (By contrast, a scratch on a die used to strike a silver dollar will appear as a *raised* line on the finished coin.)

Striking quality varies from die variety to die variety. Some are more sharply impressed than others. One often-seen variety (1795 BB-27) has weakly defined details in Miss Liberty's hair. Some especially intriguing specimens of the 1795 date have a Mint-inserted silver plug in the center of the coin.

Attributing 1795 Flowing Hair die varieties is easy to do. On the obverse, the positions of the bust, hair curls, stars, letters in LIBERTY, and date numerals in relation to each other are determinants. On the reverse, such variables as the number of berries in the wreath and their positions, the letters of UNITED STATES OF AMERICA in relation to the leaves and berries, the number of leaves below each wing of the eagle, and other features provide keys to attribution.

After a short perusal of the Easy-Finding Guide and examination of the illustrations, each variety will come to life in your eyes and will be easy to identify.

1795-1798 Draped Bust Dollars
Small Eagle Reverse

Late in the year 1795 the Draped Bust obverse with Small Eagle reverse was adopted for silver dollar coinage. Artist Gilbert Stuart, contemplating the Flowing Hair motif, remarked in 1795 that "Liberty on the other coins had run mad. We will bind it up and thus render her a steady matron." Accordingly, Stuart created what we know today as the Draped Bust obverse motif.

The new design depicted the draped bosom of Miss Liberty facing right, the word LIBERTY above, the date below, and stars to left and right, on the obverse. The reverse showed an eagle perched on a cloud within a wreath composed of an olive branch to the left and palm leaves to the right, tied with a bow at the bottom. The inscription UNITED STATES OF AMERICA surrounds, with particularly wide spacing between the words. Just two die varieties are known for the 1795 year: BB-51 and BB-52. Each is easy to find.

This style was continued through early 1798 and is similar to that used on half dimes and dimes of 1796 and 1797, quarters of 1796, and half dollars of 1796 and 1797.

Particularly interesting is the 1795 BB-51 variety with small letters on the reverse. This identical reverse die was used with six different obverses dated 1795, 1796, 1797, and 1798!

All dollars of 1796 and 1797 are of the Draped Bust obverse and Small Eagle reverse type. Silver dollars of both dates exist in several varieties. A rarity is the 1797 issue with the Small Letters reverse, BB-72, struck from the durable reverse die just discussed, first used to coin 1795 BB-51. Nearly all specimens of the 1797 BB-72 dollar are weakly defined on

The long-lived Small Letters reverse as used on certain die varieties of 1795, 1796, 1797, and 1798, shown here on a 1795 BB-51 dollar.

the reverse, due to the shallow relief of the die after it had been resurfaced (relapped). No specimens of 1797 BB-72 exist above the AU level, to my knowledge, and the best grade usually seen is VF. However, since the first edition of this book there has been wide "gradeflation" in the marketplace and with the certification services. In many series coins that were once certified as high-level AU are now certified in lower levels of Mint State.

During the first part of 1798, two varieties of silver dollars of the Draped Bust type with Small Eagle reverse were produced, 1798 BB-81 and BB-82. Coinage was quite limited, as can be estimated from the fact that there are over 30 different die varieties of 1798 silver dollars, of which just *two* have the Small Eagle reverse style. 1798 Small Eagle dollars are scarce in all grades.

1798-1804 Draped Bust Dollars
Heraldic Eagle Reverse

The most often seen early silver dollars are those of the 1798-1803 years with Draped Bust obverse and Heraldic Eagle reverse. The new reverse motif, by Robert Scot, was first employed on the 1796 $2.50 gold quarter eagle and is an adaptation of the Great Seal of the United States. The Heraldic Eagle coin motif differs in that the eagle holds arrows in its dexter claw (observer's left on the coin) and an olive branch in its sinister claw (observer's right)—the opposite of the placement on the Great Seal.

The year 1799 saw the first overdate in the silver dollar series, 1799/8. Apparently an unhardened, unused 1798 obverse die was on hand in 1799, and rather than waste the die (or harden it and then use it with the 1798 die date—this was also an early Mint practice), the timely digit 9 was punched over the earlier 8, thus producing the overdate. Including the overdate (which occurs in three die varieties, from mating the obverse die with three different reverse dies), there are 22 distinct 1799 dollar issues. This year and 1798 seem to be the most common of all early dollars, and nearly half of all known silver dollars within the 1794-1804 range known today are dated either 1798 or 1799.

The Heraldic Eagle design was continued in 1800. Popular references list several

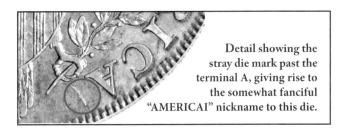

Detail showing the stray die mark past the terminal A, giving rise to the somewhat fanciful "AMERICAI" nickname to this die.

different variations within the year, including the curious AMERICAI variety which is not a diecutting error but, instead, has the terminal "I" in the form of a stray mark in that position. 1801-dated dollars include Proof novodels, popularly called "restrikes," although no originals from the dies were ever made

Among 1802 dollars the overdate 1802/1, known from five different obverse dies, is especially interesting. On many examples the undertype 1 is almost as bold as the 2.

Dollars of the year 1803 include those with small 3 in the date and one variety with large 3.

The very rare 1804-dated silver dollar, the most famous of all United States coins, was first minted for presentation and numismatic purposes circa 1831-1834 and was not intended as a regular circulating issue.

RARITY OF EARLY DOLLARS

Estimating Rarity

How rare is a given early silver dollar variety? In the present book I attempt to give rarity ratings for individual die varieties as well as for major dates and types (such as 1795 Flowing Hair dollars as a class). My estimates in the first edition were based upon the following: estimates of rarity given by Bolender and catalogers who have attributed coins in their publications; data compiled by Mark Borckardt and Bowers and Merena Galleries staff members using hundreds of auction catalogs, advertisements, and price lists (especially since about 1950, for as Bolender mentioned in his book, in earlier times dealers' attributions to Haseltine numbers were often incorrect); consultations with specialists; and my own observations. These estimates, as well as other information, have been reviewed for the present second edition.

In addition, I present what I consider to be good reasons why previously published Mint report figures and/or coinage figures in numismatic reference books for certain years, types, and varieties (*e.g.*, 1797 BB-72 with Small Letters reverse) probably are not correct.

Revised Mintage Figures

It is popular with numismatists to use published mintage figures as a guide to rarity. However, I suggest that in the field of early silver dollars, official figures are of relatively little use in this regard.

Each year the Mint kept production records of coins minted, and each year the Treasury Department made the numbers available in annual reports to the public. According to these figures, the following quantities of silver dollars were struck during the calendar years indicated:

1794: 1,758 • 1795: 203,033 • 1796: 72,290 • 1797: 7,776 • 1798: 327,536 • 1799: 423,515 • 1800: 220,920 • 1801: 54,454 • 1802: 41,650 • 1803: 85,634[1] • Total: 1,438,566

These are the figures that are published in the *Guide Book* and other standard references. I have no quarrel at all with the total of these numbers, and believe that during the time span in question, silver dollars totaling 1,438,566 coins were struck. Further, I am sure that 1,758 silver dollars must have been struck in calendar year 1794, 203,033 in calendar year 1795, and so on. However, I do have a problem with the assumption that the calendar year mintage figures equate to the dates actually struck on the coins.

For example, on the market today, the 1797 dollar is only *slightly* scarcer than the 1796 dollar. There is little difference in market prices between the two dates. Thus, it is not reasonable to assume that the mintage of 1797-*dated* dollars was only 7,776. It must have been more (or else the mintage of 1796-dated dollars must have been less than the government number). It seems to me that the original mintage of 1796-dated dollars and 1797-dated dollars must have been about the same.

As Dr. Robert Stark has suggested, it is possible—in view of the belief that large quantities of dollars were exported—that as the Mint struck silver dollars to order for bullion depositors, an exporter may have deposited a quantity of foreign coins or bullion, and received new dollars.[2] The freshly coined dollars, perhaps consisting of much or most of the production of a given die variety, could have been exported, never to enter domestic circulation, and to be lost to present-day numismatists.

In the early years it was Mint practice to keep using dies until they wore out or broke.[3] Thus, if the Mint had made up a quantity of 1797-dated dies in anticipation of a large coinage that year, but if silver deposits were insufficient, or there were other problems, and if only a few coins were minted, the serviceable dies still on hand at the end of the year would be used the following year. I believe that this happened in the majority of instances.

---

[1] 85,634 includes 19,570 struck in calendar year 1804 from earlier dated dies.

[2] Letter to the author, January 1, 1993.

[3] This policy was followed for a long time. For example, in 1827 an obverse die for the quarter dollar was made by overpunching an 1823-dated die still on hand but not used earlier. Circa 1798, the Mint used a 1795 half eagle obverse to strike coins with the Heraldic Eagle reverse (which had not been devised by 1795, thus creating a design oddity).

Of course, the Mint never stated that its production figures for early silver dollars referred to the dates actually on the coins. Numismatists have just assumed that they did. In the first edition this situation was explored in depth using the Economite Hoard (1878) and other sources, revisited for the present second edition. In *The Fantastic 1804 Dollar*, p. 50, Eric P. Newman and Kenneth E. Bressett said the following: "Obverse dies were used until they failed, and good dies were not withdrawn when the year of their dating had passed." In his *Encyclopedia of U.S. and Colonial Coins*, p. 428, Walter H. Breen stated this: "Mintage reported for 1801 consisted largely of coins dated 1800; similar backdating was the rule through 1804."

In summary, here are the official Mint figures for calendar year coinage (again) and, in parentheses, my estimates of the approximate actual mintage of coins bearing those dates.

1794 Mint figure: 1,758 (delivered); author's estimate: No change.

- 1795 Mint figure: 203,033; author's estimate: 390,000.
- 1796 Mint figure: 72,290; author's estimate: 75,000.
- 1797 Mint figure: 7,776; author's estimate: 60,000.
- 1798 Mint figure: 327,536; author's estimate: 235,000.
- 1799 Mint figure: 423,515; author's estimate: 395,000.
- 1800 Mint figure: 220,920; author's estimate: 100,000.
- 1801 Mint figure: 54,454; author's estimate: 35,000.
- 1802 Mint figure: 41,650; author's estimate: 80,000.
- 1803 Mint figure: 85,634; author's estimate: 60,000

The years 1797, 1798, and 1800 in particular are interesting relative to the use of dies in year(s) other than indicated on the dies.

CHAPTER 3
RARITY AND ITS RELATION TO PRICE

The Universal Rarity Scale

The Universal Rarity Scale uses a simple geometric progression of numbers, as 1, 2, 4, 8, 16, 32, etc. (see the right-most of each number pair), rounded off for simplicity for the higher numbers. Introduced in 1993 this has been widely used in various publications since that time. It is not copyrighted.

Universal Rarity Scale-0 = None known
URS-1 = 1 known, unique
URS-2 = 2 known
URS-3 = 3 or 4
URS-4 = 5 to 8
URS-5 = 9 to 16
URS-6 = 17 to 32
URS-7 = 33 to 64
URS-8 = 65 to 124
URS-9 = 125 to 249
URS-10 = 250 to 499
URS-11 = 500 to 999
URS-12 = 1,000 to 1,999
URS-13 = 2,000 to 3,999
URS-14 = 4,000 to 7,999

Population Estimates

Drawing from authoritative catalogs, population reports (if identifiable as to rarity, the case with certain *Guide Book* varieties such as those of 1794 and 1797), contributions by specialists, and other sources, I have derived estimates of the population of each variety in several different grade ranges. A typical variety is accompanied by an estimate summary similar to the following:

MS-65 or better: 0 (URS-0)
MS-64: 0 (URS-0)
MS-63: 1 to 2 (URS-1)
MS-60 to 62: 2 to 5 (URS-2)
AU-50 to 58: 10 to 20 (URS-5)
VF-20 to EF-45: 250 to 450 (URS-10)
G-4 to F-15: 100 to 200 (URS-8)
Total for all grades combined: 350 to 675 (URS-10)
Estimated Total Condition Census: 63-60-60-55-55-55

Estimated Condition Census

A Condition Census rating has been given for each silver dollar variety. The rating consists of listing the numerical grading of the top six specimens known, reliably reported to me, or reasonably estimated to exist in private hands. Early dollars in institutional collections (the American Numismatic Association, American Numismatic Society, Smithsonian Institution, etc.) are not included.

In some instances the Condition Census will include more than six, if the lowest number in the range has multiple coins. I will give illustrations of each instance:

1. In this hypothetical instance, it is believed that the finest known specimens of a given variety grade AU-55, AU-50, AU-50, EF-45, EF-45, EF-45, EF-40, EF-40, EF-40, VF-30, and so on downward. The Condition Census would be expressed as follows of this variety: 55-50-50-45-45-45, which relates the grade of the top six coins.

2. In this next hypothetical instance the finest known examples of a given variety are AU-55, AU-50, AU-50, AU-50, AU-50, followed by 22 grading EF-45, followed by 30 in EF-40 grade, and so on downward. In this instance the Condition Census would be expressed as follows: 55-50-50-50-50-45 (multiples).

The Condition Census has the advantage that the collector can determine at a glance the range and availability of the finest known pieces. It has the disadvantage that grading interpretations vary, and what one cataloger or expert might call MS-60, another might call AU-55 or even MS-63. Because of this, the grades, including those given by the certification services, must not be considered as absolute. Time and time again I have seen coins of the same grade and certified by the same grading service, put side by side, and to my eyes one would be materially nicer than the other.

Each year, estates come on the market, old-time collections are broken up, and coins otherwise appear that have not been available for years. Even more relevant, coins that have never been attributed will come under the scrutiny of someone familiar with die varieties, and will be identified.

Because of these, over a period of time the Condition Census numbers will rise, as more high-grade pieces are found. If EF-40 represents the lowest grade in a Condition Census today, perhaps a decade from now the lowest grade will be EF-45 or AU-50. The same is true of rarity ratings. If more coins are discovered, the rarity ratings will become more generous. Certain coins described today as having two or three known may be properly described as having four to six known later.

In other words, take my numbers with a degree of skepticism, with a grain of salt.

RARITY VS. PRICE

Factors Affecting Pricing

Early silver dollars exist in varying degrees of rarity. The pricing of a given early dollar is affected by several factors. Among those are the following:

1. Rarity as a date: If a coin is basically rare as a date—and dollars dated 1794 and 1804 are prime examples—pieces will bring strong prices as there is a great demand from date collectors.

2. Major varieties: In addition to collecting dollars by dates, many numismatists also aspire to own *major* varieties. Thus, for the 1795 coins they desire to own two examples, one of the Flowing Hair design and one of the Draped Bust type. They are not particularly concerned with subdivisions within those varieties, or whether a 1795 Flowing Hair is, for example, a BB-15 or a BB-21. All they want is a Flowing Hair coin. Such collectors often employ the *Guide Book of United States Coins* to formulate a want list as to what major varieties to acquire. Accordingly, any variety listed in the *Guide Book* draws a larger following than one that is not.

An excellent example of this is provided by the year 1797. In this instance there are three varieties known, BB-71, BB-72 and BB-73. The *Guide Book* lists three as being major. These match up with the three Bolender varieties. Accordingly, all three varieties of the 1797 date are in strong demand.

On the other hand, just two varieties are listed of 1795 Flowing Hair dollars, the style with two leaves beneath each wing of the eagle and the style with three leaves. Further subdivisions are not considered, even though 19 different die varieties of 1795 Flowing Hair dollars are known.

3. Die varieties: The dedicated specialist in early silver dollars seeks to acquire one of each BB die variety. This may or may not (and usually does not) include individual die state subdivisions within a variety, but certainly includes one of each Bolender number. Accordingly, a variety which is unique or of which just a few are known, say up to a dozen or so, will bring a strong price based upon the demand by variety collectors.

4. Other considerations: Notoriety enters the pricing structure of several early silver dollar varieties. In addition to being rare as a date, 1794 dollars are of the first year of issue. Over the years the 1794 dollar has received much publicity, thereby enhancing its desirability. Two researchers, the late Jack Collins and also Martin Logies have created specialized studies for this date alone.

The 1795 Draped Bust dollar with Small Eagle Reverse has a special demand attached to it as it is the first of its design type, a motif continued through early 1798. Similarly, the 1798 Draped Bust obverse with Heraldic Eagle reverse is more popular than would otherwise be the case as it is the first of its design type. The 1800 AMERICAI variety, with the extra "I" being caused by a stray mark from a punch, has always been in exceptional demand as it seems to be curious and interesting to many observers. The 1801-2-3 "restrikes" (actually novodels) have drawn an enthusiastic but limited following, and have brought high prices, because they represent an unusual opportunity to acquire an early-dated dollar with a high grade Proof finish.

The 1804 dollar is in a category all by itself. Fame has propelled it to the front rank of American rarities. More words, paragraphs, columns, and pages of print have been expended on the 1804 silver dollar than on any other United States coin rarity in any series. Indeed, two books have been written about this coin! Over the years, numerous collectors and dealers who do not specialize in early dollars by dates or die varieties have sought to acquire an example of the prize 1804 just to have it for enjoyment and display — a "trophy coin."

CHAPTER 4

CHARACTERISTICS OF EARLY DOLLARS AND DIES

DIE STATES AND CHARACTERISTICS

Die States

The term *die state* refers to the condition of the dies when a particular piece was struck. Specific considerations for certain die states include these: 1. The presence of pitting or rust, which on a coin appears *raised,* sometimes as a rough or grainy patch. In the humid Philadelphia summer, a die not protected by grease could rust in a matter of days.

Detail of a 1796 BB-65 dollar showing raised areas from rust on the die at ER (AMERICA) and also a piece that fell from the die.

2. Die finishing marks, which include file marks and polishing marks, are often visible as *raised* lines near the dentils. Sometimes stray finishing marks appear elsewhere. As a die was used, these marks wore away gradually.

3. Repunching marks made when a design element such as a date numeral, star, or inscription letter was punched more than once, with the second punch being slightly misaligned, as to show a doubling on the finished coin. Sometimes, repunching was done to correct an error as with the 1795 BB-21. Often such repunching traces wore away as the die was used. An example of a die-punching error is furnished by 1798 BB-118, which has the N in UNITED over a previous erroneous I.

4. Die cracks. Cracks in a die—ranging from tiny hairline cracks extending for a short distance, to massive cracks bisecting a coin, to rim breaks—usually start small,

Stray die finishing mark near a star in the left obverse field of a 1795 BB-20 dollar.

On the 1795 BB-21 dollar the 7 in the date is punched over an earlier erroneous 1.

and increase in length and prominence. Often (as in the case of 1800 BB-194, the so-called *Dotted Date*), a die crack would begin as one or a series of dots or small lumps. A die with a crack just beginning indicates an earlier state than one with the same crack more advanced, or with additional cracks. Dies deteriorated for several reasons, including being used extensively. If a die was improperly hardened during the die preparation process, it might crack after only a few coins were struck from it, thus creating a rare die variety. Theoretically, a die could acquire cracks during the preparation process, including improper hard-ening; in such an instance,

Detail of an 1799 BB-154 dollar showing a die crack at the border on the left side of the reverse.

Detail of a 1800 BB-196 dollar showing a clash mark below Liberty's neck at the top of the bosom, a feature transferred from the reverse die.

all coins struck from the die, from the first piece onward, would show the crack(s). If a piece of metal falls away from a die it is called a die break. *Caveat:* If a die with one or more cracks is relapped, these cracks may be removed, or may be diminished in prominence.

5. Die clashing. Often during the course of striking silver dollars—in fact, beginning with the initial issue in the series, 1794—the obverse and reverse dies would come together without an intervening planchet. If the impact was severe enough, the harder of the two dies (no two steel dies had exactly the same hardness) would be impressed into the softer die, and lettering, designs, etc., usually in fragmentary form, would be impressed into it. Thus, a die state of 1800 BB-192 has the incuse letters MERIC visible on the right of the obverse between the stars and the border, clashed impressions from these letters as part of AMERICA on the reverse. The letters MERIC were incuse in the reverse die; thus, in clashed form, they were

in relief on the obverse die. As they were in relief on the obverse die, they were impressed into the coin incuse (intaglio, or recessed), as noted. If a feature was incuse on a die to begin with, such as the crevices or folds in the drapery on Miss Liberty's bust, then in clashed form they would appear in relief on a coin. This happened on 1800 BB-193, Die State III, which exhibits raised traces of the drapery, now on the reverse of the coin at F in OF. Numerous other examples could be cited. Die clashing was a prime reason to relap or resurface a die.

6. Die faces not parallel. If a pair of dies was put into the coining press, with the faces not parallel, then the upper and lower dies would be closer together on one side and wider apart on the other. Coins struck from such misaligned dies would be sharper and with more prominent edge dentils (toothlike rim projections) where the dies were closer together, and lightly struck and indistinct where the dies were more widely separated. This situation occurs several times among early dollars, the most famous instance being that of *all* silver dollars dated 1794. The very rare 1798 BB-91 is another example.

Detail showing weak stars at the lower left of a 1794 dollar from the dies not being parallel in the press. All dollars of this date show this feature.

7. Resurfacing or relapping. Sometimes to extend its use, a die was resurfaced. The die used to coin 1798 BB-101 shows just 10 arrows, but earlier, when used to coin 1798 BB-96, the same die had 10 arrows and two "sticks" (arrows without heads). The die was ground down (called "relapping"), and certain shallow features were removed, including the two sticks. Relapping also caused the dentils to be smaller (and the rims of resultant coins to be lower, thus causing the coins to wear faster), and stars to be irregular or "spidery."

8. Strengthening and altering. In some instances, die features were strengthened or augmented. For example, the obverse die used to strike 1795 BB-25 had the tail of the R in LIBERTY strengthened with an engraving tool after relapping had removed some of what was already a defective R (struck from a broken punch).

9. Miscellaneous flaws. Often, early dollar dies had small flaws in certain areas, often around the borders. These were caused by improper finishing of the die, imperfections in the die steel, stray marks from an engraving tool or piece of metal (believed to be the cause for the extra I in the inscription AMERICAI on an 1800 dollar die), or in other ways. Such flaws, indented in the die, appear raised on the coins struck from

such a die. Often, such flaws wore away as the die was used. In other instances, flaws indicated die weakness and furnished the genesis for a die crack.

About Bifurcation

The term *bifurcated* was used extensively by Bolender, and refers to letters and numerals around the periphery of an early dollar which seem to be split at their bases.

Thus, the letter I, if bifurcated, will have the bottom of the vertical shaft split or forked.

During the striking process, the metal that starts to fill up the vertical shaft of the I will continue to expand outward (toward the rim) along that shaft, leaving the base of the upright unfilled. If the dies come no closer together after this happens, the letter I (in this example) will appear bifurcated. The bases of other letters will remain incomplete as well, the degree of bifurcation depending upon the depth of the strike and the shapes of the letters. Those letters with long, vertical uprights will be affected the most, and the effect will be more noticeable if there are serifs struck up at their bases.

On the other hand, if the strike is adequate and the dies continue to come closer together, the base of the shaft will ultimately fill up with the silver alloy metal, and the planchet will mold itself to the design in the dies, and outward expansion will be inhibited.

A variant type of bifurcation was caused by metal flow, when a planchet with an insufficiently upset rim (a too-flat slope up to the rim raised during the lettering of the edge on the blank planchet), or too loosely fit within the collar, was struck, and the metal in the planchet flowed outward toward the collar, especially if the strike was not deep enough to fully bring up all aspects of the design, and to fill all the die recesses. Any characters in the die near the border—and this usually meant stars, letters (especially letters with long, vertical shafts), or date numerals—would then sustain flow marks, or bifurcations, at the inner edges of the characters. Sometimes, the bifurcation process made the

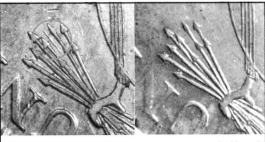

The same die was used to coin 1798 BB-107 (left) and 108. Notice the light stick or headless arrow (circled). On 1798 BB-108 (right) the die is lightly relapped removing the headless arrow.

letters around the border appear ornate or fancy, as in examples of 1799 B-8 [BB-165] examined by Bolender and found to have the letters of the word LIBERTY with extensive bifurcations. As one of many coins that could be cited, an example of 1795 BB-18 studied by the author had beveled, flattened innermost star rays, and bifurcated tops to the 1 and 9 in the date. Often, stars appear

Bifurcated letters on a 1799 BB-153 dollar.

lopsided, with the point toward the center of the coin shortened, due to the bifurcation process.

Apparently, Bolender had no clue as to what bifurcation marks really were. He must have considered them to be a product of die deterioration or perhaps repunching, for in some instances he assigned a separate sub-variety number to coins with bifurcation marks. This does not detract from his fine work, as state of the art research concerning coining processes was not sophisticated in 1950. An example is provided by Bolender's 1799 B-10 (BB-163), which has no bifurcation marks, and his Bolender-10b, which is from the same dies, "and with the letters much bifurcated."

As we understand the minting process today, a planchet which had a properly upset rim and/or was tightly fit into the collar would have minimal metal flow near the rims, and no bifurcation marks would result. If a planchet had an insufficient upset rim and was significantly smaller in diameter than the collar, then it was a candidate for bifurcation marks, as metal flow occurred in an outward direction from the center. If such a planchet was loosely placed in the dies, close to the collar on one side and distant from it on the other side, then bifurcation marks would occur on the side most distant from the collar—as the metal flow to the collar was greatest there.

Stack's catalog of the sale of the W. Earl Spies Collection, 1974, offered a specialized cabinet of early dollars described very carefully. Among the 1801-dated dollars were these three coins:

1801 [BB-211] B-1. Wide date. Small dot next to center dot. Most of the letters are not bifurcated. VF, delicate toning.

1801 [BB-211] B-1a. Dies as above. The letters are lightly but mostly bifurcated. VG.

1801 [BB-211] B-1b. Letters not bifurcated (per Bolender, in reference to his observations), but there is now a crack from the wing tip through "STA" through the clouds to first "A" of AMERICA. "Waves" through "ERICA." Fine, with some scratches across the obverse.

Per the preceding, it is apparent that a particular variety of 1801 dollar was struck with most letters *not* bifurcated. Then, a specimen was struck from the same dies, with most letters bifurcated. Then, the reverse die cracked, and in this *later* use, the coin struck from the dies was *not bifurcated.* In other words, bifurcation had nothing to do with the life or wear of the dies.

Sometimes a die pair would be used to strike many loose-fitting planchets, and many coins with bifurcated features would result. Other times, a die pair would be utilized to strike closely-fitting planchets, with no resultant bifurcation. Contrary to what Bolender stated, *the absence or presence of bifurcation does not constitute a separate die variety, or even a consistent die state.*

The same process that caused bifurcation in the vertically-oriented elements—border letters, stars and numerals—sometimes affected horizontal parts of letters and numerals as well. If at the border, the metal flow was "sliding" outward from the center, it might skim over a thin horizontal element in the die (such as the thin line at the bottom or top of the letter E or D) and fill in the serifs, but not the thin line. Thus, for example, certain specimens of 1798 BB-94 appear as if the tops of E and D in UNITED are broken; it is logical, and is a fact, that the vertical elements of these same letters are heavily bifurcated.

With regard to stars, the bifurcation process sometimes makes the point facing toward the center of the coin seem smaller or shortened. On some strikings of the Heraldic Eagle reverse, the bottoms of the stars thus appear smaller or even defective, an idiosyncrasy of the striking of the particular coin involved—and a situation not related to die preparation or a die state.

Changing Die States

As a die was used, it became worn. Typically, over a period of time, several things would happen:

1. Minute features of a die's surface, such as tiny flaws, file marks, light repunchings, etc., would wear away.

2. Stress marks would appear, most commonly in the form of die cracks, small at first, and usually starting at the border dentils and, over a period of time, extending inward, perhaps joining other cracks.

3. As a die began to fail, the cracks would become larger, and certain areas of the die would begin to sink, often at the centers, resulting in mounds, lumps, or bulges. About this time, the die would be discarded.

For a hypothetical variety of early dollar, a sequence of die states might have a history as this:

DIE STATES:

Die State I: Perfect obverse and reverse dies. No cracks.

Die State II: Perfect obverse die. Reverse develops small crack at rim above I of AMERICA.

Die State III: Perfect obverse die. Rim crack at I extends through adjacent R in AMERICA, and continues to touch eagle's wing.

Die State IV: Obverse die crack from rim through the middle of the 2nd star (stars are counted clockwise, beginning at the left of the date), continuing to edge of Miss Liberty's hair. Reverse die as III.

Die State V: Obverse die as IV. Reverse die is cracked across.

Die State VI: Obverse die as IV. Reverse with bulging at center, die cracked across, and several other cracks developing. Latest state of the dies.

When a coin of this variety is found, it may be examined to determine its die state.

Die State I represents the obverse and reverse in the condition when the first coins of the variety were struck. Unless one or both dies were broken before the first coin was struck, Die State I shows no cracks or other breaks. Die flaws, such as file marks, repunchings, etc., will be sharper in Die State I than in later states.

Die States II, III, IV, etc., represent examples of coins seen in various later stages of the life of the obverse and reverse dies.

While die state information furnishes a handy guide to various steps leading to a die's destruction or abandonment, in practice, dies did not deteriorate in finite steps, but on a continuum. Thus, one might find a coin which has, for example, the reverse die cracked across, plus one tiny die crack developing below the eagle's tail. A check with the listing will reveal that this is between Die State V and Die State VI. You have your choice of simply calling it Die State V, or being more precise, such as "an intermediate die state between V and VI, showing a small additional crack developing below the eagle's tail." In practice few catalogers are this sophisticated. In fact, for expediency's sake, most catalogers list just the variety and omit the die state. If *all* minute die states were listed, especially for a variety known to have many cracks in its later states, the listing might well run from Die State I to Die State XX or higher! In practice, only a few intervals are listed.

Die Combinations

Die combinations, called matings or marriages, saw the pairing of an obverse die with one or more reverses, or vice-versa. If a die was particularly durable, it might outlive two, three, or more mates. One particularly robust reverse die was mated with obverse dies dated 1795, 1796, 1797, and 1798!

In some instances, a die—a hypothetical obverse, for example—was mated with a reverse die, coins were struck, and then it was removed from the die and put in the die vault; let's call these the BB-1 variety. Later, it was mated with another reverse die, and more coins were struck; BB-2. Still later, it was mated with the first reverse die, and additional BB-1 pieces were made. For starters, it is known that varieties BB-1 and BB-2 exist. However, examination revealed that the reverse of certain BB-1 coins were in Die State I, and others were in a much later die state, while BB-2 coins, using the same reverse die, were in an intermediate die state. The

1802/1 BB-234 overdate.

only conclusion: BB-1 coins were struck, then BB-2 coins, then more BB-1s.

Research concerning die progression and die states of early dollars is ongoing. As interest in the series increases, and detailed notes and observations are kept concerning minute die differences, it will be possible to determine in what order many early varieties were struck. There is ample precedent for this in the series of U.S. large cents of the years 1793-1814, which have been analyzed in detail by many specialists over a long period of years.

Coin and Striking Defects

Defective planchets and/or problems in striking (except for misalignment of dies) do not constitute die states. If a coin is weakly struck at the centers, due to inadequate die spacing, this is considered to be a weak or light strike, not a specific die state.

If a planchet was filed during the preparation process, to remove excess metal to bring the disc down to the proper weight, the resultant parallel grooves indented in the surface of a finished coin do not constitute a die state. No two coins have the same adjustment marks. Similarly, planchet cracks, carbon marks and streaks (black marks and streaks resulting from an incomplete alloy mix), laminations, etc. are not die states.

Overdates

Two overdates occur among early silver dollars: 1799/8, of which one obverse die is known; and 1802/1, of which five obverse dies are known. On the other hand various other (non-overdated) dies were sometimes used in years later than the dates on them. The most obvious example is 1797, during which calendar year only 7,776 silver dollars were made—equal only to a tiny fraction of dollars made bearing the 1797 date; *q.v.*, 1797-dated dollars were made in one or more later years. No dies are known, such as 1798/7, with 1797 being the under-date. Accordingly, dollars were struck in later years from earlier-dated, non-overdate dies.

When dies were made, they were hardened (by quenching them suddenly in cold water) to strengthen the die faces and to prolong their life. Once a dated die was hardened during the normal die-making process, it could only be overdated effectively if it was annealed (softened by slow heating), after which it would have to be rehardened. Accordingly, it was easier to utilize already-hardened dies no matter what date they bore.

On the other hand, if a die had been punched with a date, say 1801, but had not yet been hardened, and if it remained on hand until 1802, it was a simple matter in 1802 to punch a 2 over the last digit of the date, and then harden the die for use.

CHAPTER 5
EASY-FINDING GUIDE
TO EARLY DOLLARS

DISTRIBUTION OF BB NUMBERS

BB Nos.

1794: BB-1.

1795 Flowing Hair: Begins with BB-11.

1795 Draped Bust: Begins with BB-51.

1796: Begins with BB-61.

1797: Begins with BB-71.

1798 Small Eagle reverse: Begins with BB-81.

1798 Heraldic Eagle reverse, Knob 9: Begins with BB-91.

1798 Heraldic Eagle reverse, Pointed 9: Begins with BB-101.

1799/8: Begins with BB-141.

1799: Begins with BB-151.

1800: Begins with BB-181.

1801: Begins with BB-211.

1802/1: Begins with BB-231.

1802: Begins with BB-241.

1803: Begins with BB-251.

1801-4 Novodels: Begins with BB-301.

How to Use the Easy-Finding Guide

The following Easy-Finding Guide is intended to make it easy to attribute a given dollar to a BB number. Use the Easy-Finding Guide by following these steps. Be sure to follow the steps in order. Do not jump ahead or skip any step. The final step in the process should yield a likely BB number for your coin. Once this number is found, then check your coin against the detailed individual listing in that variety's special section.

First, pick a Roman numeral category (I, II, or III) that fits your coin. Second, under that Roman numeral heading, pick a number (1 or 2) that fits your coin. Third, under that number, pick a letter (A, B, C, etc.) that fits your coin. When you have completed the third step, you should have a match. The BB number is given in parentheses, such as (BB-11).

Some sorting procedures will not require all three steps if there are not multiple selections. Go as far as you can.

Once you have tentatively identified the variety, check it against the text description and photographs in its section.

1794 DOLLARS

Easy-Finding Guide

1794 BB-1. From the F.C.C. Boyd and Cardinal Collections. MS-63+ (PCGS)

FLOWING HAIR TYPE: ONLY ONE VARIETY (BB-1)

1795 DOLLARS

Easy-Finding Guide

1795 Flowing Hair. BB-18. From the Eliasberg and Cardinal Collections. MS-64 (PCGS)

I and II: FLOWING HAIR TYPE:

I. TWO LEAVES BELOW EACH WING

1. **Head of '94:**
   A. Reverse: 16 berries arranged 8+8. (BB-11)
   B. Reverse: 17 berries arranged 9+8. Obverse: Star 15 partially under point. (BB-13)
   C. Reverse: 17 berries arranged 9+8. Obverse: Star 15 completely under bust point. (BB-14)

D. Reverse: 19 berries arranged 8+11. (BB-17)

E. Reverse: 19 berries arranged 9+10; berry under center of first A in AMERICA. Obverse: Bottom curl open, touches two points of star 1. (BB-12)

F. Reverse: 19 berries arranged 9+10; berry under extreme left foot of first A in AMERICA. Obverse: Star 15 partly under bust, curl almost closed, touches innermost point of star 1. (BB-16)

G. Reverse: 19 berries arranged 9+10; outside wreath berry under N. Tip of leaf under right foot of I in UNITED. (BB-28)

2. **Head of '95:**

A. Reverse: 18 berries arranged 9+9. (BB-22)

B. Reverse: 19 berries arranged 9+10, outside wreath berry under N. Tip of leaf under right foot of I in UNITED. (BB-23)

C. Reverse: 19 berries arranged 9+10; berry just about under left edge of left serif of foot of first A in AMERICA. Obverse: Star 15 distant from bust. (BB-15)

D. Reverse: 19 berries arranged 9+10; berry under right foot of first A in AMERICA. Obverse: Lowest curl is broken, interrupted by innermost point of star 1; usually seen with raised die scratch or "bar" opposite innermost part of star 4. (BB-20)

E. Reverse: 19 berries arranged 9+10, berry under right foot of first A in AMERICA. Obverse: Lowest curl touches star 1 at its innermost point. (BB-21)

F. Reverse: 19 berries arranged 9+10; berry under right foot of first A in AMERICA. Obverse: Lowest curl nearly touches star 1 at its upper left point, and firmly joins star 1 at its innermost point. (BB-24)

II. THREE LEAVES BELOW EACH WING

1. **Paired Berries Below D in UNITED:**

A. Reverse: 14 berries arranged 7+7. Obverse: Star 15 points to just below tip of bust point. Star 1 touches lowest curl. (BB-18)

B. Reverse: 14 berries arranged 7+7. Obverse: Star 15 points to slightly above tip of bust point. Star 1 pierces lowest curl and separates it. (BB-19)

2. **Paired Berries Below F in OF:**

A. Reverse: 13 berries arranged 7+6. Obverse: E in LIBERTY punched over erroneous R. (BB-25)

B. Reverse: 13 berries arranged 7+6. Obverse: Lowest curl passes through innermost tip of star 1. (BB-26)

C. Reverse: 13 berries arranged 7+6. Obverse: Raised line or "bar" behind head extends toward star 5. (BB-27)

D. Reverse: 12 berries arranged 6+6. (BB-29)

III. DRAPED BUST TYPE:

1795 Draped Bust. BB-51. From the Cardinal Collection. MS-64 (PCGS)

1. **Obverse: Bust too far left; berry under A of STATES. (BB-51)**

2. **Obverse: Bust well centered; leaf under A of STATES. (BB-52)**

1796 DOLLARS

Easy-Finding Guide

1796 BB-61. MS-61 (PCGS)

SMALL EAGLE REVERSE TYPE (AS ARE ALL):

I. SMALL LETTERS ON REVERSE

1. **Reverse: Berry under A of STATES, Obverse: Star 15 points to *middle* of bosom drapery; *lowest curl does not touch 1 of date.* (BB-62)**

2. **Reverse: Berry under A of STATES. Obverse: Star 15 points to *just above middle* of bosom drapery; bottom curl touches 1 of date. (BB-63)**

3. **Reverse: Berry under A of STATES. Obverse: 7 and 9 of date more widely spaced than 17 or 96;**

star 15 points to *near top* of bosom drapery; bottom curl touches 1 of date. Two points of star 1 touch bottom curl. (BB-66)

4. Reverse: Leaf under A of STATES. (BB-65)

II. LARGE LETTERS ON REVERSE

1. Reverse: Outside berry under T of UNITED. Outside berry under T of STATES. Without massive vertical die crack on reverse. (BB-61)

2. Reverse: No outside berry under T of UNITED. No outside berry under T of STATES. Usually (always?) with massive vertical die crack on reverse. (BB-64)

1797 DOLLARS

Easy-Finding Guide

1797 BB-73. From the Cardinal Collection. MS-63 (NGC)

SMALL EAGLE REVERSE TYPE (AS ARE ALL):

I. OBVERSE: 6 STARS ON RIGHT

1. Reverse: Large letters. (BB-71)

II. OBVERSE: 7 STARS ON RIGHT

1. Reverse: Small letters. (BB-72)
2. Reverse: Large letters. (BB-73)

1798 DOLLARS

Easy-Finding Guide

1798 Small Eagle reverse. BB-81. From the Eliasberg and Cardinal Collections. MS-62+ (PCGS)

I. SMALL EAGLE REVERSE TYPE:

1. Obverse: 13 stars. (BB-82)
2. Obverse: 15 stars. (BB-81)

1798 Heraldic Eagle reverse. BB-108. From the Cardinal Collection. MS-63 (PCGS)

II. HERALDIC EAGLE REVERSE TYPE:

1. **Knob on 9 in Date, Arc Star Pattern**
   A. Obverse: 1 in date close to but with separation from curl; 8 twice as close to bust as to dentils. (BB-94)
   B. Obverse: 1 in date virtually touches curl; 8 nearly touches bust and is distant from dentils. (BB-95)

2. **Knob on 9 in Date, Line Star Pattern**
   A. Branch stem points toward tip of eagle's tail. Large Letters reverse (larger interior space in A, etc.). Obverse: Stars 10-11 are as close to each other as stars 11 and 12. (BB-92)
   B. Branch stem points toward tip of eagle's tail. Large Letters reverse (larger interior space in A, etc.) . Obverse: Stars 10 and 11 are much farther apart than are stars 11 and 12. (BB-91)
   C. Branch stem points downward. Star ray points between B and U of PLURIBUS. Large Letters reverse (larger interior space in A, etc.) (BB-96)
   D. Branch stem points downward. Star ray points to center of B in PLURIBUS. Small Letters reverse. (Usually, but not always, seen with vertical crack bisecting right side of reverse.) (BB-93)

3. **Pointed Tail 9 in Date, Arc Star Pattern, Berry Partially or Completely Under Left Foot of A.**
   A. Reverse: *Star points to I in PLURIBUS.* (BB-102)
   B. Reverse: Arrowhead ends under right edge of serif on left foot of N. Obverse: Space between numeral 8 in date and bust. (BB-103)
   C. Reverse: Arrowhead ends under right edge of serif on left foot of N. Obverse: *Numeral 8 in date touches bust.* (BB-104)
   D. Reverse: Stars very close to or touch clouds 1 and 2. Obverse: Star 7 is farther from L than star

8 is from Y or star 13 is from bust. (BB-110)

E. Reverse: Stars very close to or touch clouds 1 and 2. Obverse: On the left, stars 1-2 and 4-5 are the closest together. On the right, stars 11-12 and 12-13 are the closest together. (BB-111)

F. Reverse: Stars very close to or touch clouds 1 and 2. Obverse: On the left, stars 5 and 6 are farther apart than are any others. (BB-112)

G. Reverse: Stars very close to or touch clouds 1 and 2. Obverse: On the left, stars 4-5 are the closest together. On the right, stars 8-9 and 11-12 are extremely close to each other. (BB-113)

4. **Pointed Tail 9 in Date, Arc Star Pattern, Berry Under Center of A.**

A. Reverse: Star points between I and B of PLURIBUS. Obverse: Star 13 is much farther from bust than star 7 is to L. (BB-107)

B. Reverse: Star points between I and B of PLURIBUS. Obverse: Star 13 is slightly closer to bust than star 7 is to L. (BB-108)

C. Reverse: Star points at center of B of PLURIBUS. Obverse: *Numeral 8 in date touches bust.* (BB-105)

D. Reverse: Star points at center of B of PLURIBUS. Obverse: Numeral 8 in date separated from bust. (BB-106)

E. Reverse: *Star points to right of B of PLURIBUS.* Star extremely close to and/or touching eagle's beak. (BB-116)

5. **Pointed Tail 9 in Date, Arc Star Pattern, Berry Partially or Completely Under Right Foot of A.**

A. Reverse: Star extremely close to and/or touching eagle's beak. Obverse: Point of star 8 is farther from lower right base of Y in LIBERTY than point of star 7 is to L in LIBERTY. Little or no space between cloud 8 and star below. (BB-117)

B. Reverse: Star extremely close to and/or touching eagle's beak. Obverse: Point of star 8 is closer to lower right base of Y in LIBERTY than point of star 7 is to L in LIBERTY. (BB-125)

C. Reverse: Star distinctly spaced away from eagle's beak. Center of A over cloud 2. Leaf tip under I. Star points to left side of B in PLURIBUS. (BB-109)

D. Reverse: Star distinctly spaced away from eagle's beak. Center of A over cloud 3. (BB-118)

E. Reverse: Star distinctly spaced away from eagle's beak. Center of A over cloud 2. Leaf tip under space between R and I. Star points to I in PLURIBUS. (BB-121)

6. **Pointed Tail 9 in Date, Line Star Pattern, Berry Under Center of A.**

A. Reverse: Star does not overlap cloud 4 or even touch it. Star points between B and U in PLURIBUS. *Large Letters reverse* (larger interior space in top of A) (BB-101)

B. Reverse: Star does not overlap cloud 4 or even touch it. Star points at B in PLURIBUS. Small letters reverse (small interior space in top of A). (BB-122)

C. Reverse: Star overlaps cloud 4. Obverse: Star 13 is more than twice as close to bust as star 7 is to L. (BB-124)

D. Reverse: Star overlaps cloud 4. Obverse: Star 13 is slightly farther from bust than star 7 is to L. (BB-123)

7. **Pointed Tail 9 in Date, Line Star Pattern, Berry Under Right Foot of A.**

A. Obverse: *Point of star 4 opposite center of middle hair ribbon.* Stars 8-9 normally spaced. Stop here, do not check the reverse. (BB-120)

B. Obverse: Point of star 4 opposite bottom tail of middle hair ribbon. Stars 8-9 almost touch. Reverse: Star points directly at center of left upright of U of PLURIBUS. Stop here, do not check the reverse further. (BB-114)

C. Obverse: Point of star 4 opposite bottom tail of middle hair ribbon. Stars 8-9 almost touch. Reverse: Center of A in STATES over junction of clouds 2 and 3. Only one star point is extremely close to cloud 8. (BB-115)

D. Obverse: Point of star 4 opposite bottom tail of middle hair ribbon. Stars 8-9 almost touch. Reverse: Center of A in STATES over cloud 3. Two star points are extremely close to cloud 8. (BB-119)

1799 DOLLARS

Easy-Finding Guide

1799 BB-164. From the Cardinal Collection. MS-65 (PCGS)

I. HERALDIC EAGLE TYPE, STARS 8X5:

1. **Obverse: Stars arranged 8 to the left and 5 to the right. (BB-159)**

II. HERALDIC EAGLE TYPE, STARS 7X6:

First, check coin to see if it matches any one listing under nos. 1 through 5 below (do not check 6 and 7 at this time).

1. **1799/8 Overdate.**
   A. Obverse: Star points protruding from below cloud 1 (15-star reverse variety). (BB-141)
   B. Reverse: Berry under right foot of final A in AMERICA. (BB-142)
   C. Reverse: Berry nearly centered under first A in AMERICA. (BB-143)

2. **1799. Upper Left Serif of U in UNITED Missing**
   A. Reverse: Die crack bisects reverse from E in UNITED to M in AMERICA. Far right edge of A over cloud 3. (BB-168)
   B. Reverse: Berry under left serif of right foot of final A in AMERICA. Far right edge of A over junction between clouds 3 and 4. (BB-157)
   C. Reverse: Berry under center of final A in AMERICA. Far right edge of A over junction between clouds 3 and 4. (BB-158)
   D. Reverse: No berries on branch. Obverse star 1 points to space between dentils. Far right edge of A over junction between clouds 3 and 4. (BB-161)
   E. Reverse: No berries on branch. Far right edge of A over junction between clouds 3 and 4. Obverse: Star 1 points to dentil. (BB-160)

3. **1799. Star 13 Touches Bust**
   A. Reverse: One star point touches cloud 4. Far right edge of A over junction between clouds 3 and 4. (BB-151)
   B. Reverse: Two star points overlap cloud 4. Far right edge of A over cloud 3. (BB-152)
   C. Reverse: Star points protruding from below cloud 1 (15-star reverse variety). (BB-153)

4. **1799. Highest Wave of Hair Under Right Side of E**
   A. Reverse: Star ray points to center of U in UNUM. (BB-154)
   B. Reverse: Arrow closest to U in UNITED does not extend beyond U. (BB-155)
   C. Reverse: Die crack bisects reverse from E in UNITED to M in AMERICA. (BB-168)
   D. Reverse: Berry under right side of final A in AMERICA. (BB-167)

5. **1799. Edge of Eagle's Neck at Middle of N in UNUM**

A. Reverse: Large letters in E PLURIBUS UNUM. Arrowhead ends below right upright of U in UNITED. Far right edge of A over cloud 3. (BB-162)

B. Reverse: Large letters in E PLURIBUS UNUM. Arrowhead ends directly below center of U in UNITED. Far right edge of A over junction between clouds 3 and 4. (BB-164)

SPECIAL NOTE: If coin does not match any of the above characteristics, 1 to 5, then (and only then), check nos. 6 and 7 below:

6. **1799. Far Right Edge of A Over Cloud 3**
   A. Reverse: Leftmost arrowhead tip ends slightly past center of bottom of U in UNITED. Star points between B and U in PLURIBUS. (BB-156)
   B. Reverse: Leftmost arrowhead tip ends opposite right upright of U in UNITED, and is closer to U than to N. Star points slightly left of U in UNUM. (BB-166)
   C. Reverse: Leftmost arrowhead tip ends closer to left side of N in UNITED than to U. Star points to center of U in UNUM. (BB-163)

7. **1799. Far Right Edge of A Over Junction Between Clouds 3 and 4**
   A. Reverse: Leftmost arrowhead tip ends opposite right upright of U in UNITED. (BB-165)
   B. Reverse: Leftmost arrowhead tip ends closer to left serif of N in UNITED than to U. (BB-169)

1800 DOLLARS

Easy-Finding Guide

1800 BB-190. From the Carter and Cardinal Collections. MS-64+ (PCGS)

HERALDIC EAGLE TYPE (AS ARE ALL):

I. FAR RIGHT EDGE OF A OVER CLOUD 3.

1. **Reverse: Leaf touches *lower right tip* of I. Raised die lump to lower right of obverse star 1. There is a space between lower right serif of F and cloud 8.**

Obverse: Second 0 in date *slightly* closer to bust than to dentil. (BB-181)

2. Reverse: Leaf touches lower right tip of I. No raised die lump to lower right of star 1. There is a space between lower right serif of F and cloud 8. Obverse: Star 8 is much closer to Y than to star 9. Second 0 in date *much* closer to bust than to dentil. (BB-182)

3. Reverse: Lower right serif of F virtually touches or does touch cloud 8. Obverse: The distances from star 7 to L, star 8 to Y, and star 13 to bust are all about equal. (BB-186)

4. Reverse: There is a space between lower right serif of F and cloud 8. Tip of arrowhead ends under center of U in UNITED. (BB-188)

5. Reverse: Berry slightly right of center under second A in AMERICA (when the coin is held with the A upright). There is a space between lower right serif of F and cloud 8. (BB-184)

6. Reverse: There is a space between lower right serif of F and cloud 8. Berry under right foot of A. Tip of arrowhead ends under right side of right upright of U in UNITED. 10 perfect arrows and *3 disconnected arrowheads.* (BB-195)

7. Reverse: Lower right serif of F virtually touches or does touch cloud 8. Obverse: The distance from star 7 to L is much greater than either the distance from star 8 to Y or star 13 to bust. (BB-187)

8. Reverse: Lower right serif of F virtually touches or does touch cloud 8. Obverse: Star 8 is significantly closer to Y than to star 9. (BB-185)

II. FAR RIGHT EDGE OF A OVER JUNCTION OF CLOUDS 3 AND 4.

1. Reverse: Tip of arrowhead ends under center of U in UNITED. Leaf touches I *below its center.* (BB-183)

2. Reverse: Tip of arrowhead ends under center of right upright of U in UNITED. Obverse: Star 7 is closer to L than star 13 is to bust. (BB-189)

3. Reverse: Tip of arrowhead ends under center of right upright of U in UNITED. Obverse: Star 7 is farther from L than star 13 is to bust. (BB-190)

4. Reverse: Tip of arrowhead is under left tip of left serif on N in UNITED. This is the AMERICAI reverse (one of two; also see BB-192). Obverse: *Point of star 1 is slightly farther from hair than point of star 7 is to L.* (BB-191)

5. Reverse: Tip of arrowhead ends under center of right upright of U in UNITED. *Berry under right foot of A in AMERICA.* (BB-196)

6. Reverse: Tip of arrowhead is under left tip of left serif on N in UNITED. AMERICAI reverse (one of two; also see BB-191). Obverse: *Point of star 1 is closer to hair than point of star 7 is to L.* (BB-192)

III. FAR RIGHT EDGE OF A OVER CLOUD 4.

1. Obverse: No raised die lumps at first 0 of date. Reverse: Tip of arrowhead opposite bottom of U in UNITED. (BB-193)

2. Obverse: Raised die lumps at first 0 of date. *Dotted Date* variety. Reverse: Tip of arrowhead opposite right side of upright of U in UNITED. (BB-194)

1801 DOLLARS

Easy-Finding Guide

1801 BB-214. From the Eliasberg and Cardinal Collections. MS-64 (PCGS)

HERALDIC EAGLE TYPE (AS ARE ALL):

1. Obverse: The distance from 1 in date to curl is about the same as the distance from star 8 to upper right serif of Y. Reverse: Arrowhead under U of UNITED. (BB-211)

2. Obverse: As preceding. Reverse: Tip of arrowhead just under edge of left serif of N in UNITED. Leaf does not touch I in AMERICA. (BB-212)

3. Obverse: As preceding. Reverse: Leaf touches base of I in AMERICA. Bottom right serif is missing on all T's in reverse legend, the result of a broken punch. (BB-213)

4. Obverse: The distance from 1 in date to curl is a tiny fraction of the distance from star 8 to upper right serif of Y. (BB-214)

1802 DOLLARS

Easy-Finding Guide

1802 BB-241. From the Starr and Cardinal Collections. MS-65 (PCGS)

HERALDIC EAGLE TYPE (AS ARE ALL):

I. 1802/1 OVERDATE.

1. Obverse: Star 1 about as close to second curl as 7 is to L. Stars 6-7 are closer than 5-6. 1 is extremely close to lowest curl and nearly touches. Reverse: One star point is near clouds 1, 7 and 8. (BB-231)

2. Obverse: Star 1 significantly closer to second curl than 7 is to L. Reverse: One star point is near clouds 1, 7 and 8. (BB-232)

3. Obverse: Star 1 about as close to second curl as 7 is to L. *Stars 5-6 are closer than 6-7*. Reverse: Two star points are near clouds 1, 7 and 8. (BB-233)

4. Obverse: Star 1 significantly closer to second curl than 7 is to L. Reverse: Two star points are near clouds 1, 7 and 8. (BB-234)

5. Obverse: Star 1 about as close to second curl as 7 is to L. Stars 6-7 are closer than 5-6. 1 is measurably separated from lowest curl. Reverse: Two star points are near clouds 1, 7 and 8.(BB-235)

II. 1802.

1. Obverse: Star 7 is much farther from L than star 8 is from Y. Lower right foot of T in LIBERTY is missing. Reverse: One star point is near clouds 1, 7 and 8. (BB-241)

2. Obverse: Star 7 is about as far from L as star 8 is from Y. Lower right foot of T in LIBERTY is not missing. Reverse: Two star points are near clouds 1, 7 and 8. (BB-242)

1803 DOLLARS

Easy-Finding Guide

1803 BB-255. From the Cleneay and Cardinal Collections. MS-63 (PCGS)

HERALDIC EAGLE TYPE (AS ARE ALL):

I. THIN TOP TO 3 (SMALL 3)

1. Reverse: Point of star touches outside of eagle's beak. Obverse: Point of star 8 is equal to or closer to bottom of Y than top of T is to top of Y. (BB-251)

2. Reverse: Top of eagle's beak comes down on point of star. Obverse: Star 7 the same distance from L as star 8 is from Y. (BB-253)

3. Reverse: Point of star touches *lower part* of eagle's beak. (BB-256)

4. Reverse: Top of eagle's beak comes down on point of star. Obverse: Star 7 is noticeably farther from L than star 8 is from Y. (BB-254)

5. Reverse: Point of star touches outside of eagle's beak. Obverse: Point of star 8 is notably farther from bottom of Y than top of T is to top of Y. (BB-252)

II. THICK TOP TO 3 (LARGE 3)

1. Obverse: *Thick top to 3 in date.* Obverse: Top of eagle's beak comes down on point of star. (BB-255)

Congrefs of the United States:

AT THE THIRD SESSION,

Begun and held at the City of Philadelphia, on Monday the fixth of December, one thoufand feven hundred and ninety.

RESOLVED *by the* SENATE *and* HOUSE *of* REPRESENTATIVES *of the United States of America in Congrefs affembled*, That a mint fhall be eftablifhed under fuch regulations as fhall be directed by law.

Refolved, That the Prefident of the United States be, and he is hereby authorized to caufe to be engaged, fuch principal artifts as fhall be neceffary to carry the preceeding refolution into effect, and to ftipulate the terms and conditions of their fervice, and alfo to caufe to be procured fuch apparatus as fhall be requifite for the fame purpofe.

FREDERICK AUGUSTUS MUHLENBERG,
Speaker of the Houfe of Reprefentatives.

JOHN ADAMS, *Vice-Prefident of the United States, and Prefident of the Senate.*

APPROVED, March the third, 1791.

GEORGE WASHINGTON, *Prefident of the United States.*

DEPOSITED among the ROLLS in the OFFICE of the SECRETARY of STATE.

Secretary of State.

Reproduction of the resolution establishing a federal mint, March 3, 1791. (From *Illustrated History of the United States Mint* by George C. Evans)

CHAPTER 6
1794 SILVER DOLLARS

MINTAGE
Calendar year, Mint report: 1,758 distributed
(from total mintage of c. 2,000)

Coinage Context

Dollars authorized: The Mint Act of April 2, 1792 authorized the production of silver dollars of 416 grains weight, with silver content of 371.25 grains, equivalent to .89243 fine. The remaining metal was to be copper, added for strength. Such coins were intended to circulate at par with Mexican and other Spanish-American silver "dollars" (of the eight reales denomination) which were common in the states at the time. Indeed, earlier the Continental Congress had denominated its paper currency in Spanish milled dollars. Although framers of the Mint Act of 1792 were not aware of it, typical Spanish-American dollars contained 65 parts silver out of a total of 72 parts, equal to .90278 fine. In practice, later assays performed at the Mint showed that finenesses of Mexican silver coins varied and were not made to any accuracy carried out to five decimal places. One specimen might be .901 fine and another .902.

A problem with the weight: Albion Cox, Mint assayer who was well versed in coinage (and who earlier produced New Jersey coppers), found that the statutory fineness of .89243 was difficult to attain, and he proposed adjusting it to the point at which the silver content of the dollar was 371.25 grains (thus achieving the amount of silver Congress wanted), but with the copper content lowered to 41 grains, thus yielding a 412.25-grain coin of .900456 fine silver (which was close to what Congress authorized over 40 years later under the Act of March 31, 1837). Congress did not agree with the Cox plan.

Mint Director David Rittenhouse then proposed to increase the silver content from 371.25 grains to 374.74, for a total coin weight of 416 grains, resulting in .90084 silver fineness. Under this proposal, unauthorized by Congress, all 1794 dollars and, it is believed, most if not all 1795 Flowing Hair dollars were minted. Each had 3.49 grains of extra, illegal silver. Depositors receiving silver dollars in exchange for bullion were thus short about 1% in value for each dollar received (see Additional Information below).

Concerning the copper with which to alloy the silver, R.W. Julian noted this: [1]

It is my opinion, based on the fact that I have yet to find in the Mint records any purchases of scrap copper after 1792, that the source of 99% of the copper alloy for the dollars of 1794-1804 was the copper coinage, either in misstruck half cents and cents or in the scissel (the remainder of the flattened copper ingot after the planchets had been punched out). Depositors usually had to wait several weeks for their coins, and very rarely obtained them within a month. For example, years later when silver coinage was heavy and regular in 1814, the delays were sometimes for several months.

Dies made: The dies for the 1794 dollar are almost certainly the work of Robert Scot, a medalist and die sinker. He had begun his career in England as a watchmaker, and had come to America, where he engaged in engraving plates for money and bills of exchange during the Revolutionary War, scales used in the office of financier Robert Morris, and plates illustrating architectural items for *Dobson's Encyclopedia,* among numerous other commissions. In 1780 he produced the dies or molds for an Indian peace medal, "Happy When United," for the state of Virginia. In 1781 his workshop was located in Philadelphia on the west side of Front Street, near the corner of Vine.

Following the death from yellow fever in the summer of 1793 of Joseph Wright (a talented artist of whom many fine things were expected), the Mint sought to add a full-time engraver to the staff. Wright had worked on and off for the Mint, and today is credited with designing the 1792 eagle-on-globe patterns and the 1793 Liberty Cap cent, both beautiful works of art.

On November 23, 1793, Secretary of State Thomas Jefferson, who was in charge of the affairs of the Mint, wrote to Robert Scot and sent him a commission to be engraver at the Mint. To Scot fell the task of cutting the dies for coinage, including the 1794 Flowing Hair dollar. In November 1794, John Smith Gardner was hired as his assistant, but by this time the initial delivery of silver dollars had been accomplished. Probably, Gardner worked on some of the 1795 and later dies.

Planchet preparation: Silver was obtained by the Mint from various depositors, who primarily brought foreign silver coins, but often furnished silver utensils and other wrought items as well. The silver was received

---

[1] Letter to the author, December 7, 1992.

by the Mint, and in due course, dollars or other coins were made from the metal and paid out. Unfortunately, the Mint did not have a bullion fund, or house account, to provide for the purchase of silver and the immediate payment in kind from earlier-minted coins on hand. Under the procedure in effect during the era of the 1794-1803 silver dollars, depositors often had to wait several days or more for their coins.

After receipt, the silver would be melted, refined, cast into ingots, rolled into bars, and then rolled and drawn into sheets the thickness of the desired planchets. Great difficulties were experienced during these processes, especially with the rolling mills, as the rollers tended to deteriorate and produce strips of metal with uneven surfaces. At one time, the Mint operations almost shut down because of rolling mill problems. The acquisition of copper with which to alloy the silver was a great challenge, and use was made of copper nails, roofing sheets, used copper cookware, and even coins and tokens. Often the copper was black or otherwise defective.

From the finished strip of the proper thickness, a small punch and die would cut out planchets one at a time. By this point in time, a great deal of effort and expense had been invested in creating each planchet. However, there was more to be done.

Adjustment marks: At the time the Mint did not have elaborate quality-control procedures in place, and it was difficult to produce planchets precisely of the required weight. Accordingly, the typical planchet was made slightly heavier than needed, and the weight was adjusted by hand filing to the correct level. Underweight planchets would have been useless, as their weight could not have been increased, and they would have had to have been discarded, to go through the entire process of melting, conversion to ingots, rolling the strip, and punching planchets again. (In 1795, the problem of underweight planchets may have been solved by plugging; see description under 1795.)

Evidence of the hand filing is seen today in the form of parallel or crisscross grooves known as adjustment marks. The majority of 1794 dollars show these marks, usually at the lower left obverse and the corresponding part of the reverse, where metal flow was not as great (due to non-parallel die alignment; in this area the dies were too far apart, little metal movement occurred, and adjustment marks on the original planchet were less likely to be obliterated).

Edge lettering: To prevent filing and clipping by the public to reduce a minted coin's weight, it was desired to ornament the edge. In this way, the removal of silver could be easily detected. For the silver dollar, lettering was applied by a machine which rolled the finished planchet between two parallel steel bars, upon each of which was half of the edge lettering inscription: HUNDRED CENTS ONE DOLLAR OR UNIT and some ornamentation.

These steel bars compressed the letters incuse into the edge of each planchet, and at the same time raised a rim around the border of each side of the planchet. Apparently, the height of the rim varied over a period of time, for some 1794-1803 dollars are known with rims that are almost flat, and others have rims that are quite high.

The raised rim did several things:

1. During the striking process, the metal could flow more easily into the toothlike notches at the edge of each die, to create dentils around the border.

2. The raised rim would protect the coin's surface from wear, and it would last longer in circulation. Coins with low rims wore quickly; those with high rims preserved their details for a greater length of time.

3. The coins would stack better, a convenience to banks, merchants, and counting houses.

In later years (beginning with the 1836 Gobrecht issues), the Mint would raise the rims on silver dollars by means of a milling machine. However, in the 1790s, whatever rim was to be raised was a by-product of the process of squeezing the edge of the coin during the lettering process.

Dollars struck: In 1793 and 1794, the largest press at the Mint was intended for striking no coins larger than a half dollar. Surviving documents indicate that Mint officials lamented the lack of a press suitable for coining silver dollars and medals. It was not until spring 1795 that one was installed.

In the meantime, a screw press suitable for coining cents and half dollars was put into service to make silver dollars. The initial coinage of the new denomination was accomplished in the first part of October 1794. The effort was not completely successful, as evidenced by surviving coins which show areas of weak striking. Apparently, just one blow of the press was used (as evidenced by the lack of double struck features on surviving pieces).

Known silver dollars dated 1794 are from a single pair of dies and are believed to have been made to the extent of, perhaps, 2,000 coins (Walter H. Breen's estimate), of which 1,758 pieces considered to be satisfactory delivered by the coiner on October 15, 1794. The remaining impressions, possibly amounting to 242 coins, rejected as being too weak, probably were kept on hand for later use as planchets. Supporting this theory is the existence of at least one 1795 silver dollar (BB-14) plainly overstruck on a 1794 dollar.

As several die states exist, the striking could not have been continuous, but was interrupted by the removal of the dies from the press for resurfacing (relapping) after clash marks were sustained early in their life (see Die States below). The silver for striking these came from ingot deposits made by Director Rittenhouse and Charles

Gilchrist. This is certain, because Rittenhouse personally received all the first coinage of dollars.[1]

The obverse and reverse die faces were not parallel, with the result that on almost all pieces surviving today the lower left obverse side appears weaker than the upper right obverse side, with corresponding weakness and strength on the opposite areas of the reverse. As the die faces remained out of parallel after having been removed from the press for resurfacing and removal of clash marks, and re-inserted in the press, the cause of the maladjustment must have been that the face of one (or, less likely, both) die was not perpendicular to its shank.

After the effort at coining dollars, the project was abandoned as a bad job, and a large supply of silver dollar planchets was put into chests for storage until a larger, satisfactory press could be installed. Thus, the mintage of 1794 dollars was much smaller than had been intended.

Reception of the dollars: So far as is known, the new 1794 silver dollars slipped into circulation and immediately began doing their duty in the channels of commerce. Despite all good intentions, when the first 1794-dated United States silver dollars reached merchants and bankers, and when their successors dated 1795, 1796, etc., did also, the Spanish-American dollars, or eight-reales pieces, were preferred over the native American product. The old eight-real coins were worth slightly more on the market than were the sparkling new United States coins with the head of Miss Liberty on one side and an eagle on the other. The reason is that the citizenry was familiar with the eight-real coins, and especially in the export trade they were welcomed worldwide. Although the new United States dollars might test properly by weight or analysis, most business was done at sight, and the new coins had yet to prove their status.

By early December 1794, a few of the new dollars had traveled north to the Granite State, where the *New Hampshire Gazette* reported the following on December 2nd:

Some of the dollars now coining at the Mint of the United States have found their way to this town. A correspondent put one into the editor's hands yesterday. Its weight is equal to that of a Spanish dollar, encircled by *Fifteen Stars,* and has the word "LIBERTY" at the top, and the date, 1794, at the bottom. On the reverse, is the *Bald Eagle,* enclosed in an *Olive Branch,* round which are the words "One Dollar, or Unit, Hundred Cents." The *tout ensemble* has a pleasing effect to a connoisseur; but the touches of the graver are too delicate, and there is a want of that boldness of execution which is necessary to durability and currency.

Numismatic historian Don Taxay viewed the 1794 dollar as unsatisfactory, noted that engraver Robert Scot's

"talents, never marked, show a rapid decline."[2] He took the position that Mint Director Rittenhouse's successor (after June 1795), William DeSaussure, did not like Scot's work, and, apparently, not his assistant Gardner's either, and in September 1795 went over the heads of Scot and Gardner to enlist an outside artist, John Eckstein, to redesign the dollar and replace the Flowing Hair motif with the Draped Bust obverse, Small Eagle reverse, type.

I, for one, disagree with Don Taxay—and find the Scot and/or Gardner work on 1794-5 Flowing Hair coins to be very attractive, not only on the early dollars, but on half cents, large cents, half dimes, and half dollars as well. Unfortunately, very few contemporary accounts survive to tell us of the contemporary public reception of the newly minted 1794 silver dollars and their use in commerce. Coins were taken for granted, and relatively little notice was taken in print concerning them.

All too often, historians judge by today's standards what happened two centuries ago. In 1794, the almighty Spanish-American dollar, showing "that boldness of execution which is necessary to durability and currency," had little in the way of aesthetic appeal. Depicting the kings of Spain and, earlier, the Pillars of Hercules and two globes, these coins had virtually no fine detailing. The dies were made quickly, and crudely. By contrast, we have it on the word of an unnamed editor of a New Hampshire newspaper that the new 1794 United States silver dollar had "a pleasing effect to a connoisseur." What more could be asked for?

Numismatic Information

Desirability of the 1794 dollar: Today, the 1794 dollar is recognized as a great classic, not only because it is rare, but because it stands as the first silver dollar produced by the fledgling Philadelphia Mint. From the inception of coin auction sales on a large scale in the 1860s, to the present day, the appearance of a 1794 silver dollar in an auction usually has provided the opportunity for the cataloger to provide an extended comment. Similarly, 1794 dollars have occupied the spotlight in numerous dealers' fixed-price lists over the years.

Charles Steigerwalt, in *The Coin Journal,* September 1880, commented as follows concerning the 1794 dollar:

The number of pieces coined in this year was not large and they have become very rare. Good specimens bringing about 50 dollars. The dies of the dollars and half dollars of this year were not sharp and the impressions are generally weak; good specimens being difficult to obtain.

When Ebenezer Locke Mason wrote *Rare American Coins: Their Description, and Past and Present Fictitious Values,* in 1887, he focused upon this coin and noted the following:

---

[1] Certain information in this paragraph is from R.W. Julian, letter to the author, December 7, 1992.

[2] *U.S. Mint and Coinage,* p. 106.

The 1794 United States silver dollar, which occupies the centre of the group in our illustration [a collage of coins at the top of the page], was authorized by an act of Congress, April 2, 1792, and was struck at the old Mint, opposite Filbert Street, in Seventh Street, Philadelphia, and is still standing. This dollar, which is considered very rare, commanded a premium of about $25 in 1860, and has steadily advanced in fictitious value from year to year, and commanded, in every condition, in 1885, the sum of three hundred dollars.

It is said that but few of the 1794 dollars were struck, and the earliest from the dies equaled Proof pieces in their glistening splendor. The British Museum contains the best known specimen of the 1794 dollar, and probably received it as a gift from our government the year it was coined.[1]

Population of 1794 dollars. The number of 1794 silver dollars known is subject to conjecture. Many pieces offered in nineteenth and early twentieth century catalogs were not illustrated, making it difficult to trace their pedigrees with certainty today. By December 1992 Jack Collins, who has made a detailed study of this date, had identified 118 different specimens by photographs. More recently, Martin Logies identified 134 distinct specimens, and estimated that the total remaining population as 140 to 150.

Mint State grades: Over the years several different specimens of the 1794 dollar have been designated as Uncirculated by various catalogers. Today, fewer than 10 coins are believed to be MS-60 or finer by current grading interpretations.

Circulated grades: Nearly all 1794 dollars seen today are in lower grades ranging from Good to Fine. Not many make the VF grade, and perhaps fewer than 15 totally are EF or better. Population report data are not particularly useful in determining the number of EF 1794 dollars known, as a number marked "EF" (or the curious "EF") are, in my opinion, only VF. There seems to have been a grade escalation in regard to this particular date.

Caveat emptor: It is apparent that possibly two dozen or more 1794 silver dollars in numismatic hands today, ostensibly normal coins exhibiting varying degrees of wear, were at one time holed, plugged, initialed, or otherwise damaged. Over the years numerous of these have been expertly repaired so as to almost defy detection. Jack Collins, in the course of his research on dollars of this date, found numerous instances of damaged pieces being described as such in auction catalogs, and then later reappearing as "undamaged" coins. The inescapable conclusion is that they were cleverly repaired in the meantime. Martin Logies has identified additional, more recent examples of these occurrences, as well as the existence of two die-struck fake 1794 dollars produced from transfer dies created from a known genuine specimen. Purchasers of 1794 dollars are urged to check pieces carefully in this regard.

One explanation for the survival of so many impaired coins is probably that bullion dealers and others were alerted to the rare 1794 dollars by coin collectors when the hobby when it its infancy in the 1840s and 1850s. While holed and damaged dollars of other dates, such as 1795, were even more common, the bullion dealers did not extract these as they passed through their hands. However, *any* dollar dated 1794 was saved, no matter what the damage was. Accordingly, a higher proportion of this date survived in damaged condition in numismatic hands than any other early dollar issue of either the Flowing Hair or Draped Bust types.

---

1 In a conversation with the author, August 6, 1992, Jack Collins stated that in the course of his research involving 1794 dollars he had learned that the specimen in the British Museum had been cleaned to the extent that it showed extensive hairlines. Perhaps Collins' assessment was overly harsh, or natural re-toning over the intervening years lessened the appearance of the cleaning, as John Dannreuther noted in his August 2006 article, "U.S. Coin Highlights in the British Museum," that during a recent visit to the Museum he examined the 1794 dollar and found it to be "an original, well-struck Almost Uncirculated example," and commented that "in the past, this coin has been reported as harshly cleaned, but if there is cleaning under the toning, it is minor."

VARIETIES

1794 BB-1

(Bolender-1, Haseltine-1)

Dollars bearing the 1794 date were struck from a single pair of dies. Nearly all seen by the author are lightly struck at the lower left of the obverse and corresponding part of the reverse. Some few pieces display a well-balanced strike and are exceedingly rare. Perhaps because there was just one variety of the year, Bolender did not assign a number to it in his 1950 book. However, specialists since then have called it Bolender-1. Haseltine's 1881 Type Table Auction did not include a specimen of the 1794 dollar; however, for completeness, he did nonetheless include a detailed description of the dies in an addendum to the catalog, identifying the variety as Haseltine-1.

Obverse: Flowing Hair design with six curls, the third curl weak on most specimens. First star close to 1 in date. Second star near first curl, but does not touch it. The head of Miss Liberty in the 1794 dollar has a fuller cheek and more pronounced jaw line than does any of 1795, and admits of consanguinity with some of the finely-detailed heads seen on large cents made early in the year 1794. Blunt tip to neck point.

No head on a 1795 dollar is *exactly* like this head, although four obverse dies of 1795, one used to coin BB-11, BB-12, and BB-13; another to produce BB-14; a third to strike BB-16, BB-17, and BB-18; and a fourth used to produce BB-28, each have a blunt tip to neck point and are more like the 1794 head than any others. If any 1795 obverses are worthy of the "Head of '94" appellation, these four are. In the 1795 Flowing Hair dollar study, below, I designate these "Head of '94" coins as Portrait I (PI) issues.

A curious fact, apparently not mentioned earlier in the literature, is that while the eight stars on the left of the 1794 silver dollar are each oriented with a point toward the dentils (as standard), the seven stars on the right are each positioned differently, unique to 1794 in the early dollar series, with two points toward the dentils (see plate).

Reverse: Eagle perched on a rock within a wreath; 21 leaves on each branch. The wreath has 19 berries, 10 on the left branch, 9 on the right. A leaf is joined to second T in STATES, and another almost touches the right corner of F in OF. "Lobster claw" leaf pair under second T of UNITED and first A of AMERICA. Eagle's wing touches R in AMERICA. Ribbons below wreath thinner and much closer together, and branch ends thinner and straighter, than on any 1795 reverse. Ribbon (not a knot) around junction of the two wreath stems. Rock under eagle's feet extends much farther to the left than on any 1795 die. This die was retired after the 1794-dated coinage and was not used in 1795.

Die States

Die State I: Perfect dies. No clash marks in fields. Cf. Neil Collection (Mehl, 1947): 1 to Amon G. Carter, Sr. to Carter Family Collection (Stack's, 1984): 207. Just this one single one specimen is known from this perfect state of the dies.

Die State II: Light clash marks in obverse and reverse fields (usually visible only on coins grading EF or better). The ends of Miss Liberty's hair locks extend farther into the field and are more detailed than on the next. End of curl approaches innermost point of star 2. Cf. Lord St. Oswald (Christie, Manson & Woods, London, 1964): 137 to A.J. Ostheimer 3rd, to the Gilhousen Collection (Superior, 1973), to Frank Andrews (temporarily, to Jonathan Hefferlin), to Newport Collection (Bowers and Ruddy, 1975): 371, via intermediaries to Jimmy Hayes Collection (Stack's, 1985): 72; Lord St. Oswald (1964):

138 to Norweb (1988): 3741; Somerset Collection (Bowers and Merena, 1992) coins; and others.

Die State III:[1] Obverse (especially) and reverse dies lightly reground, removing clash marks. The ends of Miss Liberty's lower hair locks are now shortened; the tips are missing. This is the usually seen die state.

Notes: A prooflike impression of these dies struck in copper (Judd-19) is in the National Collection in the Smithsonian Institution, a gift of Stack's (in 1954, it appeared as lot 1264 in Stack's Davis-Graves [James Davis] Collection sale, $1,400). Bolender reported a second, in copper, silver plated, but this was the American Numismatic Society's electrotype (illustrated in the Bolender book as the plate for 1794; his own coin was only VG).

A 1794-dated pattern without obverse stars (Judd-18) is from a different 1794 die, a fact first noted by Andrew W. Pollock III; earlier, it was believed that stars were added to the pattern die for use in regular coinage.

Collecting Notes
See narrative above.

Notable Specimens
Neil Specimen. SP-66 (PCGS). Description from Superior Stamp & Coin 1991: *"Prooflike and superb! This is 'The Coin,' the World's Finest 1794 Silver Dollar which has the added value of also being the only Presentation Specimen known. Although there were no 1794 Proofs officially made, there is no denying this coin received extra care when it was made."* Ex Virgil Brand Collection • James Kelly (FPL #20, 1945) • C. David Pierce • Art & Paul Kagin • Will W. Neil Collection (Mehl, 1947) lot 1, $1,250 • Amon Carter, Jr. Collection (Stack's, 1984) lot 207, $264,000 to the following • Hugh Sconyers for the American Rare Coin Fund Limited Partnership • Wayne Miller and Hoagy Carmichael Collections (Superior, 1986) lot 1173, $209,000 • An Amazing Collection of Silver Dollars (Superior, 1991) lot 699, $506,000, at which time it was certified MS-65 by PCGS • Knoxville Collection • Sold by private treaty to Jay Parrino. Graded in 2002 by NGC as MS-66 and noted as having been struck on a planchet with a mint-inserted silver plug. Subsequently, re-sold by private treaty to Steve Contursi and later re-graded by PCGS as Specimen-66 and also noted as having been struck on a planchet with a mint-inserted silver plug. Acquired via private treaty by the Cardinal Collection Educational Foundation, May 2010 for the world's record price of $7,850,000. Jack Collins

considers this to be the finest Mint State 1794 dollar (per note received by the author, December 31, 1992).

Boyd Specimen. MS-66 (PCGS). Description from Stack's Numisma '95 Sale (1995): "Gem brilliant uncirculated. A gorgeous toned satin gem." Originally from the vast holdings of Colonel E.H.R. Green; F.C.C. Boyd Collection. "World's Greatest Collection" sale, (F.C.C. Boyd, Numismatic Gallery, 1945) lot 1, $2,000 • Adolph Friedman; Charles Williams; 1949 ANA Convention Sale (Numismatic Gallery, August, 1949) lot 140, $1,800 • Beverly Hills Stamp & Coin Shop (Abe Kosoff & Max Justus) Fixed Price List, 1957 • 1958 ANA Convention Sale (Numismatic Gallery, August 1958) lot 1678, $7,750 • James Kelly • Lelan Rogers; Numisma '95 Sale (Stacks, November 1995) lot 1315, $577,500 • purchased by Jay Parrino, who had it certified by PCGS (as MS-66) • The Mint (Jay Parrino) Fixed Price List, 1996 • Stellar Collection.

Lord St. Oswald-Ostheimer Specimen. MS-66 (PCGS). Description from Gilhousen Sale: "Uncirculated." One of two 1794 dollars believed to have been obtained during a visit to Philadelphia in 1795. • Major the Lord St. Oswald, late October 1795, on his visit to Philadelphia; in the hands of St. Oswald's descendants until 1964, when it appeared as lot 137 of the Christie, Manson & Woods auction of the St. Oswald Collection • Alfred J. Ostheimer 3rd • Superior Stamp & Coin Co., 1972, • Gilhousen Collection (Superior, 1973) lot 1209, sold for $110,000 to the following, but, apparently, problems developed, and it was reacquired. • Ralph Andrews • Superior Stamp & Coin Co. • Jonathan Hefferlin for a reported $127,500. • Newport Collection (Bowers and Ruddy, 1975) lot 371, $75,000.[2] • Jimmy Hayes Collection (Stack's, 1985) lot 72, $220,000 • Private Texas collection.

Lord St. Oswald-Norweb Specimen. MS-64 (PCGS). One of two 1794 dollars believed to have been obtained during a visit to Philadelphia in 1795. • Family collection of Lord St. Oswald which was sold at auction by Christie's in London October 1964, lot 138. Sold to the following. • A.H. Baldwin & Sons and Lester Merkin, on behalf of the following. • Ambassador and Mrs. R. Henry Norweb. Norweb Collection (Bowers and Merena, 1988) lot 3741, MS-60/63. $242,000. Since graded MS-63. • "A Cabinet of Rarities" (Bowers and Merena, RCR#78, 1990) lot 129; later re-graded by PCGS as MS-64; private Southwest collector. • Additional information: The two Lord St. Oswald coins: Certainly among the very finest Mint State 1794 silver dollars are two coins sold at auction in 1964 by Christie's of London, as part of the family collection of Lord St. Oswald, who is said to have visited Philadelphia in 1795,

---

[1] A later die state has been reported with a rim break at 7th star; very late impression from the dies. Cf. Gilhousen (Superior, 1973): 1210, VF; there called one of just two reported. However, Jack Collins (in a commentary received by the author on December 31, 1992) noted that the "rim break" is believed to have been a rim bump, and no specimen is known to exist with a break at the 7th star.

[2] Details from *Walter Breen's Complete Encyclopedia of U.S. and Colonial Coins*, p. 424.

possibly in October. These coins, long forgotten with a group of other copper and silver issues dated 1794 and 1795, appeared on the market to delight and surprise numismatists, several of whom traveled from the United States to attend the London event. At the sale each 1794 silver dollar brought the American equivalent of $11,200. The first, lot 137, went to A.J. Ostheimer 3rd. The second, lot 138, was knocked down to A.H. Baldwin & Sons, Ltd., London dealers, on behalf of Hon. and Mrs. R. Henry Norweb. As to which was the better coin has been a toss-up in discussions since. Lot 137 has fewer adjustment marks but is not quite as sharp on the 1 of the date, and has a few carbon marks on the reverse. Lot 138 has more adjustment marks. Both are brilliant and lustrous, and both are from an early state of the dies showing light clash marks. (There were three other early dollars in the sale: a specimen of 1795 BB-18 and two of 1795 BB-20.) All told, the miscellaneous group of 1794 and 1795 pieces owned by Lord St. Oswald, representing an investment of less than $10 in 1795, brought the princely sum of $72,000!

Boyd Specimen (another). MS-63+ (PCGS). Description by Quality Sales 1973: "Brilliant uncirculated, choice and nearly pristine. The beautiful surfaces display a remarkable sheen, resplendent with full original mint frost. It barely falls short of absolute perfection due to a small mint abrasion on third star, otherwise without any visible blemish incurred after striking." Originally obtained from B. Max Mehl from the Virgil Brand estate in the 1930s • F.C.C. Boyd Collection duplicate • Sold privately by Numismatic Gallery at the time of the "World's Greatest Collection" sale. Stack's (Fixed Price List No. 47, 1950), $1,595 • B.M. Eubanks • Sold at auction by Quality Sales (Kreisberg-Cohen, September, 1973) lot 464, $51,000 • "Collector's Portfolio" Public Coin Auction (Abner Kreisberg Corporation, October, 1978) lot 633, $57,500 • Bowers and Ruddy (Fixed Price List No. 41, 1981), $295,000 • The Charmont Sale (Steve Ivy, August 1983) lot 3769, $121,000 • The Somerset Collection (Bowers and Merena, May 1992) lot 1300 • Sold to the following: Jeff Isaac, who had it certified by PCGS (as MS-63) in 1992. Later re-graded by NGC as MS-64 • The Cardinal Collection (American Numismatic Rarities, June 2005) lot 5, $1,150,000 • Private collector • subsequently re-acquired by the Cardinal Collection in 2008 • Pre-ANA Sale (Bowers & Merena, August 2010) lot 1005, $1,207,000 • Heritage Auctions, who had it certified by PCGS (as MS-63+) • Bruce Morelan • Legend Numismatics • Private collector.

French Specimen. MS-62+ (PCGS). Auction '84 description: "Uncirculated 60+." • Auction '84 (Paramount, 1984) lot 725, Uncirculated 60+. • L.R. French, Jr. Family Collection (Stack's, 1989) lot 2 • Gary Minsey Collection; graded by PCGS as MS-61; this coin was later graded

by NGC as MS-62, subsequently crossed-over to PCGS as MS-62, and then regarded by PCGS in June 2010 as MS-62+ • Private Midwestern collection.

Connecticut Historical Society Specimen. AU-58 (PCGS). Bowers and Merena description: "EF-45." • Many years in the Connecticut Historical Society Collection; sold in 1983 by Bowers and Merena. Described as EF with adjustment marks. • Louis B. Hungerford Collection, donated in 1926 to the Connecticut Historical Society where it resided until 1983 • Connecticut Historical Society (Bowers and Merena, April 1983) lot 736 • Auction '88 (David Akers, July 1988) lot 628 • Auction '90 (David Akers, August 1990) lot 1626 • subsequently submitted for certification and graded by PCGS as AU-55, and later by NGC as AU-58 • Fall Long Beach Sale (Heritage, October 1995) lot 6047 • Gainsborough II Sale (Superior Galleries, February 1997) lot 1288 • Private Midwestern collection • privately to the Cardinal Collection, August 2004, at which point it was re-graded by PCGS as AU-58 • private collector • Pre-FUN Elite Sale (Superior Galleries, January 2005) lot 501 • Pre-Long Beach Sale (Superior Galleries, July 2005) lot 1101 • The Hesselgesser Collection • Pre-Long Beach Sale (Ira and Larry Goldberg, May 2011) lot 867 • Century Coin Group.

Murdoch Specimen. AU-58. Empire Sale description: "Uncirculated." • Murdoch Collection (Sotheby's, London, July 1903) • George H. Earle (Henry Chapman, June 1912) lot 2667 • William Cutler Atwater Collection (B. Max Mehl, June 1946) lot 185 • Empire (Cass) Collection (Stack's, November 1957) lot 1678 • The Gibson Collection (Stack's, November 1974) lot 75 • Harry W. Bass, Jr. Collection (Bowers and Merena, May 1999) as AU-58 to MS-60: lot 2021 • Phillip Flannagan Collection (Bowers and Merena, November 2001) lot 4202, at which time it was graded as MS-61 (NGC) • Private Southeastern collection • Long Beach Sale (Heritage, June 2005) lot 6571 • Private collector; Joseph C. Thomas Collection (Heritage, April 2009) lot 2529 • subsequent to the 2009 sale, the coin was presented to PCGS for grading and assigned the grade of AU-55.

Ostheimer Specimen (another). AU-55★ (NGC). Described as following in Lester Merkin's sale: "Choice Uncirculated, obverse field prooflike (new die retaining polish), rev. frosty, faint obverse adjustment marks, two minute hidden reverse rim nicks, trivial bag marks— only one needing mention above T on obverse and that one not disturbing color, minute traces of cabinet friction from when this coin rested in a 19th century velvet display tray, above average strike, all obverse sharp but very center, borders bold, eagle's head very sharp, claws plain, part of breast feathers visible." • John F. McCoy Collection (W. Elliot Woodward, May 1864) • Joseph Zanoni (Edward D. Cogan, April 1867) • James Ten Eyck

• Mortimer Livingston MacKenzie (Edward Cogan, June 1869) lot 151 • E. Harrison Sanford, Esq. (Edward Cogan, November 1874) lot 96 • Col. James H. Taylor (W.H. Strobridge, November 1875) lot 1073 • Lorin G. Parmelee (New York Coin and Stamp, June 1890) lot 681 • H.O. Granberg • William H. Woodin • Waldo Newcomer • Col. E.H.R. Green • Jerome Kern (B. Max Mehl, May 1950) • Clint Hester • W.G. Baldenhofer; James Kelly (Fixed Price List, 1959) • Alfred J. Ostheimer 3rd (Lester Merkin, 1968) lot 224 • Stack's (Fixed Price List, Summer 1993) lot 215 • Cabinet of Lucien M. LaRiviere, Part II (Bowers and Merena, 2001) lot 324 • Jack Lee Collection (Heritage, November 2005) lot 2184 • Joseph C. Thomas Collection (Heritage, April 2009) lot 2528; subsequent to the 2009 sale, the coin was presented to PCGS for grading and assigned the grade of AU-50; upon a later re-submission to NGC the coin was assigned the grade of AU-55★ • private collector.

Austrian Specimen. AU-55. "Austrian private collection" (or possibly the Paris Mint Collection or that of the *Bibliothéque Nationale).* • Paul H. Wittlin • 1956 American Numismatic Association Convention sale conducted by James Kelly (lot 1509, fetching $8,000) • Stack's • Private owner. Sold to the following in 1975. • Stack's • Julian Leidman and Mike Brownlee • Paul Nugget • Dave Berg • Private owner • Dr. Edward Willing Collection (Bowers and Ruddy, 1976) lot 412.

The Miles Specimen. AU-50. Adjustment marks on left obverse; usual weak strike left obverse and reverse sides. • R.L. Miles, Jr. Collection (Stack's, 1969) lot 1525, AU. • "Autumn" Sale (Stack's, 1978) lot 287, AU.

Eliasberg Specimen. EF-45 (PCGS). Bowers and Merena Galleries 1997, lot 2167. Light gray and lilac surfaces. Very pleasing in all respects. Charles P. Britton Collection (Cogan, January 1883) • Fine Greek, Foreign and United States Coins (S.H. & H. Chapman, June 1889) lot 190 • E.S. Norris Collection (S.H. & H. Chapman, May 1894) lot 24 • J.M. Clapp • John H. Clapp • Clapp Estate 1942 • to Louis E. Eliasberg, Sr. (Bowers and Merena, April 1997) lot 2167 • Harry Laibstain; private collector • Old

The Neil specimen 1794 Flowing Hair dollar with mint-inserted silver plug. Graded Specimen-66 by PCGS.

West & Franklinton Collections (American Numismatic Rarities, August 2006) lot 685 • Long Beach Signature Sale (Heritage, February 2008) lot 827 • Walter Husak.

Childs Specimen. EF-40 (NGC). Bowers and Merena description, 1999: "Mottled rainbow iridescence on pale golden gray surfaces. Lightly struck on the obverse from about 6:00 to 10:00, and correspondingly on the reverse, as *always* (in our experience) seen in one degree or another for authentic specimens of this date." Walter H. Childs Collection (Bowers and Merena, August 1999) lot 439 • Warren Miller Collection of Early Dollars.

Total Estimated Population
MS-65 or better: 3 (URS-3)
MS-64: 1 (URS-1)
MS-63: 1 (URS-1)
MS-60 to 62: 1 or 2 (URS-1)
AU-50 to 58: 6 to 9 (URS-4)
VF-20 to EF-45: 35 to 45 (URS-7)
Fair-2 to F-15: 75 to 90 (URS-8)
Total for all grades combined: 135 to 150 (URS-8)
Estimated Total Condition Census: SP-66, MS-66, MS-66, MS-64, MS-63+, MS-62+

Known hoards of Mint State coins: Two pieces were in the Lord St. Oswald Collection auctioned in London in 1964, hardly a "hoard," but an interesting instance of two pieces from the same source.

Known hoards of circulated coins:[1] Dealer John Saunder owned about seven or eight at one time in the late 1880s; George H. Earle had a few in the decade or so after 1900; Dr. Charles Ruby, Fullerton, California, is believed to have had six by the late 1960s; in the 1980s an Ohio numismatist consigned about 15 pieces to Auctions by Bowers and Merena, Inc. for sale.

Commentary: The 1794 silver dollar, the first year of issue of the denomination, has always been a highly prized classic.

---

[1] Most of this information is courtesy of Jack Collins.

SUMMARY OF CHARACTERISTICS

1794

CIRCULATION STRIKES

Enabling legislation: Act of April 2, 1792

Designer: Robert Scot, with some credit due to Joseph Wright, who engraved the Liberty Cap *cent* in August 1793.

Statutory weight: 416 grains; .8924 silver, balance copper; actual fineness used (unauthorized by Congress): .900 silver, .100 copper

Melting value (silver bullion value) in year minted (discussion for all years 1794-1803):[1] Considered by Mint officials to be on a par with the Spanish dollar, and worth about $1.00 intrinsically. Silver values varied widely, and published data for prices on the London and Hamburg exchanges are not necessarily relevant for Philadelphia. Using European data, irrelevant as noted, the figure $0.907 is obtained. Again using European data (the Hamburg Exchange ratios of silver to gold), and reckoning the American gold eagle ($10) at its statutory weight of 247.59 grains gold, and the silver dollar at 371.25 grains silver, and using 1793's ratio of 15 to 1 (silver to gold) computed the yearly silver bullion value of the U.S. silver dollar as follows: 1794 (ratio: 15.37 to 1) $0.976; 1795 (ratio: 15.55 to 1) $0.964; 1796 (ratio: 15.65 to 1) $0.958;

1797 (ratio: 15.41 to 1) $0.973; 1798 (ratio: 15.59 to 1) $0.962; 1799 (ratio: 15.74 to 1) $0.953; 1800 (ratio: 15.68 to 1) $0.956; 1801 (ratio: 15.46 to 1) $0.970; 1802 (ratio: 15.25 to 1) $0.983; and 1803 (ratio: 15.41 to 1) $0.973. In 1794, the Bank of Maryland deposited in the Mint the écu equivalent of 69,692.4 ounces of silver, for which $80,715.735 was paid out, equal to $1.15 per ounce of pure silver. By this reckoning, a silver dollar (statutory weight of 371.25 grains pure silver) would have been worth $0.889. However, as R.W. Julian has pointed out,[2] there is no way to determine the exact value of silver at the Mint at the time, except to note that Mint officials always considered Spanish (later, Mexican) dollars to be worth par, or $1 in terms of a U.S. silver dollar. Values of silver in terms of gold are, as noted, not particularly relevant. "Part of the difficulty lies in the fact that, while the United States officially had a bimetallic system, in reality we had the single standard of silver, and all monetary matters were judged on this basis."

Dies prepared: Obverse: 1 (plus another, of which only a pattern striking is known, without obverse stars); reverse: 1

Circulation strike mintage, calendar year: 1,758 delivered; possibly 2,000 or so minted; Delivery figures by day: October 15: 1,758.

Estimated quantity melted: None specifically. Possibly 250 or so poorly struck 1794 dollars, from an original mintage of 2,000, were rejected as unsuitable for circulation and were used in 1795 as planchets for 1795 dollars.

Characteristics of striking: Nearly always seen lightly struck at lower left of the obverse and corresponding part of the reverse.

---

[1] In addition to the above, anyone desiring European melt-down values of U.S. silver dollars 1794-1799 can adapt them from Table 15, Jastram, *Silver: The Restless Metal*. Dollars 1794-5 are to be computed on the basis of .900 fine silver per coin, while those 1796-9 are to be computed at .8924 fine. These are *London* metal market prices translated at the fictitious exchange rate of $4.44 per £, without allowance for normal discounts and/or premiums; prices in the United States were different. I have been unable to locate any reliable yearly *domestic* figures for the 1794-1799 years. Quite probably, in New York a 1794 dollar was worth more than $0.907 in bullion value. Hamburg calculations courtesy of Andrew W. Pollock III. Michael J. Hodder provided information concerning Mint deposits.

---

[2] Letter to the author, January 2, 1993.

ADDITIONAL INFORMATION

Dickeson and the 1794 $1 (1859)

Dr. Montroville W. Dickeson included this information about the 1794 dollar in *The American Numismatical Manual*, 1859, the earliest widely-circulated text on numismatics published in America:

"1794. The first issue of the dollar, by our government, occurred in the latter part of October of this year. We are unable to furnish the exact number issued, as the mint report aggregates the sum for this and the succeeding year. As near as we have been able to learn, it was about 94,000."

Dickeson went on to say: "Of the dollar of this year we have met with but one type and four varieties, the latter of which may be determined by the variation in the size of the eagle, and the arrangement and size of the leaves in the wreath. This coin has become exceedingly rare, and fair specimens command a handsome premium."

Dickeson surely erred in regard to the multiple varieties, for later generations of numismatists have recognized just one variety of the 1794 dollar. Apparently, Dickeson may have examined worn coins, or in some other way came to a conclusion there were multiple varieties. Perhaps his notes on 1794 dollars were mixed with his notes on 1795 issues (of which many die varieties are known). He noted that his findings were "based upon the knowledge of them, which we have, with much great care and labor, been able personally to acquire."

Snowden and the 1794 $1 (1860)

The Cabinet Collection of the Mint of the United States, by Mint Director James Ross Snowden, 1860, p. 107, told of the first coinage of dollars:

The first deposit of silver bullion for coinage took place on the 18th day of July 1794. The deposit was made by the Bank of Maryland, and consisted of "coins of France," amounting to eighty thousand seven hundred and fifteen dollars seventy-three cents and five-tenths ($80,715.735.)

The first return of silver coins from the Chief Coiner to the Treasurer was made on the fifteenth day of October, and comprised 1,758 dollars. The second delivery was on the first day of December, and consisted of 5,300 half dollars. This embraced the entire silver coinage of the year. There was a small coinage of half dimes, but they were only struck as pattern pieces, for the purpose of trying the dies, and were not regularly issued.

The types were as follows: Obv. A head of Liberty, facing to the right, with flowing hair. Above was the word "Liberty," and beneath the date "1794." To the left of the effigy were eight stars, and to the right seven, fifteen in all. On the reverse was an eagle with raised wings, encircled by branches of laurel, crossed....

A Study of the 1794 $1 (1876)

The Coin and Stamp Journal, Kansas City, Missouri, January 1876, contained the following:

RARE AMERICAN COINS: We will endeavor, from the facts within our reach, to show what are our rare American coins, and their value. We do not attempt to give all the sales that have taken place, but only a few in different years. The great difference in prices brought at these sales are not caused so much by the real changes in the value of the coins, as from other circumstances, such as bad weather, numerous sales in succession, and lastly, our present hard times.[1]

THE DOLLAR OF 1794 is the first U.S. silver coin we will notice, and is, with the exception of 1804, the rarest of dollars. At the Mickley sale in 1867, the 1794 dollar brought $75.00. Described, "one of the finest dollars of this date in existence. The impression excellent and condition superb; much finer than one once sold for $285."

At the MacKenzie sale, June 23, 1869, one brought $145. Described, "This dollar is known to many collectors as the one sold in the collection of coins belonging to Mr. Zanoni, of Cincinnati, and is in my estimation the best that has ever been offered at auction, showing less marks of circulation than any other, *and very rare in this state of preservation.*" Another sold at the Fewsmith sale, Oct. 4, 1870, for $25. Described: "Good for date; obverse, head of Liberty bold and good; stars weak; date plain. Reverse, eagle and wreath well preserved; legend weak, extremely rare."

At Cauffman's sale, May 3, 1871, the price was $32. Described: "A better impression of this rare dollar than is usually found, being less injured by circulation than most of those offered at auction."

At a sale in New York, June 1, 1871, the dollar sold for the sum of $5.50. Thus described: "1794 dollar. Had it not been for an imperfection in the planchet, which has partly erased the three first figures in the date, it might have been called very good for this rare date, as in other respects there is not much to find fault with."

Sanford's sale, November 1874. Price procured was $180. Described: "This, in my opinion, is about the best impression that has ever been offered at auction. It is but little circulated and is exceedingly rare in this condition."

Parker's sale, May 5, 1875, only $30. Described: "Rather weak date, head rubbed, altogether fair for this rare piece."

At a Philadelphia sale, Jan. 25, 1875, one sold for $41. Described: '1794. Very good for this rare date; the head on obverse and eagle on reverse unusually bold; very desirable specimen; date all plain."

---

[1] QDB note: A reference to the unfavorable economic conditions which began with the Panic of 1873.

The one of Col. Cohen's collection, sold in October last, for $125. Described: "A remarkably fine impression of this date, being all but Uncirculated on obverse and reverse, and as fine, if not finer, than the one sold in Mr. Sanford's sale, and extremely rare in this condition."

The last one sold, Col. J.H. Taylor's, November 16th, brought $100. Described: "The best impression from the dollar dies of this date, and on the best planchet that I have ever seen—a remark I have often heard from others since the piece came into my hands. There has been a name engraved on the obverse and burnished out, the effect being observable, though not greatly hurtful; it is beautiful dollar, and equaled by few. Rare."

1794 $1 Sold for Face Value (1916)

The Numismatist, June 1916, page 294 reported an article from the Cincinnati *Times-Star,* April 20, 1916, which noted the following: "A silver dollar of 1794, the first standard dollar ever coined by the United States, was received at the United States Sub-Treasury Wednesday from a Louisville Bank, and it was redeemed as a one dollar Silver Certificate."

Venn on "Daddy Dollars" (1921)

The Numismatist, November 1921, contained an article, "Are the 'Daddy Dollars' Again Coming Into Their Own?" by Theodore J. Venn. The author was especially interested in the subject of coin popularity and investment and was a few decades ahead of most other writers in this field:

There was a time, far beyond the recollection of our present generation of numismatists, when our earliest silver dollars, the "dollars of our daddies," or "daddy dollars," as they were usually called, were the most popular coins among American collectors. This was years before the collecting of large United States cents became general and when these coins and the half cents still constituted our active copper circulation.

These early dollars, with their fine hair lines,[1] unquestionably made a strong appeal to the artistic eye, and many people therefore saved the few specimens that chanced to fall into their hands. From the time of their introduction in 1794 until the date of their suspension in 1803 (or 1804, as some will have it) fewer than 1,500,000 of these coins, all told, had been struck, so it will be readily seen that they could not have had much circulation among the people at large.

During the lapse of 36 or 37 years which followed prior to the resumption of silver-dollar coinage for general circulation in 1840 with a change of type, collectors eagerly sought these "daddy dollars" and paid large premiums for them. During the long hiatus the silver dollars had, so to speak, become obsolete, and many non-collectors who possessed a few of the coins became so attached to them that they refused to part with their specimens for any reasonable consideration. To some degree they had become heirlooms. And this continued for many years after the new type dollars made their appearance, for these were not "daddy dollars."

In examining early coin auction catalogs and price lists of the dealers of bygone days one will be surprised at the quotations for some of these dollars, even in Good or VG condition, as compared to what they had been bringing for about 20 years until the recent reaction in their favor set in. And the surprise will be increased when one stops to figure the vast difference between the purchasing power of money in those days and in our own.

It is difficult to attribute a cause for the decrease in interest in the early silver coinage which took place about a score or so years ago, unless it be laid to the influence of the preponderant number of collectors of copper coins who had entered the numismatic ranks within more recent years. This and a decline or absence of interest in the antique on the part of those into whose hands the "daddy dollars" had chanced to fall, thus temporarily glutting the coin market, would have been sufficient to bring about the condition that then prevailed.

The advent of so many new collectors within the past two years, however, has entirely changed the aspect of affairs and those who have been steadfast in their affection for the "daddy dollars" are about to be rewarded by seeing them once more come into their own. So many of the younger generation among the numismatists are showing a preference for these old dollars that bind us to the past that they probably will place them on a pinnacle higher than they formerly occupied, and the early silver half dollars, for which they also show a strong fancy, appear slated for deliverance from the slough of despondence in which they so long have been floundering. In fact, they have been on the upward trend for a year or more.

The numismatist who is inclined to doubt the good news need but examine his dealer's stock or make inquiries from collectors who unsuccessfully have been trying to secure some of the dates and varieties of the early dollars during the past year. Fortunately for the collector who wishes merely a specimen or two, the 1798, 1799 and 1800 still are readily procurable, but in most instances it is a different story with the other dates. A review of the auction sales of recent months also will show that the offerings have greatly decreased.

It is to be hoped the tribe of "daddy-dollar" collectors will continue to increase. Every true numismatist will be glad to learn that the shadows finally have lifted from these rare antiques that have been in partial eclipse so long.

---

[1] QDB note: A reference to the finely detailed hair strands of Miss Liberty on the 1798-1803 Draped Bust portrait.

More From Venn (1922)

The Numismatist, January 1922, carried more from Venn, under the title of "Liberty Dollars, 'Daddy' Dollars, Et Al.":

When the writer contributed a short article to the November issue of *The Numismatist* on the "daddy" dollars, he was aware there was a misconception on the part of some collectors as to which issue of United States silver dollars was really entitled to the appellation, but it is only within the past few weeks he has learned so many have been led into the delusion that the term applies to the 'Liberty-seated' dollars, the coinage of which began in 1840.

There is a slight excuse for this error, as it is partially based on custom, but custom frequently rests upon a false foundation and manages to perpetuate itself, nevertheless. Custom grows rapidly, but it is often a poor schoolmaster. For instance, custom wrongfully causes us to turn a German into a Dutchman and to shock purists with such expressions as "ain't" for "isn't," etc. Hence a small additional explanation as to the early dollars may not come amiss. The historical facts are as follows:

When coinage on the first issue of dollars, also frequently called "Liberty" dollars, was suspended, they soon went out of active circulation and few people saw any of them. When shown one of the coins, the exhibitor often was wont to remark, "These were the dollars of the daddies"—hence "daddy" dollars. Finally, to the average man, they became a mere tradition. When the later issue appeared in 1840, many of the younger generation who had heard the older issue referred to as "daddy" dollars would exclaim, "We again have the dollars of our daddies," and thus the custom grew until it finally even made some inroads on collectors, who also began to accept the term "daddy" dollars for the later issue. But this error on the part of custom does not make the earlier dollar lose any of its prerogatives—it is still the "daddy" dollar.[1]

The Hilt Theories (1980)

No discussion of the 1794 dollar would be complete without noting the revisionist theories proposed by Robert P. Hilt II in his 1980 book, *The Die Varieties of Early United States Coins.* Among his theories was that of a sharply revised mintage figure for dollars bearing the date 1794.

Hilt relates that the initial deposit of silver at the United States Mint was made by the Bank of Maryland on July 18, 1794, and consisted of 94,532 ounces of French minor coins of an inferior alloy. The Mint had but crude refining facilities at the time, and when the metal from this

deposit was brought up to the required standard the silver was imperfect. Planchets made from this batch "show splitting and craters on the surfaces," according to Hilt. However, in actuality, 1794 silver dollars were *not* made from the Bank of Maryland deposit (but were made from silver ingots deposited by Director David Rittenhouse and Charles Gilchrist).

He further related that 5,574 silver dollar planchets had been prepared by October 1794, and coinage began. Initial production consisted of 1,758 pieces, after which coinage was suspended. Hilt identified dollars from this first group by the poor striking of the stars at the lower left obverse and lightness of detail on the corresponding part of the reverse. He called these pieces Class I, and noted they were struck from perfect dies and blackened planchets. 1,758 such pieces were delivered on October 15, 1794.

He noted that Class II 1794 dollars were struck from lapped dies and blackened planchets, and that 3,810 coins were delivered on May 6, 1795. Class III 1794 dollars were struck from lapped dies and normal planchets, and 1,200 additional pieces were delivered on May 16, 1795. These figures add up to a revised total of 6,768 dollars dated 1794.

In his narrative comments, Mr. Hilt stated that after 1,758 1794 dollars were struck the dies were badly clashed and coinage was halted. He noted that survivors from this group of 1,758 are identifiable by having the stars on the lower left obverse and the corresponding area of the upper left reverse sharply struck. These were struck on a press intended for large cents, but which was put into service to make dollars [a fact which no one disputes]. Hilt suggested that when a correct large press was put into service in May 1795, lapped dies of 1794 were used, and that the lapping, intended to remove clash marks, weakened the design on the lower left obverse die on the corresponding area of the upper left of the reverse. The same writer stated that about 105 dollars of the 1794 date survive today.

Most students of the series, including the present author, believe that the weakness was caused by aligning the obverse and reverse die in a non-parallel fashion. Mr. Hilt illustrates and shows "presentation" coins from October 15, 1794 and notes that coins in the Lord St. Oswald Collection were also "presentation" pieces. I am not aware of any documentation for such presentations, or, for that matter, that anyone connected with the Lord St. Oswald Collection ever visited the Mint (the collection consisted of mixed coinage, dated *no later* than 1795, but including worn pieces as well as Uncirculated coins).

While the Hilt theories are interesting, I prefer to adhere to the commonly accepted delivery figure of 1,758 coins (plus, perhaps, 250 or so coins of defective strike held back for later use as planchets in 1795). I believe that the typical weakness of striking at the lower left of the obverse

---

[1] Notwithstanding this article, it is a fact that the Treasury Department called Liberty Seated dollars "daddies" and "daddy dollars." (See Liberty Seated section of the first edition.) However, traditionally the term was applied in numismatics to dollars of the 1794-1803 years, as Venn relates.

and corresponding area of the reverse on all known coins was due to the die faces not being parallel in the press, not, as Hilt suggests, to die resurfacing.

With regard to other early dollars, the Hilt study employs some highly interesting methods and ideas. Although I do not agree with certain of his conclusions concerning die progressions and mintage quantities, his text furnishes much excellent food for thought. (See also my comments about Robert Hilt's numbers for the 1797 BB-72 dollar, under that heading.)

The Year 1794 in History

The Whiskey Rebellion took place in western Pennsylvania when farmers on what was then the American frontier objected to a federal tax on whiskey. At the time, liquor was a medium of exchange and a store of value, as corn distilled into whiskey could be shipped more economically to eastern markets and was more easily stored and traded than grain. Tax collectors were tarred and feathered—or worse. President George Washington ordered the federal militia to stop such acts, which he called treasonous. Some Rebellion leaders were taken to Philadelphia (then capital of the United States) and tried. Two were convicted but were pardoned by the president. The Whiskey Rebellion was the first test of government power to enforce laws enacted by Congress.

On March 22, 1794 Congress forbade the states to engage in the slave trade with foreign nations. Nevertheless, the law was widely ignored, and slavers, as they were called, continued to bring their ships from Africa to ports in the southern United States. Slave markets flourished. In 1794, France declared that all slaves within its borders were free, becoming the first country in the world to make such a move.

The Battle of Fallen Timbers, August 20, 1794, was won by the government ending attacks on American settlers by Indians in the Kentucky and Ohio districts. Indians had been encouraged by the British to attack white settlers.

Jay's Treaty was signed on November 19, 1794, settling certain outstanding, unresolved disputes between the United States and Great Britain, but certain terms—including the provision that the British could search American vessels and take as prisoners any seamen of British citizenship—were met with disfavor in the United States. The Insurance Company of North America, chartered from Philadelphia, became the first United States firm to offer life insurance policies.

The Lancaster Road, financed by a $465,000 stock issue, opened to link Lancaster with Philadelphia and the Delaware River. The dirt thoroughfare, 62 miles in length, was a great success and paid dividends as high as 15% in some years. This set the tone for other toll road projects, including the Cumberland Road in 1811. In an era before canals and railroads, toll roads provided the main links between cities. Transportation was by horse and carriage. Few Americans traveled far from home. Eastern cities, mainly located on the Atlantic coast or on large inland tributaries, were connected by sailing ship routes which facilitated trade.

The membership rolls for Peale's Museum, opened in Philadelphia by portrait artist Charles Willson Peale, opened in January 1794. For the sum of one dollar, a patron could gain admission for the year. The first to subscribe was President George Washington, who bought four tickets. Exhibits in this, the first notable popular museum in America, pertained to natural history, art, and science.

Bowdoin College was founded in Maine in 1794; it would go on to have such illustrious instructors as Henry Wadsworth Longfellow and Harriet Beecher Stowe and to be recognized as a premier institution of higher learning. John Trumbull, American artist, produced his heroic-sized painting, *The Declaration of Independence,* which would become famous (and which in 1976 would be used on the reverse of the $2 bill). The first section of Thomas Paine's *The Age of Reason* was published in Paris, and solidified public opinion about Paine into two starkly opposing camps: staunch supporters, and vehement opponents. 1794 was, after all, the beginning of the Reign of Terror in France.

At the Philadelphia Mint, the emphasis was on copper coinage, and numerous varieties of half cents and large (as they would later be called) cents were struck. Half dollars and silver dollars were also made. Dies were prepared for 1794-dated half dimes but were not used until the following year. In New York City, the trading firm of Talbot, Allum & Lee issued copper one-cent pieces imported from Birmingham, England.

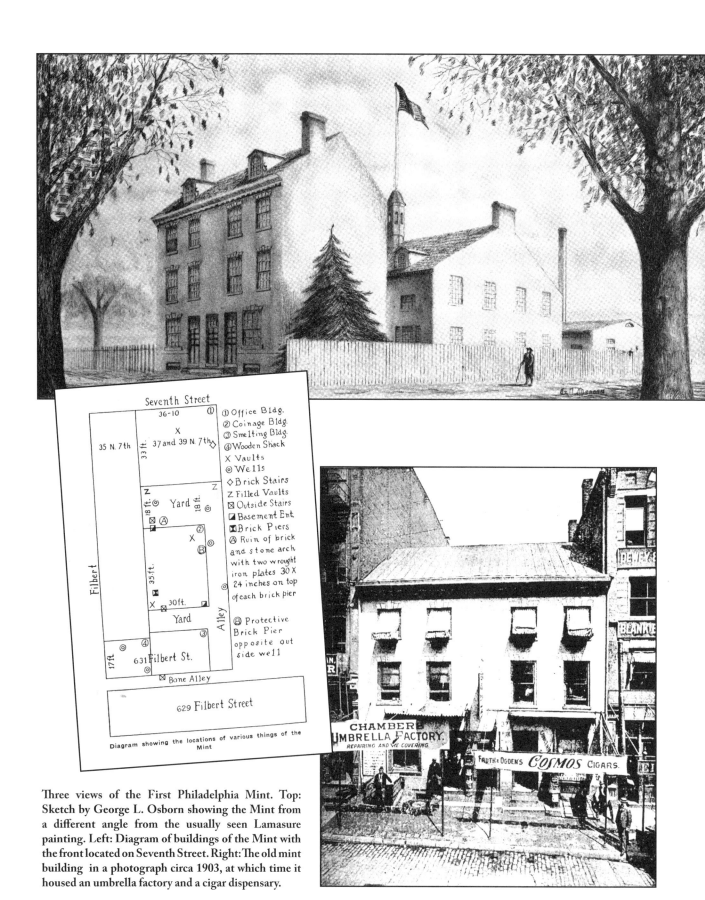

Seventh Street

36-10

① 35 N. 7th

X

33 ft.

37 and 39 N. 7th ◇

35 N. 7th

◎

Z   N   Z

18 ft.   18 ft.

Yard

⊠ Ⓐ

☑ ②

X

Ⓑ

◎

35 ft.

⊠ ☑

X   30 ft.   ☑

Yard   ③

◎ ④

17 ft.   631 Filbert St.

◎

⊠ Bone Alley

629 Filbert Street

① Office Bldg.
② Coinage Bldg.
③ Smelting Bldg.
④ Wooden Shack
X Vaults
◎ Wells
◇ Brick Stairs
Z Filled Vaults
⊠ Outside Stairs
☑ Basement Ent.
☒ Brick Piers
Ⓐ Ruin of brick
and stone arch
with two wrought
iron plates 30 X
24 inches on top
of each brick pier

Ⓑ Protective
Brick Pier
opposite out
side well

Diagram showing the locations of various things of the Mint

Three views of the First Philadelphia Mint. Top: Sketch by George L. Osborn showing the Mint from a different angle from the usually seen Lamasure painting. Left: Diagram of buildings of the Mint with the front located on Seventh Street. Right: The old mint building in a photograph circa 1903, at which time it housed an umbrella factory and a cigar dispensary.

Chapter 7
1795 FLOWING HAIR SILVER DOLLARS

Mintage (all types)
Calendar year, Mint report: 203,033
Coins bearing date, author's estimate: 390,000

1795 FLOWING HAIR SILVER DOLLARS

BB to Bolender to Haseltine Equivalents

BB Number	Bolender #	Haseltine #	Rarity	Average Grade
BB-11	B-3	H-3	URS-7	VF-29
BB-12	B-11	H-11	URS-6	VF-26
BB-13	B-9	H-9	URS-10	VF-27
BB-14	B-4	H-4	URS-10	VF-25
BB-15	B-8	H-8	URS-3	VF-22
BB-16	B-20	---	URS-3	F-14
BB-17	B-18	---	URS-1	N/A
BB-18	B-7	H-7	URS-11	VF-31
BB-19	B-19	---	URS-1	N/A
BB-20	B-2	H-2	URS-10	VF-28
BB-21	B-1	H-1	URS-12	VF-26
BB-22	B-10	H-10	URS-6	VF-28
BB-23	B-16	---	URS-2	VF-38
BB-24	B-13	H-13	URS-8	VF-36
BB-25	B-6	---	URS-10	VF-29
BB-26	B-12	H-12	URS-8	VF-20
BB-27	B-5	H-5	URS-13	VF-29
BB-28	B-21	---	URS-1	N/A
BB-29	B-22	---	URS-1	N/A

Coinage Context

Mintage figures and estimates: The government figures, per the annual Mint report, stated that 203,033 silver dollars were coined in calendar year 1795.

Based upon the number of 1795-dated dollars in the 1878 Economite hoard and the number certified today, I estimate that about 390,000 were struck bearing the 1795 date. I believe that nearly 185,000 of these were struck in later years, through 1798. Further information concerning these and other estimates may be found in Appendix II. These estimates are based upon the frequency of appearance of coins in the Economite Hoard unearthed in 1878, coins certified since 1986-7 by PCGS and NGC, and quantities believed to exist in numismatic circles today.

Walter H. Breen's estimates: Believing that Flowing Hair dollars were made at the Mint at least through early autumn 1795, and Draped Bust dollars were made after that, Walter H. Breen, in his *Encyclopedia*, has estimated that the mintage through and including October 10, 1795, consisted of Flowing Hair dollars, to the extent of 160,295 pieces, and that the last two deliveries of the year, on October 17 and 24, amounting to 42,738 coins, consisted of the Draped Bust type.

Author's estimates: As of September 2012, NGC and PCGS certified 4,326 specimens of the 1795 dollar, divided into 3,183 Flowing Hair dollars (74% of total) and 1,143 Draped bust dollars (26%).

If these percentages are applied to the 390,000 1795-dated dollars I believe were struck, the estimated mintage (rounded off) of 1795-dated Flowing Hair dollars is 290,000, and that of 1795-dated Draped Bust dollars is 100,000.

I caution the reader to remember that these estimates are simply that: estimates. As one estimate is used to create another, we have the situation of estimates being built upon other estimates, and the reliability diminishes. Because of this, all estimated figures should be taken as approximations. The way I see it, while the certification service percentages of 74% and 26% are as good as any, perhaps the truth is really 68% and 32%, or 75% and 25%, or whatever. We are dealing with *concepts*, not with mathematical precision. However, these concepts are a valuable aid to understanding the relationships among early dollar types and varieties. Further, although the relative availability of surviving Flowing Hair types and Draped Bust dollars can be observed, and coinages can be estimated from these numbers, there is no documentation that the Draped Bust dollars were first struck in autumn 1795. There is always the possibility that they could have been made later.

Number of dies used: The number of dies employed to create 1795-dated dollars is as follows:

1795 Flowing Hair, obverses: 10

1795 Flowing Hair, reverses used with this obverse style: 11

1795 Draped Bust, obverses: 2

1795 Draped Bust, reverses used with this obverse style: 2

Total: 12 obverses and 13 reverses for dollars of this year.

Die use averages: By dividing the number of obverse dies and the number of reverse dies each with the mintage figure for the appropriate design, estimates of the average number of impressions per die can be obtained. In practice, some dies lasted a long time and others broke quickly; the figures here are averages, as noted.

10 Flowing Hair obverses divided into estimated Flowing Hair coinage of 286,956 = 28,696 coins per obverse die.

11 Flowing Hair reverses divided into estimated Flowing Hair coinage of 286,956 = 26,087 coins per reverse die.

2 Draped Bust obverses divided into estimated Draped Bust coinage of 103,044 = 51,522 coins per obverse die.

2 Draped Bust reverses divided into estimated Draped Bust coinage of 103,044 = 51,522 coins per reverse die (the inclusion of the long-lived 1795 BB-51 die, which was used later, distorts this figure).

Numismatic Information

Collecting possibilities: For the numismatist interested in die varieties, 1795 Flowing Hair dollars offer 19 possibilities (or 20, if Die State I and Die State III of 1795 BB-25 are collected separately). As most early dollars on the market are unattributed, there is always a chance of finding a rare variety for a "type" price. Even when varieties are attributed—such as in sales held by the leading auction houses—rare varieties often sell for only a little more than common ones. Extremely rare varieties are an exception, however. A variety of which fewer than a dozen are known will always command wide attention. Even so, current market prices are apt to be much less than one would pay for a large cent of the same era and of comparable rarity.

Of the 19 known varieties of Flowing Hair dollars, it should be possible to acquire about half of them within a year or so. The others will be located a few at a time. If the majority of the dealer community and the NGC and PCGS certification services begin attributing dollars by die varieties, they will be advertised widely and will be easier to find. Of course, this is a two-edged sword, for then the prices of scarce and rare varieties will probably be higher than it is now.

There are only two varieties of 1795 Draped Bust silver dollars, BB-51 and BB-52. Both are readily available, and you will have no difficulty in acquiring a specimen of one or both. The 1795 BB-51, employing as it does the off-center Draped Bust on the obverse and the curious and long-lived Small Letters die for the reverse, is certainly one of the most interesting varieties in the early dollar series.

Technical Information
(Flowing Hair and Draped Bust Types)

General information: All 1795 dollars have 8 stars to the left and 7 to the right, as in 1794. This 15-star count was used on all Flowing Hair and Draped Bust dollars of 1795.

Making punches: Master dies, puncheons, or hubs (they have been known under many names over the years) were created for certain elements in the design of the 1795 (and later) dollars. For dollars of the 1795-1803 period, these punches, as I shall call them here, consisted of major design elements. Punches for the head of Miss Liberty, eagle, and much of the wreath were probably made as follows:

1. The engraver prepared a smooth, polished die surface at the end of a steel shank. A light coating of wax was applied to the surface, and a sketch of a design was transferred by rubbing or burnishing into the wax. By use of engraving tools, the craftsman cut the features of the wreath, including the branch and some leaves—intaglio (incuse) into the die. From time to time, wax impressions would be made of the engraving as it progressed, to show in raised or relief features what the wreath would look like on a finished coin. Some of the leaves were put in with punches. Finally, all details were completed, and the punch was ready for further use.

2. The die was heated slowly, then quenched in water, to harden the steel. The surfaces of the die were cleaned, and another wax impression was taken of the wreath, to be sure it was what was wanted.

3. The hardened die was placed in a screw press that operated slowly (alternatively, with a series of quick, light blows), as to squeeze the image from the hardened die into the face of another die, the second die being of soft steel (not yet hardened). The second die had a slightly conical face, rather than a flat one, to facilitate metal movement into the recesses of the hardened die.

4. The second die, with the wreath appearing raised (in relief), was inspected, and any minor changes needed were made. The second die was then subjected to the hardening process, after which it was cleaned, and was ready to use as a finished punch.

A punch could be made by engraving the design in relief, rather than in intaglio, equivalent to step 4. This was done with letter, star, numeral, and certain other punches, which were easier for the artist to create in this manner.

Any punch could be replicated by hardening it, pressing it into soft steel, hardening the soft steel, and using the just-hardened die to press into still another soft steel blank, to create a positive (in relief) copy. This would be hardened, and used as a punch. This hard-soft steel transfer process resulted in some detail being lost each time, but this loss could be compensated for by retouching.

The making of design punches, such as the portrait of Miss Liberty, the eagle, and, to a lesser extent, the wreath, was assigned to a skilled engraver. The preparation of numeral, star, leaf, letter, and other small punches was sometimes done on a contract basis with outsiders.

Earlier in this book, R.W. Julian related that Frederick Geiger had been hired in early 1794 by Director David Rittenhouse to make letter punches for coinage; his tenure as a Mint employee was brief. On October 19, 1795, Thomas Bingham, not a Mint employee, was paid $48 for 96 letter and numeral punches for use on various coin denominations.[1]

For some dies it is possible, indeed probable, that the engraver who made the motif punches was not the same engraver who made the coining die by utilizing the motif punches and adding the lettering, etc. It is presumed that over the years duplicate punches were made of letters used frequently, such as in the familiar (today) E (most frequently used letter), T, A, O, I, N, S, H, R, D, L, U, etc., sequence, although for coinage in the 1790s, the letters in commonly used inscriptions such as LIBERTY and UNITED STATES OF AMERICA were those for which duplicates were needed. Examination of 1796-7

coins reveals that two different "Small Letters" E punches were used on dollars, for example.

Making dies: An obverse die for a 1795 silver dollar was made by punching the portrait into a die blank of soft steel. Probably, LIBERTY was added next, then the stars, and finally the date.

To make a reverse die for a 1795 silver dollar, the finished eagle motif punch was used to impress the eagle design into the center of a soft steel coining die. After this was done, the wreath punch was used. Then, wreath stems, ribbon ends, and letters of UNITED STATES OF AMERICA were added, and the coining die went through the hardening process. Then it was cleaned and made ready for use in a coining press.

The classification of die varieties today is accomplished by studying the positions of these elements in relation to each other.

Classifying 1795 Dollar Obverse Die Styles (Flowing Hair type)

There were two different portrait punches used on obverse dies for 1795 Flowing Hair dollars and two different eagle punches used on reverse dies. In addition, reverses were made in two different styles of wreaths: These are described below:

PI Portrait: "Head of 1794." The Head of 1794 portrait was made from a master punch depicting Miss Liberty with rounded cheek and prominent jaw line. There is no double line under bust truncation. The bust point is blunter than on the following (Head of 1795). At the back of the head, the highest curl is thin. All of these portrait characteristics are also found on the 1794 silver dollar.

No 1795 head is *exactly* like 1794, as hair details were finished by hand. However, dollars from the PI portrait punch come quite close. It is believed that this punch die was the work of Robert Scot, on the knowledge that as of the initial delivery of 1794 dollars on October 15, 1794, Scot was the chief engraver at the Mint. (An assistant, John Smith Gardner, was hired in November 1794, and continued at the Mint intermittently until summer 1796.) The dies could have been finished by either Scot or Gardner, by punching the stars, letters of LIBERTY, and date. It is popular to suggest that the chief engraver (in this case, Scot) did the main design work, and the assistant (Gardner) did the routine job of making dies. In actuality, probably the work was divided. Once the motif punches were made (and this was done only at widely separated intervals as new designs or replacement punches were called for), the primary work for the chief engraver and his assistant was creating dies.

PII Portrait: "Head of 1795." The Head of 1795 portrait was made from a new master punch with the cheek of Miss Liberty in shallower relief than the preceding, and

---

[1] *Walter Breen's Complete Encyclopedia of U.S. and Colonial Coins*, p. 425.

the jaw line not prominent. There is a double line, sort of a flattened loop, under the center and left side of the bust truncation. Bust point sharp. At the back of the head, the highest curl is thick. It is not known who made the master hub for the Class II obverse, but John Smith Gardner may be a candidate.

Distribution of varieties:

Varieties with PI Portrait (Head of 1794, no line under truncation):

Obverse Die No. PI-1: Used to strike 1795 BB-11, BB-12, and BB-13.

Obverse Die No. PI-2: Used to strike 1795 BB-14 (although BB-14 is of the PI style, the bust point is less rounded than on the other dies).

Obverse Die No. PI-3: Used to strike 1795 BB-18, BB-17, and BB-16 (on this, the highest curl at the back of the head is slightly thicker than usually seen on PI, but thinner than usually seen on PII).

Obverse Die No. PI-4: Used to strike 1795 BB-28.

Varieties with PII Portrait (Head of 1795, line under truncation): This obverse portrait hub was used to create the majority of 1795 obverse dies as follows:

Obverse Die No. PII-1: Used to strike 1795 BB-21, BB-22, and BB-23.

Obverse Die No. PII-2: Used to strike 1795 BB-20 and BB-19.

Obverse Die No. PII-3: Used to strike 1795 BB-27.

Obverse Die No. PII-4: Used to strike 1795 BB-24, and, in original and relapped states, to strike 1795 BB-25.

Obverse Die No. PII-5: Used to strike 1795 BB-15

Obverse Die No. PII-6: Used to strike 1795 BB-26 and BB-29.

Classifying 1795 Dollar Reverse Die Styles (used with Flowing Hair type)

EI Eagle: The EI and EII eagle punches are somewhat similar to that used in 1794, but are not the same. The EI has six feathers in the eagle's tail (EII has five). On EI the left-most claw (from the observer's viewpoint) is at the top *edge* of the rock (on EII it is in from the edge). There are some slight differences in the feather details; see under the eagle's right or dexter (to observer's left) wing, for example. Both the EI and EII punches seem to be from the same engraver's hand.

EII Eagle: Five feathers in eagle's tail; leftmost claw is not on the edge of the rock.

WI Wreath, 2 Leaves Under Each Wing: The WI wreaths, of which there are several variations (as finishing work was done by hand) are stylistically similar to that used in 1794 (but are not from the motif punch used in 1794, if indeed a motif punch was used for the reverse then), and are quite different from WII (described below).

Perhaps, the 1794 wreath and 1795 WI were the work of Robert Scot, and 1795 WII was from the hand of John Gardner, although I believe that insufficient evidence is on hand to make such attributions.

WI wreaths have two leaves beneath each wing—a quick guide to identification (WII wreaths have three leaves). On the WI wreaths, the two branches to the wreath are thinner, and the leaves are smaller and less finely detailed. On the eagle's right (observer's left) wing there are two leaves at the point at which the branch crosses it. On the inside of the wreath at the top, below the single leaves at the apex, are found pairs of leaves, one on each side, drooping downward. Where the wreath branches join at the bottom, the ribbon has a knot (unlike 1794, which lacks this feature). The engraver's work on the reverse dies with WI wreath was probably accomplished in this order:

1. The eagle motif was punched into the steel blank.
2. The wreath motif was punched into the die.
3. Wreath details were added and/or strengthened, the wreath apex was completed, leaves were punched into the left side of the die where the wreath is *above* the eagle's wing, berries and their stems were added, the branch ends were added, and the lettering UNITED STATES OF AMERICA was added around the border.

WII Wreath, 3 Leaves Under Each Wing: The three known dies using WII wreaths are each quite different from the preceding WI varieties. There are three leaves beneath each wing, which is the least important consideration from a style viewpoint. The leaves are larger than on the WI wreaths, are more finely detailed, and have raised edges or outlines; overall, the wreath is more sturdy. On the eagle's dexter (observer's left) wing there are more than two leaves at the point at which the branch crosses it. The inside pairs of leaves at the top are larger and not as "droopy" as on the preceding. Where the wreath branches join at the bottom there is no knot; the junction is wrapped with a ribbon (as in 1794).

All three of the known WII wreath dies were made from the same wreath punch, which did not include the topmost part of the wreath (which was added by hand). The engraver's work on the reverse dies with WII wreath was accomplished in this order:

1. The eagle motif was punched into the steel blank.
2. The wreath motif was punched into the die.
3. Wreath details were added and/or strengthened, the wreath apex was completed, leaves were punched into the left side of the die where the wreath is *above* the eagle's wing, the branch ends were added, and the lettering UNITED STATES OF AMERICA was added around the border.

The WII wreath punch was more sophisticated than that used for WI, in that most of the berries were in place on WII as were nearly all of the final leaves (except at the apex). Thus, it is certain that WII reverse dies were made later than WI reverse dies. In general, reverses with WII wreaths appear bolder than those with WI wreaths. The structure and appearance of individual leaves in WII wreaths is similar to that on leaves on the reverse of the 1795 Draped Bust obverse, Small Eagle reverse dollars, further indicating that the WII reverse style was the latest made before the end of the Flowing Hair coinage. I believe that WII wreaths were not made before late summer or autumn 1795.

Distribution of varieties (by reverses):
Varieties with EI Eagle (6 tail feathers) and WI Wreath (2 leaves under each wing):
    Reverse Die No. EI-WI-1: Used to strike 1795 BB-21, BB-20, and BB-24.
    Reverse Die No. EI-WI-2: Used to strike 1795 BB-11.
    Reverse Die No. EI-WI-3: Used to strike 1795 BB-13 and BB-14.
    Reverse Die No. EI-WI-4: Used to strike 1795 BB-15 and BB-16.
    Reverse Die No. EI-WI-5: Used to strike 1795 BB-12.
    Reverse Die No. EI-WI-6: Used to strike 1795 BB-23 and BB-28.
    Reverse Die No. EI-WI-7: Used to strike 1795 BB-17.
Varieties with EI Eagle (6 tail feathers) and WII Wreath (3 leaves under each wing):
    Reverse Die No. EI-WII-1: Used to strike 1795 BB-18 and BB-19.
Varieties with EII Eagle (5 tail feathers) and WI Wreath (2 leaves under each wing):
    None.
Varieties with EII Eagle (5 tail feathers) and WII Wreath (3 leaves under each wing):
    Reverse Die No. EII-WII-1: Used to strike 1795 BB-25, BB-26 and BB-27.
    Reverse Die No. EII-WII-2: Used to strike 1795 BB-29

1795 Die Combinations
(Flowing Hair Type)

PI Obverse/EI-WI Reverse: 1795 BB-11, BB-12, BB-13, BB-14, BB-16, BB-17, and BB-28.

PI Obverse/EI-WII Reverse: 1795 BB-18.

PI Obverse/EII-WI Reverse: 1795 None.

PI Obverse/EII-WII Reverse: 1795 None.

PII Obverse/EI-WI Reverse: 1795 BB-16, BB-15, BB-21, BB-22, BB-23, BB-20, and BB-24.

PII Obverse/EI-WII Reverse: 1795 BB-19.

PII Obverse/EII-WI Reverse: 1795 None.

PII Obverse/EII-WII Reverse: 1795 BB-25, BB-26, BB-27, and BB-29.

BB Varieties / Portrait / Eagle / Wreath Styles

1795 BB#	Portrait	Eagle	Wreath
BB-11	I (Head of '94)	I	I (2 leaves)
BB-12	I (Head of '94)	I	I (2 leaves)
BB-13	I (Head of '94)	I	I (2 leaves)
BB-14	I (Head of '94)	I	I (2 leaves)
BB-15	II (Head of '95)	I	I (2 leaves)
BB-16	I (Head of '94)	I	I (2 leaves)
BB-17	I (Head of '94)	I	I (2 leaves)
BB-18	I (Head of '94)	I	II (3 leaves)
BB-19	II (Head of '95)	I	II (3 leaves)
BB-20	II (Head of '95)	I	I (2 leaves)
BB-21	II (Head of '95)	I	I (2 leaves)
BB-22	II (Head of '95)	I	I (2 leaves)
BB-23	II (Head of '95)	I	I (2 leaves)
BB-24	II (Head of '95)	I	I (2 leaves)
BB-25	II (Head of '95)	II	II (3 leaves)
BB-26	II (Head of '95)	II	II (3 leaves)
BB-27	II (Head of '95)	II	II (3 leaves)
BB-28	I (Head of '94)	I	I (2 leaves)
BB-29	II (Head of '95)	II	II (3 leaves)

Delivery Dates

Had dollar-minting operations been in normal order at the Mint, it would be logical to assume today that the earlier dies—PI Portrait obverses and WI Wreath reverses—would have been used first, followed by the PII Portrait and WII Wreath dies. However, after the initial delivery of 1794 dollars on October 15, 1794, dollar production was suspended, as it was felt that a larger press was needed. On October 28, 1794, Director David Rittenhouse wrote to Secretary of State Edward Randolph stating, in part: "A large parcel of blank dollars is ready for coining, waiting for a more powerful press to be finished, in order to complete them for currency." Obviously, it was intended that these blank planchets be coined into 1794-dated dollars, but as the striking of 1794 dollars had not been completely satisfactory (the coins were weak on the left side of the obverse and corresponding part of the reverse), and the dies had been damaged by clashing and relapping, it was deemed best to wait. In the meantime, large quantities of silver half dollars were struck.

Collectors of *half* dollars can be grateful that the Mint had no suitable press for silver dollars, for in the absence of dollar coinage from October 1794 through May 1795, deliveries of half dollars were frequent and massive. Depositors of silver bullion could not obtain silver dollars. Thus, they were given specimens of the largest silver denomination available, half dollars. Once silver dollar production resumed with vigor in May 1795, half dollar deliveries diminished. The last half dollar delivery of the year was on June 5, 1795, after which no half dollars were delivered until 1797 (in which year 1796- and 1797-dated halves were paid out). On the other hand, if the Mint had not obtained a suitable silver dollar press until 1798, then today 1796 and 1797 halves would be common! It is interesting how a single event, such as the availability of a coin press, dramatically affected the production and relationship of silver dollar dies of 1795, the quantities of half dollars produced late 1795 through 1797, and other situations.

By May 6, 1795, a large press was in working order, silver dollars had been struck, and a delivery of 3,810 silver dollars took place. Presumably, in the more than half year that elapsed since the last delivery of dollars on October 15, 1794, many new silver dollar obverse (dated 1795) and reverse dies had been created, probably including all three of the known PI (Head of 1794) obverses and many of the WI style reverses (but not the two known WII reverses).

When completed, these dies were coated with grease (to protect against rusting) and put in the die chest or vault, awaiting call for their use. When that call came in May 1795, the earliest dies made were not necessarily the earliest dies used. The circulation strike mintages of the *calendar year* 1795 are given below, per the research of R.W. Julian.

In addition, in *italic type*, delivery dates for $10 gold coins are given. If the same large press was employed for minting this denomination, the coinage for these deliveries would have interrupted the production of silver dollars and would have necessitated the removal of the dollar dies from the press. (Probably, half dollars were made on a smaller press—as evidenced by multiple deliveries of half dollars early in 1795, before the large-size press for dollars was installed. It may be that $10 pieces, about the diameter of a half dollar and in slightly softer alloy, were coined on a smaller press as well.)

Circulation strike mintage (combined for all 1795 dollars, Flowing Hair and Draped Bust types): 203,033 (not including pieces reserved for the Assay Commission; these are additional and are given in parentheses); Delivery figures by day: • May 6: 3,810 First delivery of silver dollars since the one and only 1794 dollar delivery on October 15, 1794. By now, a new, larger press had been installed specifically to make silver dollars • May 16: 15,268 (+3 for Assay Commission) • June 5: 10,917 (+3) • June 5 (same day): 10,430 (+2) In June, Mint Director David Rittenhouse resigned, and William DeSaussure took his place. • June 17: 10,000 (+3) • June 20: 5,986 (+3) • June 26: 6,000 (+3) • June 29: 4,000 (+3) • July 2: 5,243 (+3) • July 9: 5,000 (+3) • July 13: 7,000 (+3) • July 17: 4,500 (+3) • July 21: 6,000 (+3) • July 23: 4,876 (+3) • July 30: 1,184 (+3) • *July 31: Delivery of $10 eagles. Silver dollar coinage interrupted.* • August 10: 3,500 (+3) • *August 11 through August 21; multiple deliveries*

of eagles. Silver dollar coinage interrupted. • August 22: 4,385 (+3) • August 29: 6,500 (+3) • August 31: 1,106 (+3) • September 1: 830 (+3) New WII wreath may have been introduced about this time; in the meantime, WI wreaths continued to be used on extant dies. • *September 1: Delivery of $10 eagles. Silver dollar coinage interrupted.* • September 12: 4,260 (+3) • *September 22, 24: Deliveries of $10 eagles. Silver dollar coinage interrupted.* • September 24: 4,000 (+3) • October 3: 15,000 (+3) New Draped Bust/Small Eagle design may have been introduced about this time. • October 7: 6,000 (+3) • October 10: 14,500 (+3) • *October 10: Delivery of $10 eagles. Silver dollar coinage interrupted.* • October 17: 23,368 (+3) • *October 22: Delivery of $10 eagles. Silver dollar coinage interrupted.* • October 24: 19,370 (+3) • October 27: Resignation date of Mint Director DeSaussure; no more silver dollars minted this calendar year. • *November 27: Delivery of $10 eagles.*

The preceding deliveries demonstrate that silver dollars were coined on many different occasions throughout the 1795 year. Most deliveries were of Flowing Hair type dollars, with the later deliveries being of the new Draped Bust type. It is not known exactly when Draped Bust dollars were first delivered, nor is it known that from that point all were of the new type. I consider it likely that left-over 1795 Flowing Hair dollar dies and their appropriate reverses were also used after 1795.

When it was desired that dollars be coined, a pair of dies would be taken from the die chest or vault and placed into the press. Inasmuch as there are few instances of random mixing of dies, it was probably the usual case (with some exceptions) that a die pair would be used until one of the dies broke or otherwise became unusable. The defective die would be removed, and another die put in its place. Coining would resume. Eventually, another die would break—perhaps the newer one put in recently, or perhaps the older of the two dies. Another die would be installed. This process went on and on, creating die linking. By means of studying die states, numismatists today can determine the order of striking of certain varieties.

I assume that the earlier mintage of 1795 dollars, for the deliveries for May 1795 and a month or two afterward, were from dies with the PI (Head of 1794) obverse and the WI (two leaves under each wing) reverse. As more dies were made, these were mixed up with dies already on hand, and any semblance of logical sequence was lost. I believe that the two reverse dies with the WII style wreath (three leaves under each wing) were the last made for use with the Flowing Hair obverses, and were manufactured no earlier than late summer 1795.

Coinage in 1795 vs. later years: As noted in the introduction to the section on early dollars, it seems likely to me that tens of thousands of 1795-dated dollars were made after 1795, perhaps in 1796 but most likely in 1798. If this is the case, can it be determined which varieties were coined in 1795 and which were minted later? The answer cannot be definitive, but there are some varieties which were certainly minted in 1795. These include the following:

BB-11, BB-13, BB-14, BB-18, BB-19, and BB-21, because these varieties are known with silver alloy plugs in the center, the correction of a problem believed to have been unique to the 1795 year (see "A curious situation" below).

BB-14 (additional verification), because an example of this variety is known overstruck on a 1794 dollar, presumably one on hand early in 1795. It is believed that a couple of hundred or more defective 1794 dollars were kept at the Mint and overstruck in May 1795 when the new press became available.

BB-20 and BB-18, because these varieties were a part of the Lord St. Oswald Collection consisting of coins said to have been gathered in America in autumn 1795.

Putting together the preceding, the list of "positive" 1795 striking includes these varieties: BB-11, BB-13, BB-14, BB-18, BB-19, BB-20, and BB-21. These are a mixture of motif punch styles, verifying that these die classes were employed at the Mint in no particular order. To be specific:

BB-11: Portrait I, Eagle I, Wreath I. Earlier obverse portrait and reverse styles.

BB-13: Portrait I, Eagle I, Wreath I. Earlier obverse portrait and reverse styles.

BB-14: Portrait I, Eagle I, Wreath I. Earlier obverse portrait and reverse styles.

BB-18: Portrait I, Eagle I, Wreath II. Earlier obverse portrait and earlier eagle style with later wreath style.

BB-19: Portrait II, Eagle I, Wreath II. Later obverse portrait and earlier eagle style with later wreath style.

BB-20: Portrait II, Eagle I, Wreath I. Later obverse portrait in combination with earlier eagle motif and wreath style.

BB-21: Portrait II, Eagle I, Wreath I. Later obverse portrait in combination with earlier eagle motif and wreath style.

Arranged another way:

Earlier obverse portrait and reverse styles. BB-11, BB-13, and BB-14.

Earlier obverse portrait and earlier eagle style with later wreath style: BB-18.

Later obverse portrait in combination with earlier eagle motif and wreath style: BB-21 and BB-20.

Later obverse portrait in combination with earlier eagle motif and later wreath style: BB-19.

A curious situation:[1] Several examples of 1795 Flowing Hair dollars (including BB-11, BB-13, BB-14, BB-18, BB-19, and BB-21 varieties) have been seen with a circular

(more or less) silver plug in the center, the outline of the plug being visible at the center of the obverse and reverse.[2] The plugs were inserted before the coins were struck, as they were flattened by the dies and carry impressions of the design. Why these plugs were used is not known. It is quite possible, indeed likely, that numerous other dollars exist with central plugs, but that the flattening during the striking process was so complete that no trace remains of them today. Often, the different alloy of the central plug caused it to tone differently.

It may have been that during the weighing process, certain planchets were found to be slightly too light. Rather than go through the process of melting the planchets, casting the metal into ingots, rolling strips from the ingots, and making new planchets, it may have been deemed more expedient to drill a small hole in the center of the light-weight planchet and insert a silver plug, extending slightly above and below the planchet surface; a plug with enough extra weight to compensate for the drilled hole and also the deficiency in the original planchet weight. The planchet-with-plug was then struck by dies, flattening the plug and producing coins as observed. The Mint had the technological capability of inserting such plugs, as evidenced by the 1792 silver-center pattern cents (Judd-1).

The complicated nature of planchet making in 1801, a year not distant from the 1795 year under discussion, is illustrated by this quotation from *The U.S. Mint and Coinage:*[3]

"Voigt said that the gold and silver planchets underwent 32 operations before they were ready to receive an impression." However, the same text also noted this: "Voigt's 32 operations must have included many subdivisions, and perhaps the labor of various clerks." Even so, it is clear that planchet making was not an simple process.

A commentary upon and summary of the 1795 plugged dollars by Kenneth E. Bressett follows:[4]

Certain United States silver dollars dated 1795 are known to have a silver plug in the center of the coin. This plug was imbedded in the planchet prior to the coin being struck by regular dies. In some cases the only evidence of the plug is a tell-tale seam or discoloration at the center of the coin on one or both sides.

Just why a plug was added to these coins is a mystery. Most silver dollars of 1795 do not have such a plug, and no other dollars of any other date have been seen with this feature. As far as is now known no other coin denomination in the

---

[1] This situation was first described by the author in 1981. Tom DeLorey, Kenneth E. Bressett, and Roger W. Burdette, among others, corresponded with the author on the subject in 1991-2.

[2] As of October 26, 1992, Kenneth E. Bressett had examined three plugged specimens of BB-12, one of BB-11, one of BB-13 (plus a photograph of another BB-13), one of BB-14, and two of BB-18. Letter to the author, October 26, 1992.

[3] Don Taxay, 1966, p. 35. The discussion was part of a Mint effort to discredit one Robert Leslie, who proposed introducing roller dies ("double cylinder dies") to the Mint.

[4] Created for inclusion in this book.

regular United States series was officially altered with a plug of any kind. The only similar occurrence can be found in the 1792 silver center patterns where a silver plug was added to a copper planchet prior to striking the coin.

The 1795 dollars with silver plug have been known to a few students for the past decade, but no one has been able to determine the reason for this strange alteration to normal coinage. It is reasonable to believe that many such pieces have been overlooked in the past because of the subtle difference in appearance. The number of pieces originally made can only be roughly estimated by the availability of surviving specimens. The fact that about a dozen pieces were identified by the author in a six-month period indicates that the coinage was perhaps quite extensive.

All of the examined dollars of 1795 with plug are of the Flowing Hair type. None of the 1795 Draped Bust type pieces have been observed with this feature. Varieties seen are: BB-11, 13, 14, 18, and 21 (equivalent to Bolender-3, 9, 4, 7 and 1 respectively). Each of these varieties is also known with plentiful specimens of normally made coins without the plug. In each case the plugs were inserted before the coins were struck, as they were flattened by the dies and carry impressions of the design. The plugs average about 8 mm. in diameter and are always located in the exact center of the coin. The effect can usually be seen on both sides.

It has been suggested by Q. David Bowers that the striking sequence of 1795 dollars indicates that BB-11, 13, 14, 18, and 21 were varieties made earlier than many of the others, but no earlier than late summer 1795. It also seems likely that all of the silver plug pieces were made in 1795 and none later.

The use of multiple dies for striking plugged pieces seems to negate the possibility of the plug being used to alter the fineness of these coins. The notion of that possibility was originally suggested by the author and Roger W. Burdette, among others, because of the situation created by Mint director David Rittenhouse whereby he allowed coins to be made of an illegal standard to reconcile the strange .8924 fineness (1485/1664) mandated by Congress. A plug might have been used to correct or adjust coins found to be too far from the authorized fineness.

A simpler, and more plausible solution seems to be in the use of the plug to adjust the weight of these coins. Planchet preparation in those days was costly and time consuming. Any that were too heavy could be filed to remove excess metal, but those that were underweight had to be melted and remade into blanks. An alternate remedy may have been to cut a hole in the center of the blank, insert a plug of proper weight and then stamp the coin.

Evidence of this later theory comes from testing known pieces to ascertain the metal content of coin and plug. If plugs were added to adjust the fineness they should be lower than the basic coins which according to Rittenhouse were of a fineness higher than specified by law. If on the other hand the plugs were added to adjust the weight, they would be of a fineness similar to the rest of the coin.

Testing by spectrographic x-ray analysis showed that most of the coins with plugs were made of the same alloy both in the plug area and in the surrounding coin. One showed that the plug was of higher fineness, and one of lower fineness. Although the tests were inconclusive as to the nature and reason for being added to these coins, it seems safe to conclude that the most likely reason was to add silver to underweight planchets. Why this was done only on silver dollar blanks and only for the Flowing Hair pieces remains a mystery. Perhaps it was an experimental practice tried on the blanks that were made and stored for a time awaiting a more powerful coinage press.

By May 6, 1795, a large press was put into use and delivery of 3,810 silver dollars took place. Thereafter followed many thousands of additional pieces, some of which were surely made from the stockpile of silver dollar planchets that had been in waiting since late 1794.

Perhaps we will never know exactly why the Mint made these unusual silver plug dollars. Their existence and purpose has been hidden for nearly 200 years. Are there other coins like these in the United States series? Hopefully knowledge of these pieces will lead to still other unexplored areas of numismatics that no one before suspected. It is discoveries like these that keep the hobby alive and enjoyable.

As the known die varieties with visible plugs are distributed throughout the striking sequence (as evidenced by the inclusion of BB-18, which uses the WII wreath employed, in my opinion, no earlier than late summer 1795), it seems that the plugging process was employed from May to at least late summer. In any event, I believe that varieties known with silver plugs were struck in calendar year 1795 and not later. If the plug was inserted to correct the planchet weight, the problem must have been solved after 1795, as no later-dated dollars are known with this feature. As Kenneth E. Bressett has said, it is such situations that keep numismatics interesting.

CREATING EMISSION SEQUENCES

Facts and Assumptions

Known facts: The following is an attempt to build a die linkage and sequence of emission of 1795-dated silver dollars. Each die linkage constitutes a "striking period." If possible, the authors of this section (Q. David Bowers and Mark Borckardt) will devise a chronology for the different striking periods.

Known facts include the following:

1. BB-11, BB-13, BB-14, BB-19, and BB-21 are known with silver alloy plugs. Presumably, these were among the first varieties of 1795 dollars made.

2. BB-14 is known overstruck on a 1794 silver dollar. If unsatisfactory 1794 silver dollars had been saved as planchet stock, then BB-14 would have been one of the first 1795-dated dollars struck to use up this stock.

3. BB-18 and BB-20 are varieties known to have been included in the Lord St. Oswald Collection, which contained coins believed to have been obtained in America in autumn 1795. Thus, these varieties would have been struck in 1795.

4. When dies were placed on the presses, they remained there unless one or another die broke, at which time the useless die was removed and replaced with another. If a die became damaged and had to be relapped, it was removed from the press; in such an instance, it could have been replaced immediately after relapping, or it could be put on the shelf to await a later use. If the press was required for other purposes—such as for coining $10 gold eagles—both obverse and reverse dollar dies would be removed; when dollar coinage resumed, the mating of a particular obverse might be with another reverse, and vice-versa. However, the earlier-listed schedule of silver dollar and $10 gold deliveries show that there were more interruptions to dollar coinage than there are known dollar striking periods (see below). Thus, in some instances, dollar dies must have been removed from the press briefly, $10 coins minted, and then the same silver dollar die pair re-installed. In all instances, $10 coinages were very small, and must have taken little time to produce. If the Mint had to be closed for an extended period—such as during one of the periodic yellow fever epidemics—dies were removed from presses and taken to a vault in a bank; when coinage resumed, die mating might be different.

Reasonable assumptions: Reasonable assumptions include the following:

1. Certain obverse dies have the Head of 1794 style and were probably made earlier than those with the Head of 1795 style.

2. Certain reverse dies are of the WI wreath style of simpler design and were probably made earlier than the more ornate WII wreath style.

3. As 1795-dated obverse dies and appropriate reverse dies were not used for coinage until May 1795, because a suitable coining press was not available, these dies were not stored in the sequence in which they were made. Instead, they were kept as a mixed group.

4. When coinage of 1795-dated dollars began in May 1795, the inventory of silver dollar dies would have consisted mostly if not entirely of the earlier styles (Head of 1794 obverses and WI reverses).

5. As there are three extended die-link sequences of 1795 dollars, it is assumed that if one of these sequences had more early-type obverses and reverses than any

other die-link sequence, that sequence would have been made first.

6. Similarly, if an extended die-link sequence of 1795 dollars contained most or all late-type obverses and reverses, it would have been the last made. (Any mixed group of early- and late-type dies would fall in between.)

(Flowing Hair Type)
Striking Period 1: At the very beginning, a pattern emerges. One of the die sequences contains four coins, all of which have early characteristics. These seem to constitute the initial production of 1795-dated dollars, called Striking Period 1. These varieties are as follows:

Striking Period 1
1795 BB-11 (equivalent to Bolender 3). Believed to be the first 1795 silver dollar variety struck. • 1795 BB-12 (Bolender-11) • 1795 BB-13 (Bolender-9) • 1795 BB-14 (Bolender-4)

The rationale for assigning the foregoing varieties to Striking Period 1 is as follows:

BB-11, BB-12, and BB-13 all share a common obverse die of the Head of 1794 style. BB-13 is from a later state of the die. Therefore, it was struck after BB-11 and BB-12. All examples of BB-12 studied by the authors are weakly struck on the right side of the obverse. This is the only evidence to place BB-12 after BB-11. Should extremely high grade specimens of BB-11 and BB-12 become available for examination, die state differences may be revealed, and it is possible that the order given above could be transposed.

It is a certainty that BB-11 and BB-12 were the first two struck (although the order of the two is not certain), and then BB-13 came next. As BB-13 and BB-14 shared a common reverse die, BB-14 had to have been struck when the obverse of BB-13 failed and was replaced with a new die.

As a further indication of the early time of Striking Period 1, we note that BB-11, BB-13, and BB-14 are known to exist with a silver plug. Quite possibly, a specimen of BB-12 with a silver plug will be located.

Striking Periods 2 and 3: Striking Period 3 is the largest group of 1795-dated dollars. Striking Period 3 is related to Striking Period 2 and followed it, but not necessarily within the same time frame. Striking Period 2 probably occurred in 1795. Striking Period 3 could have occurred anytime from mid-1795 through early 1798.

If and when high-grade specimens of certain of the transitional or change-over varieties become available for comparison—namely BB-20, BB-21, and BB-24—it will be possible to determine which of the "either-or" possibilities given below is the correct one.

Striking Period 2

BB-15 (B-8) • BB-16 (B-20) • BB-17 (B-18) • BB-18 (B-7) • BB-19 (B-19) • BB-20 (B-2) At this point, the reverse of BB-20 was either: (1) Mated with an obverse to create BB-21, continuing a link to BB-22 and BB-23, and then BB-28, BB-24, BB-25 Die State I and BB-29, or (2) Mated with an obverse to create BB-24 and BB-25 Die State I, after which time the dies for BB-25 were removed from the press (and the dies for BB-29 tested), and then the reverse used to coin BB-20 was mated with an obverse to coin BB-21, then by linkage, BB-22, BB-23 and BB-28 were coined. • ---EITHER continuing to coin the following: • BB-21 (B-1) • BB-22 (B-11) • BB-23 (B-16) • BB-28 (B-21) ---OR, continuing to coin the following: • BB-24 (B-13) • BB-25 Die State I (B-6) • BB-29 (B-22)

Striking Period 3

EITHER: • BB-24 (B-13) • BB-25 Die State I (B-6) • BB-29 (B-22) — OR: • BB-21 (B-1) • BB-22 (B-11) • BB-23 (B-16) • BB-28 (B-21)

Striking Period 4: Striking period 4 stands by itself. The die pair used to coin BB-25 Die State I was removed from the press. The obverse die was relapped. The reverse was cleaned up, and extensively re-worked, including re-engraving of sections of the wreath branches, berries, and, most noticeably, the addition of a fourth leaf to the cluster of three leaves below the first S of STATES. Striking period 4 could have occurred at any time from late summer 1795 through early 1798.

Striking Period 4

BB-25 Die State III (B-6) • BB-26 (B-12) • BB-27 (B-5)

Summary of Characteristics

1795 Flowing Hair and Draped Bust Dollars

Circulation Strikes

Enabling legislation: Act of April 2, 1792

Flowing Hair type: Designer: Robert Scot

Draped Bust type: Designer: Robert Scot (after Stuart), model by John Eckstein

Statutory weight: 416 grains; .8924 silver, balance copper; actual fineness used (unauthorized by Congress): .900 silver, .100 copper; this applied to *all* 1795 dollars *actually minted in 1795*, not to any with the 1795 date but minted later; the change back to the legal standard did not occur until Elias Boudinot became director, which took place after the final delivery of silver dollars for the 1795 calendar year.

Melting value (silver bullion value) in year minted: Considered by Mint officials to be on a par with the Spanish dollar, and worth about $1.00 intrinsically (see discussion under Summary of Characteristics, 1794).

Dies prepared (Flowing Hair obverse, Eagle on Rock reverse): At least 10 obverses and 11 reverses.

Dies prepared (Draped Bust obverse, Small Eagle reverse): At least 2 obverses and 2 reverses for the Draped Bust coinage.

Circulation strike mintage (combined for all 1795 dollars, Flowing Hair and Draped Bust types), calendar year: 203,033 (not including pieces reserved for the Assay Commission; these are additional and are given in parentheses); Delivery figures by day: May 6: 3,810;[1] May 16: 15,268 (+3 for Assay Commission) • June 5: 10,917 (+3) • June 5 (same day): 10,430 (+2) • June 17: 10,000 (+3) • June 20: 5,986 (+3) • June 26: 6,000 (+3) • June 29: 4,000 (+3) • July 2: 5,243 (+3) • July 9: 5,000 (+3) • July 13: 7,000 (+3) • July 17: 4,500 (+3) • July 21: 6,000 (+3) • July 23: 4,876 (+3) • July 30: 1,184 (+3) • August 10: 3,500 (+3) • August 22: 4,385 (+3) • August 29: 6,500 (+3) • August 31: 1,106 (+3) • September 1: 830 (+3) • September 12: 4,260 (+3) • September 24: 4,000 (+3) • October 3: 15,000 (+3) • October 7: 6,000 (+3) • October 10: 14,500 (+3) • October 17: 23,368 (+3) • October 24: 19,370 (+3).

Estimated circulation strike mintage of 1795 Flowing Hair type (Breen estimates): 160,295 (on the assumption that all deliveries through and including October 10th were of the Flowing Hair type). Walter H. Breen uses the calendar year total as provided by the government as his basis.

Estimated circulation strike mintage of 1795 Draped Bust type (Breen estimates): 42,738 (on the assumption that the last two deliveries of the year, October 17th and 24th, were of the Draped Bust type). Based upon government figures.

---

[1] May 6, 1795 date from Mint records preserved in the National Archives. A receipt dated May 4, 1795, from David Rittenhouse (receipt in author's possession, 1992) states that on May 4th there were "Delivered to the Treasurer of the Mint 46,000 half dollars and 3,810 dollars of the coinage of the United States."

Circulation strike mintage of 1795-dated dollars (total of Flowing Hair and Draped Bust types) regardless of calendar year of mintage (author's estimate): 390,000 (rounded).

Estimated circulation strike mintage of 1795 Flowing Hair type (author's estimate): 391,521 x 74% = 290,000 (rounded).

Estimated circulation strike mintage of 1795 Draped Bust type (author's estimate): 391,521 x 26% = 100,000 (rounded).

Estimated quantity melted: None at any specific time; quantities were exported.

1795 Flowing Hair Dollars (all die varieties combined)
MS-65 or better: 8 to 10 (URS-5)
MS-64: 9 to 15 (URS-5)

MS-63: 30 to 50 (URS-6)
MS-60 to 62: 65 to 110 (URS-8)
AU-50 to 58: 235 to 400 (URS-9)
VF-20 to EF-45: 3,300 to 5,000 (URS-13)
G-4 to F-15: 2,400 to 3,750 (URS-13)
Total for all grades combined: 6,000 to 9,500 (URS-15)
Estimated Total Condition Census: 65 (multiples)

Commentary: 1795 silver dollars were made in quantity. The Flowing Hair type is at least twice as plentiful as the Draped Bust type and was made in many more die varieties. While some die varieties are very rare, the two major design types are readily available. Most 1795 dollars exist in worn grades from Fine to VF, indicating that they circulated widely.

1795 FLOWING HAIR

MINTAGE
290,000 (author's estimate)

VARIETIES

1795 FLOWING HAIR, BB-11

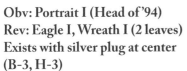

Obv: Portrait I (Head of '94)
Rev: Eagle I, Wreath I (2 leaves)
Exists with silver plug at center
(B-3, H-3)

Obverse: Flowing hair in six curls; the third one from the top *turns downward and touches* the fourth curl. Two points of first star touch the lowest curl which ends at star point. The last star or lowest one on the right is mostly under the bust, and a point nearly touches. Close date; outlines from repunching appear at top of 5 and right top of 7 (most visible on early impressions from the die).

Obverse die used to strike 1795 BB-11, BB-12, and BB-13.

Reverse: Two leaves under each wing. *The only variety with 16 berries*, eight on each branch of wreath. There are only *two berries* on left branch, between eagle's wing and ribbon bow, both on inside of wreath.

Reverse die used to strike 1795 BB-11 only.

Die States

Die State I: Perfect dies.

Die State II: A diagonal crack on the reverse extends from the lower right rim, passing adjacent to the right edge of C in AMERICA, crossing the wreath and reaching to the underside of the eagle's right wing (viewer's left). Very rare, with just three specimens currently known of this die state.

Collecting Notes

Between 50 and 75 1795 BB-11 dollars exist, making this one of the more elusive issues of the Flowing Hair type. Not that it makes any difference to its price, for BB-11 sells for not much more than a common issue, but it is at least twice as rare as a 1794 dollar. Such comparisons make interesting reading in auction catalogs.

The population of 1795 BB-11 seems to be clustered around the VF level which, of course, covers a fairly wide range (VF-20 to just below EF-40). Specimens are not easy to locate, and often a year will pass on the calendar without a single piece crossing the auction block. No truly Mint State coins are known.

The Garrett-Cardinal specimen of the 1795 BB-11 dollar with mint-inserted silver plug. Graded AU-55 by PCGS.

Notable Specimens

Atwater Specimen. AU-58 (NGC). William Cutler Atwater Collection • Frank Stirling Collection • W. David Perkins • Warren Miller Collection.

Garrett Specimen. AU-55 (PCGS) Silver Plug. Lyman H. Low's 8th Sale (June 1885) lot 59, bought at the sale by T. Harrison Garrett, Garrett Collection • Stack's (March 1976) lot 245 • unknown intermediaries • Phillip Flannagan Collection (Bowers & Merena, November 2001) lot 4204, bought at the sale by the Cardinal Collection • Cardinal Collection Sale (American Numismatic Rarities, June 2005) lot 6 • private collector; privately to the Cardinal Collection January 2006 • privately to Dr. Hesselgesser, February 2008 • The Dr. Hesselgesser Collection • Hesselgesser Collection Sale, (Ira and Larry Goldberg, September

2011) lot 5000 • May Pre-Long Beach Auction, (Ira and Larry Goldberg, May 2012) lot 1259.

Parsons Specimen. AU-50. George M. Parsons Collection sale (Henry Chapman, 1914) • M.H. Bolender Collection, 1952, lot 5. • K.P. Austin. • A.J. Ostheimer 3rd. • ANA Convention Sale (Superior, 1975) lot 790.

Ostheimer Specimen. EF-45 net. (Mint State, but damaged). Choice Uncirculated, but with initials having been lightly scratched into the obverse fields and then expertly removed; Davis-Graves Collection (Stack's, 4/54), lot 1268 • unknown intermediaries • W.G. "Farish" Baldenhofer • Milferd H. Bolender • Ostheimer Collection • A.J. Ostheimer 3rd Collection (Lester Merkin, 1968) lot 226 • Dr. Joseph A. Presley • unknown intermediaries • James A. Dolittle Collection (Bowers and Ruddy, June 1977), lot 2834 • unknown intermediaries; Pre-Long Beach Sale, (Superior, May 1999), lot 2326 • Cardinal Collection • Elite Sale (Superior, January 2002) lot 1175 • CSNS Signature Sale (Heritage, April 2002) lot 6689.

Hesselgesser Specimen. EF-40 (PCGS). "Pleasing antique gray with golden undertones throughout, decidedly noticeable die crack on the reverse"; The Dr. Hesselgesser Collection • Hesselgesser Collection Sale (Ira and Larry Goldberg, September 2011) lot 5001.

Capitol City Specimen. VF-35. Capitol City Sale (Mid American, 1985) lot 685, "VF-35/35, actually close to EF."

Total Estimated Population

MS-65 or better: 0 (URS-0)

MS-64: 0 (URS-0)

MS-63: 0 (URS-0)

MS-60 to 62: 0 (URS-0)

AU-50 to 58: 3 (URS-3)

VF-20 to EF-45: 30 to 45 (URS-6)

G-4 to F-15: 20 to 30 (URS-6)

Total for all grades combined: 50 to 75 (URS-7)

Estimated Total Condition Census: 58-55-50-45-40-35 (multiples)

1795 Flowing Hair, BB-12

Obv: Portrait I (Head of '94)
Rev: Eagle I, Wreath I (2 leaves)
(B-11, H-11)

Obverse: See description under BB-11. Now always weakly struck on the right.

Obverse die used to strike 1795 BB-11, BB-12, and BB-13.

Reverse: Two leaves under each wing. 19 berries, nine on left branch, 10 on right. *Differs from any other 19-berry reverse*, as follows: Two berries in wreath under A in STATES, the one on inside of wreath under center of A, and the one on outside of wreath under left corner of right foot of A. Only one berry in wreath under OF, and it is on the inside of wreath. Two berries, one inside of wreath, and one outside, are close together under first S in STATES, and two more close together under first A in AMERICA.

Reverse die used to strike 1795 BB-12 only.

Die States

Die State I: Perfect dies. Obverse weakly struck on the right side.

Collecting Notes

1795 BB-12 is one of the famous rarities in the 1795 Flowing Hair series. Perhaps, somewhere between 20 and 35 exist, all of which may be in circulated grades. I am not aware of any Mint State examples, or even an AU. All known specimens of the 1795 BB-12 silver dollar show significant weakness of strike at the right obverse.

My rarity estimate is tenuous for this variety. Douglas Winter suggests a population of six to 10, and less than 10 specimens have been positively identified to date.

Haseltine's specimen was only Good, and scratched in field, the only one he could find. Thus it is no wonder that in his 1881 *Type-Table*, he called it "excessively rare."

Notable Specimens

Wyatt Specimen. EF-45. Superior, 1985: 2005. "EF-45." • H.W. Blevins Collection (Superior, 1988) lot 3593, EF-40. • Dr. Robert Stark Collection.

Hesselgesser Specimen. EF-40 (PCGS). European Collection • Dr. Robert Hesselgesser Collection • Hesselgesser Collection Sale (Ira and Larry Goldberg, September 2011) lot 5002.

Willasch Specimen. EF-40 (NGC). H. Roland Willasch Collection (Superior, 1990) lot 449 • Warren Miller Collection.

Earle Specimen. VF-35 (PCGS). George H. Earle (Henry Chapman, June 1912) • M.H. Bolender Collection (M.H. Bolender, 183rd Sale, 1952), lot 13 • K.P. Austin • Baldenhofer Collection • Ostheimer Collection (Superior, August 1975), lot 806 • Jules Reiver; Jim Matthews (Heritage, July 2008) lot 1720.

Matthews Specimen. VF-25 (PCGS). J.J. Teaparty • Jim Matthews (Goldberg Coins, September 2002), lot 458 • Steve Liu (December 2005) • William Luebke (Heritage, January 2007) lot 4943.

Ivy Specimen. VF-25. • Steve Ivy, December 1979: 793, Not plated and not traced since. This may be an earlier appearance of the Matthews Specimen, or a later appearance of the Spies Specimen.

Spies Specimen. F-15. W. Earl Spies Collection (Stack's, December 1974), lot 14.

Total Estimated Population

MS-65 or better: 0 (URS-0)
MS-64: 0 (URS-0)
MS-63: 0 (URS-0)
MS-60: 0 (URS-0)
AU-50 to 58: 0 (URS-0)
VF-20 to EF-45: 5 to 7 (URS-4)
G-4 to F-15: 5 to 10 (URS-5)
Total for all grades combined: 20 to 35 (URS-6)
Estimated Total Condition Census: 45-40-40-35-25-25

1795 FLOWING HAIR, BB-13

Obv: Portrait I (Head of '94)
Rev: Eagle I, Wreath I (2 leaves)
Exists with silver plug at center (B-9, H-9)

Obverse: See description under BB-11. Sometimes seen in a late die state showing die clash marks from the wings and wreath behind Miss Liberty's head.

Obverse die used to strike 1795 BB-11, BB-12, and BB-13.

Reverse: Two leaves under each wing. 17 *berries*, nine on left branch, eight on right. A berry is on outside of the wreath midway between S and T of STATES, the only variety in which this occurs; the arrangement is similar to that used on the 1794 dollar.

Reverse die used to strike 1795 BB-13 and BB-14.

Die States

Die State I: Perfect dies. Obverse without obverse clash marks. The die state usually seen. Specimens are often seen with varying degrees of bifurcation on obverse and reverse, and somewhat indistinct dentils.

Die State II: Clash marks from the wings and the wreath are visible behind Liberty's head. Rare. Gilhousen (Superior, 1973): 1216, "almost VF," was described as from an "obverse die partly flattened and

The Cardinal specimen of the 1795 BB-13 dollar with mint-inserted silver plug. Graded AU-53 by PCGS.

roughened by severe clash marks from reverse, parts of wings and wreath being very plain behind head."

Die State III: With "additional die cracks," as described in the 1945 catalog of the F.C.C. Boyd Collection ("World's Greatest Collection").

Collecting Notes

I estimate that about 300 to 500 specimens exist of 1795 BB-13, a figure considerably more liberal than the Bolender suggestion of R-5 (31 to 75 coins, if he meant R-5 on the Sheldon Scale), or the 1881 *Type-Table* designation of "very rare." While a considerable number are now known to exist, the variety is still unknown in true Mint State quality. The finest known specimens consist of choice AU examples.

Notable Specimens

Cardinal Specimen. AU-58 (PCGS). Matthew Stickney Collection (Henry Chapman, June 1907) lot 810 • Stack's sale of April 1978, lot 712 • unknown intermediaries • Legend Numismatics • Cardinal Collection (American Numismatic Rarities, June 2005) lot 7 "A simply beautiful dollar, one that is a feast for the eyes from far arm's length and under magnification."

ANA Sale Specimen. AU-58 (NGC). ANA Signature Sale

(Heritage July 2005) lot 10236. "Struck from an early state of the dies, before the dies clashed,…this specimen is toned a light to medium gray both on the obverse and reverse."

Saunders Specimen. AU-55. Ebenezer Milton Saunders Collection, Bowers and Merena,1987) lot 371, AU-55 (ANACS).

Hesselgesser Specimen. AU-55 (PCGS). Ira and Larry Goldberg, May 2011, lot 869 • Ira and Larry Goldberg, September 2011, lot 5003. "A superior specimen blanketed with lovely golden shades on both sides."

Cardinal Specimen (another). AU-53 Silver Plug (PCGS). Northeast Numismatics • Cardinal Collection • Tangible Asset Galleries • Dr. Robert Hesselgesser Collection (Ira and Larry Goldberg, May 2011) lot 868. "Appealing multi-dimensional toning covers both sides beautifully. The Silver Plug is quite pronounced and can be easily seen with the naked eye."

Atwater Specimen. Net AU-50. (MS-60, planchet defect) Severely laminated planchet. • Atwater Collection (B. Max Mehl, 1946) lot 191. • Ostheimer Collection (Lester Merkin, 1968) lot 231. "Brilliant Uncirculated."

• The March Sale (Stack's, 1985) lot 1227. "Brilliant Uncirculated." • Rarities Sale (Bowers and Merena, August 1998) lot 219 • Pre-Long Beach Sale (Superior Galleries, September 1999) lot 1461 • Pre-Long Beach Sale (Ira and Larry Goldberg, February 2002) lot 1140.

DeCoppet Specimen. EF-45. James Kelly, 1955. "Choice EF, beautifully toned."

The March Sale Specimen. EF-45. Stack's March Sale, 1983, lot 924. "Choice EF."

Total Estimated Population

MS-65 or better: 0 (URS-0)
MS-64: 0 (URS-0)
MS-63: 0 (URS-0)
MS-60 to 62: 0 (URS-0)
AU-50 to 58: 6 to 12 (URS-5)
VF-20 to EF-45: 140 to 240 (URS-9)
G-4 to F-15: 150 to 250 (URS-9)
Total for all grades combined: 300 to 500 (URS-10)
Estimated Total Condition Census: 58-58-55-55-53 (multiples)

1795 FLOWING HAIR, BB-14

Hidden Star Obverse
Obv: Portrait I (Head of '94)
Rev: Eagle I, Wreath I (2 leaves)
Exists with silver plug at center
Exists overstruck on a 1794 dollar
(B-4, H-4)

Obverse: *Star 15 is "hidden" entirely under the bust, where Miss Liberty cannot "see" even a part of it;* the only 1795 obverse with this characteristic. Flowing hair in six curls; lowest curl ends faintly above two points

of first star, and close to one point. Close date, figures 9 and 5 closest, and the distance between the 1 and 7 about the same as between the first star and figure 1. The 9 and 5 are lightly repunched. Two center dots; the larger is higher, slightly farther to the right, and closest below ear. Star closer to date than in any other variety, about 1.5 mm.

Obverse die used to strike 1795 BB-14 only.
Reverse: See description under BB-13.
Reverse die used to strike 1795 BB-13 and BB-14.

Die States

Die State I: Perfect dies. Early impressions may have a small lump under the chin and/or die flaws near the rim opposite stars 10 and 11.

Collecting Notes

1795 BB-14 is one of the more readily available issues of the year. An estimated 350 to 550 exist in all grades combined. The specialist will have no trouble acquiring a specimen in just about any grade up to VF. At the EF level, BB-14 becomes somewhat elusive, but a specimen in this grade can usually be acquired easily with less than a year's search. AU coins are rare, and Mint State examples are very rare.

The rims on this issue are higher than most other 1795 dollars, giving them a somewhat more "modern" appearance than the typical variety of this year. Planchet adjustment marks are not often seen on BB-14. A few pieces I have seen have had black carbon streaks, the result of improper alloy mixing. Probably a batch of 1795 BB-14 dollars was made from an impure alloy melt.

The only known 1795 dollar overstruck on a previously coined 1794 is of the BB-14 variety and is described at length below. This suggests that 1795 BB-14 was probably included among the first dollars minted in 1795. As such it helps verify the varieties listed in Striking Period 1.

The Hesselgesser specimen of the 1795 BB-14 dollar with mint-inserted silver plug. Graded EF-40 by PCGS.

Notable Specimens

Parmelee Specimen. MS-62+ (PCGS). Parmelee Sale (U.S. Coin & Stamp Co., June 1890) lot 702 • Amon Carter, Jr. Collection (Stack's, 1984) lot 209, "Brilliant Uncirculated." • Dillard Collection (Heritage, 1990) lot 969, "AU-58" • Midwest collection.

October Sale Specimen. MS-62 (NGC). October Sale (Superior, 1990) lot 3713. "Premium Quality."

Boston Rarities Specimen. AU-58 (NGC). Rarities Sale (Bowers and Merena, August 2010) lot 1006. "A satiny, lustrous Choice AU" • Dr. Robert Hesselgesser Collection (Ira and Larry Goldberg, September 2011) lot 1261.

Hesselgesser Specimen. AU-55 (PCGS). Pre-Long Beach Sale (Ira and Larry Goldberg, June 2011) lot 871, "Peripheral toning exhibiting blue-green and hints of russet shades are noticeable on both sides of this almost uncirculated piece. Highly attractive and carefully preserved."

Jenks Specimen. AU-55 (PCGS). John Story Jenks Collection (Chapman, 1921) • Shore Collection (Superior 1988) lot 2176 • W. David Perkins Collection • Flannagan Collection Sale (Bowers and Merena, November 2001) lot 4205 • Cardinal Collection • Cardinal Collection Sale (American Numismatic Rarities, June 2005) lot 8 as AU-58 (PCGS), "A beautiful specimen, mostly toned in mottled shades of silver and pewter gray with some golden and coppery tones around reverse design elements" • Larry Stack • private collector • later "conserved," re-sold and re-encapsulated as AU-55(PCGS) • Long Beach Signature Sale (Heritage, September 2010) lot 4300.

Reiver Specimen. AU-55 (NGC). Lester Merkin • Garry Fitzgerald (November 1968) • Jules Reiver Collection (Heritage, January 2006) lot 23467.

Perkins Specimen. AU-53 (NGC), Struck over 1794 Dollar. Discovered in 1961 and discussed in detail by Walter Breen in *The Metropolitan Numismatic Journal*, Volume 1, Number 1, May-June 1961 • Lexington Collection Sale (Bowers and Merena, January 1994) lot 1274 • W. David Perkins • ANA Signature Sale (Heritage, August 2004) lot 6310.

Matthews Specimen. EF-45 (PCGS) Silver Plug. Rossi & Wilson Sale (Bowers and Merena, May 1997) lot 1384 • Jim Matthews (Goldberg Coins, September 2002), lot 454.

Miller Specimen. EF-45 (NGC) • Warren Miller Collection, Die State I.

Hesselgesser Specimen. EF-40 (PCGS) Silver Plug. Pre-Long Beach Sale (Ira and Larry Goldberg, June 2011) lot 870. "Pleasing antique gray tones with a trace of golden colors cover both sides."

Total Estimated Population
MS-65 or better: 0 (URS-0)
MS-64: 0 (URS-0)
MS-63: 0 (URS-0)
MS-60 to 62: 2 (URS-2)
AU-50 to 58: 10 to 20 (URS-5)

VF-20 to EF-45: 220 to 350 (URS-9)
G-4 to F-15: 120 to 175 (URS-8)
Total for all grades combined: 350 to 550 (URS-10)
Estimated Total Condition Census: 62+-62-58-55 (multiples)

1795 FLOWING HAIR, BB-15

Obv: Portrait II (Head of '95)
Rev: Eagle I, Wreath I (2 leaves)
(B-8, H-8)

Obverse: Flowing hair in six prominent curls. The second curl from the bottom points down to an inside ray of star 2. Very prominent shoulder loop. Stars 3 and 4 on the left are slightly closer together than the others. Stars 6 and 7 are slightly wider. On the right, stars 11 and 12 as well as stars 14 and 15 are closer than the rest. Star 1 touches the bottom of the lowest curl; the curl continues to almost completely close a circle. Star 8 is closer to base of L than star 9 is to base of Y. Star 15 is far from the bust, exactly 2 mm. from the bust tip. Wide date with the 1 and 7 wider apart than the other digits. The bust is high in the field, over 2.5 mm. above the 5 and under 1 mm. from LIBERTY at its closest point. LIBERTY is wide with LIB more widely spaced than the letters in BERTY.

This die bears a very close resemblance to the die used to coin BB-21, BB-22, and BB-23; especially with regard to the high position of the head and the relationship of the hair curl to the first star, and was probably created by the same person around the same time.

M.H. Bolender noted that the head is not well-centered, but too high and too far to left; however, this is neither definitive nor unique to the variety.

Obverse die used to strike 1795 BB-15 only.

Reverse: Two leaves under each wing of eagle. Nine berries on the left branch, 10 on the right branch. Two berries inside the right branch, at the eagle's tail. No letters of the legend touch any leaf. The T of UNITED touches the eagle's dexter (observer's left) wing, while the R of AMERICA appears to touch the sinister wing but actually just misses. A berry on the outside of the right branch is below the extreme left foot of the first A in AMERICA. A die scratch extends into the field from a dentil left of the first A in AMERICA.

This is one of just two 1795 reverses with two berries inside the branch near the eagle's tail (the other die is that used to coin 1795 BB-21, BB-20, and BB-24). This reverse die bears a very close relationship with the reverse used to coin 1795 BB-21, BB-20, and BB-24, and another die used to coin 1795 BB-23, and must have been prepared by the same person about the same time.

Reverse die used to strike 1795 BB-15 and BB-16.

Die States

Die State I: Perfect dies. May not exist with perfect obverse die.

Die State II: Obverse: A vertical crack extends from the hair above the forehead down to the base of the neck, extending through the tip of hair behind the eye, through the ear lobe and along the back of the neck; the crack passes through the right edge of the center dot. No traces of this crack extend beyond the portrait into the fields. Actually, this crack appears more as a change of elevation, with the surface of the portrait to the right of the crack slightly higher than the details of the hair to the left. It is possible that this is an unusual form of internal die crack, perhaps beginning at the center dot. Another possibility is that the portrait hub punch was cracked, and the crack was transferred to this working die. If this was the case, then the obverse of BB-15 would have been the last time this punch was used. The reverse shows no cracks, nor evidence of lapping.

Collecting Notes

1795 BB-15 remains a prime rarity, with only five positively identified.. M.H. Bolender wrote this in 1950:

> In 40 years the author has seen only two specimens! One of these was handled by him four times, but was recognized as the same example. Doubtless a very few others are hidden away in collections, but without any doubts, Bolender-8 is "excessively rare" as stated by Haseltine. His specimen was not in the Haseltine sale catalog of 1881, having been withdrawn beforehand and sold privately. Rarity 7.

However, Dr. Robert Stark advised that within a two-year period he saw three different specimens offered, one of which was repaired.[1]

Notable Specimens

Boyd Specimen. EF-40 (NGC). "World's Greatest Collection" (F.C.C. Boyd, Numismatic Gallery, 1945) lot 9. • 1949 ANA Sale of Adolph Freeman's Collection (Numismatic Gallery) lot 143 • M.H. Bolender Collection (Bolender, 1952) lot 9. "A little wear on high parts of hair and eagle, but VF and well-centered even impressions." • K.P. Austin. • A.J. Ostheimer 3rd • ANA Convention Sale

---

[1] Letter to the author, January 3, 1993.

(Superior, 1975) lot 801. VF-20. • H. Roland Willasch Collection (Superior, 1990) lot 446 • Jim Matthews Collection • Jim Matthews (Goldberg Coins, September 2002), lot 456, unsold • Warren Miller Collection.

Reiver Specimen. Fine Details (NCS). Discovered unattributed to Jim Matthews • privately to Jules Reiver, June 1989 • Jules Reiver Collection (Heritage, January 2006) lot 23473.

Blevins Specimen. F-12 net. (VF-25, repaired). The H.W. Blevins Collection (Superior, 1988) lot 3590. "VF-25." • Jim Matthews • East Coast collector.

Fox Specimen. VG-8 net. (VF-20, damaged). Marmaduke Fox Collection (M.H. Bolender, 1951) • Spies Collection (Stack's, 1974) lot 10. "VF, but noticeably damaged by some severe dents obverse and reverse." Bolender said he handled this coin four times. • Frank M. Stirling Collection (Heritage, February 1986) lot 1321.

Reiver Specimen (another). About Good Details (NCS), Double-Struck, Countermarked. Discovered unattributed to Jim Matthews • privately to Jules Reiver, June 1989 • Jules Reiver Collection (Heritage, January 2006) lot 23473.

Total Estimated Population

MS-65 or better: 0 (URS-0)
MS-64: 0 (URS-0)
MS-63: 0 (URS-0)
MS-60 to 62: 0 (URS-0)
AU-50 to 58: 0 (URS-0)
VF-20 to EF-45: 1 (URS-1)
G-4 to F-15: 3 (URS-3)
Total for all grades combined: 3 to 6 (URS-3)
Estimated Total Condition Census: 40-15-12-8-2

1795 Flowing Hair, BB-16

Obv: Portrait I (Head of '94)
Rev: Eagle I, Wreath I (2 leaves)
(B-20)
Obverse: Flowing hair in six curls. The lowest curl is very small and perfect, and touches the innermost point of star 1, as it continues to nearly complete a loop. Curl end is close to and extends toward innermost point on star 2. Last star partly under bust, but not as far under as BB-11, and not quite as close, but it is near. (Note: In BB-14 the last star is *entirely* under bust.) Wide date, most space between 1 and 7.

Obverse die used to strike 1795 BB-16, BB-17, and BB-18.

Reverse: See description under 1795 BB-15. Two leaves under each wing. 19 berries arranged 9x10.

Reverse die used to strike 1795 BB-15 and BB-16.

Collecting Notes

Extremely rare. Just three have been traced. First described in Lester Merkin's sale of February 1972, lot 299, by Walter H. Breen, as reprinted below.

Notable Specimens

Stirling Specimen. VF-35 (PCGS). Lester Merkin, February 1972, lot 299. "New muling of known dies. Obverse Bolender-7. Reverse Bolender-8, but finer than Bolender plate coin of that variety. Immediately identified by straight die scratch in field, like part of an extra A, left of first A in AMERICA, pointing to the nearest berry; recut C in AMERICA. Just about VF, many obv. adjustment marks. Rev. sharper than obv. and fully VF. The Bolender-8

die was formerly known only by two impressions of that variety; the present muling is superior to either of them and in addition represents a discovery linking the Bolender-8 dies with the remainder of the group (Bolender 16, 10, 17, 1, 2, 7, 19, 18, 12, 5 and 6). Identified by Walter Breen, originally obtained merely as a specimen of the date. Unpublished, to date unique." *Described as B-21 by Lester Merkin, this variety was later included in the revised Bolender reference as Bolender-20.* • Frank M. Stirling Collection. • Dr. Robert Hesselgesser Collection • Pre-Long Beach Sale (Ira and Larry Goldberg, September 2011) lot 1262.

Miller Specimen. VG-10 (NGC). Lindesmith Collection (Bowers and Merena, March 2000) lot 2051 • Cardinal Collection • Elite Sale (Superior, January 2002) lot 1179 • Warren Miller Collection.

Reiver Specimen VF Details (NCS) Holed, Damaged. Montgomery Collection (Bowers and Merena, May 1998) lot 2254 • Cardinal Collection • privately via John Haugh to Jules Reiver • Jules Reiver Collection (Heritage, January 2006) lot 23481.

Total Estimated Population

MS-65 or better: (URS-0)
MS-64: (URS-0)
MS-63: (URS-0)
MS-60 to 62: (URS-0)
AU-50 to 58: (URS-0)
VF-20 to EF-45: 1 (URS-1)
G-4 to F-15: 2 (URS-2)
Total for all grades combined: 3 (URS-3)
Estimated Total Condition Census: 35-10-4

1795 Flowing Hair BB-17

Obv: Portrait I (Head of '94)
Rev: Eagle I, Wreath I (2 leaves)
(B-18)

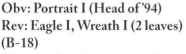

Obverse: See description under 1795 BB-16. Wide date.

Obverse die used to strike 1795 BB-16, BB-17, and BB-18.

Reverse: Two leaves under each wing. The only 1795 reverse die with 19 berries arranged 8x11. No outer berry under A in STATES.

Reverse die used to strike 1795 BB-17 only.

Notes about other die varieties called Bolender-18 in years past:

A "Bolender-18" variety different from that I list as BB-17 here, billed as a new discovery and described in the December 1952 issue of *The Numismatist*, and there called Bolender-18, was later called Bolender-21 by collectors. However, today it is called neither Bolender-18 nor Bolender-21, but an early state of 1795 Bolender-6 (now BB-25), to which refer.

The Spies Collection "Bolender-18" coin (Stack's, 1974): 19, was described as: "Unlisted in Bolender. B-13 obverse, B-12 reverse. EF and wholly prooflike, but a few very faint scratches between the 1 and 7." *This coin is now included among the listings for 1795 BB-25, die state I, while 1795 BB-17 is a different variety.*

Collecting Notes

Douglas Winter once reported that at least two are known; however, there has been no record of a second specimen for over 50 years, leaving the Eliasberg specimen as the only confirmed example.

Notable Specimens

Eliasberg Specimen. AU-58 (NGC). Bowers and Merena Galleries 1997, lot 2168, The impression is well centered on the planchet with complete border dentilation on both obverse and reverse. Although a few details

are obscured by wear, the original strike was quite strong. The stars are mostly flat. The surfaces are slightly reflective with minor handling marks visible, primarily on the obverse, and light adjustment marks which are mostly on the reverse. Pale champagne toning is blended with faint blue and lavender. Miss Liberty's cheek has a small area of light wear surrounding very small nicks and mottled toning. A small patch of discoloration is in the area of the digit 5 and star 15. The reverse has a very tiny edge bruise over the second T in STATES. The obverse die is perfect without clash marks, die cracks, or other signs of die wear. The reverse die is also perfect. This coin traces its pedigree to Henry Chapman's presentation of the George H. Earle sale in 1912. However, the cataloger, probably Chapman himself, was not aware that it was a new die variety. He described it as follows: 1795 Head resembling that used on the 1794. R. Two leaves under each wing of the eagle. Very fine. Many small nicks on obverse, and around edge of reverse may be seen many of the file marks in the planchet. Rare." It was a curious stroke of fate that only the *obverse* was pictured, as the obverse was struck from a known die. It was *the reverse that was entirely unknown to specialists.* When inspecting the Earle catalog, a later generation of scholars, including M.H. Bolender who in 1950 published his book, *The United States Early Silver Dollars from 1794 to 1803,* had no clue that this coin was anything other than ordinary! The first identification of this new, unique die combination appeared in *The Numismatist,* July 1953. By Walter Breen, "A New Variety of 1795 Silver Dollar" appeared in due course, and was illustrated, but not with an enlargement. In 1953 the text in general use in silver dollars was that by M.H. Bolender, with pieces being given "B" numbers (for Bolender). Breen, interested in early dollars, recognized that the piece listed as "B-18" by Bolender was, in fact, not a distinct die combination at all but, instead, was simply a die state of Bolender's B-6. This left the B-18 number vacant, and thus Walter reassigned it to the new discovery. Years later in 1982, when Krause Publications put out the fourth revised edition of the Bolender book, this piece was described as B-18" with the notation, "Specimen known in Eliasberg Collection." George H. Earle Collection (Henry Chapman, June 1912) lot 2671 • John H. Clapp; Clapp estate, 1942.

(See original catalog for lengthy detailed description.) • Warren Miller Collection.

Total Estimated Population
AU-50 to 58: 1 (URS-1)
Total for all grades combined: 1.
Total Condition Census: 58

1795 FLOWING HAIR BB-18

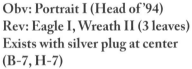

Obv: Portrait I (Head of '94)
Rev: Eagle I, Wreath II (3 leaves)
Exists with silver plug at center
(B-7, H-7)
Obverse: See description under 1795 BB-16. Wide date. Obverse die used to strike 1795 BB-16, BB-17, and BB-18.
Reverse: Three leaves under each wing. *The only 14-berry variety.* Seven berries on each branch. There is *only one* berry on left branch of wreath between eagle's wing and ribbon bow, and it is on the inside of wreath. Two berries below the D in UNITED. Conspicuous die flaws at the end of the left ribbon. E in AMERICA double punched at top.
Reverse die used to strike 1795 BB-18 and BB-19.

Die States

Die State I: Die flaws or stray marks at the end of the left ribbon; these are in the form of two tiny extensions to the ribbon, with the extension on the left being the larger of the two. The state usually seen.

Die State II: As preceding, but the smaller of the two flaws—the one on the right side of the left ribbon end—is now gone, either from die wear or light relapping. Much scarcer than preceding.

Collecting Notes

1795 BB-18 is one of the more available varieties of the year, but is hard to find in higher grades. Probably, about 500 to 800 survive. In his 1881 *Type-Table*, J.W.

Haseltine called this variety very rare. By 1950, M.H. Bolender played the rarity down to the R-4 level, which, if the Sheldon Scale was intended, meant that Bolender felt that somewhere between 76 and 200 were known. Since then, many more have been identified.

The Photographic Department of Bowers and Merena Galleries had 16 different specimens go through its hands from 1984 to 1992—hardly a situation which bespeaks rarity. Over the years, 1795 BB-18 has been readily available at auction, and many more have been shipped from dealers' inventories.

Inasmuch as a Uncirculated specimen of BB-18 appeared in the Lord St. Oswald Collection as part of a group of coins acquired in America in autumn 1795, it is certain that BB-18 was actually struck in 1795.

Notable Specimens

Bullowa Specimen MS-66 (PCGS). Catherine E. Bullowa (Coinhunter, December 2005) "Very Choice to Gem Uncirculated" • Private Texas collection.
Lord St. Oswald Specimen. MS-65 (PCGS) Silver Plug. Major Lord St. Oswald Sale (Christie's, 1964) lot 141. • Spink & Son, Ltd. • Lester Merkin, October 1973, lot 451 • Greater New York Numismatic Convention Sale, Jimmy Hayes Collection,[1] (Stack's, 1983) lot 1220, Brilliant

---

[1] Hayes, a numismatic connoisseur from Louisiana, sold his collection in the 1980s to finance a successful bid for a seat in the U.S. House of Representatives.

Uncirculated • Private Texas collection. Illustrated in *Walter Breen's Encyclopedia of United States and Colonial Proof Coins* where the author described it as a presentation piece.

Eliasberg Specimen. MS-64 (PCGS). This piece not only is of an excellent technical grade, but possesses a simply stunning, absolutely gorgeous aesthetic appeal. The specimen displays delicate lilac and gold toning over lustrous surfaces. The piece is very well struck except for the central portions, with nicely developed stars, dentils, lower hair tresses, leaves, eagle's wing feathers, and more. Some Mint-caused adjustment marks are seen at the center of the reverse. In the overall panorama of 1795 Flowing Hair dollar varieties, the BB-18 is one of the most often seen, although nearly always in a lower grade than the Eliasberg Collection coin. Among the finer high-grade examples known to us are the present Mougey Collection specimen and the so-called "Lord St. Oswald" example (which Walter Breen stated was struck circa May 6-16, 1795; the Breen commentary is now largely discredited per a later study by Michael Hodder), both

The Cardinal specimen of the 1795 BB-18 dollar with mint-inserted silver plug. Graded AU-58 by PCGS.

of which were called MS-63 in our 1993 study of early dollars, there being no others at this numerical level • Mougey Collection (Thomas L. Elder, September 1910), Choice Unc. • George Clapp. • Louis Eliasberg Collection (Bowers and Merena, April 1997) lot 2169 "MS-63" • Long Beach Signature Sale (Heritage, September 1999) lot 6478 • Michael Herring Collection (Heritage, January 2002) lot 7165 • Kevin Lipton • Legend Numismatics • Cardinal Collection (American Numismatic Rarities, June 2005) lot 9 • Jack Lee Collection • Jack Lee Estate (Heritage, January 2009) lot 3926.

Ostheimer Specimen MS-64 (PCGS) Silver Plug. Richard Boswell Winsor Collection (S.H. and H. Chapman, December 1895) lot 388 • David S. Wilson Collection (H. Chapman, March 1907) lot 366 • T. James Clarke Collection (New Netherlands, November 1956) lot 612 • A.J. Ostheimer Collection (Lester Merkin, September 1968) lot 230 • Barker/Cheek/Wayman/Robinson Sale (Stack's, October 1986) lot 102 • Hain Family Collection, Part II (Stack's, January 2002) lot 1500 • Private Texas collection.

October Sale Specimen. MS-65 (NGC) • October Sale (Superior, 1990) lot 3714. "MS-62 (NGC), Premium Quality" • ANA Signature Sale (Heritage, August 1996) lot 7950, as MS-64 (NGC) • Subsequently re-graded by NGC as MS-65.

Warns Specimen. MS-63. Warns Collection (Lester Merkin, 1973) lot 451. "Irregularly toned prooflike gem, struck from new brilliant polished dies on a brilliantly polished planchet which however does have adjustment marks."

Bolender Specimen. MS-60. Bolender Collection, 1952. • W.G. Baldenhofer • A.J. Ostheimer 3rd • Gilhousen Collection (Superior, 1973) lot 1215, "Prooflike Uncirculated." • ANA Convention Sale (Superior, 1975) lot 799 • Davenport Collection (Superior, 1977) lot 466, MS-60.

Cardinal Specimen AU-58 (PCGS) Silver Plug. Hollywood Collector • Tangible Asset Galleries • Cardinal Collection (American Numismatic Rarities June 2005), lot 10 "Evenly toned antique gray surfaces with a hint of golden undertones." • Don Willis • Dr. Robert Hesselgesser Collection Pre-Long Beach Sale (Ira and Larry Goldberg, June 2011) lot 872 • Century Coin Group.

Hesselgesser Specimen AU-58 (PCGS). Dr. Robert Hesselgesser Collection Pre-Long Beach Sale (Ira and Larry Goldberg, September 2011) lot 5008 "A superlative example of this desirable variety. Razor sharp devices and shimmering luster leave the viewer breathless while looking at this astounding creation. Tremendous pizzazz."

Total Estimated Population

MS-65 or better: 2 (URS-2)
MS-64: 1 or 2 (URS-2)
MS-63: 3 to 5 (URS-3)
MS-60 to 62: 10 to 20 (URS-5)
AU-50 to 58: 50 to 80 (URS-7)
VF-20 to EF-45: 250 to 400 (URS-10)
G-4 to F-15: 200 to 300 (URS-9)
Total for all grades combined: 500 to 800 (URS-11)
Estimated Total Condition Census: 66-65-64-64-64-63

1795 Flowing Hair, BB-19

Obv: Portrait II (Head of '95)
Rev: Eagle I, Wreath II (3 leaves)
Exists with silver plug at center
(B-19)

Obverse: Flowing hair in six prominent curls. The lowest curl is pierced and separated by the innermost point of star 1, and the curl is continued upward to almost close its loop. Wide date, the 95 closer together than the other figures. The upper left star is 2 mm. distant from L in LIBERTY, and is farther from the L than in any other variety. A diagonal "bar," actually a small die scratch, slightly more than 1.5 mm. long appears raised in the left field close to inner point of 4th star, this bar extending diagonally northwest to southeast. The position of the bar distinguishes it from BB-27, which also has a bar, but close to the 5th star.

Obverse die used to strike 1795 BB-19 and BB-20.

Reverse: See description under 1795 BB-18. Three leaves under each wing. 14 berries arranged 7x7.

Reverse die used to strike 1795 BB-18 and BB-19.

Collecting Notes

This variety, unknown to Bolender, is extremely rare. Just one specimen has been positively traced, and, perhaps, just two are known.

Notable Specimen

Stirling Specimen. VG Details (NGC) Silver Plug, Damaged. The 5th revised edition of the Bolender book, Krause Publications, 1988, p. 21, noted: "Specimen reported in the Frank Stirling Collection." The collection of the late Frank M. Stirling was dispersed during his lifetime, and this specimen of BB-19 remained with another owner for an extended time • privately via W. David Perkins to the Warren Miller Collection. At the time of its acquisition by Warren Miller, this specimen was presented to NGC for authentication and grading, and it was identified as exhibiting a Mint-inserted silver plug at its center.

Total Estimated Population

MS-65 or better: 0 (URS-0)
MS-64: 0 (URS-0)
MS-63: 0 (URS-0)
MS-60 to 62: 0 (URS-0)
AU-50 to 58: 0 (URS-0)
VF-20 to EF-45: 0 (URS-0)
G-4 to F-15: 1 (URS-1)
Total for all grades combined: 1 or 2 (URS-1); more information is needed before the Population Distribution can be completed.
Estimated Total Condition Census: Unknown

1795 Flowing Hair, BB-20

Obv: Portrait II (Head of '95)
Rev: Eagle I, Wreath I (2 leaves)
(B-2, H-2)
Obverse: See description under 1795 BB-19. Close date. Obverse die used to strike 1795 BB-19 and BB-20.
Reverse: Two leaves under each wing. A leaf ends directly below center of first S in STATES and another leaf ends just under left corner of upright of E in STATES. The wreath is delicate, leaves small, berries large. 19 berries. Paired berries opposite I in UNITED, opposite A in STATES, under leaf below O in OF, and opposite I in AMERICA, on both inside and outside of wreath. One of these large berries is below *right* corner of I in UNITED, another below left corner of I in AMERICA. This is one of just two 1795 reverses with two berries inside the branch near the eagle's tail (the other die is that used to coin 1795 BB-16 and BB-15). This reverse die bears a very close relationship with the reverse used to coin 1795 BB-15 and 20, and another die used to coin BB-23, and must have been prepared by the same person about the same time.
Reverse die used to strike 1795 BB-20, BB-21, and BB-24.

Die States
Die State I: Perfect dies. Not lapped. May not exist.
Die State II: Obverse lapped, making stars (especially on the left side of the coin) somewhat thin and spidery, and separating end of lower curl from its matrix; on all specimens seen, the curl end is discontinuous to the right of the innermost point of star 1. On some specimens, the "bar" is hardly visible.

Collecting Notes
1795 BB-20 exists to the extent of an estimated 300 to 500 specimens. Thus, the specialist will find acquiring one to be a snap. For reasons unknown today, most are in the range of Fine, rather than VF. For every situation there is an explanation, and perhaps someday it will be learned. Probably, the

manner of distribution had something to do with it; examples of 1795 BB-20 were used widely in the channels of commerce, rather than stored by banks or bullion brokers.

The variety is typically encountered in lower grades but is rare above EF. Typically, the rims are quite raised on BB-20; coins are usually well centered, with prominent denticulation on both sides. While higher grade pieces will often show excellent hair detail on the obverse, usually the eagle's breast is somewhat flat.

As it is believed that two specimens in the Lord St. Oswald Collection, sold in 1964, were acquired during a visit to America in autumn 1795, this indicates that this particular variety must have been struck at or before that time. This means that BB-20 would have had a greater opportunity to circulate (i.e., acquire wear) than a 1795-dated dollar struck in a later year such as 1798.

Notable Specimens
Eliasberg Specimen. MS-65 (NGC). George H. Earle Collection sale (Henry Chapman, June 1912) • George Clapp. Sold to the following in 1942. • Louis Eliasberg Collection (Bowers and Merena Galleries, 1997) lot 2170. MS-65. Brilliant surfaces have prooflike characteristics. While conventional wisdom has it that Proofs as we know them today were not struck at the Philadelphia Mint in 1795, this piece certainly is very *special*. Seemingly struck from dies that were polished, and on a specially prepared planchet. Brilliant surfaces have just a whisper of golden toning. One of the most beautiful early dollars in existence. Quite possibly this was a presentation piece. If any 1795 Flowing Hair dollar is worthy of being designated a *Proof,* here it is! In his 1989 book on Proof coins, p. 33, Walter Breen specifically named the Eliasberg Collection coin as possibly being a Proof presentation piece. A very nice strike overall. Very sharp on the obverse. The reverse has some lightness at the center, as is true of virtually all 1795 silver dollars, but is still a notably above average strike.

Superb, delicate golden toning on obverse and reverse. This may well be the finest known 1795 Flowing Hair silver dollar of *any* die variety. • Jay Parrino • private collector.

Heifetz Specimen. MS-65 (NGC). Heifetz Collection (Superior, 1989) lot 3815. "MS-65. Superb. • unknown intermediaries • private collector • Steve Contursi • Cardinal Collection (American Numismatic Rarities June 2005), lot 11 • Purchased at the Cardinal Sale by James Halperin for Heritage inventory stock • Long Beach Signature Sale (Heritage, June 2011) lot 3820.

Lord St. Oswald-Stack Specimen. MS-64 PL (NGC). The Lord St. Oswald Collection (Christie, Manson & Woods, London, 1964) had two specimens: lot 139 was described as "Planchet marks on both sides and some scratching in obverse field, otherwise in brilliant Mint State, very rare. The coin was sold to Norman Stack for $1,288, who put it in his personal set of U.S. coins by design types (sold privately through Eric Streiner in 1989) • Eric Streiner • The August Sale (Superior, 1991) lot 553, MS-64 • Bob Bisanz U.S. Type Set (Heritage, January 2001) lot 7186 • FUN Signature Sale (Heritage, January 2007) lot 1025.

Rothschild Specimen. MS-64 (NGC). Rothschild Collection, 68th Anniversary Sale (Stacks, October 2003) lot 1218 "Very Choice BU" • Oliver Jung • Long Beach Signature Sale (Heritage, February 2008) lot 834 • Pre-Long Beach Sale (Ira and Larry Goldberg, September 2008) lot 1216 • Pre-Long Beach Sale (Ira and Larry Goldberg,

February 2009) lot 1038 • Pre-Long Beach Sale (Ira and Larry Goldberg, January 2010) lot 11172 • Pre-Long Beach Sale (Ira and Larry Goldberg, May 2010) lot 964.

Anderson-Dupont Specimen. MS-63. Anderson-Dupont Collection (Stack's, 1954) lot 2491. "Choice Uncirculated, prooflike surface."

1973 GENA Specimen. MS-63. 1973 Great Eastern Numismatic Association Sale, lot 293. • Frank M. Stirling Collection (Heritage, February 1986) lot 1327. • Auction '86: 1207.

Lord St. Oswald-Ostheimer Specimen. MS-63. Lord St. Oswald Collection, lot 140, "A similar coin, planchet marks on both sides, some scratching on face and in field on obverse, otherwise in Mint State, very rare," went to Alfred J. Ostheimer 3rd for $2,520.

Total Estimated Population
MS-65 or better: 2 or 3 (URS-2)
MS-64: 2 or 3 (URS-2)
MS-63: 4 to 7 (URS-3)
MS-60 to 62: 4 to 7 (URS-3)
AU-50 to 58: 6 to 12 (URS-4)
VF-20 to EF-45: 200 to 325 (URS-9)
G-4 to F-15: 100 to 150 (URS-8)
Total for all grades combined: 300 to 500 (URS-10)
Estimated Total Condition Census: 65-65-64-64-63 (multiples)

1795 Flowing Hair, BB-21

Obv: Portrait II (Head of '95)
Rev: Eagle I, Wreath I (2 leaves)
Exists with silver plug at center
(B-1, H-1)

Obverse: Flowing hair in five prominent curls, with a thin faint additional curl below the third curl from the top. Innermost point of star 1 just touches lowest curl. The curl continues upward to half close the loop. Head high

and closer to LIBERTY than on most other obverses. The date is wide, with more space between 1 and 7 than other figures. The 7 in the date was repunched over an erroneous 1, prompting some to catalog the variety as 1795 over 1195. The erroneous 1 is especially visible on early die states. This die bears a very close resemblance to the die used to coin BB-15; especially with regard to the high position of the head and the relationship of the hair curl to the first star.

As is the case with the obverse used to coin BB-27, the present obverse (also used to coin BB-22 and BB-23) had the head of Miss Liberty deeply impressed into the die, causing it to be in slightly higher relief than most other varieties of the year; because of this, the hair details wore away quickly as the coins circulated.

Obverse die used to strike 1795 BB-21, BB-22, and BB-23.

Reverse: See description under BB-20. Two leaves under each wing.

Reverse die used to strike 1795 BB-20, BB-21, and BB-24.

Die States

Die State I: Perfect dies.

Collecting Notes

1795 BB-21 is a very common variety. Indeed, it is second only to BB-27 in terms of its widespread availability. I have handled well over 100 since 1953, and this is without any special effort to acquire the variety. I estimate that about 1,500 to 2,500 exist. Most of these have been bought and sold privately. However, as nearly every specialized collection has had one, many have crossed the auction block over the years.

The Hesselgesser specimen of the 1795 BB-21 dollar with mint-inserted silver plug. Graded AU-53 by PCGS.

This variety can be found well struck, with sharp centers to the stars on higher-grade examples.

1795 BB-21 is especially plentiful in lower grades, with the average being in the range of VF-20 to 35. EF specimens, while elusive, are not rare. AU specimens occasionally are seen, and a dozen or more true Mint State coins exist in private hands.

Notable Specimens

Stack Family Type Set Specimens. MS-65 (PCGS). Contained within the "Stack Family" type set were *two* extraordinary examples of the 1795 BB-21 dollar; upon presentation to PCGS, both were encapsulated at MS-65.

Jack Lee Specimen. MS-65 (NGC). Jack Lee III Collection (Heritage, November 2005) lot 2186 • Madison Collection (Heritage, January 2008) lot 2920 • Joseph C. Thomas Collection (Heritage, April 2009) lot 2533.

Auction '84 Specimen. MS-63 (PCGS) • Auction '84 (Stack's, 1984) lot 1180, "Gem Brilliant Uncirculated." • unknown intermediaries • Oliver Jung • Legend Numismatics • Private collector .

Eliasberg Specimen. MS-63 (NGC). Harlan P. Smith Sale (Chapman brothers, 1906) • Louis Eliasberg Collection (Bowers and Merena, April 1997) lot 2171. "A lovely specimen, prooflike on obverse and reverse, and quite possibly struck from lightly polished dies. Some light evidence of contact on obverse and reverse and is mostly covered by lilac, gold, and delicate blue toning—creating a coin which is a visual and aesthetic delight. The strike is quite fine, with excellent higher detail on the obverse (considering the variety), and with the reverse well defined in all areas except the very highest part of the eagle. Under magnification the striking shows some bifurcation, notable around the periphery, giving the letters an especially ornate appearance. This is an artifact of striking, not of die preparation." • Phillip Flannagan Collection (Bowers and Merena, November 2001) lot 4208 • Robert Lehmann • Cardinal Collection (American Numismatic Rarities June 2005) lot 12 • Dallas Signature Sale (Heritage, December 2005) lot 903 • Pre-Long Beach Sale (Ira and Larry Goldberg, May 2007) lot 1304 • Orlando Rarities Sale (Bowers and Merena, January 2010) lot 405.

Boyd Specimen. MS-63. "World's Greatest Collection" (F.C.C. Boyd, Numismatic Gallery, 1945) lot 2, Uncirculated.

West Coast Specimen. MS-61 (NGC) Silver Plug. Private West Coast collector • Chicago ANA Sale (Stack's Bowers Galleries, August 2011) lot 7387.

Delp Specimen. MS-60. Winner F. Delp Collection (Stack's, November 1972) lot 84 • 55th Anniversary Sale (Stack's, 1990) lot 1658. "Brilliant Uncirculated, fully prooflike."

Chapman Specimen. MS-60. Lot 9 in an early, unidentified S.H. Chapman sale • Possibly 1992-05 (Superior, 1992) lot 2101. "MS-60."

Hesselgesser Specimen. AU-53 (PCGS) Silver Plug. Dr. Robert Hesselgesser Collection • Pre-Long Beach Sale (Ira and Larry Goldberg, September 2011) lot 5010 •

Pre-Long Beach Sale (Ira and Larry Goldberg, June 2012) lot 1264.

Cardinal Specimen. AU-53 (PCGS) Silver Plug. Tangible Asset Galleries • Cardinal Collection • Private collector.

Total Estimated Population

MS-65 or better: 3 (URS-3)
MS-64: 2 to 4 (URS-2)

MS-63: 4 to 6 (URS-3)
MS-60 to 62: 8 to 12 (URS-4)
AU-50 to 58: 50 to 100 (URS-7)
VF-20 to EF-45: 850 to 1,500 (URS-11)
G-4 to F-15: 600 to 900 (URS-11)
Total for all grades combined: 1,500 to 2,500 (URS-12)

Estimated Total Condition Census: 65-65-65-64-64-63 (multiples)

1795 FLOWING HAIR, BB-22

Obv: Portrait II (Head of '95)
Rev: Eagle I, Wreath I (2 leaves)
(B-10, H-10)

Obverse: See description under BB-21.

Obverse die used to strike 1795 BB-21, BB-22, and BB-23.

Reverse: Two leaves below each wing. 18 berries arranged nine left and nine right. A berry is on the outside of the wreath opposite C in AMERICA, *and* only one berry opposite last A in AMERICA, that being on inside of wreath. Two berries on outside of wreath on right between eagle's wing and ribbon bow.

Note: Bolender said this about the reverse in his 1950 book: "10 [berries] on left branch and 9 on right. Capt. Haseltine was in error in calling this the '18-berry variety.' His specimen was a worn one, and even on Fine specimens the *19th berry shows very faintly* on the inside of left stem near last single leaf."

Notwithstanding this seemingly definitive statement, I have been unable to find the nineteenth berry on any specimen examined, or on catalog plates.

Reverse die used to strike 1795 BB-22 only.

Die States

Die State I: Perfect dies.

Collecting Notes

1795 BB-22 is a very rare variety of which only nine have been positively identified and probably no more than 25 to 50 are known. Virtually all are in lower grades through VF, a notable exception being the F.C.C. Boyd coin, later appearing on the market in other sales, which is a superb Uncirculated example. Bolender called this variety R-6 (13 to 30, if he was using the Sheldon Scale), which rating is essentially unchanged today.

In his 1881 *Type-Table*, J.W. Haseltine called this variety "excessively rare," which, presumably, means rare to excess, or rarer than it should be! A better word would have been *exceedingly*, but "excessively" seems to have insinuated itself into the American numismatic nomenclature, and over the years many catalogers have used it (in fact, catalogers on my staff have done so).

Notable Specimens

Granberg Specimen. AU-58 (PCGS). H.O. Granberg Collection • "World's Greatest Collection" (F.C.C. Boyd, Numismatic Gallery, 1945) lot 12. Uncirculated. • Bareford Collection (Stack's, 1981) lot 404. "Brilliant Uncirculated." • Jim Matthews • 400th Sale (Stack's, 1988) lot 1166, "Brilliant Uncirculated." • Subsequently graded MS-61

(NGC) • Dr. Robert Hesselgesser Collection Pre-Long Beach Sale (Ira and Larry Goldberg, September 2011) lot 5012 as AU-58 (PCGS) • Pre-Long Beach Sale (Ira and Larry Goldberg, June 2012) lot 1265.

Brooks Specimen. EF-45 (PCGS). Brooks Collection (Bowers and Merena, 1989) lot 160. "VF-30." • Jim Matthews Collection (Goldberg Coins, September 2002), lot 457.

Bolender Specimen. EF-40. Milferd Bolender Collection • Midwest collection.

1952 ANA Sale Specimen. EF-40. 1952 ANA Convention Sale (New Netherlands) lot 3099 • 1975 ANA Convention Sale (Superior) lot 805. • Mid-American, September 1985, lot 514. • H.W. Blevins Collection (Superior, 1988) lot 3592. "VF-20." • Midwest collection.

Cardinal Specimen. VF-35 (PCGS). Pre-Long Beach Sale (Ira and Larry Goldberg, May 2001) lot 843 • Cardinal Collection • Elite Sale (Superior, January 2002) lot 1177 • CSNS Signature Sale (Heritage, April 2002) lot 6688 • Albany Collection (Heritage, September 2002) lot 7746.

Miller Specimen VF-35 (NGC). J.J. Teaparty • Warren Miller Collection.

Reiver Specimen. EF-40 (NGC). ANA Sale (New England Rare Coin Galleries, August 1979) lot 1027 • Jules Reiver Collection (Heritage, January 2006) lot 23476.

LaRiviere Specimen. F-15 (NGC). Lucien M. LaRiviere Collection Sale (Bowers and Merena, May 2001), lot 2.

Matthews Specimen. F-12, Scratches. Jim Matthews Collection • ANA Signature Sale (Heritage, August 1982).

"1793" Specimen. Good Details, Countermarked. Obverse counterstamped with "1793"; Offered unattributed on eBay in 2001 and purchased by a private collector.

Total Estimated Population

MS-65 or better: 0 (URS-0)
MS-64: 0 (URS-0)
MS-63: 0 (URS-0)
MS-60 to 62: 1 (URS-1)
AU-50 to 58: 0 (URS-0)
VF-20 to EF-45: 15 to 30 (URS-5)
G-4 to F-15: 10 to 20 (URS-5)
Total for all grades combined: 25 to 50 (URS-6)
Estimated Total Condition Census: 60-45-40-35 (multiples)

1795 Flowing Hair, BB-23

Obv: Portrait II (Head of '95)
Rev: Eagle I, Wreath I (2 leaves)
(B-16)
Obverse: See description under BB-21.

Obverse die used to strike 1795 BB-21, BB-22, and BB-23.

Reverse: Two leaves beneath each wing. 19 berries, nine on left branch, 10 on right. Berries on outside of wreath include those under left side of N in UNITED, under center of first A in AMERICA, and under right side of C. One of the inside berries is below the center of M. No *berry* opposite either I on outside of wreath. *Point of third leaf on right outside of wreath under center*

of I in AMERICA. This die bears a close resemblance to that used to coin 1795 BB-21, BB-20, and BB-24, and another die used to coin BB-15 and BB-16, and was probably made by the same person around the same time.

Reverse die used to strike 1795 BB-23 and BB-28.

Die States
Die State I: Perfect dies.

Collecting Notes
Bolender said this in 1950: "Unknown to Haseltine, the author's example is a Proof, and the only specimen he has seen or heard of in forty years' collecting. Rarity 8."

The obverse was known to Haseltine in 1881, who listed it as part of his H-1 and H-10 numbers. The reverse was new to the Bolender book.

I am aware of just four specimens of this variety in numismatic hands today.

Notable Specimens

Elder Specimen. AU-58. Thomas L. Elder, sold in the 1930s to the following. • M.H. Bolender Collection (Bolender, 1952) lot 19. "Uncirculated, with Proof surface." Plate. (Reverse of this coin was used for plate II in book.)" • K.P. Austin Collection. • A.J. Ostheimer 3rd Collection. • Gilhousen Sale (Superior, 1973) lot 1218, Uncirculated. • ANA Convention Sale (Superior, 1975) lot 811. "Borderline Uncirculated with some faint obverse scratches, numerous reverse adjustment marks." • Davenport Collection (Superior, 1977) lot 468, almost MS-60.

Miller Specimen. VF Details (NGC) Double Struck. Warren Miller Collection.

PCGS CoinFacts Specimen. VG-8 (PCGS). Recently discovered specimen • private collector • Harry Laibstain.

Reiver Specimen. Fine Details (NCS). Early 1980s coin show • H. Roland Willasch, November 1989 • Jules Reiver Collection. Two light scratches cross on the obverse. • Jules Reiver Collection Sale (Heritage, January 2006) lot 23480 • William Luebke Collection (Heritage, January 2007) lot 4951.

Total Estimated Population

MS-65 or better: 0 (URS-0)
MS-64: 0 (URS-0)
MS-63: 0 (URS-0)
MS-60 to 62: 0 (URS-0)
AU-50 to 58: 1 (URS-1)
VF-20 to EF-45: 0 (URS-0)
G-4 to F-15: 3 (URS-3)
Total for all grades combined: 4 (URS-[3])
Estimated Total Condition Census: 58-12-8-8]

1795 FLOWING HAIR, BB-24

Obv: Portrait II (Head of '95)
Rev: Eagle I, Wreath I (2 leaves)
(B-13, H-13)
Obverse: Flowing hair in six curls, 3rd and 4th close together; lowest curl barely misses a point of first star, but continues on to touch and slightly pass a second point of same star. The second curl from bottom turns downward pointing to space between two points of second star. *Wide date, 79 closest.* E in LIBERTY punched over an earlier erroneous R. The Y in LIBERTY is higher than the adjacent T. Foot of R in LIBERTY shortened from a broken punch.

Obverse die used to strike 1795 BB-24 (early state) and BB-25 (early and late states).

Reverse: See description under BB-20. Two leaves under each wing.

Reverse die used to strike 1795 BB-20, BB-21, and BB-24.

Die States

Die State I: Perfect dies.

Collecting Notes

Bolender wrote this in 1950: "The author's example is probably the Haseltine specimen. Two others are known to the author, and no others have been heard of in 40 years. Rarity 7." Haseltine in 1881 considered his coin to be unique.

I believe that somewhere between 100 and 150 exist, most of which are in relatively high grades for a 1795 issue. In this regard, BB-24 is in sharp contrast to BB-26, the latter of which is usually seen in Fine. Most 1795 BB-24 dollars are in better grades such as VF or EF, or even finer.

The problem of evaluating the rarity of early dollars today in the early 1990s is akin to what large cent researchers were faced with 75 to 100 years ago, before popular references became generally available. Information in print is often contradictory. Common varieties are called rare, and rare varieties are sometimes sold for "common prices." Although the Bolender book is excellent, it has not served as a springboard for research in the silver dollar series to the same extent that Dr. William H. Sheldon's 1949 text, *Early American Cents*, did for large cents 1793-1814. Nor is there a very wide circle of friends of the early silver dollar, while, by contrast, there are at least a couple thousand or more numismatists who seek to acquire early (1793-1814) large cents by die varieties. In doing research for this book, one expert ventured the opinion that about 10 to 15 specimens of 1795 BB-24 existed, while another suggested that 80 to 100 was the correct range. As noted, Bolender knew of only three coins!

All things considered, the 1795 BB-24 dollar is an excellent variety for further research. Why are most specimens in higher grades? How many are known to exist?

Notable Specimens

Atwater Specimen. MS-60+. Atwater Collection (B. Max Mehl, 1946) lot 187. "Brilliant semi-proof just about equal to a brilliant Proof." $152.50. Sold to the following. • Louis G. Stirling, who sold it to the following. • Frank M. Stirling Collection (Heritage, Mid-Winter ANA Convention Sale, 1986) lot 1328. • Four Landmark Collections (Bowers and Merena, 1989) lot 1942. "MS-60 to 63, prooflike • Jascha Heifetz Collection (Superior, 1989) lot 2381. "MS-60+. • Auction '90 (RARCOA, 1990) lot 760. "Choice Brilliant Uncirculated." • The May Sale (Superior, 1991) lot 948, "MS-60+, prooflike."

The Baldenhofer Specimen. MS-62 (PCGS). W.G. Baldenhofer Collection. • A.J. Ostheimer 3rd Collection. • ANA Convention Sale (Superior, 1975) lot 810. "AU-50 or better." • Alex Highland Collection (Heritage, May 2001) lot 6261 as AU-58 (PCGS) • Rarities Sale (Bowers and Merena, January 2002) lot 503 • Steve Contursi • Private collector • Baltimore Sale (Bowers and Merena, March 2009) lot 3001 • Hesselgesser Collection (Ira and Larry Goldberg, September 2011) lot 5013.

Miller Specimen. AU-53 (NGC). CSNS Signature Sale (Heritage, April 2006) lot 2111 • Warren Miller Collection.

Spies Specimen. AU-50 (PCGS). W Earl Spies Collection (Stack's, December 1974) lot 18 • Gary Burghoff Collection (Superior, January 1980) lot 275, • Steve Ivy Numismatic Auctions, August 1980, lot 2500 • Brooks Collection (Bowers and Merena, June 1989) lot 162 • Jim Matthews (Ira and Larry Goldberg, September 2002), lot 460, unsold.

Orlando Specimen. EF-45 (NGC). FUN Signature Sale (Heritage, January 2004) lot 7132 as EF-45 (PCGS) • CSNS Signature Sale (Heritage, May 2004) lot 7933 as EF-45 (NGC).

The Wyatt Specimen. EF-40. Wyatt Collection (Superior, 1985) lot 2006. "EF-45+." • H.W. Blevins Collection (Superior, 1988) lot 3565, there called EF-40 • Dr. Robert Stark Collection.

Miller Specimen (another) EF-40 (NGC). Warren Miller Collection • Dr. Robert Hesselgesser Collection (Ira and Larry Goldberg, February 2007) lot 1549 • Pre-Long Beach Sale (Ira and Larry Goldberg, February 2008) lot 2834 • Pre-Long Beach Sale (Ira and Larry Goldberg, May 2011) lot 875.

Bolender Specimen. EF-40. Bolender's 183rd Sale (Bolender, February 1952) lot 17.

Rothert Specimen. EF-40. Matthew Rothert Collection (Bowers and Ruddy, November 1973) lot 919 • Davenport Sale (Superior, February 1977) lot 467.

Haseltine Specimen. EF-40. Haseltine Collection sold in 1881, untraced since.

Luebke Specimen. VF-35 (NGC). Americana Sale (Stack's, January 2004) lot 3457 • William Luebke Collection (Heritage, January 2007) lot 4952.

Reiver Specimen. VF-30 (NGC). Ex: Bland (August 1975) • Jules Reiver Collection (Heritage, January 2006) lot 23479.

Total Estimated Population

MS-65 or better: 0 (URS-0)
MS-64: 0 (URS-0)
MS-63: 1 or 2 (URS-1)
MS-60 to 62: 2 to 4 (URS-2)
AU-50 to 58: 5 to 10 (URS-4)
VF-20 to EF-45: 80 to 130 (URS-8)
G-4 to F-15: 4 to 8 (URS-3)
Total for all grades combined: 100 to 150 (URS-8)
Estimated Total Condition Census: 63-62-53-50-45-40 (multiples)

1795 FLOWING HAIR, BB-25

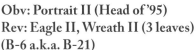

Obv: Portrait II (Head of '95)
Rev: Eagle II, Wreath II (3 leaves)
(B-6 a.k.a. B-21)

Note: Die State I of BB-25 is a new discovery not known to Haseltine and Bolender, and differs from the traditional or "old" B-6 and H-6 (for which see Die State III below). The present BB-25, Die State I, was earlier called B-18 (in 1952) and B-21 (later). What is now called B-18 is a different variety; and there is no B-21.

Obverse: See description under 1795 BB-24.

Obverse die used to strike 1795 BB-24 (early state) and BB-25 (early and late states).

Reverse: Three leaves under each wing of eagle. *13 berries,* seven on left branch, six on right. Two berries under first T in STATES, one on inside and one on outside of wreath. Die State I has three leaves visible below first S of STATES (early state of die, probably with 4th leaf depression in die filled with foreign matter). Die State III with four leaves; also used in its later state to coin BB-26 and BB-27, each of which has four leaves beneath the first S of STATES.

Reverse die used to strike 1795 BB-25 (two states; Die State I with three leaves and Die State III with four leaves under first S in STATES; presumably, one of the leaf recesses in the die was clogged, thus preventing one leaf from striking up), BB-26 (later state with four leaves under first S in STATES), and BB-27 (later state with four leaves under first S in STATES).

Die States

Die State I: Dies without cracks. Obverse die unlapped (*i.e.,* in an early state). Three leaves on reverse in the cluster below the first S in STATES. Early state of obverse and reverse dies. This die state was discovered by Frank M. Stirling of Baton Rouge, Louisiana, and was reported by M.H. Bolender in the December 1952 issue of *The Numismatist.* At the time it was considered to be from an entirely new die, and the designation "Bolender-18" was given to it (later, it became known as

Bolender-18); all this time it acquired a special aura as a great rarity, until it was realized that is was simply a die state of a standard variety known for many years. It is still very rare, but as a die state, not a separate die variety.[1/2]

Die State II. Clash marks in obverse fields.

Die State III: Obverse die relapped (*i.e.,* in a later state than Die State I). The relapping was especially severe and shortened the curls; lowest curl now ends in a point

---

[1] During the preparation of the first edition of this book, the 3-leaf and 4-leaf situation became a point of discussion when it was realized that conventional wisdom (per 5th edition of the Bolender book, and other writing) was that this reverse die was made with 3 leaves under the first S of STATES, but in a *later state,* a 4th leaf was added. As Thomas K. DeLorey and Harry Salyards, M.D. pointed out, and as the author and Mark Borckardt had been contemplating, it defied all known Mint practice of the era to add an extra leaf or similar feature to an already work-hardened die. This would have been a complicated process which hardly would have been undertaken to "fix" something as innocuous as a cluster of leaves. Mark Borckardt finally said in a note to the author, "Thou shalt not overlook the obvious"—and proposed that a piece of foreign matter clogged one leaf in the die, a basic situation which has occurred many times throughout American coinage history, and which has caused various design elements, mintmarks, etc., to be weak or to disappear.

[2] Subsequent to the publication of the first edition of this book, the Stirling discovery piece was provided to John Dannreuther for extensive evaluation and analysis, and the conclusion from his research was later published the July 2007 issue of the *PCGS Rare Coin Market Report.* Logic and "the obvious" notwithstanding, Dannreuther's careful comparisons of the Stirling Die State I specimen with a common Die State II specimen identified many more differences between the two die states than just the presence (or absence) of the fourth leaf in the cluster beneath first S in STATES. Many leaves on the right side of the wreath were noticeably re-worked, and berries were strengthened, enlarged, re-positioned, and given different stem lengths. Dannreuther summed up by saying "Knowledge is an evolution and the examination of the evidence leads to surprising conclusions. The complete reworking of already used dies had been doubted, but we now know it was done."

between two points of star, and is near star. Traces of erroneous R under E of LIBERTY now mostly ground away. An engraving tool was used to strengthen the bottom tail of R. Reverse: A fourth leaf is now seen in the cluster below the first S in STATES on the reverse; presumably, the die became unclogged. This die state used to be cataloged as Bolender-6 and Haseltine-6. Common.

Collecting Notes

•DIE STATE I: Two specimens are known to the writer. The first is Frank M. Stirling's discovery piece, which from the illustration in *The Numismatist* appears to be EF. The second is that included in Stack's sale of the Spies Collection, December 9-10, 1974, lot 19, and described as prooflike EF, with a few faint scratches between the 1 and 7 of the date.

•DIE STATE II: Transitional state. Not seen by the author.

•DIE STATE III: It is believed that 300 to 500 specimens of 1795 BB-25, Die State III, exist, most of which are in lower grades through VF. Thus, 1795 BB-25 is one of the more readily available issues of the year. The variety becomes rare in AU and better preservation.

The rims are usually indistinct in portions, with some areas appearing flattened; weakness is usually seen at the rim beginning about the 8th star and continuing over LIBE, and from the 13th star, the date, to the 1st or 2nd star; on the reverse, the weakness is most often seen at the rim above UNI and OF AME. Most specimens are weak at the obverse center in the area of Miss Liberty's ear (which is usually not visible), and on the eagle's breast.

Notable Specimens
(Die State I coins)

Stirling Specimen. EF-45 (PCGS). Frank M. Stirling Collection • Stirling Family • W. David Perkins • Dr. Robert Hesselgesser Collection (Ira and Larry Goldberg, September 2011) lot 5014 • Pre-Long Beach Sale (Ira and Larry Goldberg, May 2012) lot 1266.

Spies Specimen. EF-40. W. Early Spies Collection (Stack's, December 1974) lot 19.

(Die State III coins)

Winsor Specimen. AU-58 (PCGS). Richard Winsor Collection (S.H. & H. Chapman, December 1895) lot 390 • unknown intermediaries • Austin Collection

The Stirling-Hesselgesser specimen of the 1795 BB-25 dollar, "Three Leaves" Die State I. Graded EF-45 by PCGS.

(Bowers and Ruddy, May 1974) lot 2 • Edward B. Willing Collection (Bowers and Ruddy, June 1976) lot 1091 • Roy Harte Collection (Bowers and Ruddy, November 1977) lot 2779 • Harry Einstein Collection (Bowers and Merena, June 1986) lot 1727 • The Saunders Collection (Bowers and Merena, November 1987) lot 370 • 69th Anniversary Sale (Stack's, October 2004) lot 1878 • unknown intermediaries • Pinnacle Rarities, September 2012 • Private collector.

Frontenac Specimen. AU-58 (NGC) • Four Landmark Collections (Bowers and Merena, 1989) lot 1942, "AU-58." • The Frontenac Sale (Bowers and Merena, 1991) lot 2201. "AU-58, NGC."

Baltimore Specimen. AU-58 (NGC) • Baltimore Sale (Bowers and Merena, March 2005) lot 2001.

Yee Specimen. AU-55+ (NGC). Fred Yee Collection (Heritage, September 2012) lot 4622.

Hesselgesser Specimen. AU-53 (PCGS). Pre-Long Beach Sale (Ira and Larry Goldberg, February 2007) lot 1551, as AU-55 (NGC) • Dr. Robert Hesselgesser Collection (Ira and Larry Goldberg, September 2011) lot 5015, as AU-53 (PCGS) • Pre-Long Beach Sale (Ira and Larry Goldberg, May 2012) lot 1267

Total Estimated Population (Die State I)
MS-65 or better: 0 (URS-0)
MS-64: 0 (URS-0)
MS-63: 0 (URS-0)
MS-60 to 62: 0 (URS-0)
AU-50 to 58: 0 (URS-0)
VF-20 to EF-45: 2 (URS-2)
G-4 to F-15: 0 (URS-0)
Total for all grades combined: 2 (URS-2)
Estimated Total Condition Census: 45-40-0

Total Estimated Population (Die State III)
MS-65 or better: 0 (URS-0)
MS-64: 0 (URS-0)
MS-63: 0 (URS-0)
MS-60 to 62: 0 (URS-0)
AU-50 to 58: 10 to 20 (URS-5)
VF-20 to EF-45: 190 to 275 (URS-9)
G-4 to F-15: 100 to 190 (URS-8)
Total for all grades combined: 300 to 500 (URS-10)
Estimated Total Condition Census: 58-58-58-55 (multiples)

1795 FLOWING HAIR, BB-26

Obv: Portrait II (Head of '95)
Rev: Eagle II, Wreath II (3 leaves)
(B-12, H-12)

Obverse: Flowing hair in six curls, the *lowest curl passing through a point of first star*, and continues to right, ending in a sharp point. Second curl from bottom points downward to space between two points of second star. Hair at top is flat and lacks any "wave." Wide date, the 7 and 9 closer than other figures. Letters IB spaced too widely. Letter B leans to right, as do also the T and Y. E in LIBERTY is repunched.

Obverse die used to strike 1795 BB-26 and BB-29..

Reverse: See description under BB-25. Three leaves under each wing of eagle. With four leaves below first S of STATES (late state of die, used to coin Die State III of BB-25, the present BB-26.

Reverse die used to strike 1795 BB-25 (two states; Die State I with three leaves and Die State III with four leaves under first S in STATES; presumably, one of the leaf recesses in the die was clogged, thus preventing one leaf from striking up), BB-26 (later state with four leaves under first S in STATES), and BB-27 (later state with four leaves under first S in STATES).

Die States

Die State I: Perfect obverse die. Rare, but the most often seen die state.

Die State II: Bolender's "12a." Vertical break from the bust truncation to the border through the 7. Bolender's specimen was Stickney: 807 (Henry Chapman, 1907), and was the only one known to him. Also see 1975 ANA Convention Sale: 808 and 809.

Die State III: This state shows the die crack more clearly; crack extends from rim through the center, to Miss Liberty's ear. The centers are weak from die failure

on some. Cf. Spies (as "Bolender-12-b"); the cataloger of Gilhousen (Superior, 1973): 1217, VG-Fine, knew of only one other—the Emanuel Taylor coin. An AU-55 coin examined by the author had excellent center detail on obverse and reverse.

Die State IV: This state, sometimes cataloged as "Bolender-12b" shows a heavy lump between the 7 and the bust while the crack extends up to the ear.

Collecting Notes

1795 BB-26 is believed to exist to the extent of 100 to 150 coins, most of which are in lower grades up to and including VF. Fine grade seems to be about par for this variety, an issue which must have circulated very extensively. The variety is very rare EF and unknown in Mint State. Any specimen which grades EF or higher is Condition Census level.

In his 1881 *Type-Table*, this was one of the varieties J.W. Haseltine designated as "excessively rare."

Notable Specimens

Stirling Specimen. AU-55 (PCGS). William F. Gable Collection (S.H. Chapman, May 1914) lot 614 • unknown intermediaries • Frank M. Stirling Collection (Heritage, February 1986) lot 1322. • Ebenezer Saunders Collection Sale (Bowers and Merena, November 1987) lot 372, as "AU-55" • ANA Mid-Winter Auction (Heritage, March 1988) lot 935 • The Brooks Collection (Bowers and Merena, June 1989) lot 161, "EF-40. Bolender-12a die state." • H. Roland Willasch Collection Sale, but not part of the Willasch Collection, (Superior, May 1990) lot 450, Bolender-12a. EF-40 • James L. Moore Collection (Heritage, July 2003) lot 8117 • Cardinal Collection (American Numismatic Rarities June 2005), lot 13, as AU-55 (PCGS) • Mark Gordon Collection

(Ira and Larry Goldberg, May 2009) lot 594 • Cardinal Collection (Bowers and Merena, November 2010) lot 2192 "Die State III."

Miller Specimen. EF-45 (NGC). Lanu Balulescu • Warren Miller Collection, Die State I.

Portland Specimen. EF-45 (NGC). Portland ANA Convention Sale (Young, August 1959) lot 1648 "Magnificent blue EF B-12" • unknown intermediaries • David Lawrence Galleries • Cardinal Collection • Thaler Collection, Die State I.

Hesselgesser Specimen. EF-40 (PCGS). Dr. Robert Hesselgesser Collection (Ira and Larry Goldberg, September 2011) lot 5016 • Pre-Long-Beach Sale (Ira and Larry Goldberg, May 2012) lot 1268. "Die State III."

Elder Specimen. EF-40. Thomas L. Elder Sale, 1924. • M.H. Bolender Collection, 1952: 14. "EF."

Miller Specimen (another). VF-35. Julian Leidman • Warren Miller.

Blevins Specimen. VF-20. H.W. Blevins Collection (Superior, 1988) lot 3594. "VF-20."

Hewitt Specimen. VF-20. Lee F. Hewitt Collection (Bowers and Merena, 1984) lot 2284. "VF-20."

Million Dollar Sale Specimen. VF-20. Million Dollar Sale (Harmer, Rooke, 1969) lot 1118 • The Long Beach Convention Sale (Kagin's, February 1987) lot 1125. "VF-20."

The New Netherlands 61st Sale Specimen. VF-20. June 1970, lot 408, "VF, … shows only the most microscopic signs of the 'Bolender-12a' die crack."

Rumbel Specimen. F-15. 1952 ANA Convention Sale, O.K. Rumbel Collection (New Netherlands) lot 3100. • A.J. Ostheimer 3rd Collection (Lester Merkin, 1968) lot 232. "Almost VF. … Claimed to be ex Stickney 807, but that claim is also made for the more worn Bolender, Taylor, Kagin piece."

Total Estimated Population

MS-65 or better: (URS-0)

MS-64: (URS-0)

MS-63: (URS-0)

MS-60 to 62: (URS-0)

AU-50 to 58: 1 (URS-1)

VF-20 to EF-45: 30 to 50 (URS-6)

G-4 to F-15: 70 to 100 (URS-8)

Total for all grades combined: 100 to 150 (URS-8)

Estimated Total Condition Census: 55-45-45-40-40-40

The Stirling-Cardinal specimen of the 1795 BB-26 dollar, Die State III with advanced die cracks. Graded AU-55 by PCGS.

1795 Flowing Hair, BB-27

Obv: Portrait II (Head of '95)
Rev: Eagle II, Wreath II (3 leaves)
(B-5, H-5)

Obverse: Flowing hair in six curls, the 3rd and 4th close together; the 4th has a tiny curved "tail" extending downward, and visible on higher grade pieces. Lowest curl distant from star. A "bar" over 2 mm. long extends diagonally from close to top curl toward point of 5th star. Look for the "*bar*" *near uppermost curl.* (By contrast, BB-20 has the bar near 4th star.) Wide date, the 1 and 7 farthest apart. First star about as close to 1 as 7 is to 9. Most early die states show striking weakness at the centers.

As is the case with the obverse die used to coin BB-21, BB-22, and BB-23, the present obverse had the head of Miss Liberty deeply impressed into the die, causing it to be in slightly higher relief than other varieties of the year; because of this, the hair details wore away quickly as the coins circulated.

Obverse die used to strike 1795 BB-27 only.

Reverse: Three leaves under each wing. *13 berries,* seven on left branch, six on right. Three leaves under each wing of eagle. Two berries under first T in STATES, one on inside and one on outside of wreath. With *four leaves below first S of STATES* (late state of die, also used to coin BB-25, later state, and BB-26; the state used to strike BB-25, early state, has only three leaves).

Note: All specimens of BB-27 and BB-25 examined by Bolender showed a fine die crack from end of left stem downward, in BB-27 extending to border. However, the crack does not appear on some specimens of BB-27, nor in BB-26 nor BB-26a, indicating BB-26 was struck earlier.

Reverse die used to strike 1795 BB-25 (two states; Die State I with three leaves and Die State III with four leaves under first S in STATES; presumably, one of the leaf recesses in the die was clogged, thus preventing one leaf from striking up), BB-26 (later state with four leaves

under first S in STATES), and BB-27 (later state with four leaves under first S in STATES).

Die States

Die State I: Perfect reverse. None seen by Bolender. However, about one in 20 to 30 1795 BB-27 dollars is of this state. Usually lightly struck at the centers, even on high grade coins.

Die State II: Crack just beginning from end of the left stem to rim. Cf. Gilhousen (Superior, 1973). Common. Often lightly struck at the centers; even AU and Mint State coins are weak at the centers.

Die State III: The reverse is cracked from the end of the left stem to border; the die crack is not bold. Common. Usually better struck at the centers than Die State II.

Die State IV: Clash marks before the lip and the nose, die roughness in LIBE and at the back of the lower curls. Not seen by the author.

Die State V: Crack from top of 7 to bust. Rare. Crack from rim through star 10 to chin. Very scarce. Not seen by the author.

Die State VI: Obverse die buckles from 5:00 to 8:00 at the rim, date weakens. Rare. Not seen by the author.

Die State VII: Obverse die reground; "bar" nearly gone and stars smaller. 1975 ANA Convention Sale (Superior): 793; 1986 ANA: 4708. Very rare. (How does this compare to Die State IV?)

Collecting Notes

1795 BB-27 is by far the most common variety of 1795. A couple thousand or more exist; I estimate the population to be 2,500 to 3,500 in all grades combined. However, in his 1881 *Type-Table,* J.W. Haseltine called this variety rare if "strictly Uncirculated." In its day, this die combination may have struck 100,000 or more coins! The die steel must have been especially well tempered.

Due to the depth of the Miss Liberty portrait in the die, the resultant coins were in high relief. Because of this, the hair wore quickly at the center of the obverse, with the result that pieces grading VF or lower usually have little detail still remaining. On some (but not all) higher grade coins, usually Die State III in EF or finer preservation, the hair detail at the center of the obverse and the eagle's breast feathers are well defined. As many as 50 to 100 Mint State coins may exist.

Notable Specimens

Montgomery Collection. MS-66 (NGC). British collection. • Bowers and Ruddy Galleries • Montgomery Collection (Bowers and Ruddy, February 1976) lot 1998. "Gem Uncirculated." Pedigree: Possibly originally struck as a presentation piece, originally obtained by [us] from an overseas source, [we] subsequently sold it to its present owner who consigned it to [us]." • Foxfire Type Set Collection.

Eliasberg Specimen. MS-64 (PCGS). The striking is above average, with good detail (considering the variety) at the centers, even at the high part of the eagle's body, although not with full feather definition. The dentils frame the coin nicely, as is the case with a number of varieties of this year. The rim is somewhat flat on the dentils opposite stars 5-8. E.W. Ropes Collection (New York Coin & Stamp Co., February 1899) • J.M. Clapp • John H. Clapp • Clapp estate, 1942 • Louis E. Eliasberg Sr. Collection (Bowers and Merena, April 1997), lot 2172. Die State III, as "MS-62 or finer" • Rarities Sale (Bowers and Merena, August 1999) lot 234, as MS-64 (NGC) • Essex Palm Collection (Heritage, January 2007) lot 1023, as MS-64 (NGC) • Kevin Lipton • ANA National Money Show Signature Sale (Heritage, March 2007) lot 865, as MS-64 (PCGS).

Matlock Specimen. MS-64 (PCGS). Marvin Matlock Collection (Bowers and Merena, March 1991) lot 460 • Haig Koshkarian Collection (American Numismatic Rarities, March 2004) lot 94, as MS-65 (NGC) • Joseph O'Connor • Private collector • Liberty Collection (Heritage, August 2012) lot 5173, as MS-64 (PCGS).

2008 Pre-Long Beach Sale Specimen. MS-64 (NGC). Pre-Long Beach Sale (Ira and Larry Goldberg, September 2008) lot 1214 • Pre-Long Beach Sale (Ira and Larry Goldberg, January 2011) lot 1510 • Pre-Long Beach Sale (Ira and Larry Goldberg, May 2011) lot 876.

2009 Pre-Long Beach Sale Specimen. MS-64 (NGC). Pre-Long Beach Sale (Ira and Larry Goldberg, February 2009) lot 1039 • Pre-Long Beach Sale (Ira and Larry Goldberg, January 2010) lot 1172 • Pre-Long Beach Sale (Ira and Larry Goldberg, May 2010) lot 963.

1977 ANA Convention Sale Specimen. MS-63. ANA Convention Sale (Kagin's 1977) lot 1748.

Auction '80 Specimen. MS-63. Auction '80 (RARCOA, 1980) lot 1614.

Auction '85 Specimen. MS-63. Auction '85 (Stack's, 1985) lot 1745.

Davenport Specimen. MS-63. Davenport Collection (Stack's, 1977) lot 406.

Hall Specimen. MS-63. Hall Collection (Bowers and Ruddy, 1978) lot 1672.

Helfenstein Specimen. MS-63. Helfenstein Collection (Lester Merkin, 1968) lot 276.

Robison Specimen. MS-63. Ellis H. Robison Collection (Stack's, 1982) lot 1854. "Brilliant Uncirculated."

Ebsen Specimen. MS-63. Buddy Ebsen Collection (Superior, 1987) lot 1876.

Miller Specimen. MS-63. Hoagy Carmichael and Wayne Miller Collections (Superior, 1986) lot 1174.

Turoff Specimen. MS-63. Julius Turoff Collection (Bowers and Ruddy, 1976) lot 1028. "Gem Uncirculated."

Total Estimated Population

MS-65 or better: 1 or 2 (URS-1)
MS-64: 3 to 5 (URS-3)
MS-63: 12 to 20 (URS-5)
MS-60 to 62: 30 to 50 (URS-6)
AU-50 to 58: 100 to 150 (URS-8)
VF-20 to EF-45: 1,300 to 1,800 (URS-12)
G-4 to F-15: 1,000 to 1,600 (URS-12)
Total for all grades combined: 2,500 to 3,500 (URS-13)
Estimated Total Condition Census: 66-64-64-64 (multiples)

1795 Flowing Hair, BB-28

Obv: Portrait I (Head of '94)
Rev: Eagle I, Wreath I (2 leaves)
(B-21)

Obverse: Flowing hair in six curls, the top curl turning up at its end. The lowest curl forms a nearly closed circle, similar to only obverse 4 among the Portrait I obverse dies. Star 1 is vertically below this curl and distant, unlike obverse 4, which has star 1 joined to the lowest curl. Stars 1 and 2 have two points each approximately equidistant from this curl. The four middle curls are approximately equal in length, their tips nearly in vertical alignment. Second curl from the bottom points to the center of star 3. The date has the digit 5 leaning sharply left. LIBERTY is widely spaced with LI close, IB wider, BER close, and RTY slightly wider.

Obverse die used to strike 1795 BB-28 only.

Reverse: Two leaves beneath each wing. 19 berries, nine on left branch, 10 on right. Berries on outside of wreath include those under left side of N, under center of first A in AMERICA, and under right side of C. One of the inside berries is below the center of M. No berry opposite either I on outside of wreath. Point of third leaf on right side of wreath under center of I in AMERICA. This die bears a close resemblance to that used to coin 1795 BB-21, BB-20, and BB-24, and another die used to coin BB-15 and BB-16, and was probably made by the same person around the same time.

Reverse die used to strike 1795 BB-23 and BB-28.

Die States

Die State I: Perfect dies.

Collecting Notes

The discovery example remains the only known example of this variety, and thus the only appearance of the obverse die. With just four known examples of BB-23, the reverse die is represented by a total population of just five coins. At its first appearance at auction in 1997, it was accompanied by an envelope from B.G. Johnson noting "Not in Haseltine."

Notable Specimens

B.G. Johnson Specimen. VG-10 (NGC). Attractive uniform medium gray toning with a couple small darker splashes on the reverse. Details of Very Fine, but a number of old, toned-over fine scratches criss cross the obverse surface. B.G. Johnson Collection • B.G. Johnson Estate • "Important Coins and Banknotes" (Spink America, June 1997) lot 186 • Private collector • Rarities Sale (Bowers and Merena, August 1999) lot 235 • Cardinal Collection • Elite Sale (Superior Galleries, January 2002) lot 1180 (unsold) • Privately to Warren Miller Collection.

Total Estimated Population

MS-65 or better: 0 (URS-0)
MS-64: 0 (URS-0)
MS-63: 0 (URS-0)
MS-60 to 62: 0 (URS-0)
AU-50 to 58: 0 (URS-0)
VF-20 to EF-45: 0 (URS-0)
G-4 to F-15: 1 (URS-1)
Total for all grades combined: 1 (URS-1)
Estimated Total Condition Census: 10

1795 Flowing Hair, BB-29

Obv: Portrait II (Head of '95)
Rev: Eagle II, Wreath II (3 leaves)
(B-22)

Obverse: Flowing hair in six curls, the *lowest curl passing through a point of first star,* and continues to right, ending in a sharp point. Second curl from bottom points downward to space between two points of second star. Hair at top is flat and lacks any "wave." Wide date, the 7 and 9 closer than other figures. Letters IB spaced too widely. Letter B leans to right, as do also the T and Y. E in LIBERTY is repunched.

Obverse die used to strike 1795 BB-26 (Die State I) and BB-29.

Reverse: Three leaves beneath each wing. *The only variety with 12 berries,* six on left branch and six on right. Berries on outside of wreath include those under left side of D, under the left side of the S in STATES, and under the center of M. One of the inside berries is below the center of M. No berry opposite either I on outside of wreath. A cluster of four leaves passes over top of the eagle's right wing (viewer's left).

Reverse die used to strike 1795 BB-29 only.

Die States

Die State I: Perfect dies.

Collecting Notes

The discovery example remained the only known example of this variety for more than 10 years. In 2009 a second specimen was discovered and verified, bringing the known population to two.

Notable Specimens

Reiver Specimen. VF Details (NGC). Discovered by ANACS grader Charles Erb October 1997, and confirmed by ANACS Senior Numismatist Michael Fahey • privately to Jules Reiver via Julian Leidman, November 1997 • Jules Reiver Collection • Reiver Estate (Heritage, January 2006) lot 23482, "Surfaces toned pale gray and displaying signs of tooling or repair on the obverse" • Warren Miller Collection.

Hatfield Specimen. AG Details, Holed and Plugged. Port City Coin & Jewelry eBay auction, January 2009, as an unattributed 1795 Flowing Hair dollar • David Hatfield, who discovered the true attribution of the coin • JRCS Member #101.

Total Estimated Population

MS-65 or better: 0 (URS-0)
MS-64: 0 (URS-0)
MS-63: 0 (URS-0)
MS-60 to 62: 0 (URS-0)
AU-50 to 58: 0 (URS-0)
VF-20 to EF-45: 0 (URS-0)
G-4 to F-15: 1 (URS-1)
Total for all grades combined: 2 (URS-2)
Estimated Total Condition Census: 12-2

CHAPTER 8

1795 DRAPED BUST SILVER DOLLARS

Mintage
100,000 (author's estimate)

1795 SILVER DOLLARS
BB to Bolender to Haseltine Equivalents

BB Number	Bolender #	Haseltine #	Rarity	Average Grade
BB-51	B-14	H-14	URS-12	VF-35
BB-52	B-15	H-15	URS-12	VF-33

Coinage Context

New portrait: Conventional numismatic wisdom has it that the new Draped Bust obverse was the pride and joy of Henry William DeSaussure, Mint director since June 1795, who upon taking office stated that he wanted to do two things: circulate gold coins and improve the design of all denominations, particularly silver. Portrait artist Gilbert Stuart (best known today for his depiction of George Washington, unfinished at the bottom familiarly displayed in schoolrooms) was hired, and is said to have prepared a drawing of Mrs. William Bingham, the former Ann Willing. John Eckstein, a Providence, Rhode Island artist of uncertain ability (per Breen), translated the sketches into plaster (probably) models, which may have been Liberty head and eagle device punches, for Mint Engraver Robert Scot.[1] The record shows that on September 9, 1795, Eckstein was paid $30 for "two models for dollars."

Vattemare's suggestion: Alexandre Vattemare (November 8, 1796-April 7, 1864), born in Paris, was a showman, impersonator, ventriloquist, numismatist, and sleight-of-hand artist. The Frenchman traveled in the United States in 1838-1841 (appearing in New York City at the Park Theatre beginning October 28, 1839), and again 1847-1850. He devised an international monetary system in 1838, and proposed it to the United States Congress in 1840 and again in 1847,[2] and was a founder of the Boston Public Library.

He visited the Mint and various numismatists, and wrote *Collection de Monnaies et Médailles de l'Amérique du Nord de 1652 à 1858,* published in 1861—a wonderfully detailed account of United States coins and, especially, medals, including those of the colonial period. At the Mint he was presented with Proof sets which he later donated to the Bibliothèque Nationale in Paris. Apparently, Vattemare was viewed by some as being somewhat of a crafty scoundrel. In 1867, Matthew A. Stickney, owner of an 1804 dollar, wrote that he had to be alert when Vattemare visited him in Massachusetts, lest his guest steal the precious coin![3]

In the aforementioned *Collection de Monnaies* Vattemare suggested that the second silver dollar design of 1795 featured "the head of Liberty with the traits of Mme. [Martha] Washington." Probably, this was his own observation, and was not based upon any specific information he obtained from Mint officials.

A masterpiece: Whatever the inspiration for the portrait, and whatever the design process may have been, the obverse and reverse punches for the 1795 Draped Bust dollar far exceeded in quality anything created earlier. If Eckstein did the Draped Bust and Small Eagle device punches, he is certainly deserving of a niche in the Pantheon of numismatic notables, for the Draped Bust motif went on to be used for many years, not only in the silver dollar series, but with other denominations from the half cent to the half dollar. The Small Eagle reverse, too, is a masterpiece of intricate engraving.

The Draped Bust punch, unchanged in detail, was employed through the end of the circulating dollar coinage (which bore the date 1803).

---

[1] R.W. Julian, letter to the author, December 7, 1992.

[2] *House Document 50,* 26th Congress, first session; *Senate Misc. Document 46,* 30th Congress first session.

[3] Stickney's commentary is given under Additional Information, 1804 silver dollar, narrative of Matthew A. Stickney, 1867.

Deliveries: Walter H. Breen suggests that the mintage of 1795 Draped Bust dollars amounted to 42,738 pieces, such being taken by correlating specific deliveries in 1795 to varieties and types known today. The assumption was made that dollars of this design were struck during the last two weeks of October 1795. This figure is based on the further assumption that design and die changes were made to correspond with deliveries, whereas in actuality a die could have been replaced in the press in the midst of a day's work, and the change of type cannot be ascertained from delivery records.

On October 27, 1795, DeSaussure resigned his directorship due to illness and disaffection with his position. Elias Boudinot was his successor and took office the next day.

In his historical overview of early dollars in the present book, R.W. Julian suggests that the most likely time for the inception of Draped Bust coinage would have been October 1, 1795. If this conjecture equates with reality, and if no dollars except the Draped Bust type were minted from that point through the end of the year, and if no 1795-dated Draped Bust coinage was accomplished in later year(s), this would mean that 78,238 Draped Bust dollars were struck in the remaining days of 1795. However, as R.W. Julian points out, this is pure supposition, and it may be the case that Draped Bust coinage commenced earlier or later, that the balance of dollars coined during calendar year 1795 also included some Flowing Hair coins, and that some 1795-dated coins were made in later years as well.

My estimate, based upon ratios derived from surviving coins, is that 100,000 (within 10%) were coined. If, indeed, the production of 1795-dated Draped Bust dollars was somewhere in this range, specimens must have been struck later than calendar year 1795, for coinage would have had to have begun before autumn if it had all been accomplished in the year appearing on the coins.

With all of these "ifs," one person's guess is as good as another. However, an exposition of this kind points out the imprecise nature of mintage figures correlated to designs or dies of the period.

1795 Draped Bust dollars as a type are about two and one-half times scarcer than those of the Flowing Hair design (based upon several factors, including certification service and auction appearance data), so the mintage figures given here, if not provable as precisely correct, are probably at least proportionately accurate. It is unquestioned that the Draped Bust dollars constituted just a small fraction of the total production of 1795-dated silver dollars.

Numismatic Information

General commentary: All dates of Draped Bust obverse, Small Eagle reverse dollars from 1795 through early 1798 primarily exist in lower grades. Some die varieties are rarities in grades of EF or better.

In catalogs of years ago it was popular to call the obverse design the Fillet Head or Fillet Bust, fillet meaning ribbon and pertaining to the band tying Miss Liberty's hair at the back of her head.

Die preparation: The engraver's work on the obverse die was accomplished in this order: 1. The Draped Bust portrait of Miss Liberty was punched into the center of the blank die made of soft steel. 2. The letters of LIBERTY and 15 stars were added around the border by use of individual punches. 3. The date 1795 was punched one digit at a time below the bust.

The reverse die was made in this order: 1. The new Small Eagle on clouds motif was punched into the center of the blank die. The wreath punch, partially finished, and lacking most olive leaves and all berries and stems, and some palm leaves, was punched into the die. 3. Berries and their stems were added to the wreath, leaves were added to the olive branch and palm branch, details were added to the top of the cloud, leaves were added and/or strengthened on the cloud below the eagle's right (on observer's left) wing, and the letters of UNITED STATES OF AMERICA were punched in.

The obverse portrait punch is of high quality and is superbly engraved, with a wealth of minute detail. Whoever made it, Robert Scot or John Eckstein, was extremely skilled. The reverse punch of the Small Eagle on billowy clouds is likewise superbly done. The wreath is sophisticated as well. The left side of the wreath, with olive leaves, bears a stylistic resemblance to the WII wreath of 1795 (three leaves beneath each wing), as the individual leaf elements are similar in appearance, with raised or outlined edges.

(Draped Bust Type)

Striking Periods 5 and 6: These can be considered as a pair. I have selected 1795 BB-51 as the first made, for it has the obverse portrait off center to the left. All other Draped Bust portraits from 1795 through 1803 have the portrait centered. It could have been that this die, putatively the first, was viewed as in need of improvement; thus, later dies had the bust placed in a more central position. More importantly, many prooflike Mint State examples of 1795 BB-51 exist, while only a few Mint State coins, not prooflike, are known for BB-52. It seems logical that specimens of BB-51, representing the first use of the design in American coinage, were made for presentation.

The only argument for placing BB-52 as the first and BB-51 as the second, is that the reverse die for BB-51 was used in later years (through 1798). However, there is no indication that it was kept in the press after coining 1795 BB-51. If it had been, this could simply mean that 1795 BB-52 was struck after certain 1796-dated dollars were made from the same reverse (see 1796 section for more information concerning this die).

Striking Period 5:

BB-51 (B-14). First 1795 Draped Bust coinage. Probably occurred in late 1795; mintage included proof-like presentation coins.

Striking Period 6:

BB-52 (B-15). Second Draped Bust coinage. May have occurred any time from late 1795 to early 1798.

Availability: As a class, 1795 Draped Bust dollars are considerably scarcer than are Flowing Hair dollars. Neither of the two Draped Bust varieties, BB-51 and BB-52, is a rarity. Both are readily available in middle grade ranges. In AU or better grades, BB-51 is seen much more often than BB-52. It is believed that BB-51 was the first struck.

Estimated Total Population (both varieties combined):
  MS-65 or better: 10 to 13 (URS-5)
  MS-64: 12 to 18 (URS-5)
  MS-63: 25 to 40 (URS-6)
  MS-60 to 62: 85 to 160 (URS-8)
  AU-50 to 58: 250 to 450 (URS-10)
  VF-20 to EF-45: 1,500 to 2,500 (URS-12)
  G-4 to F-15: 450 to 700 (URS-10)
  Total for all grades combined: 2,400 to 3,800 (URS-13)
  Estimated Total Condition Census: 65 (multiples)

Characteristics of striking: See individual die variety descriptions.

Proofs: None of official record. However, some examples of 1795 Draped Bust, BB-51, are known with full Proof surfaces and may have been presentation pieces.

1795 Draped Bust, BB-51

(B-14, H-14)

Obverse: Bust of Miss Liberty facing right, the hair tied up in a ribbon at back. *The bust was not properly centered* in the die work, being placed too far to the left. *The highest wave of the hair is under the B of LIBERTY.* Lowest curl is distant from 1 in 1795. Star 1 touches curl.

Obverse die used to strike 1795 BB-51 only.

Reverse: Small Eagle, differently styled than on any of the preceding varieties. Small Letters in legend. Eagle stands on clouds. Wreath is composed of a palm branch (right) and olive branch (left), the latter with seven berries. *Berry under A of STATES;* a quick way to identify this reverse.

This reverse die is one of the most remarkable in all of American numismatics, and was mated with obverse dies bearing four different dates. The features are cut in shallow relief, and the rim is low. Thus, all impressions from the die

appear somewhat flat, a situation particularly evident on coins in VF or lower grades. The shallow relief does not materially affect the striking of higher grade coins, which often have exquisite detail, including a full complement of eagle feathers.

Reverse die used to strike 1795 BB-51; 1796 BB-62, BB-63, and BB-66 (now relapped); 1797 BB-72; and 1798 BB-81.

Die States

Die State I: Perfect dies. The only state known. The denticulation is often weak at the border, especially below the wreath. Some specimens are ever so slightly struck off center, due to alignment of the dies in the press (not to the positioning of individual planchets); these typically are weak at the bottom of the reverse, but have long, prominent dentils at the top (the situation is the opposite on the obverse, with weakness at the top border and strength at the bottom); in this situation, from stars 7 through 10 and at LIBERTY; also, as metal movement was less in such areas of light striking, planchet adjustment marks are often seen at the upper obverse.

Collecting Notes

1795 BB-51 is one of the most abundant varieties of the 1795 year and runs third only to the BB-27 and BB-21 Flowing Hair varieties. Almost certainly, well over 1,000 specimens exist. I estimate the number to be between 1,400 and 2,000.

I believe the BB-51 to be the earlier of the two Draped Bust varieties dated 1795, as evidenced by the following: 1. The Draped Bust motif on the obverse was placed slightly to the left of where it should have been; this was corrected for the next variety, BB-52, and on all later dates of the type. 2. BB-51 exists in high grades in significantly larger numbers than does BB-52, and most of these are prooflike—indicating that some may have been made as presentation specimens of the new Draped Bust obverse, Small Eagle reverse design. Indicative of the availability of the issue, at the 1993 Florida United Numismatists Convention, dealer Ed Milas had three high-level Mint State coins on display.

The striking of 1795 BB-51 is usually weak at the bottom reverse and top obverse (see details under Die States above); such coins are apt to have stars 7 through 10 weak at the centers, and the word LIBERTY slightly weak. Much rarer (about one in 10 coins) are well-centered pieces with *all* stars sharp, including full centers to stars 8 and 9 flanking LIBERTY; a "price is paid" for this sharpness, for such coins usually have the eagle's head and breast feathers less sharply detailed than on the off-center coins! Mint-caused planchet adjustment marks, when seen, are apt to be more prominent on the obverse, especially at the upper left. For some unexplained reason, more often than not these are oriented in a roughly northwest to southeast direction on the obverse.

In the course of surveying close to 200 photographs of BB-51, I did not encounter any coins with die deterioration. The reverse die, as noted, went on to later use. What happened to the 1795-dated obverse is unknown. Perhaps like the famous one-hoss shay, it performed admirably and then broke apart all at once.

The typically encountered 1795 BB-51 is in the VF range, from VF-20 to 35. Really low grade coins, such as Fair, Good, or VG, are few and far between. On the other hand, EF coins appear on the market with frequency. As a group, 1795 BB-51 silver dollars are about 30% to 50% more plentiful than BB-52 dollars, and in grades of AU or better, are much more available than BB-52 coins.

Multiple Mint State BB-51 dollars are known. Most of these have virtually full prooflike or Proof surfaces, and are sometimes cataloged as presentation pieces. Probably,

these were made upon the occasion of the first striking of the new Draped Bust obverse, Small Eagle reverse, design.

Unquestionably, the average specimen 1795 BB-51 circulated to a lesser extent that did most of its contemporaries. The reason for this is not known. Quite possibly, many were saved as souvenirs of Gilbert Stuart's Draped Bust design, a novelty at the time, a motif that would not appear elsewhere on coinage until the following year.

Research Notes

The letter punches used to impress UNITED STATES OF AMERICA into the reverse die were also used on the Small Letters reverse die of 1795 BB-52, and some (but not all) were used to create the Small Letters reverse die of 1796 BB-65. The E in the punch set used in 1795 is distinctive in that the serif at the end of the crossbar is longer at the top end than at the bottom.

An undersized copper trial piece weighing 100 grains exists and is believed to be unique. Its original purpose is unknown; it was not large enough to serve as a set-up piece for die spacing. Perhaps, it was made as a whimsy. The pedigree includes Stack's May 30, 1975 Sale: 932, earlier the Judd, Boyd, Newcomer, Woodin, and Parmelee collections, and came from W. Elliot Woodward, April 28, 1863. See Judd Appendix B where it is incorrectly designated a mint error.

Notable Specimens

Garrett Specimen. SP-66 (PCGS). J. Colvin Randall Collection (W. Elliot Woodward, 1885) lot 12, brilliant Proof. • Garrett Collection (Bowers and Ruddy, 1980) lot 680. "Choice brilliant Proof." • Jimmy Hayes Collection (Stack's, 1985) lot 73. "Choice Brilliant Proof; presentation piece." • Private Texas collection.

Eliasberg Specimen. MS-66 (PCGS). MS-67, Prooflike. Superbly, indeed, incredibly sharply struck, the very *definition* of the design. Brilliant surfaces with just a whisper of golden toning. This piece is certainly one of the very finest in existence of any issue in the entire Draped Bust series. Believed to be the very finest known specimen of 1795 BB-51, an incredibly important coin from the aspect of its preservation and also its numismatic and historical significance. Quite possibly the Eliasberg Collection specimen is a presentation coin to illustrate the first use of the Draped Bust obverse style. If any 1795 Draped Bust dollar is deserving of the *Proof* appellation, this is such a coin! George H. Earle • Henry Chapman, June 25-29, 1912 • John H. Clapp • Clapp estate, 1942 • Louis E. Eliasberg, Sr. Collection (Bowers and Merena Galleries 1997) lot 2173 • Private collector • New York Rarities Sale (Bowers and Merena, July 2002) lot 427.

Brand Specimen. MS-65 (PCGS). Virgil M. Brand estate (probable attribution). • B.G. Johnson. • T. James

Clarke Collection (New Netherlands 48th Sale, 1956) lot 614, "Uncirculated gem." • Stack's, September 1974, lot 40 • Jascha Heifetz Collection (Superior, 1989) lot 3816 • Knoxville Collection • Steve Contursi • Oliver Jung • James Lull Collection (Bowers and Merena, January 2005) lot 702, as MS-66 (NGC) • Denver ANA Sale (Bowers and Merena, August 2006) lot 2304, as MS-66 (NGC) • Private collector, subsequently re-graded by PCGS as MS-65.

Gilchrist Specimen. MS-65 (PCGS). Gilchrist Collection (Heritage, September 1999) lot 6479 • Private Midwest collection.

Superior August Sale Specimen. MS-65 (NGC). August Sale (Superior, 1991) lot 554.

Stack Family Specimen. MS-64 (PCGS). Stack Family Type Set • Joseph O'Connor • Oliver Jung • Cardinal Collection (American Numismatic Rarities, June 2005) lot 15 • Jack Lee Collection • Jack Lee Estate (Heritage, January 2009) lot 3935.

Lee Specimen. MS-64 (PCGS). Jack Lee Collection (Heritage, November 2005) lot 2187.

Ostheimer Specimen. MS-64 (NGC). ANA Convention Sale (Superior, 1975) lot 812. This sale featured silver dollars from the Ostheimer Collection • Morris Silverman Collection (Heritage, April 2002) lot 4006.

Four Landmark Collections Specimen. MS-64. Four Landmark Collections Sale (Bowers and Merena, 1989) lot 353.

Stirling Specimen. MS-64. Frank M. Stirling Collection (Heritage, February 1986) lot 1330. MS-65 obverse, MS-63 reverse."

Carter Specimen. MS-63+ (PCGS). Amon Carter, Jr. Collection (Stack's, 1984) lot 212. "Brilliant Uncirculated and wholly prooflike." • Private Midwest collection.

Alto Specimen. MS-63. Alto Collection (Stack's, 1970) lot 1059. "Brilliant Uncirculated."

Aspen Specimen. MS-63. Nelson Page Aspen, M.D. Collection (Bowers and Merena, 1989) lot 352.

Auction '85 Specimen. MS-63. Auction '85 (Stack's, 1985) lot 1748. "Brilliant Uncirculated." • Auction '87 (Stack's, 1987) lot 777.

Auction '90 Specimen. MS-63. Superior, 1990, lot 1145.

Brown University Specimen. MS-63. • Brown University Collection (Pine Tree, 1976) lot 308. "Choice Uncirculated." • Kagin's, 1977, lot 1754.

Chalkley Specimen. MS-63. Chalkley Collection (Superior, 1990) lot 2829.

Essex Institute Specimen. MS-63. Essex Institute Collection (Stack's, 1975) lot 983. "Brilliant Uncirculated."

Forrest Specimen. MS-63. S.S. Forrest, Jr. Collection (Stack's, 1972) lot 977. "Brilliant Uncirculated."

Holmes Specimen. MS-63. Milton Holmes Collection (Stack's, 1960) lot 2233. "Brilliant Uncirculated."

MANA Convention Sale Specimen. MS-63. Kagin's, 1973, lot 1300. "Acquired as Proof."

Newport Specimen. MS-63. Bowers and Ruddy, 1975, lot 375. "Brilliant Uncirculated." • Bowers and Merena, 1989, lot 1943. • Gore and Long Collections (Bowers and Merena, 1990) lot 345.

Robison Specimen. MS-63. Ellis H. Robison Collection (Stack's, 1982) lot 1855. "Brilliant Uncirculated."

Stack's Specimen. MS-63. May Sale (Stack's, 1991) lot 458. "Choice Brilliant Uncirculated."

Total Estimated Population

MS-65 or better: 5 to 8 (URS-4)

MS-64: 8 to 12 (URS-5)

MS-63: 20 to 35 (URS-6)

MS-60 to 62: 50 to 100 (URS-7)

AU-50 to 58: 200 to 350 (URS-9)

VF-20 to EF-45: 800 to 1,400 (URS-11)

G-4 to F-15: 250 to 400 (URS-10)

Total for all grades combined: 1,400 to 2,200 (URS-12)

Estimated Total Condition Census: 66-66-65-65-65-64 (multiples)

1795 Draped Bust, BB-52

(B-15, H-15)

Obverse: Draped Bust similar to last, but the *bust is well-centered* in the die. *The highest wave of the hair is under the E of Liberty.* The obverse often shows a crack at the center, which increased in size as the die was used. Lowest curl is close to 1 in 1795. Star 1 does not touch curl.

Obverse die used to strike 1795 BB-52 only.

Reverse: Similar to BB-51, but with only six berries in the olive branch. *Leaf under A of STATES;* a quick way to identify this reverse. Small letters. The finishing details of the higher areas of the clouds are quite different from those seen on BB-51, and on the present die are more boldly delineated.

Reverse die used to strike BB-52 only.

Die States

Die State I: Perfect dies. May not exist.

Die State II: Perfect obverse die. Reverse with small piece out of the die on the palm branch directly below the upright of F in OF; this flaw, appearing as a lump on the coin, has two tiny projections pointed toward the F; on worn coins, these projections are readily seen, although the lump on the leaf has been worn away. I have seen just one coin of this die state, a VF-20. On the reverse there are some scattered, raised die flaws between F in OF and the first A in AMERICA; these intensify as die use progresses.

Die State III: Small die crack or break in the hair on the obverse, to the right of and slightly higher than where the bow joins the head; this appears as a raised, triangular (with the hypotenuse vertically oriented, slightly rounded outward, and facing left) lump visible only on coins grading VF or finer. Reverse as preceding. I have seen just one coin of this die state, an EF-40.

Die State IV: Crack in hair expands considerably and now appears as a jagged, vertically-oriented lump

consisting of the triangular lump of Die State III but now with an extension upward, doubling its vertical dimension (crack visible only on coins grading VF or finer). Reverse rim develops a hairline crack beginning above D in UNITED, barely touching left bottom of first S in STATES, continuing through the branch leaves, and ending under E of STATES. Common.

Die State V: Obverse as preceding. On the reverse, a new hairline crack forms at the top right of R and continues through the tops of the letters in ICA, into the field at right. (Cf. Gilhousen: 1220, EF, there called "probably one of the last ones made, late October 1795"). Common.

Die State VI: The reverse cracks intensify, the obverse shows die rust in the fields. Not seen.

Die State VII: The obverse die crack extends up to over midway between the ribbon and the top of the head. MARCA 5/86: 1. Not seen. Very rare.

Note: The BB-52 die pairing seems to have started to fail early in its life (at least by Die State III, allowing for the possibility that the reverse lump of Die State II may have been in the original die). Large numbers of pieces seen today are from flawed dies.

Collecting Notes

The population of 1795 BB-52 is, perhaps, about 2/3 that of BB-51, but this means that enough exist that just about any motivated collector can easily acquire one. As is the case with BB-51, most specimens of BB-52 are in the range from about VF-20 to VF-35. Lower grade coins are seldom seen, and pieces in EF-40 or better grade are rare as well.

Most coins are reasonably well centered, with good details in all areas. Adjustment marks are seen much less often on specimens of BB-52, probably because the striking was better (recall that BB-51 coins with adjustment marks were usually also lightly struck in areas), and such marks were obliterated by the metal flow.

It is interesting to note that the obverse die for BB-51, thought to have been struck in larger quantities than BB-52, is known only in a perfect state, while the BB-52 deteriorated almost from the time it was first used. Similarly, the reverse used to coin the more plentiful BB-51 was not damaged in the process, and went on to be mated in later years with five other obverses; in contrast, the reverse die of BB-52 developed cracks. The difference in durability undoubtedly was caused by better hardening or tempering of the steel in the BB-51 dies.

BB-52 is considerably rarer than BB-51 in AU and Mint State categories.

Notable Specimens

Tettenhorst Specimen MS-66 (PCGS). Fully prooflike obverse and reverse, sharply struck with pale gold and brown toning. Early die state with virtually no trace of obverse die break. This specimen appears in the NGC Population Report as SP-65, and more recently in the PCGS Population Report as MS-66.

Hood Specimen. MS-65 (PCGS). Walton Hood Collection • FUN Signature Sale (Heritage, January 2007) lot 1027 • Flambeau Type Collection • Joseph O'Connor • Bruce Morelan Type Collection • Legend Numismatics • Private collector.

Cardinal Specimen. MS-65 (PCGS). Dr. Craig Morgan Collection (Bowers and Merena, November 1998) lot 259 • Phillip Flannagan Collection (Bowers and Merena, November 2001) lot 4218 • Cardinal Collection (American Numismatic Rarities, June 2005) lot 16 • Joseph C. Thomas Collection (Heritage, April 2009) lot 2536 • Joseph O'Connor • Private collector.

Boys Town Specimen. MS-65 (PCGS). Boys Town Sale (Superior, May 1990) lot 3876.

Lustig Specimen. MS-65 (NGC). 55th Anniversary Sale (Stack's, October 1990) lot 1659 • Andrew Lustig • "Amazing Collection of United States Silver Dollars" (Superior, May 1991) lot 700.

Auction '89 Specimen. MS-64 (NGC). Auction '89 (Superior, 1989) lot 664. • Superior, 1990, lot 2828. *These two appearances appear to be the same coin.*

The Orlando Specimen. MS-64 (PCGS). Orlando Sale (Superior, 1992) lot 173.

Bareford Specimen. MS-64 (NGC). Stack's, January 1958, lot 316 • Harold Bareford Collection (Stack's, 1981) lot 406. "Brilliant Uncirculated." • 68th Anniversary Sale (Stack's, October 2003) lot 2713 • Bay State Collection (Heritage, August 2009) lot 1140 • FUN Signature Sale (Heritage, January 2010) lot 2580 • CSNS Signature Sale (Heritage, April 2010) lot 2147.

Anderson-Dupont Specimen. MS-63. Anderson-Dupont Collection (Stack's, 1954) lot 2493. "Choice Uncirculated, prooflike surface."

Fairfield Specimen. MS-63. Fairfield Collection (Bowers and Ruddy, 1977) lot 103., "Choice Brilliant Uncirculated."

Carter Specimen. MS-62 (PCGS). Amon Carter, Jr. Collection (Stack's, 1984) lot 213. "Brilliant Uncirculated, slightly prooflike." • Auction '85 (Superior, 1985) lot 822. MS-63. • The December Sale (Stack's, 1986) lot 74. • H. Roland Willasch Collection (Superior, 1990) lot 456 • Private Midwest collector.

Miller Specimen. MS-60+ (NGC). U.S. Coins • Warren Miller Collection.

DeCoppet Specimen. MS-60. André DeCoppet Collection (James Kelly, 1955) "Uncirculated."

Helfenstein Specimen. MS-60. Helfenstein Collection (Lester Merkin, 1968) lot 277. "Really Mint State though not fully struck up in centers."

Marks Specimen. MS-60. Robert Marks Collection (Bowers and Ruddy 1972) lot 73. "Brilliant Uncirculated."

More Specimen. MS-60. Philip More Collection (Bowers and Ruddy, 1978) lot 451. "Brilliant Uncirculated."

Total Estimated Population

MS-65 or better: 5 (URS-4)

MS-64: 4 to 6 (URS-3)

MS-63: 5 to 7 (URS-4)

MS-60 to 62: 35 to 60 (URS-7)

AU-50 to 58: 50 to 100 (URS-7)

VF-20 to EF-45: 700 to 1,100 (URS-11)

G-4 to F-15: 200 to 300 (URS-9)

Total for all grades combined: 1,000 to 1,600 (URS-12)

Estimated Total Condition Census: 66-65-65-65-65-64 (multiples)

ADDITIONAL INFORMATION

Dickeson on 1795 Dollars (1859)

The following appeared in Dr. Montroville W. Dickeson's 1859 book, *An American Numismatical Manual:*

Those [silver dollars] coined in this year, up to September, were of the same design of the preceding year; but in the latter portion of the year, the type was changed. Of the first of these [Flowing Hair type], there are six varieties, and the second [Draped Bust type], four. In the latter, the effigy is presented with a full bust adorned with drapery; the hair is secured by a band, the bow of which is perceptible on the back of the head, and flows gracefully in ringlets below the lower part of the bust. The edge also differs slightly from the former type in the punctuation. On the reverse the eagle is smaller, apparently floating upon clouds, the wings not extending, as in the first type, beyond the circle of the wreath. Not rare, but good specimens are scarce.

Snowden's Commentary (1860)

The Cabinet Collection of the Mint of the United States, by James Ross Snowden, 1860, p. 107, told of the coinage of 1795 dollars:

In the following year (1795) a change took place in the type of the dollar. Henry Wm. DeSausure [*sic*] was appointed to the Directorship of the Mint on the eleventh of July; and it is probable that the alteration was made soon after. Mr. DeSausure resigned his office on the twenty-eighth of October following, after which date there was no further coinage of dollars during the year; and, as there is no very great difference in the degrees of rarity of the two varieties of this year, we are forced to believe that there was a large emission of the new type, which would place the date of its first coinage early in August.

The obverse has a full bust of Liberty, adorned with drapery; from beneath the hair appears a ribbon, which is tied in a bow behind. The reverse has an eagle with expanded wings, standing upon clouds, between branches of laurel and lily, crossed. Otherwise it is the same as before.

The Year 1795 in History

Congress passed the Naturalization Act on January 29, 1795, providing that naturalized citizens must first reside in the United States for five years and renounce foreign allegiances. One of the first governmental frauds surfaced this year, and involved the sale by the Georgia legislature of 35 million acres of land on the Yazoo River, in areas comprising much of Mississippi and Alabama, for $500,000 to four companies in which, it was revealed, nearly all (except just one) members of the legislature had financial interests. In 1796 a new legislature endeavored to overturn the sale, but this was not accomplished. Finally, in 1810, the United States Supreme Court decision of Fletcher vs. Peck ruled that the sale was effective. Congress appropriated $8 million to settle claims, but Georgia refused to honor the payment.

Following Indian trails, pioneer explorer Daniel Boone created the Wilderness Road, making it possible for future settlers to move west. The North West Company established Milwaukee as a trading post on Lake Michigan. On Oak Island in Mahone Bay, Nova Scotia, three boys digging beneath a tree found an old shaft leading down to ancient oak flooring, thus alerting the world to the Oak Island treasure; during the next two centuries, millions of dollars would be spent by various individuals and companies seeking treasure believed to have been hidden by pirates.

In Paris, the second part of Thomas Paine's *The Age of Reason* was published. In America, Philip Freneau's *Poems Written Between the Years 1768 and 1794* saw print. Ricketts' Circus, a group of equestrian performers from England, appeared in eastern United States cities. Among those in the audience was President George Washington. A cent-size token or store card was created, probably at the Mint, with inscriptions pertaining to Ricketts. In the Kentucky territory the James B. Beam Distilling Company was founded, and would remain in business through the twenty-first century.

David Rittenhouse of Pennsylvania served as director of the Mint from April 1792 to June 1795. Henry William DeSaussure served as director of the Mint from July 1795 to October 27, 1795. Elias Boudinot served from October 28, 1795 to July 1805. The first United States gold coins were struck—$5 and $10 pieces.

A short walk from the Mint, William Cobbett, writing under the *nom de plume* "Peter Porcupine," fanned the partisan political fires with his *A Little Plain English Addressed to the People of the United States, on the Treaty Negotiated with His Britannic Majesty.*

CHAPTER 9

1796 SILVER DOLLARS

Mintage (all types)
Calendar year, Mint report: 72,920
Coins bearing date, author's estimate: 75,000

1796 SILVER DOLLARS
BB to Bolender to Haseltine Equivalents

BB Number	Bolender #	Haseltine #	Rarity	Average Grade
BB-61	B-4	H-4	URS-12	VF-28
BB-62	B-3	H-3	URS-2	N/A
BB-63	B-2	H-2	URS-9	VF-30
BB-64	B-6	---	URS-3	N/A
BB-65	B-5	H-5	URS-11	VF-31
BB-66	B-1	H-1	URS-9	VF-25

Coinage Context

Problems of 1796: The estimated mintage of 75,000 1796-dated dollars (of various die varieties combined, each of the Draped Bust type) is less than that of the estimated mintage of 110,000 Draped Bust dollars coined with the date 1795. The estimated mintage of 75,000 is not far different from the official calendar year figure of 79,920.

My estimate of 75,000 1796-dated dollars does not suggest when these dollars were struck. It may have been the case, indeed likely, that many if not most 1796-dated pieces were struck later, in 1798. Much of the calendar year mintage of 79,920 dollars reported struck in 1796 were probably dated 1795. I believe that mintage during the first part of calendar year 1798 consisted in large part of dollars dated 1795, 1796, and 1797.

The Mint experienced various difficulties in 1796, including a yellow fever epidemic. Coinage was anything but easy.

On June 1, 1796, Tennessee was admitted to the Union as the 16th state. While other denominations reflected this, 16 stars were not used on silver dollars until 1797, which suggests that obverse dies for 1796-dated dollars were made prior to June.

Number of dies used: The number of dies employed to create 1796-dated dollars is as follows:

1796 obverses, 4

1796 reverses, 4 (includes one left over from 1795)

Die use averages: By dividing the number of obverse dies and the number of reverse dies each with the estimated mintage figure of 75,000 coins dated 1796, estimates of the average number of impressions per die can be obtained. In practice, some dies lasted a long time and others broke quickly; the figures here are averages, as noted.

4 1796 obverses divided into an estimated mintage of 1796-dated dollars of 75,000 = 18,750 coins per obverse die.

4 1796 reverses divided into an estimated mintage of 1796-dated dollars of 75,000 = 18,750 coins per reverse die (the inclusion of the Small Letters die used earlier in 1795 and used later for coinage dated 1797 and 1798 distorts this figure).

Numismatic Information

Collecting 1796 dollars: The dollars of 1796 are a little world unto themselves. There are but six varieties, four of which are readily available, and two that are exceedingly rare. *Right now* in the marketplace, only a few people in the numismatic world know that 1796 BB-62 (so rare that its very existence is controversial to some) and the 1796 BB-64 (of which just two are known) are among the most elusive die varieties of this era.

Known varieties: Dollars of 1796 are of two main obverse styles, Large Date (BB-65 only) and Small Date (BB-61 to BB-64 and BB-66), and two reverse styles, Large Letters (BB-61 and BB-64) and Small Letters (BB-62, BB-63, BB-65, and BB-66). In all instances, the 6 in the date was made by inverting the 9 punch.

Traditionally, the varieties of 1796 have been collected as follows:

1796 Small Date, Large Letters (BB-61 and BB-64).

1796 Small Date, Small Letters (BB-62, BB-63, and BB-66)

1796 Large Date, Small Letters (BB-65)

Of course, the purist and die variety collector will aspire to obtain all six die varieties, not just the three "major varieties" delineated above.

Dollars of this year are quite easy to attribute, and with the Easy-Finding Guide, above, you should have no trouble instantly identifying a 1796 die variety, even with one eye closed and one hand behind your back.

Grade possibilities. Although many hundreds, if not a thousand or more Mint State 1796 cents exist (thanks to the Goodhue-Nichols Hoard), and many dozens of prooflike Uncirculated 1796 quarters are known, Mint State dollars are few and far between. Apparently, few if any were saved as souvenirs or represented in hoards.

For a 1796 silver dollar, Very Fine is about par for a "nice" coin, although occasionally Extremely Fine and AU pieces are encountered. Mint State coins, graded by today's stringent interpretations, are sufficiently rare as to be virtually of legendary status.

Obverse dies, a chronology: There were four obverse dies made with the 1796 date. Three of these are of the so-called Small Date style, and one (BB-65) is of the Large Date. As the Large Date more closely resembles the numerals used on 1797 dollars, I assign this as the last die made.

The four obverse dies can be attributed chronologically by the state of the letter R punch used as part of the LIBERTY inscription. Characteristics follow:

BB-61, BB-62 (Small Date) die: Perfect R punch.

BB-66 (Small Date) die: Perfect R punch.

BB-63, BB-64 (Small Date) die: Lower right tip of R partially broken.

BB-65 (Large Date) die: Lower right tip of R broken.

This order of *manufacture* does not necessarily equate with the order of *use* of the obverse dies. The R on the obverse of the die used to coin 1796 BB-63 and BB-64 is about in the same condition as the obverse of the die used to coin *1795* BB-52. This probably indicates the obverse dies to coin 1796 BB-61, BB-62 and BB-66 were made prior to *1795* BB-52, and were complete except for the date. Obverse dies for 1795 BB-52 and 1796 BB-63, BB-64, complete except for the date, were made next. Finally, the obverse die for 1796 BB-65 was made; this last die could have been made in 1795, but not dated, or could have been made in 1796.

Reverse dies, a chronology: There were two major reverse letter styles used on four dies to coin 1796 dollars. These consisted of the following:

BB-62, BB-63, BB-66 (Small Letters) die left over from 1795.

BB-65 (Small Letters) die. Style of 1795, and probably made in 1795 (but not used until 1796) or in early 1796; in any event, made before the Large Letters dies.

BB-61 (Large Letters) die. New style (style of 1796). Made about the same time as the reverse die for BB-64.

BB-64 (Large letters) die. Made about the same time as the reverse die for BB-61.

The preceding probably gives the order of *manufacture* of the reverse dies, but not necessarily the order of *use*. As can be seen, 1796 BB-65 is struck from the latest-made 1796 obverse die in combination with one of the earliest reverses. The explanation is that when they were made, the dies were put "on the shelf" and not used in any particular sequence. There was no first-in, first-out policy in effect.

Coin production, *toward* a chronology: Probably, it will never be known exactly when on the calendar the various 1796-dated dollars were made. I believe that some were made in 1796, and that additional pieces were coined in calendar year 1798. Die state evidence helps us to draw some conclusions as follows:

1796 BB-61: The obverse die state on a shared die is earlier than on BB-62.

1796 BB-62: The obverse die state on a shared die is later than on BB-61. Reverse die is left over from 1795 (in early state, not relapped).

1796 BB-63: The obverse die state on a shared die is earlier than on BB-64. Reverse die is left over from 1795 (in early state, not relapped).

1796 BB-64: The obverse die state on a shared die is later than on BB-63.

1796 BB-65: Late obverse die combined with early reverse die. Not linked with any other obverse or reverse dies.

1796 BB-66: Early obverse die mated with left-over 1795 reverse die (with the reverse die now relapped, and in a later state than when used on any other 1796 dollar).

The assumption is made that at least two obverse matings with the left-over die earlier used to coin 1795 BB-51, not yet relapped, were made at the same time (rather than in a later year, such as 1798, when the same 1795 BB-51 reverse was also used, but in a relapped state). The two varieties in question are BB-62 and BB-63.

A problem arises with another mating with the 1795 BB-51 reverse, and that involves 1796 BB-66. This utilizes the left-over die earlier used to coin 1795 BB-51, but with BB-66 it is relapped. Apparently, after the coinage of 1796 BB-62 and BB-63 was completed, the reverse die was taken out of the press and relapped. At some later date it was combined with a hitherto unused obverse die.

At this point, the following chronology can be suggested. Although varieties are combined into the First Striking Period and the Second Striking Period, which of these striking periods actually occurred first is not known.

Striking Period 1:

Struck first: 1796 BB-61: The obverse die state on a shared die is earlier than on BB-62.

Struck second: 1796 BB-62: The obverse die state on a shared die is later than on BB-61. Reverse die is left over from 1795.

Striking Period 2:

Struck third: 1796 BB-63: The obverse die state on a shared die is earlier than on BB-64. Reverse die is left over from 1795.

Struck fourth: 1796 BB-64: The obverse die state on a shared die is later than on BB-63.

Striking Period 3:

Struck fifth: 1796 BB-65: Late obverse die combined with early reverse die. Not linked with any other obverse or reverse dies.

Striking Period 4:

Struck sixth: 1796 BB-66: Early obverse die mated with left-over 1795 reverse die (now in a very late, relapped state). I believe this striking period occurred in 1798.

In calendar year 1796, coinage deliveries were as follows, for a total of 72,920 pieces:

January 30: 4,550 (+2; parenthetical numbers are additional pieces for the Assay Commission) • February 13: 390 (+1) • March 30: 2,777 (0) • April 9: 2,222 (+1) • May 9: 6,354 (+3) • May 27: 378 (+1) • June 14: 10,509 (+1) • June 28: 941 (+1) • July 21: 8,750 (+3) • July 29: 1,720 (+3) • August 27: 11,485 (+3) • September 1: 1,580 (+3) • September 14: 8,391 (+3) • October 17: 8,103 (+3) • December 22: 4,770 (+3)

From the foregoing it is seen that deliveries of silver dollars were spread throughout the year. There is no known way of matching the above dates with die usage. All that can be said with certainty is that the dollars delivered were dated either 1795 (from leftover dies) or 1796.

Whether dies remained fixed in the press (the largest press at the Mint, acquired in spring 1795, was used to strike dollars) probably depended upon whether the press was needed to strike $10 gold eagles, which were struck on several occasions during the year (as gold deposits warranted).

$10 *eagle gold coins* delivered in calendar year 1796: • January 9: 1,181 • January 30: 134 • March 19: 1,169 • March 31: 116 • June 2: 2,232 • June 21: 960

Interfiling the delivery dates for silver dollars with those of $10 eagles (*italic type*) yields the following:

January 9: 1,181 ($10 gold eagles) • *January 30: 134 ($10 gold eagles)* • January 30: 4,550 (+2) • February 13: 390 (+1) • *March 19: 1,169 ($10 gold eagles)* • March 30: 2,777 (0) • *March 31: 116 ($10 gold eagles)* • April 9: 2,222 (+1) • May 9: 6,354 (+3) • May 27: 378 (+1) • *June 2: 2,232 ($10 gold eagles)* • June 14: 10,509 (+1) • *June 21: 960 ($10 gold eagles)* • June 28: 941 (+1) • July 21: 8,750 (+3) • July 29: 1,720 (+3) • August 27: 11,485 (+3) • September 1: 1,580 (+3) • September 14: 8,391 (+3) • October 17: 8,103 (+3) • December 22: 4,770 (+3)

The preceding shows that if the dollar press was used to coin $10 gold coins, there were several periods in which dollar dies could have remained fixed in the press, between dollar delivery dates. For example, after June 21, dollar dies could have remained in the press continuously.

How the "striking periods" mentioned earlier might have fit into the preceding listing of delivery dates is unknown. There is also the strong possibility that some 1796-dated dollars were struck later. If this is the case, perhaps some of the "striking periods" took place in, say, 1798. Further, as noted under the 1795 die studies, there is a distinct possibility that the dollar press, which was intended for silver dollars and large medals, was not used for $10 gold coins at all (for these were about the same diameter as the half dollar and were in softer alloy; half dollars were struck on a smaller press).

Summary of Characteristics
1796 (all varieties combined)

Circulation Strikes

Enabling legislation: Act of April 2, 1792

Designer of obverse: Robert Scot (after Stuart), model by John Eckstein

Designer of reverse: Robert Scot, model by John Eckstein

Statutory weight: 416 grains; .8924 silver, balance copper

Melting value (silver bullion value) in year minted: Considered by Mint officials to be on a par with the Spanish dollar, and worth about $1.00 intrinsically (see discussion under Summary of Characteristics, 1794).

Dies prepared: At least 4 obverse; at least 4 reverse dies, including one left over from 1795.

Circulation strike mintage, calendar year: 72,920 (for all varieties of 1796 combined, not including pieces reserved for the Assay Commission; these are given in parentheses); Delivery figures by day: January 30: 4,550 (+2) • February 13: 390 (+1) • March 30: 2,777 (0) • April 9: 2,222 (+1) • May 9: 6,354 (+3) • May 27: 378 (+1) • June 14: 10,509 (+1) • June 28: 941 (+1) • July 21: 8,750 (+3) • July 29: 1,720 (+3) • August 27: 11,485 (+3) • September 1: 1,580 (+3) • September 14: 8,391 (+3) • October 17: 8,103 (+3) • December 22: 4,770 (+3).

Estimated circulation strike mintage of 1796-dated dollars (author's estimate): 75,000 (rounded).

Estimated quantity melted: Normal quantities by export or in the normal course of Mint redemption.

Estimated total population (all varieties):
  MS-65 or better: 0 (URS-0)
  MS-64: 1 (URS-1)
  MS-63: 1 or 2 (URS-1)
  MS-60 to 62: 10 to 18 (URS-5)
  AU-50 to 58: 30 to 60 (URS-6)
  VF-20 to EF-45: 1,500 to 2,600 (URS-12)
  G-4 to F-15: 750 to 1,400 (URS-11)

Total for all grades combined: 2,300 to 4,100 (URS-13)
Estimated Total Condition Census: 64-63-62-62-61-60 (multiples)

Characteristics of striking: Varies from variety to variety. Those with the Small Letters reverse, lapped die, are always weaker on the obverse than the reverse.

Proofs: None, although a few have prooflike surfaces.

Commentary: When seen today, most 1796 dollars show ample evidence of circulation.

1796 DRAPED BUST/SMALL EAGLE

1796 Small Date, Large Letters, BB-61

(B-4, H-4)

Obverse: Small, wide date with 96 close and 6 tipped to the left. Raised "dot" die flaw over 1 in date and closest to bust, tiny extra projection or flaw extending from the space at the bottom of star 11 (these flaws are visible on all die states given below). This and the obverse used to strike BB-66 were the first two obverse dies cut in 1796, and have the lower right tip of the R in LIBERTY intact.

Also see description under 1796 BB-62 (which is equivalent to Die State III described for BB-61).

Obverse die used to strike 1796 BB-61 (early state) and BB-62 (late state).

Reverse: *Large letters* in legend. Letters AMER crowded and touch at bases. Eight plain berries in wreath. *Berry under first T in STATES.* Two leaves beneath eagle's right (to observer's left) wing, these having been added by hand in front of the cloud. From the same hub used to create 1795 BB-51 and 52, but on 1796 BB-61 not as strongly impressed, with the result that the eagle's breast feathers are not bold.

Bolender mentions a die defect in the wreath extending to the right side of the M in AMERICA and the right wing tip.

Reverse die used to strike 1796 BB-61 only.

Die States

Die State I: Early state of the 1796 BB-61 die, described above. Top curl perfect; stars normal. Curl at top of forehead in the form of three or four arcs together. Lower curl nearest date boldly defined. The usually seen obverse die state. Walter Breen, in the *John Reich Journal*, January 1987, stated that most specimens of 1796 BB-61 are of this die state, and that "over 10%" are of Die State II.

Die State II. Intermediate between I and III. Very lightly relapped *at top* of die. Top curl on head weaker and detached at right. Curl at top of forehead now appears as two arcs, connected only at their tops. Lower curl nearest date boldly defined.

Die State III: Bolender-4a, showing the same die relapping effects as 1796 BB-62. Entire die relapped since Die State II. Curl on top of head defective, now tiny and detached. Curl at top of forehead now just a faint wisp. Some stars on the right smaller, the final two or three appearing spidery. Lower curl nearest date now very weak on side nearest date. In 1950, Bolender noted this: "Extremely rare. The only specimen I have found. From the John T. Reeder Collection. Mr. Reeder purchased it from Henry Chapman's sale of the Gable Collection." Since that time, numerous specimens have come to light. Walter Breen, in the *John Reich Journal,* January 1987, stated that "over 10%" of the specimens he had seen of [BB-61] are of Die State II, and that he had started observing this die state in 1955, and after seeing over 30 coins, he stopped counting. In my experience, at least 25% of 1796 BB-61 dollars are Die State II or, mostly, III.

Collecting Notes

The 1796 BB-61 dollar is the most common variety of the year. An estimated 1,250 to 2,000 specimens exist. Most are in middle circulated grades, with VF being the median. EF coins turn up with regularity in dealers' stocks and auctions and make a nice "type" coin. In AU or better grade 1796 BB-61 is very rare. A few prooflike specimens exist, possibly made as presentation coins (cf. Walter H. Breen's Proof coins *Encyclopedia*, p. 35, where he states that he saw two pieces earlier, and "would like to see the pieces again to verify that they have the quality of surface and striking characteristic of actual presentation pieces of the period"). I am not aware of any special occasion in 1796 which would have called for prooflike silver dollars. However, prooflike quarter dollars of this date are often seen.

Due to unsatisfactory impressing of the eagle punch in the working die, specimens of 1796 BB-61 are not as well defined on the reverse as are most others of this general design type. Even AU and Mint State coins are apt to have the feathers appear "fuzzy" or indistinct. In worn grades the lack of detail on the eagle's breast feathers is even more apparent.

Notable Specimens

Kagin Reference Specimen. MS-63. The finest known may be a prooflike piece once owned by A.M. and Paul Kagin (as part of a "1796 Proof set") and later advertised by Heritage in *Coin World* in August 1986. During the 1950s and early 1960s, the Kagins displayed the 1796 set as part of the Kagin Reference Collection.

CSNS Convention Sale Specimen. MS-63. CSNS Convention Sale (Kagin's, 1979) lot 357. "Sharply struck Unc.-60++." • Kagin's, 1980, lot 885. "Choice BU-63."

Reiver Specimen. MS-61 (PCGS). Jamie McConnell, August 1972 • Jules Reiver Collection (Heritage, January 2006) lot 23487, as MS-61 (NGC) • Joseph C. Thomas Collection (Heritage, April 2009) lot 2537, as MS-61 (NGC) • Heritage inventory • Philadelphia Signature Sale (Heritage, August 2012) lot 5175, as MS-61 (PCGS).

Heathgate Specimen. MS-60 (PCGS). Margene Heathgate Sale (Superior, June 1997) lot 861 • Cardinal Collection • Tangible Asset Galleries • Private collector • Pre-Long Beach Sale (Ira and Larry Goldberg, May 2006) lot 1566.

Stack Specimen. AU-58. Norman Stack Type Set • John Whitney Walter Collection (Stack's, May 1999) lot 1782.

Aspen Specimen. AU-58. Nelson Page Aspen, M.D. Collection (Bowers and Merena, 1989) lot 358. "MS-60 to 63 • John Whitney Walter Collection (Stack's, May 1999) lot 1783.

Newcomer Specimen. AU-58 (PCGS). Waldo C. Newcomer Collection • Col. E.H.R. Green Collection. • James G. Macallister • T. James Clarke Collection (New Netherlands 48th Sale, 1956) lot 617. "Choice Uncirculated." • unknown intermediaries • Robert Lehmann • Cardinal Collection (American Numismatic Rarities, June 2005) lot 17 • Dale Friend Collection.

Eliasberg Specimen. AU-55 (NGC). Benjamin H. Collins, March 1896 (or Frossard's sale of Collins' coins) • Louis E. Eliasberg Collection (Bowers and Merena Galleries, April 1997) lot 2174 • Northeast Numismatics • Private collector.

Total Estimated Population

MS-65 or better: 0 (URS-0)
MS-64: 0 (URS-0)
MS-63: 1 or 2 (URS-1)
MS-60 to 62: 6 to 10 (URS-4)
AU-50 to 58: 15 to 30 (URS-5)
VF-20 to EF-45: 800 to 1,300 (URS-11)
G-4 to F-15: 400 to 700
Total for all grades combined: 1,250 to 2,000 (URS-12)
Estimated Total Condition Census: 63-63-61-60 (multiples)

1796 Small Date, Small Letters, BB-62

(B-3, H-3)

Obverse: Die State III of 1796 BB-61, to which refer. *Small wide date*, the 9 and 6 closer together than other figures, the top of 6 tipped more to left. The 9 is a trifle high with its top tipped too much to the right. Lowest *star on left does not quite touch hair*. Die flaw extends from space at bottom of 11th star. Raised die dot defect above 1 of date and closer to bust. The stars are small and the last two or three are spidery. Curl on top of the head defective.

This is a later state, equal to Die State III of 1796 BB-61 as noted, with relapping removing part of Miss Liberty's top curl, and some of the part of the stars in lower relief, making them appear smaller.

Obverse die used to strike 1796 BB-61 (early state) and BB-62 (late state).

Reverse: Described under 1795 BB-51, herewith repeated: Small Eagle. Small Letters in legend. Eagle stands on clouds. Wreath is composed of a palm branch (right) and olive branch (left), the latter with seven berries. *Berry under A of STATES;* a quick way to identify this reverse.

Bolender reported that some letters were bifurcated on examples he had seen of 1796 B-3 [BB-62], and thought this meant that the die had been "touched up" (however, bifurcation is an idiosyncrasy of striking, and has nothing to do with the die variety or state).

Reverse die used to strike 1795 BB-51; 1796 BB-62, BB-63, and BB-66 (now relapped); 1797 BB-72; and 1798 BB-81.

Die States

Die State I: Perfect dies. May not exist. Reverse die not relapped.

Die State I: Obverse die relapped; curl at top of head now defective, some stars appear smaller. Reverse die not relapped. This is the die state usually seen. Obverse die state

equivalent to Die State III of 1796 BB-61. Reverse die state equivalent to 1796 BB-63. 1796 BB-62 was struck before 1796 BB-66 (which I believe to have been struck in 1798). 1796 BB-61 was struck before 1796 BB-62.

Collecting Notes

Bolender wrote this in 1950: "While many 1796 dollars have been listed as [B-3; BB-62], this has been erroneously done. I have purchased a dozen or more [B-3; BB-62], every one of them wrongly attributed. Only three specimens are known to me."

The rarity of 1796 BB-62 approaches legendary proportions. In fact, it has kept out of sight so well that many specialists had never seen an example. The fifth revised edition (1988) of Bolender's *The United States Early Silver Dollars* noted the following: "Most experts now question whether this variety actually exists."

In a conversation, Jules Reiver related that over the years a dozen or more 1796 "Bolender-3" dollars have been offered to him, but without exception they were all misattributed.[1] "I don't believe that B-3 [BB-62] exists," he concluded. As late as 1999, Reiver wrote "I am going to stick my neck out. I am saying that it does not exist. Unless someone comes forth with the truth, we may never know. In any event, I've stuck out my head, so chop it off if you find a real one."[2]

Those opinions notwithstanding, a specimen had already been listed and clearly illustrated as lot 2065 of the Philip G. Straus Collection (Stack's, 1959). The cataloger, probably Norman Stack, described it as follows:

1796 B-3 [BB-62]. Small Date, Small Letters. Has diagnostic flaw in hair curl. On reverse, berry centered directly below A of STATES. An excessively rare variety, and only

---

[1] Telephone conversation with the author, December 2, 1992.
[2] *The United States Early Silver Dollars*, Reiver, 1999, page 29.

three known according to Bolender. Very Fine to Extremely Fine. After checking some of the outstanding collections of silver dollars, we learned that none have this variety represented. One specialist commented that "This is the only B-3 [BB-62] I have ever seen. Nobody I know has one." Considering the rarity of the coin, we would not be surprised to see it bring a "run-a-way price." [The coin brought $500.]

The identical specimen appeared 16 years later as lot 24 of the W. Earl Spies Collection (Stack's, 1974). The cataloger noted the following:

1796 B-3 [BB-62]. Small Date, Small Letters. The letters not bifurcated and the curl at the top of the head imperfect. One of only very few known. Probably a high Rarity-6 or perhaps 7. Very Fine to Extremely Fine. From our Straus Sale in 1959. [Realized $950.]

The preceding descriptions, particularly that in the Straus Collection sale, indicated that the cataloger for Stack's was quite certain at one time that a BB-62 existed, and that it was examined by a specialist. Yet, later experts doubted its existence. It was not until 2001, when a specimen was identified within the Vermeule Collection that the variety was finally confirmed to current numismatists. Coincidentally, just two years later, the Straus-Spies specimen re-appeared and was also verified. Since that time, no other specimens have come to light.

In recent decades, such notable silver dollar variety collection sales as Ostheimer (1968), Gilhousen (1973), 1975 ANA, and Willasch (1990) have lacked an example of this variety. It is worth noting that Bolender's own collection, auctioned in 1952, was missing the 1796 BB-62.

Notable Specimens

Straus Specimen. AU-53 (NGC). Straus Collection (Stack's, 1959) • Spies Collection (Stack's, 1974) lot 24. Letters not bifurcated, and the curl on top of the head imperfect. VF to EF • Rothschild Collection (Stack's, October 2003) lot 2715 • Warren Miller Collection.

Vermeule Specimen. F-15 (PCGS). Vermeule Collection (Stack's, November 2001) lot 421• Warren Miller Collection, then graded VF-25 (NGC) • privately to Dr. Robert Hesselgesser Collection (Ira and Larry Goldberg, September 2011) lot 5024 • Pre-Long Beach Sale (Goldbergs, May 2012) lot 1273.

The following are of unknown status: With the exception of the Straus-Spies and Vermeule coins,, *all* "Bolender-3" 1796 dollars listed in our survey fall into one of two categories: 1. The coin was misattributed based on plate examination. 2. The coin was not plated in the catalog making verification impossible.

Phoenix Specimen. VF-25. Steve Ivy, 1982, lot 998. Die dot in field above 1 in date. Tear-drop die flaws below stars 11 and 13. Non-bifurcated letters in LIBERTY. *Not plated.*

Boyd Specimen. VF-20. "World's Greatest Collection" (F.C.C. Boyd, Numismatic Gallery, 1945) lot 20. Haseltine-3. VF and very scarce. *Not plated.*

Aaron Specimen. VF-20. Steve Ivy, 1982, lot 1070. *Not plated.*

Blauvelt Specimen. VG-10. Bowers and Ruddy, 1977, lot 492, About Fine. Some marks on obverse. *Not plated.*

Hatie Specimen. VG-8. Bowers and Merena, 1983, lot 908, VG-8 or fairly close to it. Some traces of adjustment marks on obverse right field. *Not plated.*

Total Estimated Population

MS-65 or better: 0 (URS-0)
MS-64: 0 (URS-0)
MS-63: 0 (URS-0)
MS-60 to 62: 0 (URS-0)
AU-50 to 58: 1 (URS-1)
VF-20 to EF-45: 1 (URS-1)
G-4 to F-15: 1 or 2 (URS-1)
Total for all grades combined: 2 to 5 (URS-2)
Estimated Total Condition Census: 53-25-? (information incomplete)

1796 Small Date, Small Letters, BB-63

(B-2, H-2)

Obverse: *Small wide date;* all of the figures of date *evenly spaced* wide apart. 6 leans to the left. Highest wave of hair under serif at left bottom of E; second highest wave under upright of R. End of hair tress touches *only one (the innermost) point of star 1.* The curly lock closest to the date barely misses the star point to the right of the innermost point of star 1 (magnification may be necessary to tell this; on BB-66, the curly lock touches not only the tip of the innermost point of star 1, but also the point to the right of it). On BB-63, star 1 points to the space between two dentils (on BB-66 it points to a dentil). A point of star 15 points to the middle of the drapery folds (on BB-66 it points to a spot high on the drapery folds). This obverse bears a close resemblance to the obverse of BB-66, and specimens should be compared to it. The R in LIBERTY shows beginning signs of failure at the lower right tip. Of the four 1796 obverses, this die was cut next to the last.

Obverse die used to strike 1796 BB-63 (earlier use) and BB-64 (later use).

Reverse: Described under 1795 BB-51, herewith repeated: Small Eagle. Small Letters in legend. Eagle stands on clouds. Wreath is composed of a palm branch (right) and olive branch (left), the latter with seven berries. *Berry under A of STATES;* a quick way to identify this reverse. Weakly detailed at center.

Reverse die used to strike 1795 BB-51; 1796 BB-62, BB-63, and BB-66 (now relapped); 1797 BB-72; and 1798 BB-81.

Die States

Die State I: Perfect dies. Reverse die state the same as used on 1795 BB-51; no lapping yet (compare to die states of 1796 BB-66). This is the only die state seen by the author. This the same reverse die state as used to coin 1796 BB-62.

Die State II: Reverse die relapped, removing some details of the shallowest (lowest) folds in the wreath ribbon and removing about 50% of the lowest left leaf on the wreath (just below the U of UNITED). This die state was also used to coin 1797 BB-72 and 1798 BB-82. May not exist with 1796 BB-63.

Collecting Notes

An estimated 175 to 300 specimens exist of 1796 BB-63, another variety that is usually seen in lower grades. Above VF, acquisition becomes a challenge. Specimens are scarce if EF and very rare if AU. The typical example of 1796 BB-63 is not as well struck as 1796 BB-66, and is apt to show weakness at the lower center of the reverse at the eagle's tail and feet.

Centering may be irregular, but only slightly so. For example, a coin may be perfectly centered on the reverse, but have the obverse very slightly off center to the top (making the dentils very prominent at the bottom of the obverse, and weak at the top); or, conversely, a specimen may be well centered on the obverse, but have the reverse very slightly off center to the top (making the dentils very prominent at the bottom of the obverse, and weak at the top).

Notable Specimens

Eastern Specimen. MS-60. Specimen in a private Eastern collection, MS-60 (reported by Douglas Winter).

Carter Specimen. AU-58 (PCGS). Amon Carter, Jr. Collection (Stack's, 1984) lot 214. "AU." • John Whitney Walter Collection (Stack's, May 1999) lot 1780 • Private Midwest collection.

Newcomer Specimen. AU-58 (NGC). Waldo C. Newcomer. • Col. E.H.R. Green. • James G. Macallister. • T. James Clarke Collection (New Netherlands 48th Sale, 1956) lot 616. "AU-55, only a shade from Mint State." • Harold Bareford Collection (Stack's, October

1981) lot 407 • John Whitney Walter Collection (Stack's, May 1999) lot 1781 • 65th Anniversary Sale (Stack's, October 2000) lot 1138 • Cardinal Collection (American Numismatic Rarities, June 2005) lot 18 • Mark Gordon Collection (Ira and Larry Goldberg, May 2009) lot 600.

Orlando Specimen. AU-55 (PCGS). Orlando Signature Sale (Heritage, January 2010) lot 2582.

FUN Specimen AU-55 (NGC). FUN Signature Sale (Heritage, January 1999) lot 6924.

Miller Specimen. AU-53 (NGC). Jim McGuigan • Warren Miller Collection.

Total Estimated Population

MS-65 or better: 0 (URS-0)
MS-64: 0 (URS-0)
MS-63: 0 (URS-0)
MS-60 to 62: 1 or 2 (URS-1)
AU-50 to 58: 10 to 15 (URS-5)
VF-20 to EF-45: 120 to 190 (URS-8)
G-4 to F-15: 50 to 100 (URS-)
Total for all grades combined: 175 to 300 (URS-9)
Estimated Total Condition Census: 60-58-58-55-55-53

1796 SMALL DATE, LARGE LETTERS, BB-64

(B-6)

Obverse: See description under 1796 BB-63. Small, wide date.

Obverse die used to strike 1796 BB-63 (earlier use) and BB-64 (later use).

Reverse: Large letters. This variety has a reverse, unknown to Bolender, not found on any other dollar of the era. Four berries inside wreath, four berries outside. Lowest outside berry is between the N and I in UNITED. *Berry under right foot of A in STATES.*

The two specimens known are each in a reverse die state quickly identifiable by a massive vertical die crack from the rim, through the left side of O in OF, through palm branch, wing tip, palm branch again, C, then turning to the left and continuing to border. This crack strongly affects the right side of the reverse. A smaller crack goes from the bow knot, to the right, through left foot of A, bottom of C, to join larger crack. Usually, the area to the left of the crack is weakly struck. Probably, the die failed almost immediately. Discovered by Walter H. Breen in the summer of 1957.

Reverse die used to strike 1796 BB-64 only.

Die States

Die State I: Perfect obverse die. Perfect reverse die. May not exist with perfect obverse die.

Die State II: Obverse die very slightly relapped. Part of interior of lowest curl gone. Perfect reverse die. May not exist.

Die State III: Obverse die as preceding. Reverse with massive crack and smaller crack as described above. The only two specimens known are of this die state. (Of course, it is possible that intermediate states, perhaps numerous, may have existed at one time between Die State II and III.)

Collecting Notes

Three specimens are known of this variety.

The first example known to me was in the cabinet of K.P. Austin, of Salisbury, Maryland, leading specialist in the series several decades ago. It then went into the A.J. Ostheimer 3rd Collection, then to Superior's 1975 ANA Convention sale, where it appeared as lot 823 and was described as follows:

1796 obverse Bolender-2, but with a semi-unique and unlisted reverse having a long vertical die crack from the dentils at 1:00 passing left edge of O in OF, through wreath, wing tip, wreath, C of AMERICA and curving left slightly to a dentil. Was VF before someone scratched the lines across the diameter of the obverse in a wheel spoke fashion; after which someone else tried improving this piece by lightly burnishing the entire obverse. Reverse is untouched and shows the unmistakable weakness on the left three quarters of the coin due to the die failure. Damaged, but still semi-unique to date. [$850.00.]

The coin went to the collection of Jules Reiver, long-time expert and specialist in early American silver coinage. From a value viewpoint, some have considered the coin to be net VG-8. The condition of the second piece is not known to me. In a conversation, Jules Reiver related the following: [1]

I know of just a single specimen of the 1796 B-6 [BB-64], the one I own. This is a very curious coin. Some time ago I held a class on grading coins for some local schoolchildren. Some of them became quite knowledgeable. The B-6 [BB-64] has a huge die break on the back, and on the left side of the break it is very weak and worn-appearing, and on the right side it looks AU and is sharp. I would cover over the sharp part of the coin and ask a student to grade it. One of them said it was Good to Very Good, which was about right. I would then cover over that part, and resubmit the coin with the sharper part of the reverse showing, and the same person graded it as AU, which was also right.

We then had a discussion as to why a coin could be Good in one section of the surface and AU in another. The obverse of the coin is scratched up and somewhat defaced. The same student suggested that after this coin was struck, someone at the Mint examined it and saw the effects of the broken die, and said it was unfit to be released into circulation. This

Mint employee then scratched it, so it wouldn't be given out, but, somehow, it escaped. That theory sounded good to me.

Notable Specimens

Taylor Specimen. VF-35 (NGC). Emanuel Taylor Collection • Hollinbeck-Kagin Fixed Price List, ca. 1959, lot 19 • Greenwald and Jackson Collections Sale (Bowers and Merena, September 1995) lot 1249 • John Whitney Collection (Mr. 1796), (Stack's, May 1999) lot 1249 • Warren Miller Collection.

Austin Specimen. EF Details (NCS) Damaged. K.P. Austin. • A.J. Ostheimer 3rd. • 1975 ANA Convention Sale (Superior) lot 823. • Jules Reiver Collection (Heritage, January 2006) lot 23490.

Piedmont Specimen Fine Details (ANACS) Net VG-8, Plugged, Tooled, Whizzed. Piedmont Collection (Heritage, June 200) lot 7737 • Cardinal Collection (Superior, January 2002) lot 1184 • Albany Collection (Heritage, September 2002) lot 7763 • Long Beach Signature Sale (Heritage, June 2005) lot 6587.

Note: The coin listed as lot 23 of the World's Greatest Collection was incorrectly attributed and is a late die state of BB-65.

Total Estimated Population

MS-65 or better: 0 (URS-0)
MS-64: 0 (URS-0)
MS-63: 0 (URS-0)
MS-60 to 62: 0 (URS-0)
AU-50 to 58: 0 (URS-0)
VF-20 to EF-45: 1 (URS-1)
G-4 to F-15: 2 (URS-2)
Total for all grades combined: 3 (URS-3)
Estimated Total Condition Census: 35-8-8

---

[1] Commentary "transcribed" from my memory, a few minutes after my telephone conversation with Jules Reiver, December 2, 1992.

1796 Large Date, Small Letters, BB-65

(B-5, H-5)

Obverse: Large date. The "large" size of the date is not immediately obvious, but upon study, the digits are indeed slightly larger, and are in the numeral size used the following year, 1797. The 6 in date plainly shows it was double punched; this is visible at the underside of the top of the 6 and the upper inside of the bottom loop. Stars at right are very closely spaced and touch or nearly touch their neighboring stars. Highest wave of hair is below upright of E and is very indistinct, probably due to very light relapping.

As the numerals bear a close relationship to those used in 1797, this obverse die was probably the final die cut in the 1796 year. Further, the lower right tip of R in LIBERTY is broken; the latest state of any of the four 1796 obverses.

Obverse die used to strike 1796 BB-65 only.

Reverse: *Small letters. Leaf under A of STATES.* Seven large berries in wreath, and a very small eighth berry is made to show on inside stem of lowest sprig of leaves on left. Three leaves beneath eagle's right (to observer's left) wing, these having been added by hand in front of the cloud. Eagle punch impressed deeply and strongly into the working die; thus, coins from this die have much better breast feather definition than on BB-61. Wreath differs from any other variety, *several* leaves *touching letters* of legend. *Quickly identifiable by a lump at right top of I in AMERICA;* this lump *does not touch C* in the earlier state of the dies.

Note: This is the third and final Small Letters reverse die in the series The others were the long-lived die first used to strike 1795 BB-51, later 1796 BB-62, BB-63, and BB-66 now relapped, 1797 BB-72, and 1798 BB-82, and another die used to strike 1795 BB-52. The obverse of BB-65 is believed to be the latest die made bearing the 1796 date, but the reverse, the Small Letters style, is the style of 1795 and, possibly, early 1796, and was probably the first 1796 reverse cut (before the two Large Letters dies).

The reverse of BB-65 could have been made in 1795 but not used then.

Reverse die used to strike 1796 BB-65 only.

Die States

Die State I: Perfect dies; obverse not relapped; reverse without lump at I in AMERICA on reverse. May not exist.

Die State II: Obverse lightly relapped, with highest wave of hair incomplete. Reverse: Prominent lump caused by piece out of the die at the upper right outside of I in AMERICA, extending upward toward the dentils and rightward toward C, but touching neither dentils nor C. The field of the coin is bulged outward in a small area below the lump (discernible only on higher grade coins). Stars 2 and 3 are weak and are not defined at their centers, due to metal flow into the lump at I, which was opposite stars 2 and 3 when the dies were in the press. Most specimens seen are of this die state.

Die State III: As above, but the lump at I in AMERICA is now slightly larger and lightly touches the adjacent C. Scarcer than the preceding.

Die State IV: As III, but now the lump extends along the curve of the C closest to the I, and also has enlarged to the left, covering the vertical shaft of the I at one point. Scarcer than either II or III.

Die State V: Bolender-5a. The lump joins IC and extends past C. Rare.

Die State VI: The lump extends further, and there is noticeable die rust at ER in AMERICA (cf. Bowers and Merena 3/89: 1951 and others).

Note: There is really no end to the theoretical number of intermediary states. For this reason, most numismatists are content with but a single specimen of a given variety of a specific Bolender number. Collecting by die states has attracted a few numismatists over the years, primarily because Bolender gave much space to them. Today, interest in minute die state differences is minimal.

Collecting Notes

1796 BB-65 is the second most available (after BB-61) of the die varieties of the 1796 date. I estimate that 800 to 1,400 survive. While it is common in the middle circulated grades, BB-65 becomes a rarity AU or finer.

Most specimens show light striking at stars 2 and 3 (due to metal requirements to fill the defect at I opposite in the dies in the press). A few have weak striking at first T in STATES on reverse.

Notable Specimens

Texas Specimen. MS-64 (PCGS). Private Texas Collection, displayed at 2001 World's Fair of Money.

Four Landmark Collections Specimen. MS-62 (PCGS). Four Landmark Collections Sale (Bowers and Merena, 1989) lot 1951 • Dale Friend Collection • Legend Numismatics • Cardinal Collection (American Numismatic Rarities, June 2005) lot 19 • Joseph C. Thomas Collection (Heritage, April 2009) lot 2539 • Dale Friend Collection.

Flannagan Specimen. MS-62 (NGC). Privately to John Whitney Walter in 1994 • John Whitney Walter Collection (Stack's, May 1999) lot 1784 • Phillip Flannagan Collection (Bowers and Merena, November 2011) lot 4222 • Jack Lee Collection III (Heritage, November 2005) lot 2189 • Joseph C. Thomas Collection (Heritage, April 2009) lot 2540.

Alto Specimen. MS-61 (NGC). Alto Collection (Stack's, 1970) lot 1063. Brilliant Uncirculated, with a prooflike surface. • S.S. Forrest, Jr. Collection (Stack's, 1972) lot 978. • Metropolitan New York Convention Sale (Stack's, 1975) lot 154 • Queller Family Collection of Silver Dollars (Heritage, April 2008) lot 2011.

DeCoppet Specimen. AU-55. André DeCoppet Collection (James Kelly, 1955). "Practically Uncirculated, a beautiful sharp specimen."

New Netherlands 54th Sale Specimen. AU-55. New Netherlands 54th Sale, 1960, lot 1010. "Uncirculated." • Don Corrado Romano Collection (Stack's, 1987) lot 746.

Garrett Specimen. AU-55 (PCGS). Garrett Collection, Johns Hopkins University (Bowers and Ruddy, March 1980) lot 683 • Private collector.

Eliasberg Specimen. AU-53 (PCGS). John G. Mills Collection (S.H. and H. Chapman, April 1904) • J.M. Clapp; John H. Clapp; Clapp estate, 1942 • Louis E. Eliasberg, Sr. Collection (Bowers and Merena, 1997) lot 2176 • Tangible Asset Galleries • Private collector.

Flip-strike mint error. EF-40. Concerning a flip-strike specimen of Die State V, grade not stated, Bolender noted this in 1950: "Another specimen of this variety is a curious overstrike. The reverse is struck over the obverse of this variety, the date and stars showing plainly on the reverse." • Warren Miller Collection.

Total Estimated Population

MS-65 or better: 0 (URS-0)
MS-64: 1 (URS-1)
MS-63: 0 (URS-0)
MS-60 to 62: 3 to 6 (URS-3)
AU-50 to 58: 6 to 12 (URS-4)
VF-20 to EF-45: 550 to 950 (URS-11)
G-4 to F-15: 200 to 400 (URS-9)
Total for all grades combined: 800 to 1,400 (URS-11)
Estimated Total Condition Census: 64-62-62-61-58 (multiples)

1796 Small Date, Small Letters, BB-66

(B-1, H-1)

Obverse: *Small date;* the 9 and 6 closer together than other figures. Highest wave of hair under upright of E; second highest wave under and slightly to the right of the middle of R. End of hair tress touches innermost point of star 1 on its right, and continues slightly past it. The curly

lock closest to the date barely touches the star point to the right of the innermost point of star 1 (magnification may be necessary to tell this; on BB-63 the curly lock clearly misses this star point). On BB-66, star 1 points at a dentil (on BB-63 it points to the space between two dentils). A point of star 15 points to a spot high on the drapery folds (on BB-63, it points to the middle of the drapery folds).

This obverse bears a close resemblance to the obverse of BB-63, and specimens should be compared to it. This and the obverse die used to strike BB-61 and BB-62 were the first two obverse dies cut in 1796, and have the lower right tip of the R in LIBERTY intact.

Obverse die used to strike 1796 BB-66 only. I believe this obverse, although it was one of the first obverses made in 1796, was first used for coinage in calendar year 1798.

Reverse: Described under 1795 BB-51, herewith repeated: Small Eagle. Small Letters in legend. Eagle stands on clouds. Wreath is composed of a palm branch (right) and olive branch (left), the latter with seven berries. *Berry under A of STATES;* a quick way to identify this reverse.

Reverse die used to strike 1795 BB-51; 1796 BB-62, BB-63, and BB-66 (now relapped); 1797 BB-72; and 1798 BB-81.

Die States

Die State I: Perfect dies. Reverse die state the same as used on 1795 BB-51; no lapping yet (compare to die states of 1796 BB-63). May not exist with 1796 BB-66.

Die State II: Reverse die relapped, removing some details of the shallowest (lowest) folds in the wreath ribbon and removing about 50% of the lowest left leaf on the wreath (just below the U of UNITED). In the process, the border dentils were made smaller, and the rim, low to begin with, was nearly reduced to insignificance. This die state was also used to coin 1797 BB-72 and 1798 BB-82. As there was no longer much in the way of a protective rim on the reverse, this side of the coin wore away quickly in circulation. This is the only die state of 1796 BB-66 seen by the author. Thus, 1796 BB-66 was coined *after* 1796 BB-62 and BB-63. I consider it to be a strong possibility that 1796 BB-66 was coined in 1798, at or near the same time 1797 BB-72 and 1798 BB-81 were struck.

Collecting Notes

I estimate that 1796 BB-66 exists to the extent of 200 to 350 pieces, most of which are in grades from well-worn to VF, with a very occasional EF and an even more infrequent AU. No Mint State coins have been reported. The builders of other great collections were fortunate if they had a VF coin. Bolender's personal coin was VF, ex Primus C. Clark, 1932.

The typical 1796 BB-66 silver dollar is well centered and, if in a high grade, has excellent striking detail at the center of the obverse and reverse. On worn specimens, the reverse details are typically less well defined than the obverse, as the reverse, lacking a satisfactory protective rim, wore away quickly. For this reason, grading of the variety is by the obverse only.

Another mystery involving early dollars surrounds the distribution pattern of 1796 BB-66. Why are most in lower grades as compared to, for example, 1795 BB-51?

Notable Specimens

Hesselgesser Specimen. AU-58 (PCGS). September Sale (Superior, September 1975) lot 298 • Riverly Collection (Heritage, August 1998) lot 8020 • Private collector • Tangible Asset Galleries • Cardinal Collection • Private collector • Dr. Robert Hesselgesser Collection (Ira and Larry Goldberg, September 2011) lot 5027 • Werner Family Collection (Stack's Bowers Galleries, August 2012) lot 11172.

California Specimen. AU-58 (NGC). Private collector • California Numismatic Funding • Private collector.

Whitney Specimen. AU-53 (PCGS). The Kenneth C. Long Estate Collection (Bowers and Merena, May 1995), lot 1153 • John Whitney Walter Collection (Stack's, May 1999), lot 1779 • CSNS Signature Sale (Heritage, April 2002) lot 4007.

New York Specimen. AU-53 (NGC). New York Signature Sale (Heritage, July 2002) lot 8357 • ANA Signature Sale (Heritage, July 2008) lot 1736 • Internet Sale (Heritage, September 2008) lot 21314 • Houston Signature Sale (Heritage, December 2008) lot 803 • Long Beach Signature Sale (Heritage, February 2009) lot 1525 • CSNS Signature Sale (Heritage, April 2009) lot 2538.

Davis Specimen. AU-50. R. Coulton Davis • W.G. Baldenhofer • Farish-Baldenhofer Sale (Stack's) lot 432 • A.J. Ostheimer 3rd. • Gilhousen Collection (Superior, 1973) lot 1221. "Practically Uncirculated." • Superior, 1975, lot 821.

Miller Specimen. EF-45+. Warren Miller Collection.

Higgins Specimen. EF-40. Lloyd M. Higgins, M.D. Collection (Bowers and Merena, 1988) lot 2209.

Herdegen Specimen. Net VF-20 (EF-40, scratched). Herdegen Collection (Schulman, 1973). EF, with two scratches near eagle's wing, initials "H F" scratched on reverse below wreath.

Turoff Specimen. Net VF-20 (EF-40, retooled). Julius Turoff Collection (Bowers and Ruddy, 1976) lot 1079. "EF and apparently well struck, but actually reinforced by some skillful retooling on Liberty's face."

Total Estimated Population

MS-65 or better: 0 (URS-0)
MS-64: 0 (URS-0)
MS-63: 0 (URS-0)
MS-60 to 62: 0 (URS-0)
AU-50 to 58: 5 to 8 (URS-4)
VF-20 to EF-45: 100 to 200 (URS-8)
G-4 to F-15: 100 to 200 (URS-8)
Total for all grades combined: 200 to 350 (URS-9)
Estimated Total Condition Census: 58-58-53-53-50-45 (multiples)

ADDITIONAL INFORMATION

Dickeson on 1796 Dollars (1859)

The following appeared in Dr. Montroville W. Dickeson's 1859 book, *An American Numismatical Manual:* "The number coined in this year was 72,920; they are not considered rare, and may be found in good order."

Trading a 1796 Dollar (1892)

From *The Numismatist,* Volume 4, August 1892, pp. 20-21:

Echoes from a Coin Dealer's Sanctum: Mr. Henry Ahlborn, one of the oldest coin dealers in Boston, is about as keen a man for a bargain as one can find. He tells how one summer day, trade being unusually dull in his store, he started on a pick-up trip along the North Shore. Going through the old towns of Salem, Marblehead, Hamilton, and Essex, he stopped in all the country stores, and talked with many an old farmer, always with a view of finding some rare old coin. He, at last, heard of an old lady who had in her possession a number of fine old cents and silver coins.

Mr. Ahlborn paid her generous prices for the cents and some silver and was about to go away when the old lady said that she had another piece, that was a gift from her father and was made in the year he was born, but that she would not part with it for anything. He asked to see it and she brought out the finest 1796 half dollar he had ever seen. His eyes snapped, and he immediately considered how he could get possession of that half dollar.

A lucky idea struck him. He bethought himself of a fine 1796 *dollar* he had bagged that morning, and taking it out he offered to exchange it with the lady for her half dollar making prominent the fact that this was a whole dollar, while hers was only a half dollar—besides it bore the same date and was equally as good. Convinced by this reasoning, she readily made the exchange, and Mr. A. went on his way satisfied with his day's work.

He afterwards sold it to Mr. Parmelee for $150, and I think he holds it today for $350. It bears but very slight traces of circulation.

Likes 1796 and 1797 Dollars (1930)

Writing in the January 1930 issue of *The Numismatist,* Theodore J. Venn gave some investment predictions, noting that certain coins "should certainly continue to go higher [in price] if the number of collectors increases or even holds its own." Further: "In the dollar issues I favor most the coins of 1796 and 1797, also those of 1795 and 1801 and the 1799 with 5 stars facing."

The Year 1796 in History

On September 17, 1796, President George Washington delivered his Farewell Address, not orally but by publication in the *Philadelphia American Advertiser.* In it he said "it is our true policy to steer clear of permanent alliance with any portion of the foreign world." This established the isolationism that characterized much of American politics during the next century. In December, John Adams of Massachusetts was elected to the presidency on the Federalist ticket, gaining 71 Electoral College votes, as compared to 68 for Thomas Jefferson, 59 for Thomas Pinckney, and 30 for Aaron Burr. Under the provisions effective at the time, Jefferson, with the second highest number of votes, became vice president.

Tennessee, earlier a part of North Carolina, was admitted to the Union as the 16th state. Possibly because of this, certain coins (but not silver dollars) were made with 16 obverse stars—the highest standard star count to be achieved as part of any obverse design of the era. A public land act passed by the Congress on May 18, 1796 authorized the sale of U.S. government lands in minimum lots of 640 acres each at $2 per acre with payment to be made under a credit system.

Gilbert Stuart created his famous painting of George Washington, the so-called Athenaeum Head, which became the most popular of all portraits of the president; reproductions appeared in most schoolrooms in the United States. In Philadelphia, experiments with gas lighting were conducted. Billiards were a popular American recreation, particularly in the South. English astronomer Francis Baily toured the United States and reported that Norfolk, Virginia had a dozen parlors devoted to the game. English actor Joseph Jefferson appeared on the New York stage for the first time; decades later, he would become famous for his portrayal of Rip Van Winkle. Robert Burns wrote the poem, "Auld Lang Syne."

France experienced hyper-inflation, and a bushel of flour, worth the equivalent of 40¢ in 1790, rose in price to $5 (although a direct comparison is not possible, as changes in the value of money, the wage structure, etc., must be considered as well). In England, physician Edward Jenner first used inoculation effectively against smallpox, one of the world's most rampant, devastating afflictions (an improvement, vaccination, would be announced in 1798).

At the Mint, the dime and quarter dollar denominations were struck for the first time. Half cents bearing the 1796 date were made in small numbers and would become recognized as rarities, as would 1796 half dollars. $2.50 gold pieces, known as quarter eagles, were first minted. David Rittenhouse, late Mint director and president of the American Philosophical Society, died, and was eulogized by would-be Mint director Benjamin Rush in an address at the First Presbyterian Church in High Street, Philadelphia, December 17, 1796 (cf. *Essays, Literary, Moral, and Philosophical,* by Benjamin Rush, M.D., Philadelphia: Thomas and Samuel Bradford, 1798).

CHAPTER 10
1797 SILVER DOLLARS

Mintage (all types)
Calendar year, Mint report: 7,776
Coins bearing date, author's estimate: 60,000

1797 SILVER DOLLARS

BB to Bolender to Haseltine Equivalents

BB Number	Bolender #	Haseltine #	Rarity	Average Grade
BB-71	B-3	H-3	URS-12	VF-30
BB-72	B-2	H-2	URS-9	VF-23
BB-73	B-1	H-1	URS-12	VF-29

Coinage Context
(all 1797 Varieties)

An extensive coinage: In 1797 the number of stars on the silver dollar was increased to 16. The coinage is said by government reports to be the lowest of any year from 1795 to 1803, although now it is believed that the numbers given are incorrect. I believe that most or all of the mintage of 7,776 coins reported for the calendar year may have been of earlier dates, and that most coins struck from dies dated 1797 were actually made in early 1798.

It is a virtual certainty that *many more* than 7,776 silver dollars were struck with the 1797 date. I estimate the number to be 60,000 (within about 10%). As noted earlier in the present text, numerous numismatic data suggest that the mintage of 1797 must have been about on a par with that of 1796, or not significantly different. (I estimate the mintage of 1796 to have been 75,000, not far from the official government figure for the calendar year of 79,920; however, some 1796 dollars may have been struck later as well, and part of the 79,920 number may have consisted of *1795-dated* dollars.)

As the estimated 60,000 1797-dated silver dollars could not have been struck earlier than 1797, and the quantity made is almost certainly far greater than 7,776, the only remaining possibility is that they were struck later, with the calendar year 1798 being the most likely candidate.

In 1797, production problems continued at the Mint. Sporadic coinage runs for silver dollars occurred in February, late May to late June, and in August. The Mint was closed from late August to late November, due to a yellow fever outbreak. Thus, the mintage for the calendar year was very small.

Numismatic Information

Rarity: Only two obverse dies and three reverse dies were employed for silver dollar coinage bearing the 1797 date. In his 1881 *Type-Table*, J.W. Haseltine called H-1 (equal to BB-73 today) rare, H-2 (BB-72), very rare, and said nothing about the rarity of H-3 (BB-71).

As a class, 1797 dollars are slightly more elusive than are those dated 1796, although auction data belie this (but only slightly). Mark Borckardt's survey of auction appearances yielded 490 listings for 1796-dated dollars and 552 for those of 1797.

Striking quality: Among extant 1797 dollars, striking quality is often irregular. The rims are often very boldly defined (the reverse rim of BB-72 being an exception), and yet the center of the obverse and the eagle on the reverse may be weak.

Number of dies used: The number of dies employed to create 1797-dated dollars is as follows:

1797 obverses, 2

1797 reverses, 3 (including one left over from 1795-6)

Die use averages: By dividing the number of obverse dies and the number of reverse dies each with the estimated mintage figure of 60,000 coins dated 1797, estimates of the average number of impressions per die can be obtained. In practice, one die might last a long time and another might break quickly; the figures here are averages, as noted.

2 1797 obverses divided into an estimated mintage of 1797-dated dollars of 60,000 = 30,000 coins per obverse die.

3 1797 reverses divided into an estimated mintage of 1797-dated dollars of 60,000 = 20,000 coins per reverse

die (the inclusion of the long-lived BB-72 die, used also for later-dated coinage, distorts this figure).

Collecting 1797 dollars: A complete "set" of 1797 die varieties consists of but three coins, 1797 Stars 9x7, Large Letters (BB-73); 1797 Stars 9x7, Small Letters (BB-72), and 1797 Stars 10x6, Large Letters (BB-71). The total population of all 1797 dollar varieties combined is only slightly more than that for a single variety of 1795 dollar, the BB-27.

While as a class 1797 dollars are scarce, none of the three varieties is an impossible rarity. The toughest is the BB-72, but enough of these are around that an example can be found with relatively little looking. Some have suggested that it is rarer than a 1794 dollar, but I believe it to be more available.

Dollars of this date are a study in contrast. Rather than differing by some minor feature, each is almost a "type." Thus, acquiring one each of the three will be an especially fascinating pursuit. The quest is not advised for the buyer who is conditioned to want Mint State coins, or even AU pieces. Better, he turn attention to something such as Morgan or Peace dollars, where there is hope of fulfillment. A splendid goal for a set of 1797 dollars would be Extremely Fine, and Very Fine is closer to reality.

Among collectors seeking early silver dollars have been several to whom money was not a question. Even so, their collections were more likely to average below the EF grade than above it.

SUMMARY OF CHARACTERISTICS

1797 (All varieties)

Circulation Strikes

Enabling legislation: Act of April 2, 1792

Designer of obverse: Robert Scot (after Stuart), model by John Eckstein

Designer of reverse: Robert Scot, model by John Eckstein

Statutory weight: 416 grains; .8924 silver, balance copper

Melting value (silver bullion value) in year minted: Considered by Mint officials to be on a par with the Spanish dollar, and worth about $1.00 intrinsically (see discussion under Summary of Characteristics, 1794).

Dies prepared: At least 3 obverse dies, at least 3 reverse dies (including one left over from 1795)

Circulation strike mintage, calendar year: 7,776 (for all varieties of 1797 combined, not including pieces reserved for the Assay Commission; for 1797 the number of assay coins is not known); Delivery figures by day: February 28: 342 • May 26: 1,060 • June 30: 3,881 • August 13: 2,071 • August 28: 422.

Estimated circulation strike mintage of 1797-dated dollars (author's estimate): (60,000).

Estimated quantity melted: As part of exports or normal Mint redemptions.

Estimated total population (all varieties):

MS-65 or better: 1 (URS-1)

MS-64: 1 or 2 (URS-1)

MS-63: 5 to 9 (URS-4)

MS-60 to 62: 15 to 30 (URS-5)

AU-50 to 58: 60 to 90 (URS-7)

VF-20 to EF-45: 1,900 to 3,250 (URS-12)

G-4 to F-15: 725 to 1,050 (URS-11)

Total for all grades combined: 2,750 to 4,500 (URS-13)

Estimated Total Condition Census: 65-64-63 (multiples)

Characteristics of striking: Striking is irregular on 1797 dollars. Those with Small Letters reverse (BB-72) always have a weak reverse.

Commentary: Silver dollars of 1797 are nearly always encountered in lower grades. The 1797 9x7, Small Letters reverse, is one of the most famous of all early dollars.

DRAPED BUST/SMALL EAGLE VARIETIES

1797 Stars 10x6, Large Letters, BB-71

(B-3, H-3)

Obverse: 16 stars, *only six at right* facing bust. A die dot close to the bottom right of the second digit makes the date read 17.97 (some imagination is required); the last 7 is high. The star arrangement of 10 stars to the left and six to the right is unique in the dollar series.

Obverse die used to strike 1797 BB-71 only.

Reverse: Large letters in legend. 8 berries in left branch. *Leaf ends under middle of E in STATES.* Lowest berry near ribbon bow is on *outside* of wreath. Large planchet. A leaf is almost below the T in UNITED, a berry is at the right side of the first T in STATES, another leaf is past the O in OF and another leaf is very close to the R in AMERICA. Three leaves below eagle's right (observer's left) wing.

Reverse die used to strike 1797 BB-71 only.

Die States

Die State I: Obverse and reverse die perfect; neither relapped. Obverse shows the highest wave of hair fully impressed in the die, stars perfect. May not exist.

Die State II: Obverse die relapped. Highest wave of hair, under upright of B, is incomplete. Stars appear spidery and imperfect. Stars 9 and 10 have the innermost points shortened. Slightly scarcer than the following.

Die State III: Obverse die relapped as above. Reverse relapped, removing the right edges of several palm leaves on the right side of the branch. The die state usually seen.

Die State IV: Die crack develops on and just below right foot of first A in AMERICA, and on right edge of palm leaf under center of that A. Very rare.

Collecting Notes

1797 BB-71 is about tied with BB-73 in terms of availability. I estimate that 1,250 to 2,000 are known. If anything, BB-71 is very slightly scarcer than BB-73.

As is the case with dollars of the two other varieties of this year, examples of 1797 BB-71 are usually seen in lower grades. However, several have been called Uncirculated over the years. Undoubtedly, most would not merit the grade by today's stricter interpretations of standards. However, any 1797 dollar that is a candidate for being in this grade is apt to be of the BB-71 variety. In October 1990, Superior sold a coin certified as NGC MS-64, which may be the finest known.

Specimens are seen on large or slightly smaller planchets. The large-planchet coins have the obverse dentils especially boldly defined. Those on smaller planchets have narrower rims.

Notable Specimens

Eliasberg Specimen. MS-65 (NGC). Harlan P. Smith Collection (Chapman Brothers, May 1906) • J.M. Clapp • John H. Clapp • Clapp Estate, 1942 • Louis E. Eliasberg Sr. Collection (Bowers and Merena, April 1997) lot 2177. • Legend Numismatics • Phillip Flannagan Collection (Bowers and Merena, November 2001) lot 4226 • Private Midwest collection.

Smith Specimen. MS-65 (NGC). Elliot Smith Collection • J.C. Morgenthau & Co. • T. James Clarke Collection (New Netherlands, November 1956) lot 620 • Farish Baldenhofer • Milferd H. Bolender (1959, privately) • Alfred and Jackie Ostheimer Collection (Lester Merkin, September 1968), lot 243 • Unknown intermediaries •

Joseph O'Connor • Jack Lee Collection III (Heritage, November 2005) lot 2090, as MS-64 (NGC) • Private collector • Rarities Sale (Stack's Bowers, August 2011) lot 7394, as MS-65 (NGC).

Baldenhofer Sale Specimen. MS-64 (PCGS). W.G. Baldenhofer Collection • Farish-Baldenhofer Sale (Stack's). • A.J. Ostheimer 3rd Collection • Gilhousen Collection (Superior, 1973) lot 1227. "Warmly toned Uncirculated." • ANA Convention Sale (Superior, 1975) lot 843 • October Sale (Superior, 1990) lot 3715 • Private Texas collection.

Queller Specimen. MS-63 (NGC). Stack's, privately December 1982 • Queller Family Collection of Silver Dollars (Heritage, April 2008) lot 2013.

Cardinal Specimen. MS-62 (PCGS). R.L. Miles Collection (Stack's, April 1969) lot 1532 • September Sale (Stack's, September 1975) lot 299 • Portland ANA Sale (Heritage, August 1998) lot 8028 • Tangible Asset Galleries • Cardinal Collection (American Numismatic Rarities, June 2005) lot 20 • Joseph C. Thomas Collection (Heritage, April 2009) lot 2543.

1992 ANA Specimen. MS-62 (PCGS). Orlando ANA Sale (Heritage, August 1992) lot 1909, as AU-55 (PCGS) • Unknown intermediaries • Robert Lehmann • Cardinal Collection • Robert Lehmann • Private collector • Pre-Long Beach Sale (Ira and Larry Goldberg, September 2002) lot 469 • FUN Elite Sale (Superior, January 2003) lot 846 • ANA Classics Sale (American Numismatic Rarities, July 2003) lot 528 • ANA Rarities Sale (Stack's Bowers, August 2011) lot 7395 • ANA Rarities Sale (Stack's Bowers, August 2012) lot 11480.

Triple Struck Specimen. MS-61 (NGC). Rarities Sale (Bowers and Merena, September 2002) lot 346 • Pre-Long Beach Sale (Ira and Larry Goldberg, September 2003) lot 519 • Classics Sale (American Numismatic Rarities, March 2004) lot 1145 • Warren Miller Collection.

Carnegie Institute Specimen. MS-60+. Spink's Carnegie Institute Sale, 1982. The London firm of Spink & Son, Ltd. handled the Carnegie Institute (Pittsburgh)

coins on the advice of their advisor, Lester Merkin. • Jascha Heifetz Collection (Superior, 1989) lot 2390 • Auction '85 (Superior, 1985) lot 823. MS-60+.

Auction '86 Specimen. MS-60. Auction '86 (RARCOA, 1986) lot 727. "Well struck Choice Brilliant Uncirculated."

Austin Specimen. MS-60. Bowers and Ruddy, 1974, lot 16. "Choice Brilliant Uncirculated. A few normal adjustment marks." • Kensington Collection (Bowers and Ruddy, 1975) lot 1214.

Cleneay Specimen. MS-60. Thomas Cleneay (Chapman brothers, 1890), Uncirculated.

Mills Specimen. MS-60. John G. Mills (Chapman brothers, 1904), Uncirculated.

Gable Specimen. MS-60. William F. Gable (S.H. Chapman, 1914), Uncirculated.

Golding Specimen. MS-60. Golding Collection (Stack's, 1952) lot 221. • Harold Bareford Collection, (Stack's, 1981) lot 410. "Brilliant Uncirculated."

DeCoppet Specimen. MS-60. André DeCoppet Collection (James Kelly, 1955). "Strictly Uncirculated."

Robison Specimen. MS-60. Ellis H. Robison Collection, Part II (Stack's, 1982) lot 823. "Brilliant Uncirculated."

Spies Specimen. MS-60. W. Earl Spies Collection (Stack's, 1974) lot 36. "Uncirculated."

Wolfson Specimen. MS-60. Louis Wolfson Collection (Stack's, 1963) lot 1374. "Brilliant Uncirculated."

Total Estimated Population

MS-65 or better: 1 (URS-1)
MS-64: 2 (URS-2)
MS-63: 4 to 7 (URS-3)
MS-60 to 62: 10 to 20 (URS-5)
AU-50 to 58: 35 to 50 (URS-7)
VF-20 to EF-45: 900 to 1,500 (URS-11)
G-4 to F-15: 300 to 425 (URS-10)
Total for all grades combined: 1,250 to 2,000 (URS-12)
Estimated Total Condition Census: 65-64-64-63-62-62

1797 Stars 9x7, Small Letters, BB-72

(B-2, H-2)

Obverse: 16 stars, arranged nine to the left and seven to the right. Highest wave of hair, below the upright of E, is lightly defined, probably due to insufficient depth of punching of the Draped Bust motif into the die (and not due to relapping).

Obverse die used to strike 1797 BB-72 (earlier) and BB-73 (later).

Reverse: Described under 1795 BB-51, herewith repeated: Small Eagle. Small Letters in legend. Eagle stands on clouds. Wreath is composed of a palm branch (right) and olive branch (left), the latter with seven berries. *Berry under A of STATES;* a quick way to identify this reverse.

Reverse die used to strike 1795 BB-51; 1796 BB-62, BB-63, and BB-66 (now relapped); 1797 BB-72; and 1798 BB-81.

Die States

Die State I: Perfect dies (no cracks). Earliest state of the obverse; equivalent to 1797 BB-73 Die State I. Reverse die relapped, equivalent to 1796 BB-63 Die State II.

About Mintage and Rarity

How many exist? 1797 BB-72 has been subjected to widely varying estimates of rarity over the years, with some observers stating that only about 20 are known, and others ranking the population at Sheldon's Rarity-4 (76 to 200). The latter is probably closer to the truth. I believe that 200 to 300 exist today, and believe that this figure is conservative (I wouldn't bet against someone who suggested that even more than 300 could be traced). At one convention a few years ago, I purchased four specimens for stock—something that one usually can't do if only 20 are known. At that rate, one would see an 1797 BB-72 dollar only about as frequently as an 1876-CC twenty-cent piece (of which I believe that about 20 are known), but that isn't the case.

In reality, the fame of the 1797 BB-72 has been larger than reality. However, the BB-72 is still eminently desirable. It is just that quite a few more than 20 are known. In trying to track down why the issue has been listed as a *major* rarity, I concluded that the culprit is the low mintage of just 7,776 for the *calendar* year 1797. *If* only 7,776 were minted, and if 1797 BB-72 is the rarest variety of the year (which it is), then the mintage of BB-72 must have been some tiny fraction of 7,776. What might the mintage be? From that point, it was a short step to the inspection of the calendar year 1797 delivery figures by day: February 28: 342 • May 26: 1,060 • June 30: 3,881 • August 13: 2,071 • August 28: 422. The lowest figure, 342, fit the bill exactly; *q.v.,* 1797 BB-72 dollars were all delivered on February 28, 1797, and the mintage was 342. Neat idea. However, it doesn't square with the fact that nearly that many are known to exist today.

Robert P. Hilt III, in *Die Varieties of Early United States Coins,* 1980, stated that the mintage of Bolender-2 (BB-72) was not 342, but composed the entire production of 7,776 for the 1797 calendar year. He went on to suggest that if the survival rate of the issue was 1.45% of the mintage, 112 coins would exist today. He further stated that the other two varieties, Bolender-1 (BB-73) and Bolender-3 (BB-71), were struck in 1798. While I do not agree with all of the numbers, the Hilt theory comes far closer to what I consider to be the truth, than anything else I have seen in print. (I believe the mintage of 1797 BB-72 to have been in the range of 4,000 to 4,500 coins, also probably minted in 1798; I, too, believe that BB-73 and BB-71 were minted in 1798, or at least a majority of each was.)

Collecting Notes

Of all varieties of 1797, the BB-72 is at once the rarest, best known, and most sought after. This issue occupies its own niche in numismatic literature, in which listings it has been showcased as a rarity in some instances and ignored in others. Without a doubt, it is the best known die variety of the 1796-7 years combined. Indeed, it may well be the most famous variety after 1794 and before 1804.

While various catalogers over the years have ascribed great rarity to 1797 BB-72, I believe that about 200 to 300 exist today, as explained in detail above.

In this die combination, the obverse shows very prominent and bold denticulation and excellent relief. The reverse, not deeply punched to begin with, and since relapped, always appears to be very shallow and weak in comparison to the obverse, as the relapping largely destroyed what small protective rim there was initially. Part of each reverse rim dentil has been ground away. Because of the low rim, a coin whose obverse grades VF may have a reverse grading only VG. Typically, if a single grade is to be given, the grading is by the obverse only, although in the past there has been no consistency in this regard. A split grade such as VF/Fine or Fine/VG is more informative.

This Small Letters reverse die is famous in its own right, as already noted, and was mated with obverses dated 1795, 1796, and 1798, in addition to 1797.

Most known specimens of 1797 BB-72 are in grades from VG to EF, with VF being most often seen. True EF or finer coins are rarer than auction or other data suggest, as often grading has been on the liberal side for this rare variety.

Notable Specimens

Cardinal Specimen. AU-58 (PCGS). R.L. Miles Collection (Stack's April 1969) lot 1534 • unknown intermediaries • Cardinal Collection (American Numismatic Rarities, June 2005) lot 21 • Thaler Collection • Pre-Long Beach Sale (Ira and Larry Goldberg, February 2008) lot 2853.

Carter Specimen. AU-55+ (PCGS). Amon Carter, Jr. Collection (Stack's, 1984) lot 218. AU, frosty luster. • Michael Herring Collection (Heritage, January 2002) lot 7182 • Chris Napolitano • Private Midwest collection.

Reiver Specimen. AU-55 (NGC). Julian Leidman, privately February 1978 • Jules Reiver Collection (Heritage, January 2006) lot 23494.

Hesselgesser Specimen. AU-53 (PCGS). Dale Friend Collection • U.S. Coins • Cardinal Collection • Private collector • Baltimore Rarities Sale (Bowers and Merena, July 2008) lot 702, as AU-50 (PCGS) • Dr. Robert Hesselgesser Collection (Ira and Larry Goldberg, September 2011) lot 5029.

Miller Specimen. AU-50 (NGC). ANA Signature Sale (Heritage, August 1998) lot 8027 "AU-55" • Warren Miller Collection.

Albany Specimen. AU-50 (PCGS). Private collector • Cardinal Collection • Albany Collection (Heritage, September 2002) lot 7766, as AU-53 (PCGS) • Philadelphia Rarities Sale (Bowers and Merena, September 2009) lot 1089, as AU-50 (PCGS) • Fort Worth Signature Sale (Heritage, March 2010) lot 1177.

Miller Specimen (another). EF-45. Double struck reverse. Warren Miller Collection.

Ebsen Specimen. EF-45. Buddy Ebsen Collection (Superior, 1987) lot 1887.

Chalkley Specimen. EF-45. Chalkley Collection (Superior, 1990) 2839. "Early die state with two points of recut star visible below star 9 on obverse."

Eliasberg Specimen. EF-40 (PCGS). Louis E. Eliasberg Sr. Collection (Bowers and Merena, April 1997) lot 2178 • Highlander Collection • Private collector.

Aspen Specimen. EF-45/40. Nelson Page Aspen, M.D. Collection (Bowers and Merena, 1989) lot 361.

Total Estimated Population

MS-65 or better: 0 (URS-0)
MS-64: 0 (URS-0)
MS-63: 0 (URS-0)
MS-60 to 62: 0 (URS-0)
AU-50 to 58: 5 to 8 (URS-4)
VF-20 to EF-45: 120 to 170 (URS-8)
G-4 to F-15: 80 to 130 (URS-7)
Total for all grades combined: 200 to 300 (URS-9)
Estimated Total Condition Census: 58-55+-55-53-50-50

1797 Stars 9x7, Large Letters, BB-73

(B-1, H-1)

Obverse: See description under 1797 BB-72. Latest state of the die; struck after BB-72.

Obverse die used to strike 1797 BB-72 (earlier) and BB-73 (later).

Reverse: Large Letters style. 8 berries in left branch. *Leaf ends under center of upright of E in STATES.* Lowest berry near ribbon bow is on *inside* of wreath. E of STATES lightly repunched. All of the A's in the legend show a curious defect at their upper left corners. A leaf points to the left corner of the I in UNITED, another leaf points to the left corner of the first T in STATES while another leaf points to the very end of the O in OF. Another leaf is positioned away from the R in AMERICA.

Note: Immediately after 1797 BB-73 Die State IV was coined, the reverse die was mated with a 1798 obverse and used to coin specimens of 1798 BB-82, Die State I. The die cracks advanced slightly during the coinage. When coinage of 1798 BB-82 was completed, the dies were re-mated with this 1797 obverse, and additional specimens of 1797 BB-73 were struck, with the reverse being in the same state as used to coin 1798 BB-82. It is likely that all specimens of 1797 BB-73 were struck at the Mint in calendar year 1798.

Reverse die used to strike 1797 BB-73 and 1798 BB-82.

Die States

Die State I: Perfect dies (no cracks or clash marks). Obverse die with pellet-shaped raised die flaw in field below innermost point of star 9, and about 40% of the distance from the star point to the hair. Some die roughness, probably as made, between star 1 and date. Most plentiful die state.

Die State II: Obverse die has been lightly relapped, removing most of pellet flaw below star 9, and removing all but a trace of it. No obverse or reverse cracks yet. A plentiful die state.

Die State III: Bolender-1a. OBVERSE: A few delicate traces of arc-like clash marks are in the field before Miss Liberty's face and are so subtle that only high grade specimens show them; these are from the curved palm leaves on the reverse. The die has developed hairline cracks as follows: From dentil upward to outermost point of star 4, continuing through a point of star 5 to ribbon; crack from ribbon downward through hair curl, hair, bottom curl, to border. Minute crack from dentil downward to star 5. Crack from dentil through two bottom points of star 7 to ribbon. From bottom of 97 of date through bust drapery to star 15, minutely continuing through the centers of stars 14 and 13. From dentil toward (but not touching) star 15. Stars on right develop distended points toward the dentils. REVERSE: No cracks.

Die State IV: Bolender-1b. OBVERSE: As III. REVERSE: Cracks as follows: Crack in the field from the border above the upper left of D to the border above upper right of first T in STATES. Irregular vertical crack between branch and side of eagle's right (observer's left) wing. Light crack connects dentil with upper part of second T in STATES and continues downward to branch.

Die State V: Bolender-1c. Dies have clashed again. Now with severe clash marks in field front of Miss Liberty's face, especially from her nose to chin, and under ribbon behind head. Die cracks as IV, plus new cracks: From dentil through bottom of star 2 to hair; from 9th star downward to ribbon. Crack from dentil toward star 15 now touches star 15. REVERSE: Additional cracks as follows: Crack from left base of N in UNITED through leaf tip to connect with separate crack from right base of I to branch. Crack from center of E through D continuing through S, curving upward to border through T. Crack connecting dentil with upper part of second T in STATES and continuing downward to branch is now much heavier from dentil to top of T. Crack from same T

135

through ES to topmost palm leaf. Crack from tops of OF through center of AM.

Note: Specimens of 1798 BB-82 were struck from a die state intermediate between IV and V (with crack later from the center of E through D, etc., now only from E onward; without crack from left base of N in UNITED). Specimens were also struck from Die State V (the most usual die state for 1798 BB-82.

Die State VI: Die cracks advanced further from Die State V. Gilhousen (Superior, 1973): 1225 may be this state, there called "Bolender-1e," and described as "shattered and bulged;" ex Baldenhofer and Ostheimer collections.

Collecting Notes

The 1797 BB-73 dollar is usually seen with broad borders, a feature particularly noticeable on the obverse, where the dentils are prominently featured, but also to an extent on the reverse. The reverse is usually not as well defined as the obverse, due to the relatively low relief of the eagle motif. However, the breast feathers and other reverse details are usually excellent in higher grade specimens of earlier die states. Together with BB-71, the BB-73 is one of the two most available varieties of the year; both BB-73 and BB-71 are much more plentiful than BB-72.

Over 1,000 1797 BB-73 dollars are believed to exist; I estimate the population to be from 1,300 to 2,100. This variety is the most plentiful of the year, beating 1797 BB-71 by a tiny margin. Most examples of BB-73 are in the Very Fine category, although quite a few EF pieces are known as well, and come on the market frequently. Coins realistically graded AU are rare—much more so than conventional wisdom allows. True Mint State pieces are exceedingly—dare I say "excessively"?—rare. Although BB-71 is slightly scarcer than BB-73 in terms of all grades combined, in AU and Mint State, BB-71 is somewhat more available than BB-73.

Notable Specimens

Miles Specimen. MS-63 (NGC). R.L. Miles, Jr. Collection (Stack's, April 1969) lot 1533 • Stack's

BB-73: Late die state with advanced die cracks and heavy clash marks.

May 1974 Sale: 228. "Brilliant Uncirculated • Walton Hood Collection • Cardinal Collection (American Numismatic Rarities, June 2005) lot 22 • Private collector • Baltimore Sale (Bowers and Merena, November 2010) lot 2200.

Miller Specimen. MS-63 (NGC). Warren Miller Collection.

Eliasberg Specimen. AU-58 (PCGS). Die State I. Well struck and well centered, with both obverse and reverse framed by prominent dentils. Details are excellent in all areas except the very highest points of the obverse and reverse. Indeed, probably no finer striking exists. John G. Mills Collection (S.H. and H. Chapman, April 1904) • J.M. Clapp • John H. Clapp • Clapp estate, 1942 • Louis E. Eliasberg Sr. Collection (Bowers and Merena, April 1997) lot 2179 • Old West & Franklinton Collections (American Numismatic Rarities, August 2006) lot 593.

Norweb Specimen. AU-58 (PCGS). David M. Bullowa, privately on August 8, 1953 • Norweb Collection (Bowers and Merena, November 1988) lot 3750 • Unknown intermediaries • Chris Napolitano • Cardinal Collection • Robert Lehmann • Private collector.

Queller Specimen. AU-58* (NGC). Spring Sale (Stack's, April 1978) lot 716 • Queller Family Collection of Silver Dollars (Heritage, April 2008) lot 2015 • Chicago ANA Sale (Stack's Bowers, August 2011) lot 7396.

Baldenhofer Specimen. AU-58 (NGC). Farish Baldenhofer • A.J. Ostheimer • Clarke Gilhousen (Superior, October 1973) lot 1225 • Royal Oak Collection (Heritage, August 2006) lot 5290 "Terminal Die State" • Orlando FUN Signature Sale (Heritage, January 2009) lot 3940 • Joseph C. Thomas Collection (Heritage, April 2009) lot 2544 • Warren Miller Collection.

Auction '83 Specimen. AU-58 (NGC). Auction '83 (Stack's, 1983) lot 720. "Uncirculated and choice." • New York ANA Sale (Superior, August 2002) lot 1067 • Cardinal Collection • Private collector • Denver Signature Sale (Heritage, August 2006) lot 5289 • Dr. Robert Hesselgesser Collection (Ira and Larry Goldberg, September 2011) lot 5030 • Pre-Long Beach Sale (Ira and Larry Goldberg, May 2012) lot 1275.

Stack's Spring Sale Specimen. MS-60+. Spring Sale (Stack's, 1978) lot 716, MS-60+.

Bergen Specimen. MS-60. Herbert M. Bergen sale (Quality Sales, October 1979) lot 1346. • Auction '84 (Paramount, 1984) lot 729. "Uncirculated-60."

Blauvelt Specimen. AU-58. Harold Blauvelt Collection (Bowers and Ruddy, 1977) lot 493. "Sharply struck and lustrous borderline Uncirculated."

Harte Specimen. AU-58. Roy Harte Collection (Bowers and Ruddy, 1977) lot 2784. "Borderline Uncirculated, small mark at top on the obverse."

Total Estimated Population
MS-65 or better: 0 (URS-0)
MS-64: 0 (URS-0)
MS-63: 2 (URS-2)
MS-60 to 62: 1 or 2 (URS-2)
AU-50 to 58: 25 to 40 (URS-6)
VF-20 to EF-45: 900 to 1,600 (URS-11)
G-4 to F-15: 350 to 500 (URS-10)
Total for all grades combined: 1,300 to 2,100 (URS-12)
Estimated Total Condition Census: 63-63-61-58 (multiples)

ADDITIONAL INFORMATION

Dickeson on 1797 Dollars (1859)

The following appeared in Dr. Montroville W. Dickeson's 1859 book, *An American Numismatical Manual:*

It is stated that the reverse was changed in this year, and a few trial pieces struck off. We have never met with them.

This commentary is enigmatic, and apart from the standard "Small Eagle" reverse, no distinctive design is known to modern numismatists, nor has any anomalous reverse been reported in numismatic literature after Dickeson's book.

Snowden's Commentary (1860)

The Cabinet Collection of the Mint of the United States, by James Ross Snowden, 1860, p. 108, told of the coinage of 1797: "The silver coins of 1797 have *sixteen* stars—one star for each state. Tennessee, the sixteenth state, was admitted into the Union in the latter part of the preceding year."

The Year 1797 in History

John Adams was inaugurated president on March 4, 1797. Adams was to become the first president to occupy the White House (in 1800), and also the longest-lived chief executive; he died at the age of 90. What became known as the XYZ Affair came about when France declared that Jay's Treaty of 1794 amounted to American support for the British, who were enemies of France. Adams sent a delegation (Charles Cotesworth Pinckney, of South Carolina; John Marshall, of Virginia; and Elbridge Gerry, of Massachusetts) to Paris to smooth over the situation, only to learn that three members of the French Directoire,

known only as X, Y, and Z, attempted to extort money from the Americans. Pinckney and Marshall came back to report the incident, and Congress was outraged. Many members called for war, but President Adams acted as pacifist and quieted the outrage. The XYZ Affair gave rise to a slogan first used by Robert Goodloe Harper as a toast at a banquet the following year, June 18, 1798 and later used on many Hard Times (circa 1837) and Civil War (circa 1862) tokens: "Millions for defense, but not one cent for tribute."

In a 1797 meeting of the American Philosophical Society, Dr. Benjamin Rush argued that black people had skin of that color because of a disease like leprosy, and used as his "evidence" the case of a Virginia black man, Henry Moss, whose skin had lightened in color after he had moved to the North. In Philadelphia, a central water supply using water from the Schuylkill River went into operation, becoming the first such municipal system in America. (An improvement, the Philadelphia aqueduct, opened on October 19, 1801.) In the same city in 1797, an epidemic of yellow fever drove many to the countryside; at the time, the cause of the scourge was not known. Eli Terry obtained the first United States patent for a clock; it was assembled from wooden components. Charles Newbold was granted the first American patent for a plow.

In England, the Soho Mint, operated by Boulton & Watt, issued large-size copper coins, including the famous "cartwheel" twopence. The steam-powered coinage devices in use in England were far more sophisticated than anything employed at the Philadelphia Mint at the time.

Henry Wm. Desaussure   Robert M. Patterson   Robert Patterson
David Rittenhouse
Elias Boudinot   George N. Eckert   Samuel Moore

A gallery of paintings illustrating directors of the United States Mint from 1792 through 1851. (From *Illustrated History of the United States Mint* by George C. Evans)

CHAPTER 11
1798 SILVER DOLLARS

MINTAGE (ALL TYPES)
Calendar year, Mint report: 327,536
Coins bearing date, author's estimate: 235,000
About 35,000 Small Eagle
About 200,000 Large Eagle

1798 SILVER DOLLARS

BB to Bolender to Haseltine Equivalents

BB Number	Bolender #	Haseltine #	Rarity	Average Grade
BB-81	B-2	H-2	URS-11	VF-27
BB-82	B-1	H-1	URS-11	VF-29
BB-91	B-32	---	URS-5	VF-24
BB-92	B-4	H-4	URS-9	VF-39
BB-93	B-5	H-5	URS-6	VF-30
BB-94	B-3	H-3	URS-9	VF-30
BB-95	B-7	H-7	URS-8	VF-22
BB-96	B-6	H-6	URS-10	VF-33
BB-101	B-17	H-17	URS-7	VF-26
BB-102	B-20	H-20	URS-8	VF-30
BB-103	B-18	H-18	URS-4	VG-10
BB-104	B-22	H-22	URS-9	VF-28
BB-105	B-23	H-23	URS-11	VF-33
BB-106	B-19	H-19	URS-8	VF-35
BB-107	B-21	H-21	URS-10	VF-33
BB-108	B-13	H-13	URS-11	VF-32
BB-109	B-10	H-10	URS-8	VF-27
BB-110	B-16	H-16	URS-6	VF-33
BB-111	B-11	H-11	URS-10	VF-25
BB-112	B-15	H-15	URS-10	VF-34
BB-113	B-27	H-27	URS-11	EF-40
BB-114	B-26	H-26	URS-7	VF-33
BB-115	B-31	---	URS-9	VF-30
BB-116	B-30	H-30	URS-9	VF-30
BB-117	B-33	---	URS-4	N/A
BB-118	B-28	H-28	URS-10	VF-32
BB-119	B-29	H-29	URS-9	VF-26
BB-120	B-12	H-12	URS-9	VF-25
BB-121	B-9	H-9	URS-10	VF-29
BB-122	B-14	H-14	URS-10	VF-25
BB-123	B-25	H-25	URS-10	VF-27
BB-124	B-24	H-24	URS-11	VF-30
BB-125	B-8	H-8	URS-11	VF-28

Coinage Context

Designs used: The year 1798 saw the number of obverse stars decreased from 16 (used in 1797) to 13, the number that remained in effect throughout the remainder of the series. An exception is provided by BB-81, with 15 stars, an anachronism created by using a leftover undated die prepared in 1795 or early 1796 (before the 16-star format became standard following the admission of Tennessee to the Union), and dating it 1798.

Two reverse designs were employed: the older Small Eagle type (1798 BB-81 and BB-82) and the new Heraldic Eagle motif (all other 1798 varieties BB-91 to BB-125). Large numbers of 1798 dollars minted were of the Heraldic Eagle type.

As the obverses for BB-81 and BB-82 (which have old-style Small Eagle reverses) were made early in the year, and as these each have a knob to the bottom of the 9 in the date (Knob 9), it is presumed that the with-knob numeral style was also used earlier in the year for obverse dies that were mated with Heraldic Eagle reverses. Conversely, the Pointed Tail 9 issue dies are believed to have been made later.

As a date, 1798 dollars are fairly plentiful. Examples are encountered in all grades, although those in AU and Mint State must be deemed rare.

Mintage figures: Government mintage figures give 327,536 as the number of coins struck during calendar year 1798, and this is undoubtedly true. However, I suggest that about 140,000 to 150,000 of these bore earlier dates, including 1795, 1796, and 1797. I believe that much if not all of the silver dollar production from January through early May bore dates prior to 1798. This was an economy move, for it was known that once the 13-star Draped Bust obverse and the Heraldic Eagle reverse became standard, all earlier dies would become obsolete.

Similarly, I believe that the two 1798-dated varieties with Small Eagle reverse (BB-81 and BB-82) were struck during the first part of the year, quite possibly in May. After that point, with decks cleared and all obsolete dies of earlier dates and types used, the minting of 1798-dated dollars with Heraldic Eagle reverse began in earnest. By that time, at least 140,000 (estimated) earlier-dated dollars had been struck. Some 1798-dated dollars were probably struck later, some in 1799 and others in 1800. At the time, the Mint was not at all concerned with using dies during the year stamped on them.

I estimate that about 235,000 silver dollars (within about 10%) were struck bearing the 1798 date. I believe that about 35,000 were of the Small Eagle reverse type (1798 BB-81 and BB-82) and 200,000 were of the Heraldic Eagle type (all others). Coinage of these 1798-dated coins probably commenced in May 1798 and continued to 1799 and/or 1800.

Delivery dates: The delivery dates for silver dollars in calendar year 1798 are given below. Gold $10 eagles may have used the same press, but this is not at all certain. It is possible that $10 pieces were struck on a smaller press used to strike half dollars of similar diameter. The $10 delivery dates, when known, are interspersed among the dollar delivery dates below.

Causes for the removal of a pair of dollar dies from the press would have included the following: 1. Need to use the press to coin $10 pieces. 2. Need to remove a broken die. 3. Need to remove a die for relapping. 4. Closing of the Mint, as for the periodic yellow fever epidemics (at intervals 1797-1799), when dies were taken to a bank vault.

The removal of two dies at once—to make way for the coining of $10 pieces in the press, or when the Mint was closed—would have ended one striking period (see later commentary concerning striking periods). Upon re-insertion of the dollar dies, another striking period would commence.

The 327,536 dollars (bearing various dates) minted in the calendar year 1798 were delivered as follows: (not including pieces reserved for the Assay Commission; these are given in parentheses). The annotations such as "production of" represent my opinion, not proven fact:

The delivery dates are given here, with $10 gold delivery dates interspersed in *italic* type:

January 5: 30,372 (+3 for the Assay Commission) Production of 1795-7 era dollars? • *January 11: 1,648 gold $10.* • January 18: 8,770 (+3) Production of 1795-7 era dollars? • *January 20: 1,097 gold $10.* • *January 23: 1,464 gold $10.* • January 27: 4,694 (+3) Production of 1795-7 era dollars? • *January 30: 2,023 gold $10.* • February 16: 25,500 (+3) Production of 1795-7 era dollars? • *February 17: 900 gold $10.* • *February 28: 842 gold $10.* • March 23: 22,000 (+3) Production of 1795-7 era dollars? • April 4: 35,500 (+3) Production of 1795-7 era dollars? • April 14: 3,000 (+3) Production of 1795-7 era dollars? • May 4: 39,000 (+3) Production of 1795-7 era dollars(?) and some 1798 BB-81 and/or BB-82. • May 24: 10,000 (+3) Production of 1798 BB-81 and/or BB-82 Small Eagle reverse dollars. • June 11: 37,000 (+3) Some production of 1798 BB-81 and/or BB-82. Plus initial Heraldic Eagle dollars. • June 22: 15,000 (+3) Production of 1798-dated Heraldic Eagle dollars. • June 30: 7,370 (+3) Production of 1798-dated Heraldic Eagle dollars. • July 23: 3,000 (+1) Production of 1798-dated Heraldic Eagle dollars. • August 15: 32,720 (+3) Production of 1798-dated Heraldic Eagle dollars. • December 31: 44,610 (+3) Production of 1798-dated Heraldic Eagle dollars.

Numismatic Information

Die making: Working dies for 1798 dollars were probably prepared as follows:

Obverse: The bust of Miss Liberty was punched into the die, after which the letters of LIBERTY, the stars, and the digits in 1798 were all added with individual punches. In some instances, dies may have been made in advance with just the digits 179, with the final digit (8 or 9) to be added in the year it was used.

Reverse (Heraldic Eagle type): First, the Heraldic Eagle motif punch itself was made by a intaglio cutting of the eagle, shield, and ribbon design, after which a transfer master die or punch was raised (in relief), and the letters E PLURIBUS UNUM were individually punched in the ribbon. The master Heraldic Eagle punch included the eagle, clouds above the eagle, branch, leaves, and some rudiments of the lower parts of the arrows. This master punch, in relief, was punched into the center of the working die. Added separately to the working die were the letters of UNITED STATES OF AMERICA, the stars above the eagle, the olive branch, berries, the tops of the arrows, the arrowheads, and details of the lower parts of the arrows.

Attribution points for Heraldic Eagle reverse dollars: The elements on the obverse and reverse dies that were punched separately differ minutely in their placement from one another, and are a guide to attribution. The attribution points given below can be used for all varieties of the Draped Bust obverse, Heraldic Eagle reverse type dated from 1798 through 1804. Key points to check for differences include these:

KEYS TO ATTRIBUTING DRAPED BUST OBVERSE DIES:

The stars are numbered beginning to the left of the date. On the standard 13-star obverse, star 1 is to the left of the date, and star 7 is next to the L in LIBERTY. Star 8 is adjacent to the Y in LIBERTY, and star 13 is near the bust. With this in mind, star positions of importance include these:

Distance of star 1 from the date and/or the lowest curl.
Distance of star 7 from the L in LIBERTY.
Distance of star 8 from the Y in LIBERTY.
Distance of star 13 from the bust.

Often, a comparison can be made, such as "star 7 is closer to the L than star 8 is from the Y or star 13 is from the bust," etc.

The positions of the stars in relation to each other is important. For example, among stars 1 to 7 on the left, an examination may reveal that one or two pairs are very close, and another pair or two are unusually widely separated. Similarly, stars 8 through 13 on the right will usually have noticeable positional differences.

The word LIBERTY can be examined for broken letter segments, and for the spacing between letters, although such spacing differences are often hard to discern.

The highest wave of Miss Liberty's hair in relation to the letters in LIBERTY is a useful guidepost. Usually, it is under the upright of the E, but sometimes it is more under the center of the E, or, very occasionally, toward the right.

If a die has been relapped, often the highest wave of Miss Liberty's hair is indistinct or missing.

The date has several features, including the style of the numerals (Knob 9 or Pointed 9 among 1798 dollars), the shape of the 7, the distance of the numerals from each other and their alignment in relation to each other, and their distance from the lowest curl, the neck truncation, and the dentils.

KEYS TO ATTRIBUTING HERALDIC EAGLE REVERSE DIES:

Large Letters (used only in early 1798) or Small Letters (used later in 1798 and in all later years of dollars dated through 1804).

Placement of the letters in STATES OF in relation to the clouds below.

The leftmost one or two arrows and their position in relation to the UN of UNITED.

The arrow shafts, the arrowheads, and the arrow feathers, with regard to their placement, size, and appearance (note: if a die has been relapped or ground down, the arrow shafts will become thinner, and the arrowheads may be disconnected; this does not constitute a separate variety, just a separate die state).

The berries and their placement on the branch.

The end of the branch—its length, formation, and the direction in which it points.

The position of leaf tips in relation to the letters ICA in AMERICA.

The position of the first A in AMERICA in relation to the eagle's wing feathers (such differences are often minor, however).

The stars above the eagle, including the position of star point(s) in relation to the eagle's beak, the eight clouds, and to other stars. The star points in relation to the letters IBU in PLURIBUS are often used as points of differentiation.

The pattern of arrangement of the stars—arc or line.

The letters in E PLURIBUS UNUM.

ADDITIONAL ATTRIBUTION GUIDES (OBVERSE AND REVERSE):

The following additional key points can be used if needed, but are not as popular as those already mentioned.

The relationship of star points, letters, or numerals to dentils can be used to differentiate dies, but is not usually employed when more obvious differences can be found.

By means of an optical measuring device, distances and relationships of letters, stars, motifs, etc., can be measured in millimeters. To date, this has not been a popular discipline.

DIE STATES AS AN ATTRIBUTION GUIDE:

Often, a particular die variety usually or always (so far as is known) is seen with a distinctive die crack. These can be used as attribution guides. A problem develops if a coin is of an unlisted die state, without the usual die crack, or if it has a die crack which has not been recorded in the literature. I suggest that die cracks be used to verify a variety and, of course, to help determine a die state. However, in all instances other points of difference should be examined to be sure that a given variety has correct positional relationships of stars, letters, etc.

EDGE LETTERING:

Each silver dollar of this era has the edge lettered HUNDRED CENTS ONE DOLLAR OR UNIT (plus ornamentation). As photographs do not usually include edge lettering, and as the edges of coins sealed in holders cannot be examined easily (if at all), it is not easy for a scholar to gain information. In the Washington token, half cent, large cent, half dollar, and pattern coin series, edge lettering has been studied in detail, but thus far, virtually no research has been done on circulation strike dollars of the 1794-1803 dates.

Russell J. Logan has written the following:[1]

As you are well aware, the sequence in which the working dies were made is not necessarily the same as they were used.... The life of the Castaing edge lettering machine dies used for the *half* dollars [a denomination studied by Logan in detail] was approximately three times longer than either the obverse or reverse dies; consequently, the information derived from studying their emission sequence is paramount in establishing the emission order of the coins. Identifying each silver dollar edge die by its own diagnostic features and then sorting by die wear is required for a striking emission sequence of this series.

Numeral styles: There are two basic styles of 9 on the 1798 obverse dies.

Knob 9: The first and earlier numeral style is the Knob 9, which is found on 1798 BB-81 and BB-82 (the Small Eagle reverse dollars made early in the year) as well as Heraldic Eagle reverse varieties BB-91 through BB-96.

Pointed Tail 9. The second and later numeral style is the Pointed Tail 9, used on all other varieties from 1798 BB-101 to BB-125.

The underside of the curved upper part of the Pointed Tail 9 has a little "spur" or metal burr extending downward to the left, from a defect on the number punch. In 1950, M.H. Bolender noted that he had seen the spur plainly on the varieties known today as BB-104, BB-105, BB-108, BB-109, BB-112, BB-120, BB-122, and BB-123. As this spur is weak on some varieties and stronger on others, attribution should not be based upon this feature. Pointed Tail 9s, including many with spurs, are seen on all dollars dated 1799 as well.

The following commentary is by Walter H. Breen: [2]

It is known that Thomas Bingham cut a new 8 punch (small 8 for the Pointed 9 obverse coins), and that Mint Director Elias Boudinot paid him 50 cents for it on February 1, 1798; no one knows when obverses bearing it were used.

Type fonts / shield element lines: The Large Letters type punch font, first used on 1796 Draped Bust/Small Eagle dollars with Large Letters reverse, and distinguished by having slightly larger letters than used later in 1798, and in later years through 1803, was employed on two 1798 Heraldic Eagle reverse dies. These two dies each produced two varieties: 1798 BB-91 and BB-92 (from the first die) and BB-96 and BB-101 (from the other). It seems a virtual certainty that these were the first Heraldic Eagle reverse dies made in 1798, after which the Large Letters punches were abandoned in favor of the new Small Letters punches. This chronology is further borne out by their use (except BB-101) with Knob 9 obverses. BB-101—a Large Letters reverse mated with a Pointed Tail 9 obverse—indicates that dies were not always employed in the order in which they were made; this variety was struck later in the year.

Inspection will show that certain letters in the Large Letters font can be quickly recognized. The A in the Large Letters font has a larger interior space in the top than does the later Small Letters font, and is beveled at the upper left top of the letter. The S in the Large Letters font is more open, the C is larger and more open, and certain other letters display minor differences.

The two Large Letters reverses have another distinguishing feature, further strengthening the claim that they were the first made of the Heraldic Eagle type: Each vertical element in the shield is composed of *five* lines, whereas on all other 1798 reverses, and all other Heraldic Eagle reverses through the end of the early dollar series, each vertical element has just four lines.[3]

Among other features, the Small Letters font has a lopsided T, with the left serif shorter than the right. This Small Letters set of punches remained on hand at the Mint for many years, and in the 1830s it was used to create two Heraldic Eagle reverse dies as well as Draped Bust obverse dies dated 1802, 1803, and 1804.

E PLURIBUS UNUM letters: The letters in E PLURIBUS UNUM vary in their apparent size (caused by different sizes of letter punches or the depth they were punched into the ribbon) and placement on certain varieties. Points of difference include the shapes and proportions of

---

[1] Excerpted and lightly edited from a letter to the author, January 11, 1993.

[2] Breen commentaries are those either created especially for this book or are from *Walter Breen's Complete Encyclopedia of U.S. and Colonial Coins.*

[3] This five-lines characteristic was first pointed out to the author by Thomas K. DeLorey, letter dated January 13, 1993.

such letters as P, R, S, and U. Placement differences to note are the position of the U and S in PLURIBUS with regard to the edge of the eagle's neck on the left, and the placement of the N in UNUM in relation to the edge of the eagle's neck on the right. In general, letters in the motto were smaller in 1798 and 1799, and larger from 1800 onward. A challenge for the future is to catalog the Heraldic Eagle punches using this and other features.

Reverse star patterns: The arrangement of the 13 stars above the eagle's head on the reverse can be divided into two separate styles for 1798:

• **Arc star pattern:** The stars are arranged in arcs, the topmost having six stars arranged in an arc and being closest to the clouds, the second having five stars arranged in an arc concentric below the first, and the two extra stars being one to the left of the eagle's head and the other to the right. The arc pattern dies were cut earlier than the line pattern dies, it would seem from their general use in earlier die combinations. In nearly all instances, the arc patterns were punched into the die in a pleasing manner. An exception is the reverse of 1798 BB-121, which has the leftmost star in the second arc too high and out of place. The arc pattern was the standard for certain silver and gold denominations through the year 1807. On silver dollars, the arc pattern was used on some 1798 dies, as noted here, all 1799 dies except one (1799 BB-182, the reverse of which was coined from a 1798 line star-pattern die used to coin 1798 BB-123 and 1798 BB-124), and all issues from 1800 onward.

The following 1798-dated silver dollar varieties have the arc pattern to the stars:

1798 BB-94, BB-95, BB-102 to BB-113, BB-116 to BB-118, BB-121, and BB-125.

• **Line star pattern:** This "line" pattern arrangement is called the "cross" pattern by Robert P. Hilt III and Walter H. Breen. The stars above the eagle are arranged in lines that are more or less straight, with the star directly over the eagle's head being the center of a flattened X.

I recognize the line star pattern as three stars in a straight line beneath the clouds on the left, no star directly under cloud 4, and three more stars in a straight line beneath the clouds on the right; the straight lines are parallel to the cloud bottoms and are at an angle to each other. Below this pair of angled straight lines is a "peak" formed of five stars, peaking at the center (the star directly over the eagle's head). The two extra stars are arranged to the left of the eagle's head and the other to the right (as also on the arc style).

The line pattern of star arrangement appears on a few silver dollars dated 1798 and one dated 1799 (from a leftover 1798 reverse die) and on certain other denominations. Apparently, this arrangement was found to be unsatisfactory, for it was soon discontinued. To my eye, the line pattern is not as pleasing as the arc pattern. Breen

notes that the 14-star "line pattern" dies used on the 1804 quarter eagles and the 1804-1805 dimes have the same letter punches of those of 1798, suggesting they were left over. The following 1798-dated silver dollar varieties have the line pattern to the stars:

1798 BB-91 to BB-93, BB-96, BB-101, BB-114, BB-115, BB-119, BB-120, BB-122 to BB-124.

1799 BB-182 also has the line star pattern and was struck from the reverse die used to coin 1798 BB-123 and BB-124; all other 1799 dollars have the arc star pattern.

Arrows styles: The arrows held by the eagle on the reverse can be grouped into two major categories as follows:

Early Style Arrows: The four highest arrows on the right consist of, left to right, a fully developed arrow, a partially developed arrow or sometimes just a stick, and then two fully developed arrows. The three leftmost arrows consist of a stick or poorly developed arrow (which is the longest of the three), then two progressively shorter, fully developed arrows to the left. 1798 dollars with Early Style Arrows include these:

1798 BB-91 to BB-96, BB-101, BB-102, BB-107, BB-108, BB-121, and BB-125,

Late Style Arrows: The four highest arrows on the right have their arrowhead tips arranged in a gentle arc sloping downward to the right. These arrowheads are close together. The three leftmost arrows are progressively shorter, with the very leftmost arrow being significantly shorter than the two to its immediate right. 1798 dollars with Late Style Arrows include these:

1798 BB-103 to BB-106, BB-109 to BB-115, BB-116 (with some characteristics of Early Style Arrows), BB-117 to BB-120, BB-122, BB-123, and BB-124.

Sequences: Among 1798-dated Draped Bust obverse, Heraldic Eagle reverse silver dollars, there are two sequences that can be followed. The first is of the time of die manufacture, and the second is of the time of die use. Each follows a different progression.

In general, it seems that the Knob 9 obverse dies were made first, as the Knob 9 numeral is found on 1797 dies (the year before). In contrast, the Pointed 9 obverses follow the style of 1799 and later years. Among Pointed 9 obverses, those with the numerals closer together may have been made earlier.

Among the Heraldic Eagle reverses, the two dies with Large Letters were probably made first, as the punches are from the 1796-7 Large Letters font. Those with arc star patterns were made earliest (and incorporate the Large Letters font in two dies) and also latest. The line star-pattern reverses were made sometime in between.

A problem arises in that when 1798 silver dollars were struck, the use of the dies was not in the order in which the dies were made. As an example, the Large Letters reverse used to coin 1798 BB-94 and BB-95, both from early

Knob 9 obverses, was also combined with a later Pointed 9 obverse to coin 1798 BB-102. Similarly, the other Large Letters reverse was used to coin 1798 BB-121, which employs a later Pointed 9 obverse.

Using the obverses as starting points, and employing die linkage, the following "striking periods" are observed:

Striking Period 1.

1798 BB-81. Small Eagle, Small Letters reverse die of 1795.

Striking Period 2.

1798 BB-82. Knob 9 obverse. Small Eagle, Large Letters reverse die of 1797. This striking marked the end of the era of the Small Eagle reverse, which had begun in late 1795. • 1798 BB-91. Knob 9 obverse. Heraldic Eagle reverse type (as are all following). Large Letters on reverse. • 1798 BB-92. Knob 9 obverse. Large Letters on reverse. • 1798 BB-93. Knob 9 obverse. Small Letters on reverse. • 1798 BB-94. Knob 9 obverse. Small Letters on reverse. • 1798 BB-95. Knob 9 obverse. Small Letters on reverse. • 1798 BB-96. Knob 9 obverse. Large Letters on reverse. This striking probably marked the end of the use of dies with Knob 9. • 1798 BB-101. Pointed 9 obverse. Large Letters on reverse. Probably, the first use of the Pointed 9 obverse.

Striking Period 3.

Striking time indeterminate, but after Striking Period 2. This striking period could have been at any later time; it is not necessarily contiguous to Striking Period 2.

1798 BB-102. Pointed 9 obverse (as are all following). Small Letters on reverse (as are all following). To coin BB-102, the reverse die used to coin BB-94 and then BB-95 (after which it was removed from the press) was put back in the press and combined with a hitherto unused obverse. • 1798 BB-103. • 1798 BB-104. • 1798 BB-105. • 1798 BB-106.

Striking Period 4.

Striking time indeterminate, but after Striking Period 2. This striking period could have been at any later time; it is not necessarily contiguous to Striking Period 2.

1798 BB-107. To coin BB-107, the obverse die used to coin BB-102 and then BB-103 (after which it was removed from the press) was put back in the press and combined with a hitherto unused reverse. • 1798 BB-108. • 1798 BB-109. Dies were removed from the press, and then used again (see next striking period, which may not have been contiguous). Perhaps the press had to be used for other purposes in the interim.

Striking Period 5.

1798 BB-108. Additional coinage from this die pair.

Striking Period 6.

This large interrelated group was struck at an unknown time after Striking Period 2.

1798 BB-110. • 1798 BB-111. • 1798 BB-112. • 1798 BB-113. • 1798 BB-114. • 1798 BB-115. • 1798 BB-116. • 1798 BB-117. • 1798 BB-118. • 1798 BB-119. • 1798 BB-120.

Striking Period 7.

A stand-alone striking, not die linked to any other. 1798 BB-120.

Striking Period 8.

A stand-alone striking, not die linked to any other. 1798 BB-121.

Striking Period 9.

A stand-alone striking, not die linked to any other. 1798 BB-122.

Striking Period 10.

Striking time unknown, but these varieties are candidates for having been struck in 1799 or 1800.

1798 BB-123. • 1798 BB-124. • 1799 BB-182, which was used in a separate series of interrelated 1799 dollars, not *continuously* punch-linked to the 1798 group.

Striking Period 11.

A stand-alone striking, not die linked to any other. 1798 BB-125.

Summary of Characteristics

1798 Small Eagle and Heraldic Eagle

Circulation Strikes

Enabling legislation: Act of April 2, 1792

Designer of obverse: Robert Scot (after Stuart), model by John Eckstein

Designer of reverse (Small Eagle): Robert Scot, model by John Eckstein

Designer of reverse (Heraldic Eagle): Robert Scot (from the Great Seal)

Statutory weight: 416 grains; .8924 silver, balance copper

Melting value (silver bullion value) in year minted: Considered by Mint officials to be on a par with the Spanish dollar, and worth about $1.00 intrinsically (see discussion under Summary of Characteristics, 1794).

Dies prepared (Draped Bust obverse, Small Eagle reverse): Obverse: At least 2; Reverse: At least 2 (1 left over from 1795)

Dies prepared (Draped Bust obverse, Heraldic Eagle reverse): Obverse: At least 17; Reverse: At least 19.

Circulation strike mintage, calendar year: 327,536 (for all 1798 varieties combined, not including pieces reserved for the Assay Commission; these are given in parentheses); Delivery figures by day: January 5: 30,372 (+3); January 18: 8,770 (+3); January 27: 4,694 (+3) • February 16: 25,500 (+3) • March 23: 22,000 (+3) • April 4: 35,500 (+3) • April 14: 3,000 (+3) • May 4: 39,000 (+3) • May 24: 10,000 (+3) • June 11: 37,000 (+3) • June 22: 15,000 (+3) • June 30: 7,370 (+3) • July 23: 3,000 (+1) • August 15: 32,720 (+3) • December 31: 44,610 (+3).

Estimated circulation strike mintage of 1798-dated dollars (author's estimate): 235,000 (rounded).

Estimated quantity melted: Normal melting and export.

Estimated total population: Draped Bust Obverse, Small Eagle Reverse (BB-81 and BB-82)

MS-65 or better: 0 (URS-0)

MS-64: 1 or 2 (URS-1)

MS-63: 1 or 2 (URS-1)

MS-60 to 62: 6 to 12 (URS-5)

AU-50 to 58: 20 to 40 (URS-6)

VF-20 to EF-45: 850 to 1,500 (URS-12)

G-4 to F-15: 350 to 600 (URS-10)

Total for all grades combined: 1,200 to 2,500 (URS-12)

Estimated Total Condition Census: 64-63-62-60-58 (multiples)

Characteristics of striking: Varies. BB-81 always has the reverse weakly struck, due to the die characteristics.

Estimated total population: Draped Bust Obverse, Heraldic Eagle Reverse (BB-91 through BB-125)

MS-65 or better: 2 to 3 (URS-2)

MS-64: 3 to 4 (URS-3)

MS-63: 12 to 18 (URS-5)

MS-60 to 62: 50 to 85 (URS-8)

AU-50 to 58: 175 to 350 (URS-9)

VF-20 to EF-45: 5,000 to 9,000 (URS-14)

G-4 to F-15: 2,000 to 4,000 (URS-13)

Total for all grades combined: 7,000 to 14,000 (URS-15)

Estimated Total Condition Census: 65-64-64-64-63 (multiples)

Characteristics of striking: Depends upon the variety. If weakly struck, this is often observed at the center of the obverse and among the stars above the eagle on the reverse.

Commentary: 1798 silver dollars exist with two major reverse types, Small Eagle and Heraldic Eagle, of which the former is much the scarcer.

1798 Draped Bust/Small Eagle Varieties

1798 15 Stars, Small Eagle, Small Letters, BB-81

(B-2, H-2)

Obverse: *15 stars.* The only 1798 dollar with 15 stars. Undoubtedly, this die was made in 1795 or before June 1796, during which time 15 stars were standard; the die was complete except for the date. In 1798 the uncompleted die had the date added and was used to coin this variety. (Alternatively and less likely, it could have been a die cutting error similar to the 1817 15-stars cent.)

The highest wave of hair is incomplete, probably from relapping, which also caused certain lower hair curls to be incomplete. B and R in LIBERTY each tilted slightly right.

Wide numeral 8 in date; with top interior space of 8 a *horizontal oval* and the bottom a *circle;* a punch unique to this obverse, not used elsewhere in the early dollar series (not for the 8 on later dates such as 1800, 1801, etc., which have vertical oval spaces within the 8). This distinctive 8 punch was regularly used on 1798 $10 gold coins. It is possible that the obverse die was made circa 1795 but with just the first three date digits, 179, punched in; the final 8 could have been added in 1798 by selecting a punch from the wrong font. Squared-off bottom to 7.

Obverse die used to strike 1798 BB-81 only.

Reverse: Described under 1795 BB-51, herewith repeated: Small Eagle. Small Letters in legend. Eagle stands on clouds. Wreath is composed of a palm branch (right) and olive branch (left), the latter with seven berries. *Berry under A of STATES;* a quick way to identify this reverse.

This identical die, now relapped (as it had been since the coinages of 1796), was used in combination with six

obverses during its life. The definition on the reverse is weak, due to the lapping of an already shallow cut die.

Reverse die used to strike 1795 BB-51; 1796 BB-62, BB-63, and BB-66 (now relapped); 1797 BB-72; and 1798 BB-81.

Die States

Die State I: Early state without obverse relapping; highest wave of hair boldly defined. May not exist.

Die State II: Lapped obverse die; without obverse die cracks. This is the state typically encountered.

Die State III: A few pieces show extended obverse cracks (cf. 1975 ANA: 849). Very rare.

Collecting Notes

Of the two 1798 dollars with Small Eagle reverse (BB-81 and BB-82), BB-81 is the rarer by a slight amount. An estimated 500 to 800 exist. Most examples of BB-81 are seen in lower grades. VF is about par, even in some of the finest collections.

The 15-star count on the obverse (the type of '95 and '96) makes the 1795 BB-81 variety especially desirable as a major type. All other 1798 obverses, regardless of reverse type, have the standard 13 stars. The use of the much-mated Small Letters reverse die with this unusual obverse lends further interest. Here, indeed, is one of the most desirable varieties among early dollars.

Most if not all specimens of 1798 BB-81 have light striking at the centers of the topmost obverse stars. The bottom stars—especially 1, 2, 13, 14, and 15—are usually sharp. The reverse is always weaker than the obverse (an identical situation to that of 1797 BB-72), with the result that grading is by the obverse only. A coin with a VF-30 obverse typically has a reverse grading F-15 to VF-20.

Notable Specimens

Miller Specimen. MS-63 (NGC). Ostheimer Collection (Superior, August 1975) lot 849 • Warren Miller Collection. Die State III.

Eliasberg Specimen. MS-62+ (PCGS). Louis E. Eliasberg Sr. Collection (Bowers and Merena, April 1997) lot 2180. Die State II • New York Gold Mart • Private collector • Cardinal Collection • Legend Numismatics • Phillip Flannagan Collection (Bowers and Merena, November 2011) lot 4230 • Cardinal Collection (American Numismatic Rarities, June 2005) lot 23 • Private Midwest collection.

Queller Specimen. MS-60 (NGC). Stack's, privately March 1979 • Queller Family Collection of Silver Dollars (Heritage, April 2008) lot 2016 • Orlando Rarities Sale (Bowers and Merena, January 2009) lot 768.

Garrett Specimen. AU-58 (PCGS). Garrett Collection • Johns Hopkins University (Bowers and Ruddy, March 1980) lot 687 • FUN Convention Sale (Mid American, January 1987) lot 687 • Auction '87 (Superior, July 1987) lot 1812. • ANA Mid-Winter Auction (Heritage, March 1988) lot 940 • Premier Sale (Superior, January 1995) lot 939, as AU-58 (NGC) • Private collector • Cardinal Collection •

BB-81: Late die state with extended die crack from border to Liberty's throat.

Private collector • Pre-Long Beach Sale (Ira and Larry Goldberg, February 2008) lot 2866.

Carter Specimen. AU-58 (PCGS). Amon Carter Jr. Collection (Stack's, January 1984) lot • Unknown intermediaries • Private Midwest collection.

Hesselgesser Specimen. AU-55+ (PCGS). Private Western collection • Dr. Robert Hesselgesser Collection (Ira and Larry Goldberg, September 2011) lot 5031 • Pre-Long Beach Sale (Ira and Larry Goldberg, May 2012) lot 1276.

Clarke Specimen. AU-55 (PCGS). James G. Macallister. • T. James Clarke Collection (New Netherlands 48th Sale, 1956) lot 621. "Strictly Uncirculated." unknown intermediaries • Long Beach Signature Sale (Heritage, September 2007) lot 1866, as AU-58 (NGC) • Dr. Robert Hesselgesser Collection • Dale Friend Collection.

Total Estimated Population
MS-65 or better: 0 (URS-0)
MS-64: 0 (URS-0)
MS-63: 1 (URS-1)
MS-60 to 62: 3 or 4 (URS-3)
AU-50 to 58: 15 to 30 (URS-5)
VF-20 to EF-45: 300 to 525 (URS-10)
G-4 to F-15: 200 to 350 (URS-9)
Total for all grades combined: 500 to 900 (URS-11)
Estimated Total Condition Census: 63-62-60-58-58-55 (multiples)

1798 13 Stars obverse, Small Eagle reverse, Large Letters, BB-82

(B-1, H-1)

Obverse: 13 Stars (standard star count of the year), arranged 7 left and 6 right. Close date, knob 9, figures 98 close. Squared-off bottom to 7. The space between stars 6 and 7 is wider than the spaces between any stars 1 through 6. On the right, the space between stars 10 and 11 is wider than the spaces between any stars 8 through 13. Ray of star 13 points at junction of bosom and drapery.

Obverse die used to strike 1798 BB-82 (earlier use) and BB-91 (later use).

Reverse: Small Eagle, Large Letters style. Struck from the same die used to strike *1797* BB-73. Eight berries in left branch. Lowest berry near ribbon bow is on *inside* of wreath. E of STATES lightly repunched. A leaf points to the left corner of the I in UNITED, another leaf points to the left corner of the first T in STATES while another leaf points to the very end of the O in OF. Another leaf is positioned away from the R in AMERICA.

This reverse die was used earlier to strike 1797 BB-73 dollars, Die States I through IV, then removed from the press and used to strike 1798 BB-82 Die State I (with cracks slightly advanced from 1797 Die State IV) and Die State II (equivalent to 1797 BB-73 Die State V), then the striking of 1798 BB-82 dollars was discontinued, and the reverse die was re-mated with the same 1797 obverse, and additional 1797 BB-73 dollars were struck.

Reverse die used to strike 1797 BB-73 and 1798 BB-82.

Die States

Die State I: Obverse perfect (not relapped). Reverse as preceding. May not exist.

Die State II: Obverse die relapped. Highest wave of hair not fully defined. Lowest curl, near date, is incomplete. Stars somewhat spidery. REVERSE: Crack in the field from the border above the upper left of D to the border above upper right of first T in STATES. Irregular vertical

crack between branch and side of eagle's right (observer's left) wing. Light crack connects dentil with upper part of second T in STATES and continues downward to branch. Crack from right base of I (in AMERICA) to branch. Crack from center of E through D continuing through S, curving upward to border through T. Crack from same T through ES to topmost palm leaf. Crack from tops of OF through center of AM. (Equivalent to die state intermediate between 1797 Die State IV and V)

Die State III: Bolender-1a. (Equivalent to 1797 BB-73 Die State V) Obverse as preceding. Reverse with die cracks slightly advanced. Crack connecting dentil with upper part of second T in STATES and continuing downward to branch is now much heavier from dentil to top of T. Crack develops from left base of N in UNITED and goes through leaf tip to connect with earlier crack from right base of I to branch. Cf. Bowers and Merena, Somerset Collection, 1992, lot 1318.

Collecting Notes

Of the two 1798 die varieties with Small Eagle reverse (BB-81 and BB-82), 1798 BB-82 is the more plentiful, but only by a slight margin. 1798 BB-82 is the only 1798-dated dollar with 13 obverse stars in combination with the Small Eagle reverse; all others are mated with the Heraldic Eagle reverse.

An estimated 700 to 1,000 1798 BB-82 silver dollars exist. Several hundred specimens exist, most of which are Very Fine. EF examples are quite scarce, and any coin in better grade is rare. True Mint State coins are great rarities. I am not aware of any Mint State coin sold in recent years. The Thomas Cleneay listing below is "ancient history" numismatically.

Notable Specimens

Cleneay Specimen. MS-64. The Thomas Cleneay Collection gem (Chapman brothers, 1890) may be the only truly Mint State example known and is arbitrarily designated as MS-64 in the Population Distribution below.

Milwaukee ANA Specimen. MS-61 (PCGS). Milwaukee ANA Signature Sale (Heritage, August 2007) lot 1717, as AU-58 (PCGS) • Private Texas collection, subsequently re-graded by PCGS as MS-61.

Miller Specimen. MS-60 (NGC). Frank Stirling Collection (Heritage, February 1986) lot 1187 • Warren Miller Collection.

Cardinal Specimen. AU-58 (PCGS). Farish Baldenhofer Collection (Stack's, 1955) lot 970 • Lexington Collection (Bowers and Merena, January 1994) lot 1277 • Unknown intermediaries • Tangible Asset Galleries • Private collector • Tangible Asset Galleries • Cardinal Collection (American Numismatic Rarities, June 2005) lot 24 • Legend Numismatics • Naples III Collection • Don Willis • Dr. Robert Hesselgesser Collection (Ira and Larry Goldberg, May 2011) lot 883.

Thomas Specimen. AU-58 (NGC). Orlando Signature Sale (Heritage, January 2008) lot 2925 • Joseph C. Thomas Collection (Heritage, April 2009) lot 2546 • Private collector • Pre-Long Beach Sale (Ira and Larry Goldberg, September 2011) lot 1472 • CSNS Signature Sale (Heritage, April 2012) lot 5154 • Dallas ANA Money Show Sale (Heritage, October 2012) lot 4568.

Dallas ANA Money Show Specimen. AU-58 (NGC). Dallas ANA Money Show Sale (Heritage, October 2012) lot 4567.

Eliasberg Specimen. AU-55 (PCGS). John G. Mills Collection, S.H. and H. Chapman, April 27-29, 1904 • J.M. Clapp • John H. Clapp • Clapp Estate, 1942 • Louis E. Eliasberg Sr. Collection (Bowers and Merena, April 1997) lot 2181. Die State III, advanced cracks on the reverse, almost to the *shattered* state • Thaler Collection.

Queller Specimen. AU-55 (NGC). December Sale (Stack's, December 1984) lot 1082 • Queller Family Collection of Silver Dollars (Heritage, April 2008) lot 2017.

Farouk Specimen. AU-55. King Farouk Collection, Palace Collections (Sotheby's, Cairo, Egypt, 1953) • A.J. Ostheimer 3rd Collection (Lester Merkin, 1968) lot 244. "Practically Uncirculated."

Kagin Specimen. AU-55. Metropolitan Washington Convention Sale (Kagin's, 1980) lot 708. "Choice AU-55 • GENA Convention Sale (Kagin's, 1981) lot 1336 • GENA Convention Sale (Kagin's, 1982) lot 456.

DeCoppet Specimen. AU-50. James Kelly, 1955. "Practically Uncirculated."

Hollinbeck-Kagin Specimen. AU-50. September 1970, lot 884. "Nearly."

George III Counterstamp. Octagonal counterstamp with portrait of George III, impressed by the Bank of England, to use the silver dollar as one of many substitutes for British five-shilling pieces, which at the time were scarce in circulation. Howard D. Gibbs Collection, Hans M.F. Schulman, 1960: 100. Host coin EF. "There is one other specimen known, U.S. dollar 1798 in the British Museum." Oval (earlier) and octagonal (later) counterstamps were applied by the Bank of England on Spanish eight reales pieces (primarily) bearing the portrait of King Charles. Numerous counterfeit counterstamp punches were made by unauthorized parties. An oval stamp is known on a Flowing Hair 1795 dollar.[1]

Total Estimated Population

MS-65 or better: 0 (URS-0)
MS-64: 1 (URS-1)
MS-63: 0 (URS-0)
MS-60 to 62: 2 (URS-2)
AU-50 to 58: 5 to 10 (URS-4)
VF-20 to EF-45: 550 to 950 (URS-11)
G-4 to F-15: 150 to 250 (URS-9)
Total for all grades combined: 700 to 1,200 (URS-11)
Estimated Total Condition Census: 64-61-60-58 (multiples)

---

[1] Certain of this information is from Dr. Robert Stark, letter to the author, January 1, 1993.

1798 HERALDIC EAGLE VARIETIES

1798 KNOB 9, HERALDIC EAGLE, BB-91

Line star pattern on reverse.
Large Letters reverse, 5 lines in each shield element. (B-32)
Obverse: See description under 1798 BB-82. 13 stars.

Obverse die used to strike 1798 BB-82 (earlier use) and BB-91 (later use).

Reverse: Large Letters reverse from 1796 type font (larger interior space in A, open S, etc.); 5 lines in each vertical shield element. This was one of the first Heraldic Eagle reverse dies cut in early 1798. Upper part of eagle's beak touches ray of star slightly in from its tip; star points to upper left serif of U in PLURIBUS. Line star pattern. Three stars on left between eagle's beak and clouds are more in a slightly curved line than in form of a triangle. Leftmost star is puny and undersized. Two eagle claw nails show within talons. Leaf points close to left corner of I in AMERICA, and 4th outside leaf tip is under right base of R in AMERICA. *Tip of branch points to tip of rightmost tail feather* (compare to reverses of BB-117 and BB-118, the only other 1798 reverses in which this is the case). Berry fairly close to right side of serif of left foot of A. Only 10 perfect arrows, one faint arrow, and two sticks (one of which extends to below center of I in UNITED). Three rightmost perfect arrows each have other arrows on top of them, with arrowheads visible part way down shafts. Raised die defects at AT in STATES.

Reverse die used to strike 1798 BB-91 (earlier use) and BB-92 (later use).

Die States

Die State I: Obverse: Earlier state of the preceding. May not exist.

Die State II: Obverse: With failure at stars 6 and 7 and at base of L in LIBERTY. Faint die crack from ribbon to rim, between 3rd and 4th stars, another minute crack just left of 8 in date, from rim to bust, and another farther to the right, near the drapery end, from the center of a dentil.

Collecting Notes

I estimate that about 10 to 20 exist of the variety here described as BB-91. The record is not clear on these, for over the years the appellation "Bolender-32," equivalent to BB-91, has been assigned to a number of different unusual and/or otherwise unlisted issues.

This obverse was earlier mated with a Small Eagle reverse (style of 1795-8) to create BB-82, a variety minted early in 1798. Accordingly, BB-91 was probably one of the earliest varieties struck with the Heraldic Eagle reverse.

Notable Specimens

Cardinal Specimen. MS-61 (PCGS). Rarities Sale (Bowers and Merena, January 1997) lot 226 • Cardinal Collection • Privately to the San Marino Collection • Pre-Long Beach Sale (Ira and Larry Goldberg, September 2002) lot 501 • Cardinal Collection (American Numismatic Rarities, June 2005) lot 25 • Private collector • Dr. Robert Hesselgesser Collection (Ira and Larry Goldberg, September 2011) lot 5033 • Pre-Long Beach Sale (Ira and Larry Goldberg, May 2012) lot 1277.

Perkins Specimen. AU-55. W. David Perkins Collection.

Matthews Specimen. EF-40. W. David Perkins Collection • Jim Matthews Collection • Lindesmith Sale (Bowers and Merena, March 2000) lot 2066.

Kagin Specimen. EF-40. ANA Convention Sale (Kagin's, 1983) lot 2671. "EF-40 with light even wear. Accompanied with ANACS certificate grading EF-40/40 and a description as having a Bolender-1 obverse, Bolender-4 reverse." • Dr. Robert Stark Collection.

Miller Specimen. EF-40 (PCGS). W. David Perkins • Warren Miller Collection. Die State I.

Reiver Specimen. VF-35 (NGC). Baldenhofer • Ostheimer • ANA Sale (Superior, August 1975) lot 853 • Davenport Collection Sale (Superior, February 1977) lot 472 • Jules Reiver Collection (Heritage, January 2006) lot 23553.

Miller Collection (another). VF-30. John Haugh • Warren Miller Collection. Die State II.

Brooks Specimen. VF-25 (ICG). Brooks Collection (Bowers and Merena, June 1989) lot 218 "VF-20." • Unknown intermediaries • Albany Collection (Heritage, September 2002) lot 7800 • William Luebke Collection (Heritage, January 2007) lot 4967.

1997 ANA Specimen. VF-20 (PCGS). ANA Signature Sale (Heritage, July 1997) lot 6487, "terminal die state."

Boyd Specimen. VF-20. "World's Greatest Collection" (F.C.C. Boyd, Numismatic Gallery 1945) lot 59. "Haseltine-32. A reverse die crack extends from cloud under OF through 2 stars below it to right wing of eagle. VF."

Total Estimated Population

MS-65 or better: 0 (URS-0)
MS-64: 0 (URS-0)
MS-63: 0 (URS-0)
MS-60 to 62: 1 (URS-1)
AU-50 to 58: 1 (URS-1)
VF-20 to EF-45: 7 to 15 (URS-4)
G-4 to F-15: 3 to 5 (URS-3)
Total for all grades combined: 10 to 20 (URS-5)
Estimated Total Condition Census: 61-55-40-40-40-35

1798 Knob 9, Heraldic Eagle, BB-92

Line star pattern on reverse.

Large Letters reverse, 5 lines in each shield element. (B-4, H-4)

Obverse: Knob 9. 13 stars, as are all the following. Squared-off bottom to 7 (seen only on BB-81 through BB-96; used with the Knob 9). Highest wave of hair incomplete at left (see note below). Upper left star near L, but upper right star is over 1.5 mm. distant from Y. Bottom two rays on star 4 are undersized. Stars 4 and 5 more widely separated than any other stars on the left; stars 8 and 9 most widely separated and stars 9 and 10 closest of any stars on the right. Digits 7 and 9 closest in date. The 1 in date is near curl but does not touch it. Curl open for a small distance at its top. Two die "dots" appear under E in LIBERTY, and two more on bust just above drapery, showing on all Fine or better specimens. Base of R above bases of adjacent E and T. Earliest die state.

Obverse die used to strike 1798 BB-92 (earliest state; more detail to highest wave of hair than on BB-93 or BB-94), BB-93, and BB-94 (top left of 1 in date is "lumpy"; possibly the latest state). Striking order probably BB-92, BB-93, BB-94.

Reverse: See description under 1798 BB-91. Large Letters; 5 lines in each vertical shield element.

Reverse die used to strike 1798 BB-91 (earlier use) and BB-92 (later use).

Die States

Die State I: Normal dies as described above. Presumably, there are intermediate die states between this and II described below.

Die State II: A late reverse die state has a crack at the rim through the right top of the second T in STATES down through its stand, the clouds, the stars and the right (observer's left) wing to the N in UNITED and the rim below.

Collecting Notes

1798 BB-92 is somewhat elusive. I estimate that about 200 to 350 are known, only a few of which have appeared in auctions over the years. Most specimens are in VF and EF grades. Some examples are lightly struck at the centers, while others are sharply defined.

Notable Specimens

Thomas Specimen. MS-63 (PCGS). Orlando Signature Sale (Heritage, January 2006) lot 3224 • Joseph C. Thomas Collection (Heritage, April 2009) lot 2549 • Warren Miller Collection.

Queller Specimen. AU-50 (NGC). 68th Anniversary Sale (Stack's, October 2003) lot 2719 • Queller Family Collection of Silver Dollars (Heritage, April 2008) lot 2018 • Baltimore Signature Sale (Heritage, July 2008) lot 747 • Internet Auction (Heritage, September 2008) lot 23216 • Houston Signature Sale (Heritage, December 2008) lot 820 • Long Beach Signature Sale (Heritage, February 2010) lot 1253.

Baltimore Specimen. AU-50 (NGC). Baltimore Sale (Bowers and Merena, December 2004) lot 2272.

Orlando Specimen. EF-45 (ANACS). Orlando Signature Sale (Heritage, January 2002) lot 7264.

1983 ANA Convention Sale Specimen. EF-45. ANA Convention Sale (Kagin's, 1983) lot 2664.

Chalkley Specimen. EF-45. Chalkley Collection (Superior, 1990) lot 2847.

Emery-Nichols Specimen. EF-45. Emery-Nichols Collection (Bowers and Merena, 1984) lot 928.

GNA Convention Sale Specimen. EF-45. Georgia Numismatic Association Convention (Mid American, 1989) lot 1414.

Spies Specimen. EF-45. W. Earl Spies Collection (Stack's, 1974) lot 43. EF to AU.

1981 ANA Convention Sale Specimen. EF-40. 1981 ANA Convention Sale (Bowers and Ruddy) lot 2016. Rim nick above last letter of LIBERTY.

Lighthouse Specimen. EF-40. J.C. Lighthouse Collection • Bolender Collection, 1952, lot 41. "Reverse shows adjustment marks done at Mint." • W.G. Baldenhofer Collection • Farish-Baldenhofer Sale (Stack's, 1955) • A.J. Ostheimer 3rd Collection • ANA Convention Sale (Superior, 1975) lot 851. "EF-40." Faint reverse adjustment marks, as well as identifiable dent at D where the letter was hit with a blunt object."

GENA Convention Sale Specimen. EF-40. GENA Convention Sale (Kagin's, 1979) lot 371.

Hollinbeck-Kagin Specimen. EF-40. June 1970 Hollinbeck-Kagin Sale, lot 607. "EF."

New Netherlands 57th Sale Specimen. EF-40. December 1963, lot 1056. EF, usual center weakness.

Sears Specimen. EF-40. Elmer Sears. Sold to the following in 1909 • Albert Fairchild Holden Collection • Norweb Collection (Bowers and Merena, 1988) lot 3755.

Ostheimer Specimen. EF-40. Ostheimer Collection (Lester Merkin, 1968) lot 247. "EF."

New Netherlands Specimen. EF-40. New Netherlands 57th Sale, 1963, lot 1056; EF-40, weak at the centers • Dr. Charles Ruby Collection Part I (Superior, 1974) lot 1462. Strictly Extra Fine.

Beymer-Stark Specimen. EF-40. Jack Beymer, May 1985. Sold to the following • Dr. Robert Stark Collection.

Total Estimated Population

MS-65 or better: 0 (URS-0)
MS-64: 0 (URS-0)
MS-63: 1 (URS-1)
MS-60 to 62: 0 (URS-0)
AU-50 to 58: 2 (URS-2)
VF-20 to EF-45: 175 to 300
G-4 to F-15: 25 to 50
Total for all grades combined: 200 to 350 (URS-9)
Estimated Total Condition Census: 63-50-50-45 (multiples)

1798 Knob 9, Heraldic Eagle, BB-93

Line star pattern on reverse.

(B-5, H-5)

Obverse: See description under 1798 BB-92. The top of the 1 in date is straight in BB-93, as in BB-92.

Obverse die used to strike 1798 BB-92 (earliest state; more detail to highest wave of hair than on BB-93 or BB-94), BB-93, and BB-94 (top left of 1 in date is "lumpy"; possibly the latest state). Striking order probably BB-92, BB-93, BB-94.

Reverse: This variety is usually instantly identifiable by the heavy reverse vertical die crack which runs from rim to rim on *most* known specimens. Because of this crack, all examples seen are weak at the center of the reverse, but somewhat stronger in the area to the right of the crack. Line star pattern. Star is very close to the outside of point of upper part of eagle's beak; star ray points to right side of left upright of B in PLURIBUS. Right serif on foot of first T in STATES lower than left foot of adjacent A; right serif on foot of second lower than adjacent serif of E. Bases of letters AME and RI closer than ER. Berry below and distant from left side of serif of right foot of A. Only 10 arrows, and three heads additional without sticks.

Reverse die used to strike 1798 BB-93 only.

Die States

Die State I: Perfect dies without cracks. May not exist.

Die State II: Obverse die with tiny crack from rim to upper right serif of T in LIBERTY. "Virtually no breaks" on reverse. Cf. Spies Collection (Stack's, 1974), VF, there called "probably unique."

Die State III: Obverse as above. Reverse with die crack along right side of shield entirely across reverse, as described by Bolender. Crack from bottom of left upright of M in AMERICA, under M, to partly under E. Crack from border past second S of STATES (between S and bisecting crack). Die cracks up between lower right of

tail and where bisecting crack reaches bottom border. The usually seen die state.

Collecting Notes

Despite the inclusion of three specimens in the 1975 ANA Convention sale (Superior), the BB-93 variety is quite rare today. I believe that only 30 to 50 exist. In 1950, the situation was far different when Bolender wrote this: "Haseltine had found but a single specimen (Fair), and I have seen but one. Excessively rare. Rarity 7." This is the old story again: A specimen is considered rare, then collectors search for it, and additional coins come to light.

Notable Specimens

Long Sale Specimen. AU-55 (NGC). Likely from Hollinbeck-Kagin Sale, June 1970, lot 608 • unknown intermediaries • Kenneth C. Long Collection Sale (Bowers and Merena, May 1995) lot 1163 • Private collector • Long Beach Signature Sale (Heritage, June 1999) lot 6058.

Miller Specimen. AU-53 (NGC). Detroit ANA Signature Sale (Heritage, July 1994) lot 7104 • Warren Miller Collection.

Midwest Specimen. AU-50. Private Midwest collection.

Willasch Specimen. EF-45 (PCGS). H. Roland Willasch Collection (Superior, 1990) lot 476 • Jim Matthews Collection • San Marino Collection Sale (Ira and Larry Goldberg, September 2002) lot 475 • Unknown intermediaries • Dr. Robert Hesselgesser Collection (Ira and Larry Goldberg, September 2011) lot 5035.

Everson and Faught Specimen. VF-35. Everson and Faught Collections (Bowers and Merena, 1988) lot 2219. VF-30 to EF-40.

Ostheimer Specimen. VF-30 (PCGS). Colonel E.H.R. Green • Alfred J. and Jacque Ostheimer • Lester Merkin's sale of September 18, 1968, lot 248 • Jules Reiver

• Jim Matthews privately • Chicago ANA Sale (Stack's Bowers, August 2011) lot 10508.

Cardinal Specimen. VF-25 (PCGS), • Cardinal Collection • Pre-FUN Elite Sale (Superior, January 2002) lot 1186 • Private collector • Old West & Franklinton Collections Sale (American Numismatic Rarities, August 2006) lot 700.

Four Landmark Collections Specimen. VF-30/20. Four Landmark Collections Sale (Bowers and Merena, 1989) lot 1955. "Split grading is accounted for by the extremely late state of the reverse, the die having cracked longitudinally from 12:00 to 6:00. Clearly, the advanced state of the die accounts for the rarity of the combination. While the obverse strike appears to have been sharp, the reverse is indeterminable because of the advanced state of the break."

Total Estimated Population
MS-65 or better: 0 (URS-0)
MS-64: 0 (URS-0)
MS-63: 0 (URS-0)
MS-60 to 62: 0 (URS-0)
AU-50 to 58: 3 (URS-3)
VF-20 to EF-45: 18 to 25 (URS-6)
G-4 to F-15: 12 to 20 (URS-5)
Total for all grades combined: 30 to 50 (URS-6)
Estimated Total Condition Census: 55-53-50-45-35-30

1798 Knob 9, Heraldic Eagle, BB-94

Arc star pattern on reverse.

(B-3, H-3)

Obverse: Knob 9. See description under BB-92.

Obverse die used to strike 1798 BB-92 (earliest state; more detail to highest wave of hair than on BB-93 or BB-94), BB-93, and BB-94 (top left of 1 in date is "lumpy"; possibly the latest state). Striking order probably BB-92, BB-93, BB-94.

Reverse: Star distant from eagle's beak; ray of that star points to I in PLURIBUS. Arc star pattern. Three stars on left between eagle's beak and clouds form a right triangle with the hypotenuse parallel (more or less) to the top of the eagle's wing. Leaf points to space between I and R in AMERICA. Berry distant from and under left foot of A. Stem of branch curves outward.

Reverse die used to strike 1798 BB-94 (earliest state), BB-95 (intermediate state), and BB-102 (final state).

Die States

Die State I: Perfect obverse die. Straight top to 1. May not exist.

Die State II: Upper left of 1 in date is "lumpy" and somewhat distended, apparently a die break. Most examples are of this die state.

Die State III: Die crack begins on rim, goes between stars 2 and 3, and ends at a ray of star 2. The two 1798 BB-94 coins in the Spies Collection (Stack's, 1974) were of this die state, as was lot 363 in the Bowers and Merena 1989 sale of the Dr. Nelson Page Aspen Collection.

Note: Examples with bifurcated letters sometimes have ED of UNITED appear broken at top and the bottom points of many stars above the eagle are weak (due to lack of metal completely filling the voids); these are not separate die states.

Collecting Notes

In the context of 1798 Heraldic Eagle dollars, BB-94 is one of the rarer varieties. Probably, somewhat over 150 are known, most of which are in lower grades up through Very Fine. At the EF level, BB-94 is rare, and higher grade pieces are rarer still. The only Uncirculated piece I have encountered in the early literature is that in the Bolender Collection, 1952, since untraced; the grade equivalent of this coin today is not known.

Notable Specimens

Cardinal Specimen. MS-63 (PCGS). Unidentified B. Max Mehl sale, lot 11• ANA Sale (Kagin's, August 1986) lot 4733 • L.W. Hoffecker Collection (Superior, February 1987) lot 1316 • Worrell Family Collection (Superior, September 1993) lot 1297 • Unknown intermediaries • Dale Friend Collection • Legend Numismatics • Cardinal Collection (American Numismatic Rarities, June 2005) lot 26.

Bolender Specimen. MS-63 (NGC). Bolender Collection, 1952, lot 40. "Uncirculated, except for a few tiny spots, and minute nicks visible under a glass." • Private Denver collection • privately to the Cardinal Collection • New York ANA Signature Sale (Heritage, July 1997) lot 6491 • Hain Family Collection Sale (Stack's, January 2002) lot 1506 • Warren Miller Collection.

New York ANA Specimen. AU-50 (ANACS), New York Signature Sale (Heritage, July 2002) lot 8395.

Hesselgesser Specimen. AU-50 (PCGS). Pre-Long Beach Sale (Ira and Larry Goldberg, May 2011) lot 884 • Dr. Robert Hesselgesser Collection (Ira and Larry Goldberg, September 2011) lot 5036 • Pre-Long Beach Sale (Ira and Larry Goldberg, May 2012) lot 1278.

Carter Specimen. EF-45. Amon Carter, Jr. Family Collection (Stack's, 1984) lot 222. "EF and choice."

Spies Specimen. EF-45 (NGC). Double Struck. W. Earl Spies Collection (Stack's, 1974) lot 41. "Freak specimen that was double struck. Stars are undersized because of the double strike, giving a coin a most curious appearance. EF." • Warren Miller Collection.

Blevins Specimen. EF-40. H.W. Blevins Collection (Superior, 1988) lot 3641. "Obverse die crack between stars 2 and 3. EF-40."

Long Beach Sale Specimen. EF-40. Long Beach Sale (Heritage, 1989) lot 798.

Total Estimated Population

MS-65 or better: 0 (URS-0)
MS-64: 0 (URS-0)
MS-63: 2 (URS-2)
MS-60 to 62: 0 (URS-0)
AU-50 to 58: 1 or 2 (URS-1)
VF-20 to EF-45: 90 to 140 (URS-8)
G-4 to F-15: 60 to 110 (URS-7)
Total for all grades combined: 150 to 250 (URS-9)
Estimated Total Condition Census: 63-63-50-50-45-45

1798 Knob 9, Heraldic Eagle, BB-95

Arc star pattern on reverse.
(B-7, H-7)
Obverse: Knob 9. Thirteen stars. Point of 1 touches curl. The 8 is high and very nearly touches bust. Squared-off bottom to 7 (seen only on BB-81 through BB-96; used with the Knob 9). Upper right star is slightly closer to Y than upper left star is to L. Die flaw about like a comma after date. The stars on the right are thinner than those on the left. On the left, stars 1-2 and 3-4 are closer than any others. On the right, stars 10 and 11 are closer together than any others.

BB-95 is usually (always?) lightly struck at LIBERTY.

Obverse die used to strike 1798 BB-95 (early state only) and BB-96 (early state and late state).

Reverse: See description under 1798 BB-94.

Reverse die used to strike 1798 BB-94 (earliest state), BB-95 (intermediate state), and BB-102 (final state).

Die States

Die State I: Perfect obverse die. Perfect reverse die. The usual state seen.

Die State II: Perfect obverse die. Reverse die with die crack from wing to I of AMERICA to border. Faint clash mark from bust is through OF.

Die State III: Obverse with crack as in BB-96. May not exist with BB-95.

Collecting Notes

1798 BB-95 is one of the scarcer varieties of the year. Probably, about 100 to 150 survive—a far cry from the situation in 1950, when M.H. Bolender wrote the following: "This combination is extremely rare, and I have found but two specimens. Rarity 6."

Notable Specimens

Walter Specimen. AU-58 (PCGS). J.C. Morgenthau & Co. Sale, June 1942, lot 140, Uncirculated • Major Alfred Walter (New Netherlands, December 1968) lot 547, "AU." • Auction '87 (Stack's, July 1987) lot 778 • Gilbert Steinberg Collection (Superior, September 1996) lot 950 • Cardinal Collection (Heritage, April 2002) lot 6696.

Miller Specimen. EF-45 (NGC). Warren Miller Collection.

Hesselgesser Specimen. EF-40 (PCGS). Jim Matthews Collection • Harry Laibstain • William Luebke

Collection (Heritage, January 2007) lot 4971 • Dr. Robert Hesselgesser Collection (Ira and Larry Goldberg, September 2011) lot 5037 • Pre-Long Beach Sale (Ira and Larry Goldberg, May 2012) lot 1279.

Matthews Specimen. EF-40. Jim Matthews Collection • San Marino Collection Sale (Ira and Larry Goldberg, September 2002) lot 478.

Chalkley Specimen. EF-40 (NGC). Superior, 1990, lot 2849.

H.W. Blevins Specimen. VF-35. Superior, 1988, lot 4761. "Almost EF-40."

Total Estimated Population

MS-65 or better: 0 (URS-0)
MS-64: 0 (URS-0)
MS-63: 0 (URS-0)
MS-60 to 62: 0 (URS-0)
AU-50 to 58: 2 to 4 (URS-2)
VF-20 to EF-45: 55 to 85 (URS-7)
G-4 to F-15: 45 to 65 (URS-7)
Total for all grades combined: 100 to 150 (URS-8)
Estimated Total Condition Census: 58-50-45-40 (multiples)

1798 KNOB 9, HERALDIC EAGLE, BB-96

Line star pattern on reverse.
Large Letters reverse, 5 lines in each shield element. (B-6, H-6)
Obverse: Knob 9. Thirteen stars. See description under 1798 BB-95.

Obverse die used to strike 1798 BB-95 (early state only) and BB-96 (early state and late state).

Reverse: Large Letters reverse from 1796 type font (larger interior space in A, open S, etc.); 5 lines in each vertical shield element. This was one of the first Heraldic Eagle reverse dies cut in early 1798. Ray of star is near center of space between two parts of eagle's beak, but does not touch; star ray points to between B and U. Line star pattern. Leaf points to center of

I in AMERICA. Only 10 perfect arrows, and two sticks (one stick is located between the 2nd and 3rd arrow shaft from the left and the other is between the 2nd and 3rd from the right). Often found with very heavy dentils and weakness of strike at the centers. The base of the first A in AMERICA is joined solid. This is an early state of the reverse die used to coin 1798 BB-101 (when BB-101 was coined, the two sticks were no longer present). The two rightmost arrow shafts on this die state each have two heads (and thus count as four arrows), the third arrow shaft from the right is ghostlike (this style was used on other dies as well). This is the die state known to and described by Bolender.

Once relapped, the reverse die (as Die State V, described

below) was used to coin some specimens of 1798 BB-101. If Die States VI and VII exist (I have not seen them), then the reverse was re-mated with the obverse of BB-96 and used to coin additional pieces.

Reverse die used to strike 1798 BB-96 (early and late states), BB-101 (latest state).

Die States

Die State I: With perfect obverse and reverse dies, without cracks or relapping. May not exist.

Die State II: With perfect obverse and reverse dies without cracks, but with obverse die relapped; highest wave of hair incomplete, and stars spidery, as a result. Somewhat scarce, this die state seems to constitute about 20% to 30% of the population of BB-96.

Die State III: With obverse die crack from field below hair ribbon through star 1 toward 1 of date, but is interrupted with another crack below lowest curl going from crack to border; crack continues under 1, through bottom of 7, middle of 9. Reverse die still with 10 arrows and two sticks (not yet relapped). This is the most plentiful die state of BB-96.

Die State IV: As III, but crack develops on reverse at dentil over I of AMERICA. Enlarges slightly, and develops a spur extending toward R (there are several minor progressive variations of this crack under Die State IV). Reverse die not yet relapped.

Die State V: Bolender-6b. With obverse die crack now from hair ribbon through star 1 toward 1 of date, but is interrupted with another crack below lowest curl going from crack to border; crack continues under 1, through bottom of 7, middle of 9, to center of 8; advanced state of preceding. Additional hairline crack goes upward from border to bottom curl. Reverse die relapped; now with 10 arrows, but with two sticks ground away; 3rd shaft from left is discontinuous. Crack over I, with spur toward R, still visible. Perhaps 15% to 20% of BB-96 are of this die state. This die state was also used to coin 1798 BB-101.

Die State VI: Bolender-6a. Obverse crack heavier and more extended; continues from ribbon into hair curls. A crack has developed on the reverse through the arrows and N of UNITED. Constitutes a minor percentage of BB-96. Not seen by the author.

Collecting Notes

1798 BB-96 is of medium scarcity within the context of varieties of this date, with an estimated population of 500 to 800 pieces. As is true of most other dollars of this era, the VF category is the most populous. EF examples are in the distinct minority, and AU coins are rarer yet. Mint State records are for coins sold prior to the grading interpretation renaissance in 1986.

Notable Specimens

Eliasberg Specimen. MS-63 (NGC). A few tiny adjustment marks, as made. Light champagne and lilac toning over glossy, lustrous surfaces. Very well struck. Obverse framed with a particularly high rim, reverse very slightly misaligned (not unusual for BB-96; W. David Perkins reports having seen five thus, and others probably exist), and while there are dentils completely surrounding, they are bolder on the left than on the right. Die State IV. Relapping has not yet occurred on the reverse, and there are beginning traces of a crack at the top of I in AMERICA. Louis E. Eliasberg Sr. Collection (Bowers and Merena, April 1997) lot 2182 • Michael Herring Collection (Heritage, January 2002) lot 7203.

Cardinal Specimen. MS-61 (PCGS), • Cardinal Collection (American Numismatic Rarities, June 2005) lot 27.

Alto Specimen. MS-60. Alto Collection (Stack's, 1970) lot 1064. "Brilliant Uncirculated."

Robison Specimen. MS-60. Ellis H. Robison Collection (Stack's, 1982) lot 1867. Brilliant Uncirculated. Struck slightly off-center at 1:00.

Forrest Specimen. MS-60. S.S. Forrest, Jr. Collection (Stack's, 1972), lot 981. "Brilliant Uncirculated."

Willasch Specimen. AU-55. H. Roland Willasch Collection (Superior, 1990) lot 478.

Miller Specimen. AU-53 (NGC). Jim McGuigan • Warren Miller Collection.

Adams Specimen. AU-50 (PCGS). Adams Collection (Superior, 1992) lot 2110. Struck from lapped dies, but the recutting on star five in still visible."

Ebsen Specimen. AU-50. Buddy Ebsen Collection (Superior, 1987) lot 1894.

DeCoppet Specimen. AU-50. André DeCoppet Collection (James Kelly, 1955). "Practically Uncirculated."

First National Bank of Denver Specimen. AU-50. First National Bank of Denver Collection (Bowers and Merena, 1987) lot 2221 • Lloyd M. Higgins, M.D. Collection (Bowers and Merena, 1988) lot 2306.

Stark Specimen. AU-50. Dr. Robert Stark Collection. Purchased from Heritage, Douglas Winter, in March 1984.

Spies Specimen. AU-50. Double Struck. W. Earl Spies Collection (Stack's, 1974) lot 49. "Double struck with a double row of dentils, etc. Displays all of the cracks listed as Bolender-6a. AU." • Warren Miller Collection.

Total Estimated Population

MS-65 or better: 0 (URS-0)
MS-64: 0 (URS-0)
MS-63: 1 (URS-1)
MS-60 to 62: 2 to 4 (URS-2)
AU-50 to 58: 6 to 12 (URS-4)
VF-20 to EF-45: 400 to 650 (URS-10)
G-4 to F-15: 100 to 150 (URS-8)
Total for all grades combined: 500 to 800 (URS-10)
Estimated Total Condition Census: 63-61-60-55-53-50 (multiples)

1798 Pointed Tail 9, Heraldic Eagle, BB-101

Line star pattern on reverse.

Large Letters reverse, 5 lines in each shield element. (B-17, H-17)

Obverse: Wide date, the 8 just touching bust. Date is over 11.5 mm. across at bottom widest part. Upper star on left very close to L, and upper star on right is near Y. Second star ray points slightly right of dentil. The dentils to left of date are irregular.

Obverse die used to strike 1798 BB-101 only.

Reverse: See description under 1798 BB-96. Large Letters reverse, 5 lines in each vertical shield element. BB-101 is from an later state (Die State V as described under BB-96). On the BB-101 variety some berries appear without stems. Only 10 arrows, the two sticks seen on BB-96 having now been removed.

The reverse die was used to coin BB-96 dollars, reground and used to coin BB-101 Die State I dollars.

Reverse die used to strike 1798 BB-96 (early and late states), BB-101 (latest state).

Die States

Die State I: Perfect obverse die without injuries. The Spies Collection (Stack's, 1974), "Bolender-17a" from "finished dies" without obverse defects, may be Die State I. Walter Breen suggests (in his *Encyclopedia,* Breen-5379) that only one specimen may be known of this die state.

Die State II: Most known specimens have a readily visible die injury at Miss Liberty's left shoulder and another at the reverse field area near the stars. This is the state known to Bolender. Die crack just beginning over I of AMERICA. Equivalent to Die State V of 1798 BB-96. This is the usual variety of BB-101 seen.

Die State III: As preceding, but obverse die cracks along leftmost star rays (stars 2 to 5) and dentils on left side. Cf. Blevins Collection (Superior, 1988): 3680.

Die State IV: As preceding, but reverse crack now extends through letter R and into the field at the lower left

of the letter. Cf. 1975 ANA (Superior): 876.

Die State V: On the latest die state, the die swells at the left obverse field and at the corresponding area of the reverse.

Collecting Notes

1798 BB-101 is another rare variety. Probably about 70 to 120 are known, most of which are well circulated. The average grade of Fine-19 is one of just a few to dip below the VF category. A Mint State coin, if such could be found, would be regarded as a landmark item.

Haseltine's was only Good, the only one he ever found. In his 1881 *Type-Table,* he used his favorite adjective, "excessively" (which he used excessively), to describe the rarity of this variety. Bolender only ever saw one, the VF coin that landed in his collection. The fact that numerous specimens have appeared since then, is testimony to the potential "out there" for locating still more examples of erstwhile and present rarities. Only a small number of 1798-dated dollars in numismatic circles have ever been attributed to Bolender numbers.

Notable Specimens

Jim Matthews Specimen. AU-55 (NGC.). Gable and Schuyler Sale (Ben Green May 1906) • "World's Greatest Collection" (F.C.C. Boyd, Numismatic Gallery, 1945) lot 42 • Milferd H. Bolender's 183rd Sale (his personal collection), 1952, lot 64 • Charles Ruby, Gilhousen Sale Part 3 (Superior, October 1973) lot 1236 • Gainsborough Sale (Kreisberg, September 1980) lot 763 • the San Marino Collection (Ira and Larry Goldberg, September 2002) lot 491.

Miller Specimen. AU-53 (NGC). Warren Miller Collection. Die State III.

Cardinal Specimen. AU-53. (PCGS). Anaheim ANA Sale (Heritage, August 1995) lot 6511 • Cardinal Collection (American Numismatic Rarities, June 2005) lot 28 • ANA Las Vegas Sale (Bowers and Merena, October 2005) lot 7008.

Cardinal Specimen (another). AU-53. (PCGS). CSNS Signature Sale (Heritage, May 2000) lot 5005 • Cardinal Collection • Private collector • Dr. Robert Hesselgesser Collection (Ira and Larry Goldberg, September 2011) lot 5039 • Pre-Long Beach Sale (Ira and Larry Goldberg, May 2012) lot 1280.

Smith Specimen. AU-53 (NGC). Harlan P. Smith Sale (Chapman brothers, May 1906) • Col. E.H.R. Green • 1952 ANA O.K. Rumbel Sale (August 1952) lot 3133 • M.H. Bolender's 184th Sale (April 1953) lot 277 • K.P. Austin • M.H. Bolender (privately, circa 1959) • Jacque and A.J. Ostheimer (1960) • Ostheimer Sale (Lester Merkin, September 1968) lot 259 • W. Earl Spies • W. Earl Spies Sale (Stack's, December 1974) lot 80 • Jules Reiver Collection (Heritage, January 2006) lot 23522.

Luebke Specimen. AU-50 (NGC). Jeff Garrett, privately in 2004 • William Luebke Collection (Heritage, January 2007) lot 4974.

Luebke Specimen (another). EF-45 (NGC). Higgins Collection (Bowers and Merena, 1988), lot 2216 • Witham and Sansoucy Collections (Bowers and Merena, September 1992), lot 1404 • W. David Perkins • Harry Laibstain (April 2005) • William Luebke Collection (Heritage, May 2007) lot 911.

BB-101: Late die state.

Queller Specimen. EF-45 (NGC). Queller Family Collection of Silver Dollars (Heritage, April 2008) lot 2021.

Miller Specimen (another). EF-45 (NGC). FUN Signature Sale (Heritage, January 1997) lot 6268 • Warren Miller Collection. Die State V.

Hollinbeck-Kagin Specimen. EF-40. Hollinbeck-Kagin Sale, June 1970, lot 612.

Boyd Specimen. EF-40. F.C.C. Boyd Collection, 1945 • Bolender Collection, 1952 • Dr. Charles Ruby Collection.[1] • Gilhousen Collection (Superior, 1973) lot 1236. "EF."

Total Estimated Population
MS-65 or better: 0 (URS-0)
MS-64: 0 (URS-0)
MS-63: 0 (URS-0)
MS-60 to 62: 0 (URS-0)
AU-50 to 58: 5 to 8 (URS-4)
VF-20 to EF-45: 35 to 60 (URS-7)
G-4 to F-15: 35 to 60 (URS-7)
Total for all grades combined: 70 to 120 (URS-7)
Estimated Total Condition Census:
55-53-53-53-53-50

---

[1] Dr. Charles Ruby, a college professor in Southern California, collected quantity, not quality, although this specimen of 1798 BB-101 is certainly an exception. His pride and joy was his extensive holding of 1793 cents, which he showed to me when Kenneth W. Rendell and I were guests in his home in August 1958.

1798 POINTED TAIL 9, HERALDIC EAGLE, BB-102

Arc star pattern on reverse.
(B-20, H-20)

Obverse: Wide date, 11 mm. across at widest part. 1 close to curl, 8 near bust but does not touch. Two upper stars near L and Y. First star nearly 4 mm. from hair. Ray of last star points to lower edge of a dentil. The obverse displays a prominent die chip between the left side of the 9 and the bust. The bottom stand of the T in LIBERTY is repunched.

Obverse die used to strike 1798 BB-102, BB-103, and BB-107.

Reverse: See description under 1798 BB-94. From same die used to strike BB-94 and BB-95. The die crack that developed on BB-95 from right wing down through I in AMERICA to border has now become heavier. Another crack is below ER in AMERICA. The BB-102 reverse also has a number of die dots in and around the second cloud from the right plus a small crack from the O to the F in OF, to the lower part of the first S in STATES. Incused dentils (clash marks from the obverse) are often visible above ES and OF. Faint clash mark from bust is seen through OF.

Reverse die used to strike 1798 BB-94 (earliest state), BB-95 (intermediate state), and BB-102 (final state).

Die States

Die State I: Die state as described above for BB-102.

Die State II. Rim crack below eagle's tail just beginning.

BB-102: Early die state, with minor rim crack below eagle's tail.

Die State III: Later state with a heavy rim break (which in its early development is often mistaken for a bruise or a nick) below the eagle's tail, extending to the last A in AMERICA.

Die State IV: The obverse die lump midway between center of date and bust becomes heavier. Reverse rim break enlarges.

Die State V: The reverse has an extended reverse break which travels through ICA in AMERICA and nearly touches the eagle's tail. Die State V is extremely rare in any grade.

Collecting Notes

BB-102 is in the medium range of scarcity among silver dollars of 1798. Probably somewhere around 75 to 125 are known. The variety is one of only a few with an average grade below the VF level. A review of auction appearances demonstrates that here is a variety for which EF and AU are remarkable grades.

Exactly why 1798 BB-102 should be so elusive in any grade above VF is one of those mysteries that makes collecting early dollars so interesting. The answer probably lies in the method of distribution. I have no way of knowing, but perhaps most specimens were sent away from urban centers and saw hard use in the American hinterlands, which in the 1790s included just about everywhere except the Eastern coastal cities.

Notable Specimens

Hesselgesser Specimen. AU-58 (PCGS). Baltimore Signature Sale (Heritage, March 2009) lot 2338 • Dr. Robert Hesselgesser Collection (Ira and Larry Goldberg, September 2011) lot 5040.

Dallas Sale Specimen. AU-55 (NGC). Dallas Signature Sale (Heritage, November 2005) lot 5076.

Miller Specimen. AU-55 (NGC). • Warren Miller Collection.

New York Sale Specimen. AU-55 (ANACS). New York Signature Sale (Heritage, July 2002) lot 8396.

Albany Specimen. AU-53 (NGC). • Cardinal Collection • Albany Collection (Heritage, September 2002) lot 7786.

Queller Specimen. AU-50 (PCGS). Queller Family Collection of Silver Dollars (Heritage, April 2008) lot 2022 • Dr. Robert Hesselgesser Collection (Ira and Larry Goldberg, May 2011) lot 887 • Pre-Long Beach Sale (Ira and Larry Goldberg, January 2012) lot 2543.

Boyd Specimen. AU-50. "World's Greatest Collection" (F.C.C. Boyd, Numismatic Gallery, 1945) lot 45. "Barely circulated."

Kagin Specimen. AU-50. CSNS Convention Sale (Kagin's, 1979) lot 362. "Unlisted die break on edge below eagle's tail. AU-50."

Fairbanks Specimen. EF-40. Fairbanks Collection (formed by Ben Koenig) (Stack's, 1960) lot 545. "EF choice."

Ruby Specimen. VF-25. M.H. Bolender • Dr. Charles Ruby • ANA Convention Sale (Superior, 1975) lot 879. "Reverse rim break below eagle's tail. Unlisted die state."

Willasch Specimen. VF-25. H. Roland Willasch Collection (Superior, 1990) lot 496. A heavy rim cud has developed below the eagle's tail to the A in AMERICA. One area on the rim near Liberty's bust may have been worked on, as the rim pulls in at that point on the obverse and reverse. Rare die state. The break from the rim through the I of AMERICA extends to the tip of the scroll and another parallels it along the base of E and through R."

Total Estimated Population

MS-65 or better: 0 (URS-0)
MS-64: 0 (URS-0)
MS-63: 0 (URS-0)
MS-60 to 62: 0 (URS-0)
AU-50 to 58: 5 to 8 (URS-4)
VF-20 to EF-45: 40 to 70 (URS-7)
G-4 to F-15: 35 to 55 (URS-7)
Total for all grades combined: 75 to 125 (URS-8)
Estimated Total Condition Census: 58-55-55-55-53-50 (multiples)

1798 Pointed Tail 9, Heraldic Eagle, BB-103

Arc star pattern on reverse.
(B-18, H-18)
Obverse: See description under BB-102.

Obverse die used to strike 1798 BB-102, BB-103, and BB-107.

Reverse: Branch with five medium sized berries, the two top ones closest together. Leaf point below lower left corner of I in AMERICA. Star distant from eagle's beak. Arc star pattern. 13 arrows.

In 1950, Bolender wrote this: "Die break from milling down through right part of E in STATES to clouds. This break has been seen on all specimens examined. Die breaks through last S in STATES and top of OF. Light die crack from top of N to base of D in UNITED."

However, it seems that Haseltine (see below) knew of at least two coins with perfect reverse (and knew of none with die cracks). Some specimens of BB-103 were struck from this die in perfect condition, then the reverse die was combined with another obverse to create BB-104, some specimens were struck, then a crack developed through the E, during which state most specimens of BB-104 were made. Then the crack advanced to the shield, some specimens were struck, then the reverse was recombined with the first obverse die to create additional specimens of BB-103, the reverse die by now having sustained additional cracks.

Reverse die used to strike 1798 BB-103 (early and late states) and BB-104 (intermediate states).

Die States

Die State I: Perfect reverse die. Unknown to Bolender. Spies: 80 is this state. This die state is also known on 1798 BB-104. Rare die state for BB-103.

Die State II: Reverse die cracked through E of STATES. Known on 1798 BB-104. May not exist on 1798 BB-103.

Die State III: As II, but die crack now extending to shield. Known on 1798 BB-104. May not exist on 1798 BB-103.

Die State IV: Reverse with die crack from border down through right part of E in STATES to clouds. This crack has been seen on all specimens examined by Bolender. Die cracks through last S in STATES and top of OF. Light die crack from top of N to base of D in UNITED. The usual die state for BB-103.

Collecting Notes

The 1798 BB-103 dollar is an extreme rarity and shares honors with BB-117 as one of the two most elusive die combinations of the year. Apparently, only five to 10 are known, with the population most likely being toward the low end of that range. BB-103 has the lowest average auction grade of any 1798 dollar (a distinction based upon an admittedly small population).

This high rarity seems anomalous, when one considers that the progressively failing reverse die used to coin 1798 BB-103 went on to strike many examples of 1798 BB-104, and the still usable obverse later was employed to strike a large number of 1798 BB-107 dollars. If the rarity observations are accurate (and not just due to the lack of attribution of sufficient early dollars), the die marriage used to create 1798 BB-103 must have been interrupted on a whim.[1]

In writing of this variety, Bolender said the following (italics ours) in reference to the die crack on the reverse: "This break has been seen on *all* specimens examined." Usually, Bolender erred on the side of rarity; many specimens later proved to be not as rare as he said. The term *all*

[1] Information in this paragraph suggested by Harry E. Salyards, M.D., letter to the author, January 19, 1993.

seems to indicate that he saw more than one with a reverse die crack. He designates BB-103 as Rarity-8 (presumably, on the Sheldon Scale, but Bolender never said what his rarity ratings meant); if so, he felt that two or three specimens of BB-103 existed with the die crack.

J.W. Haseltine designated H-18 (now, BB-103) as "excessively rare" in his pioneering 1881 monograph on early silver dollars. Apparently, he saw multiple specimens, none of which had the reverse die crack (for he mentions under BB-104 that in this later use, the reverse die was broken through the letter E in STATES). Had he seen just one, he probably would have said so (as in the case of 1795 H-13, for example, of which he noted this: "Probably unique, as I have never seen or heard of another of this variety"). Based on this, it would seem that Haseltine had seen multiple specimens of 1798 H-18 (BB-103) without the crack.

Notable Specimens

Boyd Specimen. VF-20. "World's Greatest Collection" (F.C.C. Boyd, Numismatic Gallery, 1945) lot 43. "VF with slight edge dent."

Haines Specimen. VG-8. Ferguson Haines Collection (S.H. and H. Chapman, 1888) lot 233. "VG. Shows file marks in planchet." Possibly one of the above.

Spies Specimen. VG-8. W. Earl Spies Collection (Stack's, 1974) lot 82. "Reverse struck with unknown perfect dies. VG, with central portion very weak." • H.W. Blevins Collection (Superior, 1988) lot 3671. "VG-8."

Miller Specimen. G-6 (NGC). eBay Sale June 2000 • Cardinal Collection • Pre-FUN Elite Sale (Superior, January 2002) lot 1187 • Warren Miller Collection.

Willasch Specimen. G-4 net. H. Roland Willasch Collection (Superior, 1990) lot 494. "VG-10. Heavy scratches in the left field and another on Liberty's hair which have been buffed down. Early die state without the crack at the E of STATES on the reverse, unknown to Bolender."

Total Estimated Population

MS-65 or better: 0 (URS-0)
MS-64: 0 (URS-0)
MS-63: 0 (URS-0)
MS-60 to 62: 0 (URS-0)
AU-50 to 58: 0 (URS-0)
VF-20 to EF-45: 1 or 2 (URS-1)
G-4 to F-15: 2 or 3 (URS-2)
Total for all grades combined: 5 to 10 (URS-4)
Estimated Total Condition Census: 20-8-8-6-4

1798 Pointed Tail 9, Heraldic Eagle, BB-104

**Arc star pattern on reverse
(B-22, H-22)**

Obverse: Wide date, the 8 firmly united with bust. This die is similar to BB-101, but the upper stars, while near L and Y, are not as close to them as in BB-101; on this the 7th star points directly at the lower left serif end of L, while on BB-101 the star points slightly above the serif end. Second star points to a space between two dentils, third to left part of a dentil. Flaw on star 4. Slight die crack under Y and 8th and 9th stars, shows on some specimens.

Obverse die used to strike 1798 BB-104 (early state) and BB-105 (early and late states).

Reverse: See description under 1798 BB-103. Bolender said nothing about the die state of the reverse in the mating that created BB-104, except that BB-104 was struck "from same die as Bolender-18" (equivalent to BB-103). However, Haseltine in 1881 stated that the reverse had a die crack from the rim through the E of STATES, but said nothing about any other cracks. Some specimens of BB-103 were struck from this die in perfect condition, then the reverse die was combined with another obverse to create BB-104, some specimens were struck, then a crack developed through the E, during which state most specimens of BB-104 were made. Then the crack advanced to the shield, some specimens were struck, then the reverse was recombined with the first obverse to create additional specimens of BB-103, the reverse die by

now having sustained additional cracks.

Reverse die used to strike 1798 BB-103 (early and late states) and BB-104 (intermediate states).

Die States

Die State I: Perfect reverse die. Cf. W. Earl Spies Collection (Stack's, 1974), which had two perfect-die coins, one with regular letters and the other with bifurcated letters (which do not constitute two different die states). This state was used to coin early specimens of 1798 BB-103.

Die State II: Reverse die crack through E of STATES just beginning. Gilhousen's (Superior, 1973) is VF-35.

Die State III: Reverse die cracked through E of STATES only. The die state mentioned by Haseltine as normal for this issue. The variety usually seen.

Die State IV: As II, but now with die crack extending to shield. Cf. Spies Collection coin (Stack's, 1974), VF. Very rare. (See the Eliasberg Collection catalog for a *very* detailed description).

Die State V: With the additional cracks mentioned by Bolender for BB-103; may not exist on BB-104.

Collecting Notes

1798 BB-104 is in the middle range of availability among dollar varieties of this date. Several hundred are believed to exist, an estimated 225 to 400. Most are in lower grade ranges, but enough EF coins exist

BB-104: Late Die State III, with reverse die crack extending from E through clouds.

that a purchase opportunity will occur every few years on the auction market, and perhaps even more often privately. Above EF, specimens are very rare. The variety may be unknown in Mint State.

Notable Specimens

Queller Specimen. MS-61 (PCGS). Queller Family Collection of Silver Dollars (Heritage, April 2008) lot 2023 • Dr. Robert Hesselgesser Collection (Ira and Larry Goldberg, September 2011) lot 5041 • Pre-Long Beach Sale (Ira and Larry Goldberg, May 2012) lot 1281.

Eliasberg Specimen. AU-55 (PCGS). Die State IV. A very pleasing coin that will at once attract the specialist and delight the connoisseur. This is believed to be the very finest known example of BB-104, several orders nicer than the closest competitor known to the cataloger [Mark Borckardt], AU-50 • Harlan P. Smith Collection (S.H. and H. Chapman, May 1906) • J.M. Clapp • John H. Clapp • Clapp estate, 1942 • Louis E. Eliasberg Sr. Collection (Bowers and Merena, April 1997) lot 2183 • Jim Matthews Collection • San Marino Collection Sale (Ira and Larry Goldberg, September 2002) lot 494 • Orlando Signature Sale (Heritage, January 2006) lot 3223, as MS-62 (NGC).

Miller Specimen. AU-55 (NGC). Orlando Signature Sale (Heritage, January 2008) lot 1777 • Warren Miller Collection.

Herdegen Specimen. AU-50. R.T. Herdegen Collection (Hans M.F. Schulman, 1973). "AU."

Wyatt Specimen. EF-45+. Russell and Eudora Bell Wyatt Collection (Superior, 1985) lot 2028. "Uniformly struck on a problem-free planchet."

New Netherlands Specimen. EF-45. New Netherlands 57th Sale, 1963, lot 1065. "Identical central weaknesses as shown by the Bolender plate coin, hence, inherent in striking."

Saunders Specimen. EF-45. Ebenezer Milton Saunders Collection (Bowers and Merena, 1987) lot 3511. "EF-45."

Four Landmark Collections Specimen. EF-45. Four Landmark Collections (Bowers and Merena, 1989) lot 1957. "EF-45 to AU-50."

Total Estimated Population

MS-65 or better: 0 (URS-0)
MS-64: 0 (URS-0)
MS-63: 0 (URS-0)
MS-60 to 62: 1 (URS-1)
AU-50 to 58: 3 or 4 (URS-3)
VF-20 to EF-45: 190 to 300 (URS-9)
G-4 to F-15: 60 to 100 (URS-7)
Total for all grades combined: 250 to 400 (URS-10)
Estimated Total Condition Census: 61-55-55-50-45 (multiples)

1798 POINTED TAIL 9, HERALDIC EAGLE, BB-105

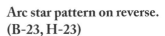

Arc star pattern on reverse.
(B-23, H-23)

Obverse: See description under 1798 BB-104. Usually lightly struck at the centers.

Obverse die used to strike 1798 BB-104 (early state)

and BB-105 (early and late states).

Reverse: Several die flaws, one between ST, another between TE, another at right of E in STATES. Curved die flaw above third upper right star on reverse. 5 small berries, the two above closest together. Leaf point is under left foot of I in AMERICA. Star distant from eagle's beak. Arc star pattern; star ray points to center of B in PLURIBUS. 13 arrows.

Reverse die used to strike 1798 BB-105 (late state) and BB-106 (early state).

Die States

Die State I: With reverse die in early state as used for BB-106. May not exist.

Die State II: Reverse die ever so slightly relapped in comparison to BB-106; now some details of cloud 3 are gone. Additional die flaws between ST, TE and the right side of the E in STATES. The usual state seen.

Die State III: Bolender-23a. As above, but obverse die now relapped, with highest wave of hair mostly gone, both bottom curls with parts missing, and stars 1 and two appearing spidery. About 20% to 30% of specimens of BB-105 are of this die state. Examples of Die State III include New Netherlands 48th Sale: 624, described as MS-60.

Collecting Notes

1798 BB-105 shares honors with BB-125 as one of the two most common varieties of the year and, indeed, one of the most common early dollars of any date. An estimated 850 to 1,500 are believed to exist. Most are in lower grades. In AU and Mint State grades it is rare.

Notable Specimens

Stellar Specimen. MS-65 (PCGS). Stellar Collection • Bruce Morelan Collection • Legend Numismatics • Private collector.

Fairbanks Specimen. MS-63. Fairbanks Collection (Ben Koenig) (Stack's, 1960) lot 548. "A superb Uncirculated specimen." • A. J. Ostheimer 3rd Collection (Lester Merkin, 1968) lot 264. Uncirculated. Planchet lightly streaked as made."

Brand Specimen. MS-63. Virgil M. Brand (presumed pedigree) • Burdette G. Johnson • T. James Clarke Collection (New Netherlands 48th Sale, 1956) lot 624.

"Strictly Uncirculated, but not quite in the 'gem' class as claimed by Mr. Clarke." Pedigreed to Virgil M. Brand through B.G. Johnson, who with Henry Chapman was one of two early appraisers of the Brand estate.

Chouinard Specimen. MS-62 (PCGS). New York ANA Sale (Superior, August 2002) lot 1071, as MS-61 (ANACS) • Richard Chouinard Collection (Heritage, January 2005) lot 30274, as MS-61 (ANACS) • Beverly Hills Rarity Sale (Bowers and Merena, September 2008) lot 379, as MS-62 (PCGS).

Hollinbeck-Kagin Specimen. MS-62 (ANACS). June 1970: 614. "Uncirculated." • Tampa FUN Signature Sale (Heritage, January 2011) lot 5620.

Terrell Specimen. MS-60. Terrell Collection (Bowers and Ruddy, 1973) lot 901 • Austin Collection (Bowers and Ruddy, 1974) lot 19. "Uncirculated."

Harte Specimen. MS-60. Roy Harte Collection (Bowers and Ruddy, 1977) lot 2785. "Brilliant Uncirculated."

Long Beach Sale Specimen. MS-60. Heritage, 1988, lot 963. "Minor edge defect, as struck, just enters the second T in STATES."

Chalkley Specimen. MS-60. Chalkley Collection (Superior, 1990) lot 2846.

Davis Specimen. AU-58. Davis-Graves (James Davis) Collection (Stack's, 1954) lot 1290. "Just a shade from Uncirculated."

DeCoppet Specimen. AU-55. André DeCoppet Collection (James Kelly, 1955). "Practically Uncirculated."

Total Estimated Population

MS-65 or better: 1 (URS-1)
MS-64: 0 (URS-0)
MS-63: 2 to 4 (URS-2)
MS-60 to 62: 8 to 15 (URS-4)
AU-50 to 58: 20 to 35 (URS-6)
VF-20 to EF-45: 600 to 1,100 (URS-11)
G-4 to F-15: 200 to 350 (URS-9)
Total for all grades combined: 850 to 1,500 (URS-11)
Estimated Total Condition Census: 65-63-63-62-62-60 (multiples)

1798 Pointed Tail 9, Heraldic Eagle, BB-106

Arc star pattern on reverse.
(B-19, H-19)

Obverse: Wide date, distant from bust. Upper left star near L. Upper and lower right stars equidistant from Y and bust. First star points to lower edge of a dentil. On the left, stars are about equally spaced. On the right, stars 12 and 13 are slightly farther apart than are other stars, which are fairly evenly spaced. Vertical die crack down through stand of E in LIBERTY, across bust through 1 of date to border.

Obverse die used to strike 1798 BB-106 only.

Reverse: See description under 1798 BB-105, actually the later state of the die.

Reverse die used to strike 1798 BB-105 (later state) and BB-106 (early state).

Die States

Die State I: Perfect obverse die. May not exist.

Die State II: Obverse die break just beginning. Cf. Blevins: 3672, described as "With the obverse crack barely visible on Liberty's hair and not yet reaching the bottom of the E in LIBERTY."[1]

Die State III: On Die State III there is the familiar bisecting crack on the obverse which runs vertically from the E in LIBERTY to the 1 in the date. The die state usually seen.

Die State IV: On State IV there is a lump below the 1 in addition to the vertical crack described above. The left side of E is beginning to crumble. The Spies coin (Stack's, 1974) is VG-F.

---

[1] Comment by Harry E. Salyards, M.D., letter to the author, January 19, 1993: "If accurate, this is interesting in that the die break apparently began in the middle (deepest recesses) of the die, and then extended to the periphery—more commonly, it is the other way around."

Die State V: This die state shows further progress of the cracks described under IV, and the obverse is beginning to bulge. Vertical die crack on head below highest hair wave.

Collecting Notes

1798 BB-106 is one of the rarer varieties of the year. An estimated 80 to 140 exist, a comfortable population large enough to assure one for the cabinet of every specialist. Most examples are in the Very Fine range. EF coins are elusive, and AU or finer pieces are exceedingly rare.

In his 1881, J.W. Haseltine called this variety very rare

Notable Specimens

Superior Sale Specimen. MS-63. September 1987 Sale (Superior) lot 2299. MS-63.

CSNS 2009 Specimen. MS-61 (NGC). CSNS Signature Sale (Heritage, April 2009) lot 2550.

Hatie Specimen. AU-55. George D. Hatie Collection (Bowers and Merena, 1983) lot 916. "Very wide date, distant from bust. With vertical break through E of LIBERTY, across bust, through 1 of date to border. Sharply struck. Choice AU-55." • ANA Mid-Winter Sale (Heritage, March 1999) lot 5167.

FUN 2007 Specimen. AU-55 (NGC). FUN Signature Sale (Heritage, January 2007) lot 5125.

Hesselgesser Specimen. AU-53 (PCGS). Dr. Robert Hesselgesser Collection (Ira and Larry Goldberg, September 2011) lot 5043.

Miller Specimen. AU-50 (NGC). Warren Miller Collection.

Herring Specimen. AU-50 (NGC). Michael Herring Collection (Heritage, January 2002) lot 7196 • Albany Collection (Heritage, September 2002) lot 7785.

Cohen Specimen. EF-45. Milton G. Cohen Collection

(Bowers and Merena, 1985) lot 523. "The obverse displays a vertical die break, probably accounting for the rarity of this die combination. Choice EF-45."

First National Bank of Denver Specimen. EF-45. First National Bank of Denver Sale (Bowers and Merena Galleries, 1987) lot 1211. "There is a tiny obverse rim nick at 1:00."

Total Estimated Population
MS-65 or better: 0 (URS-0)

MS-64: 0 (URS-0)
MS-63: 1 (URS-1)
MS-60 to 62: 1 (URS-1)
AU-50 to 58: 5 to 8 (URS-4)
VF-20 to EF-45: 60 to 90 (URS-7)
G-4 to F-15: 30 to 50 (URS-6)
Total for all grades combined: 90 to 140 (URS-8)
Estimated Total Condition Census: 63-61-55-55-53-50 (multiples)

1798 Pointed Tail 9, Heraldic Eagle, BB-107

Arc star pattern on reverse.
(B-21, H-21)

Obverse: See description under 1798 BB-102. Die lump between center of date and bust.

Obverse die used to strike 1798 BB-102, BB-103, and BB-107.

Reverse: Only 10 arrows plus a stick (headless arrow) between the 2nd and 3rd shafts from the right. Five small berries, two top ones closest together. Point of leaf under left lower tip of I in AMERICA. Star distant from eagle's beak. Arc star pattern. Die crack along right wing tip, top of AM to border above E. In the later state of this reverse (used to coin 1798 BB-108), this reverse die was relapped, and just 10 arrows are visible, but no headless stick. 1798 BB-107 was struck before 1798 BB-108.

Reverse die used to strike BB-107 (earlier state) and 1798 BB-108 (later state, lightly relapped).

Die States

Die State I: Perfect obverse die without lump. Perfect reverse die, not relapped, and *without die cracks*. May not exist.

Die State II: Obverse die between center of date and bust. Reverse not yet relapped, and with headless stick

visible among 10 arrows. With die crack along right wing tip, top of AM, to border above E.. The usual state.

Collecting Notes

1798 BB-107 falls in the scarce category among dollars of this date. About 250 to 450 are known. As is the case with any other dollar variety of this date, the potential exists for more to be discovered.

In his 1881 *Type-Table,* J.W. Haseltine called this variety very scarce. He also considered that the extra "arrow" was created simply by the die being more deeply impressed when striking specimens of BB-107, as compared to BB-108. In 1881 when Haseltine wrote his compendium, indeed even in 1950 when Bolender created his opus, very little was known in numismatic circles about die preparation and use during the era of 1794-1804 dollars.

Notable Specimens

Montgomery Specimen. MS-63. Montgomery Collection (Bowers and Ruddy, 1976) lot 1428. "Brilliant Uncirculated."

Bolender Specimen. MS-61 (NGC). Thomas Elder Sale (1923) • Charles Ruby • M.H. Bolender Collection,

1952 • Gilhousen Collection (Superior, 1973) lot 1238 • Neggen Collection Sale (Superior, 1976) lot 658 • Jules Reiver Collection (Heritage, January 2006) lot 23529.

Hesselgesser Specimen. AU-58 (PCGS). • Dr. Robert Hesselgesser Collection (Ira and Larry Goldberg, September 2011) lot 5044.

Hesselgesser Specimen (another). AU-58 (NGC). Dr. Robert Hesselgesser Collection (Ira and Larry Goldberg, February 2009) lot 1073.

Miller Specimen. AU-55 (NGC). Warren Miller Collection.

Hollinbeck-Kagin Specimen. AU-55. June 1970, lot 613. "Near Uncirculated, only barest friction."

Turoff Specimen. AU-55. Julius Turoff Collection (Bowers and Ruddy, 1976) lot 439. "Borderline Uncirculated."

Superior Auction '80 Specimen. AU-55. Auction '80 (Superior, 1980) lot 232.

1982 ANA Convention Sale Specimen. AU-55. Steve Ivy, 1982, lot 721.

Total Estimated Population

MS-65 or better: 0 (URS-0)
MS-64: 0 (URS-0)
MS-63: 1 (URS-1)
MS-60 to 62: 1 or 2 (URS-2)
AU-50 to 58: 25 to 50 (URS-6)
VF-20 to EF-45: 175 to 300 (URS-9)
G-4 to F-15: 60 to 100 (URS-7)
Total for all grades combined: 250 to 450 (URS-10)
Estimated Total Condition Census: 63-61-58-58-55 (multiples)

1798 POINTED TAIL 9, HERALDIC EAGLE, BB-108

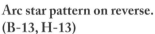

Arc star pattern on reverse.
(B-13, H-13)
Obverse: Medium wide date, 10.5 mm. across at bottom widest place. Die crack upward from right portion of L in LIBERTY. Easily identifiable by a die flaw between ray of last star and bust. Among stars on the left, 1-2, 2-3, and 5-6 are more widely separated than other stars. On the right stars 8-9 are noticeably wider apart than are any others.

The use of this obverse die is especially interesting in that it was interrupted. This die was used first to strike examples of 1798 BB-108, then BB-109 dollars were struck, then additional BB-108 dollars were coined. Die state progressions provide the telltale evidence.

Obverse die used to strike BB-108 (early and late states) and 1798 BB-109 (intermediate state; 1798 BB-109, Die State III).

Reverse: *Only 10 arrows.* 5 small berries, 2 top ones closest together. Point of leaf under left lower tip of I

in AMERICA. Star distant from eagle's beak. Arc star pattern. Die crack along right wing tip, top of AM to border above E. This is a later state of the reverse that used to have 10 arrows and a headless stick (used to coin 1798 BB-107). For the production of 1798 BB-108, the reverse die was relapped, removing the headless stick.

Reverse die used to strike 1798 BB-107 (earlier state) and BB-108 (later state, lightly relapped).

Die States

Die State I: Perfect obverse and reverse dies, not relapped. May not exist.

Die State II: Obverse crack toward border from right side of L in LIBERTY. Reverse with die relapped; headless stick no longer visible. With die crack along right wing tip, top of AM to border above E. The die state usually seen.

Die State III: Obverse now with crack from border below 17, left toward star 1. This is the die state used to coin 1798 BB-109. May not exist with BB-108.

Die State IV: Obverse now with crack from border below 17, left, now progressing through stars 1 to 5, very faint by star 5. About 20% to 30% of BB-108 dollars are of this die state.

Collecting Notes

1798 BB-108 is one of the commoner varieties of the year. I estimate that 500 to 800 survive, most of which are in grades through EF. However, AU coins come on the market with regularity. Mint State specimens are exceedingly rare.

Notable Specimens

Willasch Specimen. MS-63 PCGS). H. Roland Willasch (Superior, 1990) lot 487. Consigned by another individual to the Willasch Sale • Unknown intermediaries • Robert Lehmann • Cardinal Collection (American Numismatic Rarities, June 2005) lot 29 • Private Texas collection.

Long Beach Specimen. MS-61 (NGC). Long Beach Signature Sale (Heritage, June 1995) lot 5641 "heavy adjustment marks on reverse shield" • Baltimore Signature Sale (Heritage, July 2003) lot 8147 • Pittsburgh Signature Sale (Heritage, August 2004) lot 6329 • Orlando Signature Sale (Heritage, January 2008) lot 2927 • Chicago Rarities Sale (Bowers and Merena, April 2008) lot 489 • Long Beach Signature Sale (Heritage, September 2008) lot 2397 • Long Beach Signature Sale (Heritage, February 2009) lot 1549 • Long Beach Signature Sale (Heritage, May 2009) lot 925 • Long Beach Signature Sale (Heritage, September 2009) lot 911 • Orlando Signature Sale (Heritage, January 2010) lot 2584.

Hollinbeck-Kagin Specimen. MS-60. Hollinbeck-Kagin Sale, January 1970, lot 782. Uncirculated.

Miller Specimen. AU-58 (NGC). Warren Miller Collection.

1976 ANA Specimen. AU-58. 1976 ANA Convention Sale (Stack's) lot 1332 • Boyd, Brand and Ryder Collections (Bowers and Merena, 1990) lot 2454. AU-58.

Boyd, Brand and Ryder Specimen. AU-58. Boyd, Brand, and Ryder Collections (Bowers and Merena, 1990) lot 2453. "AU-58 to MS-60."

Gore and Long Specimen. AU-58. Gore and Long Collections (Bowers and Merena, 1990) lot 357. "AU-58 to MS-60. A tiny lamination flaw can be seen at the reverse rim at 7:00."

Kissel and Victoria Specimen. AU-58+. Kissel and Victoria Collections (Bowers and Merena, 1989) lot 389. AU-58/MS-60.

Total Estimated Population

MS-65 or better: (URS-0)
MS-64: (URS-0)
MS-63: 1 or 2 (URS-1)
MS-60 to 62: 2 to 4 (URS-2)
AU-50 to 58: 20 to 40 (URS-3)
VF-20 to EF-45: 250 to 400 (URS-10)
G-4 to F-15: 225 to 350 (URS-9)
Total for all grades combined: 500 to 800 (URS-11)
Estimated Total Condition Census: 63-61-60-58 (multiples)

1798 Pointed Tail 9, Heraldic Eagle, BB-109

Arc star pattern on reverse.
(B-10, H-10)
Obverse: See description under 1798 BB-108.

Obverse die used to strike BB-108 (early and late states) and 1798 BB-109 (intermediate state; 1798 BB-109, Die State III).

Reverse: Five small berries, the two uppermost being closest together. Arc star pattern. Star slightly distant from eagle's beak; star ray points to center of B of PLURIBUS. 13 perfect arrows, some formed better than others. Leaf points to just left of center of upright of I in AMERICA. A die flaw (chip out of die) under end of stem. *Berry under right foot of A in AMERICA* (compare to the reverse of BB-111, with the berry under the left foot). All specimens seen are lightly struck on the eagle.

Note: As the obverse was used later to coin more 1798 BB-108s, one wonders what happened to this reverse die. Why was its use interrupted. Perhaps, somewhere "out there" is a BB-109 exhibiting a sudden, massive reverse die failure.[1]

Reverse die used to strike 1798 BB-109 only.

Die States

Die State I: Obverse die without crack from right side of L in LIBERTY. May not exist.

Die State II: Obverse die with crack from right side of L in LIBERTY; without lower obverse cracks. This die state was used to coin early examples of 1798 BB-108; may not exist with BB-109.

Die State III: Obverse with die crack upward from right portion of L in LIBERTY. Light die crack from border under 7 of date to left through several stars. Centers weak. The die state usually seen.

_____
[1] This note is per the observation of Harry E. Salyards, M.D., letter to the author, January 19, 1993.

Die State IV: Centers even weaker than the preceding. Die cracks more advanced. Not seen.

Collecting Notes

1798 BB-109 is another scarce issue. I estimate that 75 to 125 exist, nearly all of which are in lower grades. Opinions concerning the rarity of this variety have been the subject of debate. Bolender suggested Rarity-4 (76 to 200 known, if he used the Sheldon Scale), which may be correct at the rarer end of the spread. Others have suggested that fewer than 30 exist. BB-109 is always weakly struck on the eagle and at the center of the bust.

Notable Specimens

Herring Specimen. MS-62 (NGC). 1998 Portland ANA Bourse • Michael Herring Collection (Heritage, January 2002) lot 7202 • Warren Miller Collection.

Boyd Specimen. AU-55. "World's Greatest Collection" (F.C.C. Boyd, Numismatic Gallery, 1945) lot 35. "Uncirculated."

Matthews Specimen. AU-53 (NGC). Steve Fischer, June 1998 • Jim Matthews Collection • San Marino Collection Sale (Ira and Larry Goldberg, September 2002) lot 481.

Hesselgesser Specimen. AU-50 (PCGS). Pre-Long Beach Sale (Ira and Larry Goldberg, May 2006) lot 3042 • Dr. Robert Hesselgesser Collection (Ira and Larry Goldberg, May 2011) lot 889 • Pre-Long Beach Sale (Ira and Larry Goldberg, January 2012) lot 2535.

Earle Specimen. AU-50. George H. Earle Collection (Henry Chapman, 1912) • Col. E.H.R. Green Collection • M.H. Bolender Collection (Bolender, 1952) lot 51. "Obverse practically Uncirculated. Reverse EF."

Hesselgesser Specimen (another). EF-45 (PCGS). Dr. Robert Hesselgesser Collection (Ira and Larry Goldberg, September 2011) lot 5046 • Pre-Long Beach Sale (Ira and Larry Goldberg, May 2012) lot 1284.

Total Estimated Population
MS-65 or better: 0 (URS-0)
MS-64: 0 (URS-0)
MS-63: 0 (URS-0)
MS-60 to 62: 1 or 2 (URS-1)
AU-50 to 58: 3 to 6 (URS-3)

VF-20 to EF-45: 40 to 70 (URS-7)
G-4 to F-15: 35 to 50 (URS-7)
Total for all grades combined: 75 to 125 (URS-8)
Estimated Total Condition Census: 62-55-53-50-50-45 (multiples)

1798 Pointed Tail 9, Heraldic Eagle, BB-110

Arc star pattern on reverse.
(B-16, H-16)

Obverse: Wide date, the most space between 9 and 8. Star 8 is slightly closer to Y than star 13 is to bust. Star 7 distant from L, and star 1 a trifle farther from curl.

In 1950, Bolender noted this: "The die broke early and so badly that very few pieces were struck, possibly not over two, as no others are known to the author. A number of pieces formerly attributed as H-16 in various catalogs and examined by the author, turned out to be incorrectly attributed. The die crack is heavy and extends from border on left near first star to right through base of lowest curl and top of 179 of date. There is a spur downward from a dentil above right part of E in LIBERTY."

Today, a perfect die coin is also known.

Obverse die used to strike 1798 BB-110 only.

Reverse: Five small berries, the two upper ones closest together. The third berry from top is attached to a leaf point. *Berry under left foot of A in AMERICA.* A leaf points to space between R and I in AMERICA. Arc star pattern. Star is distant from eagle's beak; ray points toward center of B in PLURIBUS. 13 perfect arrows, an unusually well-developed cluster. A plain die mark is always present in the back of the two highest clouds on the reverse. The first two reverse stars on the left both touch clouds. A small flaw or clash mark is present below the right ribbon.

Reverse die used to strike 1798 BB-110 (1st use), BB-111 (2nd use), BB-112 (3rd use), and BB-113 (4th and final use).

Discussion of the states of the reverse die used to strike, in this order, BB-110, BB-111, BB-112, and BB-113:

BB-110: Flaws below wing tip on the left, and under D of UNITED.

BB-111: As preceding, plus tiny crack or clash mark from left shield tip to ribbon above.

BB-112: As preceding, plus beginning of crack from branch stem end down to border.

BB-113: As preceding, plus extensive crack along border from above final S in STATES, through OF, wing tip, to border just above first A in AMERICA,

Die States

Die State I: Perfect obverse die. Two known, the 1975 ANA Convention Sale (Superior): 874, Ostheimer, Blanchard specimen, Dr. Robert Stark Collection. VF-20, and the 2004 December Baltimore Sale (Bowers and Merena): 2276, Warren Miller specimen.

Die State II: Obverse die with cracks as described by Bolender, quoted above. The usual state seen.

Die State III: Die state later than II with advanced obverse cracks. Not seen.

Die State IV: Die state advanced from III with heavy cud break seen at lower left obverse. One specimen in known, from the Willasch Collection. Mint State.

Collecting Notes

1798 BB-110 is one of the great rarities of the year 1798. Probably, no more than 30 to 50 are known. Estimates of

BB-110: Die State I with perfect obverse die.

the surviving population have varied widely, to as low as six to 12 coins. In his 1881 *Type-Table*, J.W. Haseltine called this variety very rare.

Notable Specimens

Willasch Specimen. MS-62 (PCGS). H. Roland Willasch Collection (Superior, May 1990) lot 492 • Reed Hawn Collection (Stack's, October 1993) lot 733 • Queller Family Collection of Silver Dollars (Heritage, April 2008) lot 2029 • Cardinal Collection (Stack's Bowers, August 2011) lot 7397 • W. David Perkins Collection.

Bolender Specimen. AU-55 (NGC). Numismatic Gallery, 1950 • M.H. Bolender Collection, 1952, lot 63. "EF." • ANA Convention Sale (Superior, 1975) lot 875. "EF-40." • Warren Miller Collection. Die State II.

Spies Specimen. AU-55 (NGC). W. Earl Spies Collection (Stack's, 1974) lot 79. "The break from the edge below the first star across the top of 179 is massive indeed. Spur over E very clear. Fully EF or better" • Jules Reiver Collection (Heritage, January 2006) lot 23520. Die State II.

Matthews Specimen. AU-50 (PCGS) • Gerry Wieser • Sheridan Downey, June 1990 • Jim Matthews Collection • San Marino Collection Sale (Ira and Larry Goldberg, September 2002) lot 489 • Baltimore Signature Sale (Heritage, March 2009) lot 2336 • Dr. Robert Hesselgesser

Collection (Ira and Larry Goldberg, September 2011) lot 5047, Early Die State II, with obverse crack connecting 1 an 7 of date and extending just beyond the bottom of Liberty's lowest curl.

Miller Specimen. EF-45 (NGC). Baltimore Sale (Bowers and Merena, December 2004) lot 2276 • Warren Miller Collection. Die State I.

Four Memorable Collections Specimen. VF-30. Four Memorable Collections Sale (Bowers and Merena, 1985) lot 2010 • Westchester Collection Sale (Bowers and Merena, 1987) lot 602.

Blanchard Specimen. VF-20. Rare Die State I. From a Mr. Blanchard in March 1953 • K.P. Austin Collection • A.J. Ostheimer 3rd Collection • 1975 ANA Convention Sale (Superior) • Dr. Robert Stark Collection.

Total Estimated Population

MS-65 or better: 0 (URS-0)
MS-64: 0 (URS-0)
MS-63: 0 (URS-0)
MS-60 to 62: 1 or 2 (URS-1)
AU-50 to 58: 2 to 4 (URS-2)
VF-20 to EF-45: 20 to 35 (URS-6)
G-4 to F-15: 6 to 10 (URS-4)
Total for all grades combined: 30 to 50 (URS-6)
Estimated Total Condition Census: 62-55-55-50-45 (multiples)

BB-110: Die State IV with heavy obverse die cud.

1798 Pointed Tail 9, Heraldic Eagle, BB-111

(B-11, H-11)

Obverse: Medium wide date, 10 mm. across at bottom widest place. First star about as far from curl as upper right star is from Y. The upper left star is closer to L in LIBERTY and about the same distance as last star is from bust. On the left, stars 2-3, 3-4, and 6-7 are spaced wider apart than are the others. On the right, stars 8, 9, 10, and 11 are spaced farther from each other than are stars 11-12 and 12-13. A small clash mark shows just beneath ribbon bow along two highest curls at back of head.

Obverse die used to strike 1798 BB-111 only.

Reverse: See description under 1798 BB-110.

Reverse die used to strike 1798 BB-110 (1st use), BB-111 (2nd use), BB-112 (3rd use), and BB-113 (4th and final use). See discussion of die states under 1798 BB-110.

Die States

Die State I: Obverse: Dies with clash mark as described above, but without cracks. Reverse: See discussion of die states under 1798 BB-110. Unknown to Haseltine. Cf. Davis-Graves Sale: 1285 (Stack's, 1954) VG-8. Rare.

Die State II: As above, but with mound developing below chin.

Die State III: As above, but the mound is more obvious, but hasn't yet developed into a crack.

Die State IV: Bolender-11a. With die crack under chin across three points of last star to border.

Die State V: As above, but now with another die crack across hair above ear. Scarce.

Die State VI: With the die cracks as listed by Bolender but now the upper crack is more prominent than the lower crack.

Die State VII: Bolender-11b. As last, but the die crack across hair continues across cheek, mouth, and upper ray of last star to border. This die state is always weak at the obverse center.

Die State VIII: As VII, but now with the cracks extended across the head into the field beyond, toward the L of LIBERTY.

Collecting Notes

1798 BB-111 is in the medium range of scarcity among dollars of this date. An estimated 250 to 450 exist. A perusal of auction data dramatically reveals that VF is a high grade for this issue, and that EF and AU specimens are noteworthy. The average grade of VF-25 is one of the lower figures among 1798 silver dollars. This issue circulated extensively, to say the least.

Notable Specimens

Miller Specimen. AU-55 (NGC). Warren Miller Collection. Die State II.

Chouinard Specimen. AU-55 (NGC). Richard J. Chouinard Collection (Heritage, March 2005) lot 6706. Die State VII.

Cardinal Specimen. AU-53 (PCGS). Discovered by Martin Logies in Long Beach May 1996 • Cardinal Collection (Heritage, July 1997) lot 6490 • Albany Collection (Heritage, September 2002) lot 7779. Die State II.

Reiver Specimen. AU-53 (NGC). 1979 ANA Sale (New England Rare Coin Auctions, July 1979) lot 1032 • Jules Reiver Collection (Heritage, January 2006) lot 23513. Die State VIII.

Matthews Specimen. AU-50 (PCGS). Steve Fischer, February 1998 • Jim Matthews Collection • San Marino Collection Sale (Ira and Larry Goldberg, September 2002) lot 482. Die State II.

Miller Specimen (another). AU-50 (NGC). Warren Miller Collection. Die State VII.

Auction '86 Specimen. EF-45. Auction '86 (RARCOA, 1986) lot 729. "Bold EF to AU. Perfect die state."

Brilliant and Sieck Specimen. EF-45. Brilliant and Sieck Collections (Bowers and Merena, 1992) lot 1268. "Rare die state, the obverse severely broken and buckled diagonally across from 10:00 to 4:00, with one very deep linear break extending from the center of Liberty's head to the rim above the 13th star."

MacFarland Specimen. EF-45. MacFarland Collection (Bowers and Ruddy, 1981) lot 1558. "Choice EF-45. Perfect die state."

Lighthouse Specimen. EF-40. J.C. Lighthouse Collection • Bolender, 1952, lot 53.

Boyd Specimen. EF-40. "World's Greatest Collection" (F.C.C. Boyd, Numismatic Gallery, 1945) lot 36.

Stirling Specimen. EF-40. Frank M. Stirling Collection (Heritage, February 1986) lot 1337.

Lee and Shaffer Specimen. EF-40. Lee and Shaffer Collections (Superior, 1988) lot 3140. "Sharpness of EF-40 or better."

Ostheimer Specimen. VF-35. A.J. Ostheimer 3rd Collection (Lester Merkin, 1968) lot 253. "Nearly EF."

Total Estimated Population

MS-65 or better: 0 (URS-0)
MS-64: 0 (URS-0)
MS-63: 0 (URS-0)
MS-60 to 62: 0 (URS-0)
AU-50 to 58: 6 to 8 (URS-4)
VF-20 to EF-45: 150 to 275 (URS-9)
G-4 to F-15: 100 to 175 (URS-8)
Total for all grades combined: 250 to 450 (URS-10)
Estimated Total Condition Census: 55-55-53-53-50-50

BB-111: Middle die state with prominent die crack connecting lower rays of star 13.

BB-111: Late die state with heavy die break through hair, face, obverse field and upper rays of star 13.

174

1798 Pointed Tail 9, Heraldic Eagle, BB-112

Arc star pattern on reverse.

(B-15, H-15)

Obverse: Wide date, 11 mm. across at bottom widest part. seventh star very close to L, slightly closer than figure 1 of date from curl. Last star slightly nearer bust than figure 8 is from bust. Lowest right star ray points to a space between two dentils. The L and I in LIBERTY are distant while a spike protrudes from the hair below the point of the upper curl. Interior of lower curl is shaded. On the left, space between stars 5 and 6 is greater than between other stars. On the right, star 13 is smaller than any others.

Obverse die used to strike 1798 BB-112 only.

Reverse: See description under 1798 BB-110.

Reverse die used to strike 1798 BB-110 (1st use), BB-111 (2nd use), BB-112 (3rd use), and BB-113 (4th and final use). See discussion of die states under 1798 BB-110.

Die States

Die State I: Obverse: Die perfect and not yet relapped. Reverse: Without cracks. See discussion of die states under 1798 BB-110. May not exist.

Die State II: Dies as usually seen; described above. Relapped obverse. Star 13 appears smaller than the others.

Die State III: Bolender-15a. Obverse as above. In 1950, Bolender said this: "From same dies as Bolender-15, but the stars appear smaller. Struck before the die was finished." However, today it is considered to be a later state of the dies than the regular (Die State II) BB-112 issue. This variety is always weakly struck, with the centers especially so. Reverse with a crack from the left shield point to the ribbon.

Die State IV: As preceding, but now with additional reverse crack from the right top of the first T in STATES down to the second cloud (counting from the left).

Collecting Notes

Several hundred specimens of 1798 BB-112 exist, probably about 250 to 450, placing it in the medium range of rarity among varieties of this date. Most specimens are in grades up through VF and EF. AU or finer pieces are very rare.

Notable Specimens

Cardinal Specimen. MS-62 (PCGS). Cardinal Collection (American Numismatic Rarities, June 2005) lot 30.

Thaler Specimen. MS-62 (PCGS). Long Beach Signature Sale (Heritage, September 2003) lot 7475 • Thaler Collection (American Numismatic Rarities, March 2006) lot 1026.

Miller Specimen. MS-61 (NGC) • Warren Miller Collection.

Long Beach Specimen. MS-61 (ANACS). Long Beach Signature Sale (Heritage, June 2002) lot 6459 • Portland Signature Sale (Heritage, March 2004) lot 5949.

Gettys Specimen. MS-60. Loyd Gettys Collection. • Bolender Collection, 1952 • A.J. Ostheimer 3rd Collection (Lester Merkin, 1968) lot 257.

Queller Specimen. AU-58 (PCGS). Queller Family Collection of Silver Dollars (Heritage, April 2008) lot 2030 • Dr. Robert Hesselgesser Collection (Ira and Larry Goldberg, September 2011) lot 5052.

Auction '87 Specimen. AU-50. Superior, 1987, lot 1814

Boyd Specimen. AU-50. "World's Greatest Collection" (F.C.C. Boyd, Numismatic Gallery, 1945) lot 40. "Barely circulated with nice luster." • A.J. Ostheimer 3rd Collection (Lester Merkin, 1968) lot 258. "Bolender-15a. Obverse drastically lapped."

Fairbanks Specimen. AU-50. Fairbanks Collection (Stack's, 1960) lot 544. "AU."

Newport Specimen. AU-50. Newport Collection (Bowers and Ruddy, 1975) lot 382. "Beautiful AU."

Total Estimated Population
MS-65 or better: 0 (URS-0)
MS-64: 0 (URS-0)

MS-63: 0 (URS-0)
MS-60 to 62: 3 to 5 (URS-3)
AU-50 to 58: 6 to 12 (URS-4)
VF-20 to EF-45: 135 to 220 (URS-9)
G-4 to F-15: 115 to 170 (URS-8)
Total for all grades combined: 250 to 400 (URS-10)
Estimated Total Condition Census: 62-62-61-61-60-58

1798 POINTED TAIL 9, HERALDIC EAGLE, BB-113

Arc star pattern on reverse.
(B-27, H-27)

Obverse: Close date, about 9.5 mm. at widest part. *The 8 much too high,* and out of position, top leaning to right. Identifiable by the presence of a tiny horizontal obverse die flaw at the inner point of star 12 (visible only on higher grade specimens); tinier similar flaw at star 11. Highest wave of hair incomplete, probably from a lapped die (although I have never seen an impression from an earlier, unlapped state). This same obverse die was used for numerous other varieties.

Obverse die used to strike BB-113 (1st use), 1798 BB-114 (2nd use), BB-115 (3rd use), BB-116 (4th use), BB-117 (5th use), BB-118 (6th use), BB-119 (7th and final use).

Reverse: See description under 1798 BB-110. In this combination, a light die crack extends above S, through tops of OF, right wing tip, to border above first A in AMERICA.

Reverse die used to strike 1798 BB-110 (1st use), BB-111 (2nd use), BB-112 (3rd use), and BB-113 (4th and final use). See discussion of die states under 1798 BB-110.

Die States

Die State I: Obverse: Perfect die, not relapped. Reverse: Perfect die. See discussion of die states under 1798 BB-110. May not exist.

Die State II: Obverse: With a faint crack from dentils toward center of 9 to bust. Reverse: With a light die crack above S, through tops of OF, right wing tip, to border above first A in AMERICA. Cf. Norweb: 3756. The die state usually seen.

Die State III: Perfect obverse die. Reverse dies as II, but now with additional cracks from arrowhead through the wing to STA. The Spies Collection (Stack's, 1974) had a VF example.

Collecting Notes

The 1798 BB-113 is of medium availability. I estimate that 500 to 800 exist. This is one variety of 1798 for which numerous AU and Mint State coins are known, the latter grading up through and including MS-65.

Notable Specimens
Midwest Specimen. MS-64 (PCGS). Private Midwest collection.

Eliasberg Specimen. MS-64 (PCGS) • Louis E. Eliasberg Sr. Collection (Bowers and Merena, April 1997) lot 2184 • FUN Signature Sale (Heritage, January 1998) lot 7011 • Phillip Flannagan Collection (Bowers and Merena, November 2001) lot 4244.

Garrett Specimen. MS-63 (PCGS). Garrett Collection (Bowers and Ruddy, 1980) lot 689. "Choice

Brilliant Uncirculated, MS-65." • Unknown intermediaries • Richard Allen Collection (Heritage, January 2001) lot 7191.

CSNS Specimen. MS-62 (PCGS). CSNS Signature Sale (Heritage, April 2010) lot 2154 • Chicago Signature Sale (Heritage, August 2011) lot 7248.

Norweb Specimen. MS-60+. B. Max Mehl, November 1954, lot 10 • Norweb Collection (Bowers and Merena, 1988) lot 3756. "MS-60 to 63."

Earle Specimen. MS-60. George H. Earle Collection (Henry Chapman, 1912) • Schuyler Collection • Bolender Collection (M.H. Bolender, 1952) lot 78. "Perfect dies. Uncirculated." • A.J. Ostheimer 3rd Specimen (Lester Merkin, 1968) lot 268. "Perfect dies. Uncirculated."

1953 NENA Convention Specimen. MS-60. 1953 New England Numismatic Association Convention • K.P. Austin Collection • A.J. Ostheimer 3rd Collection • Gilhousen Collection (Superior, 1973) lot 1243. "Uncirculated." • ANA Convention Sale (Superior, 1975) lot 896. "Reverse cracked. Uncirculated." • Brown Library Sale (Pine Tree, 1976) lot 312. "Choice Uncirculated." • 1977 FUN Convention Sale (Pine Tree) lot 450 • Breen III Sale (Pine Tree, 1978) lot 602. "Uncirculated."

Anderson-Dupont Specimen. MS-60. Anderson-Dupont Collection (Stack's, 1954) lot 2501. "Uncirculated."

Hollinbeck-Kagin Specimen. MS-60. Hollinbeck-Kagin June 1970, lot 616. "Uncirculated." • Hollinbeck-Kagin, November 1971, lot 1333. "Uncirculated."

Marks Specimen. MS-60. Robert Marks Collection (Bowers and Ruddy, 1972) lot 75 • Austin Collection (Bowers and Ruddy, 1974) lot 18. "Brilliant Uncirculated." • Greater New York Convention Sale (Stack's, 1987) lot 869. "Brilliant Uncirculated. Die break at upper right reverse, and a thin break from curl across throat."

Tercentenary Sale Specimen. MS-60. Kagin's Tercentenary Sale 1974, lot 1149. "Uncirculated."

Stack's Specimen. MS-60. ANA Convention Sale (Stack's 1976) lot 1334. "Brilliant Uncirculated."

Heifetz Specimen. MS-60. Jascha Heifetz Collection (Superior, 1989) lot 2392.

Willasch Specimen. MS-60. H. Roland Willasch Collection (Superior, 1990) lot 506.

Total Estimated Population
MS-65 or better: 0 (URS-0)
MS-64: 2 (URS-2)
MS-63: 1 or 2 (URS-1)
MS-60 to 62: 10 to 20 (URS-5)
AU-50 to 58: 25 to 40 (URS-6)
VF-20 to EF-45: 375 to 575 (URS-10)
G-4 to F-15: 100 to 160 (URS-8)
Total for all grades combined: 500 to 800 (URS-11)
Estimated Total Condition Census: 64-64-63-62-60 (multiples)

1798 Pointed Tail 9, Heraldic Eagle, BB-114

Line star pattern on reverse.
(B-26, H-26)

Obverse: See description under 1798 BB-113. On the BB-114 variety, *a light die crack starts at border under 9 through two inner points of first star ending in field.*

Obverse die used to strike BB-113 (1st use), 1798 BB-114 (2nd use), BB-115 (3rd use), BB-116 (4th use), BB-117 (5th use), BB-118 (6th use), BB-119 (7th and final use) .

Reverse: *Point of star touches point of upper part of eagle's beak;* star points to left side of U. Line star pattern. 12 arrows and a stick. One of these arrows, the nearest one to N, has a very small head. (Haseltine called this the 11-arrows variety.) There are five small berries, the two at top closest together. Claw close to A but not touching it. Point of leaf under center of I in AMERICA. *Die crack from shield to border below, passes through end of stem.*

Light die crack through top of ES, base of O, right cloud, right wing and ribbon, outer leaves of branch, lower part of A and stem end, thence through eagle's tail. The two upper center stars touch clouds.

Reverse die used to strike 1798 BB-114 only.

Die States

Die State I: Obverse: Faint crack from dentils through center of 9 to bust. Additional crack up through inner points of star 1 and into field toward hair ribbons. An additional crack, very faint, from dentils, adjoining first two cracks, extends through dentils to right, curving up to bust. Reverse: Perfect die without cracks. May not exist with perfect reverse die.

Die State II. Obverse: As described for Die State I (the last-mentioned faint crack will be visible only on high grade examples; cf. Bowers and Merena, Florida United Numismatists Convention Sale, 1993: 516). Reverse: Die crack from shield to border below, passes through end of stem. Light die crack through top of ES, base of O, cloud 8, right wing and ribbon, outer leaves of branch, lower part of A and stem end, thence through eagle's tail.

Die State III. Obverse: As preceding. Reverse: Now with a heavy die crack on the reverse from the upper right top of the second T in STATES into the rim.

Die State IV. Obverse: As preceding. Reverse: Later state with additional crack from top of cloud 1, down through eagle's wing, to arrows, through tail, to stem end, joining earlier crack there. Additional crack through bottom of tail.

Die State V. Obverse: As preceding. Reverse: Still later state with crack from top of E in STATES, through top of S, bottom of O, through cloud 8, wing, right side of branch, and final A in AMERICA, joining earlier cracks at stem end. Additional crack from rim above wing tip, through tops of AM of AMERICA, to border above E. Other cracks as Die State IV. The reverse die could not have functioned much beyond this point.

Collecting Notes

1798 BB-114 exists to the extent of 35 to 60 pieces, if indeed even that many, and is one of the classic rarities of the year. All or nearly all specimens are in grades from EF downward. AU and Mint State coins are very rare.

Notable Specimens

Pittman Specimen. MS-61 (PCGS). John J. Pittman Collection, Part III (Akers, May 1998) lot 1667 • Cardinal Collection • Private collector • Cardinal Collection (American Numismatic Rarities, June 2005) lot 31 • Larry Stack • Private collector • 72nd Anniversary Sale (Stack's, October 2007) lot 5195 • W. David Perkins Collection.

Queller Specimen. AU-58 (NGC). Charles Jay Collection (Stack's, October 1967) lot 166 • George F. Scanlon Collection (Stack's, October 1973) lot 1717 • Unknown intermediaries • March Sale (Stack's, March 1996) lot 500 • Queller Family Collection of Silver Dollars (Heritage, April 2008) lot 2032 • Warren Miller Collection.

Hesselgesser Specimen. AU-55 (PCGS). Discovered by Martin Logies at the 1995 ANA Convention in Anaheim • Cardinal Collection • John Haugh • Flannagan Collection Sale (Bowers and Merena, November 2001) lot 4245 • Tangible Asset Galleries • Dr. Robert Hesselgesser Collection (Ira and Larry Goldberg, September 2011) lot 5055.

Summer FUN Specimen. AU-55 (PCGS). Summer FUN Signature Sale (Heritage, July 2012) lot 3821.

Miller Specimen. AU-53 (NGC). Warren Miller Collection.

1993 FUN Convention Sale Specimen. EF-45 (PCGS). FUN Sale (Bowers and Merena, January 1993) lot 516. "EF-45 to AU-50." • Lexington Sale (Bowers and Merena, January 1994) lot 2128 • Burke Sale (Bowers and Merena, May 1994) lot 2185 • ANA Signature Sale (Heritage, August 1995) lot 6507 • Jim Matthews Collection • San Marino Collection Sale (Ira and Larry Goldberg, September 2002) lot 497.

Kagin Specimen. EF-45. 1983 ANA Convention Sale (Kagin's, 1983) lot 2667.

DeCoppet Specimen. EF-40. André DeCoppet Collection (James Kelly, 1955). "Die break on reverse not distinct. EF."

River Oaks Specimen. EF-40. River Oaks (Glenn Davidson) Collection (Bowers and Ruddy 1976) lot 698. "EF. Reverse center a bit weak as struck."

Seller Specimen. EF-40. Seller Collection (Bowers and Ruddy, 1980) lot 3280.

Total Estimated Population

MS-65 or better: 0 (URS-0)

MS-64: 0 (URS-0)

MS-63: 0 (URS-0)

MS-60 to 62: 1 (URS-1)

AU-50 to 58: 4 (URS-3)

VF-20 to EF-45: 25 to 35 (URS-6)

G-4 to F-15: 10 to 15 (URS-5)

Total for all grades combined: 35 to 50 (URS-7)

Estimated Total Condition Census: 61-58-55-55-53-45 (multiples)

1798 Pointed Tail 9, Heraldic Eagle, BB-115

Line star pattern on reverse (B-31)

Obverse: See description under 1798 BB-113.

Obverse die used to strike BB-113 (1st use), 1798 BB-114 (2nd use), BB-115 (3rd use), BB-116 (4th use), BB-117 (5th use), BB-118 (6th use), BB-119 (7th and final use) .

Reverse: *Star close to both* upper and lower points of eagle's beak but does not touch; ray points to upper outside right of B of PLURIBUS. Line star pattern. Leaf points near center of upright of I in AMERICA. Five small berries, the two upper ones closest together. Slight die crack along upper side of right wing tip. The berries are small but the one at the top right appears slightly smaller than the others. 13 arrows, with the one overlapping the third shaft from the right having a tiny head.

This reverse die, first described by Bolender in 1950, was not known to J.W. Haseltine when he wrote his *Type-Table* in 1881.

Reverse die used to strike 1798 BB-115 only.

Die States

Die State I: Obverse: Die cracks as seen on BB-116, but in a slightly earlier state. The chip on the dentil below 9 is not quite as advanced as BB-116. Sawtooth line of dentil clash marks not visible on BB-115. Perfect reverse die. May not exist with perfect reverse die.

Die State II: Obverse: As preceding. Reverse: Slight die crack along upper side of eagle's right wing tip (on left side of coin). Tiny arc line (possibly used by the engraver as a guide for

BB-115: Early Die State

punching letters) near border between S and O in OF. Slightly scarcer than Die State IV.

Die State III: Intermediate state between II and IV, not otherwise described. New Netherlands Sale 48: 55, VF-20, was called superior to the Ralph Lathrop specimen in the 1952 ANA Convention sale. The Spies Collection coin (Stack's, 1974) was cataloged as F-VF.

Die State IV: Bolender-31a. Now with extensive die cracks on reverse. Heavy crack from border down through right side of 0 to cloud; another crack from border to top of F to wing, down to cloud below, from border at right wing tip through A under MERICA across claw, stem, and tail; continuing under UNI, across bottom of TED, left wing tip, center of STA. Also four curved die cracks down from TES through stars. All seen are very weak above the eagle's head and at the corresponding obverse. The die could not have been used much longer than this die state. Slightly more plentiful than Die State II.

Collecting Notes

1798 BB-115 is known to the extent of about 175 to 300 coins, and is one of the more elusive issues of the year. Most are of Die State IV. Most are in lower grades. The auction listing for an Uncirculated piece is several decades old, and in the absence of contradictory information, I call it EF-45 in the Condition Census.

It is a small wonder that even as many as 175 or so coins are known, considering that Haseltine in 1881 did not know of the variety. It was a rarity in M.H. Bolender's eyes, and in 1950 he estimated that no more than a dozen existed of each of the two die states of which he was aware. Since then, dozens more have been discovered.

Notable Specimens

Miller Specimen. AU-58 (NGC). Warren Miller Collection.

Albany Specimen. AU-58 (NGC). Albany Collection (Heritage, September 2002) lot 7799 • Baltimore Signature Sale (Heritage, July 2003) lot 8144 • June Sale (American Numismatic Rarities, June 2006) lot 2024 • November Sale (American Numismatic Rarities, November 2006) lot 436 • J.A. Sherman Collection (Stack's, August 2007) lot 790 • Chicago ANA Sale (Stack's Bowers, August 2011) lot 10506 • Baltimore Sale (Stack's Bowers, March 2012) lot 4114 • Philadelphia ANA Sale (Stack's Bowers, August 2012) lot 11482.

Miller Specimen (another). AU-55 (NGC). Warren Miller Collection.

Queller Specimen. AU-55 (NGC). Queller Family Collection of Silver Dollars (Heritage, April 2008) lot 2033.

Stark Specimen. AU-55. Country Store, Inc., New Brighton, MN, January 1983, sold to the following • Dr. Robert Stark Collection.

Hollinbeck-Kagin Specimen. AU-50. Hollinbeck-Kagin, June 1970, lot 617. "Struck from broken dies resulting in lower portion of collar of bust and opposite portion of reverse (top right star) not being fully struck up, near Uncirculated."

DeCoppet Specimen. EF-45. André DeCoppet Collection (James Kelly, 1955). "Choice EF."

Baldenhofer Specimen. EF-45. W.G. Baldenhofer to Farish-Baldenhofer Sale (Stack's, 1955) • A.J. Ostheimer 3rd Collection • ANA Convention Sale (Superior, 1975) lot 905. "Reverse die cracks. EF-45."

Ostheimer Specimen. EF-45. W. Earl Spies Collection • A. J. Ostheimer 3rd Collection (Lester Merkin, 1968) lot 271. "EF-AU. Traces of old cleaning."

Higgins Specimen. EF-45. Lloyd M. Higgins, M.D. Collection (Bowers and Merena, 1988) lot 2310. "EF-45 to AU-50."

Willasch Specimen. EF-45. H. Roland Willasch Collection (Superior, 1990).

Total Estimated Population

MS-65 or better: 0 (URS-0)
MS-64: 0 (URS-0)
MS-63: 0 (URS-0)
MS-60 to 62: 0 (URS-0)
AU-50 to 58: 5 to 8 (URS-4)
VF-20 to EF-45: 140 to 250 (URS-9)
G-4 to F-15: 35 to 50 (URS-7)
Total for all grades combined: 175 to 300 (URS-9)
Estimated Total Condition Census: 58-58-55-55-55-50

1798 Pointed Tail 9, Heraldic Eagle, BB-116

Arc star pattern on reverse.
(B-30, H-30)
Obverse: See description under 1798 BB-113.

Obverse die used to strike BB-113 (1st use), 1798 BB-114 (2nd use), BB-115 (3rd use), BB-116 (4th use), BB-117 (5th use), BB-118 (6th use), BB-119 (7th and final use).

Reverse: The upper stars on reverse are all very *distant from clouds.* Leaf points to space between R and I in AMERICA. Arc star pattern. Point of star barely touches upper part of eagle's beak (only three arc-pattern reverse dies, those used to coin BB-116, BB-117, and BB-125 have the ray at beak); ray of star points to upper outside right of B in PLURIBUS, while another ray points to the I. 13 arrows, two being faint. Five small berries, two at top nearest together.

Reverse die used to strike 1798 BB-116 only.

Die States

Die State I: Obverse: Cracks described under BB-115 are now bolder and more advanced. Crack through 9 bold and extends into bust. Small chip on dentil below this crack. A sawtooth-like line, probably clash marks from reverse dentils, is noted from top of LIBERTY through outer points of stars 8 and 9. Cf. Bowers and Merena, Frontenac Sale, 1991: 2209. Perfect reverse die.

Die State II: Obverse as preceding. Reverse with crack from right arm of T, through ED, to eagle's wing.

Die State III: Obverse as preceding. Reverse crack continues through clouds 1-3 to base of TE, bottom half of S, to rim just left of O. Reverse with additional crack from wing on left, above first U in PLURIBUS, through star on left to cloud 2.

Die State IV: Obverse as preceding. Reverse with additional cracks: Inside of border from right of D of UNITED, along border, through tip of wing, through tops of S and T, to above A. Light crack from rim through first A of AMERICA to feather. Crack from upper right of R through ICA, faintly to stem.

Die State V: On reverse, crack continues from stem end to rim. Crack from arrow feathers, middle of U of UNITED and bases of NITE. Short crack from center of eagle's tail feathers to dentils.

Die State VI: Bolender-30a. Reverse with Crack at first A in AMERICA expanded to create a blob from top of A to border. Curiously, Bolender noted that he knew of just one coin, the VG specimen in his collection, but he called it R-6, implying that over a dozen exist.

Collecting Notes

1798 BB-116 is one of the scarcer varieties of the year. About 150 to 250 are believed to be known. Most coins are in VF or so grade. EF specimens are quite rare, and anything better is very rare.

In his 1881 *Type-Table*, Haseltine called this variety very rare.

Notable Specimens

Krugjohann Specimen. AU-58. C. W. Krugjohann Collection (Bowers and Ruddy, 1976) lot 613. "BU. Numerous die breaks (shattered dies)." • Later offered as AU-55, Robert W. Rusbar Collection (Bowers and

Merena, 1990) lot 348 • Still later as lot 1464 in the Tower Hill Collection (Bowers and Merena, September 1993).[1]

Emery-Nichols Specimen. AU-50. Emery and Nichols Collections (Bowers and Merena, 1984) lot 935. "Iridescent toning on obverse commences at the periphery in shades of pale gold, turning to hues of blue and violet toward the center. Reverse toning is not quite as vivid, though multicolored shades do highlight the sharply struck and notably clean surfaces." • Numismatic Auctions of Florida. November 1985, lot 330 • Frontenac Collection (Bowers and Merena, 1991) lot 2209, AU-50. "Particularly deeply struck, with the denticles and rims especially pronounced in most areas, most prominently around 2/3 of the reverse. Light gray and lilac toning." • Warren Miller Collection.

Hesselgesser Specimen. AU-50 (PCGS). Drew St. John Sale (American Numismatic Rarities, June 2005) lot 183 • Unknown intermediaries • Dr. Robert Hesselgesser Collection (Ira and Larry Goldberg, September 2011) lot 5058.

Newcomer Specimen. AU-50. Waldo C. Newcomer Collection as Uncirculated • B. Max Mehl • Col. E.H.R. Green Collection • T. James Clarke Collection (New Netherlands 48th Sale, 1956) lot 625. "Pronounced obverse die breaks emanating at border directly below 9 of date. Rev. All upper stars distant from clouds. Uncirculated. Neatly defined borders; comparatively well struck. Minute obverse rim bruise at right; reverse field nick (in stars) near eagle's head. Lightly toned, rose-blue iridescence. An intermediate die state, reverse crack through TED to wing described by Bolender under his Bolender-30a, but lacks the other characteristics." This was later graded AU-50 and appeared in W.G. Baldenhofer's Collection to Farish-Baldenhofer Sale (Stack's, 1955) • A.J. Ostheimer 3rd Collection • Gilhousen Sale (Superior, 1973) lot 1244. "Fine double profile. Rainbow toned Uncirculated, lustrous and sharp." • ANA Convention Sale (Superior, 1975) lot 902. "Fine double profile. AU-50, slight rainbow toning, lustrous, sharp. Tiny rim bruise opposite 10th stars is mentioned mainly for identification purposes. Fairly well centered and has some signs of obverse handling." • Santa Clara Sale (Heritage, November 2000) lot 5983, as EF-45 (PCGS) but described as "seemingly undergraded."

Stack's Specimen. AU-50. ANA Convention Sale (Stack's, 1976) lot 3451. "AU and lustrous. Purchased by the owner as Uncirculated, but there is too much of a rub on the eagle's breast and on the cheek to call it Mint State. Natural golden and iridescent toning." • Dr. Robert Stark Collection.

---

[1] Much information is from W. David Perkins, "Major Revision in CC for 1798 B30 Dollar," *John Reich Journal*, January 1995.

Willasch Specimen. Genuine (PCGS) Choice AU Details, Cleaned. H. Roland Willasch Collection (Superior, May 1990) lot 512 • Unknown intermediaries • 67th Anniversary Sale (Stack's, October 2002) lot 1272 • Brooklyn Sale (Stack's, March 2007) lot 1031 • Queller Family Collection of Silver Dollars (Heritage, April 2008) lot 2034 • Philadelphia Americana Sale (Stack's Bowers, September 2011) lot 5006.

Copper Die Trial • Unique copper die trial specimen struck from the BB-116 dies on an irregular metal scrap, discovered by metal detectorists in 2006 working on a lot adjoining the site of the first U.S. Mint in Philadelphia. Published by ANS curator Robert W. Hoge on page 39 of American Numismatic Society

Magazine, Spring 2007 • J.A. Sherman Sale (Stack's, August 2007) lot 3025.

Total Estimated Population
MS-65 or better: 0 (URS-0)
MS-64: 0 (URS-0)
MS-63: 0 (URS-0)
MS-60 to 62: 0 (URS-0)
AU-50 to 58: 8 to 15 (URS-4)
VF-20 to EF-45: 90 to 160 (URS-8)
G-4 to F-15: 55 to 75 (URS-7)
Total for all grades combined: 150 to 250 (URS-9)
Estimated Total Condition Census: 58-50-50-50-50-45 (multiples)

1798 Pointed Tail 9, Heraldic Eagle, BB-117

Arc star pattern on reverse.

(B-33)

Obverse: See description under 1798 BB-113. On this variety the highest hair curl is very weak and indistinct. The horizontal die flaws in the right field inside stars 10 and 12 are bold. A horizontal die scratch is just above the back of the head, below IB of LIBERTY.

Obverse die used to strike BB-113 (1st use), 1798 BB-114 (2nd use), BB-115 (3rd use), BB-116 (4th use), BB-117 (5th use), BB-118 (6th use), BB-119 (7th and final use) .

Reverse: Arc star pattern. Point of star almost touches upper beak (only three arc-pattern reverse dies, those used to coin BB-116, BB-117, and BB-125 have the ray at beak); ray points to right side of B in PLURIBUS. No stars touch clouds, although the last is very close. 13 perfect arrows. Lowest arrow extends just past right edge of left upright of N in UNITED. Top left berry is the smallest of 5 berries; the top right is the largest. The lowest berry is directly below the left tip of the right foot of final A. Final A does not touch claw. The first A in AMERICA

does not touch either the third or fourth feather. Point of leaf below left side of upright of I in AMERICA. From claws, branch stem angles down to the right, then back toward the left, pointing toward the tail feathers. Left base of E in UNITED higher than the base of T. Left base of E in STATES higher than base of T. Letters in AMER very close at their bases. A short die scratch extends just over 1 mm. from the right top of the shield.

Reverse die used to strike 1798 BB-117 only.

Die States

Die State I: Obverse: Cracks in about the same state as BB-116. Sawtooth-type clash marks not visible (relapped?). Perfect reverse die. May not exist with perfect reverse die.

Die State II: Obverse: As preceding. Reverse: Crack from dentils through right arm of T in UNITED, into field below left ribbon end. Another crack from dentils, connecting left serifs of M to right ribbon. The die is bulged between and joining these two cracks. Presumably, these cracks eventually joined to form Die State III. Cf. Spies Collection (Stack's, 1974) lot 111.

Die State III: Obverse: As preceding. Reverse: Heavy die crack bisects the reverse from 8 o'clock to 3 o'clock. Rust pits in shield. Cf. Spies Collection (Stack's, 1974) lot 112.

Collecting Notes

1798 BB-117, unknown to Haseltine and Bolender, shares honors with BB-103 as one of the two rarest varieties of the year. The number of specimens known is a matter of conjecture. The W. Earl Spies Collection (Stack's, 1974) had two, both EF, and both of a different die state. Just three specimens have been confirmed.

Notable Specimens

Blevins Specimen. AU-53 (PCGS. W. Earl Spies Collection (Stack's, December 1974) lot 111. "Unknown to either Bolender or Haseltine. Obverse Bolender-26, reverse is new. Fully EF." • H.W. Blevins Collection (Superior, June 1988) lot 3699 • James Matthews Collection • San Marino Collection Sale (Ira and Larry Goldberg, September 2002) lot 502.

Spies Specimen. AU-50 (NGC). W. Earl Spies Collection (Stack's, 1974) lot 112. "Reverse die crack has totally bisected the reverse from "T" to "M" in what must be the terminal state of the dies. R-8 in the Spies Collection. EF." • H. Roland Willasch Collection (Superior, 1990) lot 516. "Obverse is well struck even though a massive die crack appeared on the reverse which often renders the obverse strike weak. Reverse terminal die state—a pronounced die crack spans the reverse from the T in UNITED to the M of AMERICA. In the field below the left wing of the eagle the crack is really just a large area of swelling." • Warren Miller Collection.

Reiver Specimen. AU-50. Philip G. Straus Collection (Stack's, May 1959) lot 2083 • Jules Reiver Collection • Sold privately, and not appearing in the Heritage Sale of the Reiver Collection in January 2006. (Specimen illustrated in the 1st edition of the book.)

Total Estimated Population

MS-65 or better: 0 (URS-0)
MS-64: 0 (URS-0)
MS-63: 0 (URS-0)
MS-60 to 62: 0 (URS-0)
AU-50 to 58: 3 (URS-3)
VF-20 to EF-45: 0 (URS-0)
G-4 to F-15: 0 (URS-0)
Total for all grades combined: 5 to 10 (URS-4)
Estimated Total Condition Census: 53-50-50

1798 POINTED TAIL 9, HERALDIC EAGLE, BB-118

Arc star pattern on reverse.
(B-28, H-28)
Obverse: See description under 1798 BB-113.

Obverse die used to strike BB-113 (1st use), 1798 BB-114 (2nd use), BB-115 (3rd use), BB-116 (4th use), BB-117 (5th use), BB-118 (6th use), BB-119 (7th and final use) .

Reverse: Leaf point is slightly right of center of I in AMERICA. *Tip of branch points to tip of rightmost tail feather* (compare to reverse shared by BB-92 and BB-91, and to the reverse of BB-117, the only other 1798 reverses in which this is the case). Star distant from eagle's beak; star ray points to just left of B in PLURIBUS. Arc star pattern. 13 perfect arrows. Five medium-sized berries, the two at top closest together. A die crack begins at border above last S in STATES, and passes through center of OF, right wing, bottom of AME, up through RIC. Short crack from last A to border, another from lower outside leaf of branch past claw to stem end. Heavy crack from lower left part of shield down through claw and arrow butts. Another die crack through U and left wing. Another crack through

NITE up through TA. The left upright of N is clearly punched over a previous erroneous I.[1]

Reverse die used to strike 1798 BB-118 only.

Die States[2]

Die State I: Obverse with cracks slightly advanced from those on BB-117. Reverse die perfect. Not listed by Bolender; Stark Bolender-28a. Scarce. Auction appearances, which may include duplication, include DeCoppet (1955) VF-35, Ostheimer (1968) VF-EF, Spies (1974) VF, and 1975 ANA VF-30 dull.

Die State II: Obverse: As preceding. Reverse: Two reverse die cracks, approximately parallel, immediately to the left of the eagle's tail. Stark Bolender-28b.

Die State III: Intermediate stage(s) between II and IV; not detailed by Dr. Stark, but probably made.

Die State IV: As II, but with additional cracks from rim through U to N to arrow to second feather; rim over U through NITE to wing to STA; O

BB-118: Late die state with advanced reverse die breaks.

through F to AMERIC to rim; rim below stem to nearest A; stem to claw to leaf. Small piece of die missing in area of two approximately parallel cracks immediately to the left of the eagle's tail. The approximate die state described by Bolender for Bolender-28; Stark Bolender-28c.

Die State V: As IV, but now with larger piece of die missing to left of eagle's tail. Stark Bolender-28d. The Spies Collection coin (Stack's, 1974), F-12, damaged, had the reverse off center, indicating axial misalignment of dies; this coin may have been of this approximate die state.

Die State VI: As V, but now with entire section of die missing from area earlier within two approximately parallel cracks to the left of the eagle's tail. Crack from tip of center arrow to the 4th feather. An earlier crack, first seen on Die State II, and extending to the ribbon there, has now crossed the ribbon at P, passing through the leftmost star and extending to the 2nd cloud from the left. By this time, on the obverse clash marks are visible between the bust and the final three stars on the right. Stark Bolender-28e.

---

[1] This characteristic discovered by Thomas K. DeLorey, October 2, 1992.

[2] Robert M. Stark's article, "Die Deterioration of a 1798 Dollar (Bolender-28 Reverse)," in the *John Reich Journal*, August 1992, was used in the compilation of this information. However, Dr. Stark designates the first state, with no defects, as B-28a. I follow a different numbering sequence.

Collecting Notes

The 1798 BB-118 is of medium rarity among die varieties of the year. I estimate that 275 to 450 exist. Most of these are in lower grades through VF, although EF pieces are occasionally seen. AU or finer coins are rare.

Notable Specimens

1997 ANA Specimen. MS-64 (NGC). ANA Signature Sale (Heritage, July 1997) lot 6492 • Pre-FUN Elite Sale (Superior, January 2004) lot 461.

Boyd Specimen. MS-60. "World's Greatest Collection" (F.C.C. Boyd, Numismatic Gallery 1945) lot 54. "Uncirculated."

Hollinbeck-Kagin Specimen. MS-60. August 1970, lot 1082. "Uncirculated."

French Specimen. MS-60. French Family Collection (Stack's, 1989) lot 547. "Brilliant Uncirculated."

Stack Specimen. MS-60. James A. Stack Collection (Stack's, 1989) lot 527. "Brilliant Uncirculated."

Fairbanks Specimen. AU-55. Fairbanks Collection (Stack's, 1960) lot 550. "The early strike before the reverse die cracked, as described by Bolender. Just a shade from Uncirculated."

Miller Specimen. AU-55 (NGC). Warren Miller Collection.

Long Beach Specimen. AU-55 (NGC). Long Beach Signature Sale (Heritage, September 2005) lot 3664.

Bolender Specimen. AU-50 (PCGS). M.H. Bolender • K.P. Austin • Baldenhofer • Jacque and A.J. Ostheimer Collection (Superior, August 1975) lot 897 • Jules Reiver Collection (Heritage, January 2006) lot 23542 • William Luebke Collection (Heritage, January 2007) lot 4989 • Dr. Robert Hesselgesser Collection (Ira and Larry Goldberg, September 2011) lot 5059.

Total Estimated Population

MS-65 or better: 0 (URS-0)
MS-64: 1 (URS-1)
MS-63: 0 (URS-0)
MS-60 to 62: 6 to 10 (URS-4)
AU-50 to 58: 15 to 25 (URS-5)
VF-20 to EF-45: 160 to 250 (URS-9)
G-4 to F-15: 100 to 160 (URS-8)
Total for all grades combined: 275 to 450 (URS-10)
Estimated Total Condition Census: 64-60 (multiples)

1798 Pointed Tail 9, Heraldic Eagle, BB-119

Line star pattern on reverse.

(B-29, H-29)

Obverse: See description under 1798 BB-113.

Obverse die used to strike BB-113 (1st use), 1798 BB-114 (2nd use), BB-115 (3rd use), BB-116 (4th use), BB-117 (5th use), BB-118 (6th use), BB-119 (7th and final use) .

Reverse: Star touches lower part of eagle's beak; ray points to just left of U in PLURIBUS. Line star pattern. Five small berries, two above closest together. Leaf points under right edge of upright of I in AMERICA. 13 perfect arrows, an unusual situation.

Reverse die used to strike 1798 BB-119 (earlier state) and BB-120 (later state).

Die States

Die State I: Obverse: Die cracks similar to those on BB-118 but more advanced, now extending across bust into right field. Two short cracks from bust to last star. Additional crack from outside first star through next 3 stars and passing under the 5th, 6th, and 7th stars. The crack splits in two at this point, and both branches continue to the hair. This variety was struck shortly after BB-118. Reverse from perfect die. The variety usually seen. An AU specimen in the 1975 ANA Convention sale (Superior) had the obverse poorly centered, indicating axial misalignment.

Die State II: Obverse as preceding. Reverse with die crack through UNITED, two leftmost wing tip feathers, and ST, continuing to the top of A and above T. The die state used to strike BB-120.

Collecting Notes

1798 BB-119 is scarce. Probably about 200 to 350 exist, most of which are in lower grades through VF. EF coins are quite rare, and AU specimens are extremely rare. No Mint State coin has been seen. The one listed was sold in 1970, and may not grade as Uncirculated today.

Notable Specimens

Hollinbeck-Kagin Specimen. MS-60. Hollinbeck-Kagin, January 1970, lot 783. "Uncirculated."

Holmes Specimen. AU-55. Milton A. Holmes Collection (Stack's, 1960) lot 2243. "AU, choice."

Internet Sale Specimen. AU-55 (NGC). Exclusively Internet Sale (Heritage, July 2004) lot 11421 • Long Beach Signature Sale (Heritage, May 2009) lot 919 • Long Beach Signature Sale (September 2009) lot 907 • Baltimore Sale (Bowers and Merena, November 2009) lot 3019.

Baldenhofer Specimen. AU-50. W.G. Baldenhofer to Farish-Baldenhofer Sale (Stack's, 1955) • A. J. Ostheimer 3rd Collection • ANA Convention Sale (Superior, 1975) lot 901. "Superficially AU-50, but rubbed on the high points of the obverse."

Miller Specimen. AU-50 (NGC). September Sale (Stack's, September 2005) lot 1759 • Warren Miller Collection.

Orlando FUN Sale Specimen. EF-45 (PCGS). Orlando Signature Sale (Heritage, January 2010) lot 3542.

Miller Specimen (another). EF-45 (NGC) • Warren Miller Collection.

Saunders Specimen. EF-45. Ebenezer Milton Saunders Collection (Bowers and Merena, 1987) lot 3514. "EF-45 or finer."

Lee and Shaffer Collections Specimen. EF-45. Lee and Shaffer Collections (Superior, 1988) lot 3148. "Extremely late obverse die. Sharpness of EF-45."

Four Landmark Collections Specimen. EF-45. Four Landmark Collections (Bowers and Merena, 1989) lot 1961. "EF-45 to AU-50. Later state of the obverse die than usually seen."

Hesselgesser Specimen. EF-40 (PCGS). Dr. Robert Hesselgesser Collection (Ira and Larry Goldberg, September 2011) lot 5062 • Pre-Long Beach Sale (Ira and Larry Goldberg, May 2012) lot 1289.

Matthews Specimen. EF-40 (PCGS). Steve Fischer, October 1998 • Jim Matthews Collection • San Marino Collection Sale (Ira and Larry Goldberg, September 2002) lot 498.

Total Estimated Population
MS-65 or better: 0 (URS-0)
MS-64: 0 (URS-0)

MS-63: 0 (URS-0)
MS-60 to 62: 1 or 2 (URS-1)
AU-50 to 58: 3 to 6 (URS-43
VF-20 to EF-45: 125 to 220 (URS-9)
G-4 to F-15: 75 to 125 (URS-8)
Total for all grades combined: 200 to 350 (URS-9)
Estimated Total Condition Census: 60-55-55-50-50-45 (multiples)

1798 Pointed Tail 9, Heraldic Eagle, BB-120

Line star pattern on reverse.
(B-12, H-12)

Obverse: 17 of date close together, other figures wider apart. The date measures slightly more than 10 mm. across at the bottom widest part. Star 1 distant 3.5 mm. from curl. In date, numeral 1 is near curl, 8 far from bust. Lips of Liberty open. On the left, stars quite evenly spaced, but the space between stars 6-7 is very slightly wider. On the right, stars 10-11 most widely spaced. Star 13 points to center of a dentil.

Obverse die used to strike 1798 BB-120 only.

Reverse: See description under 1798 BB-119.

Reverse die used to strike 1798 BB-119 (earlier state) and BB-120 (later state).

Die States

Die State I: Perfect dies; no crack on reverse. May not exist. (This die state and Die State II were used to coin BB-119).

Die State II: Die crack through UNITED, two leftmost wing tip feathers, and ST, continuing to the top of A and above T. The die state usually seen.

Die State III: Obverse now shows a crack from a dentil between the 7 and the 9 to the drapery as well as other cracks from the border upward and slightly left, through the innermost rays of star 1, to the field opposite the ribbons. Another crack connects stars 11 to 13.

Die State IV: Obverse crack on right now goes from star 13 to 11 (as before), through innermost ray of star

10, to field opposite forehead. Curved arc crack from bust through bottom ray of star 15 curving to border. Additional crack from border up to drapery on right. Additional crack from border to second lowest curl on left. On reverse, new crack develops from left stand of M in AMERICA, under M and under E. A VG specimen in the Stark Collection was obtained from Jules Reiver, March 1983.

Die State V: The very rare terminal die state (cf. Gilhousen: 1233, VF) shows die failure at the drapery and the corresponding reverse plus a crack at ES OF AM.

Collecting Notes

1798 BB-120 is of medium scarcity. I estimate that about 225 to 425 exist, most of which are in circulated grades through VF. At the EF or better level BB-120 is rare.

Notable Specimens

Lee Specimen. MS-64 PCGS). Jack Lee Collection III (Heritage, November 2005) lot 2191 • CSNS Signature Sale (Heritage, April 2008) lot 2337 • Dr. Robert Hesselgesser Collection (Ira and Larry Goldberg, May 2011) lot 892.

Hesselgesser Specimen. AU-58 (PCGS). Dr. Robert Hesselgesser Collection • Private collector • Boston Rarities Sale (Bowers and Merena, August 2010) lot 1022.

Cardinal Specimen. AU-55 (PCGS). Cardinal Collection • Private collector • Long Beach Signature Sale

(Heritage, September 2010) lot 4315.

Somerset Specimen. AU-55. Somerset Collection (Bowers and Merena, 1992) lot 1321. "Lightly cleaned."

Tuttle Specimen. AU-50. Tuttle Collection (Bowers and Ruddy, 1981) lot 2980.

Miller Specimen. EF-45 (NGC). Warren Miller Collection. Die State II.

Baldenhofer Specimen. EF-45. W.G. Baldenhofer Collection, to Farish-Baldenhofer Sale (Stack's, 1955) • A.J. Ostheimer 3rd Collection • ANA Convention Sale (Superior, 1975) lot 866. "EF-45 or better."

Total Estimated Population

MS-65 or better: 0 (URS-0)
MS-64: 1 (URS-1)
MS-63: 0 (URS-0)
MS-60 to 62: 0 (URS-0)
AU-50 to 58: 3 to 6 (URS-3)
VF-20 to EF-45: 140 to 200 (URS-9)
G-4 to F-15: 85 to 135 (URS-8)
Total for all grades combined: 225 to 350 (URS-9)
Estimated Total Condition Census: 64-58-55-55-50 (multiples)

1798 POINTED TAIL 9, HERALDIC EAGLE, BB-121

"Amateur Diecutter's Reverse"
Arc star pattern
(B-9, H-9)
Obverse: Compact date, 8 close to bust, being a little nearer than 1 is to curl. Upper left star close to L and lowest right star very close to bust. On the left, stars 1 and 2, and 2 and 3, are more widely spaced than are the other stars. On the right, stars 10-11 and 11-12 are more widely spaced than are the other stars. Curl close to date is complete but is formed very delicately.

Obverse die used to strike 1798 BB-121 only.

Reverse: "Amateur Diecutter's Reverse." Star distant from eagle's beak. Arc star pattern, but amateurishly executed, with the first star in the second row out of place and too high. This is the only 1798 reverse with this "sloppy" die work. Star distant from beak. Star ray points to top of I in PLURIBUS. Five small berries, the second and third from top are closest together. Bottom end of olive branch is long and needle-like. Leaf points to lower right point of R in AMERICA. Either 12 or 13 arrows are present; two are very weak and appear to hold another stick between them; the two rightmost arrow shafts each have two heads (and thus count as four arrows), the third arrow shaft from the right is ghostlike (the three rightmost

shafts are quite similar to those on the reverse used to coin BB-96, BB-101 and certain other reverses of the era).

Reverse die used to strike 1798 BB-121 only.

Die States

Die State I: Die state as described above; perfect dies.

Die State II: Perfect dies, except for tiny vertical crack on reverse from O in OF to rim. Raised die rust marks between lowest curl and border (visible on higher grade pieces). Most BB-121 dollars are of this die state.

Die State III: Bolender-9a. Now with die cracks as follows: A crack on obverse from border up through 17 to bust. Another crack from border through two lower rays of second star. Other cracks from third to sixth stars. Reverse shows light crack through STATES OF AM. Another crack from border down through M to ribbon. Some specimens have the vertical elements of letters in LIBERTY bifurcated, or (on the reverse) even the horizontal members of the letters such as E and D in UNITED missing due to bifurcation, but this idiosyncrasy does not determine a separate die state.

Die State IV: Die cracks more advanced than preceding. Dies show rust. Cf. Spies "Bolender-9b" and possibly the Gilhousen VF coin.

Collecting Notes

1798 BB-121 has an estimated population of 300 to 500 pieces, enough that the specialist can find one with some searching, and probably will have to pay no more than a "type" price. Most specimens of BB-121 are seen in lower grade levels. The variety becomes a rarity in AU grade and extremely rare in full Mint State, if today's strict grading interpretations are used.

Notable Specimens

Long Beach Sale Specimen. MS-62 (NGC). Long Beach Signature Sale (Heritage, February 2007) lot 3610.

Cardinal Specimen. AU-58 (PCGS). Albany Collection (Heritage, September 2002) lot 7777 • Cardinal Collection (American Numismatic Rarities, June 2005) lot 32 • Don Willis • J.A. Sherman Collection (Stack's, August 2007) lot 781 • Dr. Robert Hesselgesser Collection (Ira and Larry Goldberg, May 2011) lot 893.

Cardinal Specimen (another). AU-55 (PCGS). Tangible Asset Galleries • Cardinal Collection • Private collector • Dr. Robert Hesselgesser Collection (Ira and Larry Goldberg, September 2011) lot 5065.

Miller Collection. AU-55 (NGC). Warren Miller Collection.

Reiver Specimen. AU-55 (NGC). W. Earl Spies Collection (Stack's, December 1974) lot 58 • Jules Reiver Collection (Heritage, January 2006) lot 23509.

DeCoppet Specimen. AU-55. André DeCoppet Collection (James Kelly, 1955). "Practically Uncirculated."

Mason-Dixon Specimen. AU-50. Mason-Dixon Sale, May 1957 • Alfred J. Ostheimer 3rd Collection (Lester Merkin, 1968) lot 251. "AU."

Spring Quartette Sale Specimen AU-50. Spring Quartette Sale (Bowers and Merena, 1992) lot 2578. "Struck lightly off center on both sides, with AMERICA to edge of coin on reverse."

Bauer Specimen. EF-45. Bauer Collection (Lester Merkin, 1968) lot 389. "All breaks listed by Bolender, additional break through O. EF+."

Brilliant and Sieck Collections Specimen. EF-45. Brilliant and Sieck Collections (Bowers and Merena, 1992) lot 1267.

Everson and Faught Collections Specimen. EF-45. Everson and Faught Collections (Bowers and Merena, 1988) lot 216.

Total Estimated Population

MS-65 or better: 0 (URS-0)
MS-64: 0 (URS-0)
MS-63: 0 (URS-0)
MS-60 to 62: 1 (URS-1)
AU-50 to 58: 3 to 6 (URS-3)
VF-20 to EF-45: 200 to 350 (URS-9)
G-4 to F-15: 100 to 150 (URS-8)
Total for all grades combined: 300 to 500 (URS-10)
Estimated Total Condition Census: 62-58-55 (multiples)

1798 POINTED TAIL 9, HERALDIC EAGLE, BB-122

Line star pattern on reverse.
(B-14, H-14)
Obverse: Medium wide date, 10.25 mm. across at bottom widest part. The 1 in date close to hair, 8 close to bust. Stars about equidistant from curl, L, Y, and bust, except that upper left star is a little closer to L. Ray of star 1 points to slightly left of center of a dentil. On the left there is more space between stars 6 and 7 than the other stars. On the right stars 8 and 9 have a smaller space between them than do any other stars. The highest curl on head is solid and is centered under upright of E. Some lines (die clash marks) show in field between curl

and first two stars. Interior of loop on lowest curl "shaded" with hair details.

NOTE. This obverse die closely resembles BB-124, to which refer. BB-122 is distinguishable by the fact that it has the 8 closer to the bust than does BB-124, and that the 11th and 12th stars on BB-122 are much closer together than on BB-124.

Obverse die used to strike 1798 BB-122 only.

Reverse: *Claw touches A* in AMERICA; the only 1798 reverse with this feature. Five small berries, two top ones closest together. Point of leaf under left lower point of I in AMERICA. Star just misses touching point of upper part of eagle's beak, and in worn specimens appears to touch; star ray points to center of B in PLURIBUS. Line star pattern. 13 perfect arrows. Four rightmost shafts each have two arrowheads (total of eight arrowheads there); third shaft from left is thinner than normal; fourth shaft from left is much too thick.

Reverse die used to strike 1798 BB-122 only.

BB-122: Die State II with clashed dies, but no die cracks.

Die States

Die State I: Perfect dies. No obverse clash mark. One example known in the Warren Miller Collection..

Die State II: Dies as described above for BB-122. Clash marks on obverse. Clash marks on reverse below two rightmost clouds. Raised die roughness at E of UNITED.

Die State III: Obverse die begins to fail; crack develops connecting innermost rays of stars 2 through 5. Slightly scarcer than following.

Die State IV: As above, but tiny crack now connects stars 4 and 5 near their centers. The most plentiful die state.

Die State V: As above, but reverse die now relapped, thinning and damaging some of the arrows, lightening the raised die roughness at E of UNITED, and obliterating much of the leaf under C of AMERICA. Slightly scarcer than preceding.

Die State VI: Bolender-14a. Obverse crack extends down to star 1 and up to star 7. Star 7 and L of LIBERTY weaken. Reverse die as above. Rarer than preceding.

Die State VII: Bolender-14b. With same die cracks as State VI, but the die crack on obverse is now heavier, nearly obliterating the star 7 and part of L. Bolender mentions a crack on reverse through right part of 0. Rare.

Die State VIII: Latest die state coins shows the obverse star 7 and the L in LIBERTY entirely removed by a heavy die crack.

Collecting Notes

Somewhere in the range of 350 to 550 1798 BB-122 dollars are believed to exist. The variety is very rare above EF and virtually unknown in Mint State. The distribution of available specimens is heavily weighted toward the low end of the Very Fine category.

Notable Specimens

Northeast Specimen. MS-62 (NGC). Private collector • Northeast Numismatics, advertised in *Coin World* during 1998 as MS-63 (NGC). Private collector • Long Beach Signature Sale (Heritage, February 2009) lot 1544 • CSNS Signature Sale (Heritage, April 2009) lot 2548 • Los Angeles Signature Sale (Heritage, August 2009) lot 1142. Die State IV.

Baltimore Sale Specimen. AU-58 (NGC). Baltimore Sale (Bowers and Merena, March 2007) lot 5016 • St. Louis Rarities Sale (Bowers and Merena, May 2007) lot 119. Die State IV.

Cardinal Specimen. AU-58 (NGC). RARCOA • Cardinal Collection • Private collector • Pre-Long Beach Sale (Ira and Larry Goldberg, September 2006) lot 2797. Die State II.

Orlando FUN Sale Specimen. AU-58 (NGC). Orlando FUN Signature Sale (Heritage, January 2009) lot 3941. Die State IV.

Miller Specimen (another). AU-55 (NGC). Pre-Long Beach Sale (Ira and Larry Goldberg, May 2006) lot 3039 • Warren Miller Collection. Die State II.

Hesselgesser Specimen. AU-55 (PCGS). Dr. Robert Hesselgesser Collection (Ira and Larry Goldberg, September 2011) lot 5067. Die State II.

Miller Specimen (another). AU-55 (NGC). Warren Miller Collection. Die State IV.

Garrett Specimen. AU-50. Garrett Collection (Bowers and Ruddy, 1980) lot 688.

Stark Specimen. AU-50. Stack's, September 1988. Sold to the following • Dr. Robert Stark Collection.

Hollinbeck-Kagin Specimen. AU-50. Hollinbeck-Kagin Sale, June 1970, lot 611. "Nearly Uncirculated."

Brooks Specimen. EF-45. Brooks Collection (Bowers and Merena, 1989) lot 206.

Ebsen Specimen. EF-45. Buddy Ebsen Collection (Superior, 1987) lot 1897.

Total Estimated Population
MS-65 or better: 0 (URS-0)
MS-64: 0 (URS-0)
MS-63: 0 (URS-0)

MS-60 to 62: 2 (URS-2)
AU-50 to 58: 3 to 6 (URS-3)
VF-20 to EF-45: 225 to 350 (URS-9)
G-4 to F-15: 125 to 200 (URS-9)
Total for all grades combined: 350 to 550 (URS-10)
Estimated Total Condition Census: 62-61-58-58-58-55 (multiples)

1798 POINTED TAIL 9, HERALDIC EAGLE, BB-123

"Blundered Stars Reverse."
Line star pattern (placed too high).
(B-25, H-25)
Obverse: Close date, only 9.5 mm. across at widest part. "Whisker" on chin. *Die dot* in field under chin, about one-third of the distance between neck and star 12. 1 very close to curl. Last star near bust, upper right star distant from Y, upper left star still farther from L, and first star farthest from curl.

Obverse die used to strike 1798 BB-123 only.

Reverse: "Blundered Stars Reverse" with blundered star placement; some stars overlap clouds. Perhaps, the engraver had too much rum (or "ayle," per National Archives records) while cutting this die! Two uppermost stars in center partly in clouds. Cloud 4 has two rays of a star superimposed on it at lower left; clouds 5 and 6, which overlap, are with the top ray of a star touching cloud 5, the ray to the left of it barely touching the cloud, and the ray to the right slightly overlapping cloud 6. A star touches point of upper part of eagle's beak; star ray points to right side of B in PLURIBUS. Line star pattern. *Die crack from stem* down to milling. *Small die flaws* in E of STATES, between E and S, and under S. Die crack from cloud under last S of STATES through top of O and down to base of F.

Reverse die used to strike 1798 BB-123 (earliest state), BB-124 (intermediate state, now relapped); and 1799 BB-152 (latest state).

Die States
Die State I: Bolender-25a. No cracks on obverse. On the reverse, the crack from stem end has not yet developed. Die flaws as three raised lumps extending down to the right from rays of star beneath cloud 7. Quite scarce; about 10% or so of extant BB-123 dollars are of this die state.

Die State II: Obverse still without cracks. On reverse, a tiny crack has just developed on the right side of the stem to the border, up the branch slightly from the stem end. Die cracks at star beneath cloud 7 lengthen. Only one seen.

Die State III: Obverse develops cracks completely around the border through or adjacent to stars, letters, and date. Additional crack from 1 in date to rim. Whisper of additional die crack to right of star 7. On the reverse, the die crack on the stem forms a blob at the stem end. Die cracks at star beneath cloud 7 are still larger, appear as two raised streaks, and extend to near the star beneath cloud 8. This is the usually seen die state.

Die State IV: Bolender-25b. Obverse cracks intensify. Large crack from border through two rays of star 7 to field, where another crack develops. Reverse with stem crack heavier to border. Scarcer than Die State III.

Collecting Notes
I believe that 300 to 500 examples are known of 1798 BB-123, making it in the middle range of availability. Nearly all are in lower grades through EF. AU coins are very rare.

Notable Specimens

Robertson Specimen. MS-60. J. Douglas Robertson Collection, San Diego Sale (Mid-American, 1989) lot 716. "Struck very slightly out of collar resulting in little or no denticulation at the lower obverse and the corresponding reverse."

Good Harbour Bay Specimen. AU-58 (PCGS). Good Harbour Bay Collection (Heritage, April 2010) lots 2153.

Hesselgesser Specimen. AU-55 (PCGS). St. Louis Signature Sale (Heritage, May 2005) lot 7573 • Dr. Robert Hesselgesser Collection (Ira and Larry Goldberg, September 2011) lot 5069.

Romano Specimen. AU-55. Don Corrado Romano Collection (Stack's, 1987) lot 753. "Choice AU." Romano was for many years the proprietor of the Worthy Coin Company, Boston.

Hesselgesser Specimen (another). AU-53 (PCGS). Pre-Long Beach Sale (Ira and Larry Goldberg, February 2006) lot 1660 • Pre-Long Beach Sale (Ira and Larry Goldberg, February 2007) lot 1584 • Dr. Robert Hesselgesser Collection (Ira and Larry Goldberg, February 2006) lot 1061 • Pre-Long Beach Sale (Ira and Larry Goldberg, May 2009) lot 604 • Boston Rarities Sale (Bowers and Merena, August 2010) lot 1024.

Miller Specimen. AU-53 (NGC). Dallas Signature Sale (Heritage, November 2005) lot 5075 • Orlando Signature Sale (Heritage, January 2007) lot 5108 • Warren Miller Collection. Die State III.

Essex Institute Specimen. AU-50. Stack's, 1975, lot 991. "AU."

First National Bank of Denver Specimen. AU-50. First National Bank of Denver Collection (Bowers and Merena, 1987) lot 419.

Higgins Specimen. AU-50. Lloyd M. Higgins, M.D. Collection (Bowers and Merena, 1988) lot 2308.

Miller Specimen (another). EF-45 (NGC) • Warren Miller Collection. Die State I.

Miller Specimen (another). EF-45 (NGC) • Warren Miller Collection. Die State IV.

Total Estimated Population

MS-65 or better: 0 (URS-0)
MS-64: 0 (URS-0)
MS-63: 0 (URS-0)
MS-60 to 62: 1 or 2 (URS-1)
AU-50 to 58: 5 to 10 (URS-4)
VF-20 to EF-45: 200 to 340 (URS-9)
G-4 to F-15: 90 to 150 (URS-8)
Total for all grades combined: 300 to 500 (URS-10)
Estimated Total Condition Census: 60-58-55-55-53-53

1798 POINTED TAIL 9, HERALDIC EAGLE, BB-124

"Blundered Stars Reverse."
Line star pattern (placed too high).
(B-24, H-24)

Obverse: This die resembles the obverse of BB-122 more than any other and, in fact, in 1881 was confused with it by Capt. J.W. Haseltine in his *Type-Table*. In BB-122 the 8 in date is about twice as close to bust as in BB-124. In BB-124 the 11th and 12th stars are much farther apart than in BB-122. In BB-124, the first two stars at lower left point to the center of dentils. In BB-122 the second star points to left edge of a dentil. Also in BB-122 the highest curl on head is solid and under upright of E, while in BB-124 this curl is sketchy and defective and a little more centered under E. The BB-124 obverse has three die file marks to the right of the date. This obverse was first described by M.H. Bolender in 1950.

Obverse die used to strike 1798 BB-124 only.

Reverse: See description under 1798 BB-123.

Reverse die used to strike 1798 BB-123 (earliest state), BB-124 (intermediate state, now relapped); and 1799 BB-152 (latest state).

Die States

Die State I: Perfect obverse die, without lapping. May not exist.

Die State II: Dies as described above. Obverse die relapped; highest wave of hair imperfect. No obverse die cracks. Reverse die relapped since use on BB-123; some arrows faint, leaf below C partially missing. Somewhat scarce; perhaps 20% of BB-124 dollars are of this die state. Usually seen with stars on reverse fairly well struck. May also exist with reverse die crack lighter, as in BB-124.

Die State III: As above, but with die crack just beginning at star 12; hairline crack extends to border; crack inward a short distance into the field. On the reverse, the stars above and to the right of the eagle's head are always weakly struck, due to damage and bulging at the corresponding part of the obverse; this weakness continues on all later die states. Only a few BB-124 dollars are of this state.

Die State III: Bolender-24a. Later state with die crack from neck through right field, star 12, to border. Another crack through lower four stars on right to bust. Another crack from lowest curl through top of 798 to border under point of bust. Small crack from border down to B. Die state usually seen.

Die State IV: Additional obverse crack develops from star 1 down along border to below numerals 17 in date. Another crack begins at 9, goes through upper part of 8, to border near bust. A skein of minor cracks develops between the rim and star 4. Hairline crack along border from star 1 to star 4. A few BB-124 dollars are of this die state.

Die State V: The lower right obverse eventually shatters; coins from this late state may have been struck in 1799.

Collecting Notes

BB-124 is one of the most common varieties of the year. The population is estimated to be in the range of 600 to 1,100 pieces. Specimens are plentiful from worn grades through AU. Mint State coins are very rare. Probably, some called Uncirculated years ago would merit the AU grade today.

The EF coin in the Bolender Collection (sold in 1952), earlier in the Loyd B. Gettys and Col. E.H.R. Green collections, had the reverse off center to the right; apparently, the obverse was centered; this indicates the dies were misaligned axially.

Notable Specimens

Cardinal Specimen. MS-64 (NGC). Long Beach Signature Sale (Heritage, September 2002) lot 7790 • Cardinal Collection (American Numismatic Rarities, June 2005) lot 33.

Robertson Specimen. MS-63. J. Douglas Robertson Collection, San Diego Sale (Mid-American Rare Coin Auctions, September 1989). Uncirculated.

Kagin Specimen. MS-63. Metropolitan Washington Convention Sale (Kagin's, 1980) lot 710. "Choice BU-63, die cracks at right leading to die failure at shoulder before hair strands and corresponding portion of reverse, short mark at top right reverse."

Newport Specimen. MS-60. Newport Collection (Bowers and Ruddy Galleries, 1975) lot 1044. "Beautiful Uncirculated."

CSNS Sale Specimen. AU-58 (PCGS). CSNS Signature Sale (Heritage, April 2009) lot 2547.

Queller Specimen. AU-58 (NGC). ANA Sale (Ivy, August 1980) lot 2506 • Baltimore Sale (Stack's, March 2003) lot 437 • Queller Family Collection of Silver Dollars (Heritage, April 2008) lot 2039 • Baltimore Sale (Bowers and Merena, November 2010) lot 2208.

Hollinbeck-Kagin Specimen(s). AU-58. Hollinbeck-Kagin, June 1970, lot 615. "Die failure causing some of reverse stars not to be fully struck up, virtually Uncirculated, only barest rubbing on high points." • Hollinbeck-Kagin, August 1970, lot 1081. "Uncirculated." *These may or may not be the same specimen.*

Miller Specimen. AU-55 (NGC). Warren Miller Collection.

Hesselgesser Specimen. AU-55 (PCGS). Santa Clara Bullet Sale (Heritage, November 2001) lot 1094 • Fred Miller Collection (Heritage, March 2004) lot 5948 • Pre-Long Beach Sale (Ira and Larry Goldberg, May 2006) lot 3034 • Dr. Robert Hesselgesser Collection (Ira and Larry Goldberg, September 2011) lot 5070 • Baltimore Sale (Stack's Bowers, June 2012) lot 3015.

Total Estimated Population

MS-65 or better: 0 (URS-0)
MS-64: 1 (URS-1)
MS-63: 1 or 2 (URS-1)
MS-60 to 62: 2 to 4 (URS-2)
AU-50 to 58: 10 to 20 (URS-
VF-20 to EF-45: 425 to 800 (URS-10)
G-4 to F-15: 150 to 275 (URS-9)
Total for all grades combined: 600 to 1,100 (URS-11)
Estimated Total Condition Census: 64-63-63-60-58 (multiples)

1798 POINTED TAIL 9, HERALDIC EAGLE, BB-125

Misoriented Star Reverse
Arc star pattern on reverse.
(B-8, H-8)

Obverse: Stars on right very close to Y and bust. *Long vertical die flaw in center of left obverse field* (best seen on strong VF or better pieces). Rounded-off bottom to 7. Die "dot" near edge between two dentils above left part of T in LIBERTY. 9 shows slight doubling at top. A crack from lower right part of E to hair. On the left, more space between stars 5 and 6 than between any others. On the right, more space between stars 8 and 9 than between any others. The obverse stars at the left gradually weaken from die failure, and examples can be found appearing to have only 12, 11 1/2, 11, 10 1/2, 10, or 9 stars.[1] Such pieces are sometimes sold as damaged coins as they appear, to the untrained eye, to have been plugged.

Obverse die used to strike 1798 BB-125 only.

Reverse: *Only four berries,* and these are large. The only four-berry reverse of the year. Arc star pattern. Star ray at eagle's lower beak (only three arc-pattern reverse dies, those used to coin BB-116, BB-117, and BB-125 have the ray at beak); another ray of same star points to between B and U, closer to U. *Rightmost star is misoriented and has two rays toward the top of the coin, instead of the normal vertical orientation of one ray pointing straight up and the other straight down,* the only such skewing of a star on the reverse of a 1798 dollar. Nearby star under cloud 7 is considerably tilted. 12 arrows plus one detached head; two rightmost arrows are overlaid with other arrows, with heads part way down each shaft,

as is another arrow near the middle; fifth arrow from right (on the third shaft from right, considering the doubling-up of the two rightmost arrows) is tiny and misformed. Light crack from border through upper left part of E in STATES. Point of leaf under left upright of I in AMERICA. The reverse is often weak, especially at the lower part of TED and at the right corner of the ribbon.

Reverse die used to strike 1798 BB-125 only.

Die States

Die State I: Perfect dies. May not exist.

Die State II: With die cracks as described by Bolender. Stars are weak on the obverse, and on the reverse N and E of UNITED are very weak. Most BB-125 dollars are of this state.

Die State III: Bolender-8a: With die cracks as follows: Die crack on obverse through L to ribbon. Die crack lump on lower curl to left of date. Clash marks slightly above bust line and parallel to it. REVERSE: The reverse die is now shattered with numerous cracks. A crack through top of UNIT down through ED, top of S, above TA, top of TES. Cracks through both top and bottom of OF, continue to AM, and top of ER. Another crack down through C and branch to shield. Another crack through arrow butts, eagle's tail, and stem to right. About 25% of surviving BB-125 dollars are of this state.

Die State IV: Later die state than III. On the obverse, star 5 cannot be seen, and star 7 is barely visible, due to die failure. One reverse crack starts at the lower right part of the M in AMERICA and runs to the ribbon, right shield top and the U in UNUM. A second crack begins at the top of the eagle's head and runs to the fourth cloud (counting from left to right.) UNITED is very weak, due to die buckling.

Die State V: State later than the following, with reverse die shattered and exhibiting over a dozen different cracks.

---

[1] *The Numismatist,* May 1966, printed an article by H.N. Shepherd, "New Variety 1798 Silver Dollar?" in which the author opined that his specimen of B-8 [BB-123], with just 12 stars (the 5th obverse star was missing) might be a new variety, Further: "If it is unique, it is more rare than the fabulous 1804 dollars. [The ownership of the coin is] the thrill of my life."

Hall: 1675 had the most advanced cracks of any example seen. Spies' "Bolender-8e" was described as from a "badly shattered" reverse; "there must be 15 different die breaks."

Collecting Notes

1798 BB-125 shares honors with BB-105 as one of the two most common varieties of the year and, indeed, one of the most common early dollars of *any* date. Close to 1,000 are known, and the actual number may be over that. Most specimens are in lower states of preservation from VG to VF, although EF coins are scattered throughout auction history, as are a few AU pieces. Only one Mint State coin is known to the author.

The F.C.C. Boyd ("World's Greatest Collection," 1945) and Bolender Collection (1952) specimens were each only VF. The W. Earl Spies Collection (Stack's, 1974) was notable for having five different die states of BB-125. This variety is surprisingly rare in higher grades; there must be some special story concerning how they were distributed.

Notable Specimens

Cardinal Specimen. MS-64 (PCGS). Boy's Town Sale (Superior, May 1990) lot 3877 • CSNS Signature Sale (Heritage, April 2001) lot 6566 • Robert Lehmann • Cardinal Collection • Pre-FUN Elite Sale (Superior, January 2002) lot 1185 • Legend Numismatics • Private collector.

Miller Specimen. AU-55 (NGC) Warren Miller Collection.

Richmond Specimen. AU-55 PCGS) Richmond Collection (DLRC, November 2004) lot 1450 • Jim McGuigan • Cardinal Collection (American Numismatic Rarities, June 2005) lot 34 • Private collector • Dr. Robert Hesselgesser Collection (Ira and Larry Goldberg, September 2011) lot 5071.

DeCoppet Specimen. AU-55. André DeCoppet Collection (James Kelly, 1955). Choice AU.

Eliasberg Specimen. AU-53 (NGC). Louis E. Eliasberg Sr. Collection (Bowers and Merena, April 1997) lot 2185. Die State II • Northeast Numismatics.

Cohen Specimen. AU-53. Cohen Collection (Bowers and Merena, 1985) lot 301.

Auction '87 Specimen. AU-50. Auction '87 (Superior, 1987) lot 1813.

Hall Specimen. AU-50. Hall Collection (Bowers and Ruddy, 1978) lot 1675. "AU-. Struck from shattered dies."

Newport Specimen. AU-50. Newport Collection (Bowers and Ruddy, 1975) lot 1041. "Lustrous."

Ross Specimen. AU-50. Ross Collection (Stack's, 1990) lot 401. "AU."

Total Estimated Population

MS-65 or better: 0 (URS-0)
MS-64: 1 (URS-1)
MS-63: 0 (URS-0)
MS-60 to 62: 0 (URS-0)
AU-50 to 58: 10 to 20 (URS-6)
VF-20 to EF-45: 600 to 1,075 (URS-11)
G-4 to F-15: 225 to 400 (URS-9)
Total for all grades combined: 850 to 1,500 (URS-11)
Estimated Total Condition Census: 64-55-55-55-53 (multiples)

BB-125: Middle die state, with prominent obverse die damage.

BB-125: Late die state, with advanced obverse failure.

Additional Information

Snowden's Commentary (1860)

The Cabinet Collection of the Mint of the United States, by James Ross Snowden, 1860, p. 108, told of the coinage of 1798 dollars:

In 1798…the number of stars was reduced to thirteen, being emblematic of the original thirteen states. The reverses of the dollar and dime, which were the only silver pieces coined in this year, underwent an entire change, as follows: An eagle with raised wings, bearing the United States shield upon its breast. From its beak floats a scroll, inscribed "E PLURIBUS UNUM." In the right talon it grasps a bundle of thirteen arrows, and in the left, an olive branch. Above are clouds and thirteen stars. Legend. 'UNITED STATES OF AMERICA.'

The Year 1798 in History

American resentment against France remained intense.[1] Over the objections of Vice President Jefferson, the first of four pieces of legislation known collectively as the Alien and Sedition Act, amending the Naturalization Act of 1795, was adopted, mandating 14 years of residence and a declaration of American allegiance five years before becoming a citizen. The second part of the act enabled the president to deport for a two-year period any alien considered to be dangerous to the nation. The third made it possible to arrest and deport any male aliens who were citizens or subjects of any country hostile to America.

The fourth and most blatantly offensive to human rights provided for the arrest and imprisonment of anyone who attempted to disrupt the proper processes of the government, to foment civil unrest, or to write, publish, or speak any false statement about the government, Congress, or the president. These acts were mainly the result of anti-French sentiment and a fear held by the Federalist Party that the strength of the opposing Democratic-Republican Party was increasing. Ultimately, the Alien and Sedition Act led to the dissolution of the Federalist Party.

Georgia forbade the further importation of slaves. At the time, the slave trade flourished, with many ships coming from Africa and the West Indies.

In 1798, Eli Whitney, under a government contract, used interchangeable parts to make firearms, becoming one of the first large-scale manufacturers to adopt a system of uniformity. By contrast, up to this time many machines and devices were made on an individual basis by fitting parts especially to them.

At the Park Theatre in New York, the play *Female Patriotism, or the Death of Joan de Arc* was staged. Joseph Hopkinson's play, *Hail, Columbia* was published. Among popular plays was *Speed the Plough,* by English playwright Thomas Morton; the chief character was Mrs. Grundy.

England had a poor wheat crop, and prices climbed to £12 per ton; few could afford the price, and there was widespread hunger. The "Essay on the Principles of Population," by Englishman Thomas Robert Malthus, posited that population increases geometrically while food production increases only arithmetically, a situation bound to cause starvation as the world population increases. Aloys Senefelder, a Bavarian printer, invented lithography.

---

[1] Harry E. Salyards, M.D. has furnished to the author a pamphlet titled *An Oration Spoken at Hartford…July 4th, 1798,* by Theodore Dwight. The atrocities being committed in France were outlined by Dwight, who also questioned Jefferson's patriotism.

Scenes around Philadelphia at the end of the 18th century. From top: the Franklin Library, the State House, the Arch Street ferry, and the Philadelphia Bank. (All images from *Album of American History, Volume II, 1783–1853*)

CHAPTER 12
1799/8 AND 1799 SILVER DOLLARS

MINTAGE
Calendar year, Mint report: 423,515
Coins bearing date, author's estimate: 395,000

1799/8 SILVER DOLLARS

BB to Bolender to Haseltine Equivalents

BB Number	Bolender #	Haseltine #	Rarity	Average Grade
BB-141	B-3	H-3	URS-11	EF-40
BB-142	B-1	H-1	URS-11	VF-38
BB-143	B-2	H-2	URS-10	VF-27

1799 SILVER DOLLARS

BB to Bolender to Haseltine Equivalents

BB Number	Bolender #	Haseltine #	Rarity	Average Grade
BB-151	B-13	H-13	URS-7	VF-33
BB-152	B-15	H-15	URS-10	VF-31
BB-153	B-4	H-4	URS-10	VF-26
BB 154	B 18	H 18	URS 7	VF 32
BB-155	B-19	H-19	URS-8	VF-29
BB-156	B-7	H-7	URS-10	VF-32
BB-157	B-5	H-5	URS-11	VF-33
BB-158	B-16	H-16	URS-11	VF-36
BB-159	B-23	H-23	URS-11	VF-30
BB-160	B-12	H-12	URS-11	VF-35
BB-161	B-11	H-11	URS-11	VF-31
BB-162	B-6	H-6	URS-10	VF-35
BB-163	B-10	H-10	URS-12	VF-31
BB-164	B-17	H-17	URS-11	VF-31
BB-165	B-8	H-8	URS-11	VF-29
BB-166	B-9	H-9	URS-12	VF-34
BB-167	B-14	H-14	URS-10	VF-28
BB-168	B-22	H-22	URS-10	VF-22
BB-169	B-21	H-21	URS-11	VF-27

Coinage Context
(For all 1799 varieties)

Record mintage: During calendar year 1799, the quantity of silver dollars minted reached an unprecedented 423,515. I believe many of these were dated 1798. At the time, little attention was paid to the use of dies in the year they were dated. The net coinage of 1799-dated dollars amounted to an estimated 395,000 (within 10%). Some of these may have been minted in calendar year 1800.

Among the production of 1799-dated dollars were some coined from an obverse die overdated 1799/8, although these were not the first struck.

Die making: Working dies for 1799 dollars were prepared as follows:

Obverse dies: The bust of Miss Liberty was punched into the die, after which the letters of LIBERTY, the stars, and the digits in 1799 were all added with individual punches. There were two sets of numeral punches used, each with Pointed 9:

Early style with narrow 7 and with spur at bottom of top curve of 9. Used on most obverses of 1798. Used on these 1799 varieties: BB-141, BB-142, BB-143, BB-154, BB-155, BB-156, BB-157, BB-159, BB-160, BB-161, BB-162, BB-163, BB-164, BB-166, BB-167, BB-168, BB-169.

Later style with wider 7 and without spur at bottom of top curve of 9. Space in opening at top of 9 slightly larger than on preceding. Used sparingly on 1798 varieties. Used on these 1799 varieties: BB-151, BB-152, BB-153, BB-158, BB-165.

Reverse dies: The Heraldic Eagle motif (incuse) was punched into the master die (in relief). The letters E PLURIBUS UNUM were added. The master die included the eagle, clouds above the eagle, the upper part of the olive branch, olive leaves, and arrows. (Earlier, arrow details were added by hand, but in 1799 they were punched as a group, and are thus similar from coin to coin, unlike the situation in 1798). Working dies were copied from this master die. Added separately to the working die were the letters of UNITED STATES OF AMERICA, the stars above the eagle, the lower part of the olive branch, and the berries.

The elements on obverse and reverse that were punched in separately differ minutely in their placement from one another, and are a guide to attribution. On 1799 dies, the workmanship was of a higher order than previously. Star spacing, letter alignment, and other variables are less obvious, and the attribution of certain varieties becomes more difficult.

The letters in E PLURIBUS UNUM vary in their apparent size (caused by different sizes of letter punches or the depth they were punched into the ribbon) and placement on certain varieties. Points of difference include the shapes and proportions of such letters as P, R, S, and U.

Placement differences to note are the position of the U and S in PLURIBUS with regard to the edge of the eagle's neck on the left, and the placement of the N in UNUM in relation to the edge of the eagle's neck on the right. In general, letters were smaller in 1798 and 1799, and larger from 1800 onward.

The letters in E PLURIBUS UNUM seem larger and for some letters differently proportioned on the reverses of 1799 BB-162 and BB-164, in comparison to the other reverses of the year.

Numismatic Information

The 1799/8 overdate: The overdate, from a common obverse die, occurs in three varieties created in combination with as many different reverses, known as BB-141, BB-142, and BB-143. Specimens are known in all grade levels, including Mint State, but higher grade examples are elusive.

The overdate was created from a previously unused 1798 obverse die.

Unusual dies: The curious 15-star reverse, used on BB-141 and BB-153, represents a die cutting error of the first order. The engraver punched in arc-shaped rows of stars, with seven stars in the top row (instead of six), six in the second row (instead of five), and the standard one star to each side of the eagle's head. One can imagine his wonderment when he took a wax impression of the new reverse and found it had 15 bold stars instead of 13. As by this time the die had taken much effort to create, he elected to mask his error by vastly enlarging clouds 1 and 8 to cover the leftmost and rightmost stars in the top row of seven. The job was not quite perfect, and today coins struck from this die show remnants of star points beneath the clouds,

Another interesting variety is BB-159, with the obverse stars arranged 8x5, instead of the usual 7x6.

Reverse die differences: Most Heraldic Eagle reverse dies of 1798 have the A in STATES over the junction of clouds 2 and 3, while most reverse of 1799 have the A over cloud 3. Exceptions among 1799 dies are those that have the "Reverse of '98" with the A over the junction between clouds 2 and 3: The 15-stars die used to coin 1799 BB-141 and BB-153; the line star-pattern die used to coin BB-152, which was also used to coin 1798 dollars; the die used to coin 1799 BB-162; and the die used to coin 1799 BB-168. It is presumed that these dies were made earlier in the year, closer to 1798, than the others. However, their use seems to have been scattered among other dies.

Striking sequence: 1799/8 and 1799 dollars were produced in several striking periods, two of which contain over a half dozen varieties each, and the others of which comprise one, two, or three varieties. The following striking periods are apparent.

Striking Period 1

The overdates were produced in this period, but were not the first varieties struck.

1799 BB-151 Possibly the first variety struck bearing the 1799 date. • 1799 BB-152 Line star-pattern reverse of 1798. • 1799 BB-153 • 1799/8 BB-141 (1799/8 overdate) • 1799/8 BB-142 (1799/8 overdate) • 1799/8 BB-143 (1799/8 overdate) • 1799 BB-154 • 1799 BB-155.

Striking Period 2

1799 BB-156 • 1799 BB-157 (after striking, obverse removed from press for relapping)

Striking Period 3

1799 BB-158 (1st use)

Striking Period 4

1799 BB-158 (2nd use) • 1799 BB-159 • 1799 BB-158 • 1799 BB-160 • 1799 BB-161 (relapped obverse; last preceding use was with 1799 BB-157) • 1799 BB-162 • 1799 BB-163 • 1799 BB-164

Striking Period 5

Stand-alone die pair not linked with any other. Striking time or sequence not determinable.

1799 BB-165.

Striking Period 6

Stand-alone die pair not linked with any other. Striking time or sequence not determinable.

1799 BB-166.

Striking Periods 7 and 8

A problem arises with the three remaining coins in the 1799 series, the BB-167, BB-168, and BB-169. There are two possibilities for striking periods. First, here are data concerning each: BB-167: Obverse die in earlier state than on BB-168; reverse in earlier state than on BB-169. BB-168: Obverse in later state than on BB-167; reverse not relevant as it was used only on BB-168. BB-169: Reverse in later state than on BB-167; obverse not relevant as it was used only on BB-169. Thus, BB-167 was struck earlier than BB-168, as the obverse of BB-167 is from an earlier die state. BB-167 was also struck earlier than BB-169, as the reverse of BB-167 is in an earlier die state. Thus, the striking of the three varieties could not have been continuous. There are two possibilities:

POSSIBILITY 1

Striking Period 7

BB-167 was struck first.

BB-168 was struck next, at which time the reverse die used to strike B-167 was taken out of the press, and a new reverse was employed. Both BB-167 and BB-168 use the same obverse.

Striking Period 8

BB-169 was struck next, by placing the reverse die used to coin BB-167 back in the press, and combining it with a new obverse.

POSSIBILITY 2

Striking Period 7

BB-167 was struck first.

BB-169 was struck next, at which time the obverse die used to strike B-167 was taken out of the press, and a new obverse was employed. Both BB-167 and BB-169 use the same reverse.

Striking Period 8

BB-168 was struck next, by placing the obverse die used to coin BB-167 back in the press, and combining it with a new reverse.

1799/8 and 1799 Dollars
(General Information)
Relationship of Far Right Edge of A to Cloud(s) Below:

Far right edge of A over cloud 3: (BB-141), (BB-152), (BB-153), (BB-154), (BB-156), (BB-162), (BB-163), (BB-166), (BB-168).

Far right edge of A over junction between clouds 3 and 4: (BB-141), (BB-142), (BB-143), (BB-151), (BB-155), (BB-157), (BB-158), (BB-159), (BB-160), (BB-161), (BB-164), (BB-165), (BB-167).

APOCRYPHAL VARIETY: The Boyd Collection ("World's Greatest Collection," Numismatic Gallery, 1945) lot 70 coin was described as: "(Haseltine 9a) Not listed by Haseltine. Obverse of No. 9 and reverse of No. 5." Such a variety is not known today, nor did Bolender, who attended the Boyd sale, list it in his 1950 book. This would be the equivalent of the obverse of BB-166 and the reverse of BB-157 today. Until proven otherwise, the "H-9a" is considered to be a misattribution, not a new variety.

SUMMARY OF CHARACTERISTICS
1799 (ALL VARIETIES)

CIRCULATION STRIKES

Enabling legislation: Act of April 2, 1792

Designer of obverse: Robert Scot (after Stuart), model by John Eckstein

Designer of reverse: Robert Scot (from the Great Seal)

Weight and composition: 416 grains; .8924 silver, balance copper

Melting value (silver bullion value) in year minted: Considered by Mint officials to be on a par with the Spanish dollar, and worth about $1.00 intrinsically (see discussion under Summary of Characteristics, 1794).

Dies prepared: Unknown

Circulation strike mintage, calendar year: 423,515 (for all varieties of 1799 combined, not including pieces reserved for the Assay Commission; these are given in parentheses); Delivery figures by day: February 1: 40,195 (+3) • February 25: 7,000 (+3) • March 14: 51,500 (+3) • March 28: 33,100 (+3) • April 26: 26,890 (+3) • May 23: 11,000 (+3) • June 4: 36,500 (+3) • June 28: 51,000 (+3) • July 17: 32,900 (+3) • August 23 (+3) • August 31: 31,330 (+3) • December 6: 52,100 (+3).

Estimated circulation strike mintage of 1799-dated dollars (author's estimate): 395,000 (rounded).

Estimated quantity melted: Unknown

Estimated total population: (all 1799/8 and 1799 varieties):
  MS-65 or better: 6 to 9 (URS-4)
  MS-64: 15 to 25 (URS-6)
  MS-63: 30 to 60 (URS-7)
  MS-60 to 62: 100 to 200 (URS-9)
  AU-50 to 58: 250 to 600 (URS-10)
  VF-20 to EF-45: 6,500 to 12,000 (URS-15)
  G-4 to F-15: 3,000 to 5,500 (URS-14)
  Total for all grades combined: 10,000 to 18,000 (URS-15)
  Estimated Total Condition Census: 66-65+-65 (multiples)

Characteristics of striking: Depends upon the variety. If weakly struck, this is often observed at the center of the obverse and among the stars above the eagle on the reverse.

Commentary: Many different die varieties exist for 1799, including three with the overdate 1799/8, the curious 15-stars blundered reverse die, and a variety with the obverse stars arranged 8 on the left and 5 on the right, instead of the normal 7x6 configuration.

1799/8 AND 1799 HERALDIC EAGLE

VARIETIES

1799/8 OVERDATE BB-141

15 Stars on reverse.

(B-3, H-3)

Obverse: 1799, last 9 punched over previous 8, and definitive as such; the only overdate die of the year. Last 9 of date very close to bust. Stars very close together. Letters of LIBERTY are widely spaced. Die flaws at left base of E, under RT, and above R. The same obverse die was shared to coin BB-141, BB-142, and BB-143. This die was not used to strike 1798 dollars before it was overdated.

Obverse die used to strike BB-141 (1st use), BB-142 (2nd use), and BB-143 (relapped; third use).

Reverse: *15 stars on reverse;* this is definitive, although to the uninitiated the two extra stars are not readily seen, at least at first. The two supernumerary stars are nearly lost in cloud 1 and cloud 8, and just the points show. The one protruding from the bottom of cloud 1 is the most easily seen. The result is a blundered arc pattern of stars with five (instead of six) stars in the top row, six (instead of five) in the second row, and the usual one to each side of the eagle's head, plus the superfluous star points peeking out from the bottoms of clouds 1 and 8.

The process was accomplished as follows: The engraver first punched seven stars in the top row, six in the second row, and the normal single stars to each side of the eagle's head. He then took count and realized that he had one too many stars in the top row, and one too many stars in the second row, for a total of 15. To disguise his blunder, he enlarged clouds 1 and 8, making them greatly oversized to cover up the first and last stars in the top row, reducing the count to an abnormal five (instead of the normal six), so that the abnormal six (instead of five) in the second row would not have to be altered. The normal star arrangement, top to bottom, is: 6-5-2. Before alteration, this reverse die was 7-6-2. After alteration, it was 5-6-2.

Leaf point under left upright of I in America. Die crack near border above ATES. Another crack above OF AM. The D in UNITED is repunched and there are die flaws in the right side of this letter. Far right edge of A is over cloud 3. Reverse usually not fully struck up at the center, due to sinking of the die.

Note: Die state progressions reveal that the 1799/8 overdates, which are die linked to regular 1799 dollars, were struck after certain regular or perfect date (non-overdate) pieces were made. The overdates are listed first here, following numismatic tradition.

Reverse die used to strike 1799 BB-141 (later use with 1799/8 overdate obverse) and 1799 BB-153 (earlier use with non-overdated obverse).

Die States

Die State I: Perfect dies. Reverse without cracks. May not exist.

Die State II: Early state of obverse later used to coin BB-142 and BB-143. Tiny flaw or crack above R in LIBERTY does not extend to left beyond R. Minute raised flaw at left base of E. Several raised flaws below RT. Three or four small raised areas starting to develop behind hair and above ribbon. Very tiny flaw between ray of star 7 and the bottom left of L. Reverse die with cracks.

Die State III: Obverse as preceding. Reverse with additional crack from right ribbon through AMERIC.

Die State IV: As preceding, but on reverse, a tiny additional crack develops below left upright of M to wing.

Collecting Notes

In terms of availability among overdates of this year, 1799/8 BB-141 is the most plentiful, edging out BB-142 by a healthy margin. It seems likely that about 700 to 1,200 are known today of this variety. This is nice, as it makes the interesting combination of the overdate obverse and the blundered die reverse available to all.

Examples exist in all grades through Mint State, and in terms of early dollars, is actually plentiful in the latter grade! Perhaps someone found a cache of a few dozen of them many years ago. Whatever the reason might be, it has not been recorded.

Notable Specimens

Denver ANA Specimen. MS-64 (PCGS). Denver Signature Sale (Heritage, August 2006) lot 5302 • Private Midwest collection.

RARCOA Specimen. MS-64 (PCGS). Auction '83 (RARCOA, 1983) lot 1162. "Superb gem brilliant Unc." • Auction '85 (RARCOA, 1985) lot 264. "Superb gem brilliant Unc." • Auction '86 (RARCOA, 1986) lot 731. "Superb gem brilliant Unc." • Private collector • Chicago ANA Sale (Stack's Bowers, August 2011) lot 7398 • Baltimore Sale (Stack's Bowers, March 2012) lot 4115 • Philadelphia ANA Sale (Stack's Bowers, August 2012) lot 11483.

Baltimore Sale Specimen. MS-63 (PCGS). Baltimore Sale (Bowers and Merena, November 2009) lot 3022, as MS-64 (NGC), subsequently regarded by PCGS as MS-63 • Private collector.

Austin Specimen. MS-63. Austin Collection (Bowers and Ruddy, 1974) lot 25. "Choice Brilliant Unc."

Stack's Auction '83 Specimen. MS-63. Stack's, 1983, lot 721. "Unc. and choice."

June Sale Specimen. MS-63. June Sale (Stack's, 1990) lot 400. "Choice Brilliant Unc."

Total Estimated Population

MS-65 or better: 0 or 1 (URS-0)

MS-64: 2 or 3 (URS-2)

MS-63: 3 to 6 (URS-3)

MS-60 to 62: 20 to 35 (URS-4)

AU-50 to 58: 50 to 100 (URS-7)

VF-20 to EF-45: 600 to 875 (URS-11)

G-4 to F-15: 125 to 200 (URS-9)

Total for all grades combined: 700 to 1,200 (URS-11)

Estimated Total Condition Census: 64-64-63-63-63 (multiples)

1799/8 Overdate BB-142

(B-1, H-1)

Obverse: See description under 1799/8 BB-141.

Obverse die used to strike BB-141 (1st use), BB-142 (2nd use), and BB-143 (relapped; third use).

Reverse: 13 stars above eagle. Leaf points to center of I in AMERICA. Star touches point of *lower part of eagle's beak;* ray points to the *left outside of the U* in PLURIBUS; U is usually weakly struck. Far right edge of A is over junction of clouds 3 and 4. First A in AMERICA touches third feather, and rests on fourth. Die cracked and scaled between R and I in AMERICA, above same I, and above right part of first T in STATES. Slight die crack sometimes shows through bottom of ES up to top of O, another through lower part of OF.

Reverse die used to strike 1799 BB-142 only.

Die States

Die State I: Intermediate state of obverse used earlier to coin BB-141 and later to coin BB-143. Tiny flaw or crack above R in LIBERTY now extends slightly to left beyond R. Flaw at left base of E about 50% larger than on BB-141. Several raised flaws below RT are about the same as on BB-141. Numerous small raised areas in field from area between star 7 and L, extending toward close to hair above ribbon. Very tiny flaw between ray of star 7 and the bottom left of L. Reverse die without cracks. May not exist with perfect reverse die.

Die State II: Obverse as above. Reverse die as described by Bolender, with crack between R and I of AMERICA and above I; crack above right part of first T in STATES; slight die crack through bottom of ES of STATES to top of O in OF; another crack through lower part of OF.

Die State III: Die flaws advanced at I of AMERICA; die cracked at ATES OF, wing to ribbon, and at AME. Crack from dentils to left side of O, on to junction of clouds 6 and 7. Cracks around much of the border; die shattered. New Netherlands 48th Sale: 626. MS-60, ex Waldo C.

Newcomer, Col. E.H.R. Green, James G. Macallister. This is the die state most usually seen.

Collecting Notes

1799/8 BB-142 is in the middle, rarity-wise, of the three overdate varieties of this year. I estimate that 350 to 600 are known today of this variety.

While most examples are in grades up to and including EF, a number of AU and Mint State coins have crossed the auction block. Of course, some pieces graded as Uncirculated years ago would fall into the AU category today. Interestingly, 1799/8 BB-142 is the rarest of the three overdate varieties in grades below Fine. Apparently, few ever spent an extended amount of time in circulation.

This, BB-141, and BB-143 are in especially great demand as overdates, by date collectors; the demand from variety collectors is additional. In his 1881 *Type-Table,* J.W. Haseltine called this variety very scarce.

Notable Specimens

Eliasberg Specimen. MS-65 (PCGS). Louis E. Eliasberg Collection (Bowers and Merena, April 1997) lot 2186 • Jay Parrino, who had it certified MS-66 by NGC • Private collector • Bruce Morelan, who had the coin re-graded as MS-65 (PCGS) • Legend Numismatics • Private collector.

French Family Specimen. MS-63 (PCGS). Auction '84 (Stack's, July 1984) lot 1185 • L.R. French Family Collection (Stack's, January 1989), lot 10 • FUN Signature Sale (Heritage, January 1998) lot 7017 • Cardinal Collection (American Numismatic Rarities, June 2005), lot 36 • Joseph C. Thomas Collection (Heritage, April 2009) lot 2557 • Treasures of New York Sale (Stack's, July 2009) lot 643 • March Sale (Stack's, March 2010) lot 1117.

Newcomer Specimen. MS-62+ (PCGS). Waldo C. Newcomer Collection • Col. E.H.R. Green Collection • James G. Macallister to T. James Clarke Collection

(New Netherlands 48th Sale, 1956) lot 626 • FUN Signature Sale (Heritage, January 2007) lot 1036 • J.A. Sherman Sale (Stack's, August 2007) lot 791 • Dr. Robert Hesselgesser Collection (Ira and Larry Goldberg, September 2011) lot 5073.

Carter Specimen. MS-62 (PCGS). Amon Carter, Jr. Collection (Stack's, 1984) lot 224. "Die cracks at T and RI on the reverse. Brilliant Unc. and choice." • Private Midwest collection.

Rarities Sale Specimen. MS-62 (PCGS). Rarities Sale (Bowers and Merena, August 1995) lot 175 • Robert Lehmann • Private collector • Orlando Signature Sale (Heritage, January 2004) lot 2098, as MS-63 (NGC)

Chalkley Specimen. MS-60+. Superior, 1990, lot 2860. "MS-60+."

Aspen Specimen. MS-60. Dr. Nelson Page Aspen

Collection, ANA Centennial Convention Sale (Bowers and Merena, 1989) lot 369. "MS-60 to 63."

Wolfson Specimen. MS-60. Samuel W. Wolfson Collection (Stack's, 1963) lot 1380. "Brilliant Unc."

Total Estimated Population
MS-65 or better: 1 (URS-1)
MS-64: 0 (URS-0)
MS-63: 1 or 2 (URS-1)
MS-60 to 62: 4 to 8 (URS-3)
AU-50 to 58: 10 to 20 (URS-5)
VF-20 to EF-45: 400 to 725 (URS-10)
G-4 to F-15: 80 to 150 (URS-8)
Total for all grades combined: 500 to 900 (URS-11)
Estimated Total Condition Census: 65-63-62+-62-62-60 (multiples)

1799/8 Overdate BB-143

(B-2, H-2)

Obverse: See description under 1799/8 BB-141; overdate die. Die flaws as on BB-141, plus some new die flaws in and around the date and between star seven and the L in LIBERTY extending to the hair above the ribbon.

Obverse die used to strike BB-141 (1st use), BB-142 (2nd use), and BB-143 (relapped; third use).

Reverse: 13 stars above eagle. Die crack from border down through *curved part of D* and showing at base. Leaf point is below left side of upright of I in AMERICA. Star touches lower part of eagle's beak and *just enters the mouth; ray points to right side of left upright of U* in PLURIBUS. A in AMERICA touches fourth feather, but not the 3rd. Readily distinguishable from BB-142 by its reverse crack through the curve of the D in UNITED. There is a bar, on the reverse, in the clouds below the E in STATES which may be the remnants of a mispunched letter. Die flaw between left base of N and arrowhead, next to arrowhead. Far right edge of A is over junction of clouds 3 and 4.

Reverse die used to strike 1799 BB-143 (late state) and BB-155 (early state).

Die States

Die State I: Obverse die relapped in effort to remove flaws. Lowest curl (to left of 1 in date) now partly missing and with open center. Just a trace of second curl remains as two tiny, isolated curved lines in field. Flaws below E and RT, and in field behind head are now larger than on BB-142. Reverse with crack from rim to right side of D in UNITED. Additional hairline crack from S through OF to top of wing. Die roughness at ER in AMERICA. (Slightly advanced from last die state described under 1799 BB-155.)

Die State II: Obverse as preceding. Reverse with hairline crack expanded, now through ATES, OF, wing, and top part of AME; crack becomes multiple between wing and A.

Collecting Notes

1799/8 BB-143 is the scarcest of the three overdate die

varieties of the year. I believe that 250 to 450 of this variety exist. This estimate, if accurate, makes BB-143 at least twice as elusive as BB-142 and about three times harder to find than BB-141. Equally important, unlike BB-142, the 1799/8 BB-143 variety is usually seen in lower grades. Most are VF or less. Why this is so is a mystery.

As is the case with BB-141 and BB-142, the demand for this variety is increased by the overdate feature.

Notable Specimens

Fairfield Specimen. MS-64 (PCGS). Fairfield Collection (Bowers and Ruddy, 1977) lot 1032. "Choice Unc." • Harry Einstein Collection (Bowers and Merena, 1986) lot 1730 "MS-63." • Phillip Flannagan Collection (Bowers and Merena, November 2001) lot 4249 • Private Midwest collection.

Silverman Specimen. MS-61 (NGC). Morris Silverman Collection (Heritage, April 2002) lot 4015 • Cardinal Collection • Harry Laibstain • Private collector.

FUN Sale Specimen. AU-58 (PCGS). FUN Signature Sale (Heritage, January 1998) lot 7019.

Reiver Specimen. AU-58 (PCGS). Col. E.H.R. Green Collection. • K.P. Austin Collection. • A.J. Ostheimer 3rd Collection • ANA Convention Sale (Superior, 1975) lot 910. "AU-50 or so." • Jules Reiver Collection (Heritage, January 2006) lot 23557.

Hering Specimen. AU-58 (NGC). Michael Hering Collection (Heritage, January 2002) lot 7225.

Queller Specimen. AU-58 (NGC). Queller Family Collection of Silver Dollars (Heritage, April 2008) lot 2043.

S.S. New York Sale Specimen. AU-58 (NGC). S.S. New York Sale (Stack's, July 2008) lot 4541 • Rarities Sale (Bowers and Merena, September 2008) lot 382 • March Sale (Stack's, March 2009) lot 5325.

Total Estimated Population

MS-65 or better: 0 (URS-0)
MS-64: 1 (URS-1)
MS-63: 0 (URS-0)
MS-60 to 62: 3 to 5 (URS-3)
AU-50 to 58: 5 to 10 (URS-4)
VF-20 to EF-45: 75 to 125 (URS-8)
G-4 to F-15: 175 to 310 (URS-9)
Total for all grades combined: 250 to 450 (URS-10)
Estimated Total Condition Census: 64-61-58 (multiples)

1799 BB-151

Irregular Date
(B-13, H-13)

Obverse: *Irregular date,* per traditional nomenclature, although the "irregular" feature is more notable in the telling than in the seeing. Both 9s are improperly placed, the first is tipped too far to left at top, the last 9 too far to right at top. It has been suggested by Walter H. Breen that a Draped Bust obverse die was made in 1798, but with date incomplete and as 179 only; later to be finished by adding another 9 in 1799. *A ray of star 13 touches bust.* On the left, stars 3 and 4 are wider apart than are any others.

On the right, stars 10-11 are closer together than are any others. Perfect die without cracks.

Obverse die used to strike 1799 BB-151 (first use), BB-152 (intermediate use), and BB-153 (final use).

Reverse: *Die "dot"* (rust) above E in STATES, and *die flaws* inside upper part of same letter. *Die flaws appear between and under two lower stars farthest to right.* Star is close to eagle's beak, and barely escapes touching its upper part; ray points to right side of B in PLURIBUS. Leaf points to center of I in AMERICA. A touches fourth feather of right wing. Far right edge of A is over junction of clouds 3 and 4. The upper two berries are closest and the bottom two berries are very large. All seen are weakly struck at their centers.

Reverse die used to strike 1799 BB-151 only.

Die States

Die State I: Perfect dies, including reverse die without rust. May not exist.

Die State II: As described above for BB-151. On reverse, rust spot above E in STATES. Die flaws near rightmost stars. The state usually seen.

Collecting Notes

1799 BB-151 is the rarest variety of this date and is seldom encountered in the marketplace. I estimate that only 40 to 75 are extant. The grades are spread over a wide range, rather than being clustered at, say, VF.

This is one of the few 1799 dollar varieties for which no photograph was on hand in the Bowers and Merena research files. In 1881, Haseltine rated this with his pet phrase, "excessively rare."

Notable Specimens

Cardinal Specimen. AU-58 (PCGS). Auction '87 (Stack's, July 1987) lot 779 • Gilbert Steinberg Collection (Superior, September 1996) lot 961 • Cardinal Collection (American Numismatic Rarities, June 2005) lot 37 • Warren Miller Collection.

Boyd Specimen. AU-58 (NGC). "World's Greatest Collection" (F.C.C. Boyd, Numismatic Gallery, 1945) lot 76 (tentative attribution) • A.J. Ostheimer 3rd Collection (Lester Merkin, 1968) lot 284. "Practically Unc. Indefinitely struck up in centers, elsewhere very sharp." This may be the same as: 1975 ANA Convention Sale (Superior) lot 945 EF-40, "probably ex W.G.C., Austin, Ostheimer." 1975 ANA had two others, VF-25 (ex Rev. Edward W.W. Lewis, K.P. Austin, Ostheimer), and F-15 ex A.J. Ostheimer 3rd. • Unknown intermediaries • San Francisco Rarities Sale (Bowers and Merena, August 2005) lot 674 • Long Beach Signature Sale (Heritage, February 2010) lot 1265.

Baltimore Sale Specimen. AU-53 (PCGS). Baltimore Signature Sale (Heritage, July 2008) lot 759.

Thaler Specimen. AU-50 (PCGS). Thaler Collection (American Numismatic Rarities, March 2006) lot 1037.

Jewell Sale Specimen. AU-50 (PCGS). Richard Jewell Collection Sale (American Numismatic Rarities, March 2005) lot 207.

Heritage Specimen. AU-50. ANA Convention Sale (Heritage, 1988) lot 955. • Red Bank Sale (American Numismatic Rarities, December 2003) lot 806.

Hesselgesser Specimen. EF-45 (PCGS). Warren Miller Collection • Pre-Long Beach Sale (Ira and Larry Goldberg, February 2009) lot 1079 • Dr. Robert Hesselgesser Collection (Ira and Larry Goldberg, May 2009) lot 621 • Pre-Long Beach Sale (Ira and Larry Goldberg, January 2010) lot 1184.

Reiver Specimen. EF-45 (NGC). Batchelder, March, 1968 • Jules Reiver Collection (Heritage, January 2006) lot 23578 • Queller Family Collection of Silver Dollars (Heritage, April 2008) lot 2044.

Smith Specimen. EF-45. Harlan P. Smith • Schuyler Collection. • M.H. Bolender Collection, 1952, lot 114. "Nearly Unc." • Dr. Charles Ruby Collection • Gilhousen Collection (Superior, 1973) lot 1258. "Die flaws at E of STATES. AU or better." • Neggen Sale (Superior, 1976) lot 659. • Superior, February 1981, lot 654. "EF-45 or better."

Total Estimated Population

MS-65 or better: 0 (URS-0)
MS-64: 0 (URS-0)
MS-63: 0 (URS-0)
MS-60 to 62: 0 or 1 (URS-0)
AU-50 to 58: 3 to 5 (URS-3)
VF-20 to EF-45: 20 to 40 (URS-6)
G-4 to F-15: 15 to 30 (URS-5)
Total for all grades combined: 40 to 75 (URS-7)
Estimated Total Condition Census: 58-58-53-50 (multiples)

1799 BB-152

Irregular Date
Blundered Stars Reverse
Line star pattern on reverse (only 1799 of this style).
Reverse of 1798
(B-15, H-15)

Obverse: See description under 1799 BB-151. So-called *Irregular Date.*

Obverse die used to strike 1799 BB-151 (first use), BB-152 (intermediate use), and BB-153 (final use).

Reverse: *Reverse of 1798.* Struck from the same die as BB-123 and BB-124 of the 1798 dollars. The 5 berries are the smallest of any variety of the 1799 date. A die crack joins stem end to border below. This is significant as *the only 1799 dollar with a "line pattern" of stars on the reverse* (as explained in the general introduction to 1798 dollars in this book). Most seen are very weakly struck on the reverse stars (but not as weak as on 1798 BB-124, on which the weakness was caused by an extensively damaged lower right obverse die being opposite on the coin). Far right edge of A is over cloud 3.

Reverse die used to strike 1798 BB-123 (earliest state), BB-124 (intermediate state, now relapped); and 1799 BB-152 (latest state).

Die States

Die State I: Perfect dies. No obverse cracks. Reverse always with crack from stem, as inherited from 1798 BB-123 and BB-124. May not exist without obverse cracks.

Die State II: Obverse die with hairline crack from left side of 1 in date through stars 1-4 to border opposite star 5. Bolender's personal coin was of this die state. Not seen by author.

Die State III: Obverse die with additional hairline crack from star 9 to field near star 11. Scarcer die state than the following.

Die State IV: Bolender-15a. Obverse die with further cracks: Hairline crack from center of star 4 through star 7. Separate hairline crack from center of star 7 through

LIBE. Crack from right side of R, through bottom of T, below Y, to field. Crack from Y through stars 8, 9, and 10 to bust (expansion of earlier crack from star 9 to field near star 11). 1975 ANA Convention Sale (Superior): 951 coin, EF-40, is from the Bolender and Ostheimer collections. This is the most plentiful die state of 1799 BB-152.

Collecting Notes

1799 BB-152 is among the scarcer varieties of the year, but not sufficiently rare that a nice example can't be found without undue difficulty. I believe that 300 to 500 exist.

Haseltine in his day considered this variety to be very rare. As is the case with other early dollars of which several dozen or more exist, the number of coins available exceeds the number of dedicated collectors by die varieties, thus providing the opportunity to acquire a rarity for little more than a "type" price.

Most examples of 1799 BB-152 are in lower grades. Any coin grading AU or better is especially notable. Only a few Mint State coins exist.

Notable Specimens

Cardinal Specimen. MS-64 (PCGS). Auction '85 (Stack's, July 1985) lot 1751 • Hain Family Collection (Stack's, January 2002) lot 1520 • Cardinal Collection (American Numismatic Rarities, June 2005) lot 38 • Private collector • Cardinal Collection • Dr. Robert Hesselgesser Collection (Ira and Larry Goldberg, May 2011) lot 894.

Orlando Specimen. MS-64 (NGC). Orlando Signature Sale (Heritage, January 2007) lot 1034 • Orlando Signature Sale (January 2008) lot 2932, as MS-65 (NGC) • Steve Contursi • Private collector.

Poetsch Specimen. MS-63 (PCGS). January Sale (Bowers and Merena, January 1999) lot 1174 • May Sale (Stacks, May 1999) lot 2577 • Hans Poetsch Collection (Heritage, July 2002) lot 8414 • Orlando Signature Sale

(Heritage, February 2005) lot 7328 • Dallas Signature Sale (Heritage, November 2005) lot 2193 • Joseph C. Thomas Collection (April 2009) lot 2558 • Orlando Signature Sale (Heritage, January 2010) lot 2588.

Thaler Specimen. MS-61 (PCGS). Tangible Asset Galleries • Cardinal Collection • Thaler Collection (American Numismatic Rarities, March 2006) lot 1038 • Baltimore Sale (Stack's Bowers, March 2011) lot 3198 • Chicago ANA Sale (Stack's Bowers, August 2011) lot 7401.

Pine Tree Specimen. AU-55. Suburban Washington Convention Sale (Pine Tree, 1975) lot 246. "Brilliant AU+."

Total Estimated Population

MS-65 or better: 0 (URS-0)
MS-64: 2 (URS-2)
MS-63: 0 or 1 (URS-0)
MS-60 to 62: 2 to 4 (URS-1)
AU-50 to 58: 6 to 12 (URS-4)
VF-20 to EF-45: 165 to 265 (URS-9)
G-4 to F-15: 125 to 200 (URS-9)
Total for all grades combined: 300 to 500 (URS-10)
Estimated Total Condition Census: 64-64-63-61-58 (multiples)

1799 BB-153

15 Stars on reverse
(B-4, H-4)

Obverse: *Irregular date.* See description under BB-141.

Obverse die used to strike 1799 BB-151 (first use), BB-152 (intermediate use), and BB-153 (final use).

Reverse: See description under 1799 BB-141. 15 stars; the two extra stars are identifiable only by points emanating from the bottom of clouds. Clouds 1 and 8 are oversized to hide the blunder. The stars are arranged in arcs as 5-6-2, rather than 6-5-2. Far right edge of A is over cloud 3.

Reverse die used to strike 1799 BB-141 (later use) and BB-153 (earlier use).

Die States

Die State I: Obverse die with these cracks, mostly inherited from its earlier use to coin BB-153: Hairline crack from left side of 1 in date through stars 1-4 to border opposite star 5. Hairline crack from center of star 4 through star 7. Separate hairline crack from center of star 7 through LIBE. Crack from right side of R, through bottom of T, below Y, to field. Crack from Y through stars 8, 9, and 10 to bust. Now also with hairline crack from star 1 to second curl from bottom. Reverse die without

cracks (but with some raised die flaws, as made, near D of UNITED) Scarcer die state than the following.

Die State II: Obverse now with incusation marks from reverse dentils, at obverse dentils at border from star 1 through 6, slightly toward star 7. Earlier crack from Y now extends to left to border. Crack in field opposite stars 10 and 11 begins at earlier crack, is closer to neck, and goes to bust. Crack from star 10 to border opposite star 11 (on slightly later die progression, crack extends toward field from star 10 and joins earlier crack). Crack extends from earlier crack through top of star 12 to border. The obverse die failure is responsible for usual light striking at the center of the reverse. The die could not have lasted much beyond this point. This is the die state usually seen.

Collecting Notes

I estimate that 350 to 600 examples of 1799 BB-153 are extant today, placing it in the medium range of availability within varieties of this year. Most survivors are in grades up through VF, although EF examples come on the market at intervals. In AU or Mint State, BB-153 is a great rarity. The blundered reverse die feature lends interest and value.

Reiver Specimen. AU-58 (NGC). Davenport Collection (Superior, February 1977) lot 477 • Jules Reiver Collection (Heritage, January 2006) lot 23559.

Cardinal Specimen. AU-55 (PCGS). Cardinal Collection (American Numismatic Rarities, June 2005) lot 39.

Miller Specimen. AU-55 (NGC). Warren Miller Collection.

Thaler Specimen. AU-53 (PCGS). Thaler Collection (American Numismatic Rarities, March 2006) lot 1040.

Baltimore Specimen. AU-53 (NGC). • Baltimore Sale (Stack's Bowers, June 2011) lot 4028.

Queller Specimen. AU-53 (NGC). Queller Family Collection of Silver Dollars (Heritage, April 2008) lot 2046.

Hesselgesser Specimen. AU-53 (PCGS). Dr. Robert Hesselgesser Collection (Ira and Larry Goldberg, September 2011) lot 5076.

Kagin Specimen. AU-50+. CSNS Convention Sale (Kagin's, 1979) lot 365. "Borderline Unc-50+."

Dallas Specimen. AU-50+. Dallas Auction (Heritage, 1989) lot 458. "AU (50/50+)."

Ruby Specimen. AU-50. Ruby Collection Sale, Part I (Superior, 1974) lot 1467. "Shattered obverse die, possibly later even than Gilhousen 1249. AU."

Austin Specimen. AU-50. K.P. Austin Collection • A.J. Ostheimer 3rd Collection (Lester Merkin, 1968) lot 275. "Shattered obverse. Choice Unc." • Gilhousen Collection (Superior, 1973) lot 1249. "Irregularly toned, prooflike Unc., advanced obverse cracks." • ANA Convention Sale (Superior, 1975) lot 914. "Obverse die cracks, as usual. EF-45 or better." *[Author's note: We have arbitrarily assigned the grade of AU-50 to this specimen. In 1968 it was described as Choice Unc., in 1973 as prooflike Unc. and in 1975 as EF-45 or better. We have not examined this coin to determine our 2013 grade opinion.]*

Total Estimated Population

MS-65 or better: 0 (URS-0)
MS-64: 0 (URS-0)
MS-63: 0 (URS-0)
MS-60 to 62: 0 (URS-0)
AU-50 to 58: 5 to 10 (URS-4)
VF-20 to EF-45: 225 to 400 (URS-9)
G-4 to F-15: 125 to 200 (URS-9)
Total for all grades combined: 350 to 600 (URS-10)
Estimated Total Condition Census: 58-55-53 (multiples)

1799 BB-154

(B-18, H-18)

Obverse: Star 8 farther from Y than the first star from curl, or the star 7 from L, or the last star from bust. *Highest curl on top of head is centered under right edge of E and space between E and R, the farthest right of any 1799 obverse.* Same die used for BB-155. The first three obverse stars show light repunching (visible on high grade specimens). On the left, stars 2 and 3 are much closer than are any other stars to each other; stars 4-5 and 6-7 have the widest spacing. On the right, stars 8-9 and 9-10 are more closely spaced than are the other star pairs.

Obverse die used to strike 1799 BB-154 (early use) and BB-155 (later use).

Reverse: *Heavy die crack between E and D through left wing, to top of shield, the best aid to identifying the variety (if Die State II; see Die States below).* Lighter cracks usually through TATES O, from lower part of F to top of A, from border above R, top of I, through CA, stem end, tail, up through NIT. Small point at stem end. A does not touch feathers. Leaf points below left side of upright of I in AMERICA. Point of star touches lower point of eagle's beak. The U and the T in UNITED are repunched.

Far right edge of A is over cloud 3. Usually weakly struck at reverse center. A few pieces are known with reverse die misalignment.

Reverse die used to strike 1799 BB-154 only.

Die States

Die State I: Perfect dies. Unknown to Bolender; Haseltine called it H-20, but this was eliminated by Bolender as non-existent. From one to three are known today (reported by Douglas Winter).

Die State II: Die cracks less advanced than on State III. Cf. Gilhousen (Superior, 1973), VF, called "one of the half dozen finest, exceeded by three EFs and tied or minutely exceeded by a couple of others not quite reaching EF."

Die State III: Dies as described by Bolender, above.

Die State IV: Later die state, now with a heavy crack below the left wing tip through STATES and the O in OF to the rim below; a second crack begins at the rim over the E in STATES and it then meets the crack through ED as described by Bolender.

BB-154: Die State I with perfect reverse die.

Collecting Notes

1799 BB-154 is the second rarest die variety of 1799, and is exceeded only by BB-151. I estimate that only 60 to 100 are known. Nearly all of these are in well-worn grades. A few coins described as Uncirculated came on the market years ago, but it is probable that most would grade less today. The BB-154 is an ideal example of a coin that the cherrypicker can hope to buy for a "type" price. There may come a day when most early dollars on the market are attributed to BB numbers, but until then there is always the possibility of finding something quite rare for a nominal sum.

Notable Specimens

Terrell Specimen. MS-63 (PCGS). =Terrell Collection (Bowers and Ruddy, 1973) • Austin Collection (Bowers and Ruddy, 1974) lot 27. "Unc." • Unknown intermediaries • Pre-Long Beach Sale (Superior, February 2003) lot 2170 • Cardinal Collection • Private collector • Eliasberg and Krause Collections Sale (Stack's, March 2010) lot 1118.

Hirt and Bolt Collections Specimen. MS-60. Pine Tree, 1975, lot 764. "Rainbow toned Unc., it was graded "AU" at its earlier auction appearances. First three stars obviously repunched; U and T of UNITED recut. Heavy break from rim between ED to shield; all cracks listed by Bolender, second extended through S to wing tip."

Hollinbeck-Kagin Specimen. MS-60. Hollinbeck-Kagin Sale, June 1970, lot 629. "Unc."

Miller Specimen. AU-58 (NGC). Warren Miller Collection, Die State III.

Queller Specimen. AU-58 (NGC). Rarities Sale (Bowers and Merena, August 1996) lot 207 • Queller Family Collection of Silver Dollars (Heritage, April 2008) lot 2047.

Philadelphia ANA Specimen. AU-58 (NGC). Philadelphia ANA Sale (Stack's Bowers, August 2012) lot 9338.

Fairfield Specimen. AU-58. Fairfield Collection (Bowers and Ruddy, 1977) lot 1035. "Borderline Unc."

Hesselgesser Specimen. AU-55 (PCGS). Dr. Robert Hesselgesser Collection (Ira and Larry Goldberg, May 2011) lot 895 • Pre-Long Beach Sale (Ira and Larry Goldberg, September 2011) lot 5077.

Total Estimated Population

MS-65 or better: 0 (URS-0)
MS-64: 0 (URS-0)
MS-63: 1 (URS-1)
MS-60 to 62: 1 or 2 (URS-1)
AU-50 to 58: 4 to 8 (URS-3)
VF-20 to EF-45: 40 to 65 (URS-0)
G-4 to F-15: 15 to 25 (URS-5)
Total for all grades combined: 60 to 100 (URS-7)
Estimated Total Condition Census: 63-60-60-58 (multiples)

1799 BB-155

(B-19, H-19)

Obverse: See description under 1799 BB-154. From same die as BB-154, but with die crack from border under bust, through bottom of last 9, center of 179, and first three stars on left to border. Another crack from second star to hair. The obverse is invariably quite weak.

Obverse die used to strike 1799 BB-154 (early use) and BB-155 (later use).

Reverse: See description under 1799 (1799/8) BB-143. Perfect reverse die, and also with the same crack through D in UNITED as seen on B-2. Far right edge of A is over junction of clouds 3 and 4. Reverse stars always weakly impressed.

Reverse die used to strike 1799 BB-142 (late state) and BB-155 (early state).

Die States

Die State I: Perfect obverse die. Reverse without crack. May not exist, but it could theoretically exist, unless a later example of 1799 BB-154 is discovered with obverse cracks similar to those described under Die State II.

Die State II: Obverse with crack from left side of 1 in date, extending left through stars 1, 2, and 3. Reverse without crack. Scarce die state.

Die State III: Dies described by Bolender for B-19 [BB-155]. Obverse crack expands to the right, through date, to border below drapery, and left through stars 1-3 (as before), now to border. Another crack from border through star 3 into field. Reverse without crack. The usually seen die state.

Die State IV: Obverse now with crack from star 2 to hair. Reverse now has rim crack to right side of D in UNITED. Rare die state. This may be similar to Gilhousen (Superior, 1973): 1263, a coin earlier in the Bolender and Dr. Charles Ruby collections, "With additional obverse cracks not mentioned by Bolender."

Collecting Notes

1799 BB-155 is one of the key rarities of the year. I believe that only 70 to 110 exist today. However, as of the early 1990s, there are more coins available than there are specialized collectors desiring to pay a significant premium for them; thus, specimens sell for little more than "type" prices. I see this as an advantage for anyone wishing to get involved in early dollars. Further, in recent decades, especially since the mid-1970s, many newcomers to the coin market have been conditioned to buy only Mint State coins, these being said to be of "investment quality." This leaves a vast range of VF, EF, etc., coins available to astute collectors of rare varieties, who do not have to be concerned with prices being pushed up by amateur competition from investors.

Most examples of the 1799 BB-155 dollar are in lower grades through EF. Only a few AU and Mint State coins exist.

In his 1881 *Type-Table*, J.W. Haseltine designated this variety as very rare.

Notable Specimens

Norweb Specimen. MS-62 (ANACS). Anderson-Dupont Collection (Stack's, November 1954) lot 2258 • Norweb Collection, Part III (Bowers and Merena, November 1988) lot 3760 • Matthews and Casterline Collections (Superior, May 1989) lot 3194 • Albany Collection (Heritage, September 2002) lot 7833 • Pre-Long Beach Sale (Superior, May 2003) lot 2728 • Thomas Sebring Collection (American Numismatic Rarities, January 2004) lot 141 • Cardinal Collection (American Numismatic Rarities (June 2005) lot 40.

Haskell Specimen. MS-61 (NGC). Logan Haskell Collection (American Numismatic Rarities, June 2006) lot 2033 • March Sale (Stack's, March 2007) lot 1035.

New Netherlands 53rd Sale Specimen. MS-60. 53rd

Sale (New Netherlands, June 1959) lot 1210. "Lightly toned Unc."

Davis Specimen. AU-58. Davis-Graves (James Davis) Collection (Stack's, 1954) lot 1308. "A shade from Unc. Choice."

Reiver Specimen. AU-58 (NGC). W. Earl Spies Collection (Stack's, December 1974) lot 163 • Jules Reiver Collection (Heritage, January 2006) lot 23588.

Hesselgesser Specimen. AU-55 (PCGS). Dr. Robert Hesselgesser Collection (Bowers and Merena, August 2010) lot 1040.

Miller Specimen. AU-55 (NGC). Warren Miller Collection.

Hesselgesser Specimen (another). AU-53 (PCGS).

Dr. Robert Hesselgesser Collection (Ira and Larry Goldberg, September 2011) lot 5078.

Total Estimated Population
MS-65 or better: 0 (URS-0)
MS-64: 0 (URS-0)
MS-63: 0 (URS-0)
MS-60 to 62: 2 to 4 (URS-2)
AU-50 to 58: 4 to 7 (URS-3)
VF-20 to EF-45: 45 to 75 (URS-7)
G-4 to F-15: 20 to 35 (URS-6)
Total for all grades combined: 70 to 110 (URS-8)
Estimated Total Condition Census: 62-61-60-58-58-55 (multiples)

1799 BB-156

(B-7, H-7)

Obverse: Light "waves" (die clash marks) appear at top of date between two 9's and to right, from the tops of the clouds in the reverse die. Letters in LIBERTY close. First star appears small and thin. "Pocket" (as Bolender calls it) or "cobweb" clash mark (from eagle's wing in the reverse die) under throat of Liberty shows on BB-156, BB-157, and BB-162, not always well defined. The *closest star* is the star 8 which is slightly closer to Y, than seventh star is to L. First star slightly farther from curl than last star is from bust.

In the marriage to this reverse die, the top of the 1 in the date is refinished and straight cut. A "pocket" or "cobweb" is at the throat, from die clashing with the eagle's wing in the reverse die. There are also subtle traces of die clash "waves" at top of date, especially to the right of the second 9, from the tops of the clouds in the reverse die.

Obverse die used to strike 1799 BB-156 (with clash marks), BB-157, BB-161 (now relapped), BB-162, BB-163, and BB-164.

Reverse: Point of star touches point of upper part of

eagle's beak; ray points to right edge of B in PLURIBUS. First A in AMERICA touches third feather only. Leaf points near center of upright of I in AMERICA. Clouds 1, 7 and 8 have stars penetrating into them; other clouds have stars exceedingly close or touching. Far right edge of A is over cloud 3.

Reverse die used to strike 1799 BB-156 only.

Die States

Die State I: Early state of the dies as described by Bolender, above. Obverse without cracks. Reverse without cracks. Scarce.

Die State II: Obverse as above. Reverse with hairline crack, hardly noticeable, through bottoms of RICA to stem. The die state usually seen.

Die State III: Bolender-7a. Obverse as above. Reverse now with encircling cracks, taking this path: Bottoms of RICA, through stem, eagle's tail, bottom two arrow feathers, lower part of UNITED, wing tip, to upper part of S and T; new crack commences from middle of

S, through center of T, to A, upward through A, through top of T, to border; new crack connects bottoms of ATE, goes upward through S, through upper left of S, to border; this crack connects with crack at bottom of S, touching cloud 7, splitting, and continuing, now somewhat indistinctly, through cloud 8, to wing, and downward in wing; another crack from border through top of OF, to wing tip, downward, through bottoms of AME, to join up with the RICA crack, to complete the circle. The reverse is bulged above the eagle's head. Die state significantly scarcer than the preceding. Cf. Gilhousen (Superior, 1973): 1253, later 1975 ANA Convention Sale (Superior): 923, VF.

Collecting Notes

VF and even EF coins are seen with frequency, but higher grades are virtually non-existent. I estimate that 275 to 500 exist totally, a figure which may include only one Mint State coin.

Notable Specimens

Rogers Specimen. MS-62 (NGC). Lelan Rogers Collection (Stack's, November 1995) lot 1327 • Robert Lehmann • Cardinal Collection • Private collector.

Miller Specimen. AU-58 (NGC). Warren Miller Collection.

Riverly Specimen. AU-58. Riverly Collection (Heritage, August 1998) lot 8056.

Hollinbeck-Kagin Specimen. AU-58. Hollinbeck-Kagin Sale, August 1970, lot 1086. "Virtually Unc."

Cardinal Specimen. AU-55 (NGC). Kenneth C. Long Collection (Bowers and Merena, May 1995) lot 1182 •

Cardinal Collection (Heritage, July 1997) lot 6496.

Hesselgesser Collection. AU-53 (PCGS). Dr. Robert Hesselgesser Collection (Ira and Larry Goldberg, September 2011) lot 5081.

ANA Convention Sale Specimen. AU-50. ANA Convention Sale (Kagin's, 1977) lot 1764. "Details suggest AU, or even higher."

Bebee's. AU-50. *Numismatist* advertisement, May 1953. AU.

Bebee's Specimen. EF-45. Aubrey and Adeline Bebee Collection (Bowers and Merena, 1987) lot 407. "Partially prooflike surface." • Lloyd M. Higgins, M.D. Collection (Bowers and Merena, 1988) lot 2312.

Four Landmark Collections Specimen. EF-45. Four Landmark Collections Sale, (Bowers and Merena, 1989) lot 1963. "Late state of the reverse die, the entire center appearing to bulge (actually, sinking in the die), and the die further broken through the bases of most of the letters in the peripheral legend."

Total Estimated Population

MS-65 or better: 0 (URS-0)
MS-64: 0 (URS-0)
MS-63: 0 (URS-0)
MS-60 to 62: 1 (URS-1)
AU-50 to 58: 5 to 8 (URS-4)
VF-20 to EF-45: 225 to 425 (URS-10)
G-4 to F-15: 40 to 65 (URS-7)
Total for all grades combined: 275 to 500 (URS-10)
Estimated Total Condition Census: 62-58-58-58-55-53

1799 BB-157

(B-5, H-5)

Obverse: See description under BB-156. In BB-157 and BB-162 the upper right corner is slightly indented in the 1 in date.

Obverse die used to strike 1799 BB-156 (with clash

marks), BB-157, BB-161 (now relapped), BB-162, BB-163, and BB-164.

Reverse: U in UNITED *imperfect at upper left,* the vertical element being cut off at the upper left side, taking with it the upper left serif; a defective punch was employed (used on three different dies to strike BB-157; BB-158, BB-159, BB-160, and BB-161; and BB-168). Leaf points almost under left side of upright of I in AMERICA. All six upper stars touch clouds, the two on right each having two points touching, and other four have one point touching (the star that is below clouds 2-3 nearly touches 3). Far right edge of A is over junction of clouds 3 and 4. Point of star touches point of lower part of eagle's beak; ray points directly to center of left upright of U in PLURIBUS. A touches third feather.

The reverse is similar to the die used to coin BB-158 (later, BB-159, BB-160, and BB-161), a die which must have been made about the same time, but can be easily distinguished. On BB-157, the two upper stars on the right have two points which touch clouds 7 and 8. On BB-158, etc., the upper right star has only one point which touches cloud 8.

Reverse die used to strike 1799 BB-157 only.

Die States

Die State I: Obverse die without crack. Reverse die without crack. May not exist without reverse crack.

Die State II: Bolender-5a. Obverse as preceding. Reverse with hairline crack beginning below stem, progressing to the left through the tip of the eagle's tail, UNITED, wing tip, and STA; then as the die crack continues (on slightly later states) it goes to T, then to E, the top of S, and the border. The last-named is the die state usually seen.

Die State III: Obverse as preceding. Reverse with additional cracks: Crack through bottom part of AT, below E, to top of cloud 5. Crack through AMER. Frequently seen die state.

Die State IV: Obverse as preceding. Reverse now with earlier crack through AMER now extending through IC. Crack from border, through upright of T, through cloud 2, curving left to touch star below cloud 1. The latest reverse die state seen. Scarce.

Note: Bolender said Bolender-5a has "short die cracks from lower left corner of E down to hair, and below first star." I have not seen this obverse crack on *any* die state of BB-157.

Collecting Notes

1799 BB-157 is one of the most plentiful issues of the year. About 650 to 1,000 are extant today. Despite this relative abundance, nearly all specimens are in circulated grades through VF, with a scattering of EF pieces as well. Higher grade pieces are few and far between. However, among those scattered high grade gems are a few in the MS-63 to 65 echelons, suggesting the original existence of a small hoard of this variety, long since dispersed.

Notable Specimens

Boston Specimen. MS-66 (PCGS). So-called the "Boston Dollar" as it resided with a Boston family from the time of issue until the 1960s • October Sale (Superior October 1990) lot 3716 • New York ANA Sale (Heritage, July 1997) lot 6497 • Baltimore ANA Sale (Bowers and Merena, August 2003) lot 2014 • Bruce Morelan • Private collectors • Old West and Franklinton Collections Sale (American Numismatic Rarities, August 2006) lot 710 • Orlando Signature Sale (Heritage, January 2012) lot 3292 • Bruce Morelan.

May Sale Specimen. MS-64 (PCGS). Superior, May Sale, 1991, lot 951.

Eliasberg Specimen. MS-64 (NGC). Louis E. Eliasberg Sr. Collection (Bowers and Merena, April 1997) lot 2187 • Tangible Asset Galleries • Private collector • Long Beach Signature Sale (Heritage, February 2006) lot 1622.

Hesselgesser Specimen. MS-62 (PCGS). Baltimore Sale (Stack's Bowers, March 2011) lot 3197 • Dr. Robert Hesselgesser Collection (Ira and Larry Goldberg, September 2011) lot 5082.

Robison Specimen. MS-62 (NGC). Ellis H. Robison Collection (Stack's, February 1982) lot 1870 • Spring Quartette Sale (Bowers and Merena, March 1992) lot 2580 • Warren Miller Collection.

Total Estimated Population

MS-65 or better: 1 or 2 (URS-1)
MS-64: 2 or 3 (URS-2)
MS-63: 3 to 5 (URS-3)
MS-60 to 62: 5 to 8 (URS-4)
AU-50 to 58: 15 to 25 (URS-9)
VF-20 to EF-45: 425 to 700 (URS-10)
G-4 to F-15: 200 to 325 (URS-9)
Total for all grades combined: 650 to 1,000 (URS-11)
Estimated Total Condition Census: 65-64-64-63-63-63

1799 BB-158

(B-16, H-16)
"Close 17 Obverse."

Obverse: *Left stars distant* from curl and L; star 7 is farther from L on this than on any other obverse of the year. *Right stars close* to Y and bust. This die is quickly recognized by keeping the above in mind. Numerals 1 and 7 closer together on this than on any other 1799 obverse. Star 1 is about 2 mm. distant from curl, and star 7 is just as far from the L. Star 8 is quite close to Y, and star 13 almost as near to bust. Star 6 has raised die defect or trace of extra ray to left of topmost ray (ray pointing upward).

Obverse die used to strike 1799 BB-158 only.

Reverse: U in UNITED defective at upper left part, which is cut off, due to employment of a defective U punch. Point of star touches point of lower part of eagle's beak; ray points to left serif at left side of U in PLURIBUS. Star under cloud 1 is noticeably smaller than any other. A in AMERICA rests on fourth feather. Leaf point is under left side of upright of I. Upper right star has *only one point* touching cloud 8 (whereas two points of this star touch the cloud on the BB-157 reverse). Far right edge of A is over junction of clouds 3 and 4. Berries boldly defined in branch for Die State I, with the one at top left being the smallest. Berries weaker in Die State II.

Reverse first used to strike 1799 BB-158, during which time it had its first relapping (berries weak), next coining BB-159, then BB-158 again, then, second relapping (removing berries), BB-160 and, finally, BB-161.

Die States

Die State I: Obverse and reverse with perfect dies. Early state of reverse die with all berries strong, including one at top left of branch (which later weakens). Examples are fairly plentiful.

Die State II: Berries slightly weaker, especially the one at the top left; probably from very light relapping. This is the die state used to coin 1799 BB-159. 1799 BB-158 dollars of this state are rare; I have seen just one.

Die State III: Bolender-16a. OBVERSE: Later state, after the dies came together (clashed) without an intervening planchet. Now with incuse "waves" above date caused by impression of reverse clouds on obverse die. Additional clash marks in left obverse field to right of stars 1 and 2, above bust, and between bust and star 13. Impact of clashing caused several cracks, including small crack through upper left of star 1; crack from bottom border, through drapery, upward and then curving left toward hair, then abruptly turning upward to area just to left of the front of neck. REVERSE: Incuse marks from obverse die include lower drapery line (which appears as a die crack, which it is not, through OF), and entire date 1799 between ES and OF (to see this, invert the coin; this is visible only on higher grade specimens). Berries somewhat weak as on Die State II. Scarce die state.

Die State IV: Bolender-16b. OBVERSE: Now with numerous die cracks shattering the dies. Cracks as above, plus additional cracks: From border opposite upper left of star 1, to star 2; from same spot through upper left of star 1 (as in Die State II); crack from border opposite star 2, through stars 3 to 6, past inner right ray of star 7 to field; additional crack from star 6, right and down through hair ribbon, hair, and bottom curl to border, with a couple other small cracks at the same border area; additional crack from star 5, down to end of hair ribbon, to hair; additional crack on right, from border up through drapery and bust, to field opposite star 9; border crack above stars 10 and 11 and above 12. (Some transitional pieces do not have all of the cracks fully developed.) REVERSE: As preceding. Examples are fairly plentiful.

Collecting Notes

1799 BB-158 is one of the most plentiful varieties of the year, and is readily available in most grades through AU. Mint State coins are very rare. Most auction appearances are from years ago. It is probably that some of these would only grade AU today. I estimate that 850 to 1,500 specimens of BB-158 survive in all grades combined.

Caveat emptor: J.P. Martin, of the American Numismatic Association Authentication Bureau (ANAAB), provided two counterfeit 1799 BB-158 dollars for examination. Both are Die State III of this variety. The surfaces of each displayed microscopic porosity. The rims were crisp and sharp, while the edge lettering was unusually well detailed. The edges were polished and showed microscopic scratches parallel to the rims. Both examples showed four or five raised ridges on the edge, perpendicular to the rims. On each, these were positioned at the edge device star immediately preceding H in HUNDRED. One weighed 414.8 grains, the other 419.8 grains (an authentic specimen on hand for comparison weighed 417.3 grains); the weight is apt to vary, and is not a definitive test. I recommend that any suspected example be submitted to ANAAB for checking.

Notable Specimens

Carter Specimen. MS-64+ (PCGS). Amon Carter, Jr. Collection (Stack's, January 1984) lot 225 • New York ANA Sale (Superior, August 2002) lot 1079 • Cardinal Collection • Private Midwest collection.

Johnson Specimen. MS-64 (NGC). B.G. Johnson Collection (Christie's) • Warren Miller Collection

Orlando Specimen. MS-64 (NGC). Orlando Signature Sale (Heritage, January 2009) lot 3945 • Los Angeles ANA Sale (Bowers and Merena, August 2009) lot 1655 • Pre-Long Beach Sale (Ira and Larry Goldberg, January 2011) lot 1519 • Baltimore Sale (Stack's Bowers, June 2012) lot 3021.

Hesselgesser Specimen. MS-62 (NGC). Dr. Robert Hesselgesser Collection (Bowers and Merena, August 2010) lot 1037.

Fritz Specimen. MS-60. Fritz Collection Sale (Lester Merkin, 1966) lot 307. "Gray toned Unc."

Greater New York Specimen. MS-60. Greater New York Convention Sale (Stack's, 1978) lot 182. • Greater New York Convention Sale (Stack's, 1983) lot 1222. "Brilliant Unc."

Ostheimer Specimen. MS-60. A.J. Ostheimer 3rd Collection (Lester Merkin, 1968) lot 287. "Advanced die cracks. State IV of seven known die states. RRR. Unc."

Stack's Specimen. MS-60. Stack's January 1969 Sale, lot 256. "Brilliant Unc., Struck from the terminal state of the die, showing a myriad of fine cracks all over the obverse and the double crack through 'O' of OF."

Wyatt Specimen. MS-60. Russell and Eudora Bell Wyatt Collection (Superior, 1985) lot 2039. "Late die state of Bolender-16 with numerous die cracks shattering the dies. MS-60."

Total Estimated Population

MS-65 or better: 0 (URS-0)
MS-64: 3 (URS-3)
MS-63: 1 (URS-1)
MS-60 to 62: 5 to 8 (URS-4)
AU-50 to 58: 25 to 50 (URS-6)
VF-20 to EF-45: 650 to 1,150 (URS-11)
G-4 to F-15: 175 to 300
Total for all grades combined: 850 to 1,500 (URS-11)
Estimated Total Condition Census: 64+-64-64-62-60 (multiples)

1799 STARS 8x5, BB-159

(B-23, H-23)

Obverse: *Only 5 stars* to right of bust, facing. The obverse stars are arranged eight to the left and five to the right; the only 1799 with this peculiar arrangement. The reason for this configuration is unknown. It may have been a blundered die, or the engraver may have accidentally punched the eight stars on the left after just having cut a die for a 1799 $10 gold coin (all of which have stars arranged 8x5 this year). He would then have been forced to complete the die using only five stars on the right.

Given the care taken to prepare dies at the Mint for dollar coinage this year, the 8x5 stars blunder is all the more remarkable.

Obverse die used to strike 1799 BB-159 only.

Reverse: See description under 1799 BB-158. U in UNITED defective at upper left, due to broken U punch. Now on BB-159 the upper berries are very small. Far right edge of A is over junction of clouds 3 and 4.

Reverse first used to strike 1799 BB-158, during which time it had its first relapping (berries weak), next coining BB-159, then BB-158 again, then, second relapping (removing berries), BB-160 and, finally, BB-161.

Die States

Die State I: Perfect obverse die; no crack at B and E of LIBERTY, no clash marks. Reverse as inherited from 1799 BB-158, Die State II: Die without cracks or defects. Top two of five berries in branch are weak, especially the one on the left. Scarce die state (with perfect obverse die) for BB-159.

Die State II: Obverse develops crack extending from upper left of E in LIBERTY through lower right of B into field. Reverse as preceding. This is the most plentiful die state for BB-159.

Die State III: Obverse die has clashed with the reverse, and now heavy clash marks from the clouds on the reverse can be seen as incuse "waves" above the date, additional waves are below the lowest two curls, incuse dentils are seen between drapery and border, extending to star 13; crack from star 9 to border; delicate, curved cracks in left obverse field begin at star 4 and at star 7. Reverse as preceding. Scarcer than Die State II.

Collecting Notes

1799 BB-159, with stars arranged 8x5, is exceptionally popular due to the distinctive obverse. About 500 to 900 are known, so in absolute terms the coin is not rare. However, its popularity as a type has caused specimens to sell for prices far in excess of other 1799 dollars of comparable rarity.

In a year with relatively little to offer in the way of truly notable die varieties and engraving blunders, the 1799 BB-159 is a special favorite due to its distinctive character.

BB-159: Terminal die state with advanced obverse die breaks.

Most specimens are in lower grades through VF, although EF coins are available at intervals. The literature describes certain pieces as AU or Uncirculated. It is not certain how many coins called Uncirculated years ago would qualify for this grade under today's tightened interpretations by such services as NGC and PCGS.

Notable Specimens

Brand Specimen. MS-64 (PCGS). Likely from the Virgil Brand Collection, privately to F.C.C. Boyd via B.G. Johnson circa 1943 • "World's Greatest Collection" (F.C.C. Boyd, Numismatic Gallery, 1945) lot 87. • ANA Convention Sale (Kosoff, August 1949) lot 190 • T. James Clarke Collection (New Netherlands, November 1956) lot 638 • Harold Bareford Collection (Stack's, October 1981) lot 415 • Auction '82 (Paramount, August 1982) lot 1742 • 68th Anniversary Sale (Stack's, October 2003) lot 2724 • Stu Levine, privately to the Cardinal Collection, via Joseph O'Connor, as MS-64 PL (NGC) • Cardinal Collection Sale (American Numismatic Rarities, June 2005) lot 41 • Private Texas collection.

Miller Specimen. MS-61 (NGC). Del Val Collection • Warren Miller Collection.

Kensington Specimen. MS-60. Kensington Collection (Bowers and Ruddy, 1975) lot 795. "Choice lightly toned Unc."

Carter Specimen. MS-60. Amon Carter, Jr. Collection. (Stack's, 1984) lot 226, "Brilliant Unc. The terminal state of the die, with an arc-like crack from star 1 across neck to below star 13, resulting in massive bulging of the die."

Eliasberg Specimen. AU-58 (PCGS). Louis E. Eliasberg Sr. Collection (Bowers and Merena, April 1997) lot 2188 • Dale Friend Collection • U.S. Coins • Cardinal Collection • Private collector • Dr. Robert Hesselgesser Collection (Ira and Larry Goldberg, September 2011) lot 5087 • Pre-Long Beach Sale (Ira and Larry Goldberg, May 2012) lot 1292.

Orlando Specimen. AU-58 (PCGS). Orlando Signature Sale (Heritage, January 1997) lot 321 • Long Beach Signature Sale (Heritage, February 1997) lot 772.

Queller Specimen. AU-58 (NGC). Queller Family

Collection of Silver Dollars (Heritage, April 2008) lot 2051 • Internet Sale (Heritage, May 2008) lot 62627 • Internet Sale (Heritage, August 2008) lot 23477 • Bay State Collection (Heritage, July 2009) lot 759.

Long Beach Specimen. AU-58 (NGC). Long Beach Signature Sale (Heritage, May 2008) lot 858.

Hesselgesser Specimen. AU-55 (PCGS). 2003 Baltimore ANA Bourse • Dollar Mike Collection • Private collector • Dr. Robert Hesselgesser Collection (Ira and Larry Goldberg, February 2008) lot 2885 • CSNS Signature Sale (Heritage, April 2009) lot 2559.

Total Estimated Population
MS-65 or better: 0 (URS-0)
MS-64: 1 (URS-1)
MS-63: 0 (URS-0)
MS-60 to 62: 3 to 5 (URS-3)
AU-50 to 58: 20 to 40 (URS-6)
VF-20 to EF-45: 325 to 550 (URS-10)
G-4 to F-15: 150 to 275 (URS-9)
Total for all grades combined: 500 to 900 (URS-11)
Estimated Total Condition Census: 64-61-60-60-58 (multiples)

1799 BB-160

(B-12, H-12)

OBVERSE: Described by Haseltine as from same die as H-9 (BB-166), but it is from a different die. (This new die closely resembles both BB-165 and BB-166, but the first star of BB-160 is much *farther from curl*, slightly over 2.5 mm. (Only about 2 mm. in BB-166) On the right, stars 11-12-13 are closer together than are the others.

Obverse die used to strike 1799 BB-160 only.

Reverse: *No berries.* U in UNITED defective at upper left part, which is cut off due to defective punch. Point of star touches point of lower part of eagle's beak; ray points to left serif at left side of U in PLURIBUS. Star under cloud 1 is noticeably smaller than any other. Far right edge of A is over junction of clouds 3 and 4. A in AMERICA rests on fourth feather. Leaf point is under left side of upright of I. Upper right star has *only one point* touching cloud 8 (whereas two points of the same star touch the cloud on the BB-157 reverse). No berries on branch (one tiny remnant of a stem can be seen), as the die was reground earlier (see description under 1799 BB-158).

Reverse first used to strike 1799 BB-158, during which time it had its first relapping (berries weak), next coining

BB-159, then BB-158 again, then, second relapping (removing berries), BB-160 and, finally, BB-161.

Die States

Die State I: Obverse die without cracks. Reverse relapped as inherited from BB-158. Rare die state (with perfect obverse). Only one seen.

Die State II: Obverse with tiny hairline crack extending from the lower left of the 1 in date to the field below the bottom curl. A hint of a curved hairline crack extends from the border below drapery. Reverse as preceding. Rare die state.

Die State III: Bolender-12a. Obverse cracks intensify. Crack from foot of 1 in date extends right, below 7, to border. A crack extends from the border up into the first 9, while a crosswise crack at the bottom of the first 9 goes left through the upright of 7, and right to the second 9. Curved crack from border to right now touches drapery. Crack from border between drapery and star 13 goes upward and curves to the right into field. Crack from star 12 extends to border at star 13. Reverse as preceding. A plentiful die state.

Die State IV: Bolender-12b. Obverse die cracks intensify further. Crack in right field now extends through star 9 to border. Crack from star 13 downward to border. Crack connects stars 3 to 7 with L in LIBERTY. Crack extending left from 1 in date to below lowest curl now extends farther upward, and opposite the innermost point of star 2 crosses a crack going from star 2 to the hair; original crack continues upward to end of lowest hair ribbon. Crack from border to star 1, then, somewhat split, continuing to star 2, through star 2, touching innermost ray end of star 3, to field opposite star 4. Reverse as preceding. Scarce die state. The 1975 ANA Convention Sale coin, ex Ostheimer and Bolender collections, may have been this die state, and was described as Gem Uncirculated.

Collecting Notes

1799 BB-160 is one of the more plentiful issues of the year, although it does not compare with the ready availability of the almost omnipresent BB-166 and BB-163. I suggest that about 650 to 1,150 of the 1799 BB-160 variety exist. Most are of Die States III and IV.

The reverse has no berries and is one of two 1799 varieties (the other is BB-161) lacking them. Accordingly, BB-160 has attracted the attention of a number of collectors who do not otherwise seek to acquire die varieties, thus accounting for added popularity of the issue. In his 1881 *Type-Table*, J.W. Haseltine called this variety very scarce. Obviously, it is very scarce no longer.

Notable Specimens

Newcomer Specimen. MS-65 (NGC). Waldo C. Newcomer Collection • Col. E.H.R. Green Collection. • T. James Clarke, via James G. Macallister. • New Netherlands 48th Sale, 1956, lot 634. "Bolender-12b. Shattered obverse die as described. Brilliant Unc., almost in the gem class." • Jascha Heifetz Collection (Superior, 1989) lot 3817.

"MS-67." • May Sale (Superior, May 1991) lot 701 • Baltimore Sale (Superior, July 1993) lot 547.

Flannagan Specimen. MS-64 (PCGS). Anaheim ANA Sale (Heritage, August 1995) lot 6520 • Phillip Flannagan Collection (Bowers and Merena, November 2001) lot 4257 • Jack Lee Collection III (Heritage, November 2005) lot 2192 • Joseph C. Thomas Collection (Heritage, April 2009) lot 2552.

Essex Palm Specimen. MS-63 (PCGS). Essex Palms Collection (Heritage, January 2007) lot 1032.

Deb-Ann Specimen. MS-63 (NGC). Deb-Ann Collection (Heritage, January 2009) lot 3944.

Bolender Specimen. MS-63. M.H. Bolender Collection • A.J. Ostheimer 3rd Collection • ANA Convention Sale (Superior, 1975) lot 942. "Shattered obverse. MS-60 to 65. Struck partially off center on the obverse and irregularly about the rims." • Brown Library Collection (Pine Tree, 1976) lot 314. "Shattered obverse die. Gem Unc."

Four Landmark Collections Specimen. MS-63. Four Landmark Collections Sale (Bowers and Merena, 1989) lot 1969.

Orlando Specimen. MS-63 (NGC). Orlando Sale (Superior, August 1992) lot 174.

Total Estimated Population

MS-65 or better: 1 or 2 (URS-1)
MS-64: 1 or 2 (URS-1)
MS-63: 4 to 8 (URS-3)
MS-60 to 62: 20 to 40 (URS-6)
AU-50 to 58: 35 to 70 (URS-7)
VF-20 to EF-45: 400 to 700 (URS-10)
G-4 to F-15: 200 to 350 (URS-9)
Total for all grades combined: 650 to 1,150 (URS-11)
Estimated Total Condition Census: 65-64-63 (multiples)

1799 BB-161

(B-11, H-11)

Obverse: See description under 1799 BB-156; die corrected as described under BB-163. Perfect, without cracks.

Obverse die used to strike 1799 BB-156 (with clash marks), BB-157, BB-161 (now relapped), BB-162, BB-163, and BB-164.

Reverse: *No berries.* U in UNITED defective at upper left part, which is cut off, due to the employment of a defective punch. Point of star touches point of lower part of eagle's beak; ray points to left serif at left side of U in PLURIBUS. Star under cloud 1 is noticeably smaller than any other. A in AMERICA rests on fourth feather. Leaf point is under left side of upright of I. Upper right star has *only one point* touching cloud 8 (whereas two points of the same star touch the cloud on the reverse of BB-157). Far right edge of A is over junction of clouds 3 and 4. No berries on branch (one tiny remnant of a stem can be seen), as the die was reground earlier (see description under 1799 BB-158). This is the terminal state of this die, after having mated with four obverses including this one.

Reverse first used to strike 1799 BB-158, during which time it had its first relapping (berries weak), next coining BB-159, then BB-158 again, then, second relapping (removing berries), BB-160 and, finally, BB-161.

Die States

Die State I: Obverse die without cracks. Reverse die without cracks. May not exist with unbroken reverse die.

Die State II: Bolender-11a. Large crack from left border goes past right side of D of UNITED to eagle's wing; a spur of the crack goes to the edge of the D and then downward to ribbon. Scarcer die state than the following.

Die State III: Cracks enlarge, and now crack from border goes through wing, star, eagle's head, and continues upward behind head. Crack from D to ribbon now continues downward along edge of eagle's wing to shield

(and is remarkably similar to a crack on 1799/8 BB-143). New crack goes from arrow feathers upward through UNITE to border. This die state, or a slightly less advanced version of it, is the state most often seen for BB-161.

Collecting Notes

The present population of 1799 BB-161 is believed to be about 600 to 1,100. Most of these are of Die State II, according to auction offerings, but probably most were what I call Die State III. While BB-161 is obtainable easily enough in lower grades, in AU the issue is scarce, and in true Mint State it is a notable rarity. Nearly all of the auction appearances for Mint State coins mentioned above occurred well before the revision in grading interpretations that occurred in numismatics beginning in 1986.

BB-161 has no berries in the branch on the reverse, a fact not generally known, as Milferd H. Bolender noted that it has "one tiny berry." Granted, it may have a *trace* of an erstwhile berry, but anything approaching a full berry, no. The no-berry variety has been listed in the *Guide Book* for many years, and, as such, it has drawn a circle of collectors desiring it (especially true of the better-known BB-160, which Bolender specifically noted as being berryless, but "from same die as Bolender-11," with no further explanation given).

Inasmuch as the without-berries feature on BB-161 and BB-160 was caused by relapping the die, to my mind the variety is not especially significant for that feature. Had the berries been omitted in error by the die sinker, *that* would constitute a variety worth striving for.

Notable Specimens

Davis Specimen. MS-66 (PCGS). Davis-Graves (James Davis) Collection (Stack's, 1954) lot 1302. "A shade from Unc." • A.J. Ostheimer 3rd Collection (Lester Merkin, 1968) lot 282. "Heavy breaks much more advanced than described for Bolender-11a." • Norman

Stack Type Set • Knoxville Collection • Jay Parrino • Steve Contursi • Private collector • Old West and Franklinton Collections Sale (American Numismatic Rarities, August 2006) lot 710 • Charlotte Signature Sale (Heritage, March 2007) lot 889 • Joseph C. Thomas Collection (Heritage, January 2011) lot 5621.

Sherman Specimen. MS-63 (NGC). J.A. Sherman Collection (Stack's, August 2007) lot 798 • Baltimore Rarities Sale (Bowers and Merena, July 2008), lot 706 • Pre-Long Beach Sale (Ira and Larry Goldberg, September 2008) lot 933 • Baltimore Sale (Stack's Bowers, November 2011) lot 2593.

Queller Specimen. MS-63 (ANACS). December Sale (Stack's, December 1998) lot 1405 • Baltimore ANA Sale (Bowers and Merena, August 2003) lot 2016 • Queller Family Collection of Silver Dollars (Heritage, April 2008) lot 2053 • Dr. Robert Hesselgesser Collection (Ira and Larry Goldberg, September 2011) lot 5090 • Pre-Long Beach Sale (Ira and Larry Goldberg, May 2012) lot 933.

Boyd Specimen. MS-63. "World's Greatest Collection" (F.C.C. Boyd, Numismatic Gallery, 1945) lot 73. "Similar to H-11 but reverse has die break from edge to wing and touching D in UNITED. Unc. gem." • ANA Convention Sale (Numismatic Gallery, 1949) lot 186. • Harold Bareford Collection (Stack's, 1981) lot 416. "Die break touching D of UNITED. Brilliant Unc."

Eliasberg Specimen. MS-61 (NGC). Louis E. Eliasberg, Sr. Collection (Bowers and Merena, 1997) lot 2189; *Obverse die very prominently clashed in the date area and to the left and right,* with lettering, parts of clouds, and other features visible. Studied carefully, much of the word STATES can be made out, reversed. The die has clashed twice, possibly three times, and is quite spectacular. Not described as such in the 1993 *Encyclopedia* on the subject. This is the obverse die state (with clash marks) of BB-156 and 157; now we know that *before* relapping the combination to create BB-161 occurred. Reverse is Die State III of BB-161.

Total Estimated Population

MS-65 or better: 1 (URS-1)
MS-64: 0 (URS-0)
MS-63: 1 or 2 (URS-1)
MS-60 to 62: 4 to 6 (URS-3)
AU-50 to 58: 10 to 20 (URS-5)
VF-20 to EF-45: 400 (URS-750)
G-4 to F-15: 200 to 350 (URS-9)
Total for all grades combined: 600 to 1,100 (URS-11)
Estimated Total Condition Census: 66-63-63-63-62-61-60 (multiples)

1799 BB-162

(B-6, H-6)

Obverse: See description under 1799 BB-156. The Bolender Collection specimen shows a slight crack along border opposite point of bust. Usually found weak at the centers. In BB-157 and BB-162 the upper right corner is slightly indented in the 1 in date.

Obverse die used to strike 1799 BB-156 (with clash marks), BB-157, BB-161 (now relapped), BB-162, BB-163, and BB-164.

Reverse: A in STATES touches clouds. Far right edge of A is over cloud 3. Leaf points to center of upright of I in AMERICA. Letter A touches both third and fourth feathers. Point of star touches lower part of eagle's beak; ray points to left upright of U, slightly to the left of its center. Upper stars about same as BB-157, except that the second star from the left has two points touching clouds. A very close to M, ME joined at lower part. The letters in E PLURIBUS UNUM seem larger and in some instances differently proportioned on this reverse (and also that of BB-164, from a different die).

Reverse die used to strike 1799 BB-162 only.

Die States

Die State I: Obverse die with slight crack along border opposite bust. Perfect reverse die.

Die State II: Later obverse state with an obverse crack at the bust point through the last four stars to the rim.

Die State III: Obverse as preceding. Reverse with crack from rim to cloud 7. Crack through OF to wing. Crack from bottom left of R through field to leaf. The die state usually seen.

Die State IV: Obverse as preceding. Reverse with additional crack, from ED, through wing, through STATES, to border. Scarce die state.

Collecting Notes

1799 BB-162 is of medium scarcity. I believe that 300 to 500 survive. In his 1881 *Type-Table*, J.W. Haseltine called this variety very scarce. Most specimens are in circulated grades through VF, with an occasional EF and even more occasional AU appearing on the market. Uncirculated coins are rarer yet.

Notable Specimens

Clarke Specimen. MS-64 (PCGS). Col. E.H.R. Green Collection • T. James Clarke Collection (New Netherlands 48th Sale, 1956) lot 630. "Lightly toned Unc. Obverse cracked through last four stars to bust as on Bolender-10a, Bolender-17. Reverse rusted in left field; cracked from edge between S and OF to cloud, through OF and wing, and edge to MER to branch." • FUN Signature Sale (Heritage, January 1997) lot 6276 • Long Beach Signature Sale (Heritage, February 1999) lot 6028 • Oliver Jung Collection (American Numismatic Rarities, July 2004) lot 74 • Cardinal Collection (Superior, January 2002) lot 1188 • Private collection • Chicago Signature Sale (Heritage, August 2011) lot 7249.

Cornell University Specimen. MS-63 (PCGS). Cornell University Collection Sale (Stack's, 1975) lot 910.

"Brilliant Unc." • FUN Signature Sale (Heritage, January 1997) lot 5303 • May Sale (Superior, May 2003) lot 2727 • Pre-Long Beach Auction (Ira and Larry Goldberg, May 2009) lot 614 • Los Angeles ANA Sale (Bowers and Merena, August 2009) lot 1656 • Pre-Long Beach Sale (Ira and Larry Goldberg, May 2010) lot 982 • Baltimore Sale (Stack's Bowers, March 2012) lot 4116 • Baltimore Sale (Stack's Bowers, June 2012) lot 3018.

Chalkley Specimen. MS-63. Chalkley Collection Sale (Superior, 1990) lot 2863. "Struck from a rusted reverse die."

Hesselgesser Specimen. MS-62 (PCGS). September Sale (Superior, September 1997) lot 2153 • Dr. Robert Hesselgesser Collection (Ira and Larry Goldberg, September 2011) lot 5091.

Hollinbeck-Kagin Specimen. MS-60. Hollinbeck-Kagin Sale, June 1970, lot 622. "Brilliant slightly golden Unc., reverse prooflike."

Low-Bolender Specimen. MS-60. Lyman H. Low sale 1918. • M.H. Bolender Collection, 1952, lot 93. "Unc., but a few file marks on reverse done at mint to adjust weight of planchet before striking." • K.P. Austin Collection • A.J. Ostheimer 3rd Collection (Lester Merkin, 1968) lot 277. • Gilhousen Collection (Superior, 1973) lot 1251. "Unc." • ANA Convention Sale (Superior, 1975) lot 919. "Cracked reverse. Warmly toned Unc."

Eastern Collection coin. MS-60. Coin in a private Eastern collection, Uncirculated. May duplicate another listing. (Reported by Douglas Winter.)

Total Estimated Population

MS-65 or better: 0 (URS-0)
MS-64: 1 (URS-1)
MS-63: 1 or 2 (URS-1)
MS-60 to 62: 2 to 4 (URS-2)
AU-50 to 58: 5 to 10 (URS-4)
VF-20 to EF-45: 220 to 360 (URS-9)
G-4 to F-15: 75 to 125 (URS-8)
Total for all grades combined: 300 to 500 (URS-10)
Estimated Total Condition Census: 64-63-63-62-60 (multiples)

1799 BB-163

(B-10, H-10)

Obverse: See description under 1799 BB-156. In this combination the "pocket" or "cobweb" under throat (die clash mark) has been removed by relapping the die. Upper side of 1 in date is a straight line. The Bolender Collection specimen shows a light die crack through last three stars. (Early die states do not show the obverse crack through stars 11-13.)

Obverse die used to strike 1799 BB-156 (with clash marks), BB-157, BB-161 (now relapped), BB-162, BB-163, and BB-164.

Reverse: Leaf point between left corner and left side of upright of I in AMERICA. Farthest arrow point is under right upright of N. Point of star enters eagle's mouth, and touches lower part of eagle's beak. Another point of same star points to left upright of U in PLURIBUS. Far right edge of A is over cloud 3. Most show a die crack from border through OF, bottom of AMERICA, eagle's tail, arrows, left wing, up through ST, top of AT.

Reverse die used to strike 1799 BB-163 only.

Die States

Die State I: Early state; perfect dies. No obverse or reverse cracks. Scarce.

Die State II: Bolender-10b. Obverse crack connects stars 11-12-13 but not bust (this is visible only on high grade specimens). With reverse cracks from border through OF, to wing tip, through AMERICA, through branch, through eagle's tail, through arrows,

BB-163: Die State IV, with additional reverse die cracks.

below UNITED, through wing, to S. Scarce die state.

Die State III: Obverse crack connects stars. On reverse, peripheral crack continues through first T of STATES, through top of A, to border. This is the die state usually seen.

Die State IV: Obverse crack extends to outside ray of star 10. On reverse, additional cracks develop: Vertically from border through O, between clouds 7 and 8, toward eagle's head, splits, and branch goes left through a star. Crack from wing, through right ribbon end, into field to left of branch end. Crack from branch to eagle's leg to tail. Crack from interior of branch upward to below ER. Crack from top of A, down through TES, to cloud 5, splits, two cracks go down and to the left, and one goes to right. The die could not have survived long beyond this point. Rare die state.

Collecting Notes

1799 BB-163 shares the spotlight with BB-166 as one of the two most plentiful varieties of the year. I estimate that 1,000 to 1,800 of this variety exist. Curiously, nearly all are in lower grade levels through VF, plus a few scattered EF and AU coins. The offering of a Mint State coin should be a major event (at least, once the rarity of such is widely known). This variety must have been well distributed in the channels of commerce, or there may be some other explanation why so few high grade coins were saved. In comparison, more examples of 1799 BB-166 survive in higher grades.

Notable Specimens

Eliasberg Specimen. MS-64 (PCGS). Louis E. Eliasberg, Sr.

Collection (Bowers and Merena, 1997) lot 2190. Die State II. The piece is exquisitely struck with excellent detail and is somewhat prooflike • Tangible Asset Galleries • Private Midwest collection.

St. Louis Specimen. MS-62 (ANACS). St. Louis Signature Sale (Heritage, May 2005) lot 7583.

French Specimen. MS-61 (NGC). Auction '84 (Stack's, 1984) lot 1186. "Choice Brilliant Unc." • French Family Collection (Stack's, 1989) lot 11. "Choice Brilliant Unc." • H. Roland Willasch Collection (Superior, 1990) lot 534 • Jim Matthews Collection • 1999 via Jim McGuigan, to Warren Miller Collection, Die State III.

Springdale Specimen. MS-61 (PCGS). Lake Michigan and Springdale Collections Sale (American Numismatic Rarities, June 2006) lot 2037.

Atlanta Specimen. MS-61 (ICG). Atlanta ANA Signature Sale (Heritage, August 2001) lot 6417 • Aspen Collection (Heritage, July 2008) lot 1739 • Orlando Rarities Sale (Bowers and Merena, January 2009) lot 771 • Baltimore Signature Sale (Heritage, March 2009) lot 2348.

CSNS Convention Sale Specimen. MS-60. CSNS Convention Sale (McIntire, 1988) lot 571. "MS-60. Early die state."

Heritage Specimen. MS-60. Heritage, March 1989 Sale, lot 484 "Mint State (60/60)."

Hollinbeck-Kagin Specimen. MS-60. Hollinbeck-Kagin Sale, June 1970, lot 626. "Unc."

October Sale Specimen. MS-60. October Sale (Stack's, 1990) lot 1660. "Brilliant Unc."

Total Estimated Population
MS-65 or better: 0 (URS-0)
MS-64: 1 (URS-1)
MS-63: 1 or 2 (URS-1)
MS-60 to 62: 5 to 10 (URS-4)
AU-50 to 58: 10 to 20 (URS-5)
VF-20 to EF-45: 650 to 1,250 (URS-11)
G-4 to F-15: 325 to 550 (URS-10)
Total for all grades combined: 1,000 to 1,800 (URS-12)
Estimated Total Condition Census: 64-62-61-61-61-60 (multiples)

1799 BB-164

(B-17, H-17)
Obverse: See description under 1799 BB-156. Although this obverse die was used to coin BB-156, BB-157, BB-162, BB-163, and BB-164, in its use with BB-164, the state is most similar to BB-163, with the "pocket" or "cobweb" (die clash mark) at junction of chin and neck removed by relapping the die. A die crack shows through last four stars. A faint crack is near border opposite point of bust. All seen are weak at the centers, especially on the obverse.

Obverse die used to strike 1799 BB-156 (with clash marks), BB-157, BB-161 (now relapped), BB-162, BB-163, and BB-164.

Reverse: Five *extremely large berries* in olive branch, the

largest on any 1799 dollar. The two upper berries are partly buried in the leaves. Point of star enters eagle's mouth, upper part of beak closing down on star. The point of the star almost touches lower part of beak; ray points to left edge of left serif of U in PLURIBUS. Leaf points near left corner of I in AMERICA. A does not touch feathers. Very short stem in claw; shortest stem on any 1799 reverse. Peculiar raised die flaws resembling an equal sign (=) are at an angle under the star that straddles clouds 2 and 3. An incuse die mark at the upper left corner of the leftmost cloud is present on the early die state; the second S in STATES is repunched at the inside of its lower loop. Far right edge of A is over junction of clouds 3 and 4. The letters in E PLURIBUS UNUM seem larger and in some instances differently proportioned on this reverse (and also on BB-162, a different die), in comparison to the other reverses of the year.

Reverse die used to strike 1799 BB-164 only.

Die States

Die State I: Obverse die with crack from stars 10-13 to drapery, plus tiny, lower crack from drapery end extending right about 2/3 the way to star 13. Reverse with no cracks. No more than 5% of surviving BB-164 dollars are of this die state.

Die State II: Obverse as preceding. Reverse with hairline crack beginning from right side of U, through bottom of N, extending (in two or three intermediate states) to bottom of D. Scarce die state.

Die State III: Bolender-17a. Obverse as preceding. Reverse with crack from border, then through UNITED as in Die State II, continuing though eagle's wing, then (in at least two intermediate states) to S, then to left arm of T. Many seen.

Die State IV: Obverse as preceding. Reverse with crack now continuing past ST to top of A to border. Crack from bottom of S, above clouds, to OF. Crack develops at border and goes part way through space between I and C of AMERICA, then in an intermediate state, continues across branch and into right side of shield. Small cracks develop to the left of first A in AMERICA and to the right of right ribbon loop near end. Scarce die state.

Die State V: Obverse as preceding. Reverse with crack from rim at bottom through the eagle's tail to the arrow feathers. Not seen. The description of Gilhousen (Superior, 1973): 1261 mentions the Philip Straus coin was the first of this die state reported; now possibly 8 to 12 are known. Gilhousen's (Ostheimer's) was VF-35.

Collecting Notes

As an estimated 550 to 950 specimens of the 1799 BB-164 dollar are known, examples are readily available on the market. Most are in grades through EF. AU coins are somewhat more elusive than the overall rarity might suggest. Mint State coins are great rarities.

Notable Specimens

Cardinal Specimen. MS-65 (PCGS). Dallas Sale (Heritage, December 1987) lot 712 • Unknown intermediaries • Kenny Duncan • Cardinal Collection (American Numismatic Rarities, June 2005) lot 43 • Private collector • Philadelphia ANA Sale (Stack's Bowers, August 2012) lot 11484.

Long Beach Specimen. MS-63 (NGC). Long Beach Signature Sale (Heritage, February 2012) lot 3779.

Hesselgesser Specimen. MS-62 (PCGS). Orlando Sale (Stack's, January 2007) lot 795 • Dr. Robert Hesselgesser Collection (Ira and Larry Goldberg, September 2011) lot 5093 • Pre-Long Beach Sale (Ira and Larry Goldberg, May 2012) lot 1296.

Queller Specimen. MS-62 (PCGS). Queller Family Collection of Silver Dollars (Heritage, April 2008) lot 2058.

Davis Specimen. MS-60. Davis-Graves (James Davis) Collection (Stack's, 1954) lot 1307. "Unc."

Stack's March Sale Specimen. MS-60. Stack's, March 1983, lot 935. "Brilliant Unc."

Schuyler Specimen. MS-60. Schuyler Collection • M.H. Bolender Collection. • A.J. Ostheimer 3rd Collection (Lester Merkin, 1968) lot 289. "Unc."

Essex Institute Specimen. MS-60. Essex Institute Collection (Stack's, 1975) lot 992. "Brilliant Unc."

Total Estimated Population

MS-65 or better: 1 (URS-1)

MS-64: 0 (URS-0)

MS-63: 1 (URS-1)

MS-60 to 62: 2 to 4 (URS-2)

AU-50 to 58: 10 to 20 (URS-5)

VF-20 to EF-45: 350 to 625 (URS-10)

G-4 to F-15: 175 to 300 (URS-9)

Total for all grades combined: 550 to 950 (URS-11)

Estimated Total Condition Census: 65-63-62-62-60 (multiples)

1799 BB-165

(B-8, H-8)

Obverse: Liberty with open mouth. First star is slightly farther from curl than last star is from bust, or about 2 mm. from curl. The seventh star is slightly closer to L than eighth star is to Y. There is a die chip between star 9 and the border. Star 10 is slightly repunched on its innermost ray. On the left, the stars are fairly evenly spaced. On the right, stars 10 and 11 are significantly closer than any of the others. Highest curl on top of head is centered more under *right half* of E in LIBERTY. The 1 in date is much farther from the curl, slightly over 1 mm. The letters in LIBERTY are usually seen with varying degrees of bifurcation, sometimes extensive, suggesting to Bolender that the letters were "fancy." This obverse closely resembles BB-160, to which compare.

Obverse die used to strike 1799 BB-165 only.

Reverse: Die flaws inside and to right top of final S in STATES. Far right edge of A is over junction of clouds 3 and 4. Point of star touches point of lower part of eagle's beak; ray points to left of left upright of U in PLURIBUS. Leaf points slightly right of center of I in AMERICA. AME join at lowest part. *The N in UNITED was initially cut upside down and later corrected; an extraneous serif from the error can be seen to the lower right of the N,* and appears as a line between the bottoms of N and I.

Die States

Reverse die used to strike 1799 BB-165 only.

Die State I: Obverse die without crack. Reverse with die flaws at second S of STATES, but no line cracks. About 20% or so of BB-165 dollars are of this die state.

Die State II: Bolender-8a. Obverse with die crack from border through two points of seventh star and LIB. Reverse with these cracks: Wing up through ST to above A. Crack from cloud 3 up through TES to OF. Crack from border down to second S joins other crack. Crack from CA, to stem, through tail feathers, through

arrow feathers, to U. Reverse stars are weak in this and later state. (Intermediate states of these cracks occur.) Plentiful die state.

Die State III: Bolender-8b. Obverse as II, but now with crack heavier through LIBE and extending farther. With additional crack from border above T down through TY. Reverse with additional cracks: From F through wing tip to ribbon end. From bottom of M to branch. Scarcer die state.

Collecting Notes

1799 BB-165 is one of the more plentiful varieties among dollars of this date. About 600 to 1,100 are known today. Most are in worn grades, with the norm being Very Fine. A few Mint State coins exist.

Notable Specimens

CSNS Specimen. MS-64 (NGC). CSNS Signature Sale (Heritage, April 2002) lot 4013 • Santa Clara Sale (Superior, November 2003) lot 748 • Denver Signature Sale (Heritage, August 2006) lot 5301 • Orlando Signature Sale (Heritage, January 2007) lot 1033 • Joseph C. Thomas Collection (Heritage, April 2009) lot 2554.

Auction '79 Specimen. MS-63. Auction '79 (RARCOA, 1979) lot 1032. • ANA Convention Sale (Heritage, 1988) lot 959. "MS (63/63). Choice Unc."

Hesselgesser Specimen. MS-62+ (PCGS). Frog Run Farm Sale (American Numismatic Rarities, November 2004) lot 1513 • Orlando Signature Sale (Heritage, January 2009) lot 3943 • Baltimore Signature Sale (Heritage, March 2009) 2349 • Dr. Robert Hesselgesser Collection (Ira and Larry Goldberg, September 2011) lot 5094.

Miller Specimen. MS-62 (NGC). G. Lee Kuntz Sale (Superior, October 1991) lot 2624 • Warren Miller Collection.

Queller Specimen. MS-62 (NGC). March Sale (Stack's, March 1996) lot 503 • Queller Family Collection of Silver Dollars (Heritage, April 2008) lot 2059.

Guttag Specimen. MS-62. Guttag Collection • Bolender Collection • A.J. Ostheimer 3rd Collection (Lester Merkin, 1968) lot 279. "gem Unc." • Auction '80 (Paramount, 1980) lot 799. "Gem Unc.-65." • ANA Convention Sale (Heritage, 1988) lot 958. "Mint State (62/62). Obverse has a light vertical staple scratch." (The scratch may have occurred in the 1980s, as Paramount didn't mention it.)

Boyd Specimen. MS-60. "World's Greatest Collection" (F.C.C. Boyd, Numismatic Gallery, 1945) lot 68. "A splendid Unc. example."

Fairfield Specimen. MS-60. Fairfield Collection (Bowers and Ruddy, 1977) lot 1033. "Unc. with some claims to the Choice category."

New Netherlands Specimen. MS-60. ANA Convention Sale (New Netherlands 38th Sale, 1952) lot 3163. "A very late stage of the die. Crack through LIB is

heavier and extends further. Additional break from border above T down through TY. Top of E and R defective. The reverse die is now badly shattered with numerous breaks. Unc." • W.G. Baldenhofer. • A.J. Ostheimer 3rd.

Total Estimated Population
MS-65 or better: 0 (URS-0)
MS-64: 1 (URS-1)
MS-63: 1 or 2 (URS-1)
MS-60 to 62: 4 to 8 (URS-3)
AU-50 to 58: 10 to 20 (URS-5)
VF-20 to EF-45: 400 to 725 (URS-10)
G-4 to F-15: 175 to 250 (URS-9)
Total for all grades combined: 600 to 1,000 (URS-11)
Estimated Total Condition Census: 64-63-62+-62 (multiples)

1799 BB-166

(B-9, H-9)

Obverse: Similar to BB-157, but from a different die. The stars are larger (punched more deeply into the die), making them closer together. The upper left and right stars are about equidistant from L and Y. 13th star about 1.5 mm. from bust. First star about 2 mm. from curl. On the left, stars 1 to 4 are spaced closer than are stars 4 to 7. On the right, stars 8 and 9, and 12 and 13, are spaced closer than are the other stars. Die crack below base of 1 in date on all seen.

Obverse die used to strike 1799 BB-166 only.[1]

Reverse: "Apostrophe" after final S in STATES on most (but not all) specimens. Star touches point of lower part of eagle's beak. Far right edge of A is over cloud 3. Leaf points under right side of upright of I in AMERICA. A touches third feather only. Die crack through MERIC.

Reverse die used to strike 1799 BB-166 only.

Die States

Die State I: Perfect obverse die without crack under 1. Perfect reverse die without "apostrophe" flaw after final S in STATES. Extremely rare. Not seen by author.

Die State II: Obverse die crack begins between two dentils and extends upward about halfway to base of 1 in date. Reverse with very tiny vertical "apostrophe" crack to upper right of final S in STATES. Scarce die state.

Die State III: Obverse die crack connects with bottom of 1 and enlarges. Another crack begins on bust and extends upward and to the right, touching chin, and ending in the field. On reverse. "apostrophe" crack enlarges slightly. Common die state.

Die State IV: Obverse crack through bust extends to star 10 and also downward to first 9 in date. Reverse as preceding. Scarce die state.

Die State V: Obverse die shatters. Additional crack in obverse field to left of stars 8, 9, and 10, connects with earlier crack. Crack connects stars 9 and 10. New crack from border, up through drapery, bust, field, to left side

---

[1] See note under 1799/8 and 1799 silver dollars, general information, concerning an apocryphal new variety in the Boyd Collection.

of star 12. By this time, the obverse field has a bumpy, "sandpaper" surface (observed on a Mint State coin), from extensive die rust. On the reverse, the "apostrophe" crack extends to border, as does a new crack to the left of the final S in STATES. Probably, about 10% to 20% of the specimens of BB-166 are of this die state.

Collecting Notes

1799 BB-166 and BB-163 are the most plentiful varieties of the year. It seems likely that about 1,000 to 1,800 of each are known. The population of BB-166 is distributed in a bell curve—few extremely worn ones, some VG, more in Fine grade, a cluster at VF, fewer EF, still fewer AU, and only a small number of Mint State examples. Incidentally, the same curve applies to most other early dollars, except it is sometimes truncated at the upper end. Of course, one can only guess as to how most coins offered years ago will fall into the MS-60-61-62-63, etc., distribution we know today.

Notable Specimens

Baldenhofer Specimen. MS-65 (NGC). W.G. Baldenhofer • Farish-Baldenhofer Sale (Stack's, 1955) • A.J. Ostheimer 3rd Collection • ANA Convention Sale (Superior, 1975) lot 930. "MS-60 to 65." • Unknown intermediaries • New York ANA Sale (Superior, August 2002) lot 1078 • Cardinal Collection • Private collector • Rarities Sale (Bowers and Merena, February 2006) lot 354 • Orlando Signature Sale (Heritage, January 2008) lot 2931 • Chicago ANA Sale (Stack's Bowers, August 2011) lot 7400 • Steve Contursi.

Ivy Specimen. MS-64. Steve Ivy, May 1983, lot 1762.

Saunders Specimen. MS-64. Ebenezer Milton Saunders Collection (Bowers and Merena 1987) lot 3517. "MS-64 to 65."

Franklinton Sale Specimen. MS-63 (PCGS). Old West and Franklinton Sale (American Numismatic Rarities, August 2006) lot 711 • Orlando Sale (Stack's, January 2007) lot 797 • March Sale (Stack's, March 2007) lot 1048 • J.A. Sherman Sale (Stack's August 2007) lot 774 • Pre-Long Beach Sale (Ira and Larry Goldberg, September 2008) lot 934.

Stack's Auction '90 Specimen. MS-63. Stack's, 1980, lot 258. "Brilliant Unc."

Ebsen Specimen. MS-63. Buddy Ebsen Collection (Superior, 1987) lot 1903. "Perfect obverse die. MS-63."

Dallas Specimen. MS-62 (PCGS). Dallas Signature Sale (Heritage, December 2004) lot 6372 • Long Beach Signature Sale (Heritage, February 2005) lot 7326.

(Many more Uncirculated and AU coins could be cited.)

Total Estimated Population

MS-65 or better: 1 (URS-1)

MS-64: 2 or 3 (URS-2)

MS-63: 3 to 6 (URS-3)

MS-60 to 62: 10 to 20 (URS-5)

AU-50 to 58: 40 to 80 (URS-7)

VF-20 to EF-45: 600 to 1,100 (URS-11)

G-4 to F-15: 350 to 600 (URS-10)

Total for all grades combined: 1,000 to 1,800 (URS-12)

Estimated Total Condition Census: 65-64-64-63-63-63

1799 BB-167

(B-14, H-14)

Obverse: *Two raised die flaws in field, or "tears," before eye, one very clear.* The smaller is in the field close to and opposite to the bottom of the forehead, just above the bridge of the nose. The larger and by far the most notable is in the field about 40% of the way from the nose bridge to star 9. On some lower grade coins these "tears" are not visible. Last star near bust (about 0.5 mm.) and a little closer than eighth star is to Y. seventh star farther from L, and first star nearly 2 mm. from curl. Stars 11, 12, and 13 point to spaces between dentils. Small die flaw in field to left of ray of star 8 closest to bottom of Y. The last 9 is about as near bust as star 8 is to Y. *Die flaw* from outer point of 10th star. Same obverse die used for BB-168. All examples are weakly struck on the hair.

Obverse die used to strike 1799 BB-167 (earlier use) and BB-168 (later use).

Reverse: *Die flaws* under AM, between two lower stars just back of eagle's head, between the F in OF and the wing tip, and one below the D in UNITED. Point of star touches point of lower part of eagle's beak. Another point of same star points to space between B and U of PLURIBUS. Far right edge of A is over junction of clouds 3 and 4. Leaf points to center of I in AMERICA. A does not touch feathers of right wing, but is near 3rd feather. Die crack through upper part of AME.

Reverse die used to strike 1799 BB-167 (earlier use) and BB-169 (later use).

Die States

Die State I: Perfect dies. No obverse flaws. No reverse cracks. May not exist.

Die State II: Obverse with "tears" in field before face. Reverse with flaws below first A of AMERICA, slanting downward to halfway below M. Common die state.

Die State III: Obverse as above. Reverse now with crack connecting tops of AM and extending upward toward wing. The most common die state.

Die State IV: Obverse as above. Reverse now with crack connecting tops of AME. As described by Bolender for BB-167. Scarcer than preceding.

Collecting Notes

1799 BB-167 is in the middle range of varieties of this year so far as availability is concerned. About 400 to 700 are known. Most examples are in grades of Fine and VF, with an occasional EF. Any coin finer than that is truly exceptional. This is another of many early dollar varieties that is readily available in VF grade but becomes a rarity if finer.

Notable Specimens

Sebring Sale Specimen. MS-63 (PCGS). Thomas H. Sebring Sale (American Numismatic Rarities, January 2004) lot 144 • Pittsburgh ANA Signature Sale (Heritage, August 2004) lot 6335 • J.A. Sherman Sale (Stack's, August 2007) lot 801 • March Sale (Stack's, March 2007) lot 1050.

CSNS Sale Specimen. MS-61 (ICG). CSNS Signature Sale (Heritage, April 2009) lot 872.

Chapman Specimen. MS-60. Henry Chapman • M.H. Bolender Collection, 1952, lot 115. "Unc."

Hesselgesser Specimen. AU-58 (PCGS). Dr. Robert Hesselgesser Collection (Ira and Larry Goldberg, September 2011) lot 5096 • Orlando FUN Signature Sale (Heritage, January 2012) lot 3291.

Miller Specimen. AU-58 (NGC). Warren Miller Collection.

Krugjohann Specimen. AU-58. Krugjohann Collection (Bowers and Ruddy, 1976) lot 619. "Brilliant Unc."

Miller Specimen (another) AU-55 (NGC). Warren Miller Collection, prominently double-struck.

Cardinal Specimen. AU-55 (PCGS). Tangible Asset Galleries • Cardinal Collection • Private collector • Baltimore Sale (Bowers and Merena, November 2009) lot 2629 • Orlando Rarities Sale (Bowers and Merena, January 2010) lot 416.

Baldenhofer Specimen. AU-50. W.G. Baldenhofer Collection • Farish-Baldenhofer Sale (Stack's, 1955). • A.J. Ostheimer 3rd Collection • 1975 ANA Convention Sale (Superior) lot 94.

Getty Specimen. AU-50. Getty Collection (Bowers and Ruddy Galleries, 1977) lot 536.

Getty Specimen (another). AU-50. Getty Collection (Bowers and Ruddy, 1977) lot 1695.

Stark Specimen. AU-50. New England Rare Coin Galleries, May 1979. Sold to the following. • Dr. Robert Stark Collection.

Total Estimated Population

MS-65 or better: 0 (URS-0)

MS-64: 0 (URS-0)

MS-63: 1 (URS-1)

MS-60 to 62: 1 or 2 (URS-1)

AU-50 to 58: 4 to 8 (URS-3)

VF-20 to EF-45: 250 to 450 (URS-

G-4 to F-15: 150 to 250 (URS-9)

Total for all grades combined: 400 to 700 (URS-10)

Estimated Total Condition Census: 63-61-60-58-58-58-55 (multiples)

1799 BB-168

(BB-22, H-22)

Obverse: See description under 1799 BB-167. Die flaws in field before eye as on BB-167.

Obverse die used to strike 1799 BB-167 (earlier use) and BB-168 (later use).

Reverse: *Horizontal die crack* entirely across center of reverse, from right side of E to left side of M. One arrow extends slightly past right side of upright of N. Star touches lower point of eagle's beak; ray points to left upright of U in PLURIBUS. Leaf point is slightly right of being under center of I in AMERICA. Letter A touches only third feather. U in UNITED is cut off at upper left; made from defective punch (used on three different dies to strike BB-157; BB-161, 12, 16, and 23; and BB-168). Far right edge of A is over cloud 3.

Reverse die used to strike 1799 BB-168 only.

Die States

Die State I: With perfect obverse die; reverse die not shattered. May not exist.

Die State II: Obverse with delicate crack connecting stars 11, 12, and 13. Reverse die with bisecting horizontal crack beginning at left border, right side of E, ribbon, wing, eagle's neck, wing, ribbon, left side of M, to right border. The usually seen die state.

Die State III: Obverse as preceding. Reverse is a slightly later state with blob at crack as it touches upper right of E. Scarcer than preceding.

Dies as described by Bolender for BB-168. Reverse die broken across.

Die State III: Later state with the obverse developing multiple cracks to the point of shattering. Cf. Pine Tree Auctions Sale, September 1974, lot 1028. Extremely rare. Not seen.

Collecting Notes

With a known population estimated to be in the range of 300 to 500 coins, 1799 BB-168 is at once elusive but sufficiently available that every serious specialist can own one. Most specimens are in lower grades through VF. EF coins are very rare. AU coins are extremely rare Mint State? Forget it.

Notable Specimens

Cardinal Specimen. AU-50 (PCGS). Cardinal Collection (Superior, January 2002) lot 1189 • CSNS Signature Sale (Heritage, April 2002) lot 6704.

Hesselgesser Specimen. AU-50 (PCGS). Private collector • Harry Laibstain • Dr. Robert Hesselgesser Collection (Ira and Larry Goldberg, September 2011) lot 5097 • Pre-Long Beach Sale (Ira and Larry Goldberg, May 2012) lot 1300.

Miller Specimen. EF-45 (NGC). San Francisco Signature Sale (Heritage, July 2005) lot 6554 • Warren Miller Collection.

Hesselgesser Specimen (another). EF-45 (PCGS). Dr. Robert Hesselgesser Collection (Bowers and Merena, August 2010) lot 1050 • Pre-Long Beach Sale (Ira and Larry Goldberg, May 2011) lot 900.

Aspen Specimen EF-40. Dr. Nelson Page Aspen Collection (Bowers and Merena, 1989) lot 387. "A tiny obverse rim bump is noted at 4:00."

Hollinbeck-Kagin Specimen. EF-40. Hollinbeck-Kagin Sale, August 1970, lot 1093. "Heavy die break horizontally bisecting reverse, EF (obverse not quite that; but reverse better)."

Springfield Specimen. EF-40. Springfield Collection (Bowers and Ruddy, 1981) lot 242. "Die flaws in field before eye; reverse die broken in half horizontally just above shield. Strictly EF-40, reverse more like EF-45; obverse weaker."

Chalkley Specimen. VF-35. Chalkley Collection (Superior, 1990) lot 2871. "Reverse die suffered a catastrophic horizontal crack spanning the entire die."

October Sale Specimen. VF-35. October Sale (Superior, 1990) lot 1206.

Total Estimated Population
MS-65 or better: 0 (URS-0)
MS-64: 0 (URS-0)
MS-63: 0 (URS-0)
MS-60 to 62: 0 (URS-0)
AU-50 to 58: 2 (URS-2)
VF-20 to EF-45: 125 to 225 (URS-9)
G-4 to F-15: 175 to 275 (URS-9)
Total for all grades combined: 300 to 500 (URS-10)
Estimated Total Condition Census: 50-50-45-45-40 (multiples)

1799 BB-169

(B-21, H-21)

Obverse: Star 8 much closer to Y than star 1 to curl, or star 7 to L, or star 13 to bust. Star 1 is farthest from hair. In date, numeral 1 is close to curl. Slight die roughness below first star, between milling and curl. The second star on the obverse is repunched and the obverse shows die rust which becomes extensive on the late die state. The obverse is similar in appearance to BB-154 and BB-155; identification is simplified by the reverse which reuses the 1799 BB-167 die.

Obverse die used to strike 1799 BB-169 only.

Reverse: See description under 1799 BB-167. Far right edge of A is over junction of clouds 3 and 4.

Reverse die used to strike 1799 BB-167 (earlier use) and BB-169 (later use).

Die States

Die State I: Perfect obverse die. Reverse with light crack over AME, extending slightly to the left. Raised die breaks under A and left side of M. Specimen with perfect obverse die not known to exist.

Die State II: Obverse die now with hairline crack from border, up to right through 99 to drapery. Rare early die state.

Die State III: Obverse as preceding, but now with crack from bust through field to near star 12. Reverse with crack from border above F, through wing, to AME, thus expanding earlier crack.

Die State IV: Obverse now with these additional cracks: From border up through 7 to drapery. Earlier crack from bust now extends to touch star 11. Additional crack connects bust (where flesh meets drapery) to star 13, continuing irregularly upward through all stars on the right, through TY, faintly to R. The die state usually seen.

Die State V: Later die state, as exemplified by Gilhousen (Superior, 1973): 1264, cataloged as with "the die cracks and rust marks are more advanced than Bolender mentions," otherwise undescribed.

Collecting Notes

1799 BB-169 is in the middle range of availability among the varieties of this year. 450 to 850 are believed to exist. Most are in lower grades up through EF. AU and finer coins are rare.

Notable Specimens

Harte Specimen. MS-62 (PCGS). Roy Harte Collection (Bowers and Ruddy, 1977) lot 2787. "Choice

Unc." • Unknown intermediaries • Long Beach Signature Sale (Heritage, June 1998) lot 5942 • Long Beach Signature Sale (Heritage, February 2005) lot 7327.

Holmes Specimen. MS-60. Milton Holmes Collection (Stack's, 1960) lot 2253. "Brilliant Unc."

New Netherlands 54th Sale Specimen. MS-60. New Netherlands 54th Sale, April 1960, lot 656. "Long straight obverse crack slanting up through both 9's to drapery."

Queller Specimen. AU-58 (PCGS). Rarities Sale (Bowers and Merena, January 2002) lot 522 • Rosemont Sale (American Numismatic Rarities, June 2004) lot 1120 • 69th Anniversary Sale (Stack's, October 2004) lot 1514 • Queller Family Collection of Silver Dollars (Heritage, April 2008) lot 2063 • Dr. Robert Hesselgesser Collection (Ira and Larry Goldberg, February 2009) lot 1075 • Pre-Long Beach Sale (Ira and Larry Goldberg, May 2009) lot 616 • Pre-Long Beach Sale (Ira and Larry Goldberg, September 2011) lot 5098 • Warren Miller Collection.

Dallas Specimen. AU-58 (NGC). Dallas Signature Sale (Heritage, December 2005) lot 930 • Long Beach Signature Sale (Heritage, June 2006) lot 2035.

DeCoppet Specimen. AU-58. André DeCoppet Collection (James Kelly, 1955). "Just a shade from Unc."

Hesselgesser Specimen. AU-55 (PCGS). Dr. Robert Hesselgesser Collection (Ira and Larry Goldberg, September 2011) lot 5099 • Pre-Long Beach Sale (Ira and Larry Goldberg, May 2012) lot 1301.

Hollinbeck-Kagin Specimen. AU-55. Hollinbeck-Kagin Sale, August 1970, lot 1092. "Die flaws under AM, near Unc."

Total Estimated Population

MS-65 or better: 0 (URS-0)
MS-64: 0 (URS-0)
MS-63: 0 (URS-0)
MS-60 to 62: 2 to 4 (URS-2)
AU-50 to 58: 7 to 12 (URS-4)
VF-20 to EF-45: 300 to 600 (URS-10)
G-4 to F-15: 150 to 250 (URS-9)
Total for all grades combined: 450 to 850 (URS-11)
Estimated Total Condition Census: 62-60-60-58-58-58-55 (multiples)

ADDITIONAL INFORMATION

The Year 1799 in History

On December 14, 1799, George Washington died at Mount Vernon, his Virginia home. Four days later the news reached Philadelphia. In a speech before Congress, Henry Lee described the deceased as "First in war, first in peace, and first in the hearts of his countrymen." Early the following year, speeches, eulogies, and parades were given in Washington's honor, and medallic remembrances were produced, the most famous being the varieties of cent-sized tokens made in copper, white metal, silver, and gold by Jacob Perkins of Newburyport, Massachusetts, and bearing the inscription, HE IS IN GLORY, THE WORLD IN TEARS. The memory of the first president would endure, and as one medal noted, "time increases his fame."

A census conducted by Spanish authorities in lower Louisiana revealed that there were 42,375 inhabitants, two-thirds of whom were of European extraction. The *Baltimore American* became the first publication to record Congressional debates and speeches in detail. In Dalton, Massachusetts, the Crane paper mill was established; it would later furnish sheets for the printing of bank notes and currency.

In England, chemist Humphry Davy inhaled nitrous oxide, or laughing gas, and reported that it made him insensitive to pain; the gas later came into use as an anesthetic. The first British income tax passed Parliament. In Egypt, Champollion discovered the Rosetta Stone, which had been carved with inscriptions in three different languages; when deciphered, it became the key to decoding ancient Egyptian writing.

"HIGH STREET, From the Country Marketplace, PHILADELPHIA, with the procession in commemoration of the Death of GENERAL GEORGE WASHINGTON, December 26th, 1799." (From *Album of American History, Volume II, 1783-1853*)

CHAPTER 13

1800 SILVER DOLLARS

MINTAGE (ALL VARIETIES)
Calendar year, Mint report: 220,920
Coins bearing date, author's estimate: 100,000

1800 SILVER DOLLARS
BB to Bolender to Haseltine Equivalents

BB Number	Bolender #	Haseltine #	Rarity	Average Grade
BB-181	B-1	H-1	URS-8	VF-25
BB-182	B-2	H-2	URS-6	VF-29
BB-183	B-3	H-3	URS-7	VF-34
BB-184	B-12	H-12	URS-10	VF-35
BB-185	B-20	---	URS-6	VF-23
BB-186	B-4	H-4	URS-9	VF-27
BB-187	B-16	H-16	URS-11	VF-32
BB-188	B-8	H-8	URS-9	VF-36
BB-189	B-5	H-5	URS-9	VF-28
BB-190	B-10	H-10	URS-11	VF-32
BB-191	B-11	H-11	URS-9	VF-27
BB-192	B-19	H-19	URS-11	VF-30
BB-193	B-13, B-18	H-13, H-18	URS-11	VF-32
BB-194	B-14	H-14	URS-11	VF-33
BB-195	B-15	H-15	URS-10	VF-27
BB-196	B-17	H-16	URS-11	VF-31

Coinage Context

Large mintage: The government mintage figure of 220,920 marks the last time the production of early silver dollars crossed the 100,000 mark. By this time, dollars were being exported in quantity, and it was considered futile to coin large quantities.

Die making: Working dies for 1800 dollars were prepared in the same manner as were 1799-dated dollars, to which refer. Varieties are best distinguished by noting the spatial relationships of certain features to each other.

Obverse: The bust of Miss Liberty was punched into the die, after which the letters of LIBERTY, the stars, and the digits in 1800 were all added with individual punches.

Reverse: Punched into the master die were the letters in E PLURIBUS UNUM, which can vary slightly in their placement or size (1800 BB-184 has smaller letters). The master die with the eagle punch contained the eagle, clouds, arrows, upper part of the olive branch, and inscribed ribbon. Added separately to the working die were the letters of UNITED STATES OF AMERICA, the stars above the eagle, end of the olive branch, and berries. In 1800, workmanship continued to improve at the Mint, and individual die differences become increasingly difficult to differentiate.

Die use: During the year 1800, die relapping was practiced very little. The dies were used while they were in excellent condition, after which most were discarded, even though according to standards in place a year or two before, they could have struck many more coins. Obverse and reverse dies tended to mate for the duration of their mutual lives, without ever being paired with another. Of 12 different obverse dies known for 1800, only three had more than one mate. Likewise, of 11 different reverse dies, only three had more than one partner. Because of this, the die linkages that can be constructed effectively for earlier dates do not have such an extensive counterpart here.

Quality considerations: In general, dollars of 1800 have fewer adjustment marks, planchet defects, or evidence of weak striking than do their ancestors. Quality controls must have been in place at the Mint, at least more so than previously.

Numismatic Information

Commentary: 16 die combinations are known of 1800-dated dollars, most of which do not constitute major differences, although varieties with just 12 arrows or just 10 arrows are listed in the *Guide Book* in addition to the standard with 13 arrows. The AMERICAI variety is simply a standard design with a stray mark from a punch (called a die break or crack by many catalogers) following the last letter in AMERICA, giving it a fanciful resemblance to an I. It has been suggested that this may be a remnant of an A letter in the wrong place, but I believe it is either a stray mark or was caused by a piece of foreign matter when the die was made. The AMERICAI issue, not particularly rare, has been popular over the years.

The large number of dies made vs. the number of coins produced may indicate problems with die steel or with some other aspect of the minting process.

Striking periods: There do not seem to be early and late styles of 1800 silver dollars. Thus, while striking periods can be theorized, it is not possible to place them in chronological order.

Striking Period 1
1800 BB-181. • 1800 BB-182. • 1800 BB-183. • 1800 BB-184.

Striking Period 2
1800 BB-185. • 1800 BB-186. • 1800 BB-187.

Striking Period 3
1800 BB-188. • 1800 BB-189. • 1800 BB-190. • 1800 BB-191. • 1800 BB-192.

Striking Period 4
1800 BB-193.

Striking Period 5
1800 BB-194.

Striking Period 6
1800 BB-195.

Striking Period 7
1800 BB-196.

SUMMARY OF CHARACTERISTICS

1800

CIRCULATION STRIKES

Enabling legislation: Act of April 2, 1792

Designer of obverse: Robert Scot (after Stuart), model by John Eckstein

Designer of reverse: Robert Scot (from the Great Seal)

Weight and composition: 416 grains; .8924 silver, balance copper

Melting value (silver bullion value) in year minted: Considered by Mint officials to be on a par with the Spanish dollar, and worth about $1.00 intrinsically (see discussion under Summary of Characteristics, 1794).

Dies prepared: Unknown

Circulation strike mintage, calendar year: 220,920 (not including pieces reserved for the Assay Commission; these are given in parentheses); Delivery figures by day: January 21: 24,000 (+3) • February 6: 34,000 (+3) • February 14: 29,200 (+3) • March 25: 3,500 (+1) • May 6: 2,500 (+3) • May 9: 8,220 (+3) • June 14: 11,000 (+3) • June 25: 10,850 (+3) • August 22: 23,000 (+3) • September 30: 34,000 (+3) • October 22: 6,000 (+3) • October 29: 8,300 (+3) • November 10: 5,500 (+3) • December 9: 4,000 (+3) • December 22: 7,850 (+3) • December 31: 9,000 (+3).

Estimated circulation strike mintage of 1800-dated dollars (author's estimate): 100,000 (rounded).

Estimated quantity melted: Unknown

Estimated total population (all varieties):
  MS-65 or better: 4 (URS-3)
  MS-64: 7 to 10 (URS-4)
  MS-63: 6 to 12 (URS-5)
  MS-60 to 62: 35 to 70 (URS-7)
  AU-50 to 58: 150 to 300 (URS-9)
  VF-20 to EF-45: 3,400 to 6,200 (URS-14)
  G-4 to F-15: 1,500 to 2,500 (URS-12)
  Total for all grades combined: 5,000 to 9,000 (URS-14)

Estimated Total Condition Census: 65+-65-65-64 (multiples)

Characteristics of striking: Depends upon the variety. If weakly struck, this is often observed at the center of the obverse and among the stars above the eagle on the reverse.

Commentary: Silver dollars dated 1800 are for the most part quite well struck. This is the last year dollars were made in large quantities.

1800 HERALDIC EAGLE

VARIETIES

1800 BB-181

(B-1, H-1)

Obverse: 180 close in date. TY too far apart. The 1 in date *barely misses* touching the hair. Slight *elevation* in field between lowest left star and hair due to depression in die. *Die flaws* near inside point of star 11 and also at lower outside of same star. Star 8 near Y, and star 13 near bust, the two about equidistant. On the left, stars 3 and 4 are closer together than are any others. Point of star 11 closest to border has its end bent upward, a most unusual characteristic.

Obverse die used to strike 1800 BB-181 only.

Reverse: *Leaf touches* lower right corner of serif of I in AMERICA (compare to reverse of BB-183, which touches bottom of I at a different point). Point of star touches point of lower part of eagle's beak. A in AMERICA touches only third feather. First T in STATES *is double-punched.* AME joined at lower part. A over clouds 2 and 3. Tip of arrowhead under center of U in UNITED.

Reverse die used to strike 1800 BB-181 (earlier use) and BB-182 (later use).

Die States

Die State I: Perfect dies.

Collecting Notes

This is one of the scarcer varieties of the year. I estimate that 90 to 160 exist in all grades combined.

The literature shows a confusing difference of opinion concerning rarity. In his 1881 *Type-Table* J.W. Haseltine simply noted it as being "scarce." In 1950, M.H. Bolender felt differently, and stated this: "My records over a period of 40 years show it to be extremely rare." Today in the early 1990s, it is felt that the population is somewhere in the range of 90 to 160 coins, an estimate which is large enough to provide a specimen for most advanced specialists seeking one.

Most examples are in lower grades, with VG and Fine being quite acceptable for the variety. VF coins are very rare, and any piece over VF, such as the Spies EF, would be a sure-fire Condition Census item. All seen are lightly struck at the centers.

Notable Specimens

Queller Specimen. AU-55 (PCGS). 68th Anniversary Sale (Stack's, October 2003) lot 2725 • Queller Family Collection of Silver Dollars (Heritage, April 2008) lot 2064 • Dr. Robert Hesselgesser Collection (Ira and Larry Goldberg, September 2011) lot 5101.

Cardinal Specimen. AU-53 (PCGS). Cardinal Collection (Heritage, April 2002) lot 6709.

Hesselgesser Specimen. AU-53 (PCGS). Dr. Robert Hesselgesser Collection (Ira and Larry Goldberg, September 2011) lot 5100 • Pre-Long Beach Sale (Ira and Larry Goldberg, May 2012) lot 1302.

Long Beach Specimen. AU-53 (NGC). Long Beach Signature Sale (Heritage, May 2008) lot 868 • Pre-Long Beach Sale (Ira and Larry Goldberg, September 2008) lot 939 • Baltimore Sale (Bowers and Merena, November 2008) lot 2636.

Miller Specimen. AU-53 (NGC). Warren Miller Collection.

Matthews Specimen. AU-50 (PCGS). Steve Fischer (September 1998) • Jim Matthews Collection • San Marino Collection Sale (Ira and Larry Goldberg, September 2002) lot 519.

Miller Specimen (another). EF-45 (NGC). Warren Miller Collection.

Merkin Specimen. EF-40 Details, Scratched, Cleaned (NCS). Lester Merkin, June 1972, lot 294. "EF. Planchet defect (start of a split), at final O." • Julian Leidman, 1974 • Jules Reiver Collection (Heritage, January 2006) lot 23599.

Spies Specimen. EF-40. W. Earl Spies Collection (Stack's, 1974) lot 172. "Die flaws are bold and now extend from the chin through the 11th star to edge. The "bar" at the first star is bold. EF."

Brooks Specimen. VF-35. Brooks Collection (Bowers and Merena, 1989) lot 252. "VF-35."

Total Estimated Population

MS-65 or better: 0 (URS-0)
MS-64: 0 (URS-0)
MS-63: 0 (URS-0)
MS-60 to 62: 0 (URS-0)
AU-50 to 58: 6 (URS-4)
VF-20 to EF-45: 45 to 80 (URS-7)
G-4 to F-15: 45 to 80 (URS-7)
Total for all grades combined: 90 to 160 (URS-8)
Estimated Total Condition Census: 55-53-53-53-53-50

1800 BB-182

(B-2, H-2)

Obverse: Medium wide date, figures evenly spaced. Upper point of eighth star is very close to top right tip of Y. The R in LIBERTY *is double-punched.* On the left, stars 6 and 7 are more *widely* spaced than are any of the others. On the right, stars 11 and 12 are more *closely* spaced than are any of the others.

Obverse die used to strike 1800 BB-182, BB-183, and BB-184.

Reverse: See description under 1800 BB-181.

Note: J.W. Haseltine was in error in describing this reverse as differing from No. 1. It is a crack in the die that "joins the A" to the fourth feather, and this crack continues to border. There is also a slight crack through OF to wing.

Reverse die used to strike 1800 BB-181 (earlier use) and BB-182 (later use).

Die States

Die State I: Without reverse cracks. May not exist.

Die State II: Die crack joins the first A in AMERICA to the fourth feather of the eagle, the crack continuing to

the border. Hairline crack through OF to wing. The die state usually seen.

Collecting Notes

1800 BB-182 is one of the great rarities of the year. Only an estimated 30 to 50 are known to exist. Years ago, the issue was regarded as unique. J.W. Haseltine knew of only one, and M.H. Bolender stated the same, noting that it may have been the Haseltine specimen that came under his view. Thus, when Bolender's book went to press in 1950, it was believed that there was just a single coin extant.

Since then, additional pieces have been recognized. BB-182 is not only remarkable for its rarity, but also for the fact that all known specimens show evidence of circulation. Among examples which have been reported, just two make the AU level.

Notable Specimens

Miller Specimen. AU-55 (NGC). Simon Collection (January 1989) lot 1019 • Warren Miller Collection.

Hering Specimen. AU-53 (NGC). Michael Hering Collection (Heritage, January 2002) lot 7230.

Matthews Specimen. EF-45 (PCGS). Coin Galleries Sale (Stack's, November 1997) lot 3014 • Jim Matthews Collection • San Marino Collection Sale (Ira and Larry Goldberg, September 2002) lot 520.

Cardinal Specimen. EF-45 (NGC). Discovered at the Long Beach Bourse • Cardinal Collection • Private collector • March Sale (Stack's, March 2007) lot 1053 • Dr. Robert Hesselgesser Collection (Ira and Larry Goldberg, February 2009) lot 1092 • Pre-Long Beach Sale (Goldbergs, May 2009) lot 631 • Boston Rarities Sale (Bowers and Merena, August 2010) lot 1062.

Willasch Specimen. EF-45 (NGC). H. Roland Willasch Collection (Superior, 1990) lot 555. "VF-30." • Unknown intermediaries • Evan Gale (September 2003) • William Luebke Collection (Heritage, January 2007) lot 5020.

DeCoppet Specimen. EF-40 (NGC). André DeCoppet Collection (James F. Kelly, 1955) • Jacque and A. J. Ostheimer Collection (Lester Merkin, September 1968) lot 296 • Julian Leidman, July 1973 • Jules Reiver Collection (Heritage, January 2006) lot 23600.

Goldberg Specimen. Unc Details (NGC) Cleaned. Pre-Long Beach Sale (Ira and Larry Goldberg, January 2012) lot 2555.

Queller Specimen. Unc Details (NCS) Damaged. Mid-Winter ANA Sale (Heritage, March 1997) lot 5346 • December Sale (Stack's, December 1998) lot 1410 • Queller Family Collection of Silver Dollars (Heritage, April 2008) lot 2065 • Orlando Signature Sale (Heritage, January 2009) lot 4300.

Total Estimated Population
MS-65 or better: 0 (URS-0)
MS-64: 0 (URS-0)
MS-63: 0 (URS-0)
MS-60 to 62: 0 (URS-0)
AU-50 to 58: 2 (URS-2)
VF-20 to EF-45: 20 to 25 (URS-6)
G-4 to F-15: 10 to 15 (URS-5)
Total for all grades combined: 30 to 50 (URS-6)
Estimated Total Condition Census: 55-53-45-45-45-40

1800 BB-183

(B-3, H-3)

Obverse: See description under 1800 BB-182.

Obverse die used to strike 1800 BB-182, BB-183, and BB-184.

Reverse: *Leaf touches center* of lower stand of I in AMERICA (compare to reverse of 1800 BB-181, which touches lower right of the same letter). The two upper stars on the right do not touch the clouds; the other stars each have one point touching. Point of star enters eagle's mouth, *not touching* lower part of beak. End of branch curves toward eagle's tail. AME close but do not join. A touches both third and fourth feathers. Center of A over cloud 3. Tip of arrowhead under center of U in UNITED.

Reverse die used to strike 1800 BB-183 only.

Die States
Die State I: Perfect dies.

Collecting Notes
The 1800 BB-183 dollar is rare in all grades. Only 40 to 70 are believed to exist.

The record for 1800 BB-183 is quite interesting inasmuch as until recent decades it was considered to be a prime rarity. In 1881, J.W. Haseltine knew of but a single specimen, in Very Fair condition, perhaps equal to what we would call Good or VG today. By 1950, M.H. Bolender had seen just one, a coin which he noted (in the 1952 catalog of his personal collection) as being "excessively rare, the finest known, and not found by me until 1949. Formerly in 'World's Greatest Collection.' VF, obverse edge nick at top."

Since then, others have been found, but today in the early 1990s 1800 BB-183 remains quite rare. Several dozen or so are known. Why weren't these known earlier? The answer is that by 1950, when Bolender wrote his book, only a few dealers bothered to attribute early dollars in their inventories or auction listings. Nearly all 1800 H-3 (later, BB-183) dollars were bought and sold as having no special consequence. Even today, the leading grading services—NGC and PCGS—do not attribute the early dollars that pass through their hands. Who knows, among the numerous they have certified of this date may be a few of the BB-183 variety. In his 1881 *Type-Table*, J.W. Haseltine called this variety "excessively rare."

As time goes on, the evaluation of rarity ratings will become more scientific and less empirical. My feeling is that the next decade or two will see a great interest in early dollars, and that this will bring with it a new series of studies, just as has happened in the later dollars series such as the Liberty Seated and Morgan issues.

Notable Specimens

European Specimen. MS-60. New Netherlands 48th Sale, 1956, lot 640. "Full Mint State."

Baldenhofer Specimen. AU-55. W. G. Baldenhofer • Farish-Baldenhofer Sale (Stack's, 1955) • A.J. Ostheimer 3rd Collection. • ANA Convention Sale (Superior, 1975) lot 972. "AU-50." • Superior Galleries, February 1981, lot 658, AU-50." • Auction '86 (RARCOA, 1986) lot 732. "AU."

Denver ANA Specimen. AU-55 (ANACS). Denver ANA Signature Sale (Heritage, August 1996) lot 7973.

Boyd Specimen. AU-53 (NGC). "World's Greatest Collection" (F.C.C. Boyd, Numismatic Gallery, 1945) lot 90. "EF with some wear on high spots." • M.H. Bolender Collection (Bolender, February 1952) lot 135 • W. Earl Spies Collection (Stack's, December 1974) lot 175. "EF." • Jules Reiver Collection (Heritage, January 2006) lot 23601.

Miller Specimen. EF-45 (NGC). H.W. Blevins Collection (Superior, June 1988) lot 3752 • Warren Miller Collection.

Holmes Specimen. EF-45. Milton A. Holmes Collection (Stack's, 1960) lot 2255. "EF, choice." • Don Corrado Romano Collection (Stack's, 1987) lot 756. "EF and choice."

Matthews Collection. EF-40 (PCGS). Allstate Coins • Elliot Goldman (February 1989) • Jim Matthews Collection • San Marino Collection Sale (Ira and Larry Goldberg, September 2002) lot 521 • Orlando Signature Sale (Heritage, January 2006) lot 4329, as AU-50 (ANACS).

Total Estimated Population

MS-65 or better: 0 (URS-0)
MS-64: 0 (URS-0)
MS-63: 0 (URS-0)
MS-60 to 62: 1 (URS-1)
AU-50 to 58: 5 to 8 (URS-4)
VF-20 to EF-45: 30 to 55 (URS-6)
G-4 to F-15: 5 to 8 (URS-4)
Total for all grades combined: 40 to 70 (URS-7)
Estimated Total Condition Census: 60-55-55-53-45-45

1800 BB-184

(B-12, H-12)

Obverse: See description under 1800 BB-182.

Obverse die used to strike 1800 BB-182, BB-183, and BB-184.

Reverse: A die dot inside lower part of E in UNITED, and a more prominent die flaw at lower left side of E in AMERICA. Flaw or crack like a single quotation mark or line to the upper left of U in UNITED. These things quickly distinguish this reverse from all others. *Left side of N in UNUM about in a line with edge of eagle's neck*, the only 1800 reverse for which this is true. Smallest letters in E PLURIBUS UNUM of any reverse die used this year. The berries are small. Leaf point under left side of upright of I in AMERICA. Point of upper part of eagle's beak shuts down near point of star. A does not touch feathers, and AME do not join. A over clouds 2 (partly) and 3 (mostly). Tip of arrowhead under right upright of U in UNITED. The U in UNITED is defective at its upper left corner, from a broken punch (as with 1799 BB-157, BB-158, BB-160, BB-161, and BB-168), but was hand-corrected by its engraver; thus, this is possibly one of the earliest 1800 dies. The fact that all but two 1799 reverses had small letters in E PLURIBUS UNUM also reinforces this suggestion.

Reverse die used to strike 1800 BB-184 only.

Die States

Die State I: Obverse die without cracks. Reverse die without cracks. The usual die state seen.

Die State II: Bolender-12 a. Obverse with hairline crack from star 7 to L. Reverse with a crack across top of OF and right wing tip, nearly to A. A tiny crack extends from the milling down through center of F. Some show a line through the star under cloud 8. About 20% or so of BB-184 dollars are of this die state.

Collecting Notes

The 1800 BB-184 dollar is fairly scarce. About 250 to 450 are known in all grades combined. As is the case with the majority of 1800 Bolender numbers, it is typically seen in worn grades up to and including VF. EF specimens are very rare, AU pieces are rarer yet. Just one fully Mint State piece is known today.

Notable Specimens

Cardinal Specimen. MS-63 (PCGS). October Sale (Stack's, October 1996) lot 376 • Dale Friend Collection • Legend Numismatics • Cardinal Collection (American Numismatic Rarities, June 2005) lot 44.

Green Specimen. AU-58 (NGC). Col. E.H.R. Green Collection • M.H. Bolender Collection, 1952, lot 146. Unc., Proof surface on reverse • Four Landmarks Collections (Bowers and Merena, March 1989) lot 1974 • Anaheim ANA Signature Sale (Heritage, August 1995) lot 5261 • Cardinal Collection (Heritage, August 1997) lot 6502

Queller Specimen. AU-58 (NGC). Queller Family Collection of Silver Dollars (Heritage, April 2008) lot 2066.

Hesselgesser Specimen. AU-55 (PCGS). Dr. Robert Hesselgesser Collection (Ira and Larry Goldberg, May 2011) lot 903 • Pre-Long Beach Sale (Ira and Larry Goldberg, January 2012) lot 2556.

Miller Specimen. AU-55 (NGC). Warren Miller Collection.

Reiver Specimen. AU-55 NGC). Garry Fitzgerald (November 1968) • Jules Reiver Collection (Heritage, January 2006) lot 23611.

Baldenhofer Specimen. AU-55. W.G. Baldenhofer • Farish-Baldenhofer Sale (Stack's, 1955) • A.J. Ostheimer

3rd Collection • ANA Convention Sale (Superior, 1975) lot 991. "AU-55 or so."

Brown University Specimen. AU-55. Brown University Sale (Pine Tree, 1976) lot 316. "R in LIBERTY repunched; small berries, die chip at E(R), another before U. Surfaces suggest full MS-60, but there is just enough cabinet friction on isolated details to require that we downgrade it to AU-55."

Bergen Specimen. AU-55. Herbert M. Bergen Sale (Quality Sales) lot 1356. • Auction '84 (Paramount, 1984) lot 733. "Choice AU-55."

Total Estimated Population

MS-65 or better: 0 (URS-0)
MS-64: 0 (URS-0)
MS-63: 1 (URS-1)
MS-60 to 62: 0 (URS-0)
AU-50 to 58: 10 to 20 (URS-5)
VF-20 to EF-45: 140 to 250 (URS-9)
G-4 to F-15: 100 to 175 (URS-8)
Total for all grades combined: 250 to 450 (URS-10)
Estimated Total Condition Census: 63-58-58-55 (multiples)

1800 BB-185

(B-20)

Obverse: The upper right star is in position *similar to the obverse of the 1804 dollars,* with two points almost touching Y. Therefore, as Bolender related, this variety has been used at least twice in idle fabrication of an 1804, by altering the last figure of date. The upper point of star 8 nearly touches Y at a point *below* its top, as in the 1804 dollars. Star 7 is about as near L as star 13 is from bust. Star 1 is distant, over 3 mm., from hair. On the left, star 1 is below the arc line of stars 2-7.

This obverse was not known to Haseltine when he compiled his *Type-Table* in 1881.

Obverse die used to strike BB-185 only.

Reverse: See description under 1800 BB-184.

Reverse die used to strike 1800 BB-184, BB-185, and BB-186, possibly in that order.

Die States

Die State I: Early state of obverse without bulging. Very rare, if, indeed, it exists at all.

Die State II: Bulge begins at center of obverse, especially in the left field. Die crack links stars 9 to 13. The usual state seen.

Die State III: Bulge becomes very prominent. The Spies Collection coin is VG-8.

Collecting Notes

Only about 20 to 40 are known of the 1800 BB-185, believed to be the rarest variety of the year. Bolender knew of only a single undamaged specimen of this variety, stating it was "as rare as an 1804." Since that time, other examples have come to light. Only two are known in a grade of AU or higher.

Notable Specimens

Bolender Specimen. AU-58 (NGC). M.H. Bolender Collection, 1952, lot 162. "EF." • W.G. Baldenhofer • Farish-Baldenhofer Sale (Stack's, 1955) • A.J. Ostheimer 3rd Collection • ANA Convention Sale, 1975 (Superior) lot 1003. "EF-45." • Unknown intermediaries • Bill Jones Type Collection.

Miller Specimen. AU-53 (NGC). FUN Signature Sale (Heritage, January 1998) lot 7022 • Warren Miller Collection.

Reiver Specimen. EF-45 (NGC). Jim McGuigan (February 1974) • Jules Reiver Collection (Heritage, January 2006) lot 23623.

Matthews Specimen. EF-45 (PCGS). Larry Briggs (September 1997) • Jim Matthews Collection • San Marino Collection Sale (Ira and Larry Goldberg, September 2002) lot

530 • New York Connoisseur's Sale (American Numismatic Rarities, March 2006) lot 1060 • Dr. Robert Hesselgesser Collection (Ira and Larry Goldberg, September 2011) lot 5106 • Pre-Long Beach Sale (Ira and Larry Goldberg, May 2012) lot 1304.

Willasch Specimen. VF-20. H. Roland Willasch Collection (Superior, 1990) lot 577. "VF-25. A small planchet defect is visible between third and fourth stars on the obverse and corresponding area on the reverse, only affecting the dentils. Early die state before the reverse broke at the E of AMERICA. Pedigree: Unknown, likely purchased by Mr. H. Roland Willasch as it does not appear to have come from any of the recent large Bust dollar sales."

Boyd Specimen. VF-20. "World's Greatest Collection" (F.C.C. Boyd, Numismatic Gallery, 1945) lot 108, (Haseltine-20), Not in Haseltine. Struck off center, 00 in date high, with last 0 closer to bust. Die break through E in AMERICA. VF.

Helfenstein Specimen. VF-20. Lester Merkin, 1968, lot 281. "VF. Obverse die has caved in, producing a bulge left of curls and below ribbon, accounting for immediate discard of this obverse."

Polis Specimen. VF-20. George N. Polis, M.D. Collection (Bowers and Merena, 1991) lot 2227. "VF-20.

Total Estimated Population

MS-65 or better: 0 (URS-0)
MS-64: 0 (URS-0)
MS-63: 0 (URS-0)
MS-60 to 62: 0 (URS-0)
AU-50 to 58: 2 (URS-2)
VF-20 to EF-45: 12 to 25 (URS-5)
G-4 to F-15: 8 to 15 (URS-4)
Total for all grades combined: 20 to 40 (URS-6)
Estimated Total Condition Census: 58-53-45-45-35-30 (multiples)

1800 BB 186

(B-4, H-4)

Obverse: 1 in date close to curl, and 8 tipped too much to right at top. Liberty's mouth open. 7th, 8th, and 13th stars are all equidistant from L, Y and bust, and are near. Star 1 about 2.5 mm. distant from hair.

Obverse die used to strike 1800 BB-186 only.

Reverse: *Die flaws* show at top and to right of ES, easily identifying this die which was also used for BB-187 and BB-185. *Lower right serif of F is extremely close to or touches cloud 8;* the only reverse of 1800 with this characteristic. The eagle's beak closes down on extreme point of a star. Leaf points slightly right of center of I in AMERICA. First A in AMERICA rests on wing. Letter T in UNITED *is double-punched.* A over clouds 2 and 3. Tip of arrowhead under right side of right upright of U in UNITED.

Reverse die used to strike 1800 BB-184, BB-185, and BB-186, possibly in that order.

Die States

Die State I: Perfect dies of BB-186 without obverse crack. Apparently, unknown to Bolender in 1950. Very rare. One of these is 1975 ANA Convention Sale (Superior): 973, described as "Bolender-4b," perfect dies, just one of four known; a second piece was in the same sale; both were cataloged as VF-20.

Die State II: Obverse shows slight die crack from border below 1 of date, through base of 1, upward through 8 to first 0. Another fine crack from border under first O through base of second O to bust. The usually seen die state of BB-186.

Die State III: Bolender-4a. Now with extensive die cracks on obverse. Die crack from border up through entire 1 of date and bust to 12th star. Another crack through first star to curl under ribbon. Another crack between IB touching left lower part of B down through hair. Crack along inner points of 10th to 12th stars. Always found weakly struck. Considerably scarcer than the preceding.

Collecting Notes

1800 BB-186 is one of the scarcer varieties of a year which has quite a few elusive die combinations. I estimate that only 150 to 275 are known. Quite a few of these are in grades such as EF and AU, in contrast to, for example, BB-182, which is mostly known in lower grades.

In his pioneering study in 1881, Capt. J.W. Haseltine considered it to be very rare. By Bolender's publication date, 1950, many dozens of coins had been located.

Notable Specimens

Miller Specimen. MS-61 (NGC). Warren Miller Collection.

Long Beach Specimen. MS-61 (ANACS). Pre-Long Beach Sale (Ira and Larry Goldberg, February 2008) lot 2887 • Pre-Long Beach Sale (Ira and Larry Goldberg, May 2008) lot 4015 • Dallas Signature Sale (Heritage, October 2008) lot 1094.

Reiver Specimen. AU-55 (PCGS). W. Earl Spies Collection (Stack's, December 1974) lot 178 • Jules Reiver Collection (Heritage, January 2006) lot 23603 • Dr. Robert Hesselgesser Collection (Ira and Larry Goldberg,

September 2011) lot 5107 • Baltimore Sale (Stack's Bowers, June 2012) lot 3024.

Palm Beach Specimen. AU-55 (NGC). Palm Beach Signature Sale (Heritage, March 2005) lot 6717 • Long Beach Signature Sale (Heritage, June 2005) lot 6632.

MacFarland Specimen. AU-55. Bowers and Ruddy Galleries, 1981, lot 1577. "AU-55. Intermediate die state with all of the obverse cracks listed for Bolender-4, plus the arc crack from rim to rim passing through 1, shoulder, neck and 12th star (as listed for Bolender-4a). But with no signs of the other Bolender-4a cracks (between IB or along 10th to 12th stars, or through the first star to ribbon)."

RARCOA Auction '86 Specimen. AU-55. Auction '86 (RARCOA, 1986) lot 733. "Lovely choice AU."

Ebsen Specimen. AU-55. Buddy Ebsen Collection (Superior, 1987) lot 1912. "Prooflike surfaces."

Akers Auction '88 Specimen. AU-55. David Akers, 1988, lot 629.

F.U.N. Specimen. AU-55. Florida United Numismatists Sale (Mid American, 1989) lot 608. "AU-55."

Total Estimated Population

MS-65 or better: 0 (URS-0)
MS-64: 0 (URS-0)
MS-63: 0 (URS-0)
MS-60 to 62: 2 (URS-2)
AU-50 to 58: 10 to 20 (URS-5)
VF-20 to EF-45: 120 to 220 (URS-8)
G-4 to F-15: 20 to 35 (URS-6)
Total for all grades combined: 150 to 275 (URS-9)
Estimated Total Condition Census: 61-61-55 (multiples)

1800 BB-187

(B-16, H-16)
Obverse: Close date, 1 almost touches curl. The 8 is too low, and top tipped too much to right. Last O near bust. *Die dot just to left of highest curl* on top of head. On

the left, stars 1, 2 and 3 are more widely spaced from each other than are stars 5, 6, and 7. On the right, stars 9 and 10 are more widely spaced than are any others. The ray of star 10 that is nearest to an adjacent ray of star 11 is misaligned with that ray of star 11. Die flaws *between top* of R and T in LIBERTY.

Obverse die used to strike 1800 BB-187 only.

Reverse: See description under 1800 BB-186.

Reverse die used to strike 1800 BB-184, BB-185, and BB-186, possibly in that order.

Die States

Die State I: Perfect obverse die without die crack. Reverse with some roughness between E and S of STATES. Does a perfect obverse die impression exist?

Die State II: Obverse with curved hairline crack up through right side of second 0 in date, through bust, point of chin, to star 10. Some light clash marks between stars 3 to 6 and the border. Roughness between E and S of STATES. This is the die state usually seen.

Die State III: As preceding, but roughness has developed into a prominent period-like crack between the tops of E and S.

Die State IV: As BB-187, but with die clash marks as "waves" along the top of the date. Stack's Auction '89: 1779 AU.

Die State V: Very late state. New die flaws form at the top of ES in STATES, the back of Miss Liberty's head, between the L and I in LIBERTY and stars 7 and 8. A new obverse crack is present along the dentils from below the 8 to just past the second O.

Collecting Notes

The 1800 BB-187 is about tied with BB-193 as the most plentiful variety of the year. About 700 to 1,200 are known to exist. This plethora of specimens in no way indicates that BB-187 is readily available in Mint State, for it is not. Why, no one knows.

Notable Specimens

Cardinal Specimen. MS-64 (NGC). Pre-FUN Elite Sale (Superior, January 2002) lot 1193 • Robert Lehmann Cardinal Collection (American Numismatic Rarities, June 2005) lot 45 • Dallas Signature Sale (Heritage, December 2005) lot 936 • Larry Shapiro Collection (Bowers and Merena, February 2007) lot 423 • Dr. Robert Hesselgesser Collection (Ira and Larry Goldberg, September 2011) lot 5108.

Carter Specimen. MS-62 (PCGS). Amon Carter, Jr. Collection (Stack's, January 1984) lot 231 • Auction '86 (Stack's, July 1986) lot 293 • Private Midwest collection.

1988 ANA Specimen. MS-62. Auction '79 (RARCOA, 1979) • ANA Convention Sale (Heritage, 1988) lot 965. "Mint State (62/62)."

Boyd Specimen. MS-60. "World's Greatest Collection" (F.C.C. Boyd, Numismatic Gallery, 1945) lot 102, Haseltine-16. Unc. • ANA Convention Sale (Abe Kosoff, 1949) lot 201. • Harold Bareford Collection (Stack's, 1981) lot 419. "An arc-like die crack from 10th star to the last 0 of the date. Brilliant Unc."

Royal Oak Specimen. AU-58 (PCGS). Royal Oak Collection (Heritage, August 2006) lot 5305.

Queller Specimen. AU-58 (NGC). Stack's, privately • Queller Family Collection of Silver Dollars (Heritage, April 2008) lot 2067.

DeCoppet Specimen. AU-58. André DeCoppet Collection (James Kelly, 1955). "Practically Unc."

Total Estimated Population

MS-65 or better: 0 (URS-0)

MS-64: 1 (URS-1)

MS-63: 0 (URS-0)

MS-60 to 62: 4 to 8 (URS-3)

AU-50 to 58: 25 to 50 (URS-6)

VF-20 to EF-45: 400 to 750 (URS-10)

G-4 to F-15: 275 to 400 (URS-10)

Total for all grades combined: 700 to 1,200 (URS-11)

Estimated Total Condition Census: 64-62-62-58 (multiples)

1800 BB-188

(B-8, H-8)

Obverse: Bolender said this: "Look for the die 'dot' inside lower part of R, near the left upright, in LIBERTY." This easily distinguishes this die, which was also used for BB-189. Left base of E slightly high in relation to bottom of B (this same characteristic is true of the different obverse used to strike BB-193). Mouth of Liberty closed. Star 7 is closer to L, by a tiny amount, than star 8 is to Y, and star 13 is separated from the bust even farther, and the hair from star 1 farther yet. On the left, stars 1-2 and 2-3 are closer together than are any other stars. On the right, stars 10-11 and 12-13 are wider apart than are any other stars. Stars 2-3 and 11-12 are slightly misaligned in relation to each other.

Obverse die used to strike 1800 BB-188 (earlier use) and BB-189 (later use).

Reverse: Three upper stars on right on reverse *do not touch* clouds. Three upper stars on left on reverse each have *one point* touching clouds. Leaf points slightly left of center of I in AMERICA. Star enters eagle's mouth, upper part of beak closing down on side of star point. Letter A just touches third and fourth feathers. AME do not join each other. Very large berries. A over clouds 2 and 3. Tip of arrowhead under center of U in UNITED.

Reverse die used to strike 1800 BB-188 only.

Die States

Die State I: Obverse and reverse dies without crack. The die state usually seen.

Die State II: Obverse die without cracks. Reverse with crack through AMER.

Die State III: As preceding, but reverse crack forms a tiny blob at upper right of R, and continues to border at that point.

Die State IV: As above, but with additional crack from right side of R to top of I to border above C. Crack through AMER now extends to the left through wing and F.

Collecting Notes

The 1800 BB-188 dollar is on the scarce side. Perhaps 150 to 275 survive in all grades combined. This population is far higher than the number of specialists seeking them. Thus, there will be no problem acquiring one for a "type" price.

Notable Specimens

Eliasberg Specimen. MS-64 (NGC). Louis E. Eliasberg Sr. Collection (Bowers and Merena, April 1997) lot 2191 • Tangible Asset Galleries • Private collector.

Queller Specimen. MS-62 (PCGS). Detroit ANA Signature Sale (Heritage, July 1994) lot 7121 • Premier Sale (Superior, January 1995) lot 951 • March Sale (Stack's, March 1993) lot 506 • Queller Family Collection of Silver Dollars (Heritage, April 2008) lot 2068 • Dr. Robert Hesselgesser Collection (Bowers and Merena, August 2010) lot 1056 • 75th Anniversary Sale (Stack's, November 2010) lot 4419 • Orlando Signature Sale (Heritage, January 2012) lot 3294 • Philadelphia ANA Sale (Stack's Bowers, August 2012) lot 11485.

Boyd Specimen. MS-60. "World's Greatest Collection" (F.C.C. Boyd, Numismatic Gallery, 1945) lot 95. "A very handsome Unc. coin."

Superior Auction '88 Specimen. MS-60. Superior Galleries, 1988, lot 212. MS-60.

Miller Specimen. AU-55 (NGC). Warren Miller Collection.

DeCoppet Specimen. AU-55. André DeCoppet Collection (James Kelly, 1955). "Practically Unc."

Hesselgesser Specimen. AU-53 (PCGS). Pre-Long Beach Sale (Ira and Larry Goldberg, May 2006) lot 3057 • Dr. Robert Hesselgesser Collection (Ira and Larry Goldberg, February 2007) lot 1596 • Boston Rarities Sale (Bowers and Merena, August 2010) lot

1059 • Chicago ANA Sale (Stack's Bowers, August 2011) lot 3019.

Ebsen Specimen. AU-50. Buddy Ebsen Collection (Superior, 1987) lot 1913. "Die dot inside lower part of R in LIBERTY; very large berries. AU-50+."

Higgins Specimen. AU-50. Lloyd Higgins, M.D. Collection (Bowers and Merena, 1988) lot 2222. "AU-50 (ANACS)."

Four Landmark Collections Specimen. AU-50. Four Landmark Collections (Bowers and Merena, 1989) lot 1972. "AU-50, prooflike." • Dr. Robert Stark Collection.

Total Estimated Population
MS-65 or better: 0 (URS-0)
MS-64: 1 (URS-1)
MS-63: 0 (URS-0)
MS-60 to 62: 2 to 4 (URS-2)
AU-50 to 58: 3 to 5 (URS-3)
VF-20 to EF-45: 100 to 190 (URS-8)
G-4 to F-15: 40 to 75 (URS-7)
Total for all grades combined: 150 to 275 (URS-9)
Estimated Total Condition Census: 64-62-60-60-55 (multiples)

1800 BB-189

(B-5, H-5)

Obverse: See description under 1800 BB-188.

Obverse die used to strike 1800 BB-188 (earlier use) and BB-189 (later use).

Reverse: A *die flaw* just to left of lower part of second T in STATES quickly identifies this reverse, the die also used for BB-190. Star enters eagle's mouth, the upper part of beak touching star. All the stars above firmly touch clouds, except the star under cloud 7 which is very close. Leaf points under left side of upright of I. The A touches both third and fourth feathers, AM joined at lower part. Center of A over cloud 3. Tip of arrowhead under left side of right upright of U in UNITED.

Reverse die used to strike 1800 BB-189 (earlier use) and BB-190 (later use).

Die States

Die State I: Obverse and reverse without cracks.

Die State II: Obverse with hairline crack through top of LIB. Reverse without cracks.

Die State III: Bolender-5b.[1] Obverse hairline crack

[1] B-5a was described as Bolender as having perfect dies, but bifurcated letters; I do not recognize this as a separate die state.

now extends from stars 5 through 7, through LIB, and upward past B to rim. On reverse, hairline crack connects tops of ED in UNITED.

Collecting Notes

About 200 to 350 examples of 1800 BB-189 are estimated to survive, making it one of the rarer varieties of the year. Still, enough specimens exist that the patient specialist will experience no difficulty in acquiring one. While numerous VF and EF coins exist, there is a dividing wall at that point. Why so few AU and no Uncirculated pieces are known is another of the intriguing mysteries that pervade the early dollar series.

Notable Specimens

Miller Specimen. AU-58 (NGC). William H. LaBelle Sr. Collection Sale (American Numismatic Rarities, July 2005) lot 1290 • Warren Miller Collection.

Queller Specimen. AU-55 (NGC). Queller Family Collection of Silver Dollars (Heritage, April 2008) lot 2069 • Dr. Robert Hesselgesser Collection (Ira and Larry Goldberg, May 2011) lot 906 • Pittsburgh Signature Sale (Heritage, October 2011) lot 3846.

Chouinard Specimen. AU-55 (NGC). Richard J.

Chouinard Collection (Heritage, May 2005) lot 6718.

Matthews Specimen. AU-53 (NGC). John J. Haugh (February 1998) • Jim Matthews Collection • San Marino Collection Sale (Ira and Larry Goldberg, September 2002) lot 523 • Warren Miller Collection.

Hering Specimen. AU-50 (NGC). Michael Hering Collection (Heritage, January 2002) lot 7227

Washington Specimen. EF-45. Suburban Washington Convention Sale (Pine Tree, 1975) lot 250. "Better than EF, sharpness nearer AU."

Montgomery Specimen. EF-45. Montgomery Collection (Bowers and Ruddy, 1976) lot 2002. "Attractive EF-AU."

Johnson Specimen. EF-45. Byron F. Johnson Collection (Bowers and Merena, 1989) lot 573. "EF-45."

Aspen Specimen. EF-45. Dr. Nelson Page Aspen Collection (Bowers and Merena, 1989) lot 394. "EF-45 to AU-50."

Total Estimated Population

MS-65 or better: 0 (URS-0)
MS-64: 0 (URS-0)
MS-63: 0 (URS-0)
MS-60 to 62: 0 (URS-0)
AU-50 to 58: 5-8 (URS-4)
VF-20 to EF-45: 140 to 240 (URS-9)
G-4 to F-15: 60 to 110 (URS-7)
Total for all grades combined: 200 to 350 (URS-9)
Estimated Total Condition Census: 58-55-55-53-50-45 (multiples)

1800 BB-190

(B-10, H-10)

Obverse: *Wide date, 00 very wide apart, and the 8 too low.* The eighth star is close to Y, last star not quite so near bust. Star 7 is distant from L, Star 1 still farther from hair. Die clash marks in field near stars 12 and 13, probably the cause of the relapping (a rather unusual occurrence among 1800-dated dollars) that made the highest curl on the head incomplete.

Obverse die used to strike 1800 BB-190 (earlier use) and BB-191 (later use).

Reverse: From same die as BB-189, but now with *light* die crack from leaf through C to border.

Reverse die used to strike 1800 BB-189 (earlier use) and BB-190 (later use).

Die States

Die State I: Perfect obverse die, without relapping. Reverse with hairline crack connecting tops of ED in UNITED, as inherited from earlier use coining 1800 BB-189. May not exist without relapping.

Die State II: Obverse die lapped. No die cracks. Reverse as preceding. Scarce.

Die State III: Obverse as preceding. Reverse with crack expanded at tops of NITED to border. Additional crack from border to left side of C in AMERICA to leaf. (Transitional die states exist between II and III.) Common.

Die State IV: Bolender-10a. As preceding, but now the die crack on reverse is more pronounced through C, and an additional crack extends from right ribbon end through ER. Commonest of all. 1975 ANA Convention Sale (Superior): 985, VF-30, was called Condition Census. Davis-Graves: 1315 (Stack's, 1954) is AU. Amon Carter, Jr.: 227 (Stack's, 1984) is Unc.

Die State V: As preceding, but with additional crack from border to U of UNITED Apparently, common, although not known to Bolender. Cf. 1975 ANA Convention Sale which had four coins, VF-30, VF-20 (ex Ruby Collection), another VF-20, and F-15.

Die State VI: As preceding, but with crack through U extending upward through arrows. Two new cracks, approximately parallel, through C of AMERICA to branch, the leftmost crack extending to border. Crack from wing to star above and to the right of M in UNUM.

Die State VI: As preceding, but with two approximately parallel cracks through ME of AMERICA. Crack from border to U to arrows now extends up to wing. Scarce.

Collecting Notes

Among dollars of this date, 1800 BB-190 is one of the most plentiful issues. As many as 600 to 1,100 are believed to exist. Once again, although the issue is readily available, most known specimens are in circulated grades. BB-190 is elusive AU, and in Mint State is rare.

Notable Specimens

Carter Specimen. MS-64+ (PCGS). Amon Carter, Jr. Collection (Stack's, 1984) lot 227, Bolender-10a. "Brilliant Unc." • Phillip Flannagan Collection (Bowers and Merena, November 2001) lot 4269 • Swan Family Type Collection • Joseph O'Connor • Cardinal Collection (American Numismatic Rarities, June 2005) lot 46 • Private Midwest collection.

Hering Specimen. MS-64 (PCGS). Michael Hering Collection (Heritage, January 2002) lot 7232 • Chris Napolitano • Jack Lee Collection III (Heritage, November 2005) lot 2195.

CSNS Specimen. MS-62 (PCGS). CSNS Signature Sale (Heritage, April 2012) lot 5159.

Baldenhofer Specimen. MS-60. W. G. Baldenhofer • Farish-Baldenhofer Sale (Stack's, 1955) • A.J. Ostheimer

3rd Collection • ANA Convention Sale (Superior, 1975) lot 982. "Reverse, light die break from leaf through C of AMERICA to border. MS-60."

Hesselgesser Specimen. AU-58 (PCGS). Baltimore Signature Sale (Heritage, July 2003) lot 7103 • Dollar Mike Collection • Private collector • Dr. Robert Hesselgesser Collection (Ira and Larry Goldberg, September 2011) lot 5111 • Warren Miller Collection.

Hering Specimen (another) AU-58 (PCGS). Michael Hering Collection (Heritage, January 2002) lot 7231 • Cardinal Collection • Private collector.

Thaler Specimen. AU-58 (PCGS). Thaler Collection (American Numismatic Rarities, March 2006) lot 1064.

Queller Specimen. AU-58 (NGC). Stack's, privately • Queller Collection of Silver Dollars (Heritage, April 2008) lot 2070.

(Many more AU specimens could be listed.)

Total Estimated Population

MS-65 or better: 0 (URS-0)
MS-64: 2 (URS-2)
MS-63: 0 (URS-0)
MS-60 to 62: 5 to 10 (URS-4)
AU-50 to 58: 25 to 50 (URS-6)
VF-20 to EF-45: 425 to 800 (URS-10)
G-4 to F-15: 150 to 250 (URS-9)
Total for all grades combined: 600 to 1,100 (URS-11)
Estimated Total Condition Census: 64+-64-62-60-58 (multiples)

1800 BB-191

AMERICAI Reverse
(B-11, H-11)

Obverse: See description under 1800 BB-190. All coins seen have been from relapped die.

Obverse die used to strike 1800 BB-190 and BB-191.

Reverse: AMERICAI variety (one of two AMERICAI

varieties, the other, which shares this reverse, is BB-192). After the word AMERICA, an almost vertical line, a stray mark (apparently, not a die crack), perhaps from a punch or from a stray piece of metal during the die making process, appears more or less like an "I" added. There are no serifs to the stray mark, and it takes some imagination to call it an

I, but the nomenclature has been with us for a long time, and "AMERICAI" it is. Nowhere else in the silver dollar series has a stray die mark done so much for a coin's value and desirability in the eyes of collectors.

Other characteristics: Star enters eagle's mouth; point of lower part of beak touches star lightly below point. Upper part of beak does not quite touch. Point of leaf slightly right of being under left upright of I in AMERICA. Middle berry is small and joined to a leaf point by what seems to be a die scratch. A touches third feather only, and ME almost join at bottom. Center of A over cloud 3. Tip of arrowhead under left side of left serif of N in UNITED. Usually (always?) weakly struck at the reverse center and on the stars above the eagle's head.

Reverse die used to strike BB-191 (earlier use) and BB-192 (later use).

Die States

Die State I: Perfect obverse die, without relapping. Reverse die without cracks. May not exist with obverse not showing relapping.

Die State II: Obverse die relapped. No die cracks. Reverse without cracks. The usual die state seen.

Collecting Notes

1800 BB-191 dollars survive to the extent of an estimated 200 to 350 coins, ranking it among the scarcer issues of a year with many elusive varieties. The desirability of BB-191 is greatly increased by the AMERICAI feature on the reverse, a stray mark from a punch that is in the right position to make it appear (with some imagination) as the letter I, hence AMERICAI.

Bolender called it "excessively rare" and noted that it took him 35 years to find a specimen! He went on to say that several times he found "H-11" coins (equivalent to BB-191 today), but upon inspection they invariably proved to be the plentiful H-19 (BB-192) variety struck from the same reverse die.

Notable Specimens

Carter Specimen. MS-62 (NGC). Amon Carter, Jr. Collection (Stack's, 1984) lot 228. "Brilliant Unc." • Queller Family Collection of Silver Dollars (Heritage, April 2008) lot 2071 • Warren Miller Collection.

Cardinal Specimen. AU-58 (PCGS). Private collector • Dollar Mike Collection • Cardinal Collection (American Numismatic Rarities, June 2005) lot 47 • J. A. Sherman Collection (Stack's, August 2007) lot 807 • Franklinton Sale (Stack's, January 2008) lot 601.

Miller Specimen. AU-55 (NGC). Orlando Signature Sale (Heritage, January 2006) lot 4336 • Warren Miller Collection • Baltimore Signature Sale (Heritage, July 2008) lot 776.

Ostheimer Specimen. AU-53 (PCGS). R. J. Lathrop Collection • ANA Convention Sale, 1952: 1270 • A.J. Ostheimer 3rd Collection (Lester Merkin, 1968) lot 303 • Highlander Collection • Thaler Collection (American Numismatic Rarities, March 2006) lot 1066.

Anaheim Specimen. AU-53 (NGC). Anaheim Sale (Bowers and Merena, May 2006) lot 11209.

Hesselgesser Specimen. AU-50 (PCGS). Joel Cheek Collection (Stack's, May 2002) lot 336 • Cardinal Collection • Dr. Robert Hesselgesser Collection (Ira and Larry Goldberg, September 2011) lot 5113 • Pre-Long Beach Sale (Ira and Larry Goldberg, May 2012) lot 1306.

Gaziano Sale Specimen. AU-50 (NGC). Dominic Gaziano and Papyrus Way Collections Sale (Stack's, March 2008) lot 395.

University of Rochester Specimen. AU-50. University of Rochester Collection (Bowers and Ruddy, 1980) lot 3285. "AU-50."

Gilhousen Specimen. EF-45. M.H. Bolender. • Dr. Charles Ruby Collection • Gilhousen Collection (Superior, 1973) lot 1269. "EF, lustrous, richly toned, many areas suggesting AU."

Stack's Auction '84 Specimen. EF-45. Stack's, 1984, lot 1187, "EF."

Brooks Specimen. EF-45. Brooks Collection (Bowers and Merena, 1989) lot 255. "EF-45."

Total Estimated Population

MS-65 or better: 0 (URS-0)
MS-64: 0 (URS-0)
MS-63: 0 (URS-0)
MS-60 to 62: 1 or 2 (URS-2)
AU-50 to 58: 4 to 8 (URS-3)
VF-20 to EF-45: 125 to 215 (URS-9)
G-4 to F-15: 70 to 125 (URS-8)
Total for all grades combined: 200 to 350 (URS-9)
Estimated Total Condition Census: 62-58-55-53-53-50 (multiples)

1800 BB-192

AMERICAI Reverse
(B-19, H-19)

Obverse: *Point of star 1 is closer to hair than point of star 7 is to L.* Right stars close to Y and bust. The last O in date is just as close to bust as is star 13. The 1 almost touches curl. Vertical *die* flaw below right side of first star near border. On the left, stars 1-2 and 5-6 are closer together than are other stars. On the right, stars 11-12 are farther apart than are other stars.

Obverse die used to strike BB-192 only.

Reverse: See description under BB-191. The AMERICAI variety.

Reverse die used to strike BB-191 (earlier use) and BB-192 (later use).

Die States

Die State I: Perfect dies without clash marks. Very scarce.

Die State II: Clash marks on obverse at date (from clouds on reverse), at E in LIBERTY (from eagle's tail), and Y through star 11 (MERIC incuse from reverse). Small die flaw or crack below star 1. This is the die state usually seen.

Die State III: Bolender-19a. Dies as BB-192, Die State II, but now with die crack along top of three upper left stars on obverse continuing along top of LIBE. Obverse clash marks seen on Die State II are now mostly gone (from light relapping?), but a new group of clash marks, slightly different in configuration, is seen in and around the date, and extending along the border to star 3.

Die State IV: Obverse as preceding. Reverse with additional die crack along border above U, left top of N, down through I (eventually to left ribbon end in a slightly later state). Die clash marks around date and at sides. Rare.

Collecting Notes

1800 BB-192 is one of the most populous varieties of the year. An estimated 600 to 1,100 exist. The BB-192 is by far the commoner of the two varieties with AMERICAI reverse (the other being BB-191). Examples are available in all basic grade ranges, with most being in the VF category.

Notable Specimens

Paramount Auction '85 Specimen. MS-65. Paramount, 1985, lot 1264. "Gem Unc. (65/65)."

Pittman Specimen. MS-64 (NGC). John J. Pittman Collection (Akers, May 1998) lot 1669.

Queller Specimen. MS-63 (PCGS). Four Landmark Collections Sale (Bowers and Merena, March 1989) lot 1978 • Auction '86 (RARCOA, July 1986) lot 734 • Queller Family Collection of Silver Dollars (Heritage, April 2008) lot 2072 • Pre-Long Beach Sale (Ira and Larry Goldberg, September 2008) lot 943.

Eliasberg Specimen. MS-63 (NGC). S.H. and H. Chapman, January 1900 • J.M. Clapp • John H. Clapp • Clapp estate, 1942 • Louis E. Eliasberg Sr. Collection (Bowers and Merena, April 1997) lot 2192 • Tangible Asset Galleries • Private collector.

Stack's Auction '85 Specimen. MS-63. Stack's, 1985, lot 1753. "Brilliant Unc." • Auction '86 (Stack's) lot 294. (Previous description repeated.)

Hesselgesser Specimen. MS-61 (PCGS). Chris Napolitano • Dr. Robert Hesselgesser Collection (Ira and Larry Goldberg, September 2011) lot 5114 • Pre-Long Beach Sale (Ira and Larry Goldberg, May 2012) lot 1307

Cardinal Specimen. AU-58 (PCGS). Tangible Asset Galleries • Cardinal Collection (American Numismatic Rarities, June 2005) lot 48 • Joseph C. Thomas Collection (Heritage, April 2009) lot 2561.

Dallas Sale Specimen. AU-58 (PCGS). Dallas Signature Sale (Heritage, November 2007) lot 948 • Chicago Rarities Sale (Bowers and Merena, April 2008) lot 511.

Miller Specimen. AU-55+ (NGC). Warren Miller Collection.

Total Estimated Population

MS-65 or better: 1 (URS-1)
MS-64: 1 or 2 (URS-1)
MS-63: 2 to 4 (URS-2)
MS-60 to 62: 10 to 20 (URS-5)
AU-50 to 58: 25 to 50 (URS-6)

VF-20 to EF-45: 400 to 725 (URS-10)
G-4 to F-15: 175 to 300 (URS-9)
Total for all grades combined: 600 to 1,100 (URS-11)
Estimated Total Condition Census: 65-64-63-63-63-61-58 (multiples)

1800 BB-193

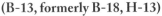

(B-13, formerly B-18, H-13)

Obverse: Star 13 slightly closer to bust than Star 8 is from Y. Star 7 is much farther from L, and the star 1 is the farthest from hair, 2.75 mm. Left base of E slightly high in relation to bottom of B (this same characteristic is true of the different obverse used to strike BB-188 and BB-189). On the left, stars 4-5 and 5-6 are more closely spaced than are the others. On the right, stars 9-10 are the most closely spaced and stars 10-11 are the most widely spaced.

Obverse die used to strike 1800 BB-193 only.

Reverse: Similar to BB-188, but A and M touch, and A in STATES is in different position; A over cloud 3 (mostly) and area between clouds 3 and 4. Tip of arrowhead under and just slightly right of center of U in UNITED.

Reverse die used to strike 1800 BB-193 only.

Die States

Die State I: Perfect dies. Obverse without cracks. Reverse without clash marks or cracks. This is the regular BB-193 variety. Three or more times scarcer than Die State III.

Die State II: First clashing. Obverse with clash marks at left side of date and stars 1 and 2, incuse impressions of clouds on reverse. No die cracks. Reverse with light clash marks at F, clouds 7 and 8, and below cloud 7, incuse impression of drapery folds. As additional strikings occur, the obverse clash marks fade away slightly. Scarce.

Die State III: (Bolender-18) Second clashing. Obverse with faded clash marks from first clashing. No die cracks.

Reverse with massive injury from second clashing. Now with raised lines through F and clouds 7 and 8 to stars below those clouds; clash marks in same position as Die State II, but now much bolder and more extensive. Die crack along top of AMERICA, extending about halfway beyond final A along the border toward eagle's tail. This "variety," actually a die state, used to be called Bolender-18, and is very common. In nearly all strikings, the 8 of the date appears "pinched" and the last two numerals appear somewhat heavier toward the bottom, undoubtedly the result of metal flow during striking.

Die State IV: Bolender-18a. Obverse die fails at stars 2 and 3, which bulge outward. An arc-like crack connects star 1 with star 4, and curves through the field just beyond stars 2 and 3. On the reverse, the metal displacement caused by the obverse bulge causes weakness at RI of AMERICA. Scarce die state.

Collecting Notes

1800 BB-193, as we know the variety today, is one of the most plentiful dollars of the year, and is about tied with BB-187 as the most common. An estimated 700 to 1,200 are known. In the present text, the population of BB-193 includes what used to be called Bolender-18, from the same dies, but a later state with clashing. Today, specialists recognize Bolender-18 as simply a later die state of BB-193.

For many years, Bolender-13 was considered to be one of the rarer varieties of 1800, while Bolender-18 was one of the more common issues. Auction data suggest that "old" B-13 coins were about three and one-half times rarer than "old" B-18 coins. As might be expected "old" B-13 coins were considered to be great rarities in high grades. The Mint State 1975 ANA Convention Sale (Superior) coin, earlier in the W.G. Baldenhofer Collection, was considered the finest known. Now come more than a half dozen records of Mint State "old" B-18 coins to dilute the desirability of the "old" B-13.

My feeling is that as time goes on, the "old" B-18 will be forgotten, and will be considered for what it really is: a die state of BB-193 [B-13]. Values will settle at the lowest common denominator, which means that Die State I of BB-193 (equal to the "old" B-13 in its entirely) may be worth slightly more than Die State III (equal to the "old" B-18), but not much more. Time will tell.

Notable Specimens

Fairfield Specimen. MS-65+ (PCGS). Fairfield Collection (Bowers and Ruddy, 1977) lot 1037, Bolender-18a. "Gem Unc."

BB-193: Late die state with advanced obverse die breaks.

Garrett Specimen. MS-65 (NGC). Garrett Collection • Johns Hopkins University (Bowers and Ruddy, March 1980) lot 693 • Andre Dawson Collection (Heritage, September 1998) lot 6826 • C.L. Lee Collection Sale (American Numismatic Rarities, September 2005) lot 530 • Orlando Signature Sale (Heritage, January 2008) lot 2933 • Joseph C. Thomas Collection (Heritage, April 2009) lot 2560.

Palm Beach Specimen. MS-63 (PCGS). Palm Beach Signature Sale (Heritage, July 2009) lot 762.

Four Landmark Collections Specimen. MS-63. Four Landmark Collections Sale (Bowers and Merena, 1989) lot 1976. "MS-63 to 64."

Denver Sale Specimen. MS-62 (PCGS). Denver Signature Sale (Heritage, August 2006) lot 5303 • Orlando Signature Sale (Heritage, January 2007) lot 5161 • Baltimore ANA Signature Sale (Heritage, July 2008) lot 1741.

Queller Specimen. MS-62 (NGC). December Sale (Stack's, December 1998) lot 1412 • Queller Family

Collection of Silver Dollars (Heritage, April 2008) lot 2073.

Baldenhofer Specimen. MS-60. W.G. Baldenhofer • Farish-Baldenhofer Sale (Stack's, 1955) • A.J. Ostheimer 3rd Collection • ANA Convention Sale (Superior, 1975) lot 993. "Clashed die reverse. MS-60."

Johnson Specimen. MS-60. B.G. Johnson • "World's Greatest Collection" (F.C.C. Boyd, Numismatic Gallery, 1945) lot 105. "H-18A. Not in Haseltine, Similar to H-18, but obverse die cracks. Unc." • A.J. Ostheimer 3rd Collection (Lester Merkin, 1968) lot 309. Bolender-18b. "Brilliant Unc."

Flannagan Specimen. AU-58 (PCGS). Phillip Flannagan Collection (Bowers and Merena, November 2001) lot 4273 • Dr. Robert Hesselgesser Collection (Ira and Larry Goldberg, September 2011) lot 5116.

Cardinal Specimen. AU-58 (NGC). Americana Sale (Stack's, January 2005) lot 2889 • Cardinal Collection (American Numismatic Rarities, June 2005) lot 47.

Hesselgesser Specimen. AU-55 (PCGS). Dr. Robert Hesselgesser Collection (Ira and Larry Goldberg, September 2011) lot 5117.

Child's Specimen. AU-55 (NGC). Walter H. Childs Collection (Bowers and Merena, August 1999) lot 454 • Warren Miller Collection.

Total Estimated Population

MS-65 or better: 2 (URS-2)
MS-64: 1 or 2 (URS-1)
MS-63: 2 to 4 (URS-2)
MS-60 to 62: 5 to 10 (URS-4)
AU-50 to 58: 25 to 50 (URS-6)
VF-20 to EF-45: 525 to 900 (URS-11)
G-4 to F-15: 150 to 250 (URS-9)
Total for all grades combined: 700 to 1,200 (URS-11)
Estimated Total Condition Census: 65+-65-63-63-62-62

1800 BB-194

Dotted Date
(B-14, H-14)

Obverse: *Dotted date,* that is, curious die breaks or cracks are visible inside and above first O in date. Tiny dot-like die breaks appear in many other places, particularly between L and I, under nose, before chin, below first star, and under the sixth and seventh stars. The steel used to make this die must have been defective. Star 8 is closer to the Y than star 13 is from the bust. Star 7 is a little farther from L, and star 1 is very distant from hair, over 3 mm. On the left, stars 2 and 3 are closer together than are any others; 1-2 and 3-4 are farther apart than are any others and are also misaligned in relation to each other. On the right, stars 8-9 are farther apart than are any others.

Obverse die used to strike 1800 BB-194 only.

Reverse: *Only 12 arrows* show plainly; the 13th arrow is much smaller and almost hidden, and appears faintly as the third shaft from the left. Leaf points to center of I in AMERICA. Point of star touches point of *lower part* of eagle's beak, and point of upper part of beak shuts down on top side of same star point. All upper stars touch clouds decidedly, except that under cloud 7 which barely misses. Die dot between second and third upper stars from right. ME touch at base. A over cloud 3 and area between clouds 3 and 4. Tip of arrowhead under right side of right upright of U in UNITED.

Reverse die used to strike 1800 BB-194 only.

Die States

Die State I: Perfect obverse die without breaks (dots). May not exist.

Die State II: Dies for BB-194 as described by Bolender. (Does an even *earlier* state, without flaws, exist?) The die state usually seen. LIBERTY usually weakly struck, especially at the tops of ERTY.

Die State III: As preceding, but with hairline crack on obverse from border up through star 1 to a short distance

in field. Die breaks (dots) at date enlarge. Crack on reverse from D through wing to S. Raised clash marks at OF from drapery creases on obverse. Scarce.

Die State III: Bolender-14a. As preceding, but now with the following die cracks. Heavy die crack under first O in date, up through left top of second O to bust. Crack through right side of last O from milling to bust. Crack from lower part of last 0, bust, and ending in right field. Light cracks in first 3 stars. Reverse die cracks also appear from border, through right top of N into field. A crack from milling to right top of E, base of D, left wing, lower part of clouds, continues in several cracks up through OF. Another crack from top of D through left wing to S. Scarcer than either of the preceding.

Die State IV: Later state than III, now with die rust on the obverse, and with failure at the rim above LIBERTY.

Collecting Notes

1800 BB-194 is another plentiful variety. About 500 to 900 are believed to survive in all grades combined. As is the case with the AMERICAI variety, the value of the Dotted Date is enhanced by die flaws, a curious situation from the viewpoint of logic. Ever since Richard S. Yeoman listed it in the *Guide Book* as a "major variety," it has been inordinately popular. Actually, there are numerous varieties of early dollars more significant than this that are not listed in the *Guide Book*.

Most known specimens of 1800 BB-194 are in lower grades. In Mint State, the issue is a major rarity, with just four specimens known.

Notable Specimens

Cardinal Specimen. MS-65 (NGC). Julian Leidman • David M. Faraday Collection (Heritage, July 1994) lot 7120 • Cardinal Collection (Heritage, July 1997) lot 6503 • Pinnacle Rarities • Dale Friend • Michael Hering Collection (Heritage, January 2002) lot 7235 • Chris

Napolitano • Cardinal Collection (American Numismatic Rarities, June 2005) lot 50.

Eliasberg Specimen. MS-64 (NGC). Harlan P. Smith Collection (S.H. and H. Chapman, May 1906) • J.M. Clapp • John H. Clapp • Clapp estate, 1942 • Louis E. Eliasberg Sr. Collection (Bowers and Merena, April 1997) lot 2193 • Jay Parrino • Rarities Sale (Bowers and Merena, August 1998) lot 234 • Michael Hering Collection (Heritage, January 2002) lot 7236 • Scottsville Collection (Heritage, April 2009) lot 2562.

Orlando FUN Sale Specimen. MS-63 (PCGS). Orlando Signature Sale (Heritage, January 2007) lot 1038 • Internet Sale (Heritage, March 2007) lot 23588 • Internet Sale (Heritage, May 2007) lot 11334 • Internet Sale (Heritage, June 2007) lot 24312 • Milwaukee ANA Signature Sale (Heritage, August 2007) lot 1720 • Baltimore Rarities Sale (Bowers and Merena, July 2008) lot 711 • Keusch, Snow and Del Zorro Collections Sale (Stack's, November 2008) lot 3737 • Eliasberg and Krause Collections Sale (Stack's, March 2010) lot 1129 • 75th Anniversary Sale (Stack's, November 2010) lot 4421.

Boyd Specimen. MS-62 (NGC). "World's Greatest Collection" (F.C.C. Boyd, Numismatic Gallery, 1945) lot 100, Haseltine-14. "An Unc. Gem, with brilliance of original mint luster. Nick on chin." • Adolph Friedman

Collection • Unknown intermediaries • Orlando FUN Signature Sale (Heritage, January 2004) lot 2099 • Tampa FUN Signature Sale (Heritage, January 2011) lot 5622.

Matthews Specimen. AU-58 (PCGS). Purchased by Jonathan Kern at the 2000 ANA Convention from a South American collector who had the coin prior to WW II • Sold to Jim Matthews privately • San Marino Collection Sale (Ira and Larry Goldberg, September 2002) lot 528 • J.A. Sherman Collection (American Numismatic Rarities, March 2006) lot 808 • Franklinton Collection Sale (Stack's, January 2008) lot 603.

Queller Specimen. AU-58 (NGC). Queller Family Collection of Silver Dollars (Heritage, April 2008) lot 2074.

Total Estimated Population
MS-65 or better: 1 (URS-1)
MS-64: 1 (URS-1)
MS-63: 1 or 2 (URS-1)
MS-60 to 62: 1 or 2 (URS-1)
AU-50 to 58: 4 to 8 (URS-3)
VF-20 to EF-45: 375 to 700 (URS-10)
G-4 to F-15: 125 to 200 (URS-9)
Total for all grades combined: 500 to 900 (URS-11)
Estimated Total Condition Census: 65-64-63-62-58 (multiples)

1800 BB-195

(B-15, H-15)
Obverse: Star 13 very close to bust; a point barely escapes touching the junction of drapery with bosom. The 1 in date is very close to curl, but does not touch. Numerals 180 in date are close, and the last 0 more distant. Star is near L. Die dot between R and T. The first star is very distant from hair, 4 mm. On the left, stars 3 and 4 are more widely spaced than are any others. On the right, stars 8-9 and 11-12 are closer together than are any other pairs. Often weakly struck on the hair.

Obverse die used to strike 1800 BB-195 only.

Reverse: *Only 10 perfect arrows* and 3 arrow heads *without sticks.* Numerous die flaws in TES and especially between last S of STATES and 0 enable quick identification. A does not touch feathers. AME join at base, the left base of M high and overlapping A. Star very close but does not quite touch eagle's beak. A over clouds 2 (part of left foot of A) and 3 (mainly). Tip of arrowhead under right side of right upright of U in UNITED.

Reverse die used to strike 1800 BB-195 only.

Die States

Die State I: Perfect dies. The obverse and (particularly) the reverse dentils are usually very long and well pronounced.

Collecting Notes

1800 BB-195 is of medium scarcity. I believe that about 250 to 450 survive. Once again, most specimens are in lower grades through VF. At the EF level BB-195 becomes rare, and AU or finer coins are very rare.

Notable Specimens

Carter Specimen. AU-58. Amon Carter, Jr. Collection (Stack's, 1984) lot 229. "AU, just a whisper from full Mint State."

Cardinal Specimen. AU-55 (PCGS). Pre-Long Beach Sale (Superior, June 2000) lot 1606 • Legend Numismatics • Cardinal Collection (American Numismatic Rarities, June 2005) lot 51 • Dr. Robert Hesselgesser Collection (Ira and Larry Goldberg, September 2011) lot 5119 • Pre-Long Beach Sale (Ira and Larry Goldberg, May 2012) lot 1310.

Long Beach Specimen. AU-55 (PCGS). Long Beach Signature Sale (Heritage, February 2009) lot 1572.

Northwest Specimen. AU-55 (PCGS). Northwest Collection (Heritage, May 2008) lot 875 • Baltimore Sale (Bowers and Merena, November 2008) lot 2635.

Austin Specimen. AU-55. Austin Collection (Bowers and Ruddy, 1974) lot 37. "Unc., some evidence of rubbing."

Newport Specimen. AU-55. The Newport Collection (Bowers and Ruddy, 1975) lot 1047. "Unc., with some very light friction on the highest parts."

Krugjohann Specimen. AU-55. The Krugjohann Collection (Bowers and Ruddy, 1976) lot 625. "AU."

Hesselgesser Specimen. AU-53 (PCGS). Dr. Robert Hesselgesser Collection (Ira and Larry Goldberg, February 2008) lot 2892.

Atlanta Sale Specimen. AU-53 ICG). Atlanta ANA Signature Sale (Heritage, August 2001) lot 6425.

Thaler Specimen. AU-50 (PCGS). Thaler Collection (American Numismatic Rarities, March 2006) lot 1069.

Miller Specimen. AU-50 (NGC). Warren Miller Collection.

Albany Specimen. AU-50 (ICG). Albany Collection (Heritage, September 2002) lot 7581.

Total Estimated Population

MS-65 or better: 0 (URS-0)
MS-64: 0 (URS-0)
MS-63: 0 (URS-0)
MS-60 to 62: 0 (URS-0)
AU-50 to 58: 5 to 10 (URS-4)
VF-20 to EF-45: 150 to 265 (URS-9)
G-4 to F-15: 100 to 175 (URS-8)
Total for all grades combined: 250 to 450 (URS-10)
Estimated Total Condition Census: 58-55 (multiples)

1800 BB-196

(B-17, H-17)

Obverse: A "collar" (clash mark) shows along neck about half the length of bust, due to clashing from the reverse die. A *line extends to left* from just above foot of 1 in date. Upper left star very distant from L, almost as far as first star is from hair, between 2 and 3 mm. 180 in date close, 1 originally cut too far to the left.

Obverse die used to strike 1800 BB-196 only.

Reverse: *Only 12 arrows.* Point of star touches point of *upper part* of eagle's beak. Leaf point is under left side of stand of I in AMERICA. Center of A over cloud 3. Tip of arrowhead under right upright of U in UNITED.

Reverse die used to strike 1800 BB-196 only.

Die States

Die State I: Without obverse clash mark or reverse die crack. Very rare.

Die State II: Obverse with clash marks visible as a "collar" at Miss Liberty's neck and bosom. This is the die state usually seen.

Die State III: Bolender-17a. As preceding, but now with additional die cracks as follows: Hairline crack at right of star 1 extends slightly into field. Crack from border to hair between star 1 and date. Tiny crack between stars 11 and 12. Reverse with prominent raised clash marks (from drapery folds) from S through OF and extending downward (called die breaks by Bolender). Die crack from border through top of A, lower part of M, to end of branch. Scarce.

Die State IV: As preceding, but now with obverse crack from star 6 to ribbon. Scarce.

Collecting Notes

The 1800 BB-196 dollar is quite plentiful. About 500 to 950 survive in all grades combined. Unlike many of its contemporaries, it is not unusual to encounter in EF. AU specimens are in the rare category, and Mint State coins are exceedingly rare.

Notable Specimens

Cohen Specimen. MS-63 (NGC). Milton Cohen Collection (Bowers and Merena, January 1985) lot 528 • Red Bank Sale (American Numismatic Rarities, December 2003) lot 811 • Cardinal Collection (American Numismatic Rarities, June 2005) lot 52 • J.A. Sherman Sale (American Numismatic Rarities, March 2006) lot 809 • March Sale (Stack's, March 2007) lot 1052.

Orlando Sale Specimen. MS-63 (NGC). Orlando Signature Sale (Heritage, January 2008) lot 2934.

Cardinal Specimen. MS-62 (PCGS). Red Bank Sale (American Numismatic Rarities, December 2003) lot

BB-196: Early die state without obverse clash marks.

812 • Chris Napolitano • Cardinal Collection (American Numismatic Rarities, June 2005) lot 53 • Joseph C. Thomas Collection (Heritage, April 2009) lot 2563.

DeCoppet Specimen. MS-60. André DeCoppet Collection (James Kelly, 1955). "Unc."

Brilliant and Sieck Collections Specimen. MS-60. Bowers and Merena, 1992, lot 1277. "MS-60/62."

Miller Specimen. AU-58 (NGC). Warren Miller Collection.

Portland Sale Specimen. AU-58 (NGC). Portland Signature Sale (Heritage, March 2004) lot 5959

Detroit ANA Specimen. AU-58 (NGC). Detroit ANA Signature Sale (Heritage, July 1994) lot 7119.

Hollinbeck-Kagin Specimen. AU-58. Hollinbeck-Kagin Sale, August 1970, lot 1094, Bolender-17a. Unc. • September 1970, lot 889, B-17A, Near Unc.

Boyd Specimen. AU-55. "World's Greatest Collection" (F.C.C. Boyd, Numismatic Gallery, 1945) lot 103, Haseltine-17. "Barely circulated.

Green Specimen. AU-50. Col. E.H.R. Green Collection. • Bolender Collection • André DeCoppet Collection (James Kelly, 1955). "Practically Unc." • A.J. Ostheimer 3rd Collection (Lester Merkin, 1968) lot 308. "Bolender-17b. R-1. AU or so."

Total Estimated Population

MS-65 or better: 0 (URS-0)
MS-64: 0 (URS-0)
MS-63: 1 (URS-1)
MS-60 to 62: 2 to 4 (URS-2)
AU-50 to 58: 5 to 10 (URS-4)
VF-20 to EF-45: 375 to 725 (URS-10)
G-4 to F-15: 120 to 210 (URS-8)
Total for all grades combined: 500 to 950 (URS-11)
Estimated Total Condition Census: 63-63-62-60-60-58 (multiples)

Additional Information

The Year 1800 in History

For much of January and February, tributes to George Washington were held in cities and towns in the various states. Mason Locke Weems, an Episcopal clergyman, published *The Life and Memorable Actions of George Washington*, which went into multiple editions, the fifth of which (published in 1806) included the fanciful tale of young Washington and the cherry tree. Much of Weems' fiction passed into popular "history." *Hymns and Odes Composed on the Death of General George Washington*, was published and included contributions from many sources, including Thomas Paine.

In the presidential election, Democratic-Republican Thomas Jefferson won 73 Electoral College votes as did Aaron Burr, followed by 65 for President John Adams and 64 for Charles Pinckney. After many more ballots, the opposition of Alexander Hamilton to Burr swung the majority to Jefferson's side in February 1801.

During the summer of 1800, the capital of the United States was moved from New York City to Washington, D.C., with 123 federal clerks participating in the move. Congress met in Washington for the first time on November 17, 1800, the same day President John Adams moved into the White House. The Executive Mansion had no plumbing, and water had to be carried from five blocks away. The Library of Congress was founded with a $5,000 appropriation for the purchase of 900 books, among which was Adam Smith's 1776 *Wealth of Nations*. The nucleus of the new library was ordered from London booksellers Cadell & Davies; 740 volumes were forwarded with an invoice of £489, 5 s., dated December 11, 1800. The 1800 census showed that Washington, D.C. had 2,464 free residents and 623 slaves. These figures were part of the decennial head count which showed a total national population of 5,308,483, including 896,849 slaves.

The Division Act of May 7, 1800 created the Indiana Territory from the western part of the Northwest Territory. The Louisiana Territory, ceded to Spain by the Treaty of Paris of 1763, was returned to France on October 1, 1800, under a secret agreement in the 1796 Treaty of San Ildefonso. France guaranteed not to transfer the territory to any country but Spain. German physician F.J. Gall founded the practice of phrenology, which would flourish in the United States at the middle of the nineteenth century.

CHAPTER 14
1801 SILVER DOLLARS

MINTAGE (ALL VARIETIES)
Calendar year, Mint report: 54,454
Coins bearing date, author's estimate: 35,000

1801 SILVER DOLLARS

BB to Bolender to Haseltine Equivalents

BB Number	Bolender #	Haseltine #	Rarity	Average Grade
BB-211	B-1	H-1	URS-11	VF-33
BB-212	B-2	H-2	URS-11	VF-29
BB-213	B-3	H-3	URS-10	VF-29
BB-214	B-4	H-4	URS-10	VF-27

Coinage Context

The price of silver: Whereas during the period 1794-1799 the intrinsic value of the silver dollar had not exceeded its face value, in 1800 the dollar became worth slightly more as bullion than face value. In 1801 a silver dollar was worth about $1.03. For this reason, mintages declined. As silver dollars continued to be worth more than face value, most (including earlier-minted coins on hand) were melted or exported. The situation was intolerable, and in 1804 production was halted.

Mintage commentary: Conventional wisdom has it that part of this mintage was dated 1800. In his *Encyclopedia,* p. 428, Walter H. Breen states this: "Mintage reported for 1801 consisted largely of coins dated 1800; similar backdating was the rule through 1804."

Die making: Die making procedures followed those employed in 1800.

On the obverse, variables include the positional relationships of the 13 stars, the word LIBERTY and its component letters, the date, and the portrait of Miss Liberty.

On the reverse, variables include the positional relationships of the letters in UNITED STATES OF AMERICA, the branch, arrows, eagle, clouds, and stars above the eagle. The reverse of 1801 BB-214 has the lower right serif of the T partially broken (from an injured or worn punch), while on the reverse of BB-213 the lower right serif or foot of the T is completely missing.

Die combinations: Two obverse dies were mated with four reverses to produce dollars dated this year. The division wasn't equal: one obverse was coupled with three different reverses to create BB-211, BB-212, and BB-213, and the other obverse was monogamous with another reverse to create BB-214 (but after its obverse "died," it went on in later years to additional unions with obverses dated 1802 and 1803 to create 1802/1 BB-233, 234, 235, and 242; 1803 BB-251 and BB-252).

Similarly, the reverse die used to coin 1801 BB-212 is one of several dies in the early dollar series employed to strike coins with more than one obverse date. Not only did it combine with an 1801 die to create BB-212, it also was used to strike 1802/1 BB-231, BB-232, and 1802 BB-241; and 1803 BB-254 and BB-255.

Of dies and year dating: Concerning the long-lived reverse dies used to create 1801 BB-212 and BB-214, BB-212 *may have been* made first, as the lower right serif of the foot of T is intact, whereas on BB-214 it is partially missing. (Made still later was the reverse to coin BB-213, with the lower right serif completely missing). However, the set of punches which contained the broken T also had duplicate(s), as evidenced by a perfect T used to make the two new reverse dies found on the 1801-1804 novodels.

Reverse die progression evidence indicates that the reverse die used to coin 1801 BB-212 (called by Bolender, Reverse A), indicates that this die was used no earlier than 1802. Similar evidence reveals that the reverse die used to strike 1801 BB-214 (Bolender's Reverse B) was not used before 1802. Thus, neither 1801 BB-212 nor 214 were coined in 1801. As obverse die progression indicates that 1801 BB-213 was struck after 1801 BB-212, this means that 1801 BB-212 also was struck after 1801. Further,

1801 BB-213 has broken T letters on the reverse, from the employment of a broken T punch. 1802 BB-241 has the same broken T on the obverse. As the 1802 obverse die could not have been made in 1801, nor would it have made sense to have made it in 1803, this isolates the year 1802 for the production of the reverse used to coin 1801 BB-213, another verification that 1801 BB-213 was struck in 1802 at the earliest.

Thus, 1801 BB-211 is the only variety dated 1801 that *might have been* actually struck in 1801! However, it too could have been struck later.

Because of this, the 54,454 silver dollars the Mint reported as having been coined in calendar year 1801 probably consisted largely of pieces of earlier dates.

Order of striking: It seems likely that the order of striking of 1801-dated dollar varieties was as follows:

1801 BB-211. Struck in 1801 or later. The only 1801-dated dollar for which there is a possibility it was actually struck in 1801.

1801 BB-212. Struck in 1802 or later.

1801 BB-213. Struck in 1802 or later.

1801 BB-214. Struck in 1802 or later.

Numismatic Information

Commentary: Four circulation strike die varieties exist, none of which is a formidable rarity. In his 1881 *Type-Table*, Capt. J.W. Haseltine said nothing of the rarity of any of the four varieties he listed (H-1 through H-4, equal to BB-211 through BB-214 today); apparently, he considered them all common. Today, as in yesteryear, the completion of a full set of 1801 dollars is a realistic goal. The 1801 is scarce as a date, as are also 1802 and 1803. The 1801 Proof novodel "restrike," made decades later, is discussed separately.

Identification of the four varieties is literally and figuratively as easy as 1-2-3 (and 4) using the Easy-Finding Guide above. Most specimens in existence today are in worn grades. It is significant to mention that as of October 1992, NGC and PCGS combined had graded just one 1801 dollar as Mint State.

Summary of Characteristics

1801

Circulation Strikes

Enabling legislation: Act of April 2, 1792

Designer of obverse: Robert Scot (after Stuart), model by John Eckstein

Designer of reverse: Robert Scot (from the Great Seal)

Weight and composition: 416 grains; .8924 silver, balance copper

Melting value (silver bullion value) in year minted: Traditionally considered by Mint officials to be on a par with the Spanish dollar, and worth about $1.00 intrinsically, but by 1801 the value had risen to about $1.03.

Dies prepared: unknown

Circulation strike mintage, calendar year: 54,454 (may include some struck from dies dated earlier; figures do not include pieces reserved for the Assay Commission; these are given in parentheses); Delivery figures by day: January 10: 6,850 (+3) • February 4: 8,483 (+3) • February 16: 9,800 (+3) • February 28: 3,500 (+3) • March 16: 5,773 (+3) • April 15: 7,350 (+3) • May 15: 1,150 (+2) • August 19: 7,040 (+3) • September 30: 3,746 (0) • December 26: 762 (+1).

Estimated circulation strike mintage of 1801-dated dollars (author's estimate): 35,000 (rounded).

Estimated quantity melted: Unknown

Estimated total population (all varieties):
MS-65 or better: 1 (URS-1)
MS-64: 1 (URS-1)
MS-63: 3 to 4 (URS-3)
MS-60 to 62: 8 to 12 (URS-5)
AU-50 to 58: 60 to 130 (URS-8)
VF-20 to EF-45: 1,100 to 2,100 (URS-12)
G-4 to F-15: 600 to 1,100 (URS-13)
Total for all grades combined: 1,800 to 3,500 (URS-13)
Estimated Total Condition Census: 65-64-63-63-63-63

Characteristics of striking: Depends upon the variety. If weakly struck, this is often observed at the center of the obverse and among the stars above the eagle on the reverse.

Proofs: Proof novodels were made decades later.

Commentary: Coinage of dollars dated 1801 was small, and specimens are scarce today. Apparently, only one variety of 1801-dated dollar, BB-211, has the possibility of being actually coined in calendar year 1801.

1801 HERALDIC EAGLE

VARIETIES

1801 BB-211

(B-1, H-1)

Obverse: *The distance from 1 in date to curl is about the same as the distance from star 8 to upper right serif of Y.* The so-called Wide Date, most space between 180, the 01 closest; this traditional nomenclature is only useful if you have a Close Date (BB-214) on hand with which to compare it. The first 1 not very close to curl. The last 1 about as far from bust as first 1 is from curl. Star 8 close to Y. Other three key stars—7, 1, and 13—are distant from L, hair, and bust. Small dot to left of center dot. Right serif of I is level with left serif of B (on BB-214, the serif of B is higher).

Obverse die used to strike 1801 BB-211 (earliest use), BB-212 (intermediate use), and BB-213 (latest use).

Reverse: *Arrowhead under U of UNITED.* Point of star almost touches point of *lower part of eagle's beak.* 13 arrows. *Ray of star points to left side of U in PLURIBUS* (the only 1801 for which this is true). A in AMERICA touches third and fourth feathers. Leaf point is under left side of upright of I in AMERICA.

Reverse die used to strike 1801 BB-211 only.

Note: As the other three varieties of 1801 dollars— 1801 BB-212, 213, and 214—were all struck in 1802 or later (see descriptions under their respective categories), this leaves 1801 BB-211 as the only candidate for a variety that *might have been* actually struck in 1801.

Die States

Die State I: Perfect dies. About 10% or so are of this die state.

Die State II: As preceding, except for a tiny hairline die crack on obverse to left of 1 in date, slanting down toward the border.

Die State III: With reverse clash marks at TED and eagle's wing, showing on high grade coins the distinct incuse impressions of obverse stars, probably stars 1 and 2, plus traces of others, as well as incusation marks from obverse dentils. This injury may have precipitated a die crack which extends through STA down through the clouds on the right, extending (in several intermediate states) to the first A in AMERICA. On worn specimens, the clash marks and crack are not easily seen. This is the usual die state encountered.

Die State IV: With reverse cracks from the rim through STA to the right wing to the first A in AMERICA to M and E to the rim. Cf. Sotheby's December 8-9, 1992: 499 (one of two pieces in the lot). Rare. Not seen.

Die State V: The latest state, of which there are several progressive stages, shows a crack from the clouds to the right wing and, finally, a large bulge at AMER. Cf. Sotheby's December 8-9, 1992: 499 (one of two pieces in the lot) was described as: "more advanced state of the die with the die crack through OF, and struck from clashed dies." Rare. Not seen.

Collecting Notes

I estimate that about 500 to 900 exist of 1801 BB-211, ranking it with BB-212 as one of the most plentiful varieties of the year. However, as a date, 1801 dollars are measurably more elusive than are those of the earlier years of the Heraldic Eagle type, up to this point in time. The BB-211 is about as available as BB-212 if all grades combined are totaled, but in higher ranges, the BB-211 is the scarcer of the two.

Quite a few AU specimens of BB-211 have crossed the auction block over the years, but at the Uncirculated level, appearances fall off sharply. In fact, only three such Mint State coins have sold in the past two decades.

Notable Specimens

Cardinal Specimen. MS-62 (PCGS). Private Arizona collector • Tangible Asset Galleries • Cardinal Collection (American Numismatic Rarities, June 2005) lot 54 • Keusch, Snow and Del Zorro Collections Sale (Stack's, November 2008) lot 3738.

Cardinal Specimen (another) MS-62 (NGC). Robert Lehmann • Cardinal Collection • Tangible Asset Galleries • Private collector • Pittsburgh ANA Signature Sale (Heritage, August 2004) lot 6343 • Rarities Sale (Bowers and Merena, February 2005) lot 1020 • Joseph C. Thomas Collection (Heritage, April 2009) lot 2564 • Philadelphia Sale (Stack's, September 2009) lot 5222 • Virginia Beach Collection (Heritage, June 2011) lot 3860.

CSNS Sale Specimen. MS-62 (NGC). CSNS Signature Sale (Heritage, April 2002) lot 4017.

Flannagan Specimen. AU-58 (PCGS). Phillip Flannagan Collection, sold privately • James Farrington Collection (Heritage, July 2002) lot 8443 • Allison Park Sale (American Numismatic Rarities, August 2004) lot 562 • J.A. Sherman Collection (Stack's, August 2007) lot 810 • Franklinton Collection Sale (Stack's, January 2008) lot 604 • 73rd Anniversary Sale (Stack's, October 2008) lot 390 • Entlich, White Oak, Gross & St. Andre Collections Sale (Stack's, March 2009) lot 5363 • 74th Anniversary Sale (Stack's, November 2009) lot 1518 • Dr.

Robert Hesselgesser Collection (Ira and Larry Goldberg, September 2011) lot 5115.

Norweb Sale Specimen. AU-58 (NGC). Norweb Collection Sale, but not part of the Norweb Collection (Stack's, November 2006) lot 451 • Minot Collection Sale (Stack's, May 2008) lot 1659 • Decatur Collection Sale (Stack's, August 2008) lot 1366.

Denver ANA Sale Specimen. AU-58 (NGC). Denver ANA Signature Sale (Heritage, August 1996) lot 7976.

Albany Specimen. AU-58 (NGC). Albany Collection (Heritage, September 2002) lot 7857.

Hollinbeck-Kagin Specimen. AU-58. Hollinbeck-Kagin Sale, June 1970, lot 635. Bolender-1a. "Die breaks on reverse with die starting to buckle at right, Unc."

New Netherlands Specimen. AU-55. New Netherlands 57th Sale, 1963, lot 1092, Bolender-1a. "Unlisted die state."

Total Estimated Population

MS-65 or better: 0 (URS-0)
MS-64: 0 (URS-0)
MS-63: 0 (URS-0)
MS-60 to 62: 3-4 (URS-3)
AU-50 to 58: 25 to 50 (URS-6)
VF-20 to EF-45: 350 to 650 (URS-10)
G-4 to F-15: 125 to 200 (URS-9)
Total for all grades combined: 500 to 900 (URS-11)
Estimated Total Condition Census: 62-62-62-58 (multiples)

1801 BB-212

(B-2, H-2)

Obverse: See description under 1801 BB-211. Now with die clash marks around date. Often struck lightly at the upper obverse.

Obverse die used to strike 1801 BB-211 (earliest use), BB-212 (intermediate use), and BB-213 (latest use).

Reverse: The point of the leftmost arrowhead is under the left edge of the left serif of N in UNITED. The point of upper part of eagle's beak touches down on a point of a star slightly back from extreme star point. Only 12 arrows show plainly (13th faintly shows, but is difficult to find). First A in AMERICA touches third feather, and is connected by die crack to fourth feather. Leaf points more towards left corner of base of I in AMERICA.

The same hub used to produce this reverse was also employed to make Reverse X and Reverse Y for the 1801-2-3-4 novodels. It had 12 arrows, instead of the correct 13. Whenever this hub was used, the 13th arrow was added by hand, always with a light impression from a separate punch.

Reverse die used to strike 1801 (intermediate state) BB-212; 1802/1 BB-231 (early state) and BB-232 (early state); 1802 BB-241 (slightly advanced intermediate state); and 1803 BB-253 (if it exists) and BB-254 (slightly advanced intermediate state), and BB-255 (terminal state).

Note: Die progression study reveals that 1801 BB-212 was struck after 1802/1 BB-231 and BB-232, but before 1803 BB-254 and 1803 BB-255; thus it was not struck before 1802.

Die States

Die State I: Perfect dies without clash marks on obverse or reverse. Scarce.

Die State II: The obverse has clash marks as follows: At top of bust are double clash marks, from two clashes, slightly misaligned between strikes; the impressions (from top of eagle's wing by UNUM on reverse) appear as a double "collar." Incusations from clouds can be seen at the date, and other incusations extend left to star 3. On the reverse, a tiny crack can be seen from the eagle's second feather to the left rim. A very light clash mark (not a die crack) from the drapery can be seen through OF. LIBERTY is often lightly struck, as is the eagle's tail, on this and Die State III (perhaps the clashing caused some misalignment of the die faces).

Die State III: Obverse die lightly relapped, removing one of the "collar" marks (now it is a single "collar"), most of the incusation marks at date and to the left, and reducing the size of a raised die line to the left of the 1 (that has

appeared since its first use on 1801 BB-211). Reverse as preceding. This is the die state most often seen.

Collecting Notes

The population of 1801 BB-212 is about 500 to 900, or about the same as 1801 BB-211. These two varieties are the two most populous of the year. However, of the four circulation strike varieties of the date, none is a rarity.

Examples are quite rare AU or finer. I know of only four Uncirculated specimens coming on the market in recent decades. The Winsor-Mills coin probably does qualify as well, and in the Condition Census I arbitrarily assign the grade of MS-63 to it.

Notable Specimens

Winsor Specimen. MS-63. Richard Winsor Collection (1895) • Mills Collection (Chapman brothers, 1904).

Snow Specimen. MS-63 PCGS). Purchased privately by Warren Snow in the 1940s • Warren Snow Collection (Stack's, November 2008) lot 3739 • Anthony Terranova • Dr. Robert Hesselgesser Collection (Ira and Larry Goldberg, September 2011) lot 5121 • Pre-Long Beach Sale (Ira and Larry Goldberg, May 2012) lot 1312.

Cardinal Specimen. MS-63 PCGS). Chris Napolitano, privately in 1996 • Cardinal Collection (Heritage, July 1997) lot 6505 • Tangible Asset Galleries • Private collector • Benson Collection Sale (Ira and Larry Goldberg, February 2002) lot 1183 • Steve Contursi and Chris Napolitano, privately to • Jack Lee Collection III (Heritage, November 2005) lot 2196 • CSNS Signature Sale (Heritage, April 2008) lot 2342 • Dr. Robert Hesselgesser Collection • Boston Rarities Sale (Bowers and Merena, August 2010) lot 1063.

Dallas Sale Specimen. MS-63 (NGC). Dallas Signature Sale (Heritage, December 2005) lot 941.

BB-212: Die State I without obverse clash marks.

BB-212: Die State III, lapped obverse die, with single "collar" clash mark.

Orlando Sale Specimen. MS-61 (PCGS). Orlando Signature Sale (Heritage, January 2012) lot 3295.

Hesselgesser Specimen. AU-58 (PCGS). Las Vegas ANA Sale (Bowers and Merena, October 2005) lot 7025 • Dr. Robert Hesselgesser Collection (Ira and Larry Goldberg, May 2011) lot 909 • Pre-Long Beach Sale (Ira and Larry Goldberg, January 2012) lot 2561.

Brooks Specimen. AU-58 (PCGS). Brooks Collection (Bowers and Merena, June 1989) lot 269 • Rarities Sale (Bowers and Merena, August 1995) lot 176.

Miller Specimen. AU-58 (NGC). Spring Quartette Sale (Bowers and Merena, March 1992) lot 2319 • Warren Miller Collection.

Boyd Specimen. AU-58. "World's Greatest Collection" (F.C.C. Boyd, Numismatic Gallery, 1945) lot 110. "Unc."

Total Estimated Population

MS-65 or better: 0 (URS-0)
MS-64: 0 (URS-0)
MS-63: 3 to 4 (URS-3)
MS-60 to 62: 1 to 2 (URS-2)
AU-50 to 58: 15 to 30 (URS-5)
VF-20 to EF-45: 325 to 625 (URS-10)
G-4 to F-15: 150 to 250 (URS-9)
Total for all grades combined: 500 to 900 (URS-11)
Estimated Total Condition Census: 63-63-63-63-61-58 (multiples)

1801 BB-213

(B-3, H-3)

Obverse: See description under 1801 BB-211.

Obverse die used to strike 1801 BB-211 (earliest use), BB-212 (intermediate use), and BB-213 (latest use).

Reverse: Point of star *touches outside* of upper part of eagle's beak. *Right foot of all T's missing*, the result of a broken punch (apparently, this die was made immediately after the die for 1801 BB-214, which has a partially broken lower right serif). A touches third feather only. 13 arrows. AM joined at base, E extremely close (Bolender said it is joined). Leaf touches I in AMERICA slightly right of center of base. Star under cloud 7 double punched (an interesting error, but a rare one; it is a wonder that more stars were not double punched c. 1798-1803).

Note: As 1801 BB-213 was struck after 1801 BB-212 (per obverse die state evidence), and as 1801 BB-212 was stuck no earlier than 1802, it follows that 1801 BB-213 was also struck no earlier than 1802.

Reverse die used to strike 1801 BB-213 only.

Die States

Die State I: Perfect dies without clash marks. Very rare.

Die State II: Obverse die perfect. Reverse with curved clash mark (from outline of bosom on obverse) above and to the right of M in UNUM; light clash mark from obverse drapery is extending from O to cloud 6 (called a die crack by Bolender).

Die State II: Reverse with massive clash marks (called die breaks by Bolender); the entire date 1801, incuse and reversed, is visible under ES O! Clash marks from obverse dentils are at border above STATES OF.

Die State II: With clash marks on reverse as described above.

Die State III: Now with a crack from the rim below the curl to the 1 in the date and another from under the curl near the rim. Die flaws between LIBERTY and the rim and scattered throughout the reverse legend.

Collecting Notes

I estimate that about 425 to 800 examples are known of the 1801 BB-213 dollar today. This is just slightly more available than BB-214, and each of these two varieties is less abundant than 1801 BB-211 and BB-212. Again, the issue is scarce in higher grades. Although a number of Mint State coins have crossed the block, most of these date from before 1986 when the change in grading interpretations took place.

Notable Specimens

Hesselgesser Specimen. MS-62 (PCGS). CSNS Signature Sale (Heritage, April 2008) lot 2341 • Dr. Robert Hesselgesser Collection (Ira and Larry Goldberg, September 2011) lot 5122 • Pre-Long Beach Sale (Ira and Larry Goldberg, May 2012) lot 1313.

Queller Specimen. MS-62 (NGC). Queller Family Collection of Silver Dollars (Heritage, April 2008) lot 2078 • Internet Sale (Heritage, May 2008) lot 64375 • Baltimore Signature Sale (Heritage, July 2008) lot 1743 • Internet Sale (Heritage, September 2008) lot 64548 • Internet Sale (Heritage, November 2008) lot 62331 • Orlando Signature Sale (Heritage, January 2009) lot 3948 • Baltimore Signature Sale (Heritage, March 2009) lot 2361.

Long Beach Sale Specimen. MS-60 (NGC). Long Beach Signature Sale (Heritage, September 2005) lot 3690 • Orlando Signature Sale (Heritage, January 2007) lot 1039 • Amherst and Waccabuc Collections Sale (Stack's, November 2007) lot 2220.

Golding Specimen. MS-60. Ex Golding Collection (Stack's, June 1952) lot 225 • Harold Bareford Collection (Stack's, 1981) lot 420, "Brilliant Unc."

Doolittle Specimen. AU-58. Doolittle Collection (Bowers and Ruddy, 1977) lot 2839. "Borderline Unc."

Austin Specimen. AU-58. Austin Collection (Bowers and Ruddy, 1974) lot 41. "Brilliant Unc."

Jarapendo Specimen. AU-55 (PCGS). Jarapendo Collection (Stack's Bowers, July 2011) lot 4043

Cardinal Specimen. AU-55 (PCGS). Cardinal Collection • Private collector • Pre-Long Beach Sale (Ira and Larry Goldberg, February 2008) lot 2895.

Flannagan Specimen. AU-55 (PCGS). Phillip Flannagan Collection, sold privately • Dr. Robert Hesselgesser Collection (Ira and Larry Goldberg, February 2009) lot 1098.

Green Specimen. AU-55. Col. E.H.R. Green. • James G. Macallister. • T. James Clarke Collection (New Netherlands 48th Sale, 1956) lot 646. "Rusted obverse die. Remarkably sharp, very close to Unc."

Kreisberg Specimen. AU-55. Abner Kreisberg mail bid sale, September 18, 1961: 1063. • A.J. Ostheimer 3rd Collection • ANA Convention Sale (Superior, 1975) lot 1009. "AU-55."

Herdman Specimen. AU-55. Herdman Collection (Bowers and Ruddy, 1977) lot 5819. "Borderline Unc."

Total Estimated Population

MS-65 or better: 0 (URS-0)
MS-64: 0 (URS-0)
MS-63: 0 (URS-0)
MS-60 to 62: 3 to 4 (URS-3)
AU-50 to 58: 15 to 30 (URS-5)
VF-20 to EF-45: 225 to 450 (URS-9)
G-4 to F-15: 175 to 325 (URS-9)
Total for all grades combined: 425 to 800 (URS-10)
Estimated Total Condition Census: 62-62-60-60-58-58-55 (multiples)

1801 BB-214

(B-4, H-4)

Obverse: *The distance from 1 in date to curl is a tiny fraction of the distance from star 8 to upper right serif of Y.* So-called *Close Date*, figures evenly spaced. The first 1 is

very close to curl, the last 1 in date distant from bust. The eighth star is about as near to Y as last star is from bust, slightly under 1 mm. Star 7 is about 1.5 mm. distant from L, and star 1 is about the same distance from curl. Right serif of I is lower than left serif of B (on BB-211 through BB-214, the serifs are level).

Obverse die used to strike 1801 BB-214 only.

Reverse: The point of the leftmost arrowhead is under the center of the left upright of the N in UNITED. There is a "spur" on the curved part of D. Leaf points under center of I in AMERICA. Point of a star touches the outside of upper part of eagle's beak slightly above beak's point. This long-lived die was mated with obverses dated 1801, 1802, and 1803. Letters T in UNITED and STATES have lower right serif partially broken. Apparently, this die was made immediately before the die used to coin the reverse of 1801 BB-213, which has the lower right serif completely missing. Die progression evidence indicates that 1801 BB-214 was struck no earlier than 1802.

Reverse die used to strike 1801 BB-214 (typically with crack from border toward cloud 6); 1802/1 BB-233 (perfect; first use of the die), BB-234 (die relapped, cloud 6 mostly missing, some arrowheads disconnected; some with clash mark from cloud 5 to border above O), and BB-235; 1802 BB-242 (spur on D from now on); 1803 BB-251 (relapped, struck before BB-252) and BB-252 (relapped, struck after BB-251).

Die States

Die State I: Perfect obverse and reverse dies without cracks.

Die State II: As above, except a tiny vertical crack begins to develop between arrows and eagle's leg feathers, closer to eagle's leg (this crack advances slightly with use of the die with other obverses). The die state usually seen.

Die State III: Tiny die crack extends diagonally to the left from border to near cloud 6. At least five to 10 times scarcer than the preceding.

Collecting Notes

About 400 to 750 specimens are known of 1801 BB-214, slightly edging BB-213 for the title of scarcest issue of the year. However, in an absolute sense, enough exist that every numismatist who wants one can have one.

Most specimens exist in lower grade levels. However, the Carter and Eliasberg specimens are particularly notable, apparently the finest known by a wide margin, at MS-65 (PCGS) and MS-64 (PCGS), respectively.

Notable Specimens

Carter Specimen. MS-65 (PCGS). Amon Carter, Jr. Collection (Stack's, 1984) lot 232. "Gem Brilliant Unc., wholly prooflike." • Private Texas collection, displayed at the 2001 Atlanta ANA Convention.

Eliasberg Specimen. MS-64 (PCGS). Die State II. David S. Wilson Collection, 1906 privately • J.M. Clapp • John H. Clapp • Clapp estate, 1942 • Louis E. Eliasberg Sr. Collection (Bowers and Merena, April 1997) lot 2194 • Legend Numismatics • Phillip Flannagan Collection (Bowers and Merena, November 2011) lot 4284 • Steve Contursi, Chris Napolitano and Robert Lehmann, jointly • Cardinal Collection (American Numismatic Rarities June 2005) lot 55 • Private Midwest collection.

Midwest Specimen. AU-58 (PCGS). Private Midwest collection.

Chicago Sale Specimen. AU-58 (PCGS). Chicago Signature Sale (Heritage, August 2011) lot 7251 • Baltimore Sale (Stack's Bowers, November 2011) lot 2608.

Ebsen Specimen. AU-58 (NGC). Buddy Ebsen Collection (Superior, May 1987) lot 1921 • Worrell Family Collection Sale (Superior, September 1993) lot 1300 • Cardinal Collection (Heritage, July 1997) lot 6504.

Hollinbeck-Kagin Specimen. AU-58. Hollinbeck-Kagin Sale, June 1970, lot 637, Close date, Unc.

Shore Specimen. AU-58. A. Bernard Shore Collection (Superior, 1988) lot 2226, Close Date. Bolender-4a. "Spur on D of UNITED. Faint reverse crack from the dentil to the right of the second S in STATES. AU-58."

Hering Specimen. AU-55 (PCGS). Michael Hering Collection (Heritage, January 2002) lot 7239 • Dallas Signature Sale (Heritage, October 2008) lot 1098 • Dr. Robert Hesselgesser Collection (Ira and Larry Goldberg, September 2011) lot 5123 • Warren Miller Collection.

Total Estimated Population

MS-65 or better: 1 (URS-1)
MS-64: 1 (URS-1)
MS-63: 0 (URS-0)
MS-60 to 62: 0 (URS-0)
AU-50 to 58: 8 to 15 (URS-4)
VF-20 to EF-45: 210 to 400 (URS-9)
G-4 to F-15: 175 to 325 (URS-9)
Total for all grades combined: 400 to 750 (URS-10)
Estimated Total Condition Census: 65-64-58 (multiples)

1801 BB-301

1801 "Proof Restrike" Dollars

No Proof dollars were struck in 1801. Generations later in the 1870s it is thought that certain Mint officials created these by combining dies made much later than 1804. Technically they are not "restrikes" as no originals were made. The proper term is *novodels*, a coin made later than the date indicated for which no originals of that date exist from the same dies. Over the years, the term *restrike* has been applied to the Proof dollars dated 1801, 1802, and 1803. However, restrike implies that originals were made, usually from the same dies, and in the instance of the 1801-2-3 Proofs, there never were original counterparts. These Proofs are believed to have been made in the 1870s, using a closed collar and beaded border process not used at the Mint during the 1801-1804 era, and were struck from newly-made dies. The reverse die was made in or about 1834 for use in making the first run of 1804-dated dollars (known as Class I today). A study of die characteristics shows that this die was first used to make Class I 1804-dated dollars, then 1802 Proofs, then 1803 Proofs, and finally 1801 Proofs. The obverse was made in the 1870s. The 1801, 1802, and 1803 dollars first appeared on the market in 1876. The weight ranges from close to 420 grains (same as the *current trade dollar* but heavier than the standard silver dollar) to slightly higher.

1801 Proof novodel: First struck at the Mint in the mid-1870s from an obverse die made in the mid-1870s and from a reverse made in the early 1830s. Intended for sale to numismatists. Struck in the same time period, but just after the 1803 novodels were struck.

Of the 1801-2-3 novodel dates, the 1801 Proof dollar is by far the rarest, although its elusive quality was not generally recognized until recent decades. Numerous collections which had an example of the 1804 lacked the 1801. It is estimated that no more than five were made. No more than two or three can be traced today. Only a few collectors have ever been fortunate to have owned one.[1]

Obverse: The obverse of the 1801 novodel is anomalous, and is stylistically different from either the original dollars of this date or the other novodels dated 1802-3-4. I believe that it was made at the Mint in the 1870s, possibly starting with a die that had received an impression of the Draped Bust punch, but no other details, in the early 1830s.

As noted in the introductory text, the differences include the following:

The 1801 has curved-top 1's in date, quite unlike the straight-top 1's of the early 1800s.

The stars on the 1801 are entirely unlike any used on original early silver dollars or the novodels of 1802-3-4. On the 1801, the stars do not have narrow, somewhat delicate points. Instead, the stars are, as Newman and Bressett relate, heavy with 60° angles to the points, somewhat like a traditional Star of David.

The letters in LIBERTY are more angular, without curves to the inside of the serifs. A different letter punch font was used to make the obverse of the 1801 novodel, in contrast to the traditional, early font (with curves to the inside of the serifs) employed on the novodels of 1802-3-4.

In addition, the obverse die has these characteristics: On the left, the stars are fairly evenly spaced, with

---

[1] For an expanded discussion and detailed history see "1801-2-3 Novodels," by R.W. Julian, and "1801-2-3-4 Dollars, by Q. David Bowers, in the first edition of this book.

excellent alignment of the star points. On the right, the star spacing is also of a high order, except that stars 11 and 12 are slightly closer together than are the other pairs. The alignment of the star points is excellent. The letters in LIBERTY are well spaced and aligned. I conclude that the die represents the work of a skilled craftsman.

As is the case with all 1801-2-3-4 novodels, the denticles on the borders are bead-like (rather than the tooth-like style used in the early 1800s).

The left tip of the highest curl is missing, a flaw caused by a broken portrait punch. This flaw also is represented on the 1804 novodels, but not the 1802 and 1803.

Obverse die used to strike 1801 Proof novodels only.

Reverse: The reverse, called "Reverse X" by Eric P. Newman and Kenneth E. Bressett, is a Mint copy of the Heraldic Eagle reverse type used to coin silver dollars of the dates 1798-1803, but is not precisely identical to any die of that era. It was made by using a Heraldic Eagle punch, and adding details including the letters of UNITED STATES OF AMERICA, stars above the eagle, and the berries and their stems. Old letter punches, the Small Letters font of 1798 or a similar set, were used; the lopsided T, with the left serif shorter than the right, is distinctive. Twelve of the arrows were part of the eagle punch (the 13th arrow, with its tiny shaft and head to the right of the two leftmost large shafts, was added by hand and differs slightly on this as compared to Reverse Y). This identical die was used to coin all 1801-2-3 novodel and Class I 1804 dollar varieties.

The A in STATES straddles clouds 3 and 4; O in OF is entirely over cloud 7. The arc star pattern is employed, as was standard after 1798. UNITED STATES OF AMERICA in the same general Small Letters font as used 1798-1803. The 12 arrows in the Heraldic Eagle punch are perfectly formed and delineated (as noted, a 13th was later added by hand), far better than any definition seen on any original circulation strike dollar c. 1798-1803.

Top right berry slightly lower on branch than top left berry. The border denticles are more bead-like (later style) than tooth-like (original style).

"Reverse X" die was used to strike 1801, 1802, 1803, and Class I 1804 novodel silver dollars.

Die States[1]

Die State I: Obverse without cracks. Reverse with tiny crack through NITED to wing tip. May not exist with perfect obverse die.

Die State II: Obverse crack at the denticle above the B in LIBERTY through that letter to the curl left of Ms. Liberty's ear, another crack from below bust through the bottom of the date through the stars on the left (description from Newman-Bressett, 1962; Kenneth E. Bressett advised the author that the illustration of the reverse of the 1801 restrike in that book was not of an 1801 but, rather, was a "stock photo" of an 1802 or 1803 reverse, mentioned here for the record). Reverse with hairline crack from top right serif of N, sloping slightly downward through ITED, and ending at the bottom of the leftmost wing tip feather Cf. Newcomer specimen.

Proof mintage: Unknown; possibly fewer than 5; in any event, fewer than any other 1801-2-3-4 novodel.

Approximate population Proof-65 or better: 3 (URS-3)
Approximate population Proof-60 to 64: 0 (URS-0)

---

[1] In the first edition of this book,, reference was made to an apparent Die State III with advanced obverse and reverse die cracks, as seen on the Amon Carter specimen. However, upon subsequent examination of the coin itself, it was determined that the anomalies seen were, in actuality, a crack in the metal planchet, running completely through, from obverse to reverse, and from the edge to near the center of the coin.

ADDITIONAL INFORMATION

Dickeson on 1801 Dollars

The following appeared in Dr. Montroville W. Dickeson's 1859 book, *An American Numismatical Manual* and told of an apparently short-lived influx of silver dollars dated 1801 appearing for sale:

> The high premiums paid for specimens of this emission, lately brought to light, and into the market, a very considerable number, and also of the emissions from 1795 to 1803, which furnished a temporary supply to collectors. Apart from this, they are getting to be scarce, and soon must again be so, as a small number coined, with the inducement to bring them out, has had the effect, we think, to develop the full supply.

The Year 1801 in History

In 1801 the United States entered a state of war—in this case undeclared—when Yusuf Karamanli, pasha of Tripoli, ordered his soldiers to cut down the American flag after the United States refused to pay tribute to Barbary Coast pirates. Several years later, on February 16, 1804, U.S. troops led by Lt. Stephen Decatur sneaked aboard the captured American ship *Philadelphia* in Tripoli harbor, attacked the guards, and set the ship afire, before rowing away to safety. In 1805, the U.S. consul in Tunis assembled a rag-tag army in Egypt, which crossed 600 miles of desert to attack Tripoli from the rear. The phrase in the *Marine Hymn*, "to the shores of Tripoli," refers to this conflict.

Thomas Jefferson was inaugurated on March 4, 1801, following his controversial election finalized on the 36th ballot by the House of Representatives on February 17.

He abolished lavish social events at the White House and dressed casually to receive visitors. To American citizens, he promised "peace, commerce and honest friendship with all nations—and tangling alliances with none." John Marshall, then secretary of state, was named chief justice of the Supreme Court. During the next 34 years his court would make several landmark decisions affecting interpretation of the Constitution.

The New York *Evening Post* was founded by Alexander Hamilton; in later decades it would become one of America's most influential newspapers. In New York City, the American Company of Booksellers was formed, and went on to sponsor five book fairs from 1802 to 1806. Congregationalist and Presbyterian religious denominations adopted the Plan of Union, which permitted them to combine their resources in frontier areas, and allow ministers from each denomination to use the same church at different times. On January 1, Parliament created the United Kingdom of Great Britain and Ireland. French inventor Joseph Marie Jacquard invented an automatic loom which used punched cards to control movements and reproduce designs; the device would continue in wide use for more than a century afterward.

At the Mint, half dollars, which had not been coined since 1797, were first produced utilizing the Draped Bust obverse design with the Heraldic Eagle reverse. The famous "Three Errors" large cent was produced, with the reverse having these blunders: UNITED appeared as IINITED, the fraction was a mathematically meaningless 1/000, and there was just one stem (instead of two) to the wreath.

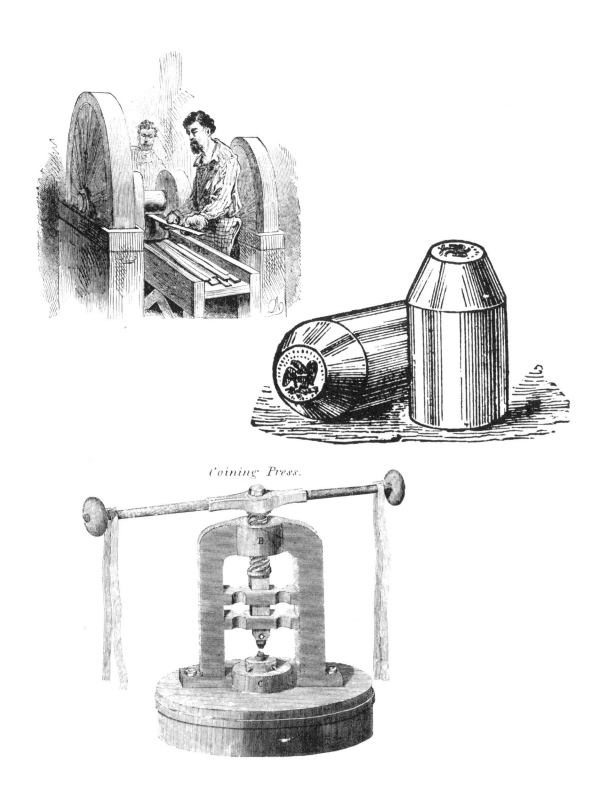

Coining Press.

Machinery and devices relating to late eighteenth and early nineteenth century coin production. From top: Rolling machine for the preparation of planchet strips, steel dies, an early hand-operated coining press of the type used at the first Philadelphia Mint beginning in 1792.

CHAPTER 15

1802/1 AND 1802 SILVER DOLLARS

MINTAGE (ALL VARIETIES)
Calendar year, Mint report: 41,650
Coins bearing date, author's estimate: 80,000

1802/1 SILVER DOLLARS

BB to Bolender to Haseltine Equivalents

BB Number	Bolender #	Haseltine #	Rarity	Average Grade
BB-231	B-1	H-1	URS-8	VF-27
BB-232	B-4	H-4	URS-10	VF-31
BB-233	B-2	H-2	URS-8	VF-26
BB-234	B-3	H-3	URS-10	VF-31
BB-235	B-9	---	URS-7	VF-31

1802 SILVER DOLLARS

BB to Bolender to Haseltine Equivalents

BB Number	Bolender #	Haseltine #	Rarity	Average Grade
BB-241	B-6	H-6	URS-12	VF-36
BB-242	B-5	H-5	URS-8	VF-30

Coinage Context

Mintage figures: Only 41,650 silver dollars were reported as having been coined in calendar year 1802. However, the proportionately large number of extant specimens indicates that many more than that must have been coined bearing the 1802 date, in 1803 and/or 1804.

Numismatic Information

Commentary: Overdates exist in close date and wide date form. The close date varieties are BB-231, 232, and 235, while the wide dates are BB-233 and 234. While wide-date and close-date terminology has been popular, these adjectives are quite arbitrary and, on their own, do little to help with identification. However, on BB-231, 232, and 235, the 0 and 2 in the date are closer together than on BB-233 and 234. None of the five 1801 undertype dies used for the overdates was ever employed for 1801-dated coinage; this can be easily ascertained by observing the position of star 13 on both 1801 dies (farther from bust) and the five 1802/1 dies (closer to bust).

While there are no legendary rarities among 1802 dollars, BB-235 is considered to be quite elusive. Only a small fraction of 1802 dollars in existence have been attributed. Thus, the possibility exists not only for finding scarce issues such as BB-235 for "type" prices, but to discover a new die variety.

1802/1 dollar die varieties are fairly difficult to attribute. As most buyers seek only the overdate, not a specific Bolender variety, relatively few coins have been attributed, as noted. Because of this, I believe that the number of known specimens of the various die varieties will increase, should collecting by varieties become more popular than it is now.

In terms of availability, 1802 BB-241 overwhelms every other die variety and is many times more plentiful. As of October 1992, NGC and PCGS have designated one 1802/1 dollar as Mint State and 10 specimens of the 1802 regular date. Presumably, most of the 10 are of the BB-241 variety.

Overdates: The year 1802 is distinguished by the presence of five different varieties of 1802/1 overdates from as many obverse dies. Just why five 1801 dies were overdated with a final 2 digit is not clear, inasmuch as at least three regular 1801 varieties (1801 BB-212, 213, and 214) were struck later than 1801, quite possibly in 1802. Perhaps, the answer is that the five known dies that were overdated had not been hardened yet in the die-making process. Thus, another digit could be stamped over the final 1 without any problem. Possibly, the other 1801 dies that were not overdated (1801 BB-212, 213, and 214) were already hardened, and were not suitable for alteration.

Striking order. Attention was not paid to striking coins in the years the dies bore. I consider it highly probable that many 1802-dated dollars were struck in 1803. The production of 1801, 1802, and 1803 dollars seems to have been done with the obverse dies mixed, as evident by the primary use of just two reverse dies with a much larger number of obverses.

Bearing the 1802 date and sharing one common reverse are 1802/1 BB-231, 1802/1 BB-232, and 1802 BB-241. Apparently, BB-231 and BB-232 were struck before 241.

Bearing the 1802 date and sharing another common reverse are 1802/1 BB-233, 1802/1 BB-234, 1802/1 BB-235, and 1802 BB-242. Die progression studies show that 1802/1 BB-233 represents the first use of this die, which was also used to coin 1801 BB-214 and 1803 BB-251 and 252, in addition to the other 1802 dollars mentioned.

If one assumes that strikings from the same reverse die occurred at the same time, this would give two "striking periods." Which one occurred first is not known. I have not had the opportunity to make detailed die studies of actual specimens of BB-235 and BB-242. If this is done at a future date, additional conclusions may be drawn. It is known that the reverse die was relapped after 1802/1 BB-233 was struck. This would have necessitated removing the reverse die from the press. Because of this, another "striking period" could have occurred after BB-233 was produced.

Striking Period 1
1802/1 BB-231 • 1802/1 BB-232 • 1802 BB-241

Striking Period 2
1802/1 BB-233 • 1802/1 BB-234 • 1802/1 BB-235 • 1802 BB-242

SUMMARY OF CHARACTERISTICS

(1802/1 AND 1802 COMBINED)

CIRCULATION STRIKES

Enabling legislation: Act of April 2, 1792

Designer of obverse: Robert Scot (after Stuart), model by John Eckstein

Designer of reverse: Robert Scot (from the Great Seal)

Weight and composition: 416 grains; .8924 silver, balance copper

Melting value (silver bullion value) in year minted: $1.03+

Dies prepared: Unknown

Circulation strike mintage, calendar year: 41,650 (all varieties of 1802 combined; may include some struck from dies dated earlier; figures do not include pieces reserved for the Assay Commission; these are given in parentheses); Delivery figures by day: January 26: 731 (+1) • March 8: 9,110 (+3) • June 22: 8,710 (+2) • August 27: 957 (+2) • November 8: 10,220 (+1) • December 8: 3,240 (+1) • December 29: 8,682 (+1).

Estimated circulation strike mintage of 1802-dated dollars (author's estimate): 80,000 (rounded).

Estimated quantity melted: Unknown

Estimated total population 1802/1 Overdate
    MS-65 or better: 0 (URS-0)
    MS-64: 1 (URS-1)
    MS-63: 2 to 3 (URS-2)
    MS-60 to 62: 4 to 8 (URS-4)

    AU-50 to 58: 20 to 40 (URS-6)
    VF-20 to EF-45: 650-1,300 (URS-11)
    G-4 to F-15: 350 to 700 (URS-10)
    Total for all grades combined: 1,000 to 2,000 (URS-12)
    Estimated Total Condition Census: 64-63-63-62+-62-62

Characteristics of striking: Depends upon the variety. If weakly struck, this is often observed at the center of the obverse and among the stars above the eagle on the reverse.

Estimated total population 1802:
    MS-65 or better: 5 to 8 (URS-4)
    MS-64: 8 to 15 (URS-5)
    MS-63: 8 to 15 (URS-5)
    MS-60 to 62: 10 to 20 (URS-6)
    AU-50 to 58: 100 to 225 (URS-9)
    VF-20 to EF-45: 1,100 to 2,100 (URS-12)
    G-4 to F-15: 300 to 600 (URS-10)
    Total for all grades combined: 2,500 to 3,000 (URS-13)
    Estimated Total Condition Census: 65 (multiples)

Characteristics of striking: Depends upon the variety. If weakly struck, this is often observed at the center of the obverse and among the stars above the eagle on the reverse.

Proofs: Proof novodels were made decades later.

Commentary: The year 1802 is remarkable for having five different overdated obverse dies.

1802/1 AND 1802 HERALDIC EAGLE

VARIETIES

1802/1 OVERDATE BB-231

(B-1, H-1)

Obverse: Close date, 02 closer than other figures. The 8 centered between 1 and O but too low. "Pocket" at throat and "collar" at neck-line, at base on most (but not all), a product of die clashing. The 1 is very close to lowest curl, but does not quite touch. A "dot" is before upper lip, under nose (visible only on high grade coins). On the left, star pairs 1-2 and 2-3 are closer together than are star pairs 5-6 and 6-7.

Obverse die used to strike 1802/1 BB-231 only.

Reverse: Same die used to coin 1801 BB-212, described earlier, but herewith repeated: The point of the leftmost arrowhead is under the left edge of the left serif of N in UNITED. The point of upper part of eagle's beak touches down on a point of a star slightly back from extreme star point. Only 12 arrows show plainly (13th faintly shows, but is difficult to find). First A in AMERICA touches third feather, and is connected by die crack to fourth feather. Leaf points more towards left corner of base of I in AMERICA.

Reverse die used to strike 1801 (intermediate state) BB-212; 1802/1 BB-231 (early state) and BB-232 (early state); 1802 BB-241 (slightly advanced intermediate state); and 1803 BB-253 (if it exists) and BB-254 (slightly advanced intermediate state), and BB-255 (terminal state).

Die States

Die State I: Perfect dies. May not exist.

Die State II: Obverse with clash marks. The state usually seen.

Collecting Notes

The 1802/1 BB-231 is very rare in all grades. Only about 100 to 175 are estimated to survive. It and BB-233 are of about equal availability. Specimens exist mainly in the lower grades, although a few AU pieces have appeared in the literature. For this variety, EF would be a notable condition. Apparently, Mint State examples are unknown.

Curiously, in 1881 Haseltine did not mention this variety or any other 1802/1 as being an overdate; this was by implication in that he called non-overdated varieties "perfect" dates.[1] H-1 (equivalent to BB-231) was called very scarce.

Notable Specimens

Cardinal Specimen. AU-58 (PCGS). Denver ANA Signature Sale (Heritage, August 1996) lot 7977 • Cardinal Collection • New York ANA Signature Sale (Heritage, July 1997) lot 6509 • Old Colony Sale (American Numismatic Rarities, December 2005) lot 1214 • Buckhead Sale (Stack's, October 2006) lot 171 • Dr. Robert Hesselgesser Collection (Ira and Larry Goldberg, September 2011) lot 5124.

Johnson Specimen. AU-58 (NGC). Burdette G. Johnson Collection • B.G. Johnson Estate (Spink America, June 1997) lot 193 • Pre-Long Beach Sale (Superior, May 1999) lot 2359 • Orlando Sale (Superior, January 2004) lot 472.

---

[1] The term *perfect date* is currently used by the *Guide Book of U.S. Coins* and certain other references to denote a date on a coin which is not overdated, notably repunched, or with some other distinctive feature.

Blevins Specimen. AU-55 (NGC). H.W. Blevins Collection (Superior, June 1988) lot 4771 • Warren Miller Collection.

Superior Specimen. AU-50. Superior Galleries Sale, September 1970, lot 1463. Toned AU.

CSNS Specimen. AU-50. CSNS Convention Sale (Kagin's, 1979) lot 370. "Choice AU-50."

Hesselgesser Specimen. EF-45 (PCGS). Diamond Collection (Heritage, January 2006) lot 4341 • Dr. Robert Hesselgesser Collection (Bowers and Merena, August 2010) lot 1070.

Houston Sale Specimen. EF-45 (PCGS). Houston Signature Sale (Heritage, December 2008) lot 849 • Long Beach Signature Sale (February 2009) lot 1579.

Stirling Specimen. EF-45. B. Max Mehl, January 1954, "Proof surface Uncirculated." • Frank M. Stirling Collection (Heritage, February 1986) lot 1341. "EF-45."

Total Estimated Population

MS-65 or better: 0 (URS-0)

MS-64: 0 (URS-0)

MS-63: 0 (URS-0)

MS-60 to 62: 0 (URS-0)

AU-50 to 58: 5 to 8 (URS-4)

VF-20 to EF-45: 40 to 70 (URS-7)

G-4 to F-15: 55 to 100 (URS-7)

Total for all grades combined: 100 to 175 (URS-8)

Estimated Total Condition Census: 58-58-55-50-50-45 (multiples)

1802/1 OVERDATE BB-232

(B-4, H-4)

Obverse: Close date, the 1 *firmly touching curl*. The 8 is tipped slightly to right. Star 13 almost touches bust near junction of drapery with bosom. Star 1 near hair, star 8 near Y, and star 7 distant from L. Base of B in LIBERTY is below base of E. On the left, star pairs 3-4 and 6-7 are farther apart than are any others. On the right, stars 8-9 are closer together (but only by a small margin) than are any others.

Obverse die used to strike 1802/1 BB-232 only.

Reverse: Described under 1801 BB-212 (repeated under 1802/1 BB-231).

Reverse die used to strike 1801 (intermediate state) BB-212; 1802/1 BB-231 (early state) and BB-232 (early state); 1802 BB-241 (slightly advanced intermediate state); and 1803 BB-253 (if it exists) and BB-254 (slightly advanced intermediate state), and BB-255 (terminal state).

Die States

Die State I: With perfect obverse die. Reverse die in early state. Scarcer than the following.

Die State II: Obverse now with a crack through the right side of the bust to near star 13. Reverse die in early state. The die state usually seen.

Die State III: Obverse with crack extending to the left to drapery. Second crack, short in length, approximately parallel and slightly below the first, develops at bosom. Reverse now with a tiny crack connecting the base of the first A in AMERICA to the third feather. Rare.

Collecting Notes

It is believed that about 400 to 750 1802/1 BB-232 dollars exist, about the same number as estimated for BB-234. Most examples are in lower grades, although AU and Mint State coins have been reported.

Notable Specimens

Queller Specimen. MS-63 (NGC). Queller Family Collection of Silver Dollars (Heritage, April 2008) lot 2080.

Generales Specimen. MS-63. Generales Collection (Stack's, 1984) lot 1254. "Choice Brilliant Unc., Wholly prooflike, has the appearance of a restrike! Some faint planchet adjustment marks."

Carter Specimen. MS-62+ (PCGS). Amon G. Carter Jr. Collection (Stack's, January 1984) lot 233 • Private Midwest collection.

Davis Specimen. MS-62 (PCGS). Davis-Graves (James Davis) Collection (Stack's, 1954) lot 1326. "Lustrous and nicely toned, but struck weakly on left side. Unlisted die breaks on obverse make this coin so much the rarer. Left side of 8 recut. Reverse has prooflike surface. Not quite in the 'gem' class. Unc." • Unknown intermediaries • Fort Worth Signature Sale (Heritage, March 2010) lot 1204.

Long Beach Sale Specimen. MS-61 (NGC). Long Beach Signature Sale (Heritage, February 2006) lot 1634 • Internet Sale (Heritage, April 2006) lot 11375 • Internet Sale (Heritage, May 2006) lot 13220.

1949 ANA Sale Specimen. MS-60. 1949 ANA (incorrectly attributed as H-1) (Numismatic Gallery, August 1949) lot 207 • Harold Bareford Collection (Stack's, 1981) lot 421. "Brilliant Unc., even steel, russet, and iridescent toning. Sharply struck even though the obverse is starting to 'mound.'"

Smith Specimen. MS-60. Elliot Smith Collection (J.G. Morgenthau & Co.) • T. James Clarke Collection (New Netherlands 48th Sale, 1956) lot 647. "Strictly Unc. Evenly centered, narrow thin border on obverse.

Sharp, uniform impressions, boldly struck throughout. Faint indications of mint adjustment marks towards the upper left obverse border. Splendid blue and pinkish gold iridescence."

Cardinal Specimen. AU-58 (PCGS). CSNS Signature Sale (Heritage, April 2001) lot 6570 • Cardinal Collection (American Numismatic Rarities, June 2005) lot 56.

Miller Specimen. AU-58 (NGC). Warren Miller Collection.

Hesselgesser Collection. AU-55 (PCGS). Thaler Collection (American Numismatic Rarities, March 2006) lot 1074 • Dr. Robert Hesselgesser Collection (Ira and Larry Goldberg, September 2011) lot 5125.

Total Estimated Population

MS-65 or better: 0 (URS-0)
MS-64: 0 (URS-0)
MS-63: 1 or 2 (URS-1)
MS-60 to 62: 2 to 4 (URS-2)
AU-50 to 58: 5 to 10 (URS-4)
VF-20 to EF-45: 275 to 500 (URS-10)
G-4 to F-15: 125 to 225 (URS-9)
Total for all grades combined: 400 to 750 (URS-10)
Estimated Total Condition Census: 63-63-62+-62-61-60

1802/1 Overdate BB-233

(B-2, H-2)

Obverse: Wide date, the *most space* between I and 8. The I farther from curl than last. Last star close to bust. Uppermost wave centered under E. On the left, star pairs 2-3 and 5-6 are closer together than are any other stars. On the right, stars 10-11 are farther apart than any others, and stars 11-12 are the closest together.

Obverse die used to strike 1802/1 BB-233 only.

Reverse: Description under 1801 BB-214, herewith repeated: The point of the leftmost arrowhead is under the center of the left upright of the N in UNITED. There is a "spur" on the curved part of D. Leaf points under center of I in AMERICA. point of a star touches the outside of upper part of eagle's beak slightly above beak's point. Called Reverse B by Bolender, this die was mated with obverses dated 1801, 1802, and 1803.

Die crack sequences reveal that 1802/1 BB-233 represents the first use of this reverse die; 1801-dated coins were struck later.

Reverse die used to strike 1801 BB-214 (typically with crack from border toward cloud 6); 1802/1 BB-233 (perfect; first use of the die), BB-234 (die relapped, cloud 6 mostly missing, some arrowheads disconnected; some with clash mark from cloud 5 to border above O), and BB-235; 1802 BB-242 (spur on D from now on); 1803 BB-251 (relapped, struck before BB-252) and BB-252 (relapped, struck after BB-251).

Die States
Die State I: Perfect dies.

Collecting Notes
Only about 100 to 175 are known of 1802/1 BB-233. Specimens appear on the market with about the same frequency as BB-231, which isn't very often. As is the case with the preceding, specimens of BB-233 are nearly always found in lower grades. AU specimens are great rarities, and it may be the case that no Mint State coins survive.

Notable Specimens
Eliasberg Specimen. AU-58 (PCGS). S.H. and H. Chapman, January 1900 • J.M. Clapp • John H. Clapp • Clapp estate, 1942 • Louis E. Eliasberg Sr. Collection (Bowers and Merena, April 1997) lot 2195 • Pre-Long Beach Sale (Superior, June 2002) lot 4400 • Dale Friend Collection.

CSNS Sale Specimen. AU-50 (PCGS). CSNS Signature Sale (Heritage, April 2010) lot 2156 • Orlando Signature Sale (Heritage, January 2012) lot 3786.

Miller Specimen. AU-50 (NGC). Warren Miller Collection.

San Francisco Rarities Specimen. AU-50 (PCGS). San Francisco Rarities Sale (Bowers and Merena, July 2005) lot 688 • 73rd Anniversary Sale (Stack's, October 2008) lot 395.

Hesselgesser Specimen. AU-50 (PCGS). Lake Michigan and Springdale Collections Sale (American Numismatic Rarities, June 2006) lot 2043 • Dr. Robert Hesselgesser Collection (Ira and Larry Goldberg, September 2011) lot 5126.

1988 ANA Specimen. AU-50. ANA Convention Sale (Heritage, 1988) lot 968. "AU (50/50)."

Long Beach Specimen. EF-45. Long Beach Exposition Sale (Heritage, 1988) lot 971. "EF (45/45)."

Earle Specimen. EF-45. George H. Earle Collection (Henry Chapman, 1912) • Schuyler Collection. • M.H. Bolender Collection, 1952, lot 170. "EF, nearly Unc."

New York Specimen. EF-40. Metropolitan New York Convention Sale (Stack's, 1967) lot 1179. "EF."

Herdegen Specimen. EF-40. R.T. Herdegen Collection (Hans M.F. Schulman, 1973). "EF."

Leavitt Specimen. EF-40. Leavitt & Co., auctioneers, 1879 • Garrett Collection (Bowers and Ruddy, 1980) lot 695. "EF-40."

Total Estimated Population
MS-65 or better: 0 (URS-0)
MS-64: 0 (URS-0)
MS-63: 0 (URS-0)
MS-60 to 62: 0 (URS-0)
AU-50 to 58: 5 to 8 (URS-4)
VF-20 to EF-45: 65 to 130 (URS-8)
G-4 to F-15: 35 to 55 (URS-7)
Total for all grades combined: 100 to 175 (URS-8)
Estimated Total Condition Census: 58-50 (multiples)

1802/1 OVERDATE BB-234

(B-3, H-3)

Obverse: Wide overdate, with *most space* between 8 and 0. Small die crack is usually seen in the field between stars 8 and 9 and Liberty's forehead. On the left, star pairs 1-2 and 6-7 are more widely spaced than are any others. On the right, stars 8 and 9 are more widely spaced than are any others.

Obverse die used to strike 1802/1 BB-234 only.

Reverse: See description under 1801 BB-214; repeated under 1802/1 BB-233.

Reverse die used to strike 1801 BB-214 (typically with crack from border toward cloud 6); 1802/1 BB-233 (perfect; first use of the die), BB-234 (die relapped, cloud 6 mostly missing, some arrowheads disconnected; some with clash mark from cloud 5 to border above O), and BB-235; 1802 BB-242 (spur on D from now on); 1803 BB-251 (relapped, struck before BB-252) and BB-252 (relapped, struck after BB-251).

Die States

Die State I: Perfect obverse and reverse dies. May not exist.

Die State II: Obverse die with small raised crack in field opposite space between stars 8 and 9 about 40% of the distance to the forehead. Reverse die relapped. Most of cloud 6 is now missing. Some arrowheads disconnected. Scarcer than the following.

Die State III: Obverse with very light clash marks (from reverse clouds) visible above and slightly to the left of the date. Obverse crack opposite stars 8 and 9 now slightly enlarged and in the shape of an oblong pellet. Reverse die relapped. Most of cloud 6 is now missing. Some arrowheads disconnected. The usual die state seen.

Collecting Notes

An estimated 400 to 750 specimens exist of the BB-234 overdate, about as many as survive of BB-232. Although several Mint State pieces are known, most are in significantly lower grades, with VF being average.

Notable Specimens

Ebsen Specimen. MS-64 (PCGS). Buddy Ebsen Collection (Superior, June 1987) lot 1922 • Hain Family Collection (Stack's, January 2002) lot 1527 • Private Texas collection.

Cardinal Specimen. MS-63 (PCGS). Private collector • Tangible Asset Galleries • Cardinal Collection (American Numismatic Rarities, June 2005) lot 57 • Legend Numismatics • Private Midwest collection.

Queller Specimen. MS-62 (NGC). Harley L. Freeman Collection, C.S.N.S. Sale, 1977. • Goshen Collection (Stack's, February 1978) lot 310. • Ellis H. Robison Collection (Stack's, February 1982) lot 1881 • Stack's, privately to Queller Family, February 1982 • Robert Michael Prescott Sale (American Numismatic Rarities, January 2006) lot 660 • Queller Family Collection of Silver Dollars (Heritage, April 2008) lot 2081 • Baltimore Rarities Sale (Bowers and Merena, July 2008) lot 714 • Pre-Long Beach Sale (Ira and Larry Goldberg, September 2008) lot 948 • Keusch, Snow and Del Zorro Collections Sale (Stack's, November 2008) lot 3740.

Hesselgesser Specimen. MS-61 (PCGS). CSNS Signature Sale (Heritage, May 2004) lot 7962 • Dr. Robert Hesselgesser Collection (Ira and Larry Goldberg, September 2011) lot 5127 • Warren Miller Collection.

Dallas Sale Specimen. AU-58 (NGC). Dallas Signature Sale (Heritage, November 2007) lot 951.

Orlando Sale Specimen. AU-58 (NGC). Orlando Signature Sale (Heritage, July 2011) lot 3748

Detroit ANA Sale Specimen. AU-58 (NGC). Detroit ANA Signature Sale (Heritage, July 1994) lot 5464 • Old West and Franklinton Collections Sale (American

Numismatic Rarities, August 2006) lot 715 • Brooklyn Sale (Stack's, March 2007) lot 1058 • Johnson Blue Sale (Stack's, August 2010) lot 607 • Baltimore Sale (Stack's Bowers, March 2011) lot 3222 • Pittsburgh Signature Sale (Heritage, October 2011) lot 3847 • Orlando Signature Sale (Heritage, January 2012) lot 3296.

Reiver Specimen. AU-55 (NGC). W. Earl Spies Collection (Stack's, December 1974) lot 223 • Jules Reiver Collection (Heritage, January 2006) lot 23632.

Stark Specimen. AU-55. Steve Ivy, November 1982. Coin has die lump in field at 2 o'clock. • Dr. Robert Stark Collection.

Total Estimated Population

MS-65 or better: 0 (URS-0)
MS-64: 1 (URS-1)
MS-63: 1 (URS-1)
MS-60 to 62: 2 to 4 (URS-2)
AU-50 to 58: 5 to 10 (URS-4)
VF-20 to EF-45: 250 to 475 (URS-10)
G-4 to F-15: 150 to 275 (URS-9)
Total for all grades combined: 400 to 750 (URS-10)
Estimated Total Condition Census: 64-63-62-61-58 (multiples)

1802/1 OVERDATE BB-235

(B-9)

Obverse: The figures of date are small and well-spaced, the 8 centered between 1 and O and not too low as in No. 1, nor tipped to right, as in No. 4. Look at the overdate 2 over 1, and observe that the left top of 1 under 2 is in line with left top and base of 2. A flaw in the die shows midway between base of B in LIBERTY and end of curl on head just beneath. Liberty has closed lips, while the mouth is open on all other overdates.

Obverse die used to strike 1802/1 BB-235 only.

Reverse: See description under 1801 BB-214; repeated under 1802/1 BB-233.

Reverse die used to strike 1801 BB-214 (typically with crack from border toward cloud 6); 1802/1 BB-233 (perfect; first use of the die), BB-234 (die relapped, cloud 6 mostly missing, some arrowheads disconnected; some with clash mark from cloud 5 to border above O), and BB-235; 1802 BB-242 (spur on D from now on); 1803 BB-251 (relapped, struck before BB-252) and BB-252 (relapped, struck after BB-251).

Die States

Die State I: Obverse die without cracks. Reverse die relapped. Tiny crack between arrows and eagle's leg (as seen on all uses of this die). Usual state seen.

Die State II: Obverse with die cracks 5:00 rim to the drapery, and the border opposite star 13 through the center of the star 12 into the field past the inner point of star 11. The first published was the New Netherlands 51st Sale coin, VF/Fine. Rare. Reverse as preceding.

Die State III: As above, but with additional obverse crack from border through 02 of date into field above 8. Rarer than preceding.

Collecting Notes

The 1802/1 BB-235 is the rarest overdate of the year as well as the rarest all 1802 varieties. Only about 50 to 90 are estimated to be known. I have found no Mint State specimen.

Unknown to Haseltine in 1881, and to other early scholars, this obverse and die combination was discovered by M.H. Bolender in the Marmaduke Fox Collection in 1950 after the plates to his book went to press, but before the text was printed. Once the variety was announced, specimens started "coming out of the woodwork," as the listing below indicates.

Notable Specimens

Miller Specimen. AU-58 (NGC), Dallas Signature Sale (Heritage, November 2007) lot 952 • Warren Miller Collection.

Cardinal Specimen. AU-53 (PCGS). Boyd E. Hayward Collection (Bowers and Merena, September 1997) lot 849 • Cardinal Collection • Pre-FUN Elite Sale (Superior, January 2002) lot 1197 • Private collector • Dr. Robert Hesselgesser Collection (Ira and Larry Goldberg, September 2011) lot 5128.

Orlando Sale Specimen. AU-50 (PCGS). Orlando Signature Sale (Heritage, January 2010) lot 3569.

Philadelphia ANA Sale Specimen. EF-45 (PCGS). Philadelphia ANA Sale (Stack's Bowers, August 2012) lot 9349.

Albany Specimen. EF-45 (NGC), Cardinal Collection, privately to • Albany Collection (Heritage, September 2002) lot 7873 • William Luebke Collection (Heritage, January 2007) lot 5043.

Baldenhofer Specimen. EF-45. W.G. Baldenhofer. • A.J. Ostheimer 3rd. • Gilhousen Collection (Superior, 1973) lot 1279, 2 over 1. "Bolender-9b, with diagnostic die

chip between curl point and B, and the crack from rim to drapery, and the second crack through 11th and 12th stars to rim. Better than EF, richly toned."

New York Connoisseur Specimen. EF-40 (PCGS). New York Connoisseur Collection Sale (American Numismatic Rarities, March 2006) lot 1078.

Stark Specimen. EF-40, edge bruise. RARCOA, 1976. Surfaces not "richly toned" (thus eliminating duplication with the Baldenhofer coin). Sold to the following. • Dr. Robert Stark Collection.

Autumn Sale Specimen. VF-35. Stack's, 1978, lot 300. "Evenly spaced date. A strong VF, nearly EF."

Newport Specimen. VF-30. Newport Collection (Bowers and Ruddy, 1975) lot 389. "VF or better."

Willasch Specimen. VF-25. H. Roland Willasch Collection (Superior, 1990) lot 596. "VF-25."

Total Estimated Population

MS-65 or better: 0 (URS-0)
MS-64: 0 (URS-0)
MS-63: 0 (URS-0)
MS-60 to 62: 0 (URS-0)
AU-50 to 58: 3 to 4 (URS-3)
VF-20 to EF-45: 45 to 80 (URS-7)
G-4 to F-15: 5 to 10 (URS-4)
Total for all grades combined: 50 to 90 (URS-7)
Estimated Total Condition Census: 58-53-50-45-45-45

1802 BB-241

(B-6, H-6)

Obverse: Close perfect date. *Wide space between 8 and 0.* The figure 2 is distant from bust. Right foot of T in LIBERTY missing. This die must have been made about the same time as the reverse for 1801 BB-213, which also displays broken T letters from the same punch.

Obverse die used to strike 1802 BB-241 only.

Reverse: See description under 1801 BB-212 (repeated under 1802/1 BB-231). Third cloud from left has a protruding spur; die flaws below E and around D in UNITED.

Reverse die used to strike 1801 (intermediate state) BB-212; 1802/1 BB-231 (early state) and BB-232 (early state); 1802 BB-241 (slightly advanced intermediate state); and 1803 BB-253 (if it exists) and BB-254 (slightly advanced intermediate state), and BB-255 (terminal state).

Die States

Die State I: Perfect obverse die. Reverse as described above. Scarce.

Die State II: Obverse die with slight crack just beginning to develop from innermost point of star 7, headed toward junction of hair and highest ribbon. Scarce.

Die State III: Obverse die lightly relapped to remove the slight crack noted under II, making bottom arm of E somewhat light, removing the outline of the neck truncation and field at the left of the truncation, and introducing flat spaces in the lower left hair curls (one of which becomes a tiny "island"). By far the commonest die state.

Collecting Notes

With an estimated population of 1,500 to 2,750 specimens, 1802 BB-241 is more plentiful than all other varieties of 1802 combined! Indeed, it is the most common variety of the 1798-1803 Draped Bust style. In terms of all dates of early dollars, only 1795 Flowing Hair BB-21 and BB-27 are of about equal availability. Mint State specimens exist in multiples, a highly unusual situation for an early dollar. The spectacular list of "notable specimens," below, must surely contain duplications; yet, the first seven specimens listed as certified Gem MS-65 are distinct and separate coins!

Notable Specimens

Eliasberg Specimen. MS-65 (PCGS). Matthew A. Stickney Collection (Henry Chapman, 1907) lot 1116 • John H. Clapp • Clapp estate, 1942 • Louis E. Eliasberg Sr. Collection (Bowers and Merena, April 1997) lot 2196 • Private Texas collection.

Starr Specimen. MS-65 (PCGS). From Europe, via "a New York dealer" • New Netherlands Coin Co.'s 48th sale, November 1956, Lot 649 • Floyd T. Starr • Starr Collection (Stack's, October 1992) lot 578 • Phillip Flannagan Collection (Bowers and Merena, November 2001) lot 4293 • Private collector • Cardinal Collection (American Numismatic Rarities, June 2005) lot 58 • Legend Numismatics • Bob Simpson Collection.

Carter Specimen. MS-65 (PCGS). Amon G. Carter Jr. Collection (Stack's, January 2004) lot 234 • Private Midwest collection.

Moores Specimen. MS-65 (PCGS). Moores Collection (Sotheby's, November 1999) lot 44.

Hood Specimen. MS-65 (PCGS). Walton Hood Collection • Rarities Sale (Bowers and Merena, January 2003) lot 426.

Lee Specimen. MS-65 (NGC) Richard Doyle Collection (Heritage, February 2000) lot 6548 • Jack Lee Collection III (Heritage, November 2005) lot 2197 • New York Connoisseur Collection (American Numismatic Rarities, March 2006) lot 1079.

Koshkarian Specimen. MS-65 (NGC). Legend Numismatics, privately March 1995 • Haig Koshkarian Collection (American Numismatic Rarities, March 2004) lot 96 • Unknown intermediaries • Baltimore ANA Signature Sale (Heritage, July 2008) lot 1746 • Baltimore Sale (Bowers and Merena, November 2009) lot 3034.

Clarke Specimen. MS-63. T. James Clarke Collection (New Netherlands 48th Sale, 1956) lot 649. "Brilliant Unc. 'gem.' Pedigree: From Europe."

Merkin Specimen. MS-63. Lester Merkin, September 1970, lot 540. "Choice Unc."

Terrell Specimen. MS-63. Bowers and Ruddy Galleries, 1983, lot 72. "Sharply struck choice Unc."

Washington Specimen. MS-63. Suburban Washington Convention Sale (Pine Tree, 1975) lot 252. "Brilliant Unc."

C.S.N.A. Specimen. MS-63. California State Numismatic Association Sale, May 1974 • Suburban Washington Convention Sale (Pine Tree, 1975) lot 253. "Unc." (This may be the same as the Terrell Collection coin.)

Fairfield Specimen. MS-63. Fairfield Collection (Bowers and Ruddy, 1977) lot 1038. "Choice Unc."

Adams Specimen. MS-63. • Edgar H. Adams. • Col. E.H.R. Green. • F.C.C. Boyd. • Auction '80, lot 1327. "Gem Brilliant Unc."

RARCOA Auction '79 Specimen. MS-63. ANA Convention Sale (Heritage, 1988) lot 967. "Mint State (62/62)."

1988 ANA Specimen. MS-63. ANA Convention Sale (Heritage, 1988) lot 974. "Mint State (63/63), prooflike. Lightly cleaned."

Heifetz Specimen. MS-63. Jascha Heifetz Collection (Superior, 1989) lot 2405. "MS-63."

Willasch Specimen. MS-63. H. Roland Willasch Collection (Superior, 1990) lot 591. "MS-63."

Many more Choice Uncirculated specimens could be listed.

Total Estimated Population

MS-65 or better: 5 to 8 (URS-4)

MS-64: 8 to 15 (URS-4)

MS-63: 8 to 15 (URS-4)

MS-60 to 62: 10 to 20 (URS-5)

AU-50 to 58: 100 to 200 (URS-8)

VF-20 to EF-45: 1,100 to 2,000 (URS-12)

G-4 to F-15: 300 to 500 (URS-10)

Total for all grades combined: 1,500 to 2,750 (URS-12)

Estimated Total Condition Census: 65 (multiples)

1802 BB-242

(B-5, H-5)

Obverse: Normal date. Base of T in LIBERTY perfect. These two characteristics, used together, are diagnostic for the variety. Star 1 over 2.5 mm. from hair curl. Star 7 close to base of L, star 8 closer to base of Y, and star 13 even closer to bust. On the left, stars 3 and 4 as well as stars 5 and 6 are closer than the other star pairs. Stars 8 and 9 on the right are closer than the others; stars 12 and 13 are wider than the others. Distance of tip of 1 to curl is 0.2 mm. 1 and 8 in date more widely spaced than the other digits. The left base of 2 is very minutely repunched.

Obverse die used to strike 1802 BB-242 only.

Reverse: See description under 1801 BB-214, repeated under 1802/1 BB-233.

Kagin's 313th Sale: 707 described a reverse with a perfect T in UNITED; this has not been verified by the author; all others seen of this reverse have a defective T.

Reverse die used to strike 1801 BB-214 (typically with crack from border toward cloud 6); 1802/1 BB-233 (perfect; first use of the die), BB-234 (die relapped, cloud 6 mostly missing, some arrowheads disconnected; some with clash mark from cloud 5 to border above O), and BB-235; 1802 BB-242 (spur on D from now on); 1803 BB-251 (relapped, struck before BB-252) and BB-252 (relapped, struck after BB-251).

Die States

Die State I: Perfect obverse die. Reverse in state as described above.

Collecting Notes

With an estimated population of only 75 to 140 specimens, 1802 BB-242 is at once the rarest (by far) non-over-dated 1802, and the second rarest (after 1802/1 BB-235)

variety of the year. In 1881, this was the only variety of 1802 that Haseltine designated as rare.

Notable Specimens

Cardinal Specimen. AU-58 (PCGS). Warren Miller, privately to • Cardinal Collection (American Numismatic Rarities, June 2005) lot 59 • Dr. Robert Hesselgesser Collection (Ira and Larry Goldberg, September 2011) lot 5131 • Pre-Long Beach Sale (Ira and Larry Goldbergs, May 2012) lot 1315.

Hollinbeck-Kagin Specimen. AU-58. Hollinbeck-Kagin Sale, June 1970, lot 539. "Unc. golden.

Miller Specimen. AU-55 (NGC). Warren Miller Collection.

Howe Specimen. AU-55 (NGC). The Bolender Collection coin from the Howe Collection, called "EF sharp" by Bolender • Superior's Ruby, Gilhousen III (1973), lot 1280 (EF+) • 1975 ANA, lot 1022 (EF-40) • February 1981 (EF/AU) • RARCOA's Auction '86, lot 736 • The obverse is plated in the Bolender book; once called the second finest known • Deb-Ann Collection (Heritage, January 2009) lot 3949.

DeCoppet Specimen. AU-55. André DeCoppet Collection (James Kelly, 1955). "Practically Unc."

S.S. New York Sale Specimen. AU-53 (PCGS). Samuel Berngard and S.S. New York Collections Sale (Stack's, July 2008) lot 4551 • Pre-Long Beach Sale (Ira and Larry Goldberg, May 2009) lot 635.

Luebke Specimen. AU-53 (NGC). Long Beach Signature Sale (Heritage, May 2003) lot 6463 • William Luebke Collection (Heritage, January 2007) lot 5045.

Thaler Specimen. AU-50 (PCGS), Thaler Collection (American Numismatic Rarities, March 2006) lot 1081.

Matthews Specimen. AU-50 (NGC). Seller Collection (Bowers and Ruddy, March 1980) lot 3278 •

Jim Matthews Collection. (Coin illustrated in the first edition of this book.) • San Marino Collection Sale (Ira and Larry Goldberg, September 2002) lot 534.

Lee and Shaffer Collections Specimen. AU-50. Lee and Shaffer Collections (Superior, 1988) lot 3164. "Sharpness of AU-55, but unfortunately, retoned."

Bolender Specimen. EF-45. M.H. Bolender Collection, 1952. • Dr. Charles Ruby Collection, Gilhousen Sale, Part III, (Superior) • California Collection Sale, (Superior) lot 1335. • Superior Galleries, February 1981, lot 665. "EF-45/AU-50." • Paramount, Auction '86, lot 1802.

Bebee's Specimen. EF-40. *Numismatist* advertisement, 1953. EF.

Herdegen Specimen. EF-40. Herdegen Collection (Hans M.F. Schulman 1973), EF.

Total Estimated Population

MS-65 or better: 0 (URS-0)
MS-64: 0 (URS-0)
MS-63: 0 (URS-0)
MS-60 to 62: 0 (URS-0)
AU-50 to 58: 8 to 10 (URS-5)
VF-20 to EF-45: 50 to 95 (URS-7)
G-4 to F-15: 25 to 45 (URS-6)
Total for all grades combined: 75 to 140 (URS-8)
Estimated Total Condition Census: 58-58-55-55-55-53 (multiples)

1802 BB-302

1802 "PROOF RESTRIKE" DOLLARS

1802 Proof novodel: First struck at the Mint in the mid-1870s from an obverse die made before autumn 1834 and from a reverse made in the early 1830s. Intended for sale to numismatists. Struck in the same time period, but just before the 1803 novodels were struck. • The mintage was probably no more than eight, of which four or five can be traced today. This may be very slightly more available than the 1803. Even the greatest collections of the past were apt to lack an example.[1]

Obverse: The 2 in date is curled at top, differing from any original obverse, and of the same "fancy" or curlicue style seen on certain 1820 half dollars (but half dollar dies were made from a smaller punch). Star 1 is about the same distance from the second curl as star 7 is from L. The star positioning is cruder than any original dollar of this date. On stars 1 to 7, *all* points closest to adjacent stars are misaligned! Obviously, whoever made this die was not accustomed to this work. On the right, the stars are aligned better, but this is ruined by something else that never occurred on an original of this date: stars 12 and 13 are so close that they actually touch at their inner points!

Highest curl centered below the E in LIBERTY. Raised border with denticles made up of truncated bead-like denticles quite unlike the toothlike denticles of original dollars of the Draped Bust type. Original 1, 8, and 0 punches from the early 1800s were used to make the die. 2 copied from one of the "Fancy 2" digits used on half dollars of the 1820s. Perfect die without cracks.

The top left curl tip is intact on the 1802 (and 1803) novodels, whereas on the 1801 and 1804 issues it is missing (due to hub damage). Thus, the 1802 and 1803 dies were made before the others.

Obverse die used to strike 1802 Proof novodels only.

Reverse: As preceding, "Reverse X." See description under 1801 Proof novodel dollar.

"Reverse X" die used to strike 1801, 1802, 1803, and Class I 1804 novodel silver dollars.

Die State

Die State I: Obverse without cracks. Reverse with hairline crack from top right serif of N, sloping slightly downward through ITED, and ending at the bottom of the leftmost wing tip feather. (Cf. Cleneay and Wilharm specimens)

Proof mintage: Probably no more than 8.
Approximate population Proof-65 or better: 2 (URS-2)
Approximate population Proof-64 or better: 2 (URS-2)
Approximate population Proof-60 to 63: 0 (URS-0)

---

[1] For an expanded discussion and detailed history see "1801-2-3 Novodels," by R.W. Julian, and "1801-2-3-4 Dollars, by Q. David Bowers, in the first edition of this book. Also see the synopsis given in the present second edition under the 1801 Proof dollar.

Additional Information

The Year 1802 in History

In April 1802, the United States learned that Napoleon Bonaparte of France had secured the return of the Louisiana Territory via a secret treaty with Spain. President Jefferson sought to buy land on the lower Mississippi River to use as a port, but the U.S. minister to France, Robert R. Livingston, was unsuccessful. In October 1802, the remaining Spanish officials in New Orleans refused to let American ships use the port. The prospect of continuing difficulties prompted Jefferson in 1803 to negotiate the purchase of the Territory from France. The Enabling Act, signed by Jefferson on April 30, 1802, provided that a territory established under the Ordinance of 1787 could become a state, once certain procedures were followed.

The U.S. Military Academy was established at West Point and opened on July 4. The Library of Congress issued what is believed to be the first catalog of books printed in America. The first version of *The New Practical American Navigator* to be published by Nathaniel Bowditch, a revision of an earlier work by J. Hamilton Moore, was distributed and would go on to many editions. One hundred merino sheep were brought to the United States and set the foundation for a textile industry using high-quality wool. E.I. Du Pont du Nemours and Company, manufacturer of gunpowder, was founded on the Brandywine River near Wilmington, Delaware. In Saratoga Springs, New York, the first lavish "grand hotel," the Union Hotel, was built by Gideon Putnam, and set the pace for the town becoming an important social center and spa during the nineteenth century. The Abel Porter & Co. brass mill began operations in Waterbury, Connecticut, a city that would become famous for its metalworking industries, including the later Scovill Works (important manufacturer of Hard Times and other tokens in the 1830s and 1840s).

British Parliament revoked the income tax initiated in 1799. Mme. Tussaud's first wax museum was opened in London; the concept would become popular, and the Tussaud name would be associated with wax museums for the ensuing two centuries. Thomas Wedgwood of England, son of famed ceramics manufacturer Josiah Wedgwood, took the world's first photographs, using paper sensitized with silver nitrate, but was unable to permanently fix the image.

CHAPTER 16

1803 SILVER DOLLARS

MINTAGE (ALL VARIETIES)
Calendar year, Mint report: 85,634
(includes 19,570 in calendar year 1804)
Coins bearing date, author's estimate: 60,000

1803 SILVER DOLLARS

BB to Bolender to Haseltine Equivalents

BB Number	Bolender #	Haseltine #	Rarity	Average Grade
BB-251	B-1	H-1	URS-9	VF-25
BB-252	B-5	H-5	URS-11	VF-31
BB-253	B-2	H-2	May not exist	N/A
BB-254	B-4	H-4	URS-10	VF-30
BB-255	B-6	H-6	URS-12	VF-28
BB-256	B-3	H-3	URS-6	VF-32

Coinage Context

Final mintage: 1803-dated dollars were the last produced during the early nineteenth century. By this time it had become profitable to export or melt newly-minted dollars, and the continued production of them would have been an exercise in futility. Had it not been for this factor, coinage undoubtedly would have continued for many years. The existence of so many worn early dollars of the 1794-1803 years is mute testimony to their success in domestic channels of commercial circulation (other dollar-sized coins, notably the Spanish-American issues, circulated very effectively as well). After the end of the Draped Bust obverse, Heraldic Eagle reverse coinage, the mantle fell to the half dollar to be the largest silver coin of the realm, a mandate the denomination filled admirably. As discussed under the 1795 silver dollars, the half dollar denomination played second fiddle to the silver dollars. When large quantities of dollars were being made, small numbers of halves were produced. When dollars were not being minted, such as from mid-October 1794 through late spring 1795, and after early 1804, production of half dollars increased tremendously.

The Mint reported that 66,063 silver dollars were minted in calendar year 1803, and 19,570 were struck in 1804. As no original 1804-dated dollar has ever been found or reliably reported, the assumption is that these 19,570 coins bore earlier dates, probably mostly 1801, 1802, and 1803 (not necessarily all dated 1803, as some have suggested).

Numismatic Information

General information: Dollars dated 1803 include those of the Large 3 and Small 3 type. Walter H. Breen believes that the Large 3 type was struck in 1804. As an aid to collecting, the *Guide Book of United States Coins* helpfully divides the coinage of 1803 into the Small 3 varieties (of which there are five) and the Large 3 (just one variety, BB-255). Milferd H. Bolender referred to these as the Thin Top and Thick Top varieties.

All six varieties considered, 1803 dollars go from the very rare (BB-253, the very existence of which is doubted by some) to the very common (BB-255, the Large 3 variety, of which well over 1,000 are believed extant).

SUMMARY OF CHARACTERISTICS

1803

CIRCULATION STRIKES

Enabling legislation: Act of April 2, 1792

Designer of obverse: Robert Scot (after Stuart), model by John Eckstein

Designer of reverse: Robert Scot (from the Great Seal)

Weight and composition: 416 grains; .8924 silver, balance copper

Melting value (silver bullion value) in year minted: $1.03-$1.04.

Dies prepared: Unknown

Circulation strike mintage for calendar year 1803, calendar year:[1] 66,044 (may include some struck from dies dated earlier; figures do not include pieces reserved for the Assay Commission; these are given in parentheses); Delivery figures by day: February 3: 7,394 (+1) • February 28: 6,153 (+1) • March 15: 8,130 (+2) • March 31: 16,000 (+2) • April 5: 2,779

(+2) • May 26: 12,100 (+2) • June 30: 1,288 (+2) • December 12: 6,380 (+2) • December 31: 5,840 (+1).

Estimated circulation strike mintage of 1803-dated dollars (author's estimate): 60,000 (rounded).

Estimated quantity melted: Unknown

Estimated total population (all varieties):

   MS-65 or better: 0 (URS-0)

   MS-64: 2 (URS-2)

   MS-63: 6 to 8 (URS-4)

   MS-60 to 62: 12 to 20 (URS-5)

   AU-50 to 58: 45 to 100 (URS-8)

   VF-20 to EF-45: 1,300 to 2,300 (URS-12)

   G-4 to F-15: 900 to 1,600 (URS-12)

   Total for all grades combined: 2,300 to 4,000 (URS-13)

   Estimated Total Condition Census: 64-64-63 (multiples)

Characteristics of striking: Depends upon the variety. If weakly struck, this is often observed at the center of the obverse and among the stars above the eagle on the reverse.

Proofs: Proof novodels were made decades later.

Commentary: Some 1803 silver dollars are believed to have been struck in 1804.

---

[1] Also see circulation strike mintage for calendar year 1804, which consisted of 19,570 coins dated prior to 1804. If the figures 66,044 and 19,570 are added, a mintage of 85,634 is obtained for 1803, a figure given in the *Guide Book* and some other texts.

1803 HERALDIC EAGLE

VARIETIES

1803 BB-251

Small 3 in date

(B-1, H-1)

Obverse: Thin top to 3 in date, right top of 3 slanting toward bust, short left tip slanting toward 0. 1 does not touch curl. Stars 8 and 13 equidistant from Y and bust respectively, and each is close. Star 8 close to Y and in the same relative position to Y as on the 1804 dollar. Liberty's mouth open.

Obverse die used to strike 1803 BB-251 only.

Reverse: Described under 1801 BB-214, repeated herewith: The point of the leftmost arrowhead is under the center of the left upright of the N in UNITED. Leaf points under center of I in AMERICA. point of a star touches the outside of upper part of eagle's beak slightly above beak's point.

Called Reverse B by Bolender, this die was mated with obverses dated 1801, 1802, and 1803.

Reverse die used to strike 1801 BB-214 (typically with crack from border toward cloud 6); 1802/1 BB-233 (perfect; first use of the die), BB-234 (die relapped, cloud 6 mostly missing, some arrowheads disconnected; some with clash mark from cloud 5 to border above O), and BB-235; 1802 BB-242 (spur on D from now on); 1803 BB-251 (relapped, struck before BB-252) and BB-252 (relapped, struck after BB-251).

Die States

Die State I: Perfect obverse die. Reverse as described above. May not exist with perfect obverse.

Die State II: Obverse with light crack from dentils through left side of R in LIBERTY to hair. Reverse as preceding. The state usually seen.

Die State III: Obverse crack at top widens and splits into two sections at bottom of R, continuing down to hair. A new crack extends from the left side of 8 in the date up into the bust. Reverse as preceding. Slightly scarcer than Die State II.

Collecting Notes

The 1803 BB-251 dollar is scarce. Probably, about 240 to 450 exist totally, just enough to make it a challenge for the advanced collector to find. EF coins are scarce, AU pieces are very rare, and Mint State specimens have not been seen.

Notable Specimens

Reiver Specimen. AU-58+ (NGC). Purchased privately in the mid-1960s along with a group of large cents • Jules Reiver Collection (Heritage, January 2006) lot 23638 • Warren Miller Collection.

Cardinal Specimen. AU-55 (NGC). Kenneth C. Long Collection (Bowers and Merena, May 1995) lot 1207 • Cardinal Collection • Displayed by John J. Haugh at the 1998 Portland ANA Convention, and inadvertently sold • James Farrington Collection (Heritage, July 2002) lot 8456 • Cardinal Collection • Private collector.

Hesselgesser Specimen. AU-50 (PCGS). Warren Miller Collection • Lake Michigan and Springdale

Collections Sale (Stack's, June 2006) lot 2045 • Dr. Robert Hesselgesser Collection (Ira and Larry Goldberg, September 2011) lot 5132.

Benson Specimen. AU-50 (PCGS). B. Max Mehl, privately May 1946 • Benson Collection (Ira and Larry Goldberg, February 2002) lot 1192.

Luebke Specimen. AU-50 (NGC). Harlan Berk, privately October 2001 • William Luebke Collection (Heritage, January 2007) lot 5046.

Matthews Specimen. EF-45 (PCGS). "Cousin" Pete Matthews, via Jim McGuigan, privately August 1999 • Jim Matthews Collection • San Marino Collection Sale (Ira and Larry Goldberg, September 2002) lot 536.

Prestera Sale Specimen. EF-45 net. ("MS-62" NTC, cleaned). Dr. Tory Prestera Collection Sale (Stack's, June 2007) lot 1192.

Forrest Specimen. EF-45 net. (AU-50, cleaned) S.S. Forrest, Jr. Collection (Stack's, 1972) lot 987. "Brilliant AU."

Brooks Specimen. EF-45 net. (AU-50, cleaned) Brooks Collection (Bowers and Merena Galleries, 1989) lot 695. "AU-50."

Holmes Specimen. EF-45. Milton A. Holmes Collection (Stack's, 1960) lot 2264. "EF, choice."

Frontenac Specimen. EF-45. Frontenac Collection (Bowers and Merena, 1991) lot 2223. "EF-45 to AU-50."

Frontenac specimen (another). EF-40 (PCGS) Frontenac Collection (Bowers and Merena, 1991) lot 2224. "EF-40 (PCGS)."

DeCoppet Specimen. EF-40. André DeCoppet Collection (James Kelly, 1955). "EF."

Hollinbeck-Kagin Specimen. EF-40. Hollinbeck-Kagin Sale, August 1970, lot 1100. "EF."

Stirling Specimen. EF-40. Frank M. Stirling Collection (Heritage, February 1986) lot 1344.

Ebsen Specimen. EF-40. Buddy Ebsen Collection (Superior, 1987) lot 1927. "EF-40."

Total Estimated Population

MS-65 or better: 0 (URS-0)
MS-64: 0 (URS-0)
MS-63: 0 (URS-0)
MS-60 to 62: 0 (URS-0)
AU-50 to 58: 5 to 8 (URS-4)
VF-20 to EF-45: 155 to 300 (URS-9)
G-4 to F-15: 80 to 140 (URS-8)
Total for all grades combined: 240 to 450 (URS-9)
Estimated Total Condition Census: 58+-55-50-50-50-45 (multiples)

1803 BB-252

Small 3 in date.

(B-5, H-5)

Obverse: Thin top to 3, the 3 too high. Figures of date all close. Stars 8 and 13 are about equidistant from Y and bust, and much closer than stars 1 and 7 are from hair and L. On the left, star pairs 2-3 and 5-6 are closest, while stars 6-7 are noticeably wider than any of the others. On the right, stars 10-11 and 12-13 are wider apart than any others, but not by much. The 3 almost touches bust, and 1 is near curl.

Obverse die used to strike 1803 BB-252 only.

Reverse: Described under 1801 BB-214, repeated under 1803 BB-251, above.

In 1803 BB-252, the reverse is found with a spur on the outside lower right of the curve of the D in UNITED. Often found weakly struck at the centers. Some strikings show heavily bifurcated letters and were considered to be a separate die state (B-5a) by Bolender.

Reverse die used to strike 1801 BB-214 (typically with crack from border toward cloud 6); 1802/1 BB-233 (perfect; first use of the die), BB-234 (die relapped, cloud 6 mostly missing, some arrowheads disconnected; some with clash mark from cloud 5 to border above O), and BB-235; 1802 BB-242 (spur on D from now on); 1803 BB-251 (relapped, struck before BB-252) and BB-252 (relapped, struck after BB-251).

Die States

Die State I: With perfect obverse die. Reverse as described above. Some strikings have bifurcated letters on the reverse and are called Bolender-5a by Bolender, but I do not consider these to be a separate die state.

Collecting Notes

With an estimated population of 500 to 950 coins, 1803 BB-252 is the second most plentiful variety of this year. Examples are known in all major grade categories. Most

are in lower grades up through VF and EF. AU examples are rare, but are seen more often than most other varieties of the date. Several high quality Mint State coins exist. In fact, in Mint State, the BB-252 is the most populous variety of the year.

Notable Specimens

Schenkel Specimen. MS-63 (NGC). Father Flanagan's Boy's Town Sale (Superior, May 1990) lot 3879 • Chris Schenkel Collection (Bowers and Merena, November 1990) lot 369 • ANA Centennial Convention Sale (Bowers and Merena, August 1991) lot 445 • Dr. Jack Adams Collection (Superior, May 1992) lot 2123.

Carter Specimen. MS-63 (NGC). Amon G. Carter Jr. Collection (Stack's, January 1984) lot 236 • New York Connoisseur Collection Sale (American Numismatic Rarities, March 2006) lot 4082.

Baltimore Sale Specimen. MS-63 (PCGS). Baltimore Sale (Bowers and Merena, July 2006) lot 1177 • Treasures of S.S. New York Sale (Stack's, July 2009) lot 664.

Long Beach Sale Specimen. MS-63 (NGC). Long Beach Signature Sale (Heritage, May 2008) lot 883 • September Sale (Stack's, September 2008) lot 4353 • Keusch, Snow and Del Zorro Collections Sale (Stack's, November 2008) lot 3743 • Treasures of S.S. New York Sale (Stack's, July 2009) lot 665 • Orlando Rarities Sale (Bowers and Merena, January 2010) lot 425 • Baltimore Sale (Bowers and Merena, November 2010) lot 2243.

Numisma'95 Specimen. MS-62 (PCGS). Numisma'95 Sale (Stack's, November 1995) lot 1335 • Keusch, Snow and Del Zorro Collections Sale (Stack's, November 2008) lot 3744 • Los Angeles ANA Sale (Bowers and Merena, August 2000) lot 1689 • Chicago ANA Sale (Stack's Bowers, August 2011) lot 7405.

Allison Park Sale Specimen. MS-61 (PCGS). Allison

Park Collection Sale (American Numismatic Rarities, August 2004) lot 565.

Miller Specimen. MS-61 (NGC). Warren Miller Collection.

Alto Specimen. MS-60. Alto Collection (Stack's, 1970) lot 1068. "Brilliant Unc."

San Diego Specimen. MS-60. Mid-American, 1989, lot 719. "MS-60."

May Sale Specimen. MS-60. Stack's, 1991, lot 593. "Brilliant Unc."

Total Estimated Population

MS-65 or better: 0 (URS-0)
MS-64: 0 (URS-0)
MS-63: 3 to 4 (URS-3)
MS-60 to 62: 5 to 8 (URS-4)
AU-50 to 58: 10 to 20 (URS-6)
VF-20 to EF-45: 275 to 550 (URS-10)
G-4 to F-15: 200 to 350 (URS-9)
Total for all grades combined: 500 to 950 (URS-11)
Estimated Total Condition Census: 63-63-63-63-62-61

1803 BB-253

Image Unavailable

(Status uncertain)
Small 3 in date.
5th Edition Bolender says: "Now believed that no such variety exists."
(B-2, H-2)

Obverse: Thin top to 3, top parallel to bust, left tip parallel to 0. The 3 is lower than other figures, and the 1 defective at top. Upper stars equidistant from L and Y. First star distant from hair. (Description from Bolender book.)

Obverse die used to strike 1803 BB-253 only.

Reverse: Same die used to coin 1801 BB-212, described earlier, but herewith repeated: The point of the leftmost arrowhead is under the left edge of the left serif of N in UNITED. The point of upper part of eagle's beak touches down on a point of a star slightly back from extreme star point. Only 12 arrows show plainly (13th faintly shows, but is difficult to find). First A in AMERICA touches third feather, and is connected by die crack to fourth feather. Leaf points more towards left corner of base of I in AMERICA.

Reverse die used to strike 1801 (intermediate state) BB-212; 1802/1 BB-231 (early state) and BB-232 (early state); 1802 BB-241 (slightly advanced intermediate state); and 1803 BB-253 (if it exists) and BB-254 (slightly advanced intermediate state), and BB-255 (terminal state).

Die States

Die State I: Description not available.

Collecting Notes

1803 BB-253 is a major rarity *if it exists*. There is no illustration of it in the Bolender book, and no one with whom I have been in contact in connection with the present book has reported owning one. The 5th edition (1988) of the Bolender book has the added phrase, "Now believed that no such variety exists." Based upon auction appearances, with some extrapolation, perhaps five to 10 exist, *if they can be found*. If it exists, 1803 BB-253 is one of the key issues among all dates of Heraldic Eagle reverse dollars. Only at infrequent intervals have specimens been listed in past auctions.

Notable Specimens

Hollinbeck-Kagin Specimen. AU-50. Hollinbeck-Kagin Sale, June 1970, lot 641. "Near Unc."

Pradeau Specimen. EF-45. Superior, 1970, lot 466. "Toned choice EF-AU."

Pradeau specimen (another). EF-40. Pradeau Collection (Superior, 1970) lot 465. Toned EF.

Boyd Specimen. VF-20. "World's Greatest Collection (F.C.C. Boyd, Numismatic Gallery, 1945) lot 121. "VF."

Haines Specimen. G-4. Ferguson Haines Collection (S.H. and H. Chapman, 1888) lot 29. Good.

Total Estimated Population

MS-65 or better: 0 (URS-0)
MS-64: 0 (URS-0)
MS-63: 0 (URS-0)
MS-60 to 62: 0 (URS-0)
AU-50 to 58: 1 or 2 (URS-1)
VF-20 to EF-45: 3 to 6 (URS-2)
G-4 to F-15: 1 or 2 (URS-1)
Total for all grades combined: 5 to 10 (URS-4)
Estimated Total Condition Census: 50-45-40-20-4

1803 BB-254

Small 3 in date
(B-4, H-4)

Obverse: Thin top to 3, top side long, and ends near bust, very close. 1 firmly touches curl. Last star almost touches bust. Stars 7 and 8 distant from L and Y. On the left stars 4-5 and 5-6 are closer together than are any of the others. On the right, stars 10-11 and 12-13 are wider apart than are any others.

Obverse die used to strike 1803 BB-254 only.

Reverse: Same die used to coin 1801 BB-212, described earlier, repeated under 1803 BB-253 above.

Reverse die used to strike 1801 (intermediate state) BB-212; 1802/1 BB-231 (early state) and BB-232 (early state); 1802 BB-241 (slightly advanced intermediate state); and 1803 BB-253 (if it exists) and BB-254 (slightly advanced intermediate state), and BB-255 (terminal state).

Die States

Die State I: Perfect obverse die. Reverse as described above.

Collecting Notes

I estimate that about 300 to 550 examples are known of 1803 BB-254, placing it squarely in the scarce or rare class. Most specimens are in lower grades, with VF being about par. Examples exist through and including the AU categories, but truly Mint State coins are extremely rare.

The pressman was doing his job well when BB-254 dollars were struck, as these are usually sharp. Higher grade pieces are sometimes seen with prooflike surfaces. However, "higher grade" in this instance is apt to mean AU, as just a handful of Uncirculated examples are known.

Notable Specimens

Midwest Specimen. MS-64 (PCGS). Private Midwest collection.

Queller Specimen. MS-64 (NGC). May Sale (Stack's, May 1991) lot 593 • Queller Family Collection of Silver Dollars (Heritage, April 2008) lot 2083 • Joseph C. Thomas Collection (Heritage, April 2009)lot 2565.

Eliasberg Specimen. MS-63 (PCGS). William M. Friesner Collection (Édouard Frossard, June 7-8, 1894) • J.M. Clapp • John H. Clapp • Clapp estate, 1942. • Louis E. Eliasberg Sr. Collection (Bowers and Merena, April 1997) lot 2197 • Legend Numismatics • Phillip Flannagan Collection (Bowers and Merena, November 2001) lot 4298 • Private Midwest collection • Privately via Chris Napolitano • Cardinal Collection (American Numismatic Rarities, June 2005) lot 60 • Private Midwest collection.

Worrell Family Specimen. MS-61 (NGC). Club Cal Neva Sale (Superior, September 1987) lot 2302 • Worrell Family Collection (Superior, September 1993) lot 1304 • Private collector • Cardinal Collection • New York ANA Signature Sale (Heritage, July 1997) lot 6512 • Private collector • 65th Anniversary Sale (Stack's, October 2000) lot 1165 • Queller Family Collection of Silver Dollars (Heritage, April 2008) lot 2084 • Internet Sale (Heritage, May 2008) lot 62629 • Internet Sale (Heritage, August 2008) lot 64379 • Dallas Signature Sale (Heritage, October 2008) lot 1102 • Internet Sale (Heritage, November 2008) lot 24283 • Long Beach Signature Sale (Heritage, February 2009) lot 1582 • Internet Sale (Heritage, March 2009) lot 22444.

Miller Specimen. AU-58 (NGC). Larry Hanks, privately • Warren Miller Collection.

Hesselgesser Specimen. AU-55 (PCGS). Dr. Robert Hesselgesser Collection (Ira and Larry Goldberg, September 2011) lot 5134.

Mid-Winter ANA Specimen. AU-55 (PCGS). Mid-Winter ANA Signature Sale (Heritage, March 1998) lot 6039.

Thaler Specimen. AU-55 (PCGS). Thaler Collection (American Numismatic Rarities, March 2006) lot 1083.

Baldenhofer Specimen. AU-55. W.G. Baldenhofer • Farish-Baldenhofer Sale (Stack's, 1955) • A.J. Ostheimer 3rd Collection • ANA Convention Sale (Superior, 1975) lot 1031. "AU-55 or better."

Hollinbeck-Kagin Specimen. AU-55. Hollinbeck-Kagin Sale, June 1970, lot 642. "Unc."

NASC Convention Sale Specimen. AU-55. NASC Convention Sale (Kagin's, 1979) lot 543. "Choice AU-55."

May Sale Specimen. AU-55. Stack's, 1992, lot 2196. "AU, near choice. Planchet notch as made at 5:00."

Total Estimated Population

MS-65 or better: 0 (URS-0)
MS-64: 2 (URS-2)
MS-63: 1 (URS-1)
MS-60 to 62: 1 (URS-1)
AU-50 to 58: 10 to 20 (URS-4)
VF-20 to EF-45: 170 to 300 (URS-9)
G-4 to F-15: 125 to 225 (URS-9)
Total for all grades combined: 300 to 550 (URS-10)
Estimated Total Condition Census: 64-64-63-61-58-55 (multiples)

1803 BB-255

Large 3 in date
(B-6)

Obverse: Thick top to 3 in date. Star 13 close to bust. Star 1 distant from hair, about 2.3 mm. On the left, stars 1-2 and 5-6 are closer than any others, while stars 4-5 are the most widely separated. On the right, the stars are remarkably evenly spaced. The 180 wide, and 3 a trifle low at base. The 3 is lightly double punched at its base and has a spur at its bottom.

Obverse die used to strike 1803 BB-255 only.

Reverse: See description under 1801 BB-212 (description repeated under 1803 BB-253).

Reverse die used to strike 1801 (intermediate state) BB-212; 1802/1 BB-231 (early state) and BB-232 (early state); 1802 BB-241 (slightly advanced intermediate state); and 1803 BB-253 (if it exists) and BB-254 (slightly advanced intermediate state), and BB-255 (terminal state).

Die States

Die State I: Perfect obverse die. Reverse as described above. The die state usually seen.

Die State II: Obverse with hairline crack, hardly discernible, connecting stars 10 and 11. This progresses (in intermediate states) to connect with star 9, then 12. About 20% to 30% of BB-255 dollars are of this die state.

Die State III: Obverse hairline crack connects all stars on the right. Scarcer than the preceding.

Collecting Notes

I estimate that about 1,250 to 2,000 specimens are known of 1803 BB-255. The 1803 BB-255 is about as plentiful as 1802 BB-241, and, like it, the 1803 BB-255 dominates its year—accounting for more coins than all other die varieties of 1803 combined. Notwithstanding all of this, in Mint State it is not the most often seen 1803 variety. That distinction goes to BB-252, for reasons not understood today.

Notable Specimens

Cardinal Specimen. MS-63 (PCGS). Thomas Cleneay Esq. Collection (S.H. & H. Chapman, December 1890) lot 951 • Unknown intermediaries • Jim Ruddy's personal collection, privately (circa 1960) to • Private Alabama collector • Cardinal Collection (American Numismatic Rarities, June 2005) lot 61 • Private collector • Cardinal Collection (Bowers and Merena, November 2010) lot 2242.

Eliasberg Specimen. MS-63 (PCGS). S.H. and H. Chapman, January 1900 • J.M. Clapp • John H. Clapp • Clapp estate, 1942 • Louis E. Eliasberg Sr. Collection (Bowers and Merena, April 1997) lot 2198 • Private Midwest collection.

Queller Specimen. MS-62 (NGC). October Sale

(Stack's, October 1986) lot 104 • Queller Family Collection of Silver Dollars (Heritage, April 2008) lot 2086 • Warren Miller Collection.

Cardinal Specimen (another). MS-61 (PCGS). Dale Friend Collection • U.S. Coins • Cardinal Collection • Private collector • Orlando Sale (Stack's, January 2009) lot 622 • Treasures of S.S. New York Sale (Stack's, July 2009) lot 667 • Chicago ANA Sale (Stack's Bowers, August 2011) lot 7406.

New England Rare Coin Galleries Specimen. MS-60, prooflike. New England Rare Coin Auction's sale of April 1980, lot 705. • New England Rare Coin Auction's sale of June 1981, lot 1311, accompanied by the text of a letter from Walter Breen in which he expressed his belief that the coin was a special presentation striking. • Auction '89 (Stack's) lot 1780, Bolender-6a. "Brilliant Unc. The dies were refinished and polished in the Mint at a time when they were in a late state and had rusted slightly."

Brand Specimen. MS-60. Virgil M. Brand Collection. • M.H. Bolender Collection, 1952, lot 181. "Sharp Unc. Pedigree: from the Brand Collection."

Gable Specimen. MS-60. Gable Collection, 1914. • M.H. Bolender Collection, 1952, lot 183. "Bolender-6b. Shows obverse die crack faintly through stars on right.

Unc., with Proof surface."

Hollinbeck-Kagin Specimen. MS-60. Hollinbeck-Kagin Sale, June 1970, lot 644. "Brilliant Unc. gem with some prooflike surface."

MANA Specimen. MS-60. 21st MANA Convention Sale (Kagin's, 1973) lot 1304. "Unc."

Smith Specimen. MS-60. Elliot Smith Collection. • Harold Bareford Collection (Stack's, 1981) lot 423. "Brilliant Unc."

(Many additional specimens certified as AU-58 by PCGS and NGC could also be listed.)

Total Estimated Population

MS-65 or better: 0 (URS-0)
MS-64: 0 (URS-0)
MS-63: 2 (URS-2)
MS-60 to 62: 5 to 10 (URS-4)
AU-50 to 58: 20 to 40 (URS-6)
VF-20 to EF-45: 700 to 1,110 (URS-11)
G-4 to F-15: 525 to 850 (URS-11)
Total for all grades combined: 1,250 to 2,000 (URS-12)
Estimated Total Condition Census: 63-63-62-61-60 (multiples)

1803 BB-256

Small 3 in date
(B-3, H-3)

Obverse: Thin top to 3, position of 3 similar to 1803 BB-251, but star 8 is more distant from Y. Close date. On the left, stars 1 and 2 are more widely separated than are any others.

Obverse die used to strike 1803 BB-256 only.

Reverse: AM touch at base. Point of star *touches* point of *lower part* of eagle's beak. Very short stem in claw. Right edge of right foot of A over edge of cloud 4 (the only such instance for a dollar of 1803).

Reverse die used to strike 1803 BB-256 only.

Note: As 1803 BB-256 stands alone without die linkage

to any other 1803 dollars, it is not possible to determine the striking sequence within the year.

Die States

Die State I: Perfect dies. Bolender noted that this variety is always weak at the center of the reverse.

Collecting Notes

The 1803 BB-256 is the second rarest die variety of the year (after BB-253, if BB-253 exists). I estimate that 30 to 60 are known. Examples seldom surface on the market. This issue is one that the specialist would be well advised to acquire in any condition, using leisure time to upgrade if the opportunity is presented.

In his 1881 *Type-Table,* J.W. Haseltine called this variety extremely rare, but did not inform the reader whether an *extremely* rare coin was more or less populous than an *excessively* rare one.

Notable Specimens

Newcomer Specimen. MS-60. Waldo C. Newcomer. • Col. E.H.R. Green. • James G. Macalllister. • T. James Clarke Collection (New Netherlands 48th Sale, 1956) lot 651. "Unc., a gorgeous first-strike."

Queller Specimen. AU-53 (PCGS). L.W. Hoffecker Sale (Superior, February 1987) lot 1338 • Queller Family Collection of Silver Dollars (Heritage, April 2008) lot 2087 • Dr. Robert Hesselgesser Collection (Ira and Larry Goldberg, September 2011) lot 5136 • Pre-Long Beach Sale (Ira and Larry Goldberg, May 212) lot 1316.

Matthews Specimen. AU-50 (PCGS). Winthrop Sale (Bowers and Ruddy, September 1975) lot 503 • Jim Matthews Collection • San Marino Collection Sale (Ira and Larry Goldberg, September 2002) lot 537.

Stirling Specimen. AU-50 (NGC). Frank Stirling Collection (Heritage, February 1986) lot 1345 • Warren Miller Collection.

73rd Anniversary Sale Specimen. AU-50 (NGC). 73rd Anniversary Sale (Stack's, October 2008) lot 401.

Herdegen Specimen. AU-50. R.T. Herdegen Collection (Hans M.F. Schulman, 1973). "AU."

Jewell Sale Specimen. EF-45 (PCGS). Richard C. Jewell Collection Sale (American Numismatic Rarities, March 2005) lot 224.

Cohen Specimen. EF-45. Milton Cohen Collection (Bowers and Merena, 1985) lot 530. "Choice EF-45, semiprooflike."

Newport Specimen. EF-40. Newport Collection (Bowers and Ruddy, 1975) lot 503. EF.

Cardinal Specimen. VF-35 (PCGS). Greenwald & Jackson Collections Sale (Bowers and Merena, September 1995) lot 736 • Cardinal Collection (Heritage, July 1997) lot 6510 • Boys Town Sale (Bowers and Merena, March 1998) lot 1441 • Michael Hering Collection (Heritage, January 2002) lot 7245.

Luebke Specimen. VF-35 (NGC). Ellesmere Numismatics, privately July 2002 • William Luebke Collection (Heritage, January 2007) lot 5050.

Reiver Specimen. VF-35 (PCGS). Thomas Werner (April 1954) • K.P. Austin • Jacque and A.J. Ostheimer Collection (Superior, August 1975) lot 1030 • Jules Reiver Collection (Heritage, January 2006) lot 23639 • Dr. Robert Hesselgesser Collection (Ira and Larry Goldberg, September 2011) lot 5137.

Total Estimated Population

MS-65 or better: 0 (URS-0)
MS-64: 0 (URS-0)
MS-63: 0 (URS-0)
MS-60 to 62: 1 or 2 (URS-1)
AU-50 to 58: 3 to 5 (URS-4)
VF-20 to EF-45: 17 to 35 (URS-6)
G-4 to F-15: 10 to 20 (URS-5)
Total for all grades combined: 30 to 60 (URS-6)
Estimated Total Condition Census: 60-53-50-50-50-50

1803 BB-303

1803 "Proof Restrike" Dollars

1803 Proof novodel: First struck at the Mint in the mid-1870s from an obverse die made before autumn 1834 and from a reverse made in the early 1830s. Intended for sale to numismatists. Struck in the same time period, but after the 1802 novodels and before the 1801 novodels. The mintage was probably no more than eight, of which four or five can be traced today. Only a few cabinets have ever included one.[1]

Obverse: Thick 3. Stars on left are much better aligned than on the obverse of the 1802 novodel. On the 1802, the spacing is fairly good, but stars 3 and 4 are wider apart than are any others. Star 1 is closer to the second curl than star 7 is to L. On the right, the stars are well spaced and aligned.

Highest curl on top of head about centered under upright of E, and next top curl centered under R. A small raised line is present just above the obverse center dot; heavy rust marks around star four and light rust marks at the 18 in the date. The die was made by using original number punches from the early nineteenth century. Raised border with denticles made up of truncated beads.

The top left curl tip is intact on the 1803 (and 1802) novodels, whereas on the 1801 and 1804 issues it is missing (due to hub damage). Thus, the 1802 and 1803 dies were

---

[1] For an expanded discussion and detailed history see "1801-2-3 Novodels," by R.W. Julian, and "1801-2-3-4 Dollars, by Q. David Bowers, in the first edition of this book. Also see the synopsis given in the present second edition under the 1801 Proof dollar.

made before the others.

Obverse die used to strike 1803 novodel dollars only.

Reverse: As preceding. See description under 1801 Proof novodel dollar.

"Reverse X" die used to strike 1801, 1802, 1803, and Class I 1804 novodel silver dollars.

Die State

Die State I: Obverse without cracks. Reverse with hairline crack from top right serif of N, sloping slightly downward through ITED, and ending at the bottom of the leftmost wing tip feather. Apparently, struck about the same time as the 1802 Proof novodel. All specimens seen have raised spots, from die rust, on and near star 4 and similar marks between the 1 and 8 in 1803, indication that the novodels were struck measurably later than the time they were prepared.

Proof mintage: Fewer than 10 (estimated)
Approximate population Proof-65 or better: 4 (URS-3)
Approximate population Proof-60 to 64: 0 (URS-0)

ADDITIONAL INFORMATION

The Year 1803 in History

Ohio became the 17th state in the Union on February 19, 1803, and the first new state which abolished slavery from the beginning of statehood; earlier, Vermont, which joined the Union in 1791, had abolished slavery under its constitution of July 1777. The Louisiana Purchase was completed at a cost of about $15 million, and added about 828,000 square miles of land to the United States. New York and Massachusetts threatened to secede from the United States in protest of Jefferson's purchase, which was made secretly.

Fort Dearborn, later known as Chicago, was established on the western shore of the lower part of Lake Michigan. Buffalo, New York was founded where the Niagara River meets Lake Erie. In May 1803, official U.S. architect Benjamin Latrobe addressed the American Philosophical Society on the subject of steam power, but was not enthusiastic about its prospects. In the meantime, great advances in steam power had been made elsewhere, particularly in England by Boulton & Watt. South Carolina resumed importing slaves to solve a labor shortage brought about

by increased need for cotton pickers; Eli Whitney's cotton gin, invented in 1792, made it possible to vastly expand the crop.

In April 1803, John James Audubon arrived from France and began banding the feet of phoebes to study their habits; later, Audubon's studies would become famous, and an elephant-folio-size collection of his bird paintings would be published. William Dunlap adapted a French play to create *The Voice of Nature*, the first popular melodrama to be produced on the American stage.

The British Passenger Act of 1803 mandated that each passenger on a transatlantic vessel have a minimum of 43 square feet of space, a law which dramatically slowed emigration from the British Isles to the United States. George Rapp emigrated to America from Germany in 1803; in 1805 he and his followers established the cooperative community of Harmony, Pennsylvania. In 1814-5 they moved to Indiana and established another Harmony; in 1825 that community was sold to British industrialist and social reformer Robert Owen, after which the Rappites founded Economy, Pennsylvania.

CHAPTER 17

1804-DATED SILVER DOLLARS

"The King of American Coins"

Of all American coins, more has been written about, theorized, and discussed concerning the 1804-dated silver dollar than any other issue. This interest dates back to 1842 when collectors first became aware that such a coin existed.

Offering an example for sale in his June 1941 sale of the William Forrester Dunham Collection, B. Max Mehl prefaced the description:

The King of American Coins:
The UNITED STATES SILVER DOLLAR OF 1804

In all the history of numismatics of the entire world, there is not today and there never has been a single coin which was and is the subject of so much romance, interest, comment, and upon so much has been written and so much talked about and discussed as the United States silver dollar of 1804.

While there may be coins of greater rarity (based upon the number of specimens known), none are so famous as the dollar of 1804! This is due to the fact that this great coin was the first coin of United States mintage to have been recognized as the rarest coin of the United States, from the very beginning of American numismatics, more than one hundred years ago. And it is today, as it always has been, the best known and most sought-after coin, not only among collectors, but among the public in general as well.

An Early Account

An early account by W. Elliot Woodward, of Roxbury, Massachusetts, was printed in the *American Journal of Numismatics*, June 1867, and gave the opinion of America's most knowledgeable, most honored auction cataloger of that era:

The dollar of 1804 is quite as rare and valuable as stated; so rare, indeed, and the few specimens existing so well known, as to make it highly improbable that a genuine one is to be found in California [a reference to a popular newspaper clipping suggesting that a Mr. Repiton, having "made an unsuccessful tender of $1,500 for one in possession of a gentleman residing in Salem, Massachusetts," had located a

specimen elsewhere]. Very few of these dollars were struck in 1804, and probably only one or two *originals* remain.

Sometime during the administration of President Jackson, a present was received from the Imaun [*sic*] of Muscat, and our government, wishing to make a proper return to that magnate, caused, amongst other things, a set of coins to be made for him, and the only dollar dies existing being those of 1804, a few pieces were struck from them, one of which was used as intended, one retained in the Mint, and one found its way to a private cabinet.

It may interest numismatists to know that the one sent to Muscat is no longer to be found. The enthusiasm with which coin collecting is pursued may be illustrated by stating the fact that a gentleman of New York City caused an investigation to be made in the palace of the Imaun in 1865, and learned that the dollar was not there, and had not been for a long time.

Of the two others known, one is in the possession of Col. M.I. Cohen, of Baltimore, and the other is in the well-known Mickley Collection. The last was obtained many years ago from the Bank of Pennsylvania and is, no doubt, one of the genuine issues of 1804.

In later years, Woodward's comments, quite sage for the time, served as a basis for the fund of information on the 1804 dollar. (The Muscat coin survived, went into the Watters Collection, then the Childs Collection, and was auctioned by Bowers and Merena later.) A later generation of scholars discounted the possibility that any 1804 dollars were indeed struck in the year 1804, and the diplomatic gift to Muscat episode was dismissed as well. As it turned out, some of Woodward's account was, in fact, quite true.

As years went on, Mint officials such as Jacob R. Eckfeldt and William E. DuBois became more numismatically knowledgeable. Indeed, Eckfeldt had been interested in coins for a long time and had kept on hand an assortment of earlier issues, primarily copper cents, to give, exchange, or sell to interested collectors.

In time, the Mint Cabinet became a reality, and an invitation was extended to coin

The first indication numismatists had that an 1804-dated dollar actually existed was from this illustration of an example in the Mint Cabinet, published in *A Manual of Gold and Silver Coins of All Nations, Struck Within the Past Century*, 1842.

collectors to make exchanges with the Mint. This cordial, open-handed practice was continued until at least the late 1850s, as evidenced by Mint Director James Ross Snowden (1853-1861) issuing a printed circular inviting trades.

On May 9, 1843, Matthew A. Stickney visited the Mint and obtained an 1804 silver dollar in an open exchange documented by letters.

Apparently, an element of cupidity entered the equation by the late 1850s during a rapid growth stage in numismatic interest. Certain Mint employees realized that the 1804-dated dollar was a rare and valuable coin indeed, and that it would be profitable to strike more examples and sell them privately, rather than in open exchange for the benefit for the Mint Cabinet.

It seems that at this time, circa the late 1850s, the reverse die used beginning in 1834 to produce earlier versions of the 1804-dated dollar could not be found, and a hitherto unused reverse die of the same design (also made in 1834), but differing in minor details, was used. Coins from this new combination were made and sold secretly, although on occasion various Mint officials were all too happy to pronounce them to be genuine original coins actually made in the year 1804, if pressed on the subject.

In time, various stories were devised by collectors and romanticists to explain why only a dozen or so examples were known of the 1804 silver dollar, in spite of the Mint report that 19,570 were made. The knowledge of the diplomatic gift sets ordered in 1834 was completely lost (Woodward's words of 1867 had been overlooked or ignored) as was knowledge of the legitimate method of distributing the earliest-made coins (also per Woodward).

Although Woodward, and years later Mehl and many others, wrote much about the 1804, the narratives were usually a mixture of fact, fiction, and supposition. It was not until the second half of the 20th century that facts were separated from fantasy, new findings were brought forth, and the story of the 1804 became known. James C. Risk, with Stack's in New York City, startled visitors to the 1962 ANA convention by exhibiting the original 1834-made King of Siam presentation set (missing the half dime and the $5 with motto), including an 1804-dated silver dollar, owned by David Spink of London. At the time *The Fantastic 1804 Dollar*, by Eric P. Newman and Kenneth E. Bressett, the first detailed scholarly treatment, was in press. A chapter titled "The Diplomatic Gift Delusion" was hastily extracted.

The book set a new high standard, after which auction offerings of 1804-dated dollars were factual. Both Newman and Bressett later wrote of the coin, including in the transcript of "A Restated Opinion on the Origin of the 1804 Dollar and the 1804 Eagle Proofs," by Eric P. Newman, from a presentation given at the Coinage of the Americas Conference, American Numismatic Society, October 30, 1993. In 1999 a book by Q. David Bowers, *The Rare Silver Dollars Dated 1804 and the Exciting Adventures of Edmund Roberts*, presented much hitherto unpublished

Unlike the regular issue early silver dollars which were minted from 1794 through 1804 at the First Philadelphia Mint, the 1804 dated silver dollars were struck in 1834 or later at the Second Phildelphia Mint which opened in 1833. (Image courtesy of George Osborn)

information including the voyage of Roberts who sailed to the far side of the world in 1835, bearing cased Proof sets with an 1804 dollar, intended as diplomatic gifts to a sultan and a king, and also to any other rulers encountered.

Minting the First 1804-Dated Dollars

Although Mint records state that 19,570 silver dollars were minted in calendar year 1804, nowhere is it stated that those coins actually bore the 1804 date. At the time it was Mint practice to keep using dies of earlier dates until they broke or wore out. Sometimes these older dies were overdated (the 1802/1 dollar is an example), but often the original dates were retained as made, quite probably because the dies had already been hardened for use, and the overpunching (overdating) procedure required that the dies be heated to a high temperature, cooled, and cleaned, a painstaking process. Thus, it is believed that the "1804" dollars struck in that calendar year bore earlier dates.

Numismatic knowledge was scarce in America in the early 1830s. The first specialized book on United States coins had yet to be written, and the Mint's own collection, the Mint Cabinet, would not be formed until June 1838, although "master coins" (Proofs) of certain issues had been saved for a number of years in anticipation of the establishment of a collection within the Mint.

On November 11, 1834, the Department of State ordered two special sets of United States coinage to be made up by the Philadelphia Mint for presentation to the King of Siam and the Imam of Muscat. These were to be fitted in special cases and to contain an example of each denomination currently in use, to form a complete set. Two other presentation sets were subsequently ordered early in 1835.

In 1834 the currently-produced denominations included the half cent, cent, half dime, dime, quarter, half dollar, gold quarter eagle, and gold half eagle. Proofs dated 1834 were made of each of these. A search of Mint records revealed that two other denominations were authorized, but had not been struck for many years. Silver dollars had been last struck in 1804 and $10 gold eagles were last struck in 1804 as well. Although the coiners of the Mint had on hand an 1804 $10 gold coin (which would later become a part of the Mint Cabinet), they had no way of knowing, as no numismatic check list had ever been printed that revealed that the silver dollars minted in 1804 were of earlier dates.

Seeking to present coins that were historically accurate, the engraver and coiner at the Mint simply made up new silver dollar and $10 gold dies bearing the 1804 date, to illustrate these coins of yesteryear, believed to have been made, but for which no specimens were on hand (and if they had

been, they would not have been with Proof finish to match the other coins in the set). For the first time, 1804-dated silver dollars were struck. It is not known today whether in 1834-1835 there was an intent to deceive or misrepresent. Some believe that there was. Others think differently. The writer is inclined toward the view that 1804 dollars were struck in 1834 as a matter of Mint business, but in later years (circa 1858 onward) became the subject of deception by Mint officials; the so-called Class II and III pieces, of which more will be said, are surely in this category.

It can be argued that in 1834 the Mint received authorization from the executive branch of the government to make complete coinage sets, and thus the $1 and $10 dies were officially authorized and made as were the coins struck from the dies. There seems to be no question that these are official United States coins.

Varieties of 1804 Dollars

Two different reverse dies were used to make the 1804-dated dollars, each mated with the same obverse. In due course, alert numismatists noted that the 1804 silver dollar occurred with two reverse die varieties:

Class I 1804-dated dollars: Reverse die with E in STATES over a cloud. Years ago these were called "Original" dollars in some catalogs. These were first officially coined in 1834 for diplomatic presentation purposes, and perhaps continued to be coined through the mid-1850s. Eight specimens are known to exist, several of which are in museums. The first example to go into numismatic hands was obtained by Massachusetts collector Matthew A. Stickney in a trade with the Mint Cabinet in 1843. This later went into the Louis E. Eliasberg, Sr. Collection and was auctioned in 1997. The Class I dollar presented to the Sultan of Muscat went into the Childs Collection and was auctioned in 1999.

Class II 1804-dated dollars: Reverse die with E in STATES over junction between two clouds. Plain edge. "Restrike." Made in 1858. Five said to have been made, three melted, one unaccounted for. Only one is known today and it is struck over a Swiss dollar-sized silver coin. It reposes in the National Coin Collection in the Smithsonian Institution.

Class III 1804-dated dollars: Reverse die as preceding. "Restrike." Lettered edge. Made circa late 1850s onward, last date of manufacture unknown, but possibly into the late 1860s or early 1870s. Six specimens are known to exist. Kenneth E. Bressett holds the opinion that all were made in 1858.[1]

---

[1] Letter to Bowers, January 22, 1997.

REGISTRY OF THE 1804 SILVER DOLLARS

This registry of known specimens is updated from the 1962 Newman-Bressett text, the Bowers 1993 *Encyclopedia,* and the 1999 Bowers book about Edmund Roberts.

CLASS I 1804 DOLLARS

So-Called "Originals"
Early Strikings Beginning in 1834

The 1804 Class I silver dollar from the Childs Collection. The finest known at MS-68 (PCGS).

1. Mint Cabinet specimen. This coin was illustrated in the 1842 book by Jacob R. Eckfeldt and William E. Dubois, *A Manual of Gold and Silver Coins of All Nations, Struck Within the Past Century,* providing the first notice collectors saw in print that an 1804-dated dollar existed, although fanciful pictures of such pieces had been published in cambists (exchange rate publications) earlier. It was the engraving of this coin that attracted the notice of Matthew A. Stickney and led to his acquisition of No. 2 below. • 1834-1838: Struck sometime during this period, by or under the direction of Chief Coiner Adam Eckfeldt. • 1838, June: Believed to have been added to the Mint Cabinet formed at this time by Adam Eckfeldt and William E. Dubois, although Alexandre Vattemare, a visiting numismatist from France this year, did not report seeing it.[1] Perhaps it had been removed for some purpose, or had not yet been added to the display. • 1842: Illustrated by Jacob Reese Eckfeldt and William E. Dubois in *A Manual of Gold and Silver Coins of All Nations, Struck Within the Past Century.* • Later years: National Coin Collection (Mint Cabinet), Smithsonian Institution, earlier on display at the Second and Third Philadelphia mints. On display in 1893 in Chicago as part of the Treasury Department exhibit at the World's Columbian Exposition. This letter dated October 4, 1945, by J.E. Graf, of the Smithsonian Institution, to 1804 dollar owner C.F. Childs, Chicago, closes the circle: "Mr. T.T. Belote, Curator

[1] Cf. John A. Nexsen in the *American Journal of Numismatics,* April 1887, quoted by Newman and Bressett, p. 92.

of History, has brought to my attention your letter to him of September 25 with reference to the 1804 dollar in the National Numismatic Collection.... We have no information whatever concerning the circumstances under which it was acquired by the Mint...."[2] • Impaired Proof due to cleaning on multiple occasions, including with silver polish, this occurring generations ago before enlightened curators were in charge.[3] 415.2 grains. Edge lettering crushed, as on two of the 1802 Proof novodels. Nicks and friction spots.

2. Stickney Specimen 1834-1843: Struck during this time, by or under the direction of Chief Coiner Adam

[2] Original letter owned by the Childs family.

[3] Farran Zerbe contributed this comment to *The Numismatist,* August 1903: [During a recent visit to the Philadelphia Mint] I found many of the silver Proof coins of late years partially covered with a white coating. On inquiry I learned that an overzealous attendant during the last vacation months when the numismatic room was closed took it upon himself to clean the tarnished coins, purchased some metal polish at a department store, and proceeded with his cleaning operation. Later, a coating of white appeared on the coins, which was now slowly disappearing. I expressed my displeasure at this improper treatment of Proof coins, and the custodian explained, "That is nothing. I have been here eight years and they have been cleaned three or four times in my time." Zerbe went on to protest that should such cleaning of Proof coins continue, in the future the Mint Collection would consist of nothing except plain planchets and badly worn coins!

Eckfeldt.[1] Most likely coined circa the mid-1830s along with the other Class I coins. • 1843: Mint Cabinet Collection duplicate. • 1843, May 9: Matthew Adams Stickney acquired the coin from the Mint Cabinet, where it was a duplicate (although not earlier publicized as such), by exchanging a 1785 Immune Columbia cent in gold and some other pieces, including "Pine-tree money," for it.[2] The token was larger than a current $5 gold piece, and for gold value alone represented a profit of several hundred percent over the face value of the 1804. • 1843-1894: Stickney Collection. Widely cited during his ownership, with numerous mentions in the *American Journal of Numismatics,* auction catalogs, and other printed material. This was the focal-point 1804 dollar for many years. • 1894-1907: Stickney's daughter. • 1907, June: Henry Chapman, auction of the Stickney Collection, June 25-29, 1907, lot 849. • 1907-1923: Col. James W. Ellsworth. Displayed at the American Numismatic Society, 1914, and illustrated on Plate 17 of the catalog titled *Exhibition of United States and Colonial Coins, January 17th to February 18, 1914.* Ellsworth's 1804 dollar and selected other coins were part of a spectacular loan and reference display that included three other specimens of the 1804 dollar. • 1923, March 7: Wayte Raymond and John Work Garrett via Knoedler & Co. The latter, a well-known dealer in paintings and art, controlled the sale of the collection, Garrett put up the money and thus had first pick of anything he wanted (but he already owned an 1804 dollar), and the remainder of the coins—constituting most of the collection—were marketed by Raymond, a dealer of excellent reputation whose star was rising rapidly. • 1923-1940: William Cutler Atwater, New York collector. • 1940-1946: William Cutler Atwater estate. • 1946: B. Max Mehl, Atwater Collection, June 11, 1946, lot 213. The Atwater Collection sale included examples of the Class I and Class III 1804 dollars. • 1946-1976: Louis E. Eliasberg, Sr. Widely exhibited at banks and at the Smithsonian Institution. The following was written by Louis E. Eliasberg, Sr. in 1956: "The dollar on exhibit is the only coin of this rare date that can be traced back to the United States Mint, where it was acquired by Mr. Stickney in 1843 in exchange for a gold IMMUNE COLUMBIA cent and several other pieces. There are six original 1804 dollars known to exist of which three including this specimen are in private collections. It is the most famous pedigreed coin in America and has only been in four collections in the past 113 years." • 1976-1997: Louis E. Eliasberg, Sr. estate. • 1997, April 6:

Cataloged and sold by Auctions by Bowers and Merena, Inc. Realized $1,815,000, a world's record price for any coin ever sold in public competition. • 1997: Spectrum Numismatics, Greg Roberts as bidder. • Private collection. • Proof-63 in the Eliasberg Collection catalog, later graded as Proof-65 by PCGS. 415.3 grains. Edge lettering crushed.

3. King of Siam Presentation Specimen. The following pedigree is conjectural before circa the 1950s: 1834, November: Adam Eckfeldt, chief coiner at the Philadelphia Mint. Coined to the order of U.S. State Department, for inclusion in a set of specimen coins for diplomatic presentation. • 1835: Placed aboard the *U.S.S. Peacock* in the custody of Edmund Roberts. • 1836, April 6: Presented by Special Agent Edmund Roberts as a gift from President Jackson for King Ph'ra Nang Klao (Rama III) of Siam; *April 6 seems to be the correct date, contrary to previously published information.* • 1836-1868: In the possession of the royal family of Siam, passing from Rama III to his half-brother, Rama IV, a.k.a. King Mongkut, who died in 1868. *The line of descent through the 1950s is conjectural.* • 1869, October 18: Following the death of his father on this date, 15-year-old Chulalongkorn became king. Known as Rama V. King Chulalongkorn died on October 23, 1910. • 19th century: Anna Leonowens, who was known as Anna of Siam (memorialized in the musical, *The King and I*). Certain of her accounts of life in Siam, including certain aspects of her relationship with Rama IV, have been proved fictional by scholars.[3] Thus, the pedigree leap from this point to David F. Spink is highly conjectural. In 1962, Newman and Bressett commented (italics added): "No *facts* have been disclosed concerning how the set left Siam or where it has reposed over the years." • Believed to have been descended through the Leonowens family. • 1950s: Two older ladies who were believed by David F. Spink to have been descendants of Anna Leonowens, brought the set to Spink & Son of London. The half dime and the with-motto 1834 $2.50 gold coin were missing from the set by this time. • 1950s-1979: Owned by David F. Spink, personally, with no benefit to the firm (which caused some dissension among firm members). As Spink was an owner of the firm, he had the right to do this. Displayed at

---

[1] Chief Coiner Adam Eckfeldt also seems to have been the one person on the Mint staff circa 1834 who had an interest in older-dated (*i.e.,* numismatically interesting) coins.

[2] Newman and Bressett, *The Fantastic 1804 Dollar,* devote a chapter to the transaction.

[3] For example, Michael Smithies, *Descriptions of Old Siam,* 1995, p. 189: "Anna Leonowens led two lives, a fact only recently discovered; three lives, if one includes the grossly erroneous version shown in the film *The King and I....* Given that so much of what she wrote in her recollections of Bangkok cannot be relied upon, and her travels outside of the capital non-existent (her supposed journey to Angkor is a fabrication), selections from her most famous work have to be handled gingerly...." Leonowens was in Siam during the reign of King Mongkut (Rama IV), the successor to the King of Siam who had received a set of United States coins in 1835. Leonowens (1831-1915) gave her birth date as 1834.

the American Numismatic Association Convention, 1962, there becoming the center of much interest and attention. • 1979: Lester Merkin, agent for David F. Spink. At the time, Lester received some criticism from Spink & Sons staff members, although Lester was simply acting as agent for David F. Spink. The price of the set was $1 million, although the eventual transaction also involved some coins taken in trade.[1] • 1979-1989: Elvin I. Unterman, Garrison, NY. Exhibited at the Smithsonian Institution, 1983. • 1987: Lester Merkin, agent for Elvin I. Unterman. • 1987, October 14: Bowers and Merena, King of Siam Sale, lot 2209. The set was reserved by the consignor; reserve not met. • 1989, October 18: Stack's, agent for the owner. Sold on this date. • 1989-1990: The Rarities Group (Martin B. Paul) and Continental Rarity Coin Fund I (Greg Holloway) • 1990, May: Superior Galleries. Included in the catalog titled as the Father Flanagan Boys Town Sale, May 27-29, 1990, lot 3364. • 1990-1993: Iraj Sayah (Los Angeles investor and coin dealer; traded under the name Unigold) and Terry Brand (Los Angeles industrialist) • 1993: Superior Galleries, auction of January 31 and February 1, 1993, lot 1196. Sold to Dwight Manley, on the staff of and

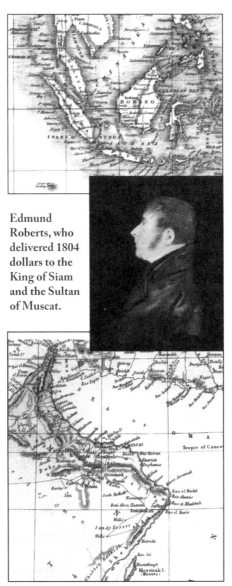

Edmund Roberts, who delivered 1804 dollars to the King of Siam and the Sultan of Muscat.

bidding for Spectrum Numismatics, Santa Ana, California. • 1993 to 2005: Private Western collection. On public display as part of the Treasures of Mandalay Museum in the Mandalay Bay Resort & Museum in Las Vegas, NV, beginning on March 3, 1999 (grand opening date of the Resort) • Sold by Ira & Larry Goldberg Coins & Collectibles of Beverly Hills, California, to Steven L. Contursi, President of Rare Coin Wholesalers of Dana Point, California on November 1, 2005, as part of the fabled King of Siam Proof set for the record price of $8.5 million. • Private collector. • Details of this specimen: Proof-67 (PCGS grade). 415.5 grains. Edge lettering crushed.

4. Sultan of Muscat Presentation Specimen. 1834, November: Adam Eckfeldt, chief coiner at the Philadelphia Mint. Coined to the order of U.S. State Department, for

inclusion in a set of specimen coins for diplomatic presentation. • 1835: Placed aboard the *U.S.S. Peacock* in the custody of Edmund Roberts. • 1835, October 1: Presented by Special Agent Edmund Roberts to the following: • 1835-1856(?). Sayyid Sa'id-bin-Sultan (a.k.a. the Sultan of Muscat) in cased presentation set of 1834. At the time the Sultan (popularly but incorrectly called Imaum or Imam) of Muscat was the most prominent factor in commercial trade in the northern and western reaches of the Indian Ocean. • 1856 to 1867 or 1868: Exact dates and intermediaries unknown. Possibly in the hands of a London numismatist by the latter time. • 1867 or 1868 to 1917: Charles A. Watters, Liverpool, England. By this time the coins were no longer in their original presentation case.[2] Watters acquired the 1804 dollar in 1867 or 1868, possibly from a source in London, this per a letter from Watters, June 27, 1879, to Jeremiah Colburn. • 1917, June 14-15: Messrs. Glendining & Co., Ltd., London, sale of Part II the Watters Collection. Lot 227, the 1804 dollar, was sold on June 15 for £330. "Excessively rare, in perfect condition, considered one of the finest specimens known." Other silver coins representing a partial presentation set of 1834 were sold separately. • 1917-1918: Henry Chapman. Displayed at the 1917 ANA Convention in Rochester, NY. Sold by Chapman on June 20, 1918, for $2,500 (a rather nice mark-up) to Virgil M. Brand • 1918-1926: Virgil M. Brand. • 1926-1933: Virgil M. Brand estate. • 1932, November 18: Appraised for $3,500 by Burdette G. Johnson.[3] • 1933, November 1 to Armin W. Brand, via the Brand estate division.[4] • 1933 November, or later, but by 1942: Traded by Armin W. Brand to his brother, Horace

---

[1] David Enders Tripp, letter to author, April 14, 1999. Tripp and Merkin were very close friends for many years.

[2] Ebenezer Locke Mason, Jr., American coin dealer, claimed that C.A. Watters saw this coin in the window of a pawnshop and bought it for 12 shillings. Mason stated that it had been owned earlier by a Mr. Walters, a wealthy corn merchant of Liverpool. Later, Mason withdrew the story, indicating that the account had been confused. This and several other comments, some contradictory, have since been discredited.

[3] Well known St. Louis dealer, at 408 Olive Street. Later in the decade Johnson was involved in the appraisal of the Col. E.H.R. Green estate (see biographical notes in Appendix II).

[4] David Enders Tripp, letter to author, April 14, 1999.

Louis Philip Brand. • 1942-1945: On consignment from Horace Louis Philip Brand to Charles E. Green and Ruth Green. Offered in *The Numismatist,* April 1942, p. 348. • 1945, August 10: Sold by Horace Louis Philip Brand and his former wife Erna M. Brand to Ruth and Charles E. Green, price $3,150.[1] Advertised in *The Numismatist,* September 1945, p. 998 • 1945, October 1: F. Newell Childs recommended that his father, Charles Frederick Childs, buy the coin. Sold by R. Green and C.E. Green to the following, for $5,000. Paid for the next day.[2] • 1945 to 1952: Charles Frederick Childs for his son, Frederick Newell Childs. • 1952: Given with the Childs coin collection to Charles Frederick Childs II, age eight, whose father, F. Newell Childs, acted as custodian. • 1952-1999: C.F. Childs II and family. • 1999, August 30: Walter H. Childs Collection sale, Auctions by Bowers and Merena, Inc. Sold to the following for a world's record auction price at the time for *any* coin, $4,140,000. Held at the Park Lane Hotel, New York City, the Childs Collection sale drew hundreds of participants as well as worldwide television (ABC, CBS, NBC, CNN, Fox, Reuters, etc.) and press coverage. • 1999, August 30: Brent Pogue and his father, Mack Pogue, whose winning bid was handled at the sale by dealer David W. Akers. • Gem Proof-68 (PCGS). 416.7 grains. Edge lettering crushed. Blue and iridescent toning. Lightly struck at certain star centers. The finest-quality specimen of the 1804 dollar.

5. Dexter Specimen. 1834-1840s, circa. Struck sometime during this period, by or under the direction of Chief Coiner Adam Eckfeldt. Most likely coined circa the mid-1830s along with the other Class I coins. • 19th century: Unknown intermediaries, perhaps someone connected with the Mint or, likely, a descendant. • 1884, circa: S. Hudson Chapman and Henry Chapman, Jr., known as the Chapman brothers, Philadelphia coin dealers. Apparently "laundered" through the following, to disguise its having come from the Chapmans. • 1884, October 14: Adolph Weyl sale, Berlin, Germany, lot 159. • 1884-1885: Chapman brothers, who bought their own coin, but now it had an exotic, if contrived pedigree to a German cabinet. • 1885, May 14-15: Chapman brothers sale, lot 354. Described by the Chapmans as a "great gem." • 1885: J.W. Scott, Scott Stamp & Coin Company. Per the Chapman brothers description in their 1885 sale, this was said: "S.H. and H. Chapman purchased October 1884, at a sale in Berlin,

and resold to a Mr. Scott, a dealer in coins,[3] for $1,000 at their Philadelphia sale, in May 1885." Scott was agent for the following. • 1885-1899: James Vila Dexter, Denver, Colorado. In his infinite wisdom, Dexter seems to have taken a "D" punch and counterstamped his initial on a cloud on the reverse. • 1899-1903: Dexter estate. • 1903, November 5: Roland (a.k.a. "Rollin") G. Parvin, Union Deposit & Trust Co., Denver, executor of the Dexter estate. Sold on this date, after much correspondence with the numismatic community. • 1903-1904: H.G. Brown, Portland, Oregon • 1904, October 11: Lyman H. Low, Part I of the Brown Collection, lot 431. • 1904-1939: William Forrester Dunham, Chicago. Exhibited by Dunham including at the February 4, 1910, meeting of the Chicago Numismatic Society • 1939-1941: B. Max Mehl, who purchased the Dunham collection for his inventory. • 1941, June 3: B. Max Mehl, Dunham Collection, lot 1058. Sold privately to Charles M. Williams, price $4,250, before the "auction" took place; Williams also bought another rarity, the 1822 $5, from the Dunham sale privately beforehand, and had his pick of anything else he wanted.[4] • 1941-1949: Charles M. Williams, Cincinnati, Ohio. • 1949: Abe Kosoff (via Numismatic Gallery) and Sol Kaplan, purchasers from Williams. • 1949-1981: Harold Bareford. • 1981, October 22-23: Stack's, Bareford Collection, lot 424. • 1981-1985: RARCOA (Ed Milas), Chicago, Illinois. • 1985-1989: Leon Hendrickson and George Weingart. • 1989, July 7: RARCOA, Auction '89, lot 247. • 1989-?: American Rare Coin Fund, L.P., Hugh Sconyers, financial manager, Kevin Lipton, numismatic manager. • 1990s, early: Northern California collector. • 1993, July: Superior Galleries sale. Reserve not met; returned to consignor • 1994, May 30-31: Superior Galleries sale. • 1994: Harlan White, proprietor of the Old Coin Shop, San Diego, California. • Private Southeastern collection. • Stack's 65th Anniversary Sale, October 2000, lot 1167, which realized $1.84 million. • Private Texas collection. • Proof-65 (PCGS). 415.8 grains. Edge lettering crushed. D counterstamped on a cloud on the reverse.

---

[1] Per commentary from R. Green, signed by R. Green and C.E. Green, to C.F. Childs, part of invoice to Childs dated October 2, 1945; also, original invoice from Brand to the Greens, copy given to C.F. Childs by the Greens.

[2] "Oct. 2 1945" is the amended date on the invoice from Green. Another document, dated October 2, states the sale took place (was confirmed) on October 1. Apparently, payment was made on October 2.

[3] The Chapman description of "a Mr. Scott, a dealer in coins," seems casual and distant; in fact, at the time Scott was one of the best known dealers in the rare coin field.

[4] Although an "auction catalogue" was published, Mehl sold many things before the sale, often *long before,* but listed them in the catalog anyway, and later published the "prices realized." The numismatic community was none the wiser until in later years the story came to light through several channels. The present writer (in a study of the John Work Garrett papers), Donald M. Miller (of Indiana, Pennsylvania, who noticed the curious situation that multiple tokens were pedigreed to the same single Dunham sale lots, and in addition to this unusual situation, some had been invoiced prior to the Dunham sale), and Abe Kosoff (who told of Charles M. Williams having had his pick of the Dunham delicacies before the auction), were among those piecing together the story.

6. Parmelee Specimen. 1834 to 1840s: Most likely coined circa the mid-1830s along with the other Class I coins, by or under the direction of Chief Coiner Adam Eckfeldt. • 1840s, late, to 1868: In the possession of the acquirer, then to an unknown "lady," allegedly bought from the Mint by a person unknown, for face value during the administration of James Knox Polk, 1845-1849. If so, this was a trade with the Mint Cabinet or an official, the details of which are not known today. • Alternatively, there is this somewhat related account in *Counterfeit, Mis-Struck and Unofficial Coins,* by Don Taxay, page 82: "In 1868 a specimen [of the rare 1804 dollar] was purchased by E.H. Sanford from an elderly lady who claimed to have obtained it (for the price of one dollar) from the Mint during Polk's administration." The "aged lady" gave the coin to her son, per the story, and the coin was sold to E. Harrison Sanford (see below) • 1868: Owned by the son of the above mentioned lady, but apparently sold by May 1868. • 1868-1874; E. Harrison Sanford. • 1874, November 27: Edward D. Cogan, Sanford Collection, lot 99. • 1874-1890: Lorin G. Parmelee. During this time he also bought and sold the Cohen coin (No. 8 below) • 1890, June: Offered for sale by Ed. Frossard in *Numisma,* apparently on consignment from Parmelee. • 1890, June 25-27: New York Coin & Stamp Company, Parmelee Collection, lot 817. • 1890-1891: Byron Reed. • 1891-1980s: Omaha City Library, Omaha, Nebraska. • 1980s to date: Transferred in the 1980s for display to Western Heritage Museum, Omaha, currently known as the Durham Western Heritage Museum. • Proof-63, flat stars. 416.1 grains (cf. Lawrence J. Lee, curator of preceding).[1] Later (1999) certified as Proof-64 by ICG. Friction in fields. Edge lettering crushed.

7. Mickley Specimen. 1834-5, circa: Probably struck sometime during this period, by or under the direction of Chief Coiner Adam Eckfeldt. • 1830s or 1840s: Possibly traded or sold to a numismatist or other collector, or placed into circulation by someone at the State Department after its presentation set was returned as undelivered. • 1850s: Henry C. Young, a teller for the Bank of Pennsylvania, c.1850, supposedly retrieved from a deposit at face value. • 1859, prior to, until 1867: Joseph J. Mickley. • 1867, October 28: W. Elliot Woodward, Mickley Collection, lot 1696. The April 1868 issue of the *American Journal of Numismatics* stated the buyer was Cogan, but William A. Lilliendahl seems to have owned it in the meantime, perhaps acquiring it via

Cogan as his agent. Indeed, the next (May 1868) issue of the same journal noted: "Since the sale of Mr. Mickley's genuine and original piece of this denomination to Mr. Lilliendahl, last fall, and its subsequent acquisition by Mr. Appleton.…" • 1867: Edward D. Cogan, briefly if at all. • 1867-1868: William A. Lilliendahl, who bought it at the Mickley sale, later selling it to the following for cash and some coins • 1868, February: Edward D. Cogan, who around this time became quite interested in the history of the 1804 dollar. Traded to the following in the same month. • 1868-1903: William Sumner Appleton. • 1903-1905: William Sumner Appleton estate. • 1905-1970: Massachusetts Historical Society. • 1970, October 23-24: Stack's, Massachusetts Historical Society Collection, lot 625. • 1970-1974: Chicago private collection. • 1974, January: Bought by Stack's, agent for the following. • 1974-1993: Reed Hawn. • 1993, October 13-14: Stack's, Reed Hawn Collection, lot 735. • 1993 to 2008 David Queller Collection. • April 2008, Heritage Galleries sale of the Queller Collection, lot 2089, there graded Proof-62 (NGC) • Joseph C. Thomas Collection. • Earlier graded as Proof-50. 416.4 grains. Edge lettering crushed

8. Cohen Specimen. 1834-5, circa: Probably struck sometime during this period, by or under the direction of Chief Coiner Adam Eckfeldt. • 1830s-1860s: Unknown intermediaries. • 1865, circa: Purchased "over the counter" at the exchange office of Edward Cohen, Richmond, Virginia. • 1865-1875: Col. Mendes I. Cohen, Baltimore, Maryland. • 1875, October 15: Edward D. Cogan, Cohen Collection, lot 535. • 1875-1876: Henry S. Adams, Boston, Massachusetts. • 1876, November 1: Edward D. Cogan, Adams Collection, lot 356. • 1876-1878: Lorin G. Parmelee. Sold by Parmelee after he bought the Sanford Collection coin, No. 6 in the above list. • 1878: Henry G. Sampson, dealer intermediary. • 1878-1906: Major William Boerum Wetmore, New York City, New York. • 1906, June 27-28: Chapman brothers, Wetmore Collection, lot 208. • 1906, June: Chapman brothers (bought for inventory) • 1906, summer: Thomas L. Elder. Bought for inventory from one of the Chapman brothers, who had dissolved their partnership. Sold in July 1906 to the following. • 1906-1921: James H. Manning, Albany, New York. • 1921, May 17: B. Max Mehl, Manning Collection, lot 778. • 1921-1922: Elmer S. Sears. • 1922: B. Max Mehl, who sold it to the following. • 1922-1952: Lammot DuPont (as he capitalized his name) • 1952-1994: Willis H. du Pont (as *he* capitalized his name). Included in the armed robbery of the du Pont coins in Florida, October 5, 1967. Recovered on April 23, 1993, in Zurich, Switzerland. • 1994: Donated to the American Numismatic Association where it is one of the foremost attractions of the ANA Museum VF-30. 410.2 grains. Many nicks and scratches. Edge lettering crushed.

---

[1] The Newman-Bressett text, *The Fantastic 1804 Dollar,* gave a lighter weight taken from an earlier listing, not a current weighing.

Class II 1804 Dollars

"Restrikes" Circa 1858

The unique 1804 Class II silver dollar. Proof. (Image courtesy of the Smithsonian Institution)

1. Mint Cabinet specimen. Smithsonian Institution. This unique specimen of the Class II 1804 dollar was struck circa 1858-1859, over an 1857-dated Bern (Switzerland) shooting taler. Note: The *American Journal of Numismatics*, April 1878, stated that five of these were made in 1858, and that four had been sold to numismatists; these were retrieved later by the Mint. Three are said to have been melted, and one is unaccounted for. Mint Cabinet Collection (circa 1858-9 to date) • Proof. 381.5 grains. Plain edge; high wire rim. Reverse slightly misaligned; 0 in date aligned with the second T in STATES.

Class III 1804 Dollars

"Restrikes" Circa 1858 or Later

The Idler Specimen 1804 Class III silver dollar. MS-62. (Image courtesy of the American Numismatic Association)

1. Berg Specimen. 1858-1872: Believed to have been struck at the Philadelphia Mint during this time period. • 1875(?): Captain John W. Haseltine, Philadelphia dealer. • 1870s (popularly, 1875): Koch & Co., Vienna. • 1876, circa: J.W. Haseltine was a likely "intermediary," although no facts are known. The story goes that Haseltine found it in the possession of Koch & Co., and bought it for his inventory or for the following client. • 1876, circa-1883: O.H. Berg, Baltimore, Maryland. • 1883, May 23-24: J.W. Haseltine, Berg Collection, lot 568. • 1883: George W. Cogan, agent for Thomas Harrison Garrett. • 1883-1888: Thomas Harrison

Garrett, Baltimore, Maryland. • 1888-1919: Thomas Harrison Garrett estate and Robert Garrett. • 1919-1942: John Work Garrett, who lived at Evergreen, the home of his father. Evergreen was subsequently given to The Johns Hopkins University. • 1942-1980: The Johns Hopkins University, Baltimore, Maryland, under the curatorship of Sarah Elizabeth Freeman,[1] Carl W.A. Carlson, and Susan Tripp. The coin was kept at Evergreen for a long period of time, but was later taken with most of the rest of the Garrett Collection to a bank vault in downtown Baltimore for safekeeping. • 1980, March 26-27: Bowers and Ruddy Galleries, Garrett Collection, lot 698. • 1980: The partnership of Pullen & Hanks (William Pullen and Larry Hanks) in combination with Santa ("Sam") Colavita, the latter having a 1/3 interest.[2] • 1980-1982: Sam Colavita, New Jersey rare coin dealer, who purchased the interest of Pullen & Hanks on April 17, 1980. For a time it was offered for sale through Texas dealer Ed Hipps.[3] • 1982, February 6: Pullen & Hanks, Long Beach Collector Series I Sale, Long Beach, lot 1076, but not sold. • 1982: Owned by Sam Colavita, but continued on consignment with Pullen & Hanks, who in the same year transmitted it by private treaty to the following.[4] • 1982-1984: Mike Levinson, Houston, Texas, who traded eight acres of land in El Paso, Texas, for it. • 1984-1986: Pennsylvania private collection. • 1986, June 24-25: Included as an added consignment in the Harry Einstein Sale, Bowers and Merena, lot 1736. • 1986: Rarities Group, Inc. (Martin B. Paul) • 1986, November: American Coin Portfolios (Dan Drykerman), agent for the following. • 1986 to: Private New York state collector, Mrs. Sommer.[5] • Accompanied by Martin Logies and Melissa Karstedt, Mrs. Sommer delivered this specimen to the Numismatic Guaranty Corporation January 2005, at which time it was encapsulated as PR-55 (NGC).[6] Subsequently traded to a private Southern California

collector. 402.8 grains. Edge lettering blundered and doubled in areas. Double struck on reverse. Reverse slightly rotated (0 in date is aligned with the second T in STATES).

2. Adams Specimen. 1858-1872: Believed to have been struck at the Philadelphia Mint during this time period. • 1875-1876: Captain John W. Haseltine, Philadelphia dealer. • 1876, January: "The first time Haseltine exhibited this coin was while waiting for the beginning of the sale of the Jewett collection in New York City, January 24-28, 1876. He offered this coin for $600 and said that it came from an old collection in England."[7] • 1876, March 30: J.W. Haseltine, "Centennial Coin and Curiosity Sale" I, lot 194. Haseltine himself seems to have been the buyer (bidding on his own coin) • 1876: Remained in the possession of J.W. Haseltine.[8] • 1876-circa 1880: Phineas Adams, Manchester, New Hampshire. • 1880, circa: Henry Ahlborn, Boston coin dealer, • 1880-1913: John P. Lyman, Boston, Massachusetts, who bought this as part of a "full set of dollars."[9] Consigned with the rest of his collection to the following. • 1913, November 7: S. Hudson Chapman, Lyman Collection, lot 16. • 1913-1932: Waldo C. Newcomer, Baltimore, Maryland. Displayed at the American Numismatic Society, 1914, and illustrated on Plate 17 of the catalog titled *Exhibition of United States and Colonial Coins, January 17th to February 18, 1914.* • 1932: B. Max Mehl, on consignment from Newcomer. • 1932-1936: Col. Edward H.R. Green. • 1936-1943, circa: Col. Green estate. As of March 1943, the 1804 dollar was still in the Green estate, which was being administered by the Chase National Bank, New York City.[10] • 1943, circa-1946: A.J. Allen, Plainfield, New Jersey, for a reported $3,200. • 1946: Frederick C.C. Boyd, East Orange, New Jersey. Boyd must have acquired it for the satisfaction of having owned this famous rarity, holding it but briefly after which he put it up for sale. • 1946: Numismatic Gallery (Abe Kosoff and Abner Kreisberg), on consignment from Boyd. • 1946-1949: Percy A. Smith, Portland, Oregon. Sold privately to the following. • 1949-1950: B. Max Mehl, who had it in his inventory

---

[1] Author of the 1964 work, *Medals Relating to Medicine and Allied Sciences in the Numismatic Collection of The Johns Hopkins University.*

[2] P. Scott Rubin (letter, April 6, 1999) provided certain information relating to the ownership of this specimen in the 1980s.

[3] Newman and Bressett, "The Fantastic 1804 Dollar: 25th Anniversary Follow-up," p. 169.

[4] P. Scott Rubin (letter, April 6, 1999) noted that while negotiations were in progress with Mike Levinson, Rubin also had an interested buyer waiting in the wings. Levinson bought the coin, and the matter ended.

[5] Newman and Bressett, "The Fantastic 1804 Dollar: 25th Anniversary Follow-up," p. 169.

[6] Numismatic Guaranty Corporation press release, February 1, 2005.

[7] Newman and Bressett, *The Fantastic 1804 Dollar*, p. 130. The Jewett sale was conducted by a competitor, Edward D. Cogan; thus, the offering may have been a breach of professional etiquette (which in any event was lightly observed at the time, indeed, as often now).

[8] P. Scott Rubin (letter, April 6, 1999) noted that he and the late Norman Stack had discussed the pedigree of this coin, and that Stack had located a named and priced copy of the 1876 catalog in which Haseltine was listed as the buyer.

[9] Newman and Bressett, *The Fantastic 1804 Dollar*, p. 130.

[10] Per a letter copy from Alexander A. McKenna, second vice president of the bank, to Eric P. Newman, March 17, 1943 (copy furnished to author; also letter from Newman to author, April 13, 1999).

by October 1949. • 1950, May 23: B. Max Mehl, Golden Jubilee Sale (Jerome Kern and other collections), lot 804. • 1950s: Amon G. Carter, Sr., Fort Worth, Texas. • 1950s-1982: Amon G. Carter, Jr. • 1982-1984: Amon G. Carter, Jr. family. • 1984, January 18-21: Stack's, Carter Collection, lot 241. • 1984: John Nelson Rowe III, agent for the following. • 1984-1989: L.R. French, Jr., Texas numismatist, • 1989, January 18: Stack's, L.R. French, Jr. Family Collection, lot 15. • 1989: Rarities Group, Inc. (Martin B. Paul) • 1989: National Gold Exchange (Mark Yaffe), Tampa, Florida. • 1989: Heritage Rare Coin Galleries. • 1989-November 1993: Indianapolis collection.[1] In May 1992, the owner commissioned Farmington Valley Rare Coin Co., New Hartford, Connecticut (Tony Scirpo, owner), to find a buyer. At this time the coin was certified as EF-45 by PCGS. • 1993, November: Acquired by a private buyer. Midwest collection. • 1998: David Liljestrand. • 1998: National Gold Exchange and Kenneth Goldman. • 1998: Legend Numismatics, Inc. (Laurie Sperber) • EF-45 (PCGS) per earlier listings; later regraded. • Phillip Flannagan Collection • 2001, November, Bowers and Merena Sale of the Phillip Flannagan Collection, lot 4303, as AU-58 (PCGS), which realized $874,000 • Donald Kagin • 2003, July, Bowers and Merena ANA Sale, lot 2026, which realized $1,207,500 • Kevin Lipton • Privately to Joseph C. Thomas, via Heritage Numismatics • 2009, April, Heritage Auction's Sale of the Joseph C. Thomas Collection, lot 2567, which realized $2.3 million • John Albanese • Private collector. • 416.25 grains. Edge lettering fairly sharp. 0 in date aligned with the second T in STATES. Currently graded Proof-58 (PCGS).

3. Davis Specimen. 1858-1872: Believed to have been struck at the Philadelphia Mint during this time period. • 1870s: Probably somewhere in Philadelphia, perhaps in the custody of J.W. Haseltine (a conjecture) • 1877, October 23: William E. Dubois, curator of the Mint Cabinet, sold this coin through J.W. Haseltine, this being the date of Haseltine's invoice.[2] • 1877-1883: Robert Coulton Davis, Philadelphia pharmacist and numismatic scholar. • 1883: Capt. John W. Haseltine. • 1883-1888: George M. Klein, Vicksburg, Mississippi. • 1888, May 21-25: W. Elliot Woodward, 95th sale, Vicksburg Collection (Klein Collection) Part I, lot 1940. • 1888: J. Colvin Randall, agent for Robert Coulton Davis (who had owned the coin earlier) • 1888: Robert Coulton Davis. • 1888-1890: Robert Coulton Davis estate. • 1890: Capt. John W. Haseltine. • 1890-1897: John M. Hale, Philipsburg,

Pennsylvania. • 1897-1950: John M. Hale family. • 1950: R.H. Mull, Philipsburg, Pennsylvania. • 1950, May 11: Parke-Bernet Galleries, catalog of the George Singer Collection (gold and enamel boxes, etc.). Cataloged by Charles M. Wormser." The silver dollar was offered as lot 221, "The lot is the property of Mr. R.H. Mull of Philipsburg, Pennsylvania." • 1950: Mrs. Fullerton, agent for her father, Henry P. Graves. • 1950-1952: Henry P. Graves. • 1952-1954: Henry P. Graves estate. • 1954, April 8-10: Stack's, Davis-Graves Sale, lot 1333. • 1954-1960: Ben H. Koenig, New York numismatist. • 1960, December 10: Stack's, Fairbanks (Koenig) Collection, lot 576. Sold to the following. • 1960-1963: Samuel Wolfson, Jacksonville, Florida. • 1963, May 3: Stack's, Wolfson Collection Sale, lot 1394. • 1963-1971: Norton Simon, California entrepreneur, sold by private treaty via Stack's to the following. • 1971, November 21, onward: James H.T. McConnell, Jr. • EF-40. 415.9 grains. Edge lettering doubled and blundered in places. 0 in date aligned with the second T in STATES.

4. Linderman Specimen. 1858-1872: Believed to have been struck at the Philadelphia Mint during this time period. • 1870s-1879: Mint Director Henry R. Linderman, who may have been present at its creation. As might be expected, this specimen was not artificially worn. It was kept with its original Proof surface (as was just one other, under somewhat similar circumstances; see the Idler specimen below). Linderman died on January 27, 1879. • 1879-1888: Linderman estate. • 1887, June 28: Lyman H. Low, cataloger of the Linderman Collection offered via a catalog bearing this date. However, the entire collection was withdrawn due to a pending federal inquiry as to the legality of certain coins within. The catalog is the same as published by J.W. Scott, February 28, 1888 (see below), by which time Low was a Scott employee.[3] • 1887, July 1: Emily Linderman, widow of the late Mint director, swore an affidavit concerning the 1804, noting, in part: "The said Dr. Linderman told deponent that he had obtained the 1804 dollar in his collection, that it was an original, that it was of great rarity, there only having been twelve or fourteen struck, that it was one of the finest, if not the finest specimen in existence, that he had paid for it in installments, not feeling able to pay for it all at one time." Mrs. Linderman may not have been aware that this was a lie. • 1888, February 28: J.W. Scott, Linderman Collection, lot 40. "A beautiful sharp Proof…. The finest known specimen of this valuable coin. This piece has the advantage over the few existing specimens, in being the property of the late director of the Mint,

---

[1] Certain information provided by Anthony Michael ("Tony") Scirpo, letter, September 19, 1999.

[2] Writing on October 19, 1908, Haseltine recalled in a letter to H.O. Granberg: "I sold it originally to Mr. Davis." Quoted in *Mehl's Numismatic Monthly,* April 1909, p. 59.

[3] Certain information courtesy of P. Scott Rubin, letter, April 16, 1999.

Dr. Linderman, which alone is a guarantee of its being struck in the U.S. Mint. It is from the same dies as that in the Mint cabinet."[1] Of course, this statement is quite curious, as widow Emily Linderman had sworn that her husband had bought it "in installments," obviously trying to give the impression that at the time it had come from someone outside of the Mint! This catalog is essentially the same as the Lyman H. Low catalog of June 28, 1887, described above, except now certain items have been withdrawn. • 1888-1910: James Ten Eyck, Albany, New York. • 1910-1922: James Ten Eyck estate. • 1922, May 2: B. Max Mehl, Ten Eyck Collection, lot 394. Called a restrike by Mehl, but accompanied by the 1887 affidavit from Dr. Linderman's widow Emily stating that it was an original. • 1922-1952: Lammot DuPont, Wilmington, Delaware. • 1952-1994: Willis H. du Pont, although for half of this period the coin was not in du Pont's possession, having been stolen in an armed robbery at the du Pont home in Florida, October 5, 1967. In May 1981, Mark Koenigsberg, of the El Paso, Texas, firm of Pullen & Hanks, received a telephone call from a woman who stated she had an 1804 dollar. This set into motion a sequence of events, in which the American Numismatic Association Certification Service played a central part, which resulted in the recovery of the coin on March 16, 1982.[2] • 1982-1994: On loan exhibit to the American Numismatic Association Museum, Colorado Springs. • 1994 to date: Donated to the Smithsonian Institution in 1994. • Proof-63. 413.52 grains. Blundered edge lettering.

5. Driefus-Rosenthal Specimen. 1858-1872: Believed to have been struck at the Philadelphia Mint during this time period. • 1870s-1893: Location unknown. Said to have been owned by a freed slave and his son, probably just a nice story (see February 15, 1894, account below) • 1893: W. Julius Driefus, Alexandria, Virginia. • 1893-1894: Isaac Rosenthal, Philadelphia scrap iron dealer. • 1894, February 15: Philadelphia Mint Superintendent Oliver C. Bosbyshell, agent for Col. Ellsworth. A letter stating that it was genuine was signed by Bosbyshell, Mint Cabinet curator R.A. McClure, and, for good measure, Chief Engraver Charles E. Barber (none of whom had any more than light numismatic credentials). "This dollar has been subjected to the most severe scrutiny in the Mint, and all of [the] experts are entirely satisfied that it is [a] genuine dollar struck in the year 1804. ..."[3] A letter of the same date from Bosbyshell to Ellsworth told this:

"The 1804 Silver Dollar purchased by me for you today, from W. Isaac Rosenthal of 190 Berks Street, this City, came into his possession in the following manner: A Mr. Julius Driefus, Nos. 3 & 4 South Wharves, Alexandria, Va., does business for Mr. Rosenthal, and borrowed money from him. Mr. Driefus met with a colored man who had the dollar for forty years—that he received it from his father, who was a freedman—the father kept the dollar because it either was the date of his birth, or the date he became a freedman—Mr. Rosenthal cannot remember which. I am promised a more circumstantial account, and will transmit it to you as soon as I receive it. ..." • 1894-1923: Col. James W. Ellsworth. Displayed at the American Numismatic Society, 1914, and illustrated on Plate 17 of the catalog titled *Exhibition of United States and Colonial Coins, January 17th to February 18, 1914.* • 1923: Wayte Raymond and John Work Garrett via Knoedler & Co. • 1923-1924: Wayte Raymond and John Work Garrett. • 1924: Guttag Brothers, agent for Farran Zerbe. • 1924-1928: Farran Zerbe, Money of the World exhibit, which was displayed widely, primarily in bank lobbies. • 1928-1978: Chase National Bank Collection, which became known as the Chase Bank Money Museum, in later times as the Chase Manhattan Bank Money Museum. Curators included Vernon L. Brown, Don Taxay, Caroline Harris, and Gene Hessler. • 1978 to date: American Numismatic Society. • In February 1978, *The Numismatist* reported: "The American Numismatic Society, one of the largest coin museums in the world, has acquired its first example of the rare U.S. '1804 Dollar' from the Chase Manhattan Bank Money Collection through a special loan/gift arrangement. Silver dollars dated 1804 are one of the most publicized and sought after rarities in the United States series. No genuine coins of this type are known—all were created surreptitiously by U.S. Mint employees in 1834 and again in 1858. The specimen, now at ANS Headquarters, was made in 1858 and first appeared in 1894, accompanied by a document attesting to its genuineness as an issue struck in 1804, signed by the then Mint superintendent, O.C. Bosbyshell; C.E. Barber, engraver of the Mint; and R.A. McClure, Curator of the Mint Numismatic Collection. This document, acquired with the coin by the Chase Manhattan Bank Money Collection, accompanies the dollar. Under the terms of the loan/gift arrangement, the Chase Manhattan Bank has placed its entire interest in the coin with the ANS for a period of 10 years with the expressed intention, by resolution of the board of directors, to donate the specimen to the ANS by the end of the loan period. In announcing this agreement, David Rockefeller, chairman of Chase Manhattan Bank, said, 'I am personally very pleased that a portion of our coin collection will be transferred to the ANS.' Along with the

---

[1] An untrue statement; the Mint Cabinet coin (No. 1 in the present list) is from a different reverse die.

[2] Newman and Bressett, "The Fantastic 1804 Dollar: 25th Anniversary Follow-up," pp. 170-172 includes details of the recovery operation.

[3] Newman and Bressett, *The Fantastic 1804 Dollar*, p. 140.

'1804 Dollar,' the ANS has received a choice collection of coins and paper money from the Chase Manhattan Bank Money Museum, including one of two known examples of the 1792 quarter-dollar pattern, struck in white metal. The value of the specimens involved in this loan/gift arrangement is in excess of $200,000." • EF, some nicks. Weight 415.48 grains. Edge lettering blundered and doubled in places. 0 in date aligned with the second T in STATES.

6. Idler Specimen. 1858-1872: Believed to have been struck at the Philadelphia Mint during this time period. • 1870s: Collection of William K. Idler, Philadelphia. • 1870s-1907: Captain John W. Haseltine, Philadelphia dealer. Kept for many years, this was "his" specimen. Appropriate to the situation, this specimen was not artificially worn, but was retained with its original Proof finish. • 1907-1908: Capt. John W. Haseltine and his protégé and partner, Stephen K. Nagy. Billed as the Idler specimen, after Haseltine's father-in-law, William K. Idler. • 1908-?: Henry O. Granberg, Oshkosh, Wisconsin. Displayed at the American Numismatic Society, 1914, and illustrated on Plate 17 of the catalog titled *Exhibition of United States and Colonial Coins, January 17th to February 18, 1914.* (On July 14, 1913, *another* "1804" dollar owned by Granberg, this one a fake, was featured in an auction sale by B. Max Mehl, but withdrawn, only to reappear in print in *The Numismatist* in 1937, then to disappear again.) • 1909, April: J.W. Haseltine's article, "Interesting Facts Regarding the 1804 Dollar" was published in *Mehl's Numismatic Monthly*, April 1909, and adapted from a letter written by Haseltine to H.O. Granberg, October 19, 1908. • Excerpts: "Complying with your request, I will state that the 1804 dollar that you have, came from the collection of the late Wm. Idler of this city. It not having been known to collectors previously is not strange that knew him. He was a very reticent man and never cared to tell anyone about this collection or to show it, even to his own sons. It is a genuine silver dollar of that date, struck at the United States Mint, the obverse from the same die all the others known were struck from There are several varieties of reverse to the 1804 dollar, but no variety of obverse.... About the Idler dollar, the mere fact that it has not so even of a surface, being slightly convex on one side, and concave on the other, is greatly in its favor, as it only carries out the fact that they were not so particular in early times how they struck the coins, and I think it was owing to the planchet being a trifle too broad for the collar. It is exactly the same obverse as the one at the U.S. Mint. There is *positively no authority or data known* for anyone to state that there were any re-strikes of this dollar, excepting the ones with the plain edge.... There is no authority for the statement that the Berg dollar was struck between 1860 and 1869, and I defy anyone to give any proof of it. Forty

years ago I knew that Mr. Idler had an 1804 dollar, and he bound me to secrecy in reference to it, as he made his electrotypes from it. • Mr. Chapman classifies the Davis dollar as 'one of the originals.' It carries with it a certificate from the U.S. Mint to that effect. He says that he does not know where it is, but I do. I sold it originally to Mr. Davis, and my recollection of it is that it is identical with the Idler dollar. The weight of the Cohn [sic] dollar is 410¼ grains. The weight of the Idler dollar is 411 and fraction grains. Restrike, plain edge, 381 and 5/8 grains.... Do not pay any attention to anyone calling the Idler dollar 'bogus' or 'fake' or insinuating that it is not from the 1804 dollar dies.... Now in closing I will stake my reputation that the Idler 1804 dollar is a genuine and original 1804 dollar struck from the dies at the United States Mint. Yours truly, JOHN W. HASELTINE." • ?-1940: William Cutler Atwater, New York City. • 1940-1946: William Cutler Atwater estate. • 1946, June 11: B. Max Mehl, Atwater Collection, lot 214. The Atwater Collection sale included examples of the Class I and Class III 1804 dollars. • 1946-1947: Will W. Neil. • 1947, June 17: B. Max Mehl, Neil Collection, lot 31. • 1947-1972: Edwin Hydeman, York, PA, merchant; owner of Wiest's Department Store. • 1961, March 3-4: Abe Kosoff, Edwin Hydeman Collection, lot 994; bought back by the consignor, although publicity was given out that the coin had sold for $29,000. The catalog included this information: "It is worthy to note that we have had the Hydeman Collection in our hands for some time. During this period negotiations were in progress, which if successful, would have transferred the entire collection into new hands. It was while negotiations were proceeding, that this cataloger was approached with an offer of $50,000 for the Idler 1804 dollar. Of course, we had not authorization to sell one coin, nor could we jeopardize the negotiations. Several other serious collectors inquired about the possibility of negotiating for this rarity and, in each instance, we were forced to discourage further pursuit along these lines. Now, of course, the coin is on the block…" • 1961-1972: On consignment to Abe Kosoff, or perhaps bought by him at the 1961 sale. Included in *Illustrated History of U.S. Coinage,* 1962, fixed price list, lot 45b. Advertised by Kosoff in *The Numismatist,* January 1972. This offering consisted of items from the Dr. J. Hewitt Judd Collection plus recent additions from other sources. • 1972: World-Wide Coin Investments, Ltd., Atlanta, John B. Hamrick, Jr., and Warren E. Tucker. Sold by private treaty to the following. • 1972-1974: Bowers and Ruddy Galleries, Inc., acquired the specimen in October 1972. First offered for sale in *Rare Coin Review* No. 19. • 1974: Continental Coin Galleries, Minneapolis, Minnesota (Kent M. Froseth and Chuck Parrish) • 1974-1979: Mark Blackburn. Subsequently offered for sale by Continental Coin Galleries, which had owned it earlier. "[The specimen was] later rumored to have gone to the Swiss Bank

Corporation in Zurich."[1] • 1979: Larry Demerer, professional numismatist. • 1979, February: Superior Galleries, agent for Dr. Jerry Buss, Los Angeles sports team owner. • 1979-1985: Dr. Jerry Buss. Acquired the coin in February 1979. • 1985, January 28-30: Superior Galleries, Buss

Collection, lot 1337. • 1985-1991: Aubrey and Adeline Bebee, Omaha, Nebraska. • 1985-1991: On loan to the American Numismatic Association. Subsequently donated by Mr. and Mrs. Bebee. • 1991 to date: American Numismatic Association Museum, Colorado Springs. • Proof-62. 411 grains. Rust on eagle's head. Weakly struck at centers. Sharpest edge lettering of any 1804 dollar (per Newman-Bressett).

---

[1] Newman and Bressett, "The Fantastic 1804 Dollar: 25th Anniversary Follow-Up," p. 172.

CHAPTER 18

HISTORICAL MARKET PRICES FOR EARLY DOLLARS

The following survey of prices realized at selected auction sales and offerings in fixed price lists and advertisements shows the changes in descriptions for varieties and the advance of values over a long period of years from the 1850s to modern times. This is not a comprehensive listing. Rather, it illustrates early silver dollars that have been part of various American cabinets over the years.

In each instance, coins are listed in order by date and variety. In the actual auction catalogs the order may have been different. There were no grading standards in effect during the 19th century, and one cataloger's Extremely Fine (EF) might be equal to another's Uncirculated (Unc.). In general, coins listed as Poor, Fair, or Good would be designated higher grades today. However, at the other end of the scale the opposite is true; for coins listed as Unc. today, many would be called EF or AU.

As is readily apparent from the auction, fixed-price, and advertising listings, there was no such thing as a standard price for a given early silver dollar sold during a particular time. Prices varied, often greatly. Even a casual perusal of the early dollars in collections auctioned during the 19th and early 20th century will demonstrate that few cabinets contained coins of uniformly high quality, and that Uncirculated pieces were represented only occasionally. I mention this now, as sometimes there is the misconception that old-time collections were laden with nothing but sparkling Uncirculated and Proof gems.

The first sophisticated cataloging of an important offering of early dollars was that in Milferd H. Bolender's descriptions of his own coins sold in his sale of February 23, 1952. New Netherlands Coin Company's American Numismatic Association Convention sale followed a few months later, in August, and featured detailed cataloging by John J. Ford, Jr. The year 1952 represents the jumping-off spot for truly knowledgeable, authoritative cataloguing of early dollars and other early series, although many later sales by various firms were cataloged hastily.

Most catalogs from about 1950 onward had detailed narrative for many of the coins noted below in a summarized or excerpted manner. Consulting the original catalogs is advised if you are interested in further information.

A.C. Kline Collection (1855):

1795 Flowing Hair, Fine. $1.70 • 1795 Flowing Hair, Fine. $1.70 • **1796** VF. $1.50 • 1797 VF. $1.63 • **1798** Thirteen stars—small eagle, scarce, VF. $1.05 • 1798 Fifteen Stars, Small Eagle, scarce, VF. $1.05 • **1799** Six Stars Facing, scarce, VF. $1.05 • **1800** Six Stars Facing, scarce, VF. $1.25 • **1801** Six Stars Facing, scarce, VF. $1.25 • **1802** Six Stars Facing, scarce, VF. $1.05 • **1803** Straight 3, VF. $1.05.

Joseph N.T. Levick Collection (Edward Cogan, December 1859):

1794 Very rare, Poor. $5.50 • **1795** Flowing Hair, Fine. $1.25 • 1795 Flowing Hair, Fine. $1.25 • 1795 Fillet Head [Draped Bust], Fine. $1.38 • **1796** Fine. $1.25 • **1797** [No grade given]. $1.38 • **1798** Thirteen Stars, Small Eagle, scarce, Fine. $1.87 • 1798 Fifteen Stars, Small Eagle, scarce, Fine. $2 • 1798 Reverse of 1799, Large Eagle, Fine. $1.10 • **1799** Five Stars facing, scarce, Fine. $2.25 • 1799 Six Stars Facing, Fine. $1.15 • **1800** VG. $1.25 • **1801** Fine. $1.30 • **1802** Fine. $1.30 • **1803** Straight 3, Fine. $1.30.

New York Sales (1859):

1794 Very rare, Fair. $7.25 • **1795** Flowing Hair, Fine. $1.15 • 1795 Flowing Hair, VF. $2.40 • 1795 Fillet Head, [no grade given] $1.20 • **1796** VF. $1.63 • **1797** [no grade given] $1.12 • **1798** Thirteen Stars, Small Eagle, scarce [no grade given] $1.50 • 1798 Fifteen Stars, Small Eagle, scarce [no grade given] $1.50 • 1798 Reverse of 1799, Large Eagle [no grade given] $1.25 • **1799** Five Stars Facing, scarce, Good. $2.10 • 1799 Five Stars Facing, scarce [no grade given] $1.12 • 1799 Six Stars Facing, scarce [no grade given] $1.62 • **1800** VF. $5 • **1801** VF. $1.25 • **1802** VF. $1.75 • **1803** Straight 3, Good. $1.70 • 1803 Crooked 3, Good. $1.75.

Edward Cogan Sale (1860):

1794 Very rare, Poor. $9.50 • **1795** Flowing Hair, VF. $5 • 1795 Flowing Hair, Fine. $1.05 • 1795 Fillet Head, Fine. $1.10 • **1796** VG. $1.30 • **1797** [no grade given] $1.80 • **1798** Thirteen Stars, Small Eagle, scarce [no grade given] $2 • 1798 Fifteen Stars, Small Eagle, scarce [no grade given] $2 • 1798 Reverse of 1799, Large Eagle, Fine. $1.40 • **1799** Five Stars Facing, scarce, VF. $2.87 • 1799 Six Stars Facing.

$1.20 • **1800** Fine. $1.10 • **1801** Good. $1.55 • **1802** VF. $1.40 • **1803** Straight 3, VF. $1.50.

William J. Jenks Collection cataloged by Edward D. Cogan, sold by Bangs & Co., April 12-13, 1877, offered a nice run of authentic dollars 1794-1803 plus a phony 1804. Jenks, a prominent 19th century collector, is not to be confused with the even better known John Story Jenks, whose collection was auctioned nearly a half century later.

1794 Fine impression. Head Fine, stars on the left flattened, those on the right much better; Liberty and date very distinct. $60 • **1795** Flowing Hair. Unusually fine impression, barely circulated. $11 • **1795** Flowing Hair. Head somewhat rubbed, but Fine. $6.25 • 1795 Flowing Hair. About same condition (Fine). $5.50 • 1795 Flowing Hair. Much more circulated. $2.50 • 1795 Fillet Head. Fine bold Unc. specimen. $8 • 1795 Fillet Head. Head a good deal rubbed. $2.25 • **1796** Large Date. VF. Barely circulated. $3 • **1797** Six Stars Facing. Head rubbed. $3.50 • **1798** Large Eagle. Barely circulated. $4 • 1798 Large Eagle. Barely circulated. $3.25 • 1798 Barely circulated. $2.50 • 1798 Fair. $4 • **1799** VF. Barely circulated. $4 • 1799 VF. $3.13 • 1799 Fine. $2.50 • **1800** VF. $3.55 • 1800 Nearly VF. $2.75 • **1801** Fine Bold impression. Little circulated. $6.50 • 1801 A good impression, but weaker struck. $3 • **1802** Very little circulated. $4.50 • **1802/1** A beautiful impression, but barely circulated. $10 • **1802** Another. About as fine in condition. $5.50 • **1803** Very strong impression. In VG condition for date. $4.50.

J.W. Haseltine's sale of January 15-17, 1879 marked the auction debut of the curious Proof novodel 1801-2-3 dollars later called "restrikes" by numismatists.

Lot 282. **1801** Brilliant Proof; sharp bold impression; exceedingly rare in this condition. $25 • Lot 283. **1802** Brilliant Proof; very sharp impression; equally rare as the preceding. $25 • Lot 284. **1803** Brilliant Proof; sharply struck; also an exceedingly rare dollar. $25 • (The preceding dollars have never before been offered at auction in Proof condition, and are the finest I have ever seen.[1])

J.W. Haseltine's sale of his own collection, June 24-25, 1880, included these two Proof dollars, not described as "restrikes." George Cogan was the buyer of each. Obviously,

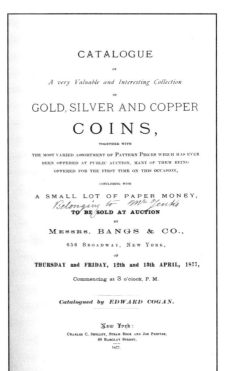

CATALOGUE
OF
A very Valuable and Interesting Collection
OF
GOLD, SILVER AND COPPER
COINS,
TOGETHER WITH
THE MOST VARIED ASSORTMENT OF PATTERN PIECES WHICH HAS EVER
BEEN OFFERED AT PUBLIC AUCTION, MANY OF THEM BEING
OFFERED FOR THE FIRST TIME ON THIS OCCASION,
CONCLUDING WITH
A SMALL LOT OF PAPER MONEY,
Belonging to Mr Jenks
TO BE SOLD AT AUCTION
BY
MESSRS. BANGS & CO.,
656 BROADWAY, NEW YORK,
ON
THURSDAY and FRIDAY, 12th and 13th APRIL, 1877,
Commencing at 3 o'clock, P. M.

Catalogued by EDWARD COGAN.

New York:
CHARLES C. SHELLEY, STEAM BOOK AND JOB PRINTER,
65 BARCLAY STREET,
1877.

Haseltine was engaging in a marketing program for these early-dated Proofs.

Lot 982. **1802** Brilliant Proof; everything sharp and boldly struck; no scratches in field; in fact, a perfect dollar of this date; excessively rare in this condition, only two others known. $16 • Lot 983. **1803** Brilliant Proof; sharp and beautiful; a companion piece to the preceding and equally rare; only two others known. $18.

The Robert Coulton Davis Collection sold by the New York Coin & Stamp Co., January 20-24, 1890.

1794 Stars flat as usual; but a much finer and stronger impression than usually offered; has been neatly plugged at lower point of bust, but barely perceptible; hair only worn on highest portions; Fine for date. $52 • **1795** Naked Bust [Flowing Hair]; strong, sharp and beautiful Unc. specimen; very rare in this condition. $16.75 • 1795 Naked Bust; Unc. strong and sharp; but milling not so well struck up as on preceding. $11 • 1795 Draped Bust; strong and sharp impression; barely if any circulated. $9.75 • **1796** Small Date; Unc., sharp and brilliant impression; a beauty in every respect; very rare. $42 • 1796 Small Date; Fine; not much circulated. $3.60 • 1796 Large Date; VF; barely touched by circulation, stars, etc.; sharp, the finest specimen we have seen. $16.50 • **1797** 6 Stars on Right; Brilliant Unc.; sharp in every particular; as it dropped from the die. $40 • 1797 7 Stars on right; sharp Brilliant impression; as handsome as when it left the die; very rare in this condition. $36 • **1798** Small eagle, 15 stars; we believe this to be the finest known specimen; a splendid Unc. piece. $52 • 1798 Small eagle, 13 stars; VF and sharp impression; barely touched by circulation; rare in this condition. $10 • 1798 Heraldic eagle; sharp impression; nearly Unc. $2.50 • 1798 VG. $1.25 • **1799** 5 Stars on right; VF and sharp; a splendid impression; barely if any circulated. $17.25 • **1799/8** VF and sharp; almost Unc. $3 • 1799 VF and sharp; nearly equal to an Unc. piece. $3.50 • 1799 VF and sharp; barely circulated. $1.75 • **1800** So-called "Comet" variety; a strong, sharp and beautiful Unc. piece. $6.50 • 1800 Perfect die; sharp bold impression; a light nick in field; otherwise a Brilliant Unc. impression. $3.60 • 1800 Cracked die; sharp, Unc. and brilliant. $3 • **1801** Unc. and sharp; rare in this condition. $5.25 • **1802/1** Stars sharp; VF. $3.25 • **1802** Few minute nicks; otherwise sharp, Unc. and brilliant. $4.10 • 1802 Duplicate; equally fine. $3.60 • **1803** Large 3; sharp and barely circulated; rare. $3.25.

---
[1] The implication seems to be that although these are the first to be auctioned, Haseltine had seen additional specimens.

Charles Steigerwalt's fixed price list, October 1890.

1794 Unc. Sharp bold impression. When shown at the Parmelee sale it was pronounced by all to be much superior to the Parmelee specimen which sold for $225.[1] $200 • **1794** Fine. An unusually even impression: stars, head and date well struck, as is also the reverse. $85 • **1795** Flowing Hair. Unc., Brilliant mint luster. Beautiful specimen. $25 • 1795 Flowing Hair. A beautiful specimen. Barely touched. Mint luster. $15 • 1795 Fillet Head. Unc., Proof surface. $75 • 1795 Fillet Head. Shows scarcely a trace of circulation. Sharp and with considerable mint luster. $30 • 1795 Fillet Head. Almost equal to last. $20 • **1796** Large Date. Quite Fine. $5 • 1796 Small Date. VF. $7.50 • **1797** Seven Stars Facing, VF. $7.50 • 1797 Six Stars Facing. Unc., Brilliant mint luster. $35 • **1798** Fifteen Stars. Small Eagle. Fine. $10 • 1798 Thirteen Stars. Small Eagle. VF. $7.50 • **1799** Five Stars Facing. Fine. $5 • **1799/8** But little worn. $3 • **1800** Barely circulated. Considerable luster. $3.50 • **1801** VF, considerable luster. $7.50 • **1802/1** Barely touched on most prominent parts. Mint luster. $10 • **1803** Could be called Unc. Sharp, handsome, with semi-proof surface. A beauty. $15.

Scott's Catalog of Gold and Silver Coins, 1893.

1794 dollar (unpriced, indicating great rarity) • **1795** With two leaves below each wing, Fair $2.50, Good $3.50 • 1795 With three leaves below each wing, Fair $2.50, Good $3.50 • 1795 Draped Bust, Fair $2.75, Good $3.75 • **1796** Small Date, Fair $3.00, Good $4 • 1796 Large Date, Fair $3.00, Good $4 • **1797** 16 Stars (6 facing) Fair $3.00, Good $4 • 1797 16 Stars (7 facing), Fair $3.00, Good $4 • **1798** 15 Stars (7 facing), Fair $6.50, Good $10 • 1798 13 Stars (6 facing), Fair $5.00, Good $8.50 • 1798 Without knob to 9, Fair $2.25, Good $3 • 1798 Knob to 9, Fair $2.25, Good $3.50 • **1799/8**, Fair $2.25, Good $3 • **1799** 13 Stars (5 facing), Fair $4.00; Good $6.50 • 1799 13 Stars (6 facing), Fair $2.00, Good $2.75 • **1800** Fair $2.75, Good $3.50 • **1801** Fair $3.00, Good $4 • **1802/1**, Fair $2.75, Good $3.50 • **1802** Fair $2.85, Good $3.75 • **1803** Small 3, Fair $3.00, Good $4 • 1803 Large 3, Fair $3.00, Good $4 • **1804** "The dies for this coin are known to have existed, and from them it is believed about 20 impressions have been taken, but we do not think that any were struck in the year the coins are dated, hence we class them as restrikes. The dies were destroyed in 1869."

---

[1] For Steigerwalt to show his coin at a sale conducted by a competitor (New York Coin & Stamp Co.) seems to have been a breach of numismatic etiquette.

COLLECTION
OF
UNITED STATES COI[NS]
OF
M. A. BROWN, ESQ.
CATALOGUED BY
S. H. & H. CHAPMAN
April 16 and 17, 1897

SILVER COINS OF THE UNITED STATES—DOLLARS.   17

COLORADO.
269   $2½. 1860 Head of Liberty. Type of regular U. S. coin. CLARK & CO. on diadem. R. Eagle, PIKES PEAK GOLD DENVER 2½ D. Very fine. Nick on edge.

JAPAN.
270   Quarter Obang. Oval plate with chrysanthemums at ends and two tablets of characters. R. Three characters incused. Perfect specimen of this curious coinage. 22x13½.

SILVER COINS OF THE UNITED STATES.
DOLLARS.
271   1795 Head resembling that used on the dollar of 1794. Very fine. Rare.
272   1795 Large head evenly spaced from stars, date and LIBERTY. R. Three leaves under wings of eagle. Sharp impression, deep milling.
273   1795 Head. Lower curl touches first star. R. Two leaves under wings of eagle. Very good.
274   1795 Bust draped and hair tied by a fillet. Very fine. Scarce
275   1796 Small date. R. Large letters. Very good. Scarce.
276   1796 Small date. R. Small letters. Very good. Scarce.
277   1796 Large date. R. Small letters. Very good. Scarce.
278   1797 Six stars before the bust. R. Large letters on rev. Uncirculated. Beautiful mint lustre. Almost invisible, very light scratches on rev. From the Winsor Collection, No. 400. $30.
279   1797 Seven stars before bust. R. Large letters. Very fine. From Winsor Collection, No. 399.
280   1797 Seven stars before bust. R. Small letters. Very good. Very rare.
281   1798 13 stars. R. Small eagle. Very fine. Splendid, bold, sharp impression. Superior to those usually obtainable. From Winsor Collection, No. 402. $15.
282   1798 15 stars. R. Small eagle. Small pin head hole on ribbon on rev. Very fine. Very rare. From Winsor Collection, No. 401.
283   1798 13 stars. R. Large eagle. Close date. Very fine.
284   1798 13 stars. R. Large eagle. Wide date. 8 touches bust. Very fine.
285   1799 over 1798. Extremely fine. Sharp impression.

S.H. and H. Chapman's sale of the M.A. Brown Collection, April 16-17, 1897.

1797 Six stars before the bust. Large letters on reverse. Uncirculated. Beautiful mint luster. Almost invisible, very light scratches on reverse. From the Winsor Collection, No. 400. $30 • 1797 Seven stars before bust. Rev. Large letters. VF. From Winsor Collection, No. 399. $5 • 1797 Seven stars before bust. Rev. Small letters. VG. Very rare. $3.50 • **1798** 12.00 13 stars. Rev. Small eagle. VF. Splendid, bold, sharp impression. Superior to those usually obtainable. From Winsor Collection, No. 402. $15 • **1799** 6 stars before bust. Even 99 the 7 high. Uncirculated. Sharp impression. Slight file marks in planchet on eagle's neck on rev. Mint luster. From Bispham Sale, 1880. $18 • **1800** Die cracked in date and up the sides. Uncirculated. Splendid, sharp impression, with Mint luster. Rarely seen in this condition. From Winsor Sale, No. 410. $15 • **1801** Uncirculated, only the faintest touch of cabinet friction obv. Reverse semi-proof. Superb specimen, sharp impression. $20 • **1802/1** Extremely Fine. Mint luster. $5 • **1802** Perfect date. Uncirculated. Sharp, even, superb impression with mint luster. From Winsor Sale, No. 413. $18 • **1803**. Large date. Uncirculated. Magnificent, sharp, even impression with Mint luster. The finest specimen of this date we know of. A superb coin and extremely rare in this condition. $23.50.

Charles Steigerwalt's fixed price list, April 1904, included these early dollars:

1795 Flowing Hair. About all circulation is on the masses of hair and eagle's breast. Brilliant mint bloom. $15 • 1795 Fillet Head. Unc.; slight Proof surface. One slight mar shows as edge nick. $17.50 • **1796** Large Date. VF. $7 • 1796 Small

Date. VF. $6 • **1797** Seven Stars Facing. VF. $5 • 1797 Six Stars Facing. VF. $5 • **1798** 15 Stars. Small Eagle. About VF. $8 • 1798 13 Stars. Small Eagle. VF. $6 • 1798 Large Eagle. Wide Date. $3.25 • 1798 Large Eagle. Compact Date, 8 high. Practically Unc. $3.50 • **1799** Five Stars Facing. EF. $8.50 • 1799 "High 9." Barely touched, slight Proof surface. $4.50 • 1799 Wide Date. Barely touched, mint bloom. $4 • 1799 Date more compact. Practically Unc. $4.50 • 1799 Last 9 low. EF. $4 • **1800** Faint circulation. Brilliant mint bloom. $5 • 1800 "AMERICAI" variety. EF. $4.50 • 1800 Dotted Date. EF. $4.50 • **1801** VF. $7.50 • 1802 EF. $6 • **1802/1** EF. $6 • **1803** Large 3. EF, slight Proof surface. $7 • 1803 Small 3. VF. $6.

Henry Chapman's sale of the Matthew Adams Stickney Collection, June 25-29, 1907. This magnificent cabinet, begun in the first half of the 19th century, contained many outstanding pieces, and many mediocre coins as well. The Chapmans went to some length to describe the varieties but for some reason did not elect to use Haseltine numbers, which would have simplified the process. Selections:

1794 Fine. Extremely rare. $190

1795 Head with intent expression on face, curl between points of first star. Rev. Three leaves under each wing of eagle. EF, only the slightest cabinet friction. Mint luster. $12 • 1795 Large head, curl high in field between stars. The variety with short bar in die behind head. Rev. as last. VF. $4.30 • 1795 Large head, curl passes through star; die cracked from edge through 7 of date up into the head. Rev. As last. Good. Rare die. $2.50 • 1795 Large head, curl passes through star and curls up towards bust; similar but different from last. Rev. Two leaves under each wing of eagle. VG. $3.10 • 1795 Large head, curl touches and stops at point of star. Rev. As last. VG. $2.75 • 1795 Small head far from LIBERTY, curl touches two points of star, and point of bust almost touches star. Rev. Two leaves under each wing, different die from preceding. EF. Mint luster. $9.50 • 1795 Type with bust in left of the field. VF. $8.50.

1796 Large Date. Rev. small letters in legend. VF. Rare. $9.50.

1797 Six stars before bust, ten behind it. Rev. large letters in legend. EF. Sharp stars, and a very superior example in every way. Mint luster. $13 .

1798 Close date, high 8; 7x6 stars. Heraldic eagle. Unc. Sharp, even impression with brilliant mint luster. $18 • 1798 Wide date, the 8 touches bust. Rev. Stars grouped three, line of five, and line of six far from clouds. EF. $6.25.

1799 8x5 stars. EF. Sharp impression. Mint luster. $20 • 1799 7x6 stars. Rev. each star of upper row of stars touches a cloud. Unc. Mint luster. Sharp impression. $4.50 • 1799 Even date. Rev. no berries on laurel branch. Unc. Only the slightest cabinet wear on bust. Mint luster. $4.50.

1800 Dotted O in date, due to small flakes out of the die. EF. Mint luster. $5.25.

1802 Perfect Date. Unc. Sharp, even impression. Mint luster. Perfection, and while I have seen several superb dollars of this year, yet I feel this is the finest specimen. A gem. $15.50 • 1802 Same dies as last. EF. Sharp, beautiful impression. Mint luster. $6.50.

1804 Original.... The present piece which Mr. Stickney received May 9, 1843 from the U.S. Mint at Philadelphia, it being a duplicate, in exchange for other coins one of which was an impression in *gold* of the 1785 Immune Columbia and which coin has remained to this day as the *only* example known. This 1804 dollar has never been out of Mr. Stickney's possession and so carefully guarded by him that few persons were ever even allowed to see it. $3,600.

B. Max Mehl's sale of the P.H. Griffith Collection, March 20, 1912, featured unusually detailed descriptions for the era.

1794 Fine for coin. Left part of coin weakly struck, but every letter, star and figure is plain. A very light immaterial dent on obverse edge and a pin-point nick in field before liberty head. Much better than usually found. $122.

1795 Head of '94. Very light scratches in field before head. Fine, with strong impression. Rare variety, seldom found so choice. $3.50 • 1795 Variety with two leaves under wings. Last curl between points of star. Good. Scarce. $3.80 • 1795 New type with Liberty facing right. 15 stars. EF, near Unc., with beautiful semi-proof surface. $5.40.

1796 date. Rev. Small letters in legend. Variety with small die break between I C in AMERICA. EF, bold impression, with some mint luster. $7.35.

1798 Heraldic eagle. Even date, large 8, very near but does not touch bust, knobless 9. About Unc., original mint luster. $3.50.

1802 Perfect Date. About Unc. with bright semi-proof surface. Only the highest portions showing slight wear which is undoubtedly due to cabinet friction. Perfectly centered and good strong impression. Extremely rare and valuable so choice. $4.80.

1803 Small 3. EF, semi-proof surface, perfectly centered. $5.25 • 1803 Large 3. Near Unc., unusually strong impression, considerable mint luster. $3.50.

Henry Chapman's sale of the George H. Earle Collection, June 25-29, 1912. Note that four specimens of the 1794 dollar are offered.

1794 EF. Sharp, bold, even impression. Stars before head sharp; those behind bold, but not centered. Slight hairmarks or abrasion in field. Light charcoal drift mark [carbon impurity] in planchet from edge at first star in a circle embracing the first and second stars to the edge. $620.00 • 1794 Fine. Bold impression, though stars behind head are flat, the first one weak. Date well struck up. Slight drift mark in planchet from head to right. Two slight dents on obverse edge and a larger one on reverse. $140 • 1794 Good. Stars behind head weak, as usual, as also UNITED STATES on reverse. Slight defect in planchet between first and second stars. $80 • 1794 Good. Stars behind head very weak, but rest of the obverse well struck. Field behind head has been rubbed down. Some scratches and edge dents. Rev. STATES very weak. Pin-point nicks on eagle's legs. $87

1795 Tall head, similar to last. Rev. Two leaves under each wing. Shows considerable planchet file marks on head. Body of eagle not up. EF. Mint luster. $18.50 • 1795 Small, low head, curl touches two points of first star. Rev. Two leaves under each wing. Unc. Mint luster. Die frosted around head. Rev. Pin scratches across eagle. $45 • 1795 Short Head. Rev. Two leaves under each wing. Surface around head frosted. Small nick on chin. EF. $6 • 1795 Beautiful head, showing center dot under ear; lower curl passes through first star. Rev. Two leaves under each wing. Proof, showing very slight abrasion. Sharp, even impression. $43 • 1795 Head in center of field. Curl free of stars. Small cut in the die back of the head. Small scratch before eagle. Three leaves under each wing of eagle. Unc. Br. mint luster. Milling around edge not struck up on half of the circumference, also shows some of the planchet file marks. $22 • 1795 As last. Unc. The very slightest abrasion. Sharp, even impression. $10.50 • 1795 Curl just touches tip of star. Rev. Two leaves under each wing. Unc., the faintest hairmarks. Mint luster. Sharp, with broad milling. $29 • 1795 Draped bust of Liberty in left of field, the hair tied by a fillet. Rev. Eagle in wreath on clouds. Uncirculated, brilliant. The faintest abrasion. Mint luster. $62.50.

1797 Stars 10x6. Rev. Large letters in legend. Unc. Minute nick on throat. Sharp for this date, even impression. Mint luster. $17 • 1797 As last. Very slightest planchet file marks on head. $5.50.

1799/8 Rev. 13 small stars, first one just emerging from cloud. EF. Mint luster. Planchet shows fine drift marks. $6.50

1799 Six stars. Unc. Stars sharp. $8 • 1799 Six stars. Unc. Two minute nicks on obverse. $6 • 1799 Large Stars. Reverse shows planchet file marks in center. Unc. Sharp. Mint luster. $5.50 • 1799 Close Date. Obverse die shattered. Unc. Sharp. Mint luster. $12.

1800 Perfect Date. Unc. Three stars not up, two behind and one before bust, owing to sinking of the die, which also shows around right edge of reverse. Mint luster. $16.

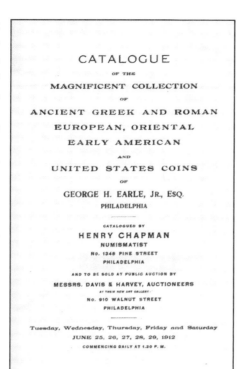

CATALOGUE
OF THE
MAGNIFICENT COLLECTION
OF
ANCIENT GREEK AND ROMAN
EUROPEAN, ORIENTAL
EARLY AMERICAN
AND
UNITED STATES COINS
OF
GEORGE H. EARLE, JR., ESQ.
PHILADELPHIA

CATALOGUED BY
HENRY CHAPMAN
NUMISMATIST
No. 1348 PINE STREET
PHILADELPHIA
AND TO BE SOLD AT PUBLIC AUCTION BY
MESSRS. DAVIS & HARVEY, AUCTIONEERS
AT THEIR NEW ART GALLERY
No. 910 WALNUT STREET
PHILADELPHIA

Tuesday, Wednesday, Thursday, Friday and Saturday
JUNE 25, 26, 27, 28, 29, 1912
COMMENCING DAILY AT 1.30 P. M.

1801 Unc. Sharp, even impression. Mint luster. A magnificent example and extremely rare in this preservation. $45

1802 Perfect Date. Unc. A few microscopic nicks. Mint luster. Sharp, even impression. $7.75 • 1802 As last and in almost same condition, the mint luster slightly chafed. $7.50.

1803 Large Date. Unc., a few microscopic nicks on bust. Sharp, even impression, with broad milling. Remarkable specimen and very rare in such beautiful preservation. $30.

B. Max Mehl's sale of the Charles H. Conover Collection, May 6, 1914.

1794 Good to VG $39 • **1795** Type as last, three leaves below eagle's wing. EF and sharp, every star filled; perfectly centered and an unusually bold impression. $5.40 • **1799** Perfect Date. Unc. Brilliant mint bloom. Perfectly centered and well struck. Every star filled. $12.50 • **1800** Perfect die. Unc. Mint luster. Every star filled and well struck. Broad milled border. $13.75 • **1801** EF, with considerable mint luster. Very nearly Unc. $7.80 • **1803** Large Date. EF with semi proof surface. Well centered and sharp. $5.75.

The Arthur C. Nygren Collection sold by B. Max Mehl, November 30, 1914.

1794 Strictly Fine; VF for coin. While left portion is not struck up as bold as the balance yet it is one of the best impressions of this excessively rare dollar that has passed through my hands. Far above average, and excessively rare in this condition. $132 • **1795** Type as 1794. Practically Unc.; considerable mint luster. Very bold impression. Only the highest portions show some traces of wear. $5.75 • 1795 Unc. Extremely rare. $6.75 • **1796** Large date. EF, nearly Unc., with considerable mint luster. Sharp, nearly every star filled. $8 • **1798** Practically Unc., with considerable mint luster. Every star sharp. $3.50 • **1799/8** Only faintest touch of circulation. Sharp, with mint luster. $3.60 • **1800** Unc. Brilliant frosty mint surface. Sharp and well struck. Every star filled. $8.25 • **1801** EF, considerable mint luster. $4.60 • **1802** EF, sharp; some mint luster. $4 • **1803** Unc. Brilliant mint bloom. The highest portions and field very slightly rubbed. A sharp and perfectly centered specimen. $7.

Henry Chapman's sale of the Clarence S. Bement Collection, May 29, 1916.

1795 Head in center, lower curl cuts through first star, small bar just inside fourth star. Rev. Two leaves under each wing; 9 berries and 22 leaves on left branch; 10 berries and 22 leaves on right branch. Unc. Mint luster. Perfect, even, sharp impression. $67 • 1795 Draped bust of Liberty in left of field. Rev. Small eagle on clouds in wreath. Unc., the slightest microscopic abrasion. Mint luster. Sharp, even brilliant impression. $65 • 1795 Draped bust of Liberty in left of field. Rev. Small eagle on clouds in wreath. Unc., the slightest microscopic abrasion. Mint luster. Sharp, even, brilliant impression. $65 • 1797 6 stars before bust, 10 behind it. Unc. Beautiful specimen with mint luster. Very faint hairmark in field. Minute dent on reverse edge. $20 • 1799 6 stars before bust, low 99. Unc., the slightest abrasion in field. Very slight depression in milling over BE. Small stars. $5.50 • 1802 Perfect Date. Unc., the slightest abrasion. Sharp, even impression. Mint luster. $8.10.

Thomas L. Elder's sale of April 13-14, 1917, contained these early dollars:

1795 Fillet. Unc., Proof surfaces. $5 • 1796 EF and sharp. $14 • 1799/8 Choice About Unc. $11 • 1799 Sharp, Unc., with brilliant Proof surface. $15 • 1799 Almost Unc. $4.50 • 1799 VF. $3.70 • 1800 Almost Unc. $6.75 • 1801 Sharp impression. Unc., bright. $18 • 1803 Unc., some Proof surface. $12.

The H.O. Granberg Collection sold by B. Max Mehl July 16, 1919.

1794 Weakly struck on left hand side, as usual. Good to VG. $41 • 1795 EF, nearly Unc., sharp with mint luster. $7.35 • 1795 Beautiful semi-proof, almost equal to a brilliant Proof. $16 • 1795 Slightest touch of circulation, sharp with mint luster. $5 • 1795 EF, considerable mint luster. $7 • 1795 Proof. A pin point nick on reverse edge. $21 • 1795 Fillet Head. Unc., sharp, with brilliant mint bloom, slight purple surface. A magnificent coin. $16 • 1796 VF, considerable mint luster. $4.25 • 1797 AU with bright mint luster. $4.65 • 1798 Unc., bright mint luster. $8.40 • 1798 Unc., mint luster. $8.40 • 1798 Beautiful sharp Unc. specimen. $9.25 • 1798 EF, nearly Unc., mint luster. $3.60 • 1799 EF, sharp, with considerable mint luster. $11.50 • 1799 Unc., broad milled borders on reverse. $10.25 • 1799 Unc. Sharp with brilliant mint luster. $10.25 • 1800 Unc., perfectly centered. Sharp. Bright mint luster. $8.40 • 1800 EF, nearly Unc. with bright mint luster. $4 • 1801 Practically Unc., sharp. Fine, hardly noticeable pin point

nicks on obverse. $5 • 1801 Restrike. Perfect brilliant Proof. $42 • 1802/1 EF, bold impression. Considerable mint luster. $4.35 • 1802 Unc., frosty mint surface, perfectly centered. $6.25 • 1802 Restrike. Beautiful brilliant Proof. $42 • 1803 Small 3 in date. AU, some mint luster, fine impression. $4 • 1803 EF, sharp, stars on left just a trifle flat. $3.75 • 1803 Restrike. Beautiful perfect brilliant Proof. $38.25.

B. Max Mehl's sale of the James Ten Eyck Collection, May 2, 1922, included many notable early dollars highlighted by an 1804 that "slept," perhaps because America was in an economic recession.

1794 Fine to VF for coin. Three small nicks on reverse edge. While the coin, as usual, is not struck very bold but on this specimen every star and date is well struck and nearly perfectly centered. By far above the average of this extremely rare coin. $94.50. • 1795 Obverse similar to last, reverse three leaves under eagle's wing. Variety with stars distant from point of bust and last curl. Unc., with beautiful mint luster. $26 • 1802/1 Practically Unc., with mint luster, reverse, almost brilliant. Rare so choice. $10.50. • 1804 Dollar.... Proof; nearly full brilliancy. Excessively rare and valuable. $840.

John Zug advertised these early silver dollars in the August 1933 issue of *The Numismatist:*

1795 Flowing Hair, 2 leaves, EF $15.00; VF $10.00; Fine $7.50 • 1795 Flowing Hair, 3 leaves, EF $15.00; VF $10.00; Fine $7.50 • 1795 Fillet Head, Unc. $25.00; EF $12.50; VF $10 • 1796 Large Date, small letters, VF $12.50; Fine $8.50 • 1796 Small Date, large letters. EF $12.50; VF $10 • 1796 Small Date, small letters, EF $22.50; Fine $10 • 1797 6 Stars Facing, EF $15.00; VF $12.50; Fine $8.50 • 1797 7 Stars Facing, Unc. $50.00; EF $17.50; VF $12.50 • 1798 Small Eagle, 15 Stars, VF $15.00; Fine $10 • 1798 Small Eagle, 13 Stars, Unc. $50.00; VF $17.50; Fine $12.50 • 1798 Large Eagle, EF $8.00; VF $6.00; Fine $4 • 1799/8 EF $10.00; VF $8.00; Fine $6 • 1799 5 Stars Facing, EF $12.50; VF $10.00; Fine $7.50 • 1799 6 Stars Facing, no berries, VF $7.50; Fine $5 • 1799 6 Stars Facing, 5 Berries, Unc. $15.00; EF $7.50; Fine $4.50 • 1800 Unc. $15.00; EF $10.00; VF $7.50; Fine $6 • 1800 Dotted Date variety, Fine $7.50 • 1800 AMERICAI variety, Unc. $20.00; Fine $7.50 • 1801 Unc. $35.00; EF $17.50; VF $12.50; Fine $7.50 • 1802/1, EF $10.00; VF $7.50; Fine $6 • 1802

Perfect Date, EF $10.00; VF $7.50; Fine $6 • **1803** Small 3. EF $12.50; VF $8.50; Fine $6.50 • 1803 Large 3. Unc. $15.00; VF $7.50; Fine $6.

J.C. Morgenthau & Co.'s sale of the J.C. Lighthouse Collection, February 18-19, 1936. Cataloged by Wayte Raymond and James Macallister.

1794 Good. Usual weakness in striking, but all of date shows. Several light dents on obverse and several edge nicks on reverse, but still a better specimen than often obtainable. Very rare. $86 • **1795** Head type. EF, only slight evidence of circulation. Three leaves under eagle's wing. $25 • 1795 Bust type. Head to left of center. Unc. except for a few immaterial edge dents. $21 • **1799/8** Unc. $21 • 1799/8 Unc. $18.50 • **1802/1** Unc., beautiful dollar. $23.

J.C. Morgenthau & Co.'s sale of December 21, 1937.

1794 VF, an unusually good specimen of this rare date. Very rare. $250 • **1795** Head similar to 1794. Three leaf variety on reverse. Unc., superb piece with mint luster. Rare. $41 • 1795 Another type of the three leaf variety. Superb Mint State, almost a Proof. Very rare. $55 • 1795 Two leaf variety. Brilliant Mint State. Superb. $41 • 1795 Bust type. Sharp Unc. with Br. Proof surface. One of the most beautiful early dollars we have seen. $60 • **1796** Large Date. Unc., mint luster. Very rare condition. $30 • **1797** Stars 9+7. EF and sharp. Scarce. $17 • **1798** Large eagle. Unc., very choice. $10.50 • **1799/8** EF. Practically Unc. Rare. $15 • **1799** Stars 7+6. Unc. $12 • 1799 Stars 8+5. AU, handsome Proof surface. Very rare. $20 • **1801** Unc., sharp with mint luster. Rare. $26 • **1802** Unc., very sharp. $16 • **1803** Large 3. Unc., prooflike. $22.50 • 1803 Small 3. AU, Proof surface. $15.

B. Max Mehl's sale of the William Forrester Dunham Collection, June 3, 1941.

1794 There is only one type and variety of this, the first issue of our dollar. Fine to VF. A planchet depression from about the middle of neck to edge. The stars on left not as bold as those on right; the legend on reverse also not as boldly struck on left. Without the planchet mark, the coin would have been at least a $350.00 specimen. A most acceptable specimen of this rare dollar. Far above the average. Cost $190.00 about 30 years ago. $217.50.

1795 Small head type; star touching bust. Reverse, two leaves under wings. EF with considerable mint luster. Very rare: The rarest 1795 dollar, and extremely rare in this choice condition . Originally purchased from Henry Chapman at $50.00. $30 • 1795 Head type. Reverse, three leaves under wings. Magnificent Unc. specimen; sharp and perfect in every respect. A gem, and as such, very rare and valuable. Just about as perfect as the day it dropped from the press. $67.50 • 1795 Second type, bust. Reverse, eagle on clouds. Just a shade from Unc.; highest portions show slight

cabinet friction, but with brilliant mint luster. Said to have cost $50.00. $30 • 1795 Bust type. Variety with bust closer to left; star on right does not touch bust, and star on left has two points touching curl. EF, with considerable luster; perfectly centered. Very scarce. $13.50.

1796 The extremely rare variety with small date and small letters. VF, with considerable mint luster. Catalogs at $35.00, but difficult to obtain at this price, especially so choice. $27

1800 Perfect die. Just a shade from Unc. with considerable mint luster. Rare so choice. Cost $20.00 over 20 years ago. $9.60 • Perfect die. Variety with stars close to bust and curl. Reverse, legend close to clouds. Just a shade from Unc., with frosty mint surface. Quite rare so choice; in fact far more so than is generally recognized. $11.10.

1801 Unc., frosty mint surface. Perfectly centered and struck, with every star filled. A rarity in this remarkable condition. Certainly far more rare than an Unc. cent of this year which is worth at least $50.00. $21.

1802 Perfect Date. Struck from the dies of the 1804 dollar, but at a later date. It is the same dies as the "King of American coins." The 2 in date is entirely different than that of any other 2 of this date dollar. Raised borders. Perfect Brilliant Proof. Just as rare as the second issue or so-called restrikes of the 1804 dollar of this variety [which sold for] $840.00 about 19 years ago. Since then a specimen sold at private sale for $1,500.00. While this date, 1802, is not as desirable as the 1804, but as mentioned before, it is just as rare and should bring well into the three-figure mark. A gem, and of highest interest. $127.50.

1803 Small 3 in date. Highest portions show slight cabinet friction, otherwise Unc. with semi proof surface. A beautiful specimen of this rare variety. Listed at $15.00 in VF condition. This one should be worth a great deal more. $15.75.

The "World's Greatest Collection" (F.C.C. Boyd Collection) sold by Numismatic Gallery, May 11-12, 1945, included an important group of early silver dollars, among which were an Uncirculated 1794 and a complete set of 1801-2-3 novodel "restrikes." Unfortunately for today's readers, the catalog descriptions were bare-bones, no historical information or pedigrees were given, and readers were left with little beyond variety and grade. Further, when a variety was unlisted by Haseltine—as several were—the catalogers did not describe the new dies or combinations in detail. As if this were not enough to digest, the researcher today does not know how many coins were attributed correctly. Plates in the catalog indicate that what was described as a 1797 H-2 was actually an H-3, and what was described as an H-3 was really an H-2, perhaps a simple case of transposition. 1798 H-16 was illustrated with what appears to be an H-15. A new variety described as 1796 H-6 was in actuality a die state of H-5. Selections from a much wider offering of mostly well-worn coins:

1794 Unc. $2,000.

1795 H-1. Unc. $145 • 1795 H-5. EF, much mint luster. $85 • 1795 H-6. About EF. $50 • 1795 H-10. Unc. $150.

1796 H-1. VF. $55 • 1796 H-2. VF; well centered. $60 • 1796 H-3. VF. $65 • 1796 H-4. VF or better. Nice luster. $55 • 1796 H-5. An EF example with much luster. Slightest wear on high spots. $100 • 1796 H-6. Unlisted in Haseltine. VF. $50.00. [Actually a late state of H-5]

1797 H-1a. Fine. $35 • 1797 H-2. Fine to VF. $37.50. [Illustrated with an H-3] • 1797 H-3. VF. $40.00. [Illustrated with an H-2]

1798 H-2A. Not in Haseltine. VF. $65 • 1798 H-6a. Not listed in Haseltine. Fine. $20 • 1798 H-10. Slight wear on reverse. Unc. $35 • 1798 H-11. EF, nice luster. $35 • 1798 H-15. Barely circulated with nice luster. $45 • 1798 H-16. Unc. $120.00. [The plate in the catalog is not an H-16, and appears to be an H-15 • 1798 H-20. Barely circulated. Cabinet friction on high spots. $20 • 1798 H-27. Barely circulated. $60 • 1798 H-28. Unc. $60.

1799 H-1. Unc. $75 • 1799 H-3. Unc. $75 • 1799 Slight cabinet friction on head. Choice. $50 • 1799 H-8. Unc. $45 • 1799 H-9. Unc. $70 • 1799 H-9a. [Described as obverse of H-9, reverse of H-5.] Light scratches across head. VF. $17.50 • 1799 H-11a. Unc. $70 • 1799 H-23. Barely circulated. $70.

1800 H-7. VF. $45 [Purchased by M.H. Bolender, who found it to be a late state of H-5.] • 1800 H-8. Unc., slightest edge nick. $45 • 1800 H-10. VF. $25 • 1800 H-11. EF. $45 • 1800 H-12. EF, with much luster. $40 • 1800 H-14. Unc., brilliant of original mint luster. Nick on chin. $70 • • 1800 H-16. Unc. $55 • 1800 H-17. Barely circulated. $45 • 1800 H-18a. Unc. $55.

1801 H-2. Unc. with cabinet friction on high spots. Brilliant. $85 • 1 1801 Brilliant Proof restrike. $225.

1802 H-6. Barely circulated. $47.50 • 1802 Brilliant Proof restrike. $210.

1803 Brilliant Proof restrike. $210.

The William Cutler Atwater Collection sold by B. Max Mehl, June 11, 1946.

This holding was one of the great American cabinets dispersed in the middle of the 20th century. Among early dollars there were many outstanding pieces. Both varieties of 1804 dollars were included.

1794 Unc., just the barest touch of cabinet friction, with frosty mint luster. Perfectly centered; an unusually bold impression. $1,575 • 1794 Strictly VG, Fine. $380 • **1795** Brilliant semi-proof; almost a brilliant Proof. Sharp and perfect in every respect with full brilliant Proof surface. Just the slightest die hairlines on head and a faint, very light, mark between 5 and first star on right. $152.50 •

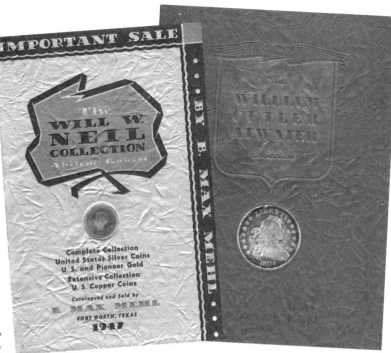

1795 Perfect Unc. Sharp and well centered, full mint luster. $137.50 • 1795 Unc. with frosty mint luster. Stars are sharp and bold, with deep milled border. $132.50 • 1795 Unc., frosty mint surface. Just the barest touch of cabinet friction. $85 • 1795 AU, with frosty mint luster. Two planchet defects. $45 • 1795 EF, well struck and perfectly centered. $52.50 • 1795 EF, sharp; just a shade from Unc. $48 • 1795 A beautiful perfect Unc. specimen with magnificent mint luster. Well struck, sharp and perfect in every respect. $157.50 • 1795 Strictly Unc. with full brilliant mint luster. $51.35 • **1796** EF with mint luster; just a shade from Unc. Two of the lower stars on left are not as bold as the others which are sharp. $40.35 • **1797** Practically Unc. with frosty mint surface. Stars are sharp. $85 • 1797 Just a shade from Unc., with frosty mint luster. Well centered and struck. $85 • **1798** EF with frosty mint surface; just a shade from Unc. $32.50 • **1799/8** Unc. with frosty mint surface. Well struck and centered. $67.50 • **1799** Practically Unc. with frosty mint surface. Unusually bold impression. $33.50 • 1799 Unc. with full mint luster. $70 • 1 • **1800** VF obverse with nearly Unc. reverse. Considerable frosty mint luster. $20 • **1803** Unc., with beautiful semi-proof surface. Reverse almost equal to a brilliant Proof. $85 • 1803 Unc. with beautiful full brilliant mint luster. $147.50 • **1804** Stickney coin. Original. [Lengthy description omitted here.] Shows very faint hair marks, otherwise EF brilliant and with slight Proof surface. $10,500 • 1804 Second type. Idler specimen. [Lengthy description omitted here.] No grade listed. $2,875.

The Will W. Neil Collection sold by B. Max Mehl, June 17, 1947.

1794 Probably the finest known specimen!... Beautiful Unc. specimen. Some short file marks in the die on upper obverse right edge. Usually, as is well known, the 1794 dollar comes with the stars on left and corresponding side on reverse weakly struck. This specimen is undoubtedly a very early impression of the die, as the stars on left are just about as bold as those on right, and the legend on reverse is perfect and well struck. Hardly the slightest touch of cabinet friction. $1,250 • **1798** 1798 Just a shade from Unc. $31 • **1801** [Proof restrike] Perfect Brilliant Proof. Raised borders and instead of milling, borders are of small dots. $300 • **1802** [Proof restrike] Perfect brilliant Proof gem. $300 • **1803** Sharply struck. Doubt if this coin has ever been in circulation, as only the highest portions show slight cabinet friction and the coin retains much of its original mint luster, iridescent surface. $67.50 • 1803 [Proof restrike] Perfect Brilliant Proof. $300 • **1804** King of American Coins. [Lengthy description abbreviated here.] Idler specimen. [No grade given] $3,125.

The Dr. Christian A. Allenburger Collection, sold by B. Max Mehl, March 23, 1948.

1794 Fine or VF for this coin. It is far above the average of specimens of this rare dollar usually found. Catalogs $600.00 and has record for that amount and higher. In much demand. $455.

1795 Head type. Point of star equal with point of bust. Star on left cuts through curl. Reverse, two leaves under wings. Beautiful sharp Unc. specimen $86 • 1795 Type similar to last but trifle smaller head. Star at right below point of bust and last curl touches two points of first star at left. Reverse, two leaves under wings. EF with considerable frosty mint surface. Rare variety in very rare condition. $40 • 1795 Dollar. Type of 1794, small head. Variety with star at right just barely under point of bust. Star at left, one point barely touches small curl. Reverse, three leaves under wings. A beautiful semi-proof. Just the slightest touch of cabinet friction. $65 • 1795 Type similar to last. Small head. Stars distant from point of bust and curl. Three leaves under wings on reverse. Perfect Unc. specimen. Sharp with full brilliant mint luster. Every star filled. Variety with tiny die break back of head. Light short hairline on cheek, hardly noticeable. A beautiful coin. Very rare and valuable. Record $137.50 for an equal specimen. $75 • 1795 Second or bust type. Variety with curl touching two points of star. Reverse, seven berries in wreath. Beautiful brilliant semi-proof. The obverse shows just the slightest touch of cabinet friction. As near a Proof of this early dollar as I have ever seen. Every star is sharp and fully struck. Superior to the Unc. specimen in my sale of the great Atwater Collection where the coin brought $157.50. $167.50.

1796 Large date and small letters on reverse. Dot die break at IC in AMERICA. EF with considerable mint luster. Well centered and struck. Record up to $50.00 for equal specimens. $48.50 • 1796 Small Date and small letters. The coin

shows very light nicks on obverse, probably due to having been handled with other coins, otherwise the coin shows but the slightest cabinet friction. At first glance the coin looks like a Proof I classify it here as EF with semi proof surface. It is next in beauty to the specimen I sold in my sale of the Roe Collection where the coin brought $175.00. $36.

1797 Variety with six stars to right of bust and 10 to left. Reverse, large letters in legend. Beautiful Unc. specimen. $105 • 1797 Variety with seven stars to right of bust and nine to left. Reverse, large letters. EF, nearly Unc. Unusually bold impression with every star sharp, fairly broad milled borders. Rare so choice. Said to have cost $75.00. $55 • 1797 The extremely rare variety with small letters in legend of reverse. Strictly Fine. Can easily be classed as VF for this coin. $41.

1799 The rare variety with five stars to right of bust and eight stars to left. Practically Unc. Almost full mint luster. $97.50 • 1799 Six stars to right and seven to left. The date is over '98. Very plain overdate. Practically Unc. with frosty mint surface. Variety with light die breaks through legend on reverse, with almost full mint luster. $30.00. • 1799 Perfect Date. Star on reverse touches lower part of beak. Faint die breaks on obverse. Nearly Unc. $12.50 • 1799 Six stars to right. Variety with stars trifle smaller and sharply cut. Stars on reverse smaller. Unc. with raised milled borders. 36.50 • 1799 Perfect Date, struck low. Light die breaks through date. Nearly Unc. $40.

1800 Variety with top lock of hair in single curl with few thin hairs above. Practically Unc. with mint luster. 90.

1802/1 Wide date. $31.

1802 Perfect Date. Beautiful brilliant Unc. specimen. Just about as perfect as the day it was minted. $115.

1803 Large 3 in date. EF with mint luster. Very scarce so choice. The coin is not far from Unc. $22.50.

The Bolender Collection of early dollars, M.H. Bolender's 183rd Sale, February 23, 1952.

This sale featured Bolender's reference collection used to describe and illustrate his book on early dollars, and thus is one of the most important in the annals of the series. Nearly all of the Bolender Collection coins were acquired by K.P. Austin, of Salisbury, Maryland, who in turn later sold them with the balance of his collection to Alfred J. Ostheimer, 3rd.[1] In due course, most of the Ostheimer coins were sold either in Lester Merkin's 1968 sale of the Ostheimer Collection or the 1973 Gilhousen Sale conducted by Superior.

Bolender's descriptions of the dies are omitted in the listing below, as they duplicate those in his book. However, his pedigrees and interesting, chatty comments are retained, as are the references to the plates in his book. The Bolender Collection catalog represents the most detailed published up to this date.

---

[1] Per author's conversation with Jules Reiver, December 2, 1992.

1794 [BB-1] VG. Lower stars on left are weak as usual. Rare. $425.

1795 [BB-11] B-3. Flowing hair. Strictly VF, sharp even impressions. Plate. (Both obverse and reverse of this very coin used in book for illustrations on plate I.) Geo. M. Parsons Coll'n. $70 • 1795 [BB-12] B-11. Flowing Hair. VF. Excessively rare variety, and the only one I have found. Haseltine's specimen was only "Good" and scratched in field, the only one he could find. A specimen listed in an important sale a few years ago as H-11 was purchased by me, but turned out to be H-2, and there was no H-11 in the sale. From the Earle sale, and later in the Schuyler Coll'n. Plate. (Reverse illustrated on plate II in the book on dollars.) $150 • 1795 [BB-13] B-9. EF, even impressions. Frosty surface around head. Very rare variety. From the Parsons sale by H. Chapman 1914. Plate. (Reverse used for illustration in my book.) $90 • 1795 [BB-13] B-9a. VF. Very rare. From Col. Green Collection, later in the Gettys Collection. $72.50 • 1795 [BB-14] B-4. Flowing Hair. EF, bold and sharp, with some prooflike surface. The edge below date and corresponding edge on reverse show a very slight planchet defect. A splendid example for this scarce variety, from the Col. Green Coll'n., later in the [Loyd B.] Gettys Collection. This piece superior to the one shown on plate in my book, as it was recently purchased to improve my collection. $70 • 1795 [BB-15] B-8. Flowing Hair type. A little wear on the high parts of hair and eagle, but VF and well-centered even impressions. Excessively rare. From the "World's Greatest Collection" sale. In my 45 years as a collector and dealer, I have seen only two specimens! However I handled one of these four times. Haseltine had seen but one, and it was not in his Type-Table sale catalog of 1881, having been withdrawn from the sale and sold privately. Plate. $165 • 1795 [BB-20] B-2. Slight wear on high portions of hair, and some adjusting marks on high part of eagle, done at mint in correcting planchet weight. EF, sharp stars. Plate. (This coin illustrated on plate I in the book.) From the Newcomer Collection. $85 • 1795 [BB-21] B-1. Flowing hair. EF, considerable luster, sharp even impression. Plate (refers to the Bolender book on silver dollars, where this identical coin was used for both obverse and reverse plates). From the great Stickney Coll'n. later in Schwab Collection. $70 • 1795 [BB-22] B-10. Flowing Hair. Fine. Purchased from Guttag Bros., New York dealers many years ago. Plate. (Reverse shown on plate II.) $85 • 1795 [BB-23] B-16. Unc., with Proof surface, a few trivial nicks under a glass. Beautifully toned, and a magnificent example, and one of the rarest of all dollars. Rarity-8, the only specimen known, and I believe it to be unique! Purchased by me at an Elder sale in New York 20 years ago. A prominent collector who was also in attendance bid against me, and it brought seven times the starting bid, and a new record for a 1795 dollar. The competition was

the sensation of the entire auction sale. It is certainly worth more than any other dollar of this date. Plate. (Reverse of this coin was used for plate II in book.) $440 • 1795 [BB-24] B-13. Flowing Hair. Several file marks on reverse done at mint to reduce planchet weight, but strictly VF and without doubt it is the finest of the three known specimens. Haseltine had met with only a single specimen, and called it "probably unique." This piece is probably the Haseltine specimen, as its condition would indicate, and was later in the Col. Green Collection. Plate. (Obverse shown on plate I.) $190 • 1795 [BB-25] B-6. Flowing hair. Some faint file marks appear on eagle's breast, done at mint to reduce planchet weight. EF. From the Lighthouse Collection. Plate. (Both obverse and reverse of this coin shown on plate I in the Bolender book on dollars.) $60 • 1795 [BB-26] B-12. Flowing hair. EF, mint luster close to letters, stars, and wreath. Extremely rare, From Elder sale, New York 1924. Finest of the few known specimens. Plate. (Obverse shown on plate I.) $110 • 1795 [BB-26] B-12a. Fine. This piece was lot 807 in the great Stickney sale held by Henry Chapman in 1907, and Mr. Chapman there described the break. Mr. Stickney was the first great collector in America. The only specimen I have ever seen. $110 • 1795 [BB-27] B-5. Flowing Hair. VF, slightly scratched in right obverse field. A.M. Smith Collection. $44 • 1795 [BB-51] B-14. Draped Bust. This piece was purchased as "Unc." but with magnifying glass you can see a pin-point nick before nose, and slight rubbing on highest point of eagle's breast. It is a beautiful example, with considerable mint luster. From the Lighthouse Collection. Plate. (Both obverse and reverse plates in my dollar book are from this very coin.) $70 • 1795 [BB-52] B-15. Draped Bust. EF, very nearly Unc. A beautiful dollar, sharply struck, splendid impressions. Bought from Henry Chapman, Philadelphia dealer, many years ago. Plate. (This coin used for both obverse and reverse in my book on early dollars.) $72.50

1796 [BB-61] B-4. EF, splendid impressions. From the Treadway Collection in 1924. Plate. (This coin used for both obverse and reverse in book.) $60 • 1796 [BB-61] B-4a. VF. Ex. rare. The only specimen I have found. Formerly in the Gable Collection sold by Chapman, bought by John T. Reeder whose grand collection I purchased in 1940. Plate. (Obverse shown on plate II.) $70 • 1796 [BB-63] B-2. VF, sharp impressions. From Geo. M. Parsons Collection. 1914. Plate. (This coin used for both obverse and reverse illustrations on plate II in my book on dollars.) $55 • 1796 [BB-64] B-5. Strictly VF. Formerly in the great Stickney Collection sold by H. Chapman in 1907, then going to the Schwab Collection where I obtained it. Plate. (This coin used for both obverse and reverse illustrations on plate II in my book on dollars.) A specimen only slightly better sold for $100 in the "World's Greatest Collection" sale in 1945. $77.50

• 1796 [BB-65] B-5a. Curious overstrike. The date and several stars and features of obverse appear on the reverse. VF. From the Col. Green Collection, later in the Gettys Collection, from whom I purchased it a few years ago for $50. $42 • 1796 [BB-65] B-5a. EF, bold even impressions. From the John G. Mills Collection sold by the Chapman brothers in 1904. $56 • 1796 [BB-65] B-5b. The die lump is very small, does not touch C in AMERICA, and touches only the right top of letter I. Early impressions from the dies. EF, choice and beautiful dollar, with considerable mint luster. Very rare state of the die break, and only recently acquired by me, since the book's publication.[1] $52.50 • 1796 [BB-66] B-1. VF. P.C. Clark Collection. Plate. (Obverse shown on plate II.) $60.

1797 [BB-71] B-3. Large planchet. EF, strong sharp impressions. The Stickney piece, later in the Schwab Collection. $55 • 1797 [BB-71] B-3a. Smallest planchet. EF, beautiful even impressions, well-centered, even border milling all round both sides, barely Unc. Newcomer Collection. $62.50 • 1797 [BB-71] B-3b. Letters only slightly bifurcated. VF. From Gettys Collection. $45 • 1797 [BB-72] B-2. Fine. Very rare. Plate. (Reverse shown on plate III.). $80 • 1797 [BB-73] B-1. Perfect dies. EF, strong impressions, but a little off center. From Treadway Collection sold in 1935 by Elder. (Both obverse and reverse shown on plate III.) $61 • 1797 [BB-73] B-1a. EF, splendid impressions, considerable luster. From the Newcomer Collection. $56 • 1797 [BB-73] B-1b. EF, and as choice as the last. From the Col. Green Collection. $56 • 1797 [BB-73] B-1c. Advanced states of the die breaks, with numerous additional cracks, from 9th star down to ribbon, neck through chin, right field to 12th star, and others. EF, a beautiful piece. Jewett Collection. $57.50.

1798 [BB-81] B-2. VF. Very rare, Plate. (Both obverse and reverse shown in book.) A.M. Smith Collection. $65 • 1798 [BB-81] B-2a. Fine and very rare. From Gettys Collection, formerly in Col. Green Collection. $47.50 • 1798 [BB-82] B-1. EF. Reverse struck off center to the right. Bought from Henry Chapman. Rare and in demand for type sets. $65 • 1798 [BB-82] B-1a. Very rare. EF. From Col. Green Collection. Plate. (This coin was used for illustrations of both obverse and reverse in plate III.) $77.50 • 1798 [BB-92] B-4. EF. Reverse shows adjustment marks done at Mint. From Lighthouse Collection. Plate. (This coin used for reverse of Plate IV.) $110 • 1798 [BB-93] B-5. Fine. Excessively rare, This is the better of the two known specimens. Haseltine's piece was only Fair. Plate. (Reverse of this coin illustrated on plate IV.) $65 • 1798

[BB-94] B-3. Unc., except for a few tiny spots, and minute nicks visible under a glass, and the reverse die was worn making UNUM weak in motto. Beautiful sharp impressions, mint luster on obverse, and full Proof surface on reverse. Recently obtained from same collection as last. Very rare so choice. $50 • 1798 [BB-95] B-6. VF. Strictly VF. From Treadway Collection, sale by Elder in 1935. Plate. (This coin was used for both obverse and reverse plates in the dollar book.) $32 • 1798 [BB-95] B-7. Obverse VF, Rev. Fine. Col. Green Collection. $29.50 • 1798 [BB-96] B-6a. Obverse VF. Reverse Fine. Very rare. Schuyler Collection. $25 • 1798 [BB-96] B-6b. Curiously double-struck on both sides. Obverse VF, Rev. Fine. $30 • 1798 [BB-101] B-17. VF. Excessively rare, Haseltine's specimen was only Good, the only one he ever found. The piece in this sale is the finest of the three known. From the Gable and Schuyler collections. Plate. (Both obverse and reverse shown in book on plates IV and V.) $31 • 1798 [BB-102] B-20. Obverse VF. Rev. Fine. From Lyman H. Low in 1916. Plate (Obverse). Rare variety. $21 • 1798 [BB-104] B-22. Obverse VF, Rev. Fine. Rare variety. From Col. Green Collection and bought of B.G. Johnson. Plate. (Reverse of this coin used for plate V.) $28 • 1798 [BB-105] B-23. EF, strong even impressions. Well-centered with complete border millings. P.C. Clark Collection. Plate. (Both obverse and reverse shown on plates IV and V). $36 • 1798 [BB-105] B-23a. EF. Elder sale 1925. Plate. (Obverse and reverse used for plates in book.) $34 • 1798 [BB-106] B-19. VF. From Col. Green Collection. Plate. (Obverse plate IV). $35 • 1798 [BB-107] B-21. EF; file marks on obverse done at mint to reduce planchet weight. Some mint luster. Rare variety. Elder sale 1923. Plate (Obverse). $30 • 1798 [BB-108] B-13. VF, nicely toned piece. From Gettys Collection, formerly in Col. Green Collection. Plate. (Reverse shown on plate V.) $22.50 • 1798 [BB-109] B-10. Obverse practically Unc., beautiful impression. Rev. EF Rare variety. From Earle sale, later in Col. Green Collection. Plate (This coin used for both obverse and reverse in book.) $37.50 • 1798 [BB-110] B-16. EF. Purchased from the Numismatic Gallery in 1950. Plate. (Obverse shown on plate IX.) $65 • 1798 [BB-111] B-11. VF. Plate. From Col. Green Collection. $36 • 1798 [BB-111] B-11 a. EF. Scarce. Lighthouse Collection. $31 • 1798 [BB-111] B-11 b. Fine. From the Gable and John T. Reeder Collections. $26 • 1798 [BB-112] B-15. Reverse EF, usual weakness at upper part of eagle in this variety. Gettys Collection. Plate. (Obverse shown on plate IV.) $39 • 1798 [BB-112] B-15 a. EF. Ex. rare. Cost $60 four years ago. $37.50 • 1798 [BB-113] B-27. EF, only slight signs of circulation, considerable mint luster. Sold in same condition at World's Greatest Collection sale in 1945 at $60. Plate. (Obverse). $36 • 1798 [BB-113] B-27a. Unc., sharp impressions. From Earle sale, then in the Schuyler Collection. $52 • 1798 [BB-114] B-26. VF. Col. Green

---

[1] QDB note: Actually, this die state is very common. Apparently, Bolender did not pay much attention to this variety.

Collection. Plate. (Both obverse and reverse). $32.50 • 1798 [BB-115] B-31. VF, well-toned. Plate (Reverse). From Col. Green Collection. $39 • 1798 [BB-115] B-31a. VF. St. Louis Stamp & Coin Co. Plate (Reverse). Excessively rare, $37.50 • 1798 [BB-116] B-30. EF, magnificent sharp and even impressions. Formerly in the Stickney and Schwab Collections. Plate. (Reverse.) $46 • 1798 [BB-116] B-30a. VG. I don't know where I found this one, but it's the only one I have seen. $16.50 • 1798 [BB-116] B-30b. Fine. From Col. Green and Gettys collections. Cost. $35. $26 • 1798 [BB-118] B-28. Obverse VF, Rev. Fine. Elder sale 1924. Plate. (Both obverse and reverse of this coin on plates IV and V in book.) $22 • 1798 [BB-119] B-29. VF. From Elder sale 1929. Plate. (Both obverse and reverse of this coin used for plates IV and V.) $27.50 • 1798 [BB-120] B-12. EF, but a few stars on reverse are always weakly struck in this rare variety, because of high relief of bust. A.M. Smith Collection. 1935. Plate. (This coin used for obverse and reverse illustrations in the book on silver dollars.) $36 • 1798 [BB-120] B-12a. Fine; slight edge dent on obverse near first star, and some stars hardly show on reverse, peculiar to this variety. Rare. $12.50 • 1798 [BB-121] B-9. EF. Plate. (Both obverse and reverse of this coin shown on plates III and V in the book.) $34 • 1798 [BB-122] B-14. EF, struck a little off center to right. From P.C. Clark Collection. Plate. (This coin used for both obverse and reverse plates in book.) $27 • 1798 [BB-122] B-14a. VF. Ex. rare, Col. Green Collection. $31 • 1798 [BB-122] B-14b. VF and very rare. This is Lot 61 of "World's Greatest Collection" sold by Numismatic Gallery in 1945. $26 • 1798 [BB-123] B-8. VF. Plate. (This coin illustrated on plate III, obverse, and plate V, reverse, in my book.) The specimen in World's Greatest Collection was in same condition, and sold in 1945 for $35. $26.50 • 1798 [BB-123] B-8. VG, two edge dents. Very rare. $17.50 • 1798 [BB-124] B-25. Fine. A rare variety. From St. Louis Coin & Stamp Co. Plate. (Obverse). $24 • 1798 [BB-124] B-25a. Fine. A.M. Smith Collection. $24 • 1798 [BB-124] B-25b. EF, choice piece. Lighthouse Collection. Plate. (Obverse). Rare. $46 • 1798 [BB-125] B-24. EF, reverse struck off center to right. Mint luster near letters, stars, etc. From Col. Green and Gettys collections. Plate. (Both obverse and reverse of this coin shown on plates IV and V.) $32.50 • 1798 [BB-125] B-24a. VF. Bought from Henry Chapman. $24.

1799/8 [BB-141] B-3. EF, sharp even impressions. From the great Earle sale, later in the Schuyler Collection. Plate. (Both obverse and reverse of this coin used for plates VI and VII in my book on dollars.) Extremely rare, Value $90. $52.50 • 1799/8 [BB-142] B-1. EF. Very rare, From Lighthouse Collection. Plate (Reverse). $37.50 • 1799/8 [BB-142] B-1a. Unc., sharp and beautiful impressions, except for on high part of eagle and around some stars on reverse. Frosty surfaces. From Col. Green Collection. $60

• 1799/8 [BB-143] B-2. VF; dent on left wing of eagle. Lacking in "World's Greatest Collection Sale." From Treadway sale by Elder 1935. Plate (reverse). $27.50.

1799 [BB-151] B-13. Nearly Unc., just slight friction on highest portions of hair and eagle. Finely toned, considerable mint luster. Perfect dies. From Harlan P. Smith and Schuyler collections. Plate. (Reverse shown on plate VII.) $37 • 1799 [BB-152] B-15. EF, the obverse practically Unc., with mint luster. Both sides are struck a little off center. A very rare variety, Just slight die crack through first 4 stars toward date. Bought from [Burdette G.] Johnson, St. Louis [Stamp & Coin Co.]. Plate. (Reverse). $42.50 • 1799 [BB-152] B-15a. VG. Rare. $16 • 1799 [BB-153] B-4. EF, nicely toned piece, with considerable mint luster. Rare variety. From Col. Green Collection, later in Gettys Collection. Plate. (Obverse used for plate VI.) $43 • 1799 [BB-154] B-18. VF, weakness on upper part of eagle. From Col. Green Collection. Plate. (Both obverse and reverse of this identical coin shown on plates VI and VII in book.) $38 • 1799 [BB-155] B-19. EF, struck a little off center, but sharp and very rare variety. Also came from Col. Green Collection. $32.50 • 1799 [BB-156] B-7. EF, some luster. A.M. Smith Collection. Plate (Reverse). $38 • 1799 [BB-156] B-7a. VF. From Lloyd Gettys Collection. $32.50 • 1799 [BB-157] B-5. EF, sharp even impressions, beautifully toned, with considerable luster. From the Harlan P. Smith sale by Chapman brothers in 1906, later in the Schuyler Collection. Plate. (Reverse shown on plate VII.) $27 • 1799 [BB-157] B-5a. EF. Col. Green Collection. $30 • 1799 [BB-158] B-16. EF, slightly rubbed on highest parts. Considerable mint luster. A.M. Smith Collection. Plate. (Both obverse and reverse shown on plates VI and VII.) $32 • 1799 [BB-158] B-16a. Same condition as last. A nice choice coin. Col. Green Collection, later in Gettys Collection. $30 • 1799 [BB-158] B-16b. EF, slight wear on highest parts. Extremely rare in this most advanced state of die breaks. From Elder sale 1924. $30 • 1799 [BB-158] B-16c. EF, some mint luster, nice impressions. Gettys Collection. $55 • 1799 [BB-158] B-16d. EF, some mint luster. Sharp impressions. Col. Green Collection. $32.50 • 1799 [BB-159] B-23. EF, nearly Unc., with sharp even impressions. From the Col. Green Collection. Very rare. Plate. (Both obverse and reverse on plates VI and VII.) $55 • 1799 [BB-160] B-12. VF. Col. Green Collection. Plate. (Obverse) $26 • 1799 [BB-160] B-12a. See plate for obverse of this identical coin on plate VI in book. EF, magnificent impressions. $72.50 • 1799 [BB-160] B-12b. EF. Rare. P.C. Clark Collection. Plate. (Obverse of this very coin shown on plate VI.) $75 • 1799 [BB-161] B-11. VF. Reeder Collection. Plate. (Reverse.) $29 • 1799 [BB-161] B-11a. EF, sharp even impressions. Considerable mint luster. Rare. From Parsons and Schuyler Collections. $27.50 • 1799 [BB-161] B-11b. VF. Bought from B.G. Johnson. Rare. $22 • 1799 [BB-162] B-6. Unc., but a few file marks on reverse done at mint to adjust weight of planchet before striking, and usual weakness at UNUM on ribbon. Attractive color and mint luster. Lyman H. Low sale 1918. Plate. (Both obverse and reverse used for plates VI and VII in book.) Very rare variety. $57.50 • 1799 [BB-162] B-6a. Unc., magnificent sharp even impressions. Highest portions of eagle on reverse are very slightly rubbed. Nearly full mint luster. This coin came from the convention sale of the California State Numismatic Association held last spring in Santa Cruz, where it was knocked off at $85. $90 • 1799 [BB-163] B-10-c. VF. Elder sale 1936. Strong even impressions. $22 • 1799 [BB-163] B-10. VF. From Elder sale 1936. Plate. (Both obverse and reverse of this coin shown on plates VI and VII.) $24.50 • 1799 [BB-163] B-10a. VF, bold even impressions. $25.50 • 1799 [BB-163] B-10b. Fine. From Lighthouse Collection. $20 • 1799 [BB-164] B-17. EF, nearly Unc., considerable mint luster, prooflike surface on reverse. Schuyler Collection. Plate. $34 • 1799 [BB-164] B-17a. EF, mint luster. From Gettys Collection. $34 • 1799 [BB-164] B-17b. VF. Col. Green Collection. $25 • 1799 [BB-165] B-8. EF, considerable mint luster. P.C. Clark Collection. Plate. (Both obverse and reverse shown on plates VI and VII in book.) $31 • 1799 [BB-165] B-8a counterstamped by Ephraim Brasher, New York City merchant, famous for his Brasher gold doubloons. With counterstamp EB in depressed rectangle, on top part of head. VG, and the only one known. Ex. rare. From the celebrated Dunham Collection. $42.50 • 1799 [BB-165] B-8a. VF, possibly better, as there is some luster close to stars and letters. Bought from Guttag Bros. many years ago. $26 • 1799 [BB-165] B-8b. Obverse Fine, reverse VG. Very rare state. $18.25 • 1799 [BB-166] B-9. Unc., beautiful impressions, except for slight friction on reverse center. Finely toned, mint luster. Early impressions. From Elder sale in 1924. Plate. (Plate VI and VII show both obverse and reverse of this identical coin.). $41.50 • 1799 [BB-166] B-9a. EF, sharp even impressions, nearly Unc., mint luster. From the Gable Collection, later in the Reeder Collection. $38.50 • 1799 [BB-166] B-9b. VF. Col. Green Collection. $22 • 1799 [BB-166] B-9c. Some file marks on reverse done at Mint to reduce planchet weight. Sharply struck, Unc., with mint luster. Schuyler Collection. $51 • 1799 [BB-167] B-14. Unc., strong impressions, reverse struck somewhat off center to right as usual with this variety. Mint luster. Bought from Henry Chapman over 30 years ago. Plate. (See plates VI and VII for both obverse and reverse illustrations of this very coin.) $45 • 1799 [BB-168] B-22. Obverse Fine, reverse VF. Ex. rare variety, From the Schwab Collection. Plate. (Reverse). $28.50 • 1799 [BB-169] B-21. EF, only slightly touched by wear on highest parts. Bought from Henry Chapman 30 years ago. Plate. (Obverse). $45.

1800 [BB-181] B-1. Fine. Very rare. Plate. (Obverse). $21 • 1800 [BB-182] B-2. Fine. Excessively rare, R From the

"World's Greatest Collection" sale by Numismatic Gallery in New York in 1945 at $45. Probably the Haseltine specimen, and the only one I have ever seen. $38.75 • 1800 [BB-183] B-3. Excessively rare, the finest known, and not found by me until 1949. Formerly in "World's Greatest Collection." VF, obverse edge nick at top. Plate. (Reverse). $42.50 • 1800 [BB-184] B-12. Unc., Proof surface on reverse. Col. Green Collection. $51 • 1800 [BB-184] B-12a. VF. From Lyman H. Low sale 1916. Plate. (Obverse) $22.50 • 1800 [BB-185] B-20. Obverse new, not known to Haseltine. The upper right star is in a position similar to the obverse of the 1804 dollars, with two points almost touching Y. This variety of the 1800 dollar is just as rare as a genuine 1804 dollar, and just as hard to find, which prevents its being used in idle fabrication of an "1804" by altering the date, but it has been done at least twice. EF, sharp even impressions, well toned. Plate. (Obverse). The only piece known to me. $175 • 1800 [BB-186] B-4. VF, strong impressions, some luster. From same collection as last. Plate. (Obverse). $32.50 • 1800 [BB-186] B-4a. VF, and from same collection as two preceding. W.G.C. sale in New York 1945. Very rare. Plate. (Obverse). $26 • 1800 [BB-186] B-4b. Recently obtained, it was formerly in Col. Green Collection. VF, except weak on upper right part of eagle, ribbon, and a few stars on right on reverse. V. rare. $27.50 • 1800 [BB-187] B-16. EF, sharp even impressions. From Earle sale, later in Schuyler Collection. Plate. (Both obverse and reverse seen on plate VIII.). $31 • 1800 [BB-187] B-16a. EF, sharp even impressions. From Gettys Collection. $28.50 • 1800 [BB-187] B-16b. VF. From H. Chapman in 1930. $24 • 1800 [BB-188] B-8. EF, sharp even impressions. H.P. Smith and Schuyler collections. Plate. (Both obverse and reverse of this very coin shown on plate VIII.) $35 • 1800 [BB-189] B-5. EF, some luster. Rare. Bought from B.G. Johnson. $36 • 1800 [BB-189] B-5a. VF, and very rare variety. Plate. (Reverse) $26 • 1800 [BB-189] B-5b. VF, nicely toned, some mint luster. Col. Green Collection. Ex. rare. $31 • 1800 [BB-189] B-5c. VF. Newcomer Collection. $24 • 1800 [BB-190] B-10. VF and sharp. From Col. Green Collection. (One of biggest collections of U.S. coins ever assembled). $23.50 • 1800 [BB-190] B-10a. EF. Col. Green Collection. $31 • 1800 [BB-191] B-11. VF. Purchased from Ben's Stamp & Coin Co. in Chicago. Plate. (Both obverse and reverse shown on plate VIII.) $32.50 • 1800 [BB-192] B-19. VF, sharp, and well-centered. Plate (obverse), bought from Johnson, St. Louis. $25 • 1800 [BB-192] B-19a. VF, nice even impressions. Schwab Collection. $24 • 1800 [BB-192] B-19b. EF, sharp even impressions. The AMERICAI variety. From Elder sale in 1927. $32.50 • 1800 [BB-193] B-18. EF, some luster near stars and letters. A.M. Smith Collection. Plate. (Plate VIII shows both obverse and reverse). $39 • 1800 [BB-193] B-18a. EF, finely toned piece. From the

Fox Collection. $31 • 1800 [BB-194] B-14. VF, nicely toned piece, some mint luster. Treadway Collection. Plate. (See plate VIII in my book on dollars for both obverse and reverse of this identical coin.) $26 • 1800 [BB-194] B-14a. VF. Lighthouse Collection. $29 • 1800 [BB-195] B-15. VF, sharp and bold impressions. From Elder sale 1924. Plate. (Both obverse and reverse shown on plate VIII.). $25 • 1800 [BB-196] B-17. EF. Formerly in Stickney Collection, then in Schwab Collection. Plate. (See plate VIII for both obverse and reverse of this coin.) $47.50 • 1800 [BB-196] B-17a. VF, strong sharp impressions. $23 • 1800 [BB-196] B-17b. EF. Col. Green Collection. $32.

1801 [BB-211] B-1. Only slight signs of circulation, strong impressions, mint luster. From Howe Collection. Plate. (Obverse and reverse of this coin shown on plate IX in book on dollars.) $42.50 • 1801 [BB-211] B-1a. EF, edge very slightly nicked on reverse. From Col. Green Collection. $41 • 1801 [BB-212] B-2. EF, a little wear on high parts of hair. Some mint luster. From Lighthouse Collection. Rare. $45 • 1801 [BB-213] B-3. EF, sharp even impressions, nearly Unc. From Col. Green and Gettys collections. $42 • 1801 [BB-214] B-4. EF, sharp even impressions. Superb example of this very rare variety, From the Treadway Collection sale by Elder in 1935. Plate. (Obverse on plate IX). $80 • 1801 [BB-214] B-4a. EF. V. rare. From Col. Green Collection. $41.

1802/1 [BB-231] B-1. EF, sharp even impressions. Well-toned piece. From Newcomer Collection. Plate. (Obverse). $37.50 • 1802/1 [BB-232] B-4. EF, struck a little off center to left. Very rare variety. From Gable and Reeder collections. Plate. (Obverse) $39 • 1802/1 [BB-233] B-2. EF, nearly Unc., considerable luster, sharp impressions. From Earle sale, then in Schuyler Collection. Plate. (Obverse of this very coin shown on plate IX). $41 • 1802/1 [BB-234] B-3. EF, magnificent impressions. From the Brand Collection $42.50 • 1802/1 [BB-235] B-9. A new variety which I discovered in 1950 when I purchased the Marmaduke Fox collection of United States coins. Unknown to Haseltine, and to me also until 1950. See my book for description. The plates for the book had already been completed when this coin was found, hence not shown on plate. Strictly Fine. May be unique. $155.

1802 Bolender-8. The Proof restrike. Brilliant and sharp perfect Proof. From the "World's Greatest Collection" sale by the Numismatic Gallery in New York in Jan. 1945. Plate. Just as rare as the 1804 dollar, but not as valuable because of the date. In very few of the great collections of the past, there was none in the great Stickney sale, although there was the 1804. $275 • 1802 [BB-241] B-6. Unc., except for light cabinet friction. From the Brand Collection. Plate. (Obverse and reverse of this very coin illustrated on plate IX in book.) $65 • 1802 [BB-242] B-5. EF, sharp even impressions, some Proof surface. From Howe Collection. Plate.

(Both obverse and reverse of this piece used for plate IX in book.) Extremely rare variety, Worth $85. $37.50.

1803 [BB-251] B-1. VF, nicely toned, and well centered. Very rare. Newcomer Collection. Plate. (Obverse) $40 • 1803 [BB-252] B-5. EF, nearly Unc., some luster. Sharp even impressions. Very rare variety. From the Brand Collection. Plate. (Obverse). $40 • 1803 [BB-252] B-5a. VF. Treadway Collection. Very rare. $37.50 • 1803 [BB-254] B-4. VF, sharp even impressions, nicely toned coin. From Gable Collection, then in Reeder Collection. Plate. (Obverse) $40 • 1803 [BB-255] B-6. Sharp Unc., beautiful mint luster, and some Proof surface. Strong sharp impressions. From the Brand Collection. $105 • 1803 [BB-255] B-6a. EF, beautifully toned. Col. Green Collection. $65 • 1803 [BB-255] B-6b. Unc., with Proof surface. Very rare. From Gable Collection. Plate. (Obverse on plate IX). $80.

Stack's sale of the Davis-Graves Collection, Part I, April 8-10, 1954.

Offered was an unusually fine group of silver dollars, beginning with a particularly well struck 1794 and ending with a specimen of the rare 1804.

1794 [BB-1] Stars struck up on left—unusually so. Handling defects on both sides, slight edge dent below 14th star. This is a VF coin but for these small imperfections. We grade it Fine (and well above average for the year). The rarest of the early dollars struck for circulation. $600

1795 [BB-21] B-1 Head of 1794. Two leaves under each wing. Well struck and centered with wide, serrated borders. This is not quite EF; prooflike surface. $70 • 1795 [BB-27] B-5. Wide date, common variety. Diagonal bar close to top curl toward fifth star; large planchet, three leaves under each wing. Free of usual defects. About Unc. $70 • 1795 [BB-51] B-14. Fillet bust; small eagle reverse. A beauty—but for slight wear on eagle's breast a truly Unc. dollar. We grade this About Unc. $65 • 1795 [BB-52] B-15. Fillet bust. Well struck, reverse with mint luster. About Unc. $80.

1796 [BB-61] B-4. Very nice specimen with some mint luster. Without usual handling marks. Light scratches in left field (done at mint). About Unc. $140.

1797 [BB-73] B-1. The rare perfect dies—these dies broke early. Not well struck; showing only very little wear; well centered. EF. $100.

1798 [BB-105] B-23. Beautiful specimen with full mint luster. Just a shade off Unc., struck weak in center. $35 • 1798 [BB-108] B-13. Struck slightly off center. Equalization marks on shield (done at mint, as said before). Much mint luster. Choice specimen. About Unc. $55 • 1798 [BB-113] B-27. Retaining much mint luster and showing only the slightest, if any, wear. Well struck up and centered. Not quite Unc. $60.

1799/8 [BB-142] B-1. This beauty, with its mint luster, is just a shade from Unc. Shows none of the defects usually found on these heavy coins. $85 • 1799/8 [BB-142] B-1a. Well struck and lustrous. Unc. $110.

1799 [BB-155] B-19. Slight rubbing on high points. Lustrous, and a shade from Unc. $61 • **1799** [BB-161] B-11a. Sharp, well-centered lustrous specimen, showing "waves" above date where clouds from reverse die are incused. A shade from Unc. $70.

1800 [BB-190] B-10a. Showing a minor bruise below first star; slight rubbing on high spots. Beautiful prooflike surface, nicely toned and struck. Just about Unc. $50 • **1800** [BB-191] B-11. AMERICAI variety. Lustrous, well-struck and centered example, showing little or no handling defects or wear of any sort, is no doubt the finest specimen known. EF. $130 edge bruises under date. Reverse more lustrous than obverse; usual handling defects. Choice VF. $40.

1801 [BB-212] B-2. Planchet defect on rim at first star; edge bruise below bottom curl. Fine to VF. $27.50 • **1801** [BB-213] B-3. Beautiful, well struck and centered specimen of high quality. Minor edge bruise at sixth star and slight bag defects take nothing away from this lustrous, Unc. dollar. $85 • **1801** [BB-214] B-4. About Unc., showing only slight rubbing on bust and light scratches in hair. $50.

1802/1 [BB-232] B-4. The rare close overdate. Lustrous and nicely toned, but struck weakly on left side. Reverse has prooflike surface. Unc. $105 • **1802/1** [BB-234] B-3. Sharp, lustrous strike, well centered, cabinet friction on high spots. A shade from Unc. $110.

1802 [BB-241] B-6. Sharp, bluish gold, Unc. specimen. Slight nick on forehead. $85 • **1802** [BB-242] B-5. Evenly worn and well centered; light scratch above bust. Well above average. Choice VF, a shade from EF. $42.50.

1803 [BB-251] B-1. Was cleaned and is now starting to tone. Evenly worn; edge bruises. VF-EF. $45 • **1803** [BB-252] B-5. VF, with some mint luster. $50 • **1803** [BB-255] B-6. Well struck and centered, with much mint luster. Choice EF. The slightest signs of friction keep this piece out of the Unc. class. $110.

1804. R. Coulton Davis specimen. [Lengthy description omitted here.] $8,000.

Stack's sale of the Anderson-Dupont Collection, November 11-13, 1954.

1794 [BB-1] Strictly Fine to VF. Usual weakness at left stars and tops of UNITED STATES. Minute attempted puncture near third star. Few pinpoint nicks; adjustment marks around reverse border. $625 • **1795** [BB-20] B-2. Unc., prooflike surface. Usual reverse adjustment marks. $210

• **1795** [BB-52] B-15. Choice Unc., prooflike. $200 • **1798** [BB-81] B-2. Unc., full mint luster, but weakly struck on center obverse and reverse. $160 • **1798** [BB-82] B-1a. AU. Faintest traces of friction; considerable luster. $125 • • **1798** [BB-113] B-27. Unc. Weakly struck on reverse borders. $80 • **1799/8** [BB-141] B-3. Unc., full mint luster. $117.50 • **1799** [BB-157] B-5a. Unc., nearly equal to last, but a trace of friction on eagle's breast, and two tiny nicks on drapery. Adjustment marks through LIBERTY. $100.

The DeCoppet Collection, sold by James Kelly, April 29-30, 1955, with the Central States Numismatic Society convention, was one of the most comprehensive holdings of early silver dollars auctioned up to that time. Relatively little publicity was given to the sale at the time, and since then few scholars have been aware of the cabinet.

1794 [BB-1] EF, coin shows marks of having been repaired at 14th star on obverse and back of F in OF on reverse. $600.

1795 [BB-13] B-9. Flowing Hair. Choice EF, beautifully toned. $107.50 • **1795** [BB-27] B-5. Flowing Hair. Unc. $135 • **1795** [BB-51] B-14. Bust type, well struck. Practically Unc. with considerable mint luster. $87.50 • **1795** [BB-52] B-15. Bust type. Unc. and just as perfect as the day struck. Original mint luster. $115.

1796 [BB-61] B-4. Small date, large letters on reverse. Practically Unc. with considerable mint luster, really a beautiful coin. $90 • **1796** [BB-61] B-4a. Excessively rare variety. VF plus. $70 • **1796** [BB-65] B-5. Large Date. Practically Unc., a beautiful sharp specimen. $70.

1797 [BB-71] B-3a. Stars 10x6, smaller planchet. This rare variety is strictly Unc. Original luster and beautifully toned. $115

1798 [BB-82] B-1a. Both obverse and reverse are double struck. Practically Unc. with some mint luster. $42.50 • **1798** [BB-82] B-1a. VF. $65 • **1798** [BB-95] B-6. Large eagle as are all of the 1798 [BB-105] B-23. Wide Date. Practically Unc. Very slight adjustment marks. $71 • **1798** [BB-116] B-30. Close Date. This is one of the finest specimens known of this very rare variety. EF, well struck. $75 • **1798** [BB-120] B-12. This rare variety is well struck and the stars on reverse sharper than usual. VF plus. $42.50 • **1798** [BB-121] B-9. Compact Date. Practically Unc. and well struck, beautifully toned. Really a gem dollar. $120 • **1798** [BB-123] B-8. However shows some cracks on reverse as on B-8a, Rarity-5, Close

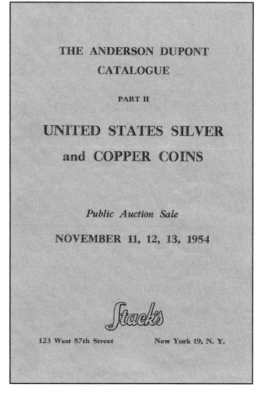

THE ANDERSON DUPONT
CATALOGUE

PART II

UNITED STATES SILVER
and COPPER COINS

Public Auction Sale

NOVEMBER 11, 12, 13, 1954

Stack's

123 West 57th Street   New York 19, N. Y.

date, four berries in branch. Choice AU. $51.

1799/8 [BB-141] B-3. Practically Unc., well struck. $55 • 1799/8 [BB-142] B-1. Practically Unc., beautifully toned. $55 • 1799/8 [BB-142] B-1a. Practically Unc. $85.

1799 [BB-156] B-7a. EF, well struck. Considerable mint luster. $60 • 1799 [BB-158] B-16a Practically Unc. with considerable mint luster. $60 • 1799 [BB-159] B-23. Unc. with beautiful, lustrously toned surface. Very slight scar below bottom curl of hair. $110 • 1799 [BB-160] B-12a. Practically Unc. $52.50 • 1799 [BB-160] B-12b. Unc. with some mint luster. $115 • 1799 [BB-161] B-11b or 11c. Practically Unc., some mint luster. $75 • 1799 [BB-162] B-6. Practically Unc., well struck. $60 • 1799 [BB-169] B-21. Rare variety, well struck and just a shade from Unc. Some mint luster. $62.50.

1800 1800 [BB-187] B-16. Practically Unc., well struck with lustrous prooflike surface. A gem coin. $60 • 1800 [BB-188] B-8. Practically Unc. A beautiful, well struck coin. $67.50 • • 1800 [BB-190] B-10a. Practically Unc. $42.50 • 1800 [BB-191] B-11. Ext. Fine, well struck, considerable mint luster. $90 • 1800 [BB-192] B-19b. AMERICAI. A choice practically Unc. specimen. $47.50 • 1800 [BB-193] B-18. Well struck and practically Unc. $43 • 1800 [BB-196] B-17a. A beautiful Unc. specimen with original mint luster. $110 • 1800 [BB-196] B-17a. Practically Unc. $65.

1801 [BB-212] B-2. Practically Unc., beautifully toned. $77.50.

1802 [BB-241] B-6. Practically Unc. $82.50 • 1802 [BB-242] B-5. Practically Unc. $105.

1803 [BB-252] B-5. Practically Unc. $90 • 1803 [BB-255] B-6. Well struck and practically Unc. Prooflike surface. $55.

The T. James Clarke Collection, with additions, sold by New Netherlands Coin Company (48th Sale), November 1956.

1794 [BB-1]. Close to EF; from a wear viewpoint, fully VF-35. $625.

1795 [BB-13] B-9. Strictly EF. $130 • 1795 [BB-18] B-7. F Only slightest friction on hair above ear and eagle's breast separate this from Unc. $115 • 1795 [BB-21] B-1. Strictly EF, closer to AU. $135 • 1795 [BB-27] B-5. EF. Liberty's hair softly, yet boldly struck; eagle, at breast and high points, flat as usual. $52.50 • 1795 [BB-51] B-14. Called "Unc. Gem" and the "Finest Known" by Mr. Clarke. $240 • 1795 [BB-51] B-14. Strictly EF. $65.

1796 [BB-61] B-4. Choice Unc. $225 • 1796 [BB-63] B-2. full AU-55, only a shade from Mint State. $320.

1797 [BB-71] B-3. Only a hair's breadth from full Unc. $155 • 1797 [BB-72] B-2. Obverse a strong Fine, reverse weak (as always found upon this RRR variety). $170 • 1797 [BB-73] B-1. Strictly EF, the obverse with strong claims to AU-55. $67.50.

1798 [BB-81] B-2. Strictly Unc. $285 • 1798 [BB-95] B-7. Strictly VG - called "Fine for coin." $32.50 • 1798 [BB-105] B-23a. Strictly Unc., but not quite in the "gem" class as claimed by Mr. Clarke. $135 • 1798 [BB-116] B-30. Pronounced obverse die breaks emanating at border directly below 9 of date. Unc. $165 • 1798 [BB-121] B-9. VF. $32.

1799/8 [BB-142] B-1a. Lustrous, iridescent Unc. $95 • 1799/8 [BB-142] B-1a. The reverse from even a more advanced die state. (Should be B-1b.) Flaws at I in AMERICA and breaks at ATES OF particularly prominent and advanced. While only VF plus, parts of this later impression are far superior to the last. $47.50 • 1799/8

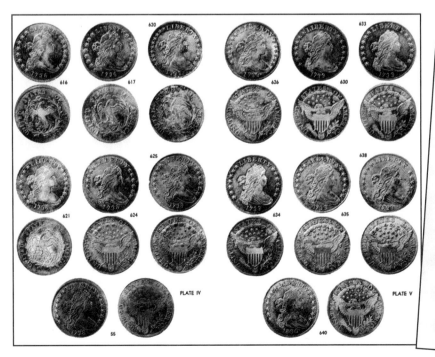

PLATE IV   PLATE V

[BB-143] B-2. Die break through D, as mentioned by Bolender, plus several other light cracks. Abt. EF and choice. $82.50.

1799 [BB-153] B-4. Fully VF. $57.50 • 1799 [BB-158] B-16. About Unc. $75 • 1799 [BB-159] B-23. Choice Unc. $260 • 1799 [BB-160] B-12a. Unc. $77.50 • 1799 [BB-160] B-12b. Similar to last; shattered obverse die as described. Brilliant Unc., almost in the "gem" class. $340 • 1799 [BB-161] B-11b. Strictly VF. $50 • 1799 [BB-162] B-6a. Lightly toned Unc. $180 • 1799 [BB-164] B-17. Fully EF. $24 • 1799 [BB-164] B-17b. Similar to last; reverse die cracked clearly from border through UNITED, left wing, up through ST. An additional crack, among others, at the base of ATES. (See lot 125, Bolender's 183rd sale.) Not quite full Unc. $72.50 • 1799 [BB-166] B-9. About Unc. $42.50.

1800 [BB-181] B-1 Misstruck freak; off-center with border 1/8" deep at lower left obv. and upper left rev. VF plus. $32.50 • 1800 [BB-183] B-3. Full Mint State. $460 • 1800 [BB-187] B-16. EF. $70 • 1800 [BB-187] B-16. With unpublished obverse die crack clearly visible from border below last O in date, through drapery and bust, to tenth star. EF. $70 • 1800 [BB-190] B-10. Very close to, but not quite Unc. $66 • 1800 [BB-192] B-19a. Strictly EF. $42.

1801 [BB-211] B-1. EF, closer to AU. $125 • 1801 [BB-213] B-3. Rusted obverse die; same as last Remarkably sharp, and very close to Unc. $75.

1802/1 [BB-232] B-4. Strictly Unc. $172.50 • 1802/1 [BB-232] B-4. Short undescribed obverse break from top of bust line to last star, as upon the last. Close to EF, evenly and strongly struck. $62.50.

1802 [BB-241] B-6. Brilliant Unc. "gem." $150 • 1802 [BB-241] B-6 Unc., but hardly as desirable as last. $75.

1803 [BB-255] B-6a. Better than EF, cleaner than the last. $62.50 • 1803 [BB-255] B-6a. Unc., but not pristine. $95 • 1803 [BB-256] B-3. Unc., a gorgeous first-strike. $450.

Stack's sale of the Samuel W. Wolfson Collection, May 3-4, 1963, included a rare 1804 dollar as well as many other notable coins:

1794 [BB-1] Strictly Fine and sharp. Usual weakness on left side of coin both obverse and reverse which is characteristic of this date. Liberty head on obverse very sharp. $2,000 • **1795** [BB-51] B-14. Bust type. EF, lustrous. $245 • 1795 [BB-51] B-14. EF, sharp. $250 • **1797** [BB-71] B-3. Br. Unc., full mint bloom. Usual weak strike in center of coin. $600 • 1797 [BB-73] B-1. About Unc. 350 • **1799/8** [BB-141] B-3. A lustrous, highly toned example, nicely struck. Unc., fairly well centered. $260 • 1799/8 [BB-142] B-1. 13 Stars. Br. Unc., sharply struck. Full mint bloom, deep serrated borders. $435 • **1799** [BB-159] B-23. Perfectly centered, sharply struck, almost full mint luster. About Unc. $300 • 1799 [BB-166] B-9. Lustrous About Unc. example, with almost full mint luster. $100 • **1800** [BB-192] B-19.

AMERICAI. Just a shade from Unc., delicately toned, full mint luster. $125 • **1801** [BB-213] B-3. Wide Date. EF, lightly toned. Sharp strike. $120 • **1802/1** [BB-234] B-3. Wide EF. Light toning. $90 • **1802** [BB-241] B-6. Close, perfect date. EF. $150.

Lester Merkin's sale of the A.J. Ostheimer, 3rd Collection, September 18-19, 1968. The 1968 Merkin sale contained many fine coins, but many of Ostheimer's best—such as the Uncirculated 1794 bought at the Lord St. Oswald Collection sale at Christie, Manson & Woods in 1964, and an Uncirculated 1795 [BB-20] B-2 from the same event—were not included. The 1794 and other treasures were sold privately in 1972 to Superior Stamp & Coin Company, Inc., which the next year auctioned the coins as part of the Gilhousen offering. Who knows where the 1795 [BB-20] B-2 went (it was in neither the Ostheimer nor the Gilhousen listings).

1794 [BB-1] B-1. Overall better than Fine, struck somewhat more strongly than average on a planchet showing light adjustment marks (mostly on obv.) and various lamination defects and splits near date, one of them visible also on edge and outer rim above second T. Comparatively clean surfaces, in some areas suggesting VF or better; two or three pinpoint nicks, of no importance. Pin scratch in 9. All of legend and stars clear, though 7 and tops of STATES are weak. $2,700.

1795 [BB-11] B-3. Brilliant Unc. 1,250 • 1795 [BB-13] B-9b. Brilliant Unc., needle sharp strike, full breast feathers, full curls, full claws. Full frost. Severe planchet defect on bust, long sliver-like lamination defect at N of UNITED. $1,350 1795 [BB-18] B-7. Really Unc., frosty, exceptionally clean surfaces, not fully struck up. Gray and blue tone, reverse iridescent. Obverse slight planchet defects. $1,800 • 1795 [BB-21] B-1. 1795 over 1195. Choice Unc., obverse field prooflike, reverse frosty. Faint obverse adjustment marks, two minute hidden reverse rim nicks, trivial bag marks. Minute traces of cabinet friction. Above average strike. $2,500 • 1795 [BB-27] B-5. Borderline Unc., obverse well above AU, reverse fully Mint State and choice. Faint cabinet friction. Many adjustment marks at left and central obverse; tiny reverse rim nick. $1,500 • 1795 [BB-51] B-14. Almost Unc. Iridescent steel, blue and dull gold tone; frosty surfaces, many reverse adjustment marks. Above average strike. Hidden reverse border dent. $2,000 • 1795 [BB-52] B-15a. About Unc. $550.

1796 [BB-65] B-5b. Large date, small letters. AU or so, peacock blue and lilac iridescence over mint frost. $425.

1797 [BB-71] B-3. Stars 10x6. Choice Unc. Tiny spots and streaks, evidently in planchet before striking; minute bag marks. $900 • 1797 [BB-73] B-1b. Stars 9x7, large letters. EF, usual weak uneven strike, with much mint luster and iridescence; clean surface. $425.

1798 [BB-105] B-23a. Pale golden toned Unc. Struck sharply except in centers. Planchet lightly streaked as made. $420 • 1798 [BB-112] B-15 . Golden and dull violet Unc., weak strike, the weakness in centers as usual. $660 • 1798 [BB-113] B-27a. Frosty, lightly toned Unc., light bag marks. $1,800 • 1798 [BB-120] B-12. Marked EF, this is nearly that level in sharpness, with surfaces showing mint luster and some streaky gray tone. Condition Census. $160 • 1798 [BB-121] B-9. Nearly About Unc., one of three finest known. $330 • 1798 [BB-122] B-14b. Really EF, lustrous, but weakly struck from injured, buckled and lapped dies. $330.

1799/8 [BB-142] B-1. About Unc., pale gold tone, frosty, bold but uneven strike. $240 • 1799/8 [BB-143] B-2a. Unpublished advanced die cracks. AU, uneven and rather indefinite strike, frosty pale gold tone. $250.

1799 [BB-151] B-13. High Practically Unc. Mint frost with iridescent cool tone; light adjustment marks on reverse; trivial handling marks. $600 • 1799 [BB-152] B-15a. Almost More or less Unc., irregular blue toning, uneven and somewhat weak strike. $310 • 1799 [BB-153] B-4a. High Irregular date with 15 reverse stars; shattered obverse. Choice Unc., weak in centers but with splendid luster and prooflike surface; irregular toning and tarnish, natural streakiness and almost no bagmarks. $800 • 1799 [BB-156] B-7a. EF, choice, lustrous, gray toned, clean and almost free of bagmarks. Condition Census level. $210 • 1799 [BB-158] B-16c. Unc., peacock blue and antique gold toning with sunset overtones; planchet defect at U; small rim dent on either side. $650 • 1799 [BB-158] B-16e. Golden and violet toned Unc., traces of cabinet friction, sharper strike than usual. $380 • 1799 [BB-159] B-23. Low Five Stars Facing. About Unc. plus. Lustrous, sunset toned. $270 • 1799 [BB-160] B-12a. No Berries. About Unc., plus. Faintest traces of cabinet friction and a few minor handling marks on either side. Almost full mint frost. Condition Census level. $360 • 1799 [BB-161] B-11b. Faintly iridescent pale gray toned choice Unc. Excellent sharp strike; one or two bag marks short of gem level. $1,000 • 1799 [BB-162] B-6b. High Iridescently toned Choice Unc. Faint reverse adjustment marks; almost free of bag marks. Unusually bold strike. $475 • 1799 [BB-164] B-17. Largest berries. Unc., magnificent prooflike surfaces; faint obverse cabinet friction, reverse superior and with full breast feathers, though weak at parts of right wing as usual. Beautiful iridescent toning. Light reverse adjustment marks. $450 • 1799 [BB-165] B-8b. R-2, this die state RR. Frosty, iridescently toned gem Unc. Weak in central obverse, and above eagle's head, elsewhere needle sharp. $750 • 1799 [BB-166] B-9b. Iridescent golden toned Unc., a couple of faint pin scratches short of gem grade. Advanced die cracks. $410.

1800 [BB-187] B-16. High EF-AU. $190 • 1800 [BB-188] B-8a. VF, some mint luster; defective planchet with many cracks; tiny rim nick either side. $120 • 1800

[BB-189] B-5a. High VF, uneven strike, some luster, light warm tone, pleasing natural gloss. $200 • 1800 [BB-193] B-18b. Brilliant Unc., peripheral tone, part of cheek and adjacent hair not up. Extremely rare with obverse cracks in stars. $340 • 1800 [BB-196] B-17b. AU or so, dull gold toning, some mint luster; reverse superior to obverse. $240.

1801 [BB-211] B-1b. High AU. Condition Census level. $380 • 1801 [BB-212] B-2a. EF-AU, brilliant, doubtless cleaned long ago, lightly bag marked. Condition Census level. $380 • 1801 [BB-214] B-4. Close Date. EF plus, highly lustrous, peripherally toned, cleaned long ago. Condition Census level. $330.

1802 [BB-241] B-6. Normal date divided 18 02. Slightly short of Unc., having light slide marks on cheek and bust; evidence of old cleaning. $425.

1803 [BB-255] B-6. Large 3. More or less Unc., prooflike surface, struck from repolished dies. Exceptional. $450.

The Gilhousen Collection sold by Superior Galleries, October 1973. This magnificent offering, sold under the pseudonym of Clarke Gilhousen, included outstanding coins from a specialized collection of silver dollars formed by Alfred J. Ostheimer, 3rd.

1794 [BB-1] Frosty, gray toned Uncirculated, one of the sharpest strikes ever reported. Date, all stars, all of back hair, feathers and leaves, dentils at left on both sides, and letters in UNITED STATES—all the details which normally come weak or illegible on 1794 dollars,—are here unusually bold. Minor field handling marks, one reverse rim dent; some adjustment marks (as made) near borders. Light clash marks but no rim break. One of two finest known. [From the Lord St. Oswald Collection, Christie's, London, 1964, Lot 138; to Alfred J. Ostheimer, 3rd; description condensed] $110,000 • 1794 [BB-1] A second, with the clash marks mostly faded out and with the beginnings of the exceedingly rare rim break at 7th star. VF and a far above average strike, the normally weak details at left being bold (except for tips of some dentils and the very tops of UNITED STA). $12,500 • 1794 [BB-1] A third. Intermediate die state, with plain clash marks but no rim break. Some areas of Fine sharpness, others of VF, but a large lamination defect behind head (as made) and about 1/3 the area of left reverse is covered by small pit marks. Usual strike with weak left stars and date, UNITED STATES hardly legible, dentils at left not discernible. $5,250.

1795 [BB-18] B-7. Richly toned prooflike Uncirculated, somewhat soft strike. Light handling marks near lowest curls. Believed to be by a small margin finest of four top examples of this variety. Ex Bolender, W.G. Baldenhofer, Ostheimer. Pictured (obverse and reverse) on the Bolender plates. $9,000 • 1795 [BB-23] B-16. Obverse of the regularly seen B-1; reverse with single outer berry at C, berry below upright of M. The variety was discovered by M.H.

Bolender 30 years ago, remaining unique to the present day. A lovely borderline Uncirculated specimen with some faint obverse scratches, numerous reverse adjustment marks and lovely iridescent toning. Full breast feathers, though with a small round nick on them. Ex Bolender, K.P. Austin and A.J. Ostheimer. (Pictured on the Bolender plates). $13,000 • 1795 [BB-25] B-6. The regularly seen 3 leaves reverse as on the common Bolender-5 but with the rarer obverse die immediately identifiable by top of Y too high. Better than VF, with much mint luster near letters, stars, and devices. Traces of old cleaning, couple of small light rim dents either side. Many obverse adjustment marks, as made. Unknown to exist in full Mint State, and a grossly undervalued coin, at least 10 times scarcer than the B-5. Early die state, no clash marks. $825 • 1795 [BB-26] B-12b. Three leaves. E repunched, I B too far apart, reverse of B-5, B-6; but the extremely rare state III, later than any known to Bolender, with heavy break from rim through 7 (a horizontal lump between 7 and the break) and extending up to near ear. VG/Fine, some of the central obverse weakness undoubtedly because of die failure. $675 • 1795 [BB-51] B-14. AU and richly toned with much of its original mint surfaces still intact. Central reverse adjustment marks. Ex Bolender, K.P. Austin and A.J. Ostheimer. Pictured obverse and reverse on the Bolender plates. $5,000 • 1795 [BB-52] B-15a. With the rare reverse advanced die cracks not known to Bolender (rim above D through S and leaves below TAT, and at tops of ICA); advanced rust marks in fields. EF, sharp, lustrous, with warm irregular toning. Probably one of the last ones made, late October 1795. $2,500.

1796 [BB-65] B-5. Large date, small letters. AU, mostly deeply toned and lustrous, but with four or five similar light areas of rubbing. Not known to exist in full Mint State. Ex Baldenhofer, Ostheimer. $6,500 • 1796 [BB-66] B-1. Practically Uncirculated, deeply toned but with much mint luster, light cabinet friction in very center of reverse, many central obverse adjustment marks. Very rare and long known as the unequaled finest of this variety. Ex R. Coulton Davis, Baldenhofer, Ostheimer. $5,000.

1797 [BB-71] B-3c. Warmly toned Uncirculated, a number of reverse scratches on eagle. Well struck, frosty and beautiful. Probably the finest known. Ex Baldenhofer, Ostheimer. $6,250 • 1797 [BB-72] B-2. Obverse almost VF and may qualify at that level; reverse better than Fine, probably should be graded as VF in terms of actual wear. This great rarity was struck from a very worn reverse die, and the reverse weakness is absolutely characteristic. (Compare 1798 B-2 below, which is struck from the same reverse die, and which though AU and lustrous still shows abnormal weakness in the same places as this coin.) Clean surfaces suggestive of VF, with only minimal handling marks. One of the top six specimens known, out of possibly 20 survivors of only 342 minted, February 28, 1797. $1,550 • 1797 [BB-73] B-1e. AU, deeply

and irregularly toned, lustrous, with several tiny rubbed places. The most advanced die state known, shattered and bulged. Ex Baldenhofer, Ostheimer. $6,750.

1798 [BB-81] B-2a. With the extended obverse scratches. AU, deeply toned with flashes of original mint brilliance; unusually sharp strike; a couple of small rubbed places, less noticeable than on some of the earlier pieces in this group. One of two finest known of this well-known variety. Ex Lester Merkin, November 1965, Ostheimer. $5,100 • 1798 [BB-82] B-1a. VF or better. $560 • 1798 [BB-95] B-6. Reverse solid base to first A of AMERICA. Struck before the die was cracked or reground. VF, lustrous, warmly toned, with few minute handling marks, mostly on obverse. Very scarce. $445 • 1798 [BB-95] B-7. Same type. Same obverse, reverse with normal A. VG. One of possibly six known, all in worn condition. The first time one of this variety has been publicly auctioned, to our knowledge, in the last 20 years. $485 • 1798 [BB-101] B-17. Very wide date, dentils weak and widely spaced at bottom and left; reverse of Bolender-6b reground, berries almost invisible. EF, lustrous, iridescently toned. One of three finest known. Ex Boyd, WGC, Bolender, Ruby. $1,050 • 1798 [BB-102] B-20a. Rim break below tail. Nearly EF, weak in centers. Mint luster and iridescent toning. Very rare break, unknown to Bolender at the time of writing his book, but presumably known to him later as this piece is ex Bolender, Ruby. $475 • 1798 [BB-104] B-22a. With the beginning of the break down through E of STATES (usually without break). VF or better, centers not well up; tiny rim dent near 9th star. Very scarce, much more than Bolender realized. $260 • 1798 [BB-107] B-21. Borderline Uncirculated, really full Mint State but too many plain adjustment marks in central obverse. Frosty, with beautiful iridescent tone. Finest known and unequaled. Approached only by three AUs. Ex Bolender, Ruby. $1,800 • 1798 [BB-111] B-11 b. Very rare break across head and field almost taking out last star. Fine or better for the coin, central obverse weakness unquestionably due to the advanced die failure. Probably one of the last made from this die. $280 • 1798 [BB-113] B-27. Very deeply toned Uncirculated, sharply struck and believed finest known. Ex K.P. Austin, Ostheimer. $5,750 • 1798 [BB-115] B-31a. Extremely rare shattered die. EF, the reverse seemingly VF but its weakness is definitely from die failure. Unusually broad border. Mint luster and iridescent toning. One of three finest known of this famous Ex Bolender plate coin. $775 • 1798 [BB-116] B-30. Fine double profile. Rainbow toned Uncirculated, lustrous and as sharp as this variety comes. Very rare, and long known to be finest of the variety. Ex Baldenhofer, Ostheimer. $5,300 • 1798 [BB-120] B-12a. Unpublished shattered die. Obverse cracked between 79 up to drapery, from rim through first star, and from rim at lower right stars. Reverse crack described for B-12 now extends through dentils through dentils over ES OF AM; an obverse crack through drapery has occasioned massive die failure, weakening drapery and rendering opposite stars (behind eagle's head) illegible. Better than VF for coin. the only one we have heard of. $725 • 1798 [BB-121] B-9a. Shattered and rusted dies. Some areas suggest EF sharpness as do some surfaces, which display mint luster, but this dollar is weaker in centers especially on reverse, possibly from die failure. Overall grade of VF. Very scarce. $360 • 1798 [BB-122] B-14a. than VF, some areas suggest EF, mint luster. Iridescent tone. Rare die state, rarer condition; only one full EF has ever been reported (Miles Collection). This is probably one of three top examples. $575 • 1798 [BB-124] B-25b. Rare shattered die state. Sharpness of About Fine, surfaces suggest a higher grade; deep gray tone. The weaknesses are from extensive die failure. Ex Kreisberg sale, November 19, 1962, Lot 1172, Ruby. $320 • 1798 [BB-125] B-24a. Scarce advanced cracks. Obverse nearly EF, lustrous and iridescently toned, reverse VF, weakly struck. $475.

1799/8 [BB-141] B-3. Very deeply toned Uncirculated, faintest suggestion of cabinet friction in one or two tiny places on reverse. Equal overall at least to the Miles and Taylor examples; has been called finest known. Ex Baldenhofer, Ostheimer. $5,300 • 1799/8 [BB-142] B-1a. Unlisted shattered reverse die state. VF, a rather weak soft strike as on the others seen from this die state (Clarke, Davis-Graves specimens). Many times rarer than the early state described by Bolender. $430.

1799 [BB-151] B-13. 13-star reverse showing die flaws at E of STATES. Surfaces of AU or better, much mint luster and only minor handling marks (three on rims, not very noticeable). Touches of cabinet friction consistent with a grade above EF. Extremely rare, underrated by Bolender; a full One of three top examples, apparently tied for second finest though of the three (this one, the Austin and the Taylor-Baldenhofer coins)_ there is at most 5 points spread in grade; the other 6 or 7 now known are in Good to Fine. The earliest variety of the year, its obverse a leftover from 1798 though with date originally minus final digit; die break progressions prove that this preceded Bolender-15, Bolender-4 and the three overdates. Ex Bolender, Ruby. $1,200 • 1799 [BB-153] B-4. Irregularly toned, prooflike Uncirculated, weakly struck in centers but much better struck elsewhere. Advanced obverse cracks. Finer of only two Uncirculated examples reported. Rare in all grades, very rare above VF. Ex K.P. Austin, Ostheimer, via Lester Merkin auction, September 1968, Lot 275. $4,500 • 1799 [BB-154] B-18. Early state with only the first and last breaks mentioned by Bolender. Better than VF, traces of mint luster, with its quota of minute handling marks. Edge planchet defects (as made) left of date and extending to above E of STATES. Very rare, a high R-6 though possibly not quite One of the half dozen or so finest, exceeded by three EFs and tied or minutely exceeded by a couple of others not quite reaching EF. Ex Fairbanks 562, Ruby. $450 • 1799 [BB-155] B-19a. With additional obverse cracks not mentioned by Bolender. Better than VF, some traces of luster, gray toning. Very rare. Ex Bolender, Ruby. $375 • 1799 [BB-156] B-7d. Unlisted shattered and buckled reverse dies, one of two latest states seen. Seemingly VF, under a glass some areas display no more wear than would be consistent with EF grade, with plenty of mint luster. One of only three seen in this die state. Ex Bolender, Ruby. $525 • 1799 [BB-157] B-5a. AU plus, deep iridescent toning and mint brilliance, but a plain old scratch

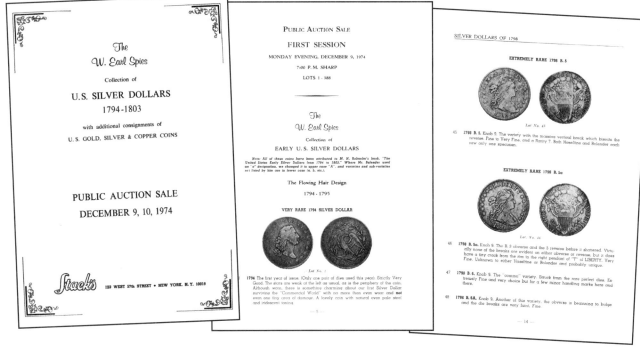

from nose to 10th star. Ex Bolender, Ruby. $1,150 • 1799 [BB-158] B-16b. Shattered obverse die, clashed reverse, one of the later die states covered by this number. EF to AU. As fine as the variety comes, exceeded in the earlier and commoner die states by one or two with minutely fewer signs of handling, but so far as we know unsurpassed in the rare late die states. Ex Bolender, Ruby. $1,050 • 1799 [BB-159] B-23. Almost EF. Early die state, before the clash marks on the bulge developed. Rare and extremely popular type coin. $425 • 1799 [BB-160] B-12b. Surfaces suggest a grade of AU or better, with plenty of mint luster and lovely iridescent toning, but there is enough cabinet friction to suggest EF grade. A splendid piece, one for the type collector. Ex Bolender, Ruby. $875 • 1799 [BB-161] B-11b. The reverse breaks much extended and with others not mentioned by Bolender. Nearly VF, irregularly toned, several small rim dents. This was the discovery specimen and the die state remains very rare. Ex O.K. Rumbel collection, 1952 ANA Convention Sale, Lot 3172, Ruby. $375 • 1799 [BB-162] B-6a. Warmly toned Uncirculated, sharp except in centers (where adjustment marks show on reverse); minute rim nicks. Said to be finest known of this rare variety. Ex Bolender, K.P. Austin, Ostheimer. Pictured (obverse and reverse) on the Bolender plates. $5,500 • 1799 [BB-163] B-10b. Greatly advanced die breaks, the break through O heavy. More or less EF, much mint luster even in those areas of fields where even brief circulation would have obliterated it; fails to qualify as AU or better only because of a little too much cabinet friction on three or four of the highest places. Few small plain bag marks on either side, more on reverse than on obverse. Light traces of old cleaning. Well struck for this rare advanced die state, which is unusual. $1,300 • 1799 [BB-164] B-17b. Advanced die cracks on reverse (at OF and IC) unknown to Bolender at time of writing. Close to EF, softly struck, with some luster (mostly on reverse) and some signs of old cleaning, now toning down naturally. Very rare, first reported in the Philip Straus estate, fewer than a dozen seen in all. Ex Bolender-Ruby. $575 • 1799 [BB-166] B-9c. Shattered obverse die unknown to Bolender at time of writing. Almost VF, two or three small rim nicks either side. This die state very rare. Ex Bolender, Ruby. $425 • 1799 [BB-167] B-14. VF and scarce; some mint luster, deep irregular iridescent tone, and obverse shows central adjustment marks, as made. Scarce and important as only one full EF has been seen to date, nothing above. Ex Bolender, Ruby. $350.

1800 [BB-188] B-8b. Advanced crack through AMERIC unmentioned by Bolender. Much frosty mint luster with warm irregular tone, but a little too much cabinet friction to qualify as full EF, though some areas do suggest this grade. Reverse struck from worn dies and grades VF. Important, as only two are now known that will grade EF or higher. $675 • 1800 [BB-189] B-5. Better than VF, faint traces of

luster, warm gray tone, minute handling marks; some parts suggest EF grade. Rare and important, probably one of the top three or four examples; only one full EF is known, and the other top specimens differ from this only by a point or two. $625 • 1800 [BB-191] B-11. The rarer of the two "AMERICAI" varieties. EF, lustrous, richly toned, many areas suggesting AU. Tied for finest known with one other, and may even be a point or two finer Ex Bolender, Ruby. $650 • 1800 [BB-193] B-18d. Extremely rare advanced breaks unknown to Bolender. Almost EF. B-18 with clashed dies but without any die breaks is common, but with any of the extra breaks it is a great and unappreciated rarity. (Same dies as "Bolender-13." the latter, extremely rare, before dies clashed.) Ex Bolender, Ruby. $775.

1801 [BB-214] B-4. Choice VF. By a small margin, scarcest of the collectible 1801s. This is in the Condition Census; apparently only one full Uncirculated is known. Ex Bolender, Ruby. $650.

1802/1 [BB-232] B-4a. Early state of unlisted crack through bust to 13th star. EF, much mint luster, lovely iridescent tone; tiny rim nick on either side. Very scarce. Ex Bolender, Ruby. $575 • 1802/1 [BB-235] B-9b. With the diagnostic die chop between curl point and B, and the crack from rim into drapery, and the second crack through 11th and 12th stars to rim. Better than EF, richly toned; one of two top examples of this extreme rarity. Ex Baldenhofer, Ostheimer. $1,300.

1802 [BB-241] B-6. Sharp but bagmarked AU cleaned years ago and now with natural sunset tone, which effectively conceals most of the faint scratches. Ex Baldenhofer, Ostheimer. $2,000 • 1802 [BB-242] B-5. Wide normal date. EF/AU, some original prooflike surface, warm light iridescent tone. Reverse with full breast feathers. Tied with one other for second finest of this R-7; possibly the most undervalued single coin in the *Guide Book*. Obverse pictured on the Bolender plate. Ex Bolender, Ruby. $1,600.

1803 [BB-251] B-1. Small 3. VF. Rare, none known above EF. Ex Bolender, Ruby. $325 • 1803 [BB-255] B-6a. Large 3. EF-45. This variety, and the 1802 Bolender 6 which immediately preceded it, doubtless made up the 19,570 dollars actually struck in 1804. Ex Baldenhofer, Ostheimer. $1,500.

The W. Earl Spies Collection sold by Stack's, December 9-10, 1974, comprised a truly memorable cabinet of early dollars by specialized die varieties, including numerous examples of die states not mentioned in the Bolender book.

1794 [BB-1] The first year of issue. (Only one pair of dies used this year.) Strictly VG. The stars are weak at the left as usual, as is the periphery of the coin. $3,100.

1795 [BB-12] B-11. Two Haseltine's was only Good and scratched in the field. Bolender only saw one specimen! This lovely coin is Fine and perfect but for one old small reverse edge ding. This could possibly be the finest known. $850 • 1795 [BB-15] B-8. , but noticeably damaged. Bolender that he has seen only two specimens in 40 years! $575 • 1795 [BB-17] B-18. Unlisted in Bolender. The obverse is B-13, the reverse B-12. EF and wholly prooflike, with but a few very faint scratches between the 1 and 7. $1,050.

1796 [BB-61] B-4a. EF, with some prooflike surface. Beautiful iridescent toning. Bolender states that he only knows of one specimen, the Gable-Reeder specimen. A few others have been discovered since that statement, still it is a most important coin. $750 • 1796 [BB-62] B-3. VF to EF. From our Straus Sale in 1959. $950.

1798 [BB-94] B-3. Knob 9. A freak specimen in that it was double struck. The stars are now undersized because of the double strike, giving the coin a most curious appearance. At least EF, and probably a trifle better. $550 • 1798 [BB-96] B-32. Unknown to Bolender or Haseltine. A new variety having the obverse of B-6 (Knob 9) and the reverse of B-17 (10 arrows). The rim break over the "I" in AMERICA clear. Here again, a new discovery in excellent condition. EF, with a few insignificant marks on the obverse. The only other specimen we know of is the Straus coin originally given by the B-33 number and now changed by us to accommodate the discovery B-33 and B-33A in this sale). $525.00. [This is known today as BB-96.] • 1798 [BB-96] B-6b. Knob 9. Double struck with a double row of dentils, etc. About Unc., delicate iridescent toning. Really a very beautiful coin. $675 • 1798 [BB-101] B-17. Another great rarity of which only two were ever seen by Bolender. EF with mint luster and delicate iridescent toning. $430 • 1798 [BB-110] B-16. Fully EF or better with mint luster and prooflike surfaces. One of the most exciting coins of this collection! $625.

1799 [BB-162] B-6. A choice EF to AU, pale iridescent toning. $550 • 1799 [BB-163] B-10c. About Unc., full frosty mint luster. $625 • 1799 [BB-164] B-17b. About Unc. Struck on a glossy planchet which has a minor area of porosity on the obverse. $550 • 1799 [BB-165] B-8a. As above, but the delicate crack from "LIB" can be seen, the flaws now more extended on the reverse. About Unc. and frosty. $825.

1800 [BB-191] B-11. Bolender states, "Excessively rare." Fine to VF. $320.

1801 [BB-211] B-1c. About Unc., lustrous with pale steel toning. $675.

The Austin Collection, Bowers and Ruddy Galleries, May 31 and June 1, 1974, contained these early dollars.

This collection was the property of a Midwestern numismatist and had no relation to the holdings of well-known early dollar specialist K.P. Austin, of Salisbury, Maryland.

1794 [BB-1] EF with adjustment marks, particularly

around the reverse border. There is some slight and normal weakness of striking on the left side, as always seen with this issue. $20,000.

1795 [BB-25] B-6. Brilliant Unc., virtually flawless fields. Slight friction on the very highest points. $5,250 • 1795 [BB-27] B-5. AU. $3,100 • 1795 [BB-52] B-15. Draped Bust, Small Eagle. Unc., slight rubbing. prooflike fields. $3.

1796 [BB-61] B-4. EF-AU, sharp. Tiny pinpricks, very minor adjustment marks. $1,025 • 1796 [BB-61] B-4. Small Date, Large Letters. Unc. $1,800 • 1796 [BB-65] B-5. AU. $1,700.

1797 [BB-71] B-3a. Draped Bust, Stars 10 left and 6 right. Large Letters. Choice BU. $10,000.

1798 [BB-105] B-23. Unc. $2,300 • 1798 [BB-113] B-27. BU, sharply struck. A gem coin. $9,750.

1799/8 [BB-142] B-1. 13 Reverse Stars. AU, small planchet flaw at right side border. $550.

1799 [BB-154] B-18. Unc. Very minor rubbing. $2,000 • 1799 [BB-166] B-9a. Brilliant Unc. $2,500 • 1799 [BB-169] B-21. AU. $900 .

1800 [BB-195] B-15. 10 arrows on reverse. Unc., some evidence of rubbing. $2,200.

1801 [BB-213] B-3. BU, some rubbing. $3,000.

1802 [BB-241] B-6. Choice BU. Very minor marks visible with glass. $3,200 • 1802 [BB-241] B-6. Close Date. AU. $2,000.

Superior Stamp & Coin Company's ANA Convention Sale, August 19-23, 1975, contained an outstanding listing of early dollars, a number of which had been sold two years before in the same firm's Gilhousen Collection Sale. Most of these were owned earlier by Mr. and Mrs. A.J. Ostheimer, 3rd, who for much of the previous 15-year period had endeavored to build a truly memorable collection of early dollars. Cataloging was by Jon Hanson.

1794 [BB-1] From Superior's Charles L. Ruby Part I sale, Lot 1446: Intermediate die state, dies clashed but as yet without the rim break at 7th star. VF, $9,500.

1795 [BB-18] B-7. EF-45. $1,350 • 1795 [BB-18] B-7. Richly toned prooflike Unc., somewhat soft strike. 6,500 • 1795 [BB-21] B-1. 1795/1195. B-1. AU-55. Condition Census. $3,300 • 795 [BB-23] B-16. Unique. A lovely borderline Unc. specimen with some faint obverse scratches, numerous reverse adjustment marks and lovely iridescent toning. Full breast feathers, though with a small round nick on them. $7,750 • 1795 [BB-24] B-13. AU-50 or better, brilliant obverse with a lustrous toned reverse. The obverse shows many microscopic handling marks, some minor rubbing, and a crescent like scratch on Liberty's jaw, reverse with many adjustment marks. $3,300 • 1795 [BB-27] B-5. MS-60 to 65. $8,750 • 1795 [BB-51] B-14. AU, richly toned with much of its original mint surface still intact. $3,800 • 1795 [BB-51] B-14. MS-65. Iridescent gray toned uniformly on the obverse with uneven tones and partially light pearl tone on reverse. Full original mint luster, well struck, beautiful and a "gem" example. Good centering, but there are a few tiny nicks on the rims, the most noticeable at 2:00 on the reverse. $9,200 • 1795 [BB-51] B-14. Not quite MS-60. $4,250.

1796 [BB-65] B-5. About Unc., mostly deeply toned and lustrous, but with four or five similar light areas of rubbing. Not known to exist in full Mint State. A lustrous EF-45 at best, but unusually well struck up at the centers. $1,750 1796 [BB-66] B-1. Practically Unc., deeply toned but with much mint luster, light cabinet friction in very center of reverse, many central obverse adjustment marks. $1,850.

1797 [BB-71] B-3. 16 stars. 10x6; large letters. AU-50, lightly toned, and lustrous. $3,800 • 1797 [BB-71] B-3. VF-20, well-toned, iridescently so about the devices. Well struck, centered and very clean, save for a few microscopic edge bruises. $800 • 1797 [BB-71] B-3b. Really AU-50, lustrous, but a rather dull pale color and rubbed on the high spots. Irregularly struck up about the obverse rims. Condition Census level. $1,750 • 1797 [BB-71] B-3c. Warmly toned Unc., a number of reverse scratches on eagle. Well struck, frosty and beautiful. $4.

1798 Unlisted. Reverse of Bolender 4; obverse B-1. [Coin] different from B.4 as follows.... Fine-15, clean, but with the usual amount of handling marks we would expect on a coin of this grade. $1,300 • 1798 [BB-81] B-2a. Extended obverse die cracks. About Unc., deeply toned with flashes of original mint brilliance; unusually sharp strike; a couple of small rubbed places, less noticeable than on some of the earlier pieces in this group. $3,000 • 1798 [BB-113] B-27. Reverse cracked. Very deeply toned Unc., sharply struck and believed finest known. An MS-60, the deep toning is partly iridescent and conceals full, nearly flawless, lustrous mint surface. A good strike, the silhouette of Liberty's chin, lips, and nose is outstanding. Not perfectly centered. $3,500 • 1798 [BB-114] B-26. VF-30, poorly struck up at centers, but relatively clean and attractive. High Condition Census. $425 • 1798 [BB-119] B-29. AU-50, but rubbed on the high points of the obverse. Bluish toning around part of the edges, clean, and partly lustrous. Obverse very poorly centered. $1,250 • 1798 [BB-120] B-12a. Unpublished shattered die, Better than VF for coin. $500.

1799/8 [BB-141] B-3. MS-60 or so, frosty with a touch of golden about the devices, and lustrous.

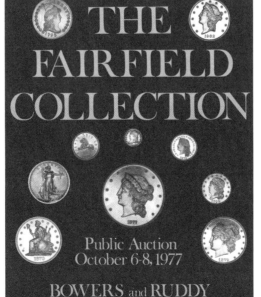

Excellent surfaces with minimal handling marks. Not fully struck up in the center portions of the reverse as usual for this variety. $5,000 • 1799/8 [BB-141] B-3. Very deeply toned Unc. Faintest suggestion of cabinet friction in one or two tiny places on reverse. Not quite MS-60, but nicer looking than the cleaned Miles example. $1,600.

1799 [BB-152] B-15. High Not quite AU-50, dull frosty tone with a speck here and there of iridescent tone. $975 • 1799 [BB-157] B-5a. Almost Unc. plus, deep iridescent toning and mint brilliance, but a plain old scratch from nose to 10th star. $1,050 • 1799 [BB-159] B-23. Low AU-50. $1,250 • 1799 [BB-160] B-12b. Shattered obverse. MS-60 to 65, fully lustrous, partly brilliant, but mostly with an even grayish tone. Struck partially off center on the obverse and irregularly about the rims. 3,800 • 1799 [BB-163] B-10b. More or less EF. $950 • 1799 [BB-167] B-14. AU-50. 925 • 1799 [BB-169] B-21a. High AU-50, frosty and lustrous. Obverse unevenly struck, but better centered than the reverse. There is a scratch on the latter's side form the clouds just above the eagle's head. $900.

1800 [BB-183] B-3. AU-50, well-toned, struck, and has highly polished surfaces. $1,150 • 1800 [BB-184] B-12. AU-55 or so. $1,650 • 1800 [BB-192] B-19. AMERICAI. AU-50, heavily toned with highly glossy surfaces, and partly lustrous. Minor evidence of handling and a single spot on Liberty's neck at hair curl. $1,350 • 1800 [BB-193] B-13. Clashed die reverse. MS-60, fully lustrous and iridescently toned. $1,800.

1801 [BB-213] B-3. AU-55. $1,450.

1803 [BB-255] B-6a. Overall near to almost Unc. than to EF, much mint luster irregular gray tone, few minute rim nicks; few border adjustment marks. $735 • 1803 [BB-255] B-6a. Virtually MS-60, dark iridescent toning, and fully lustrous with a sparkling cartwheel effect. Minor signs of handling a few microscopic rim nicks, and not fully struck up on the high points. $1,350 .

The Fairfield Collection, Bowers and Ruddy Galleries, October 6-8, 1977.

1795 1795 [BB-21] B-1. AU. $5,250 • 1795 [BB-27] B-5. Flowing Hair, Small Eagle. Gem Unc. $13,000 • 1795 [BB-27] B-5. Flowing Hair, Small Eagle. Three Leaves. Borderline Unc. $7,250 • 1795 [BB-52] B-15. Draped Bust, Small Eagle. Choice BU. $10,000 • **1799/8** [BB-143] B-2. Choice Unc. $4,200 • **1799** [BB-154] B-18a. Borderline Unc. $1,650 • 1799

[BB-165] B-8. Unc. $4,200 • **1800** [BB-190] B-10. AU. $1,450 • 1800 [BB-193] B-18a. Gem Unc. $10,000 • **1802** [BB-241] B-6. Choice Unc. $5,750.

The Bowers and Ruddy Galleries sale of the Garrett Collection (The Johns Hopkins University), March 26-27, 1980.

1794 [BB-1] B-1. VF-30 with some burnishing in the fields. $40,000.

1795 [BB-14] B-4. AU-50. Full borders. The usual adjustment marks are hardly noticeable and the details are outstanding. Most of the original mint frost is evident. $15,000 • 1795 [BB-27] B-5. Choice AU-55. $27,500 • 1795 [BB-51] B-14. Draped Bust. Choice Brilliant Proof. The obverse and reverse have a full Proof surface. $170,000 • 1795 [BB-51] B-14. Draped Bust. Choice AU-55. $19,000.

1796 [BB-61] B-4. Choice EF-45. Well centered and well struck. $6,750 • 1796 [BB-65] B-5. AU-50. Extremely sharply struck. Ample evidence of original luster. $9,500.

1798 [BB-81] B-2. AU-50. $9,000 • 1798 [BB-113] B-27. Heraldic Eagle reverse. Choice Br. Unc., MS-65. Well centered, well struck, and nearly fully brilliant. $65,000 • 1798 [BB-122] B-14. AU-50. $4,000.

1799/8 [BB-142] B-1. Overdate. AU-50. $5,250.

1800 [BB-193] B-18. Choice AU-55. 34,000.

1801 [BB-213] B-3. AU-50. $4,500.

1804 King of American Coins. [Lengthy description omitted here.] From T. Harrison Garrett, earlier from O.H. Berg, John Haseltine. EF-40. Class III style. $400,000.

Stack's sale of the Amon G. Carter, Jr. Family Collection, January 18-21, 1984,

included one of the finest quality cabinets of early silver dollars ever to cross the auction block. Gems abounded, and notable coins ranged from the first in the list, a magnificent 1794, to the last, the rare 1804. A complete of 1801-2-3 Proof "restrikes" was included as well.

1794 [BB-1] Silver dollar. Probably the finest known specimen. Unc. [Description from the Will W. Neil Collection sale repeated here.] $264,000.

1795 [BB-13] B-9. EF, iridescent toning mixed with pale golden toning. $5,500 • 1795 [BB-14] B-4. Two leaves below each wing. The last star entirely under the bust. Br. Unc., full frosty mint luster. Certainly in the Condition Census for the variety. $15,400 • 1 1795 [BB-21] B-1. Two leaves below each wing of the eagle. AU and a "gem." Perfect surfaces and edges, prooflike and slightly frosty which gives an overall satiny appearance. Lovely peripheral toning. $14,300 • 1795 [BB-51] B-14. Draped Bust, Small Eagle. The bust far to left. Br. Unc. and wholly prooflike. Some tiny marks in the field but indeed second only to the incredible Garrett specimen. Exceptionally well struck, with pale russet-iridescent toning. $23,100.00. • 1795 [BB-52] B-15.

Draped Bust. The bust is centered and, by far, aesthetically more pleasing. Die break in hair before the fillet. Br. Unc., slightly prooflike, a couple of minuscule reverse rim nicks. Well struck, with very attractive peripheral toning. $24,200.

1796 [BB-63] B-2. Small date, small letters. AU and a beauty with some prooflike surfaces. Lovely pale russet toning with iridescence about the edges. $13,200.

1797 [BB-72] B-2. AU, frosty luster. The reverse only shows the weakness but shows no signs of wear. This certainly is one of the finest extant and, by far, surpasses the beautiful coin in our March 1983 sale. $6,600 • 1797 [BB-73] B-1a. Stars 9x7, large letters. AU, full frosty mint luster. An exceptionally attractive coin and certainly far above average for this date. $5,500.

1798 [BB-81] B-2. AU. Full frosty mint bloom and exceptionally well struck. The eagle is weak, as usual, . $6,600 • 1798 [BB-105] B-23a. Heraldic eagle. Very wide date. AU, frosty mint luster, and nicely struck. Condition Census. $4,125.

1799/8 [BB-142] B-1. Die cracks at T and RI on the reverse. Br. Unc. and choice. A prooflike specimen with exquisite golden and pale iridescent toning. 8,250.

1799 [BB-158] B-16a. Intermediate die state. Lacks second reverse crack at OF and crack to 5th and 6th stars. Choice Br. Unc., blazing luster. Virtually as struck. $18,700 • 1799 [BB-159] B-23b. S Br. Unc., frosty and satiny, with iridescent and russet toning. The terminal state of the die, with an arc-like crack from star one across the neck to below star 13, resulting in a massive bulging of the die. Without question, the finest known of this die state. $9,350.

1800 [BB-187] B-16a. Close date. Most letters are bifurcated. The die breaks are advanced, with multiple areas of swelling. AU, blue and iridescent toning. $6,050 • 1800 [BB-190] B-10a. Wide date. Br. Unc. Frosty and satiny, with considerable prooflike surface, mostly on the reverse. A simply splendid coin from any point of view. $7,150 • 1800 [BB-191] B-11. Br. Unc., with just a tiny rub or two on the high points. This is undoubtedly the finest known. $9,900 • 1800 [BB-195] B-15. AU, just a whisper from full Mint State. $7,700.

1801 [BB-214] Gem Br. Unc., wholly prooflike. At first glance one might think they were looking at the restrike because of the prooflike surface, strike, and edges. $20,900 • 1801 Bolender-5. "Restrike." Br. Proof. The obverse with an arc-like crack from the B through the hair as well as the usual cracks through the bottom of the date and the first eight stars. The reverse with the mirror of that crack. Delicate pale gray and golden russet toning. Obverse: Same as adopted design but the 1's have a curved top. Tip of top curl missing. Reverse: Same as used with the Class I 1804 Dollar. Ex Will W. Neil Collection, B. Max Mehl, June 17, 1947, Lot 28. $55,000.

1802/1 [BB-232] B-4. Br. Unc., full blazing luster with splendid satiny surfaces. $7,700.

1802 [BB-241] B-6. Br. Unc. and a pristine example.

$33,000 • 1802 Bolender-8. "Restrike." Br. Proof. A gem with superb russet-golden and iridescent toning. Obverse: Same as adopted design but the 2 differs from the other 1802 dies because the tip of the upper end of the 2 ends in a vertical position rather than in a horizontal position. Reverse: Same as used with the Class I 1804 Dollar. Ex Neil Collection, Lot 29. $60,500.

1803 [BB-252] B-5. Small 3. AU, sharply struck about its periphery. $9,350 • 1803 [BB-254] B-4. Small 3. Strictly VF and, as a type, the scarcest. $935 • 1803 [BB-255] B-6. Large 3. Only one die variety. AU and a lovely coin with nearly full prooflike surfaces. $5,500 • 1803 Bolender-7. "Restrike." Br. Proof. A gem with exquisite cobalt blue and golden iridescent toning. Obverse: Same as the adopted design with the large 3. Some rust spots on and around the 4th star. Reverse: Same as used with the Class I 1804 Dollar. Ex Neil Collection, Lot 30. $68,750.

1804 Class III. Extremely Fine. $198,000.

Superior Galleries' sale of the Hoagy Carmichael and Wayne Miller Collections, January 27-28, 1986. Included were several outstanding early dollars, most notably the Neil-Carter 1794 in Mint State.

1794 [BB-1] MS-63. Prooflike surfaces. Adjustment marks (file strokes are noted on the obverse rims). There is some weakness of strike around the periphery and the corresponding part of the reverse. This magnificent coin exhibits a blending of multicolored toning; a mixture of steel blue, violet and naturally grayish-golden tone. This is the Amon G. Carter coin, January 1984, Lot 207; previously from B. Max Mehl's Will W. Neil Collection, 1947. $209,000 • **1795** [BB-27] B-5. MS-63. $8,800 • 1795 [BB-51] B-14, Draped Bust. AU-55. $4,840.

The Bowers and Merena sale of the Norweb Collection, November 14-15, 1988. Offered were many important early dollars. The 1794 is one of the two Unc. pieces from the Lord St. Oswald Collection.

1794 [BB-1] B-1. MS-60/63. Believed to be second or third finest known. The obverse and reverse are of nearly full brilliance, modified by just a whisper of light gray toning. Stars on the left side of obverse are lightly struck, and at that point some mint-caused adjustment marks can be seen. The portrait of Miss Liberty is needle-sharp. The reverse is well struck, save for the tops of the letters in the area of TED STA. $242,000.

1795 [BB-20] B-2. AU-58 to MS-60, prooflike. Light golden toning blends to gunmetal blue at the borders, with

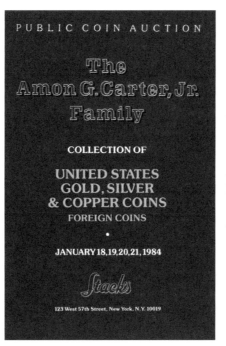

areas of silver and gold in between. $7,700 • 1795 [BB-27] B-5. Three leaves beneath each wing. AU-50. Silver and iridescent toning. A lustrous, sharply struck example. $9,900.

1797 [BB-73] B-1. AU-55. Bright, brilliant surfaces. Well centered and struck, with a broad rim of dentils serving to "frame" the interior devices. Much mint luster still survives, particularly in protected areas. $7,260.

1798 [BB-113] B-27. Heraldic Eagle. MS-60 to 63. Gorgeous bright silver surfaces, accented on the obverse by splashes of light gold. $33,000.

1799/8 [BB-141] B-3. AU-58. Lustrous, frosty with most original mint surface still visible. Bright silver surfaces accented with areas of light gray and gold. $10,450 • 1799/8 [BB-142] B-1. AU-50. Mottled medium lilac and gray surfaces. $8,250.

1799 [BB-155] B-19. AU-50. Bright silver surfaces accented with splashes of gold. $9,350.

1802 [BB-241] B-6. AU-58. Sharply struck, well centered, and very lustrous with delicate heather toning. $9,075 • 1802 Proof Restrike. B-8. Proof-65. The fields are toned a beautiful mixture of iridescent electric blue and gold. Just six to 10 specimens are known. $71,500.

Superior Galleries sale of the H. Roland Willasch Collection (with additions), **May 27, 1990.** Mr. Willasch was a well-known collector of die varieties. Many of the coins are said to have been cleaned on a periodic basis. Thus, prices were lower than uncleaned coins would have realized at the time. The reader is referred to the Willasch catalog for more information.

The Bowers and Merena sale of the Louis E. Eliasberg, Sr. Collection, Part II, April 6-8, 1997. Mr. Eliasberg collected *Guide Book* varieties and sought the finest. The following are part of the only complete collection of United States coins ever formed, from the 1793 half cent to the 1933 double eagle. The catalog includes descriptions far expanded beyond the brief notice for each coin given here.

1794 BB-1, EF-40. Tiny mark in field behind head, opposite space between stars 3 and 4. An above average strike, but with usual lightness at lower left of the obverse and at the corresponding part of the reverse (due to non-parallel die surfaces; characteristic of all known examples), the latter section showing some mint-caused adjustment marks. Probably Ex E.S. Norris Collection, S.H. and H. Chapman,

May 17, 1894; J.M. Clapp; John H. Clapp; Clapp estate, 1942. $66,000.

1795 Flowing Hair Type of '94, Two Leaves Reverse. BB-17, "B-18." Rarity-8, Unique. EF-45. The only 1795 Two Leaves reverse with 11 berries on the right branch. George H. Earle Collection, Henry Chapman, June 25-29, 1912, Lot 2671; John H. Clapp; Clapp estate, 1942. $52,800 • 1795 Flowing Hair Type of '94, Three Leaves Reverse. BB-18, B-7. MS-63. $61,600 • 1795 Flowing Hair Type of '95, Two Leaves Reverse. BB-20, B-2. MS-65. Full prooflike surface on both sides. Possible Proof presentation piece. A very nice strike overall. Very sharp on the obverse. Superb, delicate golden toning on obverse and reverse. George H. Earle Collection, Henry Chapman, June 25-29, 1912; John H. Clapp; Clapp estate, 1942. $93,500 • 1795 Flowing Hair Type of '95, Two Leaves Reverse. BB-21, B-1. AU-58. A lovely specimen, prooflike on obverse and reverse, and quite possibly struck from lightly polished dies. Some light evidence of contact on obverse and reverse and is mostly covered by delightful lilac, gold, and delicate blue toning—creating a coin which is a visual and aesthetic delight. $18,700 • 1795 Flowing Hair Type of '95, Three Leaves Reverse. BB-27, B-5. Die State III. MS-62 or finer. The surfaces are a delightful mixture of light lilac and gold, another Eliasberg coin that is absolutely incredible in its beauty. E. W. Ropes Collection, New York Coin & Stamp Co., February 28, 1899; J.M. Clapp; John H. Clapp; Clapp estate, 1942. $77,000 • 1795 Draped Bust Left obverse. Small Eagle, Small Letters reverse. BB-51, B-14. MS-67, Prooflike. Superbly, indeed, incredibly sharply struck, the very definition of the design. Brilliant surfaces with just a whisper of golden toning. This piece is certainly one of the very finest in existence of any issue in the entire Draped Bust series. Believed to be the very finest known specimen of 1795 BB-51, an incredibly important coin from the aspect of its preservation and also its numismatic and historical significance. Quite possibly the Eliasberg Collection specimen is a presentation coin to illustrate the first use of the Draped Bust obverse style. If any 1795 Draped Bust dollar is deserving of the Proof appellation, this is such a coin! George H. Earle; Henry Chapman, June 25-29, 1912; John H. Clapp; Clapp estate, 1942. $308,000.

1796 Small Date, Large Letters. BB-61, B-4. Die State I. AU-55.

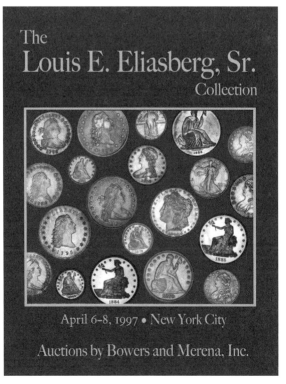

The
Louis E. Eliasberg, Sr.
Collection

April 6-8, 1997 • New York City

Auctions by Bowers and Merena, Inc.

Light golden toning over somewhat prooflike surfaces. Some splashes of blue are around the rims. Quite well struck and well defined in all areas except the very highest points at the center. Benjamin H. Collins, March 1896 (or Frossard's sale of Collins' coins, March 2-3, 1897), the records are not clear; J.M. Clapp; John H. Clapp; Clapp estate, 1942. $12,100 • 1796 Small Date, Small Letters. BB-63, B-2. VF-30. John G. Mills Collection, S.H. and H. Chapman, April 27-29, 1904; J.M. Clapp; John H. Clapp; Clapp estate, 1942 $4,400 • 1796 Large Date, Small Letters. BB-65, B-5. Die State II. AU-50. Lilac and gray toning mottled with areas of silver and gold. Somewhat prooflike, especially when held at a certain angle to the light. The piece is well centered, attractive, and exhibits a nice strike. John G. Mills Collection, S.H. and H. Chapman, April 27-29, 1904; J.M. Clapp; John H. Clapp; Clapp estate, 1942. $9,900.

1797 Stars 10x6. BB-71, B-3. Die State III. MS-63. A superb specimen, a highlight of the present sale, a coin of an unbelievable quality. The strike is excellent, with the features in all areas (including the hair strands and with each feather in the eagle's breast) visible either in outline or detailed form, except for a very small part on the neck. Silvery, highly lustrous fields with delicate champagne toning at the center changes to light gold at the rims with splashes of electric blue. Harlan P. Smith Collection, S.H. and H. Chapman, May 8-11, 1906; J.M. Clapp; John H. Clapp; Clapp estate, 1942. $176,000 • 1797 Stars 9x7, Small Letters. BB-72, B-2. VF-30. From J. Colvin Randall, May 1894; J.M. Clapp; John H. Clapp; Clapp estate, 1942. $6,160 • 1797 Stars 9x7, Large Letters. BB-73, B-1. prior to relapping. Tiny raised pellet in field opposite ninth star. On the reverse under high magnification MS-60. A delightful coin with heather and gold toning over silvery, lustrous surfaces. Well struck and well centered, with both obverse and reverse framed by prominent dentils. Details are excellent in all areas except the very highest points of the obverse and reverse. Indeed, probably no finer striking exists. $52,800.

1798 15 Stars on Obverse, Small Eagle, Small Letters. BB-81, B-2. Die State II. AU-58. Another delightful specimen. From a condition viewpoint, the piece challenges Mint State and is perhaps conservatively designated AU-58. The fields are light gray with splashes of gold and, toward the rims, electric blue. From an aesthetic viewpoint it is a visual treat. $26,400 • 1798 13 Stars on Obverse, Small Eagle. BB-82, B-1. Die State III. AU-50. Light silver and heather surfaces with splashes of sea green, gold, and electric blue. John G. Mills Collection, S.H. and H. Chapman, April 27-29, 1904; J.M. Clapp; John H. Clapp; Clapp estate, 1942. $15,400 • 1798 Heraldic Eagle. Knobbed 9. BB-96, B-6. Die State IV MS-60. A few tiny adjustment marks, as made, are hidden in the design features. Light champagne and lilac toning over glossy, lustrous surfaces. Very well struck. Obverse framed with a particularly high rim, reverse very slightly misaligned. $17,600 • 1798 Heraldic Eagle. Wide Date, 13 Arrows. BB-104, B-22. Die State IV. AU-58. A very pleasing coin that will at once attract the specialist and delight the connoisseur. This is believed to be the very finest known example of BB-104, several orders nicer than the closest competitor known to the cataloger, Harlan P. Smith Collection, S.H. and H. Chapman, May 8-11, 1906; J.M. Clapp; John H. Clapp; Clapp estate, 1942$9,350 • 1798 Heraldic Eagle. Close Date. BB-113, B-27. Die State II. MS-61. Light golden and gray toning on the obverse changes to splashes of blue at the rims. The reverse is gunmetal blue with hints of iridescence. $33,000.

1799/8 Overdate. 13 stars on reverse. BB-142, B-1. The cracks at the die at I of AMERICA are quite incredible and are unlike what are typically seen on a MS-63. A lovely specimen, believed to be the finest known. $77,000.

1799 BB-157, B-5. Die State III. MS-62. A delightful combination of high grade and gorgeous aesthetic appeal. $29,700 • 1799 8x5 Stars. BB-159, B-23. Die State II. AU-55. John G. Mills Collection, S.H. and H. Chapman, April 27-29, 1904; J.M. Clapp; John H. Clapp; Clapp estate, 1942. $7,700 • 1799 Variety without berries in reverse wreath. BB-161, B-11a. MS-61. A gorgeous piece, comfortably within the Condition Census and among the top two or three finest known. $12,100 • 1799 BB-163, B-10. Die State II. MS-64. A superb specimen of almost unbelievable quality, a piece which must have been very carefully preserved since the very day of issue! $77,000.

1800 BB-188, B-8. Die State II. MS-63. Far and away the finest known to us, head and shoulders above the closest competition from a numerical viewpoint and, it goes without saying, from an aesthetic viewpoint as well. Still another marvelous opportunity for the connoisseur and specialist. $46,200 • 1800 AMERICAI. BB-192, B-19. Die State I. MS-62. A pleasing mixture of lilac and gold toning with splashes of blue at the rims. Well struck and nicely detailed. S.H. and H. Chapman, January 1900; J.M. Clapp; John H. Clapp; Clapp estate, 1942. $33,000 • 1800 Dotted Date. BB-194, B-14. Die State IV. MS-63. Medium gold, gray, and magenta toning over lustrous, frosty surfaces. Hints of electric blue and magenta at the rims. Harlan P.

Smith Collection, S.H. and H. Chapman, May 8-11, 1906; J.M. Clapp; John H. Clapp; Clapp estate, 1942. $77,000.

1801 BB-214, B-4. Die State II. MS-62. A superb specimen, the second finest known to us of the variety BB-214, and quite possibly among the very finest 1801 silver dollars of any variety. Lustrous, silver surfaces at the center have delicate gold toning, changing to medium gold toward the borders, then electric blue and iridescent hues. David S. Wilson Collection, 1906 privately; J.M. Clapp; John H. Clapp; Clapp estate, 1942. $55,000.

1802/1 Wide overdate. BB-233, B-2. AU-58 or finer. A close challenge to Mint State, with the reverse easily attributable to that level. Another splendid coin with delicate lilac toning at the center changing to gold and blue at the rims. Well struck and nicely framed by the dentils. This is the finest BB-233 known to us in auction citations. S.H. and H. Chapman, January 1900; J.M. Clapp; John H. Clapp; Clapp estate, 1942. $20,900.

1802 Narrow Date. BB-241, B-6. MS-64. A superb specimen with light lilac and gray toning over lustrous and somewhat golden surfaces. Satiny and smooth, a gem piece of simply exquisite character. Matthew A. Stickney Collection, Henry Chapman, June 25-29, 1907, Lot 1116; John H. Clapp; Clapp estate, 1942. $165,000.

1803 Small 3. BB-254, B-4. MS-62. Medium golden toning with hints of light gray. Magenta around the rims, and among the dentils some splashes of gunmetal blue. The finest known specimen of the BB-254 variety. William M. Friesner Collection, Édouard Frossard, June 7-8, 1894; J.M. Clapp; John H. Clapp; Clapp estate, 1942. $31,900 • 1803 Large 3. BB-255, B-6. MS-62. Somewhat proof-like. Another delightful early dollar, the last in the circulation strike series here offered. Light golden toning with splashes of lilac and, at the rim, sea green and gunmetal blue. A simply outstanding coin which, to our knowledge, is the second finest known to exist. S.H. and H. Chapman, January 1900; J.M. Clapp; John H. Clapp; Clapp estate, 1942. $35,200.

1804 (See chapter about the 1804 silver dollar). $1,815,000.

The Collections of Phillip Flannagan, Dr. Robert I. Hinkley, Dr. John C. Wong, and Tree Many Feathers, Bowers and Merena Galleries, November 29 through December 1, 2001, contained the outstanding early dollar collection of Phillip Flannagan, assembled with the assistance of Laura Sperber of Legend Numismatics.

1794 BB-1. Flowing Hair MS-61 (NGC). From our sale of the Harry W. Bass, Jr. Collection, Part I, May 7-9, 1999, there as Lot 2021, uncertified and described as AU-58 to MS-60. $207,000.

1795 BB-11. AU-55 with Silver Plug (PCGS). $41,400 • 1795 BB-21. MS-63 (NGC). Ex: Eliasberg. $43,700 • 1795 BB-52. Draped Bust. MS-65 (PCGS). $140,875.

1796 BB-65. MS-62 (NGC). Ex: Whitney. $48,300.

1797 BB-71. MS-65 (NGC). Ex: Eliasberg. $178,250.

1798 BB-81. Small Eagle, 15 Stars. MS-62 (PCGS). $80,500 • 1798 BB-82. Small Eagle, 13 Stars. AU-50 (PCGS). $11,500 • 1798 BB-113. MS-64 (PCGS). 48,300.

1799/8 BB-143. MS-64 (PCGS). 66,700.

1799 BB-160. MS-64 (PCGS). $52,900.

1800 BB-190. MS-64 (PCGS). $78,200 • 1800 BB-193. AU-58 (PCGS). $9,430 • 1800 BB-194. AU-55 (PCGS). $6,670.

1801 BB-213. AU-53 (PCGS). $8,050 • 1801 BB-214. MS-63 (PCGS). Ex: Eliasberg. $78,200.

1802/1 BB-232. EF-45 (PCGS). $3,450 • 1802 BB-241. MS-64 (PCGS). Ex: Starr. $96,600 • 1802 BB-241. VF-20 (PCGS). Double Struck. $9,200 • 1802 BB-302. Restrike. Proof-64 (PCGS). $120,750.

1803 BB-254. MS-63 (NGC). Ex: Eliasberg. $43,700.

1804 Class III, so-called "Restrike" Proof-58 (PCGS). Ex: Adams-Carter. $874,000.

The Cardinal Collection, American Numismatic Rarities, June 30, 2005, contained what was then (and remains as of the publication date) the all-time finest "Major Variety" collection of early dollars within the registry sets of PCGS and NGC, assembled by Martin Logies.

1794 BB-1. Flowing Hair. MS-64 (NGC). Ex: Boyd. $1.15 million.

1795 Flowing Hair. BB-11. AU-55 with Silver Plug (PCGS). Ex: Garrett. $50,600 • 1795 BB-13. AU-58 (PCGS). Ex: Stickney. $64,400 • 1795 BB-14. AU-58 (PCGS). Ex: Shore. $43,700 • 1795 BB-18. MS-64 (PCGS). Ex: Mougey-Eliasberg. $195,500 • 1795 BB-18. AU-58 with Silver Plug (PCGS). $66,700 • 1795 BB-20. MS-65 (NGC). Ex: Heifetz. $230,000 • 1795 BB-21. MS-62 (PCGS). Ex: Earle-Eliasberg. $71,875 • 1795 BB-26. AU-55 (PCGS). Ex: Gable-Stirling. $48,300 • 1795 BB-27. MS-62 (PCGS). Ex: Benson. $66,700 • 1795 Draped Bust. BB-51. MS-64 (PCGS). Ex: Stack-Jung. $126,500 • 1795 BB-52. MS-65 (PCGS). Ex: Morgan-Flannagan. $322,000.

1796 BB-61. AU-58 (PCGS). Ex: Newcomer-Clarke. $48,300 • 1796 BB-63. AU-58 (NGC). Ex: Newcomer-Green-Clarke-

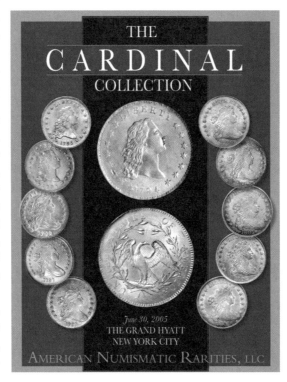

Bareford-Whitney. $29,900 • 1796 BB-65. MS-62 (PCGS). Ex: Four Landmark Collections. $78,200.

1797 BB-71. MS-62 (PCGS). Ex: Miles. $77,050 • 1797 BB-72. AU-58 (PCGS). Ex: Miles. $69,000 • 1797 BB-73. MS-63 (NGC). Ex: Miles-Hood. $89,700.

1798 Small Eagle. BB-81. MS-62 (PCGS). Ex: Eliasberg. $103,500 • 1798 BB-82. AU-58 (PCGS). Ex: Baldenhofer-Lexington. $78,200 • 1798 Heraldic Eagle. BB-91. AU-58 (PCGS). $27,600 • 1798 BB-94. MS-63 (PCGS). Ex: Hoffecker-Worrell. $39,100 • 1798 BB-96. MS-61 (PCGS). $27,600 • 1798 BB-101. AU-53 (PCGS). $12,650 • 1798 BB-108. MS-63 (PCGS). $64,400 • 1798 BB-112. MS-62 (PCGS). $23,000 • 1798 BB-114. MS-61 (PCGS). Ex: Pittman. $41,400 • 1798 BB-121. AU-58 (PCGS). $20,700 • 1798 BB-124. MS-64 (NGC). $69,000 • 1798 BB-125. AU-53 (NGC). Ex: Richmond. $8,050.

1799/8 BB-141. MS-62 (PCGS). Ex: Albany. $29,900 • 1799/8 BB-142. MS-63 (PCGS). Ex: L. R. French. $75,900.

1799 BB-151. AU-58 (PCGS). Ex: Auction '87. $23,000 • 1799 BB-152. MS-64 (PCGS). Ex: Hain. $71,300 • 1799 BB-153. AU-55 (PCGS). $11,500 • 1799 BB-154. (ANACS). Ex: Norweb. $17,250 • 1799 BB-159. MS-64 (PCGS). Ex: Brand-Bareford. $143,750 • 1799 BB-160. AU-55 (PCGS). $9,200 • 1799 BB-164. MS-65 (PCGS). $120,750.

1800 BB-184. MS-63 (PCGS). $48,300 • 1800 BB-187. MS-63 (PCGS). $59,800 • 1800 BB-190. MS-64 (PCGS). Ex: Carter. $115,000 • 1800 BB-191. AU-58 (PCGS). $17,250 • 1800 BB-192. AU-58 (PCGS). $43,700 • 1800 BB-193. AU-58 (NGC). $14,950 • 1800 BB-194. MS-64 (PCGS). Ex: Faraday. $71,300 • 1800 BB-195. AU-55 (PCGS). $19,550 • 1800 BB-196. MS-63 (NGC). Ex: Cohen. $41,400 • 1800 BB-196. MS-61 (PCGS). $32,200.

1801 BB-211. MS-62 (PCGS). $57,500 • 1801 BB-214. MS-64 (PCGS). Ex: Clapp-Eliasberg. $143,750.

1802/1 BB-232. AU-58 (PCGS). $29,900 • 1802/1 BB-234. MS-63 (PCGS). $66,700.

1802 BB-241. MS-65 (PCGS). Ex: Starr-Flannagan. $247,250 • 1802 BB-242. AU-58 (PCGS). Ex: Miller. $25,300.

1803 BB-254. MS-63 (PCGS). Ex: Freisner-Clapp-Eliasberg. $64,400 • 1803 BB-255. MS-63 (PCGS). Ex: Cleneay-Ruddy. $82,800.

Appendix 1
ERRORS AND CURIOSITIES

The United States Mint today adheres to very strict quality control standards, especially with those offerings intended for collectors. Indeed, the overall quality of modern Proof coins is such that today's collectors have become so accustomed to perfection that they might return to the Mint anything that falls short of Proof-70 status. Such was not always the case. In the days of the early Mint, the focus was on the efficiency and economy of production, and coins were intended entirely for use in circulation. Consequently, dies that were poorly made or had cracked or broken from use were kept in use and utilized as long as possible, and imperfect planchets were deemed perfectly acceptable as long that they were within legal tolerances of precious metal content. Similarly, poorly or oddly struck coins were readily released to circulation.

Most commonly, one portion or another of the coin's design might be weakly struck, or the coin might be struck just a touch off-center, but in some instances the coin might be an extreme oddity, featuring a variety of peculiar and unintended strike characteristics. Such errors are actively sought and highly prized by today's collectors. Examples might include coins that are double-struck with a lateral shift between strikes, double-stuck on center with rotation between strikes, double struck on one side only, double-struck with the planchet flipped over between strikes and with distinct obverse and reverse strikes on both sides, and even triple struck specimens. Following are some examples of these most curious pieces, including a truly extraordinary triple-struck "Starburst" and eye-catching flip-over double-struck "Stargazer."

DOUBLE STRIKE WITH LATERAL SHIFT

1802 BB-241. VF-25 (NGC)

Double Strike with Rotation

1799 BB-166. EF-45 (NGC)

One-Sided Double Strike

1803 BB-252. F-12 (NGC)

Triple Strike with Starburst Effect

1797 BB-71. MS-61 (NGC)

"Stargazer" Double Strike with Rotation and Planchet Flip-Over

1799 BB-159. VG-8 (NGC)

EARLY SILVER DOLLARS IN THE NATIONAL NUMISMATIC COLLECTION

SMITHSONIAN INSTITUTION
CIRCULATION STRIKES 1794-1803

The following is an inventory of the attributed early silver dollars in the National Numismatic Collection at the Smithsonian Institution under the directorship of Dr. Richard Doty, noted scholar and researcher in the field. The inventory was prepared and grades assigned by Jeff Garrett in cooperation with Dr. Doty and Karen Lee.

The Mint Cabinet was instituted in the summer of 1838 with a grant of $1,000 from Congress plus a yearly stipend of $300. Jacob Reese Eckfeldt and William E. Dubois were the curators. The production of early dollars had long since ceased, and none had been saved at the Mint. In ensuing years early dollars were acquired from deposits at the Mint, by trade or purchase from collectors, and by donations. In 1923 the Mint Cabinet was transferred to the Smithsonian Institution and put on display in the "Castle" building on the Mall. Later, it was moved to the new Museum of American History a short walk from the White House. Today, as noted, it is known as the National Numismatic Collection and is a national treasure.

1794	BB-1. EF.
1795	BB-25 (B-6). Flowing Hair. 3 Leaves. EF+/AU-50. .
1795	BB-25 (B-6). Flowing Hair. 3 Leaves. Nice VF.
1795	BB-27 (B-5). Flowing Hair. 3 Leaves. Nice EF. Impaired but with excellent eye appeal.
1795	BB-27 (B-5). Flowing Hair. 3 Leaves. AU-50. Counterstamped as an advertisement HOUCK'S PANACEA by a Baltimore seller of patent medicine.
1795	BB-18 (B-7). Flowing Hair. 3 Leaves. Mint-inserted silver plug. EF. Boldly double struck. A landmark coin.
1795	BB-20 (B-2). Flowing Hair. 3 Leaves. EF. Impaired.
1795	BB-21 (B-1). Flowing Hair. 3 Leaves. Fine. Bump on rim.
1795	BB-51 (B-14). Draped Bust. EF+. Impaired.

1795	BB-51 (B-14). Draped Bust. VF.
1795	BB-52 (B-15). Draped Bust. Nice EF.
1795	BB-51 (B-14). Draped Bust. MS-64. A gift of well-known dealer Lester Merkin. The first use of the Draped Bust motif on American coinage.
1796	BB-61 (B-4). VF. Slightly off center.
1796	BB-65 (B-5). AU-55.
1797	BB-73 (B-1). EF.
1797	BB-73 (B-1). AU-50. Impaired.
1798	BB-114 (B-26). EF. Damaged, Impaired.
1798	BB-82 (B-1). EF.
1798	BB-82 (B-1). VF.
1798	BB-81 (B-2). VF. Impaired.
1799	BB-166 (B-9). VF+.
1799	BB-163 (B-10). EF-40.
1799	BB-159 (B-23). VF. Counterstamped.
1799	BB-159 (B-23). AU-55.
1799	BB-169 (B-21). EF-45.
1799	BB-155 (B-19). VF. Impaired.
1799	BB-161 (B-11). AU-55.
1800	BB-192 (B-19). MS-60.
1800	BB-190 (B-10). VF. Impaired.
1800	BB-189 (B-5). VF.
1800	BB-181 (B-1). VF.
1802	BB-232 (B-4). 1802/1. EF-45.
1802	BB-232 (B-4). 1802/1. MS-63.
1803	BB-255 (B-6). VF.
1803	BB-254 (B-4). AU-50.

Credits:
Smithsonian National Numismatic Collection
Jeff Garrett for compiling the list

BIBLIOGRAPHY AND SOURCE NOTES

Unpublished Sources
(National Archives)
Record Group 104, Bureau of the Mint:[1]
Bullion Journals, 1794–1805.

Bullion Ledgers, 1794–1872.

General Correspondence, 1793–1804.

Letter Books: 1795–1804.

Silver Deposited for Coinage, 1794–1804.

Waste Books, 1794–1804.

Published Sources
Adams, Edgar H. and William H. Woodin. *U.S. Pattern, Trial and Experimental Pieces*. New York: American Numismatic Society, 1913.

Adams, John Weston. *United States Numismatic Literature. Volume I. Nineteenth Century Auction Catalogs*. Mission Viejo, CA: George Frederick Kolbe Publications, 1982. A masterful compilation of auction catalogs of the nineteenth century, with biographical sketches of the professional numismatists involved.

———— *United States Numismatic Literature. Volume II. Twentieth Century Auction Catalogs*. Crestline, CA: George Frederick Kolbe Publications, 1990. Companion volume to the foregoing.

American Numismatist, The. Paterson, NJ: C.E. Leal, 1886-1887.

Attinelli, Emmanuel J. *Numisgraphics, or a List of Catalogs in Which Occur Coins or Medals, Which Have Been Sold by Auction in the United States*. New York: 1876.

Auction Prices Realized. Iola, Wisconsin: Krause Publications, Inc., 1980s and 1990s.

Auctions by Bowers and Merena, Inc., NH, 1982-1983. Auction catalogs and prices realized.

Bolender, M.H. *The United States Early Silver Dollars from 1794 to 1803*. Freeport, IL: published by the author, 1950.

Bolles, Albert S. *The Financial History of the United States from 1774 to 1885*. Three volumes. New York, 1879–1894.

Bowers and Merena Galleries, Inc. Wolfeboro, NH. Various catalogs, 1983-2003.

Bowers and Ruddy Galleries, Los Angeles, California. Various auction catalogs, 1972-1982.

Bowers, Q. David. *A Buyer's Guide to the Rare Coin Market*. Wolfeboro, NH: Bowers and Merena Galleries, Inc., 1990.

———— *Coins and Collectors*. Johnson City, NY: Windsor Research Publications, 1964.

———— *High Profits from Rare Coin Investment*. 13th Edition. Wolfeboro, NH: Bowers and Merena Galleries, Inc., 1991.

———— *The American Numismatic Association Centennial History*. Wolfeboro, NH: Bowers and Merena Galleries, Inc. on behalf of the American Numismatic Association, 1991. Two volumes.

———— *The History of United States Coinage*. Los Angeles, California: Bowers and Ruddy Galleries, Inc., 1979; later printings by Bowers and Merena Galleries, Inc., Wolfeboro, NH.

———— *Virgil Brand: The Man and His Era*. Wolfeboro, NH: Bowers and Merena Galleries, 1983.

Breen, Walter H. *"Walter Breen's Encyclopedia of U.S. and Colonial Proof Coins, 1792-1977*. Albertson, New York: FCI Press, 1977. Many die descriptions are from this source, via Breen, a contributor to the present work.

———— *Walter Breen's Complete Encyclopedia of U.S. and Colonial Coins*. Garden City, NY: Doubleday, 1988. Many die descriptions are from this source, via Breen, a contributor to the present work.

Bullock, Charles J. Ph.D. *Essays on the Monetary History of the United States*. New York: The Macmillan Company, 1900.

Bullowa, David M. "Gilbert Stuart and the Silver Dollar." Article in *The Numismatist*, March 1942. The author notes that in 1861 Mint Director James Ross Snowden credited Stuart with the 1795 Draped Bust dollar design, based upon information furnished by a descendant of the artist, and muses if this information might be correct.

Carlson, Carl W.A. "Tracker: An Introduction to Pedigree Research in the Field of Rare American Coins." Article in *The American Numismatic Association Centennial Anthology*. Wolfeboro, NH: Bowers and Merena Galleries, Inc. (for the ANA), 1991.

Carlson, Carl W.A. and Michael J. Hodder, editors. *The American Numismatic Association Centennial Anthology*. Wolfeboro, NH: Bowers and Merena Galleries, Inc. on behalf of the American Numismatic Association, 1991.

Carothers, Neil. *Fractional Money*. New York: John Wiley & Sons, 1930.

Carruth, Gorton. *The Encyclopedia of American Facts & Dates*. Eighth edition. New York: Harper & Row, Publishers, 1987.

Certified Coin Dealer Newsletter, Torrance, California. Various issues of the 1980s onward.

Christie, Manson & Woods, Ltd. Catalog of English, Foreign and Important American Coins, the Property of Major the Lord St. Oswald, M.C., removed from Nostell Priory, Wakefield, Yorkshire. Offered a group of United States coins believed to have been acquired in a visit to the United States in autumn 1795.

Clain-Stefanelli, Elvira Eliza. "Old Friends—Common Goals: The Evolution of Numismatics in the United States."

---

[1] Philadelphia Mint unless noted otherwise. These documents were examined by R.W. Julian.

Article in *The American Numismatic Association Centennial Anthology*. Wolfeboro, NH: Bowers and Merena Galleries, Inc. (for the ANA), 1991.

Coin & Medal Bulletin. New York City: Edgar H. Adams and Wayte Raymond, April 1916 to March 1917.

Coin and Stamp Journal, The. Kansas City, Missouri: March 1876 issue. A feature article, "Rare American Coins," discussed certain silver dollars.

Coin Collectors' Journal, The. New York: Scott & Company, various issues of the 1870s and 1880s.

Coin Dealer Newsletter, Torrance, California, various issues 1963 to date.

Coin World. Sidney, OH: Amos Press, *et al.,* 1960 to date.

Coin World Almanac. Third edition. Sidney, OH: Amos Press, various editions.

Coin World Comprehensive Catalog and Encyclopedia of United States Coins. Sidney, Ohio: Amos Press, Inc., 1990.

COINage magazine. Ventura, California: Miller Magazines, Inc. Various issues 1970s to date.

Coinage Laws of the United States 1792-1894. Modern foreword to reprint by David L. Ganz. Wolfeboro, NH: Bowers and Merena Galleries, Inc., 1991.

Coins Magazine. Iola, Wisconsin: Krause Publications, various issues 1962 to date.

Collins, Jack. *1794: The History and Genealogy of the First United States Dollar.* (Manuscript)

Comparette, T.L. *Catalog of Coins, Tokens, and Medals in the Numismatic Collection of the Mint of the United States at Philadelphia, Pennsylvania.* "Prepared under the direction of the Director of the Bureau of the Mint." 3rd Edition. Washington: Government Printing Office, 1914.

Conoclast, I. (Pseudonym: "Iconoclast") "Believes Dollars Coined In 1804." Article in *The Numismatist,* August 1937.

Crosby, Sylvester S. *Early Coins of America.* Boston, 1878.

Davis Charles E. *American Numismatic Literature, An Annotated Survey of Auction Sales 1980-1991.* Lincoln, MA: Quarterman Publications, Inc., 1982.

Dickeson, Montroville Wilson. *The American Numismatical Manual.* Philadelphia: J.B. Lippincott & Co., 1859. (1860 and 1865 editions were slightly retitled as *The American Numismatic Manual.*)

DuBois, William E. *Pledges of History: A Brief Account of the Collection of Coins Belonging to the Mint of the United States, More Particularly of the Antique Specimens.* Philadelphia: C. Sherman, Printer, (1st Edition) 1846; New York: George P. Putnam, 2nd Edition, 1851.

Dye, John S. *Dye's Coin Encyclopaedia.* Philadelphia: Bradley & Company, 1883.

Eckfeldt, Jacob Reese and William Ewing DuBois. *A Manual of Gold and Silver Coins of All Nations, Struck Within the Past Century.* Philadelphia: Assay Office of the Mint, 1842. Important as the first significant book on coins

to be published in the United States. Items of interest include: p. 36: "[George Washington] took a lively interest in the national coinage. The Mint was repeatedly noticed in his messages to Congress. It was his practice, whilst President, to visit the institution frequently, the seat of government being then at Philadelphia." Plate II illustrates silver dollars of the two major types of 1795 and, for the first time in an American publication, the silver dollar of 1804.

Evans, George G. *Illustrated History of the United States Mint.* Philadelphia: published by the author, editions of 1883, 1885, 1889, 1893. Successor to the A.M. Smith work on the Mint. (Among other activities, Evans was an issuer of encased postage stamps years earlier during the Civil War.)

Forecaster, The. Investment newsletter published by John Kamin, Tarzana, CA. Issues consulted from 1962 to date.

Gengerke, Martin. *American Numismatic Auctions.* 8th edition. Woodside, NY: published by the author, 1990.

Gillilland, Cory. "Public Opinion and the Nation's Coinage." Article in *The American Numismatic Association Centennial Anthology.* Wolfeboro, NH: Bowers and Merena Galleries, Inc. (for the ANA), 1991.

Gouge, William M. *A Short History of Paper Money and Banking in the United States.* Philadelphia: T.W. Ustick (printer), 1833.

Haseltine, John W. (actually the work of J. Colvin Randall, who received no credit line). *Type Table Catalog of United States Dollars, Half Dollars, and Quarters.* Philadelphia, November 1881.

Heritage Numismatic Auctions, Inc., Heritage Auctions, Dallas, Texas. 1980s to date. Auction catalogs and prices realized.

Hickcox, J.H. *An Historical Account of American Coinage.* Albany, New York: published by the author, 1858.

Hilt, Robert P., II. *Die Varieties of Early United States Coins.* Omaha, NE: R.T.S. Publishing Company, 1980.

Historical Statistics of the United States: Colonial Times to 1970, U.S. Department of Commerce, Bureau of the Census, Washington, D.C., September 1975.

Hodder, Michael and Q. David Bowers. *The Norweb Collection: An American Legacy.* Wolfeboro, NH: Bowers and Merena Galleries, Inc., 1987.

Homans, I. Smith, Jr. *The Book of Coins.* Philadelphia: J.B. Lippincott & Co., 1878. Compendium of charts, essays, etc., from various sources, not well organized, but with some metal prices, etc., of use.

Jameson, J. Franklin, Ph.D. *Dictionary of U.S. History. 1492-1899.* Boston: Puritan Publishing Co., 1898 (*sic*) edition.

John Reich Journal. Organ of the John Reich Collector Society. Ypsilanti, MI: JRCS, various issues of the 1980s to date.

Jones, George F. *The Coin Collectors' Manual* (subtitle: *Containing a Description of the Gold, Silver, Copper and Other Coins, United States, Together With an Account of Actual Sales in Philadelphia and New York, Designed as a Guide Book for*

Coin Collectors. Philadelphia: Edward Cogan, 1860. Gives auction records for silver dollars (and other coins).

Jones, John F. "The 1804 United States Dollar." Article in *The Numismatist,* January 1938.

Judd, Dr. J. Hewitt. *United States Pattern, Experimental and Trial Pieces.* Racine, WI: Whitman Division of Western Publishing Company, 1959 (Revised editions through the 6th, 1977). Today, *United States Patterns,* Whitman Publishing LLC, Atlanta, GA. Edited by Q. David Bowers.

Julian, R.W. "Limited Census of Certain Early U.S. Coins." Article in *The Numismatist,* June 1963, p. 790.

——— "Another Look at the 1804: Origin of the 1804 Dollar." Article in *The Numismatist,* January 1970.

——— "Origin of the 1804 Dollar—II." Article in *The Numismatist,* December 1970.

——— "The Illegal Dollars of 1794-95." Article in *Coins* magazine, March 1978.

Kreisberg, Abner and Jerry Cohen. Quality Sales. Various auction catalogs. Beverly Hills, CA: 1970s and 1980s. (Some sales cataloged with the assistance of Jack Collins.)

Krueger, Kurt R. Iola, Wisconsin. 1980s and 1990s. Auction catalogs and prices realized.

Linderman, Henry R. *Money and Legal Tender in the United States.* New York, 1877.

Linett, Dana. La Jolla, California. 1980s to date. Auction catalogs and prices realized.

Logan, Russell J. "Condition Census Pre-Turban Bust Dollars." Article in the *JRCS Journal,* October 1990.

Mason, E(benezer) Locke. *Rare American Coins: Their Description, and Past and Present Fictitious Values.* Boston: Percival Gassett, 1887.

Logies, Martin A. *The Flowing Hair Silver Dollars of 1794,* Sunnyvale, California, Cardinal Collection Educational Foundation, 2004.

Mason's Monthly Illustrated Coin Collector's Magazine. Philadelphia and Boston: Ebenezer Locke Mason. Various issues of the 1860s, 1870s, and 1880s.

McIntire Numismatic Auctions, Inc. Jacksonville, Arkansas. 1980s. Auction catalogs and prices realized.

Mehl's Numismatic Monthly, Fort Worth, Texas: B. Max Mehl, issues of 1908 and 1909.

Merkin, Lester. Various auction catalogs. New York: 1960s and 1970s. (Most were partially or wholly cataloged by Walter H. Breen.)

Mickley, Joseph J. *Dates of United States Coins, and Their Degrees of Rarity.* Philadelphia: published by the author, July 1858.

Mid-American Rare Coin Auctions, Inc. Lexington, KY. 1980s and 1990s. Auction catalogs and prices realized.

New Netherlands Coin Co., Inc. Various auction catalogs. New York: 1951-1970 consulted. (Cataloged by John J. Ford, Jr., Walter H. Breen; later by Don Taxay and G. Jon Hanson.)

Newman, Eric P. "Diagnosing the Zerbe 1804 and 1804 Dollars." Article in *The Numismatist,* October 1961. The author concluded that the 1804 was an alteration from 1802 B-4 (BB-232), and the 1805 was an alteration from 1803 B-6 (BB-241).

——— "Keeping Up With the 1804 Dollar History." Article in *The Numismatist,* March 1970.

Newman, Eric P. and Kenneth E. Bressett. *The Fantastic 1804 Dollar.* Racine, Wisconsin: Whitman Publishing Company, 1962.

——— "The Fantastic 1804 Dollar: 25th Anniversary Follow-Up, " *Coinage of the Americas Conference.* New York City: American Numismatic Society, 1987.

Newman, Eric P., and Don Taxay. "An Answer to 1804 Dollar and Eagle Challenges." Article in *The Numismatist,* February 1970.

NGC Census Report. Parsippany, NJ, later Sarasota, FL. Numismatic Guaranty Corporation of America, various issues 1980s to date

Niles' Weekly Register. Baltimore: H. Niles, 1811-1847.

Numismatic and Antiquarian Society of Philadelphia, Proceedings. Philadelphia, Pennsylvania: Printed for the Society, 1865-1891.

Numismatic Gallery. Various auction catalogs. New York (1940s) and Beverly Hills, CA (later dates). (Mostly cataloged by Abe Kosoff.)

Numismatic News. Iola, WI: Krause Publications, 1952 to date.

Numismatist, The. The American Numismatic Association. Colorado Springs, CO (and other addresses), various issues 1888 to date.

Orosz, Joel J. "Robert Gilmor, Jr. and the Cradle Age of American Numismatics." Article in *Rare Coin Review* No. 58, Bowers and Merena Galleries, Inc., 1985. A very revealing article concerning a pioneer American collector and his relationship with the Mint.

Ostheimer, Alfred J., 3rd. "Contemporary 1804, 1805 Silver Dollars Authenticated." Article in *The Numismatist,* June 1961. (Later discredited by Eric P. Newman in an article, "Diagnosing the Zerbe 1804 and 1804 Dollars" in the same periodical, October 1961.)

Pacific Coast Auction Galleries, Inc., Santa Barbara, California. 1980s and 1990s. Auction catalogs and prices realized.

Paramount International Coin Corporation (and other related names), Englewood, Ohio (and other addresses), 1960s through 1980s. Auction catalogs and prices realized.

PCGS Population Report, The. Newport Beach, California: Professional Coin Grading Service, Inc. Various issues, 1980s to date.

Perkins, W. David. "The 1800 B-13 Bust Dollar—Some Thoughts on Rarity." Article in the *JRCS Journal,* April 1992.

Prime, W.C. *Coins, Medals, and Seals.* New York: Harper & Brothers, Publishers, 1861.

Rare Coin Company of America (RARCOA), Chicago (later Willowbrook), Illinois. Ed Milas. 1970s through 1990s. Auction catalogs and prices realized.

Raymond, Wayte. "A Descriptive List of Die Varieties of Early United States Silver Coins." Series of articles in the *Coin & Medal Bulletin*. New York: Edgar H. Adams and Wayte Raymond, 1916. Includes a brief descriptive listing based upon the Haseltine *Type Table*.

Reiver, Jules. "Varieties of Early United States Silver Coins." Article in the *John Reich Journal,* January 1986. The author notes that he is aware of 18 die varieties of Flowing Hair dollars (1794: 1; 1795: 17), 13 of Draped Bust dollars with Small Eagle reverse (1795: 2; 1796: 6; 1797: 3; 1798: 2), and 85 of Draped Bust dollars with Heraldic Eagle reverse (1798: 31; 1799: 22: 1800: 16; 1801: 4; 1802: 7; 1803: 5).

Risk, James C. "1804, the Continuing Story." Article in *The Numismatist,* August 1970.

Risk, James C. "Further Thoughts About the Class I 1804 Dollar and Eagle." Article in *The Numismatist,* November 1969, reprinted by Coin Galleries (with a 1970 copyright date).

Ruddy, James F. *Photograde.* Los Angeles: Bowers and Ruddy Galleries, Inc.; Wolfeboro, NH: Bowers and Merena Galleries, Inc. Various editions 1970 to 2000s.

Scott's Standard Catalogs. No. 4. Silver and Gold Coins. New York: The Scott Stamp & Coin Company, Ltd., 1893.

Sellers, Charles Coleman. *Mr. Peale's Museum.* New York: W.W. Norton & Company, Inc. 1980. Contains information about Franklin Peale, the Philadelphia scene, etc.

Shaw, W.A. *The History of Currency 1252 to 1896.* London: Wilsons & Milne, Second Edition. London, 1896.

Smith, A.M. *Illustrated History of the U.S. Mint.* Philadelphia: A.M. Smith, 1881.

Snowden, James Ross. *A Description of Ancient and Modern Coins in the Cabinet Collection at the Mint of the United States.* Philadelphia: J.B. Lippincott & Co., 1860.

Spink, David F., and James C. Risk. "New Facts About An Old American Coin." Article in *The Numismatic Review,* Stack's, Vol. III, No. 5, 1962.

Stack's, New York City. 1935 onward. Auction catalogs and prices realized.

Stack's Bowers Galleries, Irvine, California and other locations. Auction catalogs 2011 to date.

Stark, Robert M. "Die Deterioration of a 1798 Dollar (B-28 Reverse)." Article in the *John Reich Journal,* August 1992.

Stewart, Frank H. *History of the First United States Mint, Its People and Its Operations.* Philadelphia: Frank H. Stewart Electric Co., 1924.

Sumner, William G. *A History of American Currency.* New York: Henry Holt and Company, 1874.

Superior Galleries, Beverly Hills, California. 1970s through 1990s. Auction catalogs and prices realized.

Taxay, Don. *Counterfeit, Mis-Struck and Unofficial U.S. Coins.* New York: Arco Publishing Company, Inc., 1963.

———— *Scott's Comprehensive Catalog of United States Coinage.* New York: Scott Publications, 1970 (cover date 1971; largely based upon information supplied by Walter H. Breen[1]). (Revised Edition 1976 updated by Joseph Rose and H. Hazelcorn.)

———— *United States Mint and Coinage.* New York: Arco Publications, 1966.

Trager, James. *The People's Chronology.* New York: Holt, Rinehart & Winston, 1979. This provided an important source for general historical background information.

United States Mint, Bureau of the Mint, *et al. Annual Report of the Director of the Mint.* Philadelphia (later, Washington), 1795–1990. Note: Reports were on a calendar year basis through 1856, then in 1857 they went to a fiscal year (July 1 through June 30 of the following year) basis. The 1857 report is transitional and covers only January 1 through June 30, 1857, a period of six months.

Vermeule, Cornelius. *Numismatic Art in America.* Cambridge, MA: Belknap Press, Harvard, 1971.

von Bergen, William. *The Rare Coins of America.* Boston, Massachusetts: Numismatic Bank, 5th edition, 1891. A general buying list giving prices paid for United States and other coins, including silver dollars.

Wallechinsky, David and Irving Wallace. *The People's Almanac.* Garden City, New York: Doubleday and Company, 1975.

Winter, Douglas. Series of articles in *The John Reich Journal,* beginning in 1986, with updated commentary re Bolender die varieties.

Yeoman, R.S. *A Guide Book of United States Coins.* Whitman Publishing Company (and Western Publishing Company, Inc.), Racine, Wisconsin, now Whitman Publishing LLC, Atlanta, GA. Various editions 1946 to date. Kenneth E. Bressett, editor.

Zerbe, Farran. "False Rarities." Article in *The Numismatist,* March 1944. Describes fake 1804 and 1805 dollars.

---

[1] Walter H. Breen, letter to the author, March 2, 1992.

INDEX

(Notable Specimens sections are not indexed)